More praise for

ALL HOPPED UP AND READY TO GO

"A chronicle covering 50 years of music originating and emanating from all boroughs during the period NY held near total sway over the sounds we move to on the dance floor scooped up on 78 rpm shellac and later 45 or 33 rpm vinyl and building memories to last a lifetime. From Tin Pan Alley songwriters to jazz, rhythm and blues, the Brill Building, folk, doo wop, rock & roll, dance, rap, and hip-hop, it's all there and more in Tony Fletcher's *All Hopped Up and Ready to Go.*"
                        —Seymour Stein, co-founder and CEO, Sire Records

"A history we've needed for years. Anyone who ever joined the dots that lead from the Ronettes to Johnny Thunders—or from Dizzy Gillespie to DJ Kool Herc—will surely welcome Tony Fletcher's splendid biography of the Big Apple's long and fecund musical life."
                        —Barney Hoskyns, author of
            Waiting for the Sun: A Rock & Roll History of Los Angeles

"A thorough and well-researched book filled to the brim with entertaining and insightful details on the interrelated history of innovative music nurtured in New York City."   —Tommy Ramone

"Tony Fletcher digs through archaeological layers of musical arcana with an eye for New York's history as it is continually evolving and ever illuminating, each era its own neighborhood, each scene its own celebration."
                        —Lenny Kaye

"From jazz to punk, from mambo to disco, *All Hopped Up and Ready to Go* offers a giant slice of the Big Apple at its musically ripest. In this illuminating, richly researched survey of midcentury Manhattan, Tony Fletcher shows that New York is the one place in America that truly lives up to the ideal of the melting pot. . . . Virtually an independent city-state, New York has also long been a magnet for nonconformists from across the land, a haven and playground for bohemians and hustlers, extremist artists and maverick entrepreneurs. *All Hopped Up* is their riveting story."

—Simon Reynolds, author of
Rip It Up and Start Again: Postpunk 1978–1984

ALL
HOPPED
UP AND
READY
TO GO

ALL HOPPED UP AND READY TO GO

. . .

*Music from the Streets of
New York 1927–77*

TONY FLETCHER

W. W. NORTON & COMPANY

NEW YORK   LONDON

Frontispiece: The first-ever concerts to use the words "Rock 'n' Roll" were promoted by disc jockey Alan Freed in New York in 1955. His Easter Revue at the Brooklyn Paramount sold 97,000 tickets in just one week.

For information about permission to reproduce selections from this book, write to Permissions, W. W. Norton & Company, Inc., 500 Fifth Avenue, New York, NY 10110

For information about special discounts for bulk purchases, please contact W. W. Norton Special Sales at specialsales@wwnorton.com or 800-233-4830

Manufacturing by Courier Westford
Book design by Ellen Cipriano
Production manager: Devon Zahn

Library of Congress Cataloging-in-Publication Data

Fletcher, Tony.
All hopped up and ready to go : music from the streets of New York, 1927–77 / Tony Fletcher. — 1st ed.
p. cm.
Includes bibliographical references and index.
ISBN 978-0-393-33483-8 (pbk.)
1. Popular music—New York (State)—New York—History and criticism.
2. Popular music—Social aspects—New York (State)—New York—History—20th century. 3. New York (N.Y.)—Social life and customs 20th century.
I. Title.
ML3477.8.N48F54 2009
781.6409747'10904—dc22

2009020630

W. W. Norton & Company, Inc.
500 Fifth Avenue, New York, N.Y. 10110
www.wwnorton.com

W. W. Norton & Company Ltd.
Castle House, 75/76 Wells Street, London W1T 3QT

1 2 3 4 5 6 7 8 9 0

To Noel,
who learned to express himself
in song before he could do so in words.
May your love of music never die.

CONTENTS

INTRODUCTION

I was halfway through my first two-hour interview with the guitarist, producer, songwriter, journalist, and author Lenny Kaye, about as educated and
enthusiastic a student and participant of the New York City music scene as
anyone could ask to meet. We had reached the point in our conversation
where we were talking about the New York Dolls and why, despite their considerable influence over both the short and the long term, they had imploded
so quickly, barely making it through two albums.

"New York is a city that's not going to tell you no," said Kaye, which I
thought to be perhaps the most perceptive—and oddly poetic—single sentence I had heard during thousands of hours spent discussing my subject
matter over a five-year period. "It's only you who can tell you when you have
to go home and go to bed. So unless you have a great sense of personal
responsibility, you can get lost here." He was only partly alluding to the various problems that brought the New York Dolls to their knees, which is why
he went on, "It's not *just* the usual sex and drugs, etc. You can be so swamped
by the amount of cultural material. Where does your art end? How do you
define *this*? Are you going off on some wacky side road? All of these things
come into play."

Indeed they do. When I set off on the idea of writing a musical history
of New York City, I envisioned a book that would start with the vaudeville
impresario Tony Pastor and trace the birth of the American music business
to the back rooms of the German and Irish beer halls along the lower
Bowery—home of the original b-boys—in the years directly after the Civil
War. By the time I had sold the idea to a publisher, half my initial research
appeared to have been thrown out the window, and we had settled on a book

that would begin eighty years later, after World War II, and end at the present day—in a New York City whose music scene, I felt then (and still believe now), had been rejuvenated by a fresh influx of musicians and entrepreneurs in the aftermath of that great New York tragedy, 9/11.

And about halfway through the process of actually writing it, I realized I had almost split the difference. *All Hopped Up and Ready to Go* starts in 1927, in the midst of the Jazz Age. It ends in 1977, a year marked in New York by the blackout, "Son of Sam," a heated mayoral election, the opening of Studio 54, Paradise Garage, and Disco Fever, and the release of debut or second albums by the Ramones, Blondie, Television, Talking Heads, Richard Hell & the Voidoids, and Suicide.

Why those fifty years? Well, both start and end dates are major musical peaks, and the period in between covers the vast middle of the twentieth century, a period of explosion in popular music unlike any other. Besides, to delve back much farther than 1927 would necessitate recounting the birth of jazz itself, a subject so deep, so wide, and so well covered that I prefer to consider it already told. To travel much later than 1977, especially allowing for the growth of hip-hop from so-called novelty to predominant musical format, would have involved so much more detail that it would have demanded another book.

Indeed, there already is another book. It's lying in bits and bytes on my hard drive. I admit that, per Kaye's comment, I found myself absolutely swamped by the amount of cultural material available while researching this project, and I freely confess that I headed off on many a "wacky side road." New York is a city of vast wonder, and so much information is embedded and entwined in its short history that it's all too easy to pull the writer's equivalent of a club kid's all-nighter, and binge on the excessive possibilities.

But it's all part of the process of getting to the heart of the story, that of the many musical genres that have emerged from the New York streets. Music scenes have always fascinated me. And I have always believed that those scenes arise not out of vacuums but out of a specific set of social and economic (and of course musical) circumstances. Those that I write about in this book—from Cubop to hip-hop, from disco to punk—were very much a product of New York City. They could not, and did not, happen anywhere else, at any other time.

It should come as no surprise that New York has nurtured so many musical cultures. No other city undergoes such constant transformation with every new generation of immigrants; no other city can claim to be so powerfully driven by capitalism and yet so obsessed with community; no other city lures so many talented outsiders willing to risk total failure for such a small chance of success. And in no other city do so many millions of people from so many hundreds of different nations live cheek by jowl in such a confined mass, distilling and absorbing each other's cultures, creating in the process a melting pot—not just of the demographics that New York is so famous for but, crucially, of ideas too.

Other books have detailed the growth of the specific cultures or genres that I've identified in individual chapters. But no book, to my knowledge, has tried to weave these different cultures together and attempted to show, for example, how the entrepreneurs who popularized the mambo were the same ones who then cornered the vocal harmony/rhythm and blues scene. Or how the almost exclusively black hip-hop culture that everyone knows was born in the Bronx was directly related to a predominantly gay disco scene in downtown Manhattan. How glitter rock could not have happened as it did without the Ridiculous Theater, which itself would not have been what it was but for the reassuringly libertarian presence of Max's Kansas City. How the Lower East Side rock scene was a direct product of the area's thriving movements in poetry, filmmaking, avant-garde music, and experimental theater. How punk and disco emerged not so much in opposition to as in tandem with each other. And how the thorny issue of race raises its head frequently, but rarely between the musicians themselves, who appear, from the start, drawn to New York's music scene in large part because it offers an opportunity for social as well as musical harmony.

In drawing these connections and identifying my characters, I discovered that just about every scene revolves around three groups of players. First, there are the young musicians who set about formulating their own sound, consciously or otherwise, out of their geographical and social circumstances. Next, usually, there's the nightclub owner who either opens a space specifically to promote this music or otherwise embraces it at a venue that exists already but needs the business. Finally, there are the independent record company entrepreneurs who, being similarly enthusiastic, either establish new labels for the benefit of the music or turn existing imprints over to it. You'll find this three-cornered foundation in chapters on Afro-Cuban jazz and Cubop, on folk music several times over, on the mambo, the male harmony vocal groups, the Lower East Side rock scene, punk rock, and hip-hop. (And you'll find exceptions in chapters on the Brooklyn songwriters, the girl groups, and the birth of disco, all for patently obvious reasons.)

For the most part, I have tried to close out each chapter around the point that the scene in question hits the mainstream, which is usually when the major labels come in to market the music to the masses and inevitably water it down in the process. (For all that New York is the home of the American music business, these major record companies have typically removed them-selves so far from the streets that it quite caught me by surprise to realize that Bob Dylan, almost alone of the musicians in this book, never served an independent label apprenticeship.) By then, as far as I am concerned, the story has been told, and all that's left to do is count the number of record sales and ask: who made all the money?

That question took me off on many fascinating tangents that I ultimately realized were not part of the main narrative. Rather than list them all here, I invite you to visit my Web site, www.ijamming.net, where I will post addi-tional endnotes, host video links, and offer musical playlists for those who would like to read, watch, and listen in more detail.

Squeezing such a large time frame into a few hundred pages has inevita-bly involved picking and choosing my movements, and I am bound to disap-point some people by what I have left out. I followed the Latin scene as far as the mambo in the 1950s, but backed off at the point that it mutated into the bugaloo and salsa, even though there is a great story waiting to be written about the Latin funk of "El Barrio." As I wrote about the disco scene of the early seventies, it dawned on me (too late for this book) that nobody has ever done justice to the great soul, funk, and R&B bands of the early seventies New York metropolitan area: Crown Heights Affair, Fatback Band, Kool & the Gang, Brass Construction, B.T. Express, and more. Doo-wop fans will be unhappy to know that I cover in detail the mostly black groups of Harlem and the Bronx in the fifties, but offer very little about the mostly white groups of Brooklyn, Queens, and Staten Island in the sixties; I can only say that I felt the story had been told by that point. I interviewed several of the singer-songwriters who came to prominence in the sixties but could not get as excited about that aspect of the Greenwich Village scene as about the one that thrived, outdoors and independently, in Washington Square Park for decades. The avant-garde minimalism of John Cage, La Monte Young, and others is barely touched upon. Neither is modern jazz, another minefield of a massive subject. As I picked my scenes, I kept coming back to three key questions. Was the movement emanating from the streets? Was it unique to New York? And was the music offering something new? I needed an affirmative to all those questions to justify the chapter.

I could, at this point, tell my own story: how I came to New York from London, fell in love with the city, decided to move to Manhattan, and endured the familiar struggles of making rent as a freelancer while simultaneously having the time of my life. But I prefer to relay the account of an interviewee, one whose story is just beyond the time frame of this book, but in whose experiences I recognized some of my own—perhaps because, among the few people I interviewed, he also came to New York City from another country. François Kevorkian arrived in New York City, on a flight from France, in September 1975, at the age of twenty-one. He carried with him $300 in cash, a short-term tourist visa, and little else but his deeply ingrained love of jazz, which he knew he could satiate only by moving to the Big Apple. He spent his first night in the city at the YMCA on 34th Street, sleeping alongside Vietnam vets. It cost him $8. He spent a considerable chunk more of his savings on a bicycle to get around town; when he went to see Miles Davis in Central Park during his first week in the city, someone cut the lock and stole it.

Kevorkian refused to let that baptism of theft bring him down, nor was he deterred by having arrived in the midst of the city's bankruptcy. His memories of his early days in the city remain, instead, almost unanimously positive. New York, he said, "was too good to be true. Yes, there were economic problems and all this crime, but these things were secondary to me. I never paid attention to it." Looking for his inroad into jazz, he picked up a Musicians Union handbook in a midtown music store and found that it listed the home phone numbers for many of his idols. He called several of them, "and they were all so pleasant and sweet, and so welcoming," as he recollected. He saw the great Tony Williams advertising drum lessons in the *Village Voice*, and signed up—something he could never have even contemplated living in Strasbourg. Walking through Manhattan during his first month, he got talking to a friendly face and was invited to an after-work dance party on Church Street. There he discovered that, unlike those in France, the New York DJs used *two* turntables *and* a mixer and that they could actually cue in one record from their headphones while the other one was playing. Kevorkian had never seen anything like that before. (Nor, at that point, had many of the hip-hop DJs in the South Bronx.)

From that chance encounter, Kevorkian found himself taking off on what *could* have been some wacky side road—but for the fact that, in New York City's often serendipitous manner, it allowed him to create and establish his own niche. Within a year, he was immersed in the thriving discotheque scene, a resident at the club Galaxy 21—playing jazz drums on the dance floor to accompany the music that the DJ Walter Gibbons spun from the booth up above. A year after that, he was hired as an A&R man by the pioneering disco record label, Prelude, "on the strength of a five-minute conversation." And around the same time, having worked on his own DJ skills via promotions at the Hotel Diplomat, a seedy midtown location that shows up in more music scenes than you might initially presume, he found himself hired as the actual resident DJ for the main competitor to Studio 54. That club was called New York, New York. You could forgive François Kevorkian for humming a certain Frank Sinatra song. You could also understand why, thirty years later, having become an institution in the city's ever-thriving dance music underground, Kevorkian might still say of his first years in New York, "I'd never seen a place in my entire life where I witnessed so many instances of the generosity and the goodness of the human spirit."

For if New York, as Lenny Kaye put it, is a city that's not going to tell you no, then that must mean, as François Kevorkian discovered, that it's a city that wants to say yes—that any idea will be entertained, and anyone with a positive attitude and the requisite determination can find his or her calling. Over the years, this uniquely New York attitude has created many musical movements that have gone on to create an impact around the globe. This is their story.

ALL
HOPPED
UP AND
READY
TO GO

MARIO GETS DIZZY
IN NEW YORK

magine, if you will, New York City in June 1927, as seen through the eyes of a visitor. Just sixteen years old, his name is Mario Bauzá, he hails from Havana, Cuba, and he is a precociously talented clarinet player who has come to America as part of the pianist Antonio María Romeu's seven-piece orchestra, which is recording in New York at the invite of the Victor label. This is an overdue mark of respect for Romeu, a white Cuban of French descent, now forty-nine years old. And it is the opportunity of a lifetime for the teenage clarinetist.

New York City that summer is in the peak of what Scott Fitzgerald has recently coined "the Jazz Age," reveling in its status not only as a center for the music but as the unofficial capital of the New World. Elsewhere in America, great moral battles are being fought between modernists and traditionalists, liberals and conservatives, integrationists and separatists, "wets" and "drys"; but in New York, which with its seven million people is by far the most populous city in America, such cultural confrontations seem moot. The stock market is rising and sexual mores are loosening further with every passing day, the city's myriad races are forced by proximity to mingle if not always to socialize, and modernism is near enough a religion, with new skyscraper hotels opening on an annual basis, each attempting to outgild its predecessor: the Shelton Towers one year, the Ritz-Carlton the next, the Sherry-Netherland as Bauzá makes his visit. As for Prohibition, the law of the land that bars the distribution and sale of alcohol, in New York it is a standing joke: the city is home to some ten thousand speakeasies, and its ruling official, the carousing James Walker, is proud to be known as "the Night Mayor."

The Saturday after Mario Bauzá completes his two-day recording session with Romeu, June 11, New York can be found booming in every direction the visitor cares to look. On Broadway, Ziegfeld's *Rio Rita* is christening the theater just opened in the impresario's name. In the Bronx, at Yankee Stadium, Babe Ruth hits the nineteenth and twentieth home runs of what will become a record-breaking season total of sixty, helping the Yankees to the 1927 World Series, which they will win in a sweep. And in Queens, tens of thousands attend the fifty-ninth Belmont Classic, the highlight of the New York racing calender, won by Chance Shot in just over two and a half minutes.

Back in Manhattan, the streets of Fifth Avenue are being prepared for a ticker-tape parade in honor of Charles Lindbergh, who, just three weeks earlier, had taken off from a muddy field on Long Island to become the first man ever to fly an airplane solo, nonstop, across the Atlantic—a feat that, in claiming the lives of several aviators before him, had seemed beyond human capabilities. The exact number who throng the streets to welcome Lindbergh in Manhattan on June 13 is never fully determined, but it is estimated to be in the millions: Lindbergh may not be a native New Yorker, and the airport from which he departed may have been just outside the five boroughs, but New York knows how to stake a claim on heroes. In fact, just a few months later, a new dance will emerge from the jazz ballrooms of Harlem, named the Lindy Hop—supposedly because, when a champion local dancer called "Shorty" George Snowden is asked by a reporter to explain his "Breakaway" moves during a dance marathon, he replies, "We flyin'—just like Lindy did."

Harlem is itself flying in June 1927, in the midst of the New Negro movement—or what will later be called the Harlem Renaissance, an explosion in literature, art, music, theater, and politics. For the teenage Bauzá, Harlem is an eye-opener, a vision of how black people like him can live in the middle of a white society. Bauzá has had something of a rare upbringing: raised by wealthy white Spanish godparents unable to produce children of their own, afforded a private education as a result, he is a musical prodigy, having first played for the Havana Philharmonic at the age of nine. He has the prospect of a career in a Cuban orchestra to look forward to, but his opportunities for actual leadership remain limited in a country that, despite gaining independence from its Spanish colonists at the turn of the century, thanks largely to a black revolutionary army, has subsequently repressed its dark-skinned majority.

The United States, too, is segregated in 1927, with Jim Crow laws and lynching still prevalent in the South, while New York has enough discrimination, both legal and otherwise, to cause concern for any fan of the jazz music that is doing so much to cross color lines. But this only makes Harlem's status— as the "black metropolis"—all the more remarkable. Barely fifty years earlier, Harlem had still been a remote, northern Manhattan village, but after the extension of the elevated train from downtown saw first a building boom of elegant town houses, and then a bust when the growth of ever less fanciful tenement buildings outstripped demand, a young black entrepreneur named Philip Payton had, in 1904, established the Afro-American Realty Company with the specific intent of filling Harlem's empty building with black residents. A steady stream of discontented blacks had already begun filtering north from the San Juan Hill neighborhood in the West Fifties and lower Sixties, after long-troubled relations with the Irish had culminated in vicous attacks in 1900; Payton was essentially speeding up the process.

The resettling of Harlem was not without its own racial confrontations, and the Afro-American Realty Company overreached and collapsed, but its goals were realized more quickly than even Payton had dared dream: within a decade, fifty thousand blacks had settled in an area of Harlem that stretched from 130th Street north to 143rd Street, and from Seventh Avenue east to Madison. Crucially, black churches and other social institutions made the move too, and as black-owned newspapers, restaurants, and hotels all opened for business, Harlem became its own city within a city—with all the extremes of wealth and poverty, of conservatism and liberalism, of piety and vice, that any other city might be expected to encompass. The speed of this growth and, by extension, its pervasive overcrowding would return to haunt Harlem many times over in coming years, but in 1927 this seemed of little concern to all but those at the bottom of the pile. Rather, the "New Negro" movement was reaching its zenith as the writers Zora Neale Hurston, Langston Hughes, and Countee Cullen, artists Aaron Douglas and Palmer Heyden, actors Paul Robeson and Josephine Baker, to name a few, all met with acclaim, from whites as well as blacks. As Hughes wrote of the era, his pen certainly in his cheek, "Some Harlemites thought the millennium had come. They thought the race problem had at last been solved through Art plus Gladys Bentley."

A "bulldagger," in the parlance of the era, Bentley could be found nearly every night at the Clam House, located in the infamous heart of Harlem's nightlife—Jungle Alley, a blocklong stretch of clubs that ran both sides of 133rd Street from Lenox to Seventh Avenue, catering mostly to white "Negrophiliacs" who journeyed uptown in cavalcades, some with good intentions to share the "genuine" Negro experience, others out on what they openly admitted were "slumming parties." Dressed in white tuxedo and top hat as she played piano and sang, adding particularly bawdy lyrics to the popular tunes of the day and flirting with the white women in the audience, the 250-pound Bentley proved so popular with the visiting "rollers" that she soon found herself living on Park Avenue, with her own maids and chauffeur. You could easily see Langston Hughes's point.

Elsewhere on Jungle Alley, at places like Tillie's Chicken House, Mexico's, and Pod's and Jerry's, a visitor could theoretically catch the great stride pianists of the era in performance: Willie "the Lion" Smith, Fats Waller, and James P. Johnson, whose compositions "The Harlem Strut" and "Go Harlem" further celebrated the area's glowing reputation. Speakeasies in all but official name, these clubs were especially popular with the Negrophiliacs for their ability to stay open all night and serve endless amounts of barely disguised liquor in a city that supposedly had a 3 a.m. curfew and a ban on alcohol.

Barely a block farther up Seventh Avenue stood the elite Harlem nightclubs Smalls Paradise and Barron Wilkins's Exclusive Club, each named for their charismatic owners. Ed Smalls ran a gambling operation in the back of his basement operation at 135th Street, but the majority of customers came for the front-room entertainment. From opening night in 1925 through the following decade, that meant the pianist Charlie Johnson and his Paradise Band, who epitomized the trend for "Harlem orchestra music"—though the waiters, Charleston-dancing their way through the hundreds of jazz fans to serve Chinese food to an integrated audience, were also part of the attraction. Smalls could be found on hand at his venue most every night; by June 1927, Barron Wilkins could not. Having started out as promoter of "tango tea" dances to become the proud sponsor of black baseball teams and boxers, a power broker whose club, wrote Count Basie, "was where a lot of downtown"—read white—"politicians, entertainers and sporting-life people liked to hang uptown," and which had given Duke Ellington his first break back in 1923, Wilkins had been shot dead outside his club in 1925, reputedly over nonpayment to his bootlegger.

Wilkins's untimely demise symbolized the extent to which Prohibition-era Harlem was beholden to gangland interests, and nowhere was this more evident than at the famed Cotton Club, on Lenox Avenue and 142nd Street, from where the white, English-born mobster proprietor Owney Madden reputedly controlled 90 percent of Harlem's lucrative storefront liquor traffic. The Cotton Club had developed its reputation as the "Aristocrat of Harlem" by presenting jungle-flavored floorshows, accompanied by some of the nation's most esteemed black jazz orchestras, to an exclusively white audience. Within such blatant segregation there existed further color coding, for the Cotton Club was meticulous about hiring what it called "Copper-Colored" (or, as the street term had it, "high yaller") "gals" who, in addition to having light black skin, had to fit specific size and weight requirements.

The Cotton Club opened in 1923 with the orchestra of Fletcher Henderson, whose role in bringing the New Orleans–born cornetist Louis Armstrong from Chicago contributed indelibly to New York's usurping those two cities to become the nation's jazz capital. In December 1927, Duke Ellington's Orchestra assumed house band status at the Cotton Club, where it prospered, for the next four years, during which period the Cotton Club's only real rival was Connie's Inn, on 131st Street and Seventh Avenue. Owned by a pair of Jewish German immigrants who also prohibited nonwhite customers, Connie's clientele was disparagingly described by the black Harlem newspaper the *New York Age* as "Slummers; Sports; 'coke' addicts, and high rollers of the White race who come to Harlem to indulge in illicit and illegal recreations."

All the more reason, then, to celebrate the Savoy Ballroom, a block south of the Cotton Club. From the moment it opened, late in 1926, the Savoy proved itself the immediate stomping ground of all serious jazz dancers, (mostly) black and (some) white alike. Its egalitarian status was due in large part to its size: extending a full block from 140th to 141st Street, with a stage at either end, its 10,000-square-foot sprung wood dance floor—"The Track"— could contain thousands of people at a time. Fletcher Henderson opened the Savoy, just as he had the Cotton Club. In fact, just a couple of weeks before Bauzá's arrival in New York, Henderson—a pianist who first came to New

York from Georgia to study chemistry—engaged in one of the Savoy's legendary "battles," pitting his "sweet"-sounding orchestra, with a young Coleman Hawkins among the reeds, against those of King Oliver, Fess Williams, and the young drummer Chick Webb, who would play a major role in Bauzá's future.

A truly adventurous visitor to Harlem, if not fully satiated by all this live entertainment, might try and secure himself an invitation to one of the neighborhood's rent parties. There, so rumor had it of events initially promoted out of financial necessity, the pianists Johnson, Waller, and Smith could also be found, supposedly in their element, providing the musical entertainment as dozens, even hundreds of locals crammed into their neighbors' apartments. For a nominal fee, partygoers could dance, drink, eat, be merry, and, with luck, help their neighbors keep the landlord from serving an eviction notice—at least for another month.

Bauzá, already obsessed with American jazz, which he heard by way of daily broadcasts on Cuban radio, did his best to take all of this in across his eleven-day stay. Thanks to his cousin Rene Endreira, a trumpet player who lived in Harlem and showed him "how black people had developed their own community in New York City," Bauzá subsequently claimed to have seen, during his visit, Fletcher Henderson in Harlem (presumably at the Savoy) and Duke Ellington (by some accounts), and to have attended Small's Paradise as well as Harlem's esteemed black variety theaters, the Lincoln and the Lafayette. Through Endreira, who played for a band called the Santo Domingo Serenaders, "made up of Dominican, Cuban, Panamanian and West Indian musicians," Bauzá observed that Afro-Caribbeans like himself could be accepted in New York as jazz musicians. (This made total sense to Bauzá. Jazz, he intrinsically understood, was a sibling to the Cuban *danzon*: both were descended from the slave ships of West Africa via the port of New Orleans.) And at the Paramount Theater in midtown, he witnessed Paul Whiteman, the most successful orchestra leader of his era, who attracted the greatest white musicians of the twenties. Whiteman's European modifications of American jazz incurred the wrath of the purists, but for the classically trained Bauzá, the notion that the two forms could coexist was life-changing. "When I saw (Frankie) Trumbauer play so beautifully I was completely amazed," he said of the saxophonist's solos on George Gershwin's newly composed

"Rhapsody in Blue." "The orchestration, the sounds . . . I went everyday to see all four shows."

Having experienced these musical riches, the sixteen-year-old returned to a Cuba that, despite its abundance of musical talent, lacked recording studios and record companies. A Cuba where the president, an avowed fan of the Italian Fascist dictator Mussolini, was in the process of amending the new constitution to afford himself an additional six years of unelected power. A Cuba where heavy restrictions had been placed on Abakuá and Yoruba cultural celebrations of African roots, typically manifested during carnival season by costumed parades and legions of percussion. No surprise, then, that, once back in Havana, Bauzá switched to the alto saxophone, the better to play American jazz in the style of Trumbauer and Hawkins, and told everyone that he would be moving to New York once he turned eighteen. "This," he said later, meaning New York City, jazz, a multiracial musical society, "is what life had in store for me."

Bauzá kept his promise, moving to New York in April 1930, just shy of his nineteenth birthday. He arrived, by ship, alongside Justo "Don" Azpiazu and his Havana Casino Orchestra, who had come to perform at various RKO theaters in New York. The timing was surely no coincidence. Having a popular Cuban orchestra in town afforded Bauzá a peer group as he acclimatized himself in New York; and, assuming he did not have a legal right to stay in the United States, it may have been that much easier for him to gain entry as a working musician in their company.

Certainly, the arrival of Azpiazu's orchestra was keenly anticipated. Prohibition had made Cuba a popular tourist destination in the 1920s, a place where wealthy Americans could drink, gamble, and whore to their heart's delight (enriching American mobsters in the process), and they brought home with them an enthusiasm for the Latin American rhythms they heard performed in Havana's casinos, cafés, and hotel ballrooms. At the same time, immigration to New York from the Latin countries of the Caribbean, most notably Puerto Rico but also Cuba and the Dominican Republic, was on the increase, providing a healthy indigenous crowd for any authentic touring act. At RKO's flagship theater, the Palace in midtown, the Havana Casino Orchestra became an overnight sensation, thanks to its new arrangement of a recent Havana hit, "El Manisero" ("The Peanut Vendor"). The Cubans referred to it as a *prégon* (vendor's call), but Americans saw it as pure vaudeville, what with the vocalist Antonio Machín, dressed in the title role, throwing peanuts to the audience while shouting "Mani!"

Victor Records brought the Havana Casino Orchestra into the studio barely two weeks after that debut midtown show, recording a Spanish vocal version of "El Manisero" that was an immediate hit with white Americans. These record buyers weren't interested in studying how the syncopated rhythms of the claves, maracas, and congas linked both to each other and those of the piano and double bass; they weren't focused on how the pianist's left hand played a Cuban *tumbaó* pattern familiar from Argentinean tango and American ragtime. All they understood was that these multiple parts, when topped by a casually syncopated horn line and a vocal melody easily memorized even when sung in a different language, came together to provide an almost involuntarily infectious whole. "El Manisero" became even more popular when Louis Armstrong covered it, and Hollywood built the 1931 movie *Cuban Love Song* around the song, by which time Americans had adopted a term for their new musical obsession: the "rhumba." This was not the *rumba* of specific Cuban sound, movement, and even location but a catch-all that allowed Americans to sweep up and incorporate in one easily pro-nounced (and exotic-sounding) word just about everything that had a clave rhythm: the *danzon*, its vocal successor the *son*, and, yes, the *rumba* itself.

Mario Bauzá did not share in Azpiazu's sudden success. Upon his arrival that spring, he moved in with his cousin Endreira in Harlem, where he encountered not just the inevitable homesickness but an abrupt reality check. The black self-determination he had so admired during his working holiday of three years earlier, he quickly discovered, was largely the product of dis-crimination all too familiar from his upbringing in Cuba. Harlem, he now grasped, had become a black city within a city largely because black people were not equal citizens elsewhere in New York. Bauzá suffered doubly at the hands of this discrimination, given that he was dark enough to be perceived as a Negro by white people, yet not recognized by Harlem's Negro jazz musi-cians as one of their own.

In addition, this was no longer the New York City that had seemed so assuredly prosperous in 1927. The Chrysler Building, arguably the finest of all New York skyscrapers, and at the time the tallest building in the world, may have opened for business on 42nd Street the month after Bauzá arrived, and the Empire State Building may have been rising even higher already down on 34th, but the stock market crash of October 1929 had exposed the fault lines in the American economy, putting a firm halt to the Roaring Twenties two months before the calendar made it official. President Hoover could assert that "the economy is fundamentally sound" as often as he liked, but working and unemployed folk knew otherwise. The depression was about to hit, and Harlem in particular would be left reeling: its black population, crammed into barely two square miles, had already soared to 200,000 people, and fully half of them were living on relief.

Bauzá, then, had little time to waste if he wanted to make a name for himself. He hooked up with Alberto Socarras, a fellow dark-skinned Cuban three years his elder and of remarkably similar circumstances. Having overcome his own hurdles as an immigrant, Socarras, credited with playing the first flute solo on a jazz record, introduced Bauzá around town, and the teenager took whatever work he could get—a job with a Broadway arranger here, a jazz violinist there, and a ragtime pianist when the opportunity arose. But none of it was lucrative, nothing carried the cachet of recording and performing with the great Antonio María Romeu.

That was until the summer of 1931 when Antonio Machín, who had seized on the success of "The Peanut Vendor" to form his own quartet, found himself with a Victor recording session looming and in need of a new trumpet player. Legend—always a tempting fallback—has it that Bauzá persuaded Machín to buy him a trumpet and promptly mastered it in two weeks. Truth, however, was that Bauzá had taken lessons back in Cuba before settling on the saxophone and knew his way around the instrument well enough to avoid embarrassment; even so, his ability to master brass as well as woodwind spoke to his innate talent, and with it, his career took off. That same year found him playing at the Savoy Ballroom for the first time, with Hy Clark's Missourians, who were shortly to become Cab Calloway's orchestra, and at the Central Park Hotel with the jazz elder Noble Sissle.

The Great Depression had a devastating effect on the American recording industry (among other setbacks, record companies ceased their regular field trips to Cuba), but, if anything, it served to increase Harlem's enthusiasm for entertainment, and especially the popularity of the swing orchestras, which fulfilled the audiences' escapist demand for dance music during desperate times. The Savoy Ballroom thrived as the "home of happy feet," and as the undisputed headquarters of the Lindy Hop, throughout the 1930s, setting a new attendance record of 4,600 people in October 1932, at the very height of the depression when, in what was advertised as a "breakfast dance," Cab Calloway and Fletcher Henderson battled Chick Webb to a draw. Webb suffered from spinal tuberculosis that stunted his growth at barely four feet, yet it failed to prevent him from becoming known as the greatest and most influential drummer of his generation. A renowned bandleader, he made his home for the next several years at the Savoy—and when his eleven-piece band found itself in need of a new trumpet player in 1933, he awarded Mario Bauzá the job.

Until this point, Bauzá had been alternating between his Cuban upbringing and his passion for American jazz. Given the boom in the former genre, Bauzá could surely have continued to find work with his countrymen, but even as the Cuban émigré Xavier Cugat set up shop at the Waldorf-Astoria in 1931—where he would stay for the next fifteen years—Bauzá found the Latin groups in New York pandering to the same color coding as in Havana. "Every time I seen it," said Bauzá, who challenged racism in all its forms, "the Latin bands was lily-white. . . . Musicians of my color, they had no opportunity in those bands." The music came similarly watered down for white tastes, especially that of Cugat and his orchestra. And so, when he joined Chick Webb, Bauzá turned his back on that world. For the rest of the 1930s, he would play almost exclusively with black jazz musicians.

The transformation required some education. Webb, who could not read music but was famed for his photographic memory of it, took Bauzá aside for personal training. "I'm going to teach you to pronounce your phrases like an American Negro," the trumpet player recalled being told by his bandleader, whom he described as "an incredible teacher and drummer." Having learned what he called the "differences in *language* between Cuban music and jazz," then without forgetting his expertise in the former, he concentrated his talents on the latter. The rewards came almost immediately. When Webb recorded his theme song "Stompin' at the Savoy" for Columbia in May 1934, Bauzá was granted the first solo. Not an outstanding solo, perhaps—just a few seconds' extemporization with the mute firmly in place—and certainly not one that revealed Bauzá's Cuban roots to the listening audience, but a mark of authority nonetheless. And when Webb's musical director Edgar Sampson vacated that position in 1936, Bauzá was appointed to the role, one that made him responsible for providing arrangements, writing up charts, and, in tandem with Webb, allocating soloists and acquiring new musicians. It had taken him six years, but he was now, to all intents and purposes, on top of the jazz world, in the very heart of Harlem. He celebrated his good fortune by returning to Havana to marry, and then bring back to New York with him, his teenage sweetheart, Estella Grillo.

Playing with Chick Webb, both on records and onstage, Bauzá found himself in the midst of the jazz action as the word "swing" changed, through the course of the 1930s, from verb to adjective to noun, groove taking precedent again over European adherence to melody. Credit for this transition was due in large part to Fletcher Henderson, at Roseland in midtown, and his former arranger Don Redman, at Connie's Inn in Harlem. Each man built up his orchestra until, thirteen or fourteen pieces strong, it contained whole sections (brass, reeds, rhythm) that could play "riffs" in unison, or otherwise distribute themselves across the different notes of a chord, as they engaged in call-and-response with the other sections, building like a Cuban-flavored bolero as they went along. Better yet for jazz fans who had worn out their Paul Whiteman records listening to short bursts of the cornetist Bix Beiderbecke's solos, there was space within and around these extended riffs for soloists to break out and let loose; Henderson was known for allowing every band member take a turn on the stand.

Chick Webb built up his orchestra to a similar size in the mid-1930s, adding the legendary vocalist Ella Fitzgerald in 1935 and the equally acclaimed saxophonist and vocalist Louis Jordan in 1937. Yet Webb would not enjoy enduring fame as a "swing" bandleader commensurate with his popularity at the time. As the titles to his better recordings of the early swing era, like "Go Harlem," "I Can't Dance (I Got Ants in My Pants)," and "King Porter Stomp" suggested, Webb's forte was the stage. Certainly, at the Savoy, Chick Webb reigned supreme. In his regular "battles" against visiting orchestras, he was, by all accounts, defeated only once—and that by Duke Ellington. Even Count Basie, rarely given to musical modesty, noted, "The only time we were bothered was when we played opposite a little guy called Chick Webb," though this choice of wording indicated perhaps more about Webb's posthumous obscurity than his contemporary fame.

Webb had learned how to compensate for his physical limitations with showmanship and skill: he performed on a custom-built Gretsch kit of improbable size given his stature, including a 28-inch bass drum (the front of which was painted with his signature caricature), a Chinese cymbal, and a snare drum hand-built by the concert drummer Billy Gladstone. Said his fellow jazz drummer Louie Bellson, "If you were looking at him from the front, all you saw was a mop of hair and his sticks flying up in the air." Webb's accentuated, syncopated style—a relief and a release from the simple backbeat of almost every jazz drummer before him—had a profound influence on virtually everyone who saw him. Benny Goodman's drummer Gene Krupa once told Louie Bellson, "I'm going up to play opposite Chick Webb and get a drum lesson."

Krupa was white, good-looking, and flashy, all of which helped him become that much more successful than Webb. In early March 1937, during his solos on "Sing Sing Sing," Krupa caused pandemonium in the aisles at midtown's Paramount Theater, bringing swing music very much into the white mainstream. As a result, up to ten thousand people tried to gain entry to the Savoy on May 11, when Goodman's orchestra went up against Webb's. As Bauzá recalled, Webb told his musicians not to bother showing up for work the next day if they missed as much as a single note. They didn't fail him. At the end of the night, Goodman's group congratulated Webb's orchestra on its home court victory. "Krupa goes to Chick like an embarrassed little kid," recalled Bauzá, "and bows down to him with the sticks in his hand and says . . . man, you're the king." Or, as Krupa put it, "I was never cut by a better man."

Just weeks later, in early July, Goodman's group recorded "Sing Sing Sing," Krupa embarking on some nine tom-tom interludes that stretched the recording to over eight minutes. Its release was broken up over two sides of a 78 rpm single, a first in popular music. The recording became Goodman's most renowned of the era, trumping his own fine version of "Stompin' at the Savoy"—which grew more closely associated with the white clarinetist than with the black drummer who had pioneered it.

Indeed, Goodman was credited not just with popularizing swing but, as far as many people were concerned, with inventing the genre. This was part of a continuing process of endemic racism, which in the world of jazz music had already been played out at least twice before: once, in 1917, when the all-white, misnamed Original Dixieland Jazz Band was the first to be granted a recording session; and again in the 1920s, when Paul Whiteman became a superstar for pouring European traditions into this most African American of music. Yet it's worth noting that Goodman and Krupa had crossed the color line back in 1935 by hiring first Teddy Wilson and then Lionel Hampton, at a time when such integration was unheard of—and it was primarily for this reason that they were invited to play at the Savoy. Not just any band of white guys got to go up against Chick Webb.

Back in Havana, political chaos had given way to further repression: after 1933, Cuba went through six heads of state and several rounds of vicious bloodletting in the space of one year, only to end up with the military dictatorship of Fulgencio Batista. With that violence coming on top of the repeal of Prohibition and then the Great Depression in the United States, Americans had stopped visiting the island, and the economy had grown stagnant. Black Cubans were no better off than ever. And so, in 1937, having acquired success and security in New York City, Mario Bauzá invited his wife Estella's brother, Frank "Machito" Grillo, to follow suit. Like Bauzá, Estella and Frank had enjoyed a comparatively comfortable upbringing in Havana, their father a cigar maker who also owned a general store or two. And like Bauzá, they had music in their blood: their sister Graciella established herself as a singer (and also moved to New York at some point in the 1930s), and by 1937 the twenty-five-year-old Frank had created his own reputation as a front man, singing and playing maracas for El Sexteto Naçional, at the Havana Montmartre.

But, like Bauzá, Grillo was dark-skinned and therefore, frustrated by the racism that extended from the politicians all the way down through the Cuban music business, found himself intrigued by his brother-in-law's assurance that in New York "the black man is left alone." And so he emigrated to America, moving in with Estella and Bauzá. "American blacks who were living in Harlem had all established themselves," Grillo later observed, referring to the likes of Fletcher Henderson and Duke Ellington, who lived in comfort in the Sugar Hill enclave. Capitalizing on New York's ongoing fascination with Cuban music, Machito was soon to be found singing for leading groups at the Havana Madrid nightclub on Broadway. Within a year, he was recording not just with some of New York's most renowned Latin *conjuntos* and *cuartetos* but with Xavier Cugat himself. No wonder he later said he found "so much happiness" in Harlem; his own assimilation appeared charmed.

John Birks Gillespie—"Dizzy" to all who subsequently knew him— also arrived in New York City that year. A self-taught musician, the youngest of nine children, he had been raised in poverty in Cheraw, South Carolina, where he was beaten regularly by a father who had died when John was nine years old. Under such circumstances, he had been forced to fend for himself, initially with his fists and, later, with a knife; he rarely left home without a blade in his pocket. Fortunately, this did not prevent him from putting priority on his music, and by the time he hit New York at age nineteen, he had earned himself a reputation for his harmonic invention on the trumpet, along with the nickname, which he'd picked up in Philadelphia, his last port of call, for his comic antics and wayward personality. Gillespie came to New York on the promise of a job in Lucky Millinder's band, and when he found that the gig was already taken, he decided to stay nonetheless, moving in with an older brother already living in Harlem. "Trying to survive in New York without any job was risky," he later wrote in his autobiography, "but it was the only way to make the big time in jazz."

Nineteen thirty-seven was a particularly difficult year in which to do so. New York had been in the grips of the Great Depression for over five years, and Harlem was fast losing its cachet. Its population now approached half a million, yet new arrivals continued to pour in from the Caribbean and the Deep South (people like Grillo and Gillespie), convinced that even depression-era Harlem offered greater hope than the endemic racism and abject poverty of home.

Statistics suggested otherwise. Unemployment in Harlem hovered around 50 percent. Death from tuberculosis ran four times higher than in New York City as a whole, and cancer rates twice as high—yet Harlem had only one hospital. With blacks excluded from living in many other parts of Manhattan, landlords were free to price gouge, and rents were often double those even of the famously poor Lower East Side. Rent parties were for those who knew how to throw them: most tenants who couldn't pay their way took in lodgers, only to find that many were of uncertain backgrounds and engaged in nefarious activities, which served to instill mistrust in a previously tight-knit community. The apartments themselves were squalid, frequently lacking heat, hot water, or bathing facilities. And though New York's mayor, Fiorello La Guardia, had set about a series of reforms in tandem with President Roosevelt's New Deal, progress was slow. No new school had been built in Harlem in twenty-five years, and only one new playground throughout the 1930s. The impact of the New York Housing Authority, established in 1934, was negligible: the Harlem River Houses, the area's first public "projects," which opened in 1937, were funded not by the city but by the federal government.

Even the lifting of Prohibition in 1933 had proved damaging to Harlem, for with it went much of the allure surrounding the speakeasies of Jungle Alley. A riot in 1935, sparked by rumors that a Puerto Rican shoplifter had been beaten to death, targeted white shopkeepers, which further drove down the tourist business; the Cotton Club responded by moving to midtown. A black playwright (Langston Hughes with his long-running *Mulatto*) and black actors (the entire cast of Gershwin's *Porgy and Bess*) may have conquered Broadway, but in Harlem itself the renaissance was over.

Dizzy Gillespie's older brother James proved typical of Harlem's teeming masses: one among tens of thousands who had moved to New York City from the rural South during the 1930s, he was working as a tray boy in midtown, earning just $12.50 a week, half of which went to rent for his one-room apartment. Once Dizzy came to stay, another couple of dollars went to food money for his younger brother, who would repay him by heading out most nights to the Savoy Ballroom, only a block away, and coming home in the dawn hours, usually "with some little chick with him," forcing James to sit in the park until it was time to go to work again.

In other words, his brother's hardships be damned, Dizzy was having the time of his life. He had both sufficient charisma and chops to get himself invited onstage at the Savoy, sitting in on occasion with Teddy Hill, whose former trumpet player Roy Eldridge had strongly influenced his emotionally charged style of playing. The supreme accolade came when he shared the bandstand with Chick Webb. "He must have really liked the way I sounded," said Gillespie, "because he never let nobody sit in, in his band, but me."

It was through jamming onstage with Webb at the Savoy that Gillespie met Bauzá. "I thought he was the greatest thing I had ever heard," Bauzá later stated, noting that, even then, "he came with a new approach and confirmations and a different pattern than the old jazz." The two trumpeters struck up an immediate friendship based on mutual respect: Bauzá for Gillespie's iconoclastic approach to melody, Dizzy for Mario's arranging skills and Latin roots. From here on, Gillespie and Bauzá would rarely stray far apart from each other, socially or musically, becoming one of the most influential and yet undercelebrated partnerships of modern music. Gillespie later said, "Mario was like my father" (though presumably not the one he grew up with), and certainly it's hard to imagine Gillespie's career following anything like the arc that it did without Bauzá's help.

In 1938, Bauzá, who could prove as passionately hotheaded as any other jazzman, left Webb's orchestra after an argument with the Savoy's manager, Charlie Buchanan, over wages. (The following year, Webb succumbed to complications from his spinal tuberculosis, when he was just thirty-four. Ella Fitzgerald took over the orchestra's leadership.) Bauzá filled in with the swing pioneers Fletcher Henderson and Don Redman before being hired by Cab Calloway—and when another trumpet vacancy arose in that orchestra, he helped Gillespie get the job.

By rights, this should have been the pair's dream gig. Calloway—he of "Minnie the Moocher" fame, a Cotton Club residency, and multiple movie appearances, and beloved by audiences for his incorporation of (watered-down) congas and rhumbas (for which the addition of Bauzá provided some authenticity)—led the highest-paid black orchestra in jazz: $80 a week each at the Cotton Club, $100 on tour. Not for them the degradations of Jim Crow America: Calloway and company traveled in their own Pullman coach, with three full-time valets. It was a job most musicians held on to for dear life. But Bauzá and Gillespie were not most musicians, and they chafed at what they took to be the complacency of their elders in the group, who seemed content to perform a version of jazz so mainstream that it might as well have been white. Nor did Calloway afford his musicians the kind of freedoms they took for granted onstage at the Savoy; a keen disciplinarian who maintained a professional distance from his employees, he referred to Bauzá as an "Indian." Other orchestra members dismissed Bauzá's Latin rhythms as "horse music."

This did not prevent Bauzá from stamping his influence on Calloway's music: the difference in rhythmic authenticity between "The Conga-Conga," recorded just before Bauzá joined, and "Chili Con Conga," recorded just after, proved as much. Gillespie, too, made his mark with Calloway, assuming both writing and arrangement credits for "Pickin' the Cabbage," which, as recorded in the spring of 1940, saw Dizzy take an extensive solo and, with it, a major step toward industrywide recognition. But for the most part during their time together in Calloway's orchestra, Bauzá and Gillespie preferred each other's company, along with that of the rhythm section: the bassist Milt Hinton and drummer Cozy Cole. Cole joined the trumpeters in their shared hotel rooms on tour, where Bauzá said that he taught them "how to feel some of the simpler Cuban rhythms." Gillespie, said Bauzá, citing an early example of the vocal style that would later become a genre, "would sing the drum patterns using nonsense syllables, like 'oop-bop-sh'boom.' "

Gillespie duly credited Bauza with teaching him "the importance of Afro-Cuban music." But he and Cole were among the few jazz musicians to show interest. "In those days, those American musicians didn't have the slightest idea about Latin music," said Bauzá, who, having played in four of the leading black swing groups, knew what he was talking about. "The rhythms were too complicated for them."

If the two complementary forms of music were going to meet again, then the introduction would have to come from Latin musicians. Not surprisingly, Bauzá led the way. He and his brother-in-law Frank Grillo, who was approaching his thirties and keen to lead his own group already, first formulated the idea of a full-sized jazz orchestra playing strictly Cuban music in 1939. But it wasn't until late the following year that Bauzá, otherwise still working with Calloway, committed himself to the idea.

The orchestra was unveiled as "Machito and His Afro-Cubans." Said Bauzá, "I am black, which means my roots are in Africa. Why should I be ashamed of that?" Still, the name was stunning for its audacity. "Afro-Cubans," a term still not in wide use in their home country, spoke to the dark-skinned Cuban people, those who took pride in their African roots, who were not willing to see their culture repressed, their drums outlawed, their people discriminated against. It stood in defiance of the American perception of Cuban music as the watered-down rhumbas and congas of Duke Ellington, Xavier Cugat, and Cab Calloway alike. And it provided a nationalist rallying call for the increasing number of Cubans in America, as well as a declaration of shared roots with American Negroes, for whom the term "African American" was, similarly, a long way from being commonplace. The Latin percussionist Bobby Sanabria was among those who recognized the pivotal importance of all this. The naming of the Afro-Cubans, he proclaimed, was "one of the bravest acts in the history of the civil rights movement."

As Harlem became a black residential area in the early twentieth century, the streets to its southeast had remained predominantly Jewish over to Lexington Avenue, and then Italian on out to the East River. That demographic changed once Puerto Rico became a U.S. territory in 1917 and its inhabitants, granted citizenship in the process, began a steady exodus to the American mainland in search of better living standards. Pockets of Puerto Ricans began settling in East Harlem, soon joined by Cubans and other Spanish-speaking immigrants. The metamorphosis of the community was most keenly felt around 110th Street and Fifth Avenue, where the Photoplay Theater changed its name in 1931 to El Teatro San José, and where the Jewish catering hall the Park Palace found itself increasingly hired out for Latino dances under the name of the Park Plaza—as for the Afro-Cubans' debut. By that point, some 45,000 Puerto Ricans lived in the neighborhood, in addition to Cubans, Dominicans, Panamanians, and others. New Yorkers took to calling the neighborhood the Latin Quarter, or Spanish Harlem. The residents referred to it simply as El Barrio.

The first generation of Puerto Ricans "lived by their folkways," said Gabriel Oller, who arrived in the city as a child in the first wave, in 1917 itself, and would become an important figure in the Latin Quarter's musical evolution. "They spoke Spanish, they ate Spanish food only." Integration was slow and gradual. "Although there were some problems with other people, we became friendly neighbors with Jews, who learned to speak Spanish," said Oller. "The Jewish people were our only outside influence." But this new generation of young Latinos in El Barrio then learned to bond with the neighboring black youth of Harlem—especially where dance music was concerned. The Latinos would travel to the Savoy Ballroom en masse for Sunday afternoon matinee shows, before coming back over to the Park Plaza for Sunday evening dances, often bringing black friends from Harlem with them. Still, until the 1940s, there had never been a musical group from one side of Harlem that consciously incorporated sounds from the other.

Machito's Afro-Cubans changed all that—especially after Mario Bauzá left Cab Calloway's orchestra in 1941 to join his brother-in-law's band full-time, a partnership they would maintain for the next thirty-five years. With Bauzá's input, Machito's orchestra soon featured the saxophones, trumpets, piano, and bass that were common to jazz music, but also the timbals, bongo, and maracas that were prevalent in Cuban bands. Significantly, Machito and Bauzá then added the deep tones of the conga drum, making theirs the first orchestra to bring this arsenal of percussion together. Still viewed in Cuba as a tribal carnival instrument, the province of the Abakuá, and unsuitable—even undignified—for large bands, the conga created additional percussive power behind the Afro-Cubans' strings and brass, increasing the group's rhythmic appeal. The Afro-Cubans readily played not just traditional American *son* and *rumba* but the rhumbas and congas that had been so popular with Americans over the past decade, all of which were infused by Bauzá with the melodies, harmonies, and phrasing he had acquired from his years alongside the nation's leading jazz musicians. "Our idea was to bring Latin music up to the standard of the American orchestras," Bauzá stated.

Machito, never as forthright in public as his brother-in-law, with whom he endured a famously productive but occasionally brittle relationship, also admitted the primary influence of American jazz on the Afro-Cubans, citing not just Duke Ellington and, surprisingly, Glenn Miller but two of the great Savoy orchestras. "From Count Basie and Chick Webb we learned to respect musical knowledge," he said. "When you join Afro-Cuban music with good musical knowledge, the result is very exciting music." The Afro-Cubans would serve as a house band at La Conga in midtown Manhattan for several years, steadily building a reputation as the most advanced, adventurous, and frenzied Latin orchestra in New York. That spirit was captured in their first recording session, in June 1941, for Decca, most notably on the exuberant "La Rumbantela," though the most important moment was surely the chorus refrain of "Afro-Cubans" on the gently paced rhumba "Yambu," all the more relevant for a dance said to be directly descended from Congo's *baile yuka*. The following year—by which point America was at war—they returned to the Decca studios with that much more confidence, and Machito's own composition "Sopa de Pichon," sung by the bandleader in a *guajira* style (a peasant or country form of Cuban music), became an overnight hit with the New York Latin music audience.

It would be pleasing to state that the speed at which the Afro-Cubans found themselves recording for a major label was due entirely to the orchestra's live reputation and Decca's foresight. But responsibility lay largely with the ongoing battle between the conservative American Society of Composers, Authors and Publishers (ASCAP) and the radio stations that paid fees to the society for the right to broadcast its members' music. Frustrated by ASCAP's monopoly, the CBS and NBC networks had launched their own society, Broadcast Music Incorporated (BMI), in 1939, and promptly set about signing writers who were not tied to ASCAP—which included, not so coincidentally, many of color. Then, when the radio stations' contract with ASCAP expired at the end of 1940, the broadcasters refused to renew it, turning overnight either to compositions in the public domain or to those they had stockpiled with BMI. This was a boon to jazz and Latin musicians, as it was to those playing blues, gospel, and country, all of whom suddenly found themselves gaining national radio exposure previously denied them by ASCAP's monopoly and, thanks to their membership with BMI, getting paid for it, too. Seizing on the prospect of easy airplay, the record companies set about signing BMI-affiliated acts with a vengeance—and for an all too brief period, "minority" artists like the Afro-Cubans were in vogue.

The success of their initial Decca recordings quickly brought Machito's group the opportunity to back Miguelito Valdés, considered at the time perhaps the greatest singer in Latin American music. Valdés and Machito had been in the same Havana group in the late 1920s, and Bauzá, as was his nature, had made the introductions when Valdés, increasingly frustrated with his country's continued caste system, arrived in New York from Cuba in 1940. Quickly hired by Xavier Cugat, Valdés became known as "Mr. Babalu" for his definitive version of that song in 1941—though a contemporary recording of "Anna Boroco Tinde" was just as big a hit in Spanish Harlem. But then he and Cugat had a clash of egos, and Valdés joined the bill with the easygoing Machito, at La Conga and in the Decca studio. On their July 1942 session—twenty-four songs in just three days—Valdés "sounds like he just got out of jail and is letting it rip," wrote Ned Sublette, in *Cuba and Its Music*. This was particularly true on the Chano Pozo composition "Nagüe," a simple series of repeated refrains about a "brother" being questioned for setting foot in the wrong neighborhood in search of a girl—a subject that Pozo, with his upbringing in the Havana *solar*, was surely familiar with. "Nagüe"'s groove, however, was not so straightforward, rather an archetypal example of complex interpolating Latin rhythms, the kind that American jazz musicians struggled to get their heads around. But as led by Mario Bauzá, the Afro-Cubans' horn section swung like the finest of Savoy orchestras.

A Puerto Rican teenager, Tito Puente, played timbals on several of the Miguelito Valdés tracks, his inclusion one of several examples of Machito and Bauzá reaching across island demarcations. Indeed, at a time when the growing influx of Cubans in El Barrio was causing occasional confrontations, Machito's marriage in 1941 to a Puerto Rican woman, Hilda, proved highly pivotal, demonstrating that New York Latinos of all nationalities could bond together—all the more so as they began to create a new, New York form of Latin music.

"As a kid in Spanish Harlem, I was not interested in the Puerto Rican *trios* or my family's folkloric music," wrote Max Salazar, a Latin music historian himself born in Spanish Harlem to Puerto Rican parents. "But when I heard Miguelito Valdés sing 'Anna Boroco Tinde' . . . and then the following year we heard Machito's 'Sopa de Pichon.' . . . Forget it, that was it. We were Latinos again, and that just made us proud."

2

CUBOP CITY AND ALL THAT JAZZ

n January 1942, a twenty-one-year-old Charlie Parker blew into New York, from Kansas City, for a residency at the Savoy with Jay McShann's Orchestra. A self-taught alto sax player, whose overwhelming talent and generous heart failed to fully balance his famously troubled soul, Parker could coax previously unimagined melodies, harmonies, and rhythms from his instrument—an ability that can be traced to his familiarity with, and love of, the twelve-bar blues. Bird—short for Yardbird, a name he acquired in a midwestern touring incident—"could play anything," said McShann, "because, primarily, Bird was the greatest blues player in the world."

That winter, when the Savoy shut up shop for the night, Parker would wander a few blocks south to join the after-hours jam sessions at Monroe's Uptown House, on 134th Street and Seventh Avenue, where Barron's Exclusive used to be. A basement club opened in the late 1930s by the local entrepreneur Clark Monroe ("the dark Gable" to his friends, he was also Billie Holiday's brother-in-law), the Uptown House attracted the type of white, A-list movie stars and musicians who had rarely been seen in Harlem since the heyday of the Cotton Club. Parker had played Monroe's before, in 1939, when he arrived in New York on his own, a teenage hopeful like Bauzá and Gillespie (and so many others) before him. But, intimidated perhaps by the wealth of talent at the Uptown House, he had failed to make a firm impression and had taken, instead, to visiting Dan Wall's Chili House, on Seventh Avenue and 139th Street. There the guitarist Biddy Fleet would invert the guitar chords of jazz standards, and Parker learned to abandon the original tune to "Cherokee" and instead use the higher intervals of the chords to create new melodic lines. Some have called this the first stirrings of a new style of jazz; but there were few around to witness it, and Parker headed home to Kansas City, somewhat defeated.

In New York the second time around, Parker's name carried considerably more weight, his solo on "Cherokee" at the Savoy marking him as a rising star. Accordingly, he fitted in much easier with the jam sessions at Monroe's, where he recalled Count Basie's tenor sax player Don Byas, "playing everything there was to be played," and Vic Coulsen, "a trumpet man . . . playing things I'd never heard." This, he said, "was the kind of music that caused me to quit McShann and stay in New York." Others heard that McShann had in fact sacked Parker for his already worrisome drug habits; either way, Bird stayed behind when McShann moved on, taking up semipermanent residence at Monroe's, where he flourished in the nonconformist setting. The pianist Allen Tinney noted that when musicians from the big white swing bands of Glenn Miller and Harry James stopped by, "they would say, 'What the heck are these guys playing?' Because it was different."

While many of the musicians came to Monroe's from their stints at high-paying ballrooms like the Savoy, others came direct from the other great Harlem jam joint, the saxophonist Henry Minton's club. Located in the Cecil Hotel on 118th Street, and closing at a regular hour, Minton's Playhouse gathered steam in late 1940 with the hiring of Teddy Hill, whose own orchestra had recently disbanded, as manager of the house band. Hill excelled in his new role, bringing in the same drummer, Kenny Clarke, he had fired from his own orchestra for throwing too many syncopated "bombs" into the then rigid format of the swing arrangement. Clarke in turn brought in the guitarist Charlie Christian from Benny Goodman's group; it's a sign of how they turned the jazz "rules" around at that venue that a live recording from Minton's of "Topsy" by the pair was later renamed "Swing to Bop."

Also to be found at Minton's most nights was Thelonious Monk. An obsessive and determined pianist whom Hill often had to throw out in order to lock up the club, Monk set out in jazz "to play [his] own chords." At Minton's, deconstructing jazz standards (e.g., "I Got Rhythm") until they had become his own compositions (e.g., "Round Midnight"), he did just that. Honing in on the sound of the minor-sixth chord, and then anchoring it with the sixth in the bass, he came up with what was called the half-diminished chord, which soon found its way into other musicians' arrangements.

Clearly, the regulars at Monroe's and Minton's were united by a desire to explore uncharted territory. For though the big swing orchestras continued to dominate the jazz scene, commanding the biggest bookings and selling the most records, they had grown large and unwieldy, with individual creativity stifled under the weight of set arrangements. Star vocalists were increasingly taking the place of star instrumentalists, and as stasis set in among the older musicians, it was no surprise that the younger ones increasingly preferred the freedom of the after-hours "cutting contests" against their peers to the ensemble riffs of their paid performances.

Not that such moonlighting was actively endorsed. "Cab [Calloway] frowned on the idea of guys going out blowing," said Dizzy Gillespie. "But I went anyway. Shit, fuck Cab! I was thinking about my own development. When we were in New York, after the show, I'd go to Minton's and then to Monroe's Uptown House and jam until 7:00 in the mornings."

Calloway and Gillespie were soon to part company anyway. In September 1941, after a concert in Connecticut, Calloway accused Gillespie of throwing a spitball at him onstage. ("Dizzy was a devil," said Calloway; "if something like that happened, you couldn't look at nobody but Dizzy.") Gillespie protested his innocence, but when Calloway reputedly slapped him, the trumpet player instinctively drew his blade. After he was fired, word went out that he had actually stabbed the bandleader; it was never proven.

Unapologetic, certainly undeterred, Gillespie threw himself into a new phase as a hyperactive New York City freelancer, and a permanent presence at one or another of the Harlem jam spots. "There's a big question about which place had the most memorable influence on the music," said Gillespie. "The rhythmic aspect was Minton's, the harmonic aspect was Monroe's Uptown House—it could be divided up that way." It could also be noted that Parker held court at Monroe's, and Gillespie, certainly earlier in the night, at Minton's—where, during its heyday, there were sometimes as many as thirty musicians trying to get onstage. Gillespie, exemplifying both his leadership role and his penchant for mischief, began inviting a coterie of his closest jamming friends to his Harlem apartment, where they rehearsed purposefully complex chord progressions and key changes to otherwise familiar songs. Back at Minton's, they'd fall into these unfamiliar arrangements whenever they needed to rid the stage of an overconfident and unwelcome visiting musician. As the jam sessions became manageable again, under Gillespie's influence the quality of the playing grew ever more technical, ever farther away from swing, and ever closer to a new form of New York jazz.

Dizzy Gillespie and Charlie Parker had met in Kansas City in 1940, during a Cab Calloway tour. Hearing the saxophonist "was similar to a laser," said Gillespie (in a hotel room after his show), and though the pair did not meet again until Parker came to New York in 1942, they immediately picked up their relationship at Minton's and Monroe's, becoming fast friends. At the end of the year, they were hired together for a lengthy tour by the veteran pianist Earl "Fatha" Hines, who was enjoying considerable commercial success with his blues-based singer Billy Eckstine. Over the next nine months, just as Gillespie and Bauzá had shared a stage and hotel rooms together, influencing and teaching each other, now Dizzy and Bird played together both onstage and off.

Hines recalled each of them having a photographic mind, able to take something they'd just studied in the other's exercise book and insert it straight into a live set—an achievement all the greater given that Parker switched from alto to tenor sax especially for this tour. Not that the aging bandleader necessarily understood what he was hearing from his young charges: "It was getting away from the melody a lot," Hines noted, though this is difficult to prove, as there are virtually no recordings of either Dizzy or Bird, or Billy Eckstine himself, playing with the Earl Hines Orchestra.

This loss has commonly been blamed on twin calamities that befell the music industry. One was brought on by America's entry into World War II: the U.S. government commandeered shellac, the primary ingredient in records, for the manufacture of munitions. The other was brought on by the American Federation of Musicians (AFM). James Petrillo, the union's combative president, had long argued that by allowing their recordings to be played on radio stations that otherwise relied on live performances, professional musicians were sacrificing long-term livelihoods for short-term gain. Throughout the 1930s, both the Federal Radio Commission (which became the Federal Communications Commission in 1934) and the NBC and CBS networks appeared to have agreed, and artists on the scale of Paul Whiteman had issued their records with the warning "not licensed for radio broadcast." But a court case brought in 1940 found no legal basis for such a restriction, and an FCC policy that required stations to identify the playing of prerecorded music was rescinded. Hoping to stem this evident shift in the tide, from August 1942 Petrillo had the AFM withhold licenses for recordings until the major record companies agreed to compensate the union with a royalty on every record. Despite government intervention—indeed, despite the American Federation of Labor's pledge not to strike while America was at war—Petrillo kept his word.

The major labels were reduced to releasing a cappella vocal sessions (as with Frank Sinatra), or records featuring instruments not covered by AFM membership: the harmonica, ukulele, and so on. Decca, the smallest of the three major labels, succumbed to the AFM in late 1943, but RCA Victor and Columbia did not submit until a year later, in 1944. Victory ultimately belonged to the union—though not to those musicians like Gillespie and Parker who were unable officially to record at such a prolific and experimental period in their careers. Yet while the lack of Hines Orchestra recordings is consistently mourned by jazz aficionados, it could be argued that the ban enabled his band members' new sound to better incubate itself, sharpening its edge so that it would explode on the marketplace fully formed, appearing for most listeners as if out of nowhere.

Certainly, the core members of the Hines Orchestra enjoyed themselves so much that they soon headed back out on tour—but this time the leader was Eckstine himself, whose popularity as a jazz blues singer had grown close to that of a matinee idol. Gillespie, in his first role as musical director, promptly hired Charlie Parker to lead the reeds; during its first year together, the Eckstine orchestra also attracted—though not all at the same time, the war taking its toll on consistency—Sarah Vaughan, Art Blakey, Dexter Gordon, Howard McGhee, Oscar Pettiford, and Fats Navarro. This extraordinary group of talent has lent the Billy Eckstine band a similarly retroactive "legendary" status, along with a frustration that, on those occasions when it did hit the studio, it was to serve as a backing band for Eckstine's ballads rather than as showcase for the musicians' own new styles. Still, Gillespie later complimented Eckstine as "probably the best band leader I had. He understood the music, he was a supporter of the music, a supporter of your inventing."

The singer recalled battles with his booking agency over his new musical direction: "They didn't stop to realize that I was already hooked into this thing," he said, calling it "a feeling among a nucleus at that time of younger people, of hearing something else." Certainly his orchestra had a galvanizing effect on young black audiences as it toured the country, a teenage Miles Davis proving sufficiently energized by witnessing Dizzy and Bird together in St. Louis—and sitting in with them, too—that he promptly moved to New York City to be "where all these bad musicians were."

Yet such tours were not the norm during the war years. Along with shellac, the government commandeered the rubber needed for new tires and, early in 1943, banned all "nonessential" driving, by which time fuel rationing had been in effect on the East Coast for months and the use of private buses completely forbidden. The overall result was that jazz players generally avoided touring, setting up shop in a major city—New York if possible—where they could bounce from paid evening residencies to all-night jam sessions and back again, assuming they weren't drafted in the process.

With all this talent concentrated in Manhattan, the locus of jazz now shifted from Harlem to midtown. The change had been a long time coming: as far back as 1936, Milt Gabler of the Commodore Records store on 42nd Street had moved his Sunday afternoon jam sessions into the Famous Door on 52nd Street between Fifth and Sixth Avenues. Soon enough, the surrounding basement bars began imitating Gabler's parties, and the block became known as Swing Street. By 1942, with wartime dollars flooding into midtown in the form of off-duty servicemen, talent scouts from the clubs on 52nd Street were frequenting Minton's and Monroe's, luring the best talent downtown. If there was a tipping point, it came in 1943, when none other than Clark Monroe moved his house band to the Spotlite. With Minton's the only jam venue of note left in Harlem, most musicians, even those who lived uptown, followed the flow of money to Swing Street.

Dizzy Gillespie was prominent among them. After his tour with Eckstine, he embarked on a monthlong 52nd Street booking with Duke Ellington. However, he found the senior musicians impossibly aloof, and it would be his last engagement with the old guard. Instead, Gillespie formed his own band, in partnership with the bassist Oscar Pettiford, for a residency at the Onyx, also on 52nd Street; he asked Charlie Parker to join them, but Bird, recently remarried and drifting from D.C. to Kansas City and Chicago, taking a growing heroin addiction with him, either didn't get the telegram or simply didn't bother to respond.

Even without Bird's participation, the Gillespie-Pettiford group, with Max Roach on drums, solidified a number of arrangements that became standards of the new jazz movement, the titles mixing allegiance to their new surroundings ("52nd Street Theme") with playful humor (the meaningless "Salt Peanuts"). Pettiford helped compose many of these tracks, but it was Gillespie, a born leader, who imbued them with originality. "Of all the people who were taking part in this revolution, Dizzy was the one who really intellectualized it," said the Onyx group's pianist, Billy Taylor.

But Gillespie did so in a deliberately primitive—or perhaps one should say pronounced—manner. "Dizzy had to hum everything to everybody to get them to see what he was talking about," recalled their sax player, Budd Johnson. Scat singing the melodies, much as he had the Latin rhythms he learned from Bauzá while on tour with Calloway, Gillespie repeatedly returned to the phrase "be-bop," and a track by that name entered the Onyx Club band's set list late in 1943.

Bebop was the term by which the new jazz announced itself after the war, but, stressed Kenny Clarke, in a complaint common to musical pioneers through the ages, "We never labeled the music." Still, a hilarious story by Woody Herman's drummer, Dave Tough, demonstrates just how revolutionary the Onyx quintet sounded: "As we walked in, these cats snatched up their horns and blew crazy stuff. One would stop all of a sudden and another would start for no reason at all. We never could tell when a solo was supposed to begin or end. Then they all quit at once and walked off the stand. It scared us."

It was meant to. Tough, it should be noted, was white. The bebop pioneers were exclusively black, and implicit in the development of their new, technically brilliant music was racial pride, a determination to demonstrate the arrival of the black musician as a genius on his *own* terms, not those of the white patrician. Their battle was not so much about equality or acceptance as about *rights*. If at times bebop proved overly intellectual, technical, or confrontational—and perhaps, as witnessed by Dave Tough (who himself would embrace bebop), all three at once—there's every evidence to suggest that such attributes were, initially, necessary for the culture's advancement.

Meantime, the music trade at large took note of how these younger black musicians were abandoning bigger orchestras for the security and sanctity of what was labeled "the cocktail market." The stages at the back of the 52nd Street basement clubs were barely big enough for a handful of musicians; the tables themselves scarcely catered to fifty people. In such close quarters, the audience had no opportunity to dance; people were forced to lean in and listen.

Besides, a citywide cabaret law, introduced back in the midtwenties in an attempt to legislate the inevitable by-products of Prohibition, ensured that not just any old club could feature dancing (by three or more people). For that, the venue needed a license, and the city was never widely disposed to distribute them freely. Such a law—which already seemed arcane even as it went into effect—might not have carried much weight in Harlem, but midtown clubs, especially those prominently situated on 52nd Street, could less afford to ignore it. They also had to adhere to a cabaret tax introduced in the spring of 1944, ostensibly to raise further wartime funds, though perhaps also to deter people from too much hedonism while America's youth was dying by the thousands overseas: this tax imposed a hefty surcharge on venues that offered acting, singing, or dancing. Crucially, however, instrumental music was exempted, a boon for the future beboppers. Of equal importance, as 52nd Street filled with black jazz musicians working in smaller, more self-contained units, the club owners gradually relaxed their color restrictions, at first only for the musicians who liked to stop in and hear one another's sets on break, but steadily to include black paying customers, too. White servicemen from other parts of America, where the races did not sit together at the same table or on the same bandstand, occasionally instigated violence, but there was simply too much nervous energy in Manhattan during wartime for the island to stay segregated.

Machito's Afro-Cubans spent much of the war just a couple of blocks from Swing Street, at La Conga Club, on 51st Street. In the first few months of 1943, the Afro-Cubans' lineup was ruptured by multiple draft calls, including that of Machito himself. The front man hired a reputable Puerto Rican replacement for his vocals, brought in his sister Graciela as additional singer, and left the group in the highly capable hands of his brother-in-law. No sooner had he departed in May than his musicians,

ad-libbing around the melody of "El Botellero," came up with a new song during their weekly Monday rehearsal. An observer declared it as good as
tanga—slang for marijuana—and under that name, the new number was
introduced at La Conga the following week. When Machito returned on
leave just a couple of weeks later, he discovered that "Tanga" was both opening and closing the set.

It should not have been hard to understand why. "Tanga" was, by all
accounts, the first truly Afro-Cuban jazz composition, a natural summation
of the group's goals. Written in *son clave,* it brought timbals, bongos, congas,
and maracas together in typically infectious manner, making it an immediate
hit with the Latin dancers; yet it was also punctuated by bold, abrasive, arguably discordant brass parts straight out of the new jazz that was being formulated on nearby 52nd Street. This was culture clash of the most emphatic
kind, one that could have happened only in New York—and it might have
had a greater and more immediate impact had it not been written in the
midst of the recording ban.

Machito and his Afro-Cubans were already too established to risk breaking the AFM strike, at least under their own name; besides, their career had
been well served when Decca had rushed them in, under the wire, to record
those twenty-four sides backing Miguelito Valdés. But the same rules did not
apply to the hundreds of Latin musicians lower down the ladder, who were
energized by the Afro-Cubans, or to the entrepreneurs who established labels
to record them. Sidney Siegel, owner of a furniture and record store called,
with appropriate deference to old and new East Harlem, Casa Siegel, established Seeco Records, signing up dozens of (mostly) Puerto Rican musicians
who recorded, in midtown studios, after hours and behind locked doors—just
in case a rep from Local 802 came snooping around. Casa Siegel served as
both retailer and distributor, exporting the releases, sometimes by the thousands, back to Puerto Rico, where there were plenty of record players but no
recording industry. Gabriel Oller did much the same with his Spanish Music
Center store in the middle of El Barrio, at 110th Street and Fifth Avenue,
launching SMC Records. As Seeco and SMC established a healthy financial
base, Spanish Harlem began to reverberate to the sound of its own music.

West on 125th Street, the Rainbow Music Shop had been sponsoring
Saturday Swing Concerts at the Savoy Ballroom, for which Dizzy Gillespie
had joined Coleman Hawkins, the renowned tenor sax player recently

returned from self-imposed exile in London. The Rainbow now parlayed this sponsorship into a February 1944 recording session to launch a label, Apollo, the name of which traded, disingenuously, off the renowned theater down the block. Hawkins, seizing the opportunity to reestablish himself and fully aware of what was going on downtown, brought to the studio the very cream of 52nd Street, including Vic Coulsen, Ray Abrams, Oscar Pettiford, Max Roach, Don Byas, Budd Johnson—and Dizzy Gillespie.

Was this the first bebop session? Many believe so, pointing to two of the six sides in particular. A Gillespie composition originally commissioned by the swing clarinetist Woody Herman, "Woody 'n' You" provided ample opportunity to elaborate on Thelonious Monk's half-diminished chord. Initially, its melody was performed in unison by the familiar swing band sections; but with his solo, Gillespie gradually introduced "off" notes, the unusual harmonic extremes that were often heard as "mistakes" in the early days of bebop. This idea was elaborated on a week later, and with more distinctive results (though with the same musicians), on Hawkins's "Disorder at the Border," which took the familiarity of the blues and, via the solos traded by Hawkins and Gillespie, introduced notes, rhythms, and harmonies not previously considered part of that genre.

Like any new independent label—but especially during World War II—Apollo struggled with distribution, and word spread slowly of the artistic imagination contained in these recordings. But once the AFM ban was fully lifted, at the end of 1944, along with an easement on shellac supplies now that the Allies controlled the Pacific, independent jazz labels established themselves from coast to coast, seizing on the major companies' slow response to the new music. In January 1945, Gillespie entered the studio as bandleader for the first time, recording for the Manor label; the next month, he and Charlie Parker made their studio debut together for Guild; and in May, the pair consolidated their recording reputations by leading Dizzy's All Star Quintet through "Shaw' Nuff," "Hot House," and a frenetic but playful version of "Salt Peanuts" for Guild, each of which became bebop standards. That November, Gillespie was guest on Charlie Parker's adaptation of his beloved "Cherokee" for Savoy; by this point, six years since he first began improvising new melodies to it at Dan Wall's Chili House with Biddy Fleet, Parker had rendered the piece so personal, and this landmark recording rewrote the original so completely, that it was given a new title: "Koko."

The market could barely keep up with the pace. Gillespie's January recordings of "Salt Peanuts" and "Bebop" saw release only in the summer, long after he and Parker had launched a residency together, at the Three Deuces on 52nd Street, making up for Bird's no-show at the Onyx the preceding year with what Dizzy later called "the height of the perfection of our music." At the same time, they also appeared in a couple of concerts together at Manhattan's Town Hall, a move intended to confirm the credibility of their original style.

Whatever the environment, Parker and Gillespie drove each other to fresh musical heights during their performances together that year. "Every time they got on the stand, it was competitive," said the trombonist Trummy Young. "They loved one another. But they would try to extend each other to make a move. And to me, it was a thrilling thing. . . . Bird had such a prolific mind. You could play a song, and he could play a counter melody to it right away without ever—not even think about it."

Indeed, Gillespie and Parker demonstrated such an intrinsic understanding of each other that "they used to play lines together just like each other," said Miles Davis. "You couldn't tell the difference." Proof exists on the studio recording of "Koko," on which the pair played almost impossibly complex chromatic riffs in apparent unison, defying generations of imitators and acolytes to match them note for note.

Their residency at the Three Deuces put them at the very center of the jazz world, yet Gillespie could not bear to stand still; he had a missionary zeal to spread his gospel and wanted the acclaim for doing so. Twice over the next year, he and Charlie Parker left the relative sanctuary of New York behind. Their "Hep-sations 1945" tour found Gillespie leading a big band for the first time, but rather than the intended concert halls, it was booked into ballrooms in the Deep South. Dizzy's carefully self-cultivated image—goatee, horn-rim glasses, and jive patter, all of which made him an icon of cool in New York— could not compensate for his inexperience and stiffness as a front man, and the audiences found they could not dance to the complex rhythmic patterns, unorthodox harmonies, and dissonant solos. As a result, says Gillespie's biographer Alyn Shipton, "The Hep-sations of 1945 marks the moment that jazz formally ceased to be the music of black social dance."

That December, Gillespie took his quintet, including Parker and the drummer Al Haig, out to Los Angeles, where their eight-week residency at

Billy Berg's proved a disaster, the full house giving way to empty seats within a matter of days. On the West Coast, the "attitude" that had enabled Gillespie to carve out his niche in New York was now seen as "arrogance." Gillespie could afford to wax philosophical about the experience years later. "It was very new music and California was a very long way off," he said. "They were behind the evolution. Only the guys from New York that were out there knew what was happening with the new music." Still, matters were hardly helped by Parker's growing heroin addiction; the world's most influential (and argu-ably most brilliant) sax player was clearly in decline. When the residency concluded, Parker stayed on in California, where he eventually suffered a mental breakdown and was institutionalized for several months. Gillespie, Haig, and the others returned to New York in February 1946; they were in a Manhattan studio recording "A Night in Tunisia" for RCA Victor's *New 52nd Street Jazz* album—the first bebop compilation in everything but name—so quickly that it was as if they'd hoped that nobody had noticed their absence.

That same spring of 1946, there came to New York a Cuban who would have an indelible impact on Dizzy Gillespie's music—and with it, the whole field of Afro-Cuban jazz. Directly descended from West African slaves, the son of a shoeshine boy, Chano Pozo's Havana childhood had been one of poverty and crime, his teen years spent in and out of reform schools. Yet he rose from these desperate beginnings to become an accom-plished singer and dancer, the composer of the Cuban classics "Blen, Blen, Blen," "Parampampin," and "Nagüe." And he was highly revered for his tal-ents on the conga drums, especially when performing the music of the Congolese Abakuá during the five-week carnival period. Pozo pronounced himself a practitioner of the African Yoruba faith, cloaking himself in the imagery of its thunder god Shangó, which in the Cuban Santería religion (a blend of Yoruba and Catholicism) took refuge in the disarming guise of Saint Barbara. Yet he never formally accepted Santería.

The black-skinned Pozo, both fiercely bellicose and shamelessly flam-boyant, spent the money he acquired (primarily from his songwriting) on clothes, cars, women, and cocaine. In 1943, hearing about popularity of "Nagüe" in America, as recorded by Machito and Miguelito Valdés, he demanded cash from his music publisher; when he didn't get it, he trashed the office and vowed to return the next day. An armed bodyguard was waiting and, when Pozo attacked him, responded with three bullets, one of which lodged permanently in the percussionist's lower spine. This did not stop Pozo from working, but when Machito's Afro-Cubans came to Havana for a week-long engagement in 1945, Pozo concurred with Mario Bauzá that his talents would be better served—and his safety more likely guaranteed—in New York City.

On the night he arrived, in May 1946, Valdés introduced Pozo onstage at La Conga. But though Pozo had expected to find work in Manhattan with his fellow Afro-Cubans, Machito already had a conga player. Pozo, whose English was almost nonexistent, found himself playing instead as one of a trio of drummers for the leading black dancer and choreographer Katherine Dunham on her Bal Nègre revue, which included a piece she had premiered the preceding year, named for what she had discovered from her travels was "probably the strongest of the African gods," Pozo's adopted Shangó.

The struggling Pozo was soon joined in New York by his friend Arsenio Rodriguez, the celebrated *tres* guitarist, singer, and composer. Like Pozo, Rodriguez was a member of the Abakuá; he could trace his ancestry through his grandfather's slave ship journey directly back to the sect's Congolese roots. Renowned in Cuba for leading the first *conjuto* to include the conga drum, Rodriguez had been blinded in childhood after being kicked by a mule. He came to New York primarily because he had heard of an operation that might restore his eyesight: the Afro-Cubans were part of an all-star benefit concert at the Hotel Diplomat, on 43rd Street, to raise money for his visit. When he subsequently learned that his blindness was inoperable, he went home and immediately wrote the enduring "La Vida es un Sueño," or "Life Is But a Dream."

Rodriguez and Pozo had recorded with Valdés shortly before Valdés left for fame and fortune in New York. Appropriately then, Valdés implored Gabriel Oller, who had moved his business to the corner of 52nd Street and Sixth Avenue and launched a second label, Coda Records, to make the most of this temporary alignment of great talent. Oller obliged, and in February 1947 Pozo and Rodriguez collaborated in two classic sessions for Coda: one, an all-star percussion group recording authentic Havana rumbas, the other with members of the Afro-Cubans, featuring the up-and-coming Puerto

Rican Tito Rodriguez (no relation to Arsenio) as featured singer. Three
Chano Pozo compositions were recorded at the second session, of which
"Rumba en Swing" was a response of sorts to Woody Herman's "Bijou (Rumba
à la Jazz)," distending midway through a relatively tame piece of Latin dance
into a wild percussion *montuno*. (The session was credited to the Chano
Pozo Orchestra.) These recordings survive as notable testimony to Pozo and
Rodriguez's influence on Afro-Cuban music; they also capture the Machito
Orchestra at a time when it could do no wrong. Just a month earlier, the
Afro-Cubans had lined up alongside Stan Kenton's Orchestra at Town Hall,
the first time Latin and jazz groups had appeared on the same bill at a formal
concert. Kenton—a white bandleader who fitted neither the old swing formula nor quite the new bebop sound, instead calling his music "progressive
jazz"—was quick-witted enough to borrow Machito's rhythm section for his
March 1947 hit recordings of "The Peanut Vendor" and a tribute song, additional payment of sorts, entitled "Machito."

The popularity of Herman's and Kenton's forays into Afro-Cuban music
did not sit well with Dizzy Gillespie, whose knowledge of jazz history saw
him inherently opposed to the process by which white musicians, if not
always maliciously, appropriated and resold (to white audiences) the sounds
of black and now Latin musicians, frequently leaving the originators languishing in semi-obscurity. Still pushing his own big band concept, but now
wary of leaving 52nd Street for any length of time, he was busy squeezing up
to sixteen musicians of his Dizzy Gillespie Orchestra onto the stage at the
Spotlite. He also rearranged his own composition "Bebop" into the yet more
frenetic "Things to Come," which, when recorded in the summer of 1946,
served as an epiphany for a young bandleader in Havana of Cuban-Irish par-
entage. "If this is the shape of things to come," Chico O'Farrill asked himself,
"how in the hell am I going to cut it?" His answer? Step up the quality of his
own band in Havana, incorporate some of these bebop jazz elements into the
Latin rhythms, and plan his own journey to New York to witness this phenomenon in person.

Yet, for all his influence and growing fame at the Spotlite, Gillespie recognized that his big band was losing the essence that had first made jazz so
popular. The most common complaint against bebop, after all, was the hardest to deny: that you couldn't dance to it. He called on his old friend Mario
Bauzá for advice—and Bauzá immediately recommended the underemployed

and overqualified Chano Pozo. In September 1947, Pozo made his performing debut with Gillespie at Carnegie Hall on a bill that saw Dizzy reunited with Charlie Parker and that also starred Ella Fitzgerald. There, on Manhattan's most celebrated concert stage, Pozo stunned the highbrow audience with the power and precision (and, many felt compelled to note, the primal nature) of his conga drumming and his West African chanting on a two-part piece entitled, with the utmost clarity of intent, "Cubana Be/Cubana Bop."

Dizzy's bassist Ray Brown quit soon after—though not because—Pozo arrived, noting later that while he appreciated the Cuban's playing on Latin numbers, it "didn't sit real good with me on every song." His replacement Al McKibbon took a more casual approach: "To hear a drum played by hand was new to me. . . . I'm from the Midwest." For his part, Gillespie called Pozo "the greatest percussionist I ever heard." As touring became more palatable again in the postwar climate in which Gillespie was now a cult star, he, McKibbon, and the drummer Kenny Clarke—back in the fold after three years in the service—were among those to whom Pozo handed out various drums on the bus and, communicating through a mutually shared pigeon language, showed how Afro-Cubans could keep several polyrhythmic phrases going at once. "We'd sing and play all down the highway," recalled Gillespie with fondness.

Their creative zeal emboldened, the Dizzy Gillespie Orchestra recorded eight songs for RCA Victor in December 1947. "Manteca" was the hit—a bright, brassy tune that could best be labeled Afro-Cuban swing. Gillespie allowed that the Pozo composition was "dynamite" and "probably the largest selling record I ever had." More ambitious, however, was the recording of "Cubana Be/Cubana Bop," which built considerably upon the version intro-duced at Carnegie Hall. "Cubana Be" started out all conga and drums, quickly leading into an unusual modal brass theme composed by George Russell, before bringing up a particularly chromatic Dizzy solo; "Cubana Bop" opened with Pozo chanting, leading a call-and-response of the song's title over his congas, before a collision of horns and piano intruded on their dissonant march toward the finale. Gillespie may not have been first to capi-talize on his own love of Latin rhythms in jazz, but he had delivered a defini-tive statement.

The word "Cubop" now caught on as a hip, yet perfectly accurate, descriptive for this fusion of sounds, and over the next couple of years, cross-fertilization proved an ongoing, continual creative process. Late in 1948, Norman Granz, a jazz aficionado who had founded Clef Records (and would later launch the premier jazz label Verve), brought the sax players Charlie Parker and Flip Phillips together with Machito's orchestra to record half a dozen pure Cubop cuts that were grouped on the album *Machito Jazz with Flip and Bird*. That these were the Afro-Cubans' first studio recordings to be marketed to a white audience since the Decca sessions of 1942 spoke to how, in the wake of the various wartime strikes and shortages, and with ASCAP welcomed back into the fold alongside BMI, the major music industry had once again abandoned minority tastes and focused on the mainstream.

But better late than never: with Phillips in shining form, the percussion given plenty of space to percolate, and aided by Granz's industry influence, "Tanga" became a major hit on jazz radio, setting a public standard for Afro-Cuban jazz five years after the song had actually been written. Parker's chance to glow came on the two-part "No Noise" and "Mango Mangue," his solos wafting dreamily in and around the up-tempo Latin dance rhythms. Granz also produced Clef/Mercury sessions for Machito's Afro-Cubans without the bebop musicians, resulting in the party anthems "Gone City," "Bop Champagne," and the Mario Bauzá composition "Cubop City." Twenty years after Bauzá had first come to New York hoping to marry the Afro-Cuban music of his homeland with that of American jazz, he had gone several steps further, helping to broker an entire movement of music that included the two greatest brass players of his generation.

Unfortunately, Cubop City proved too much for Chano Pozo. In November 1948, the percussionist set off on an American tour with Gillespie's orchestra. When his precious congas were stolen in Raleigh, North Carolina, he returned to New York, initially intending to purchase another pair. Once back in Harlem, however, he told Miguelito Valdés that he planned to wait out the tour rather than deal with the constant discrimination he experienced down south. On December 2, he bought some marijuana from Eusebio "El Cabito" Muñoz, a decorated war veteran who doubled as a local numbers runner and drug dealer. Dissatisfied with its quality, he accosted Muñoz outside the Rio Bar, on Lenox Avenue and 111th Street, and demanded his money back. When he wasn't obliged, he slapped the seller around a few times. Then he went inside the bar for a drink.

Pozo had not learned his lesson from back in Havana. Muñoz returned to the Rio with a loaded gun. As he later explained in court, his street reputation could not survive the humiliation of being beaten in public. Inside the bar, Muñoz confronted Pozo and, in the ensuing dispute, shot him dead.

Dizzy Gillespie later remarked of Pozo that he was a "roughneck" to the core, and that was proven by the circumstances of his death. But Gillespie loved Pozo, and, having allowed the Cuban to leave his tour and return to New York, he felt some guilt, if not actual responsibility, for the percussionist's demise. The man who had once stood accused of slicing Cab Calloway with a blade now became a strict disciplinarian, firing anyone he even suspected of drug abuse. He was kept unpleasantly active in this capacity, as up-and-coming jazz players convinced themselves that the path to Charlie Parker's greatness lay not in his talents but in his addiction to heroin.

In the meantime, it was left to Valdés and Mario Bauzá, who together had so fervently welcomed Pozo to New York not two years earlier, to identify his body, which was then returned to Cuba. On December 4, 1948, the day before Pozo's funeral, Cuban followers of Santería celebrated the Feast of Saint Barbara, and her Yoruba guise as Shangó. The thunder god whom Pozo had successfully brought alive in his music had, claimed many Santeros— Chano's sisters among them—punished the great percussionist for wrapping himself in the religion without committing to it. In New York, less superstitious fans of Afro-Cuban jazz merely mourned how, at the very moment this new music was receiving international acclaim on a par with its partner bebop, one of its leading lights had been killed on the streets of Harlem— and all for a dime bag of *tanga*.

3

THE HARLEM
HIT PARADE

The early 1930s found Manhattan's 125th Street in a state of flux. As one of the major cross-streets above Central Park, 125th had long been a base for theaters, from the Gotham on the East Side to the Alhambra on the West, which changed hands almost as regularly as they switched formats: from musicals to movies, variety to vaudeville, minstrelsy to burlesque. At the bottom of the artistic ladder, burlesque took risqué comedy and dance, stripped it almost naked, and dangled it at the very limits of the law. Along the way, it became the most popular and the most profitable form of working-class entertainment; there was no shortage of pretty young women willing to strip-tease down to their nipple pasties for income during the depression, just as there was no lack of voyeuristic men able to find the very small change it cost to go see them.

The two biggest burlesque names in New York could both be found on the same block of 125th Street, between Seventh and Eighth Avenues. Hurtig & Seamon operated out of the grand old Harlem Opera House, built for Oscar Hammerstein in 1889; the Minsky brothers, widely credited with establishing New York burlesque in their original theater on the Lower East Side, worked from the Apollo Theater, just a few doors down.

Times, however, were changing. The black metropolis was expanding steadily southward from central Harlem, forcing theater owners on the western half of 125th Street, via the politics of commerce if not necessarily of personal beliefs, to begin admitting black customers. And burlesque was up against a backlash. Outraged clergy and other guardians of morality had long decried burlesque's popularity in the community, and in former congressman Fiorello La Guardia, widely tipped to become New York's new mayor in the 1933 elections, they had found an ally. After the death of Billy Minsky in 1932, his brothers surrendered to the inevitable and closed up Minsky's Burlesque, leaving the twenty-year-old Apollo Theater in search of a new outfit.

In stepped Sydney Cohen, who already owned several moviehouses and theaters around Harlem. With venue manager Morris Sussman, Cohen decided to refurbish the 1,800-capacity Apollo as a family-friendly variety theater featuring black entertainers, and one that would admit black custom-ers. Unveiled in January 1934, the subtly renamed but completely revamped 125th Street Apollo Theater—the Apollo of future renown—would, prom-ised Cohen, offer "a revolutionary step in the presentation of stage shows."

This did not sit well with Leo Brecher, who had maintained his own presence on 125th Street for over a decade, at both the Harlem Opera House and the Loew's Theater, next door to the Apollo. Brecher also owned the Lafayette Theater, on Seventh Avenue and 131st Street, where, since 1925, his manager Frank Schiffman had promoted shows by Duke Ellington, Noble Sissle, and Bessie Smith—and all to black audiences. Brecher now moved Schiffman back to the Harlem Opera House and declared a promotional war, one keenly followed by New York's leading black newspaper, the *Amsterdam News*. When Cohen's Apollo promoted itself as "America's Finest Colored Theatre," Brecher's Opera House responded with the "Greatest Show Value in Harlem." When the host Ralph Cooper took his popular Wednesday night amateur show from the Lafayette Theater to the Apollo, and began broadcasting it on WMCA, Brecher and Schiffman launched a Tuesday night equivalent, broadcast on WNEW.

By May 1935, the competition was hurting both venues, and Schiffman and Sussman announced a merger at a press conference. But when the Harlem Opera House was promptly converted into a movie theater, with Schiffman taking over operations at the Apollo, it was evident that this was in fact a takeover—and when Sydney Cohen died of a heart attack at the end of the year, Brecher promptly bought out Cohen's interests and rewarded Schiffman with a half share of the new enterprise. The Apollo Theater at 253 West 125th Street now advertised itself as "The Only Stage

Show in Harlem." The competition thoroughly vanquished, no one argued the claim.

Brecher and Schiffman, clearly, were tough businessmen who would take whatever steps necessary to vanquish the opposition. And their survival instincts were such that they were almost begrudgingly admired for underpaying their talent. But in the difficult climate of depression-era Harlem, they were equally determined that the Apollo provide maximum entertainment for the lowest admission price. The week of April 24, 1936, offered a good example: for just fifteen cents before noon, rising to fifty cents for the prime Wednesday and Saturday night shows, audiences at the Apollo were treated to the preeminent song-and-dance team Buck and Bubbles, the "Father of the Blues" W. C. Handy (once turned away from the Cotton Club for his skin color, even though his flagship composition "St. Louis Blues" was part of the floorshow), the tap dancers Chuck and Chuckles, and the great blues singer Bessie Smith, along with a movie (intended to "clear the house"), and a chorus line. The era's big jazz stars were also frequent attractions at the Apollo: in September 1936, Louis Armstrong and the Duke Ellington Orchestra were back-to-back headliners.

The Apollo's commitment to value explained its immediate local success, but it was an involvement in the community that ensured the audience's long-term loyalty. A decade at the Lafayette had steeped Schiffman in race relations. He almost exclusively employed local people of color at a time when most theaters in New York refused to hire blacks at all. He was personally involved in helping break down the color barrier in the restaurants and stores along 125th Street, and he signed the Apollo on to any number of local and national progressive charities and organizations.

The relationship between Jewish businessmen and black entertainers is a recurrent and increasingly controversial theme throughout the history of the New York music scene. It's worth noting at the outset, then, that in the early 1930s there was little or no conflict between the Jewish people in Harlem and either the blacks or Latinos who gradually came to dominate the neighborhood. The essayist Roi Ottley was emphatic on this subject, writing in 1943, in New World A-Coming, "Anti-Jewish sentiment among Negroes . . . is a very recent manifestation, perhaps about ten years old." He blamed Harlem's "back-to-Africa" leader Marcus Garvey for introducing the "Jewish question," while noting also the impact of the depression, the rise of

Hitler's anti-Semitism, the arrival of Jewish refugees, and anti-white sentiment in Harlem that could be expressed only against those with whom black people interacted: Jewish shopkeepers and businessmen.

That so many Jewish people found themselves operating small businesses was itself a direct result of discrimination. Barred as they were from the "white-collar" enterprises on Wall Street, the entrepreneurs among them were drawn instinctively into the world of movies, music, and theater. In addition, those Jewish New Yorkers who tended toward left-wing politics (and it was a majority) found themselves ideally positioned to advance the cause of racial integration via their involvement in entertainment. And so, if it could be posited, honestly, that the Jewish businessman and the black entertainer each took from the other what they needed to succeed, it should also be stated, more generously, that given their shared ostracism from mainstream society, they had more in common than many would like to believe.

At Schiffman and Brecher's Apollo, whites continued to make up a substantial minority of the audience, but Harlemites quickly came to view the theater as their own. Early on weekends and holidays, when admission was at its cheapest, local adolescents would head up to the private playground of the second balcony, where they would stay all day; down in the stalls, mothers would bring their babies in lieu of finding a sitter; whole families would attend the major performers dressed to the nines. And as the venue's reputation for breaking and establishing talent spread nationwide among black entertainers, the give-and-take between audience and performer became the stuff of legend.

This was exemplified on Wednesdays—Amateur Night, which Ralph Cooper continued to host. The format was simple enough: a steady stream of mostly unproven talent—singers, musicians, comedians, dancers—would take the stage through the course of the evening, and audience applause would determine the winner. This was no different from the talent shows in any number of schools, churches, community halls, and theaters all over the country. But no other venue had as its judges the vociferous Apollo audience, which became as much a part of the theater as the acts on stage, engaging in famously exuberant and explicit call-and-response dialogue with the performers. If audience members liked an act, they'd shower it with praise, roaring their appreciation and echoing the performer's words as if at church. But if they didn't, the cutting insults from the resident drag queens in the side boxes, and the catcalls and choruses of boos from the stalls, echoed in a disturbingly high pitch from the balconies, would rise in volume and intensity until "Porto Rico"—the stagehand Norman Miller in disguise—emerged from the wings with his toy gun to put the act out of its misery.

Still, the potential rewards of Amateur Night far outweighed the risk of humiliation, for the audiences on Wednesdays included important talent agents, and a number of white celebrities and other society types who otherwise rarely now came to Harlem. The winner was additionally rewarded with inclusion on the Wednesday night one-hour broadcast on WMCA, an invitation to return the following week, and maybe even a place on an upcoming revue. Given that early Amateur Night successes included Sarah Vaughan, Ella Fitzgerald, Ruth Brown, and Bill Kenny of the Ink Spots, it was no wonder that the Apollo rapidly became known as the place not only to see the biggest contemporary stars in black showbiz but, on Wednesdays, the venue at which to choose the stars of the future. No wonder, also, that the Apollo turned over a million tickets a year. And no wonder that in 1942, when the music trade magazine *Billboard* decided to compile a chart to rank popular music as sold in the "Negro" community, the editors named it the Harlem Hit Parade.

As it turned out, *Billboard* was about fifteen years too late in latching onto Harlem. Trouble was brewing in the black metropolis, which was growing ever more isolated from the bigger city around it. The tensions had become evident in November 1941, when the stabbing death of a fifteen-year-old white boy near Central Park (by two teenagers and a twelve-year-old, all from Harlem) allowed the New York newspapers to sensationalize the new fashion for "mugging"; a similar killing days later in Morningside Park helped suggest that Harlem youth were out of control. The nation appeared to come together a few weeks later when the Japanese attacked Pearl Harbor and America entered the war. But not everyone shared the feeling of unity. A gathering of sixty of the nation's most prominent black leaders during that year's troubled holiday season concluded, soberly, "The colored people are not whole-heartedly and unreservedly all out in support of the present war effort."

There was good reason for such reticence. Blacks, after all, had joined the Great War in epic numbers, expecting an improvement in their status as gratitude. The Harlem horn player and Clef Club founder James Reese Europe took his vast orchestra with the 369th Infantry Regiment to France, intoxicating the Europeans with his jazz music while the "Hell Fighters," as the regiment was known, became celebrated for their bravery. But though the 369th received a parade up Fifth Avenue from Washington Square Park to Harlem upon return, progress elsewhere appeared, if anything, to reverse itself. The Ku Klux Klan was revived, Jim Crow laws solidified, and the U.S. Navy even enacted a new policy that excluded blacks from certain branches of the service.

Now, in the lead-up to America's entry into this new world war, minority races, in New York as elsewhere, had been virtually shut out from employment in the defense industries. The New York–based Brotherhood of Sleeping Car Porters, the most powerful black union in the country, threatened a march on Washington in protest, and it was called off only at the very last moment when President Roosevelt, fearing blood on the streets of the capital if the black marchers came up against the city's white police force, issued an executive order banning discrimination in the defense program. Yet segregation and discrimination persisted in the armed services themselves, leading to deadly riots in boot camps from the Deep South to Fort Dix, in New Jersey. The slurring of "the yellow-skinned Jap" further cooled enthusiasm for a fight by people who themselves had long been judged on their color—as did, it must be noted, the carefully prepared propaganda of the Nazis and Japanese alike, which promised the American black man that he would gain from an Axis victory.

Harlem, not surprisingly, became a prominent East Coast battleground. In the summer of 1942, nonresidential servicemen on leave were banned from the area, after an outbreak of syphilis was reported. Then, in April 1943, the Savoy Ballroom was busted for prostitution and ordered closed for six months as penalty. Harlemites were furious. For seventeen years, the Savoy had enjoyed world renown, not only for booking the finest jazz bands in America but as that rare venue where people of all colors shared the dance floor. (The Harlem Renaissance writer George Schuyler had courted his white future wife there.) If there were indeed prostitutes seeking business on the dance floor, argued the Savoy's defendants, they could also be found at nightclubs and ballrooms up and down New York. The city's first black councilman, Adam Clayton Powell Jr., went so far as to declare of the Savoy's closing that "Hitler has scored a Jim-crow victory in New York."

While Harlem seethed, the wider city set out, in the seemingly noble words of Parks Commissioner Robert Moses, "to induce insurance companies and savings banks to enter the field of large-scale slum clearance." But when, in May 1943, the Metropolitan Life Insurance Company agreed to build the 80-acre Stuyvesant Town, between East 14th and 20th Streets, with rental priority given to returning war veterans, blacks were excluded from the application process. Moses backed Met Life's decision, stating in a *New York Times* interview that black infiltration of white areas led to "a drop in values [and] deterioration of buildings." He went on to assail "Negro leaders who will accept nothing but complete social equality," holding them responsible for "the stories of unrest among our colored citizens."

Moses's comments were published less than two months after "zoot suit" riots in Los Angeles, in which white servicemen had targeted young Mexican-Americans, and barely six weeks after a race riot in Detroit, triggered by that city's own war machine discrimination, had left thirty-four people dead. Moses should hardly have been surprised when, hours after his interview hit the stands, on the sweltering midsummer night of Sunday, August 1, his "stories of unrest" turned into a reality.

The final spark came at the Braddock Hotel, on 126th Street, just behind the Apollo, where a twenty-six-year-old private, Robert Bandy, in the company of his mother, stepped into an argument between a white policeman and a young black woman. The rights and wrongs of the altercation were less relevant than the result: nightsticks were drawn, then guns, and the policeman shot Bandy in the shoulder. While he was taken to hospital for treatment, word spread of a black soldier shot dead by a white policeman—in front of his mother, no less—and the streets of Harlem erupted in a two-day spree of arson and looting, in which the neighborhood's white-owned stores were the primary targets. By the time the rioting was quelled, 6 people lay dead, 185 had been injured, and 550 arrested, and fifteen hundred stores reported damage. The riots left 125th Street a sea of broken glass, burned-out cars, and looted stores—with the notable exception of the Apollo Theater, which, so accounts had it, had been cordoned off from attack by a line of local black residents.

Forty years after the event, Frank Schiffman's son Jack, raised in the environs of the Apollo, lamented, "The riot of 1943 engendered fear [of Harlem] that has remained unshakable." One of its major effects, he noted, "was that the many whites who had been traveling uptown to see the show at the Apollo no longer went." It hardly helped that Clark Monroe immediately closed his Uptown House and moved to the Spotlite on 52nd Street. The *Amsterdam News* noted in an editorial the week after the riot, "It's time for Harlem to quit kidding itself. . . . Harlem never has lived up to its reputation. Harlem is, and has been for years, in a bad way."

Yet the riots served to bring attention to Harlem's long-standing social problems, and Mayor La Guardia, in his third term and acclaimed for his handling of the riot by (most) blacks and whites alike, set about addressing some of the chronic complaints, opening an office to investigate high food prices, launching education and housing programs, and beginning a drive to recruit more black policemen. At the same time, his aggressive efforts to bring war contracts to the city bore fruit: the dangerously high unemployment of 1942, which had kept some 400,000 New Yorkers on the streets and helped fuel the anger in Harlem, was almost entirely eliminated by late 1943. By the time the war ended, in 1945, the city's economy had returned to something like full strength. And the youth of Harlem, caught up in the mood of postwar optimism, were about to reaffirm their impact on the hit parade.

n the aftermath of the war, the big swing orchestras quickly fell by the wayside, unable to meet their considerable payrolls as attention switched instead to the smaller jazz groups of the beboppers, the manageable dance combos led by stars like Louis Jordan, and the swing orchestras' solo singers, who were increasingly stepping out on their own. None did so as impressively or emphatically as Tommy Dorsey's former front man Frank Sinatra, who provoked the first reported "pop riot" in Manhattan, on Columbus Day 1944, when 30,000 "bobby-soxers"—screaming teenage girls on holiday from school—showed up at the Paramount Theater to claim just 3,600 seats.

Sinatra was admired in Harlem, too, but he could not match the popularity of such black vocal groups as the Mills Brothers and the Ink Spots. The former originated in Ohio in the 1920s before moving to New York City, where their ability to emulate instrumental sounds alongside their vocal harmonies helped them become the first black group with ready appeal among white listeners. The Ink Spots, though its original members all hailed from Indianapolis, had a more defined connection with Harlem: after moving to New York, they acquired the lead tenor Bill Kenny (and with him, commercial success) in 1935 when he won Amateur Night at both the Apollo and the Savoy. (Moe Gale, a partner in the Savoy, was also the group's manager.) The Ink Spots were firm favorites in Harlem, but after their sentimental hit "If I Didn't Care" in 1939, they also played midtown hotels like the Waldorf-Astoria, the first vocal harmony group to straddle the two markets simultaneously. By the end of the war, the familiar sound of Kenny's mildly melancholy tenor over his partners' soothing harmonies rendered the Ink Spots the most popular vocal group in the country.

It may have been with Bill Kenny's success story in mind that Leonard "Zeke" Puzey, a nineteen-year-old tenor born and bred in Harlem, followed his friends' urging and registered for the Apollo Amateur Night in 1945. Puzey was not blinded by ambition, however. He'd occasionally sung onstage in high school; he lived near the Apollo; he attended the theater when a vocal act on the bill caught his attention; he listened to *Harlem Amateur Hour* on the radio like thousands of other local kids. For him, trying out for Amateur Night was not so much a risk as a natural part of growing up.

When Puzey's date finally came around, he chose to sing the ballad "There's No You," made famous by Frank Sinatra a couple of years earlier. Accompanied by the Apollo's house band, Puzey put fear of the audience out of his mind. "Naturally I'm a little nervous, a little concerned," he recalled. "But I'm in it now, may as well do the best I can." Puzey exuded a quiet confidence, and he may have even anticipated the crowd's warm response, since he was a popular local teen, but he was genuinely shocked to find himself that night's winner.

The response from the local talent scouts was immediate. Puzey was quickly summoned to the Evans Booking Agency, which had an office right on 125th Street. There he was introduced to fellow vocalists Warren Suttles and Jimmy Ricks, with the suggestion that they had the makings of a group. At someone's invitation, Jimmy Ricks opened his mouth to sing, and out came the deepest, yet most graceful voice Puzey had ever heard.

"I thought, *My God*, what is this we have here? Let's *go* with it."

• • •

Warren Suttles and Jimmy Ricks, each in his late teens as World War II ended, typified the many thousands who migrated from the South during the war years. Suttles, from Alabama, was a fanatical baseball player and an impressive baritone. After being drafted, he taught illiterates to read and write in boot camps throughout the South and was encouraged to stay on in the service. Instead he moved up to New York, where, he said, "the main advantage for me was not having to run into the prejudice everywhere you go. Down south you couldn't use the white bathroom, you couldn't use the white this or that." He had a famous baseball-playing uncle (George "Mule" Suttles) he hoped to follow into the Negro Leagues, but Mule was running a bar by the time the teenager got to Harlem, and Warren followed suit, waiting tables at the Four Hundred Tavern, on 148th Street.

There he met James Thomas Ricks, who hailed from a family of Georgian cotton pickers, all of whom sang both in the fields and in the church. "Ricky," gifted with a three-octave voice of particular resonance in the bass register, moved of his own accord to New York in his late teens and soon found himself in the Melodeers, whose career looked promising until its lead singer Herb Kenny was unexpectedly offered a place in his brother Bill's Ink Spots. As the Melodeers disbanded, Jimmy Ricks took to waiting tables, also at the Four Hundred.

Suttles's and Ricks's primary musical influence was the Delta Rhythm Boys from New Orleans, whose sophisticated interpretation of Duke Ellington's "Take the A Train" had hit big in 1941. Less overtly "pop" than the Mills Brothers and Ink Spots, less obviously gospel than the Charioteers or the Golden Gate Jubilee Quartet, and celebrated as pioneers of the early forties form of African American swing known as jive, the Delta Rhythm Boys were especially noted for their bass singer Lee Gaines. Jimmy Ricks, it turned out, had one of the few voices around that could reach similarly low notes.

With Suttles playing piano, the three young vocalists began working up the Delta Rhythm Boys' hit song "Darktown Strutter's Ball," soon adding its companion piece "Darktown Poker Club." The Evans Agency then delivered a fourth member, Ollie Jones, who came armed, unusually for young vocal groups of the day, with a worthy, self-composed ballad, "Lullaby." For no particular reason, the new group settled on the name the Ravens, not knowing that they were starting one of the biggest trends in popular music history. More important at the time was their partnership with the arranger and pianist Howard Biggs, who felt sufficiently impressed to introduce them to Ben Bart, a former partner of Moe Gale's who not only was the Ink Spots' new manager but had also just established the Hub Recording Company.

Independent record labels were, as already noted, increasingly visible by the end of the war, promoting the new strands of black music that the major labels, still playing catch-up from the AFM strike, proved painfully slow at discovering for themselves. Operating without major distribution, these labels sold instead into mom-and-pop record stores, like Bobby's Record Shop, opened by a young South Carolina native, Bobby Robinson, shortly after the war, just down the road from the Apollo. It was said to be the first black-owned business on 125th Street.

In the spring of 1946, the Ravens, with Biggs, recorded half a dozen sides for Hub that represented an interesting detour from the tried-and-true vocal group formula. "Lullaby," complete with introductory guitar vamp, began as an innocuous pop ballad in the Ink Spots style, sung in a high tenor by Leonard Puzey—but then, halfway through, Jimmy Ricks announced himself with a bold "doo doo doo doo doo doo" that sailed around the edges of the subsequent verse before briefly taking the lead. On "Honey" and the Howard Biggs composition "Bye Bye Baby Blues" (an extension of the pop jazz standard "Bye Bye Blues"), Ricks then stepped fully to the forefront, singing forcefully and fluently far above and beyond the swinging harmonies, and way over a jazzy piano, rendering the distant guitar and drums almost superfluous. Not even Lee Gaines had attempted anything quite so forceful.

The recordings were not big sellers: Hub lacked distribution much beyond New York City. But the cuts were hits on the Harlem jukeboxes, and Bart was able to book the Ravens into local venues like the Baby Grand, before securing, in December 1946, their placement on a charity bill at the Harlem Apollo alongside Stan Kenton and Nat King Cole. With the confidence that is a gift of youth and the assurance that comes from playing to a hometown audience, the Ravens opened that night with "My Sugar Is So Refined," which they had imbued on their Hub recording with a more rhythmic feel than Johnny Mercer's hit version. Puzey sang lead through most of the song in a delicate tenor, until Ricks took over on the sweet "sugar" 's manner of drinking tea: "With just two fingers / while she sticks out three." As

Puzey gesticulated to the crowd with his own outstretched fingers, Ricks's booming voice brought the audience members instantaneously to their feet.

Puzey called it "the most exciting day" of his life, partly because of his next move: "There was a dance at the time called the applejack, and I used to put some applejack steps into the breaks and spin around and wind up at the mike just when it was time for me to sing a note. And that really floored the people, they just loved that." The applejack steps were not rehearsed, he insisted, "but they blended right in with what we were doing, so we kept it in the act." The result was another defining characteristic of the Ravens' set. "The Mills Brothers, the Ink Spots, they were the main groups," Puzey acknowledged, "but they didn't have any choreography like we had."

Events moved quickly for the Ravens after that. They were nominated "Best New Singing Group" by the listeners of "Symphony" Sid Torin's influential WHOM radio show, *After Hours*; Ollie Jones was replaced—amicably— as top tenor by Maithe Marshall; and Ben Bart sold their record contract to Al Greene's National label, enabling the Ravens' recording career to begin in earnest. When, that spring of 1947, Jimmy Ricks stepped to the fore on a particularly bluesy update of the popular *Show Boat* ballad "Ol' Man River," as popularized by Paul Robeson, the result was not just the group's first hit but a crucially important and influential record, near enough a template for a new form of music. Though they never saw any royalties, the Ravens were frequently told that it had sold a million copies nationwide.

The chart on which "Ol' Man River" scored so well had recently been renamed Race Records, in acknowledgment that black music made primarily for a black audience was growing rapidly beyond connotations with a Harlem that was itself slipping out of vogue. Jerry Wexler, a *Billboard* writer who would himself retire that term four years later, thought it "a wonderful designation. . . . When a black man in Harlem said 'I'm a race man,' he meant to say that he identified terrifically with his roots, his color, his place in society and his Negritude."

The Ravens continued to cover songs made famous by white composers and singers, but with a keenly black spirit, bringing the pop and race audiences ever closer together. They also championed more overtly "blues" and "rhythm" numbers; re-released on Cincinnati-based King Records, "Bye Bye Baby Blues" became a big Race Records hit, as did another Biggs composition, "Write Me a Letter," on which Ricks's loping voice proved so effective that it crossed the song over into the pop charts. "We had a bona fide basso and a bona fide top tenor," said Suttles of the Ravens' recipe for success. "It was hard to find a basso that could carry a melody—and Ricky could carry a damn melody. And there might have been tenors that sang better than Maithe [Marshall], but none of them were as sweet."

These voices were never better showcased than on the Ravens' 1948 holiday single. On "Silent Night," Marshall took the soprano lead with almost funereal solemnity, only for Ricks to cut in with a bass so deep it was hard to believe the notes existed. "White Christmas" was recorded to a more sprightly rhythm, and the roles were reversed, Ricks announcing himself in his unique low-end style, with Marshall taking over halfway through and several octaves higher. Both were major hits on the Race Records chart, with "White Christmas" setting the standard for many a later version.

Yet, as the Ravens became steadily more successful, Jimmy Ricks's star power, ego, and greater remuneration served to alienate him from the other members of the group. Suttles and Marshall each quit, rejoined, and quit again, Puzey spent two years in the Army, and Ricks left the group once in 1954 and for good in 1956. The Ravens' creative heyday effectively ran from 1947 to 1950, when they were a regular attraction at the Apollo, toured with Cab Calloway, and recorded with Benny Goodman, and when, such was their celebrity, Puzey was temporarily engaged to the singer Ruth Brown.

Significantly, their last recording for National, early in 1950, before moving on to the major labels Columbia and Mercury, was also one of their most influential. On "Count Every Star," Ricks's vocal introduction returned to the "doo doo doo doos" as first announced four years earlier on "Lullaby"; repeated later in the song, with the two tenors now offering equally phonetic accompaniment, and Marshall's feminine soprano riding high over the top, it saw the Ravens give the first pure example of what would, in later years, come to be known as the doo-wop ballad. At the time, however, it was called "rhythm and blues."

That term came into everyday use (at least among white people) when, in 1949, *Billboard* decided that Race Records was too color-conscious a term, and asked its staff members to offer an alternative. Jerry Wexler described for the BBC how, despite his fondness for the term "race," he "came up with a handle [he] thought suited the music well—'rhythm and blues.' . . . It defined a new genre of music."

But many refute Wexler's claim to invention. "In 1949, when *Billboard* changed the name of its black pop-music chart from 'race' to 'rhythm & blues,'" wrote Nelson George in *The Death of Rhythm & Blues*, "it wasn't setting a trend, but responding to a phrase and feeling the independent labels had already made part of the vocabulary." Leonard Puzey recalled of the Ravens' early days, "We were using the term rhythm & blues, always."

"The start of rhythm and blues was 'Ol' Man River,'" Warren Suttles said emphatically some sixty years after the single's release. "*We* started rhythm and blues." His assertion makes sense from the perspective that the Ravens predated the terminology's most popular era; but for all their influence on vocal groups in the Northeast, the Ravens lacked one element that would prove integral to rhythm and blues' arrival as a new musical form: gospel.

From its early twentieth-century origins, when the major churches had relocated to northern Manhattan along with their congregations, Harlem had been a seat of great gospel singing. In the years immediately following World War II, as vocal groups began to emerge on the streets, gospel quartets from rival churches frequently "battled" each other at the Golden Gate Ballroom, on Seventh Avenue. There the Thrasher Wonders, the Brooklyn Crusaders, and others regularly bowed down to the greatest gospel group in the Northeast: the Mount Lebanon Singers, from the church of the same name on 132nd Street.

The popularity of the Mount Lebanon Singers could be traced in no small part to the impeccable credentials of Clyde McPhatter, born in North Carolina in 1932, to a minister father and a church organist mother, with five chorister siblings. By the time the family moved to Harlem, around 1946, Clyde's voice had broken, gifting him a soaring tenor capable of a phenomenal melisma—the stretching of a single syllable over several notes. He was also strikingly handsome, and the combination made him the obvious star of the Mount Lebanon Singers. The quartet, which also featured David and Wilmer Baldwin (brothers of the Harlem novelist James Baldwin) and Charlie White, toured the East Coast regularly in the late 1940s, despite Clyde's tender years.

The only problem with McPhatter's gospel singing? He didn't believe in it. "It was never explained to me what religion was all about," he later complained. "It was nothing but another word for discipline. You know, 'God don't like this,' or 'God don't like that.' So one day I said, 'God damn it!' and my father beat the hell out of me." McPhatter's rebellion was hardly unique. With more money available to young people in the postwar years, it was becoming a lot harder for parents to control their children by, quite literally, putting the fear of God into them. And with vocal music proving increasingly popular on the streets and stoops of Harlem, local gospel singers like McPhatter increasingly sought out secular singing opportunities.

The most obvious location was the Apollo, on a Wednesday. McPhatter entered Amateur Night in 1949, singing Lonnie Johnson's R&B hit "Tomorrow Night" and, unsurprisingly, given what we know about his voice, placed first. This brought him to the attention of Billy Ward, a pianist and former chorister working with the Broadway agent Rose Ann Marks on assembling a vocal group, the Ques. The seventeen-year-old McPhatter brought Charlie White with him, and they were teamed up with two of the International Gospel Singers. The new Ques immediately took first place at the Apollo Amateur Night, and did so again on the *Arthur Godfrey's Talent Scouts* on CBS television in October 1950, singing "Goodnight Irene," a Leadbelly song currently on top of the pop charts as sung by the New York folk group the Weavers. Cincinnati's King Records, now firmly established in the field of rhythm and blues, promptly snapped them up to launch its new subsidiary, Federal, but insisted on a more palatable name, and the Ques became the Dominoes.

Federal sent the group straight into the studio, and something unprecedented took place. On the Ward-Marks ballad "Do Something for Me," McPhatter sang lead with the gospel delivery of his church upbringing, giving full range to his melismas in the process. But his words were most certainly not dedicated to the Lord. Alternately begging and hustling the object of his affections, he vowed not to "sleep a wink tonight, unless you come over and treat me right," a proposition that required "teasing me" and "squeezing me" until his love would come "tumbling down." At first, the other Dominoes harmonized politely in the background—until a middle-eight unison that suggested they were no less amorous than their leader. This was not just secular music; it was *sexual* music, and it went top ten on the R&B charts. Just as the Ravens, who suddenly sounded tame by comparison, were beginning to fracture, Harlem had itself a new hit group.

Ward and Marks improved on this early success with "Sixty Minute

Man," for which the bassist Bill Brown took lead. The switch was surely in imitation of Jimmy Ricks's popularity, but the Ravens had never dared sing material like *this*. To a jaunty rhythm accentuated by a prominent electric guitar lead, Brown not only repeated the "teasing" and "squeezing" but also talked of "rocking" and "rolling"—the lyrical euphemism for sex that had been working its way into rhythm and blues records in the South and the West. He then grew yet more bold: his sixty minutes, Brown emphasized, would climax with fifteen minutes of "blowing my top," a promise of prowess for his sweetheart addressed to anyone whose "old man ain't treating you right." It was risqué stuff, banned from many radio stations, and of course the American kids loved it: "Sixty Minute Man" spent fourteen weeks atop the R&B charts, that genre's biggest-selling single of 1951. In the process, it climbed to the top 20 of the pop charts, one of the first notable rhythm and blues crossovers.

In his book *Big Beat Heat*, John A. Jackson attributes that crossover to racial stereotypes, saying that Brown comes across as a "slow-witted, sexually obsessed black man," whose "braggadocio" is so "blatantly overstated" that white kids would feel more amused than threatened. There's truth to this: Brown's basso did not have the depth or resonance that rendered Jimmy Ricks's voice so persuasive, and "Sixty Minute Man" is, for all its lyrical audaciousness, at heart a novelty record. That might explain why Marks and Ward returned to Clyde McPhatter and the subject of the Dominoes' debut single for the follow-up, "That's What You're Doing to Me"—although they kept the "rock and roll" couplet and further enlivened the arrangement with hand-claps, blues piano, and a raw sax solo.

Then came "Have Mercy Baby," and it stood R&B on its head. The arrangement was strictly twelve-bar blues, jumping with energy unmatched by any of the other East Coast vocal groups. (The Orioles from Baltimore had by now superseded the Ravens in popularity, yet heard alongside the Dominoes, they sounded as if from a previous generation.) A sax came forward to introduce the song, and took a lengthy solo halfway through that positively rang with echo. As for the vocals, always the Dominoes' calling card, McPhatter switched roles; this time he was repentant, as if apologizing for the content of previous singles. Bringing the gospel tradition of "mercy" to the studio, the tenor admitted that he was a "good-for-nothing" who'd "lied" and "cheated," and he begged for forgiveness. He even broke down in mock tears at the song's conclusion; depending on one's view, that put the single either over the edge or over the top. Regardless, "Have Mercy Baby," another number one hit, became the second-biggest-selling R&B single of 1952. The Dominoes, it seemed, were unstoppable; there were few young males in Harlem who didn't wish for some of what Clyde McPhatter had.

Truth was that, materially, McPhatter had very little. Billy Ward was a former army captain, and he treated the Dominoes like conscripts. He paid them what seemed a comfortable $100 a week, but out of this they had to provide their uniforms, their hotels, and their food. Then there were the fines: $50 for any band member who left his hotel at night, double for a band member who failed to report another member for doing so. Worse yet for the singers, the group's name was changed after the success of "Have Mercy Baby" to Billy Ward and His Dominoes, as if a throwback to the big swing bands. Ward even took to introducing the act's star as Clyde Ward.

One by one, band members quit or were fired. McPhatter reached his breaking point in the spring of 1953. The singer, who complained that when he came home to Harlem, where he was an idol, "half the time [he] didn't have enough money for a Coca-Cola," probably realized that his voice was worth more than Ward was paying him and handed in his notice. But it's possible that Ward fired the star for multiple infractions and insolence, given that McPhatter's replacement turned out to be a young Jackie Wilson, one of the greatest R&B singers America ever produced. Either way, McPhatter was absent on May 6, 1953, the night Billy Ward and His Dominoes played Birdland in midtown, and Atlantic Records' Ahmet Ertegun came by, specifically to hear "Have Mercy Baby."

Ertegun, the D.C.-raised son of a Turkish diplomat, a man of impeccable taste and considerable intelligence whose owl-like expression of ancient wisdom masked both a sense of mischief and opportunism, had established Atlantic in New York in 1947 with the former National Records A&R man Herb Abramson and his $2,500 seed money, plus a $10,000 loan from a dentist. Consummate music fans—"among the most cultivated cognoscenti in the City," said their future partner Jerry Wexler—Ertegun and Abramson promptly burned through their funding with a series of marginal releases on the periphery of jazz, R&B, and country before hitting it big in 1949 with "Drinking Wine Spo-Dee-O-Dee," by Stick McGhee. This was a cover of McGhee's own recording on an even smaller label, Harlem Records, which could not press enough records to keep up with demand. Atlantic was learning how to succeed in business—and fast.

Ertegun next signed the vocal group the Clovers, from his Washington, D.C., hometown, and wrote their debut hit, "Don't You Know I Love You," which topped the R&B charts in early 1951. Atlantic soon had another number one, "5–10–15 Hours," by Ruth Brown, seen as something of an answer record to "Sixty Minute Man." Ertegun always had his eye on Clyde McPhatter, whom he called "the most soulful singer in rhythm and blues." Noting his absence from the Dominoes that night at Birdland, and hearing that the departure was permanent, Ertegun tracked McPhatter down at once and offered his label's services. Atlantic was known for paying rare care and attention to its artists. Songs were chosen carefully, arrangements rehearsed endlessly, sessions produced meticulously. And though few people, label bosses included, were getting seriously rich in those early days of rhythm and blues, the acts on Atlantic received something they couldn't get elsewhere: royalties. McPhatter agreed to sign.

Rather than take him solo, Atlantic built a new group around McPhatter, recruited from the Mount Lebanon Singers. The first recording session yielded a future hit, "Lucille," but otherwise failed to deliver the feel that Ertegun had hoped for, and the recordings were shelved while McPhatter was persuaded to assemble a fresh lineup. He called on members of the Thrasher Wonders and, over Atlantic's objections, called them the Drifters.

It was August 1953, and Wexler had just joined Atlantic as a partner (Herb Abramson having been drafted into the Army), when the group emerged from the studio with five songs, of which the Jesse Stone composition "Money Honey" was the obvious standout. The instrumentation was much the same as had accompanied McPhatter in the Dominoes, but the performance was tighter, the sax no longer surrounded by echo, and the beat more defined, allowing for some syncopation. The backing quartet enunciated clearly nonsensical words: "ooh bop sh-bop," which echoed the bebop "language" of the preceding decade but also hinted at a coming vocal form. And McPhatter's own voice soared, his lyrical attention, per the title, now focused on the need to pay the rent, and therefore as much concerned with his lover's financial status as her libido. Nowhere near as wild as "Have Mercy Baby," but the sound of a music maturing confidently, "Money Honey" rose straight to number one on the R&B charts.

McPhatter, still barely twenty-one years old, had now found fame in not one but two Harlem groups. As the Drifters went on to become one of the most familiar names in rhythm and blues, legions of city high school kids followed McPhatter's lead, turned their back on their own church roots and embraced secular music with nothing less than a vengeance. They would find no shortage of listeners—or of businessmen waiting to sign them up. Rhythm and blues, in its most simplistic of vocal forms, was set to become the sound of the city streets.

4

THE VILLAGE TO THE
LEFT OF NEW YORK

n the same way that Harlem maintained a specific identity within the crowded confines of Manhattan, so did Greenwich Village, six miles to the south. From its earliest days as a rural hamlet, a remote safe haven for the wealthy from the yellow fever epidemics that ravaged the city below Wall Street, Greenwich Village stood distinct from the rest of the island. Because of this history, because its layout of meandering alleys and side streets was already established by the time the outgrowth reached its borders, the city agreed (though only *after* the new Ninth Avenue had been cut through the private Chelsea Estate) to spare an area from Sixth Avenue west to Ninth, and Houston Street north to 14th, from further imposition of its much vaunted new grid system. For many years thereafter, neither Sixth nor Seventh Avenue—nor Fifth Avenue to this day—cut all the way through Greenwich Village, affording it an enduring semirural quiet quite unlike any in the rest of the city.

Confirmation of Greenwich Village's elite status came when the old execution site and potter's field just to its east was converted, in the late 1820s, into the elegant Washington Square parade grounds: grand town houses arose on all four sides, and from the square's northern tip, Fifth Avenue quickly declaimed its way up Manhattan as the new address of choice for New York's upper class. Even though the area to the south of the square was simultaneously besieged by tens of thousands of European immigrants, the Village maintained a stellar reputation as "the American Ward . . . a liberal model of cleanliness, good citizenship and self-respect."

That changed in the early twentieth century, as the wealthier inhabitants of old Greenwich Village gradually gave up their town houses for new homes away from lower Manhattan's rampant overcrowding. Converted into attractive and affordable apartment buildings, the area was quickly occupied by writers, painters, poets, and radicals, drawn not only by the European-style street structure but by the abundance of cafés and bars, restaurants and stores that sprang up especially to cater for them. These newcomers took to calling their neighborhood simply "the Village," a name long abandoned by its otherwise dominant Italian population, and they bestowed on themselves the title of "bohemians." Initially used specifically for Gypsies from the Czech region of Bohemia, the word became shorthand in nineteenth-century French literature for a refusal to conform to society's expectations: the poet Alfred Kreymborg, who came to the Village in 1904 at the age of twenty-one, described bohemianism simply as "being independent and being oneself." To this end, the Village simultaneously attracted a significant homosexual and lesbian population, and a reputation for political activism. By 1913, it was firmly established as the headquarters for New York's leftists, housing a variety of organizations and publications that included the Liberal Club on MacDougal Street; Mabel Dodge's weekly salons at her 23 Fifth Avenue mansion; and the editorial offices on Greenwich Avenue of the socialist magazine the *Masses*, whose editor Max Eastman was for a time Dodge's lover.

Local bars, of which there was never any shortage, proved equally popular meeting places. The Grapevine, on Sixth Avenue and 11th Street, a popular social club of the nineteenth century where early bohemians stopped in to hear neighborhood news, gave us the expression "heard it through. . . ." And when, during Prohibition, the Village's nook-and-cranny cafés and clubs were transformed into speakeasies, the phrase to "be 86'd" from a bar (i.e., ejected) was born at the unmarked Chumley's, which would toss revelers out back of its 86 Bedford Street exit when word came of a raid on its Barrow Street entrance.

The Village's abundance of hidden gathering spaces and its predilection for good times amid political discussion made it a popular late night Prohibition-era destination for jazz and blues musicians—the downtown equivalent of Harlem, complete with the requisite jam sessions and high-roller "slumming" parties. Crime families operated most of these venues during Prohibition, but following the law's repeal, legitimate nightclubs began to flourish. Max Gordon opened the Village Vanguard in 1935 in an old basement speakeasy on a triangular block created when Seventh Avenue was finally extended below Greenwich Avenue in the 1910s. Seating just 123 people, the smoky, dingy but ever-bustling Vanguard provided an instantly popular stage for the Village's hard-drinking poets, and soon expanded into jazz, blues, comedy, and all-round variety: the future Hollywood actress Judy Holliday and her teenage friends launched themselves at the Vanguard as the Revuers, in 1939.

That same year Café Society opened on nearby Sheridan Square. Its proprietor, Barney Josephson, intended the name as ironic comment on the newly popular term for wealthy nightclub habitués; his intent, however, was to create nothing less than "the first inter-racial nightclub in America." Such an ambition might have been deemed unnecessary by Harlem venues that had long welcomed black and white customers alike, but Josephson was downtown, where segregation was the norm, and at Café Society he did indeed push both to integrate Village audiences and to challenge their expectations. This was never more evident than when he introduced the jazz singer Billie Holiday, one of the Café Society's first headliners, to Abel Meeropol, a high school English teacher who, under the pseudonym Lewis Allan, was also a prolific and political lyricist—and, like many who held court in the Village during that time, an ardent Communist. After seeing a photograph of a double lynching in the South, Meeropol had been inspired to write a hauntingly evocative lyric, "Strange Fruit," and, in this case, to compose a melody for it also. With Josephson's encouragement, and despite the singer's initial reluctance to embrace politics, Holiday introduced it into her set in 1939. Such was the instant publicity surrounding a song that referenced, among other stark couplets, a "black body swinging in the Southern breeze," she was soon ending the night with it, Josephson drawing further attention by ensuring that the lights were dimmed, that waiters stopped serving, and that a total hush descended on the audience. Those who took umbrage to the lyrics—and there were plenty—were asked to leave.

Holiday had been brought to Café Society in the first place by another Village resident, John H. Hammond Jr. Born into wealth as a scion of the Vanderbilt family, Hammond attended Carnegie Hall concerts at a young age (his parents had a private box for the New York Philharmonic), but preferred the music he heard the servants (black, naturally) play in their quarters on their Columbia Grafanola. The record that changed his life was James P. Johnson's "Worried and Lonesome Blues," which John bought in 1922, at age twelve; his musical perspective was similarly enriched by witnessing the great blues singer Bessie Smith, at the peak of her vocal powers and popularity, at the Alhambra Theater in Harlem a few years later. By the late 1930s, having followed a path through black music from fan to critic to producer, Hammond had engineered Bessie Smith's final recordings, "discovered" Billie Holiday when she was seventeen, arranging her first studio session, and brought the Count Basie Orchestra to New York. A self-confessed "dedicated radical," he had also committed himself to fighting racial segregation and discrimination—not just in the music world, but everywhere he encountered it.

This was no small task, even for a Vanderbilt, but Hammond did his best, encouraging, as an early example, his future brother-in-law Benny Goodman to hire Teddy Wilson and Lionel Hampton, which opened the door to interracial jazz groups. Of his many contributions to popular music, the greatest—the one without which it is that much harder to imagine the history that followed—came in December 1938, when he promoted the first of two annual "From Spirituals to Swing" concerts at Carnegie Hall. Hammond's intent here was not just to lay out the chronology of African American popular music but to demonstrate that music's artistic integrity on a par with white, European classical music. With an admirable display of taste in a wide range of styles, he brought in the gospel choirs the Golden Gate Quartet and Mitchell's Christian Singers, his childhood idols Bessie Smith and James P. Johnson, the boogie-woogie pianists Pete Johnson and Albert Ammons, the jazz groups of Count Basie and Sidney Bechet, and, to represent the southern folk blues, Big Bill Broonzy "from a plantation in Arkansas" (his original choice, Robert Johnson, had just died), and a near-blind harmonica player, Sonny Terry, from Georgia. In the wake of the concert's success, he then brought many of these performers downtown to headline at a Café Society now proudly billing itself as "the wrong place for the right people." Thanks to the efforts of Hammond and Josephson, traditional American black music found a home for itself in the heart of Greenwich Village.

And yet it was none other than Hammond, at the time still Holiday's producer at Columbia Records, who later complained that "the beginning of the end for Billie was 'Strange Fruit,' when she had become the darling of the left-wing intellectuals," presumably excusing himself from that demographic. Hammond so disliked "Strange Fruit" that he gave Holiday a temporary release from her Columbia contract to record it, in April 1939, for Milt Gabler and his independent Commodore label instead. It ultimately became a musical milestone—but Gabler always noted that it was the single's other side, "Fine and Mellow," that garnered the jukebox play. "Strange Fruit" was not the kind of song that lifted your spirits.

As for Hammond's insistence on what she should and shouldn't sing, Billie Holiday's comment on the subject revealed the distance in New York music circles between the patron and the patronized: "Aw, John's square, John's just rich, John wants to run my life, tries to tell me and everybody else what to do."

Alan Lomax, one of many performers playing at the Forrest Theater, on 49th Street, on March 3, 1940, remembered the benefit concert that night as nothing less than "the beginning of the American folk song revival." Given that the bill included not just the popular actor-singer Burl Ives, the former Kentucky miner's wife Aunt Molly Jackson, and the Golden Gate Quartet but also four musicians of profound future impact who were in a room together for the first time—Leadbelly, Josh White, Pete Seeger, and Woody Guthrie—it would be churlish to deny Lomax his hyperbole.

Organized and hosted by the actor Will Geer, the benefit had been named a "Grapes of Wrath Evening" for the John Steinbeck novel—and recently released movie—that highlighted the plight of American migrant workers fleeing the prairie dust bowls for low-paid work in California. The only one of the performers who had firsthand experience of this was the twenty-seven-year-old Guthrie, who had endured a calamitous upbringing in Oklahoma—he lost a sister in a house fire, and then his mother to an asylum after she set his father ablaze—which manifested itself in a prolific outpouring of monumental and mostly radical musical verse, additional talents for drawing and prose, and a copious thirst both for alcohol and for travel, along with a steadfast refusal to adhere to the most basic of marital or parental duties. He had made his journey from the Oklahoma Dust Bowl to California in 1937, and the experience had inspired him to throw his considerable energy behind the migrant workers' struggle in words, music, and action. Geer had befriended Guthrie in California and extended the invitation to come stay with him in New York, where Geer was starring in a production of *Tobacco Road* at the Forrest.

Guthrie arrived in the city for the first time that February, residing with the Geers until his habits proved too unsettling for a family with a young baby, after which he took a room at the cheap Hanover Hotel, near Times Square. Guthrie liked to sleep with his boots on and to eat standing up—lest he ever get too comfortable in one place, he explained—but was not, by any stretch, the ignorant Okie migrant of the kind typically caricatured by the Californians. He had hosted a radio show in Los Angeles, published his own songbooks, and, during the past year, written a regular column, "Woody Sez," for the Communist newspaper there, *People's World*. Manhattan's boundless displays of wealth therefore no more impressed him than did its barely hidden squalor. Quite the opposite: disturbed by what he considered the dishonestly optimistic tone of the New York–based immigrant Irving Berlin's "God Bless America," which he had heard relentlessly in its hit version by Kate Smith as he traveled east, he set about a response on the Hanover Hotel's writing paper.

Initially, Guthrie ended his verses with a subtle but important variation on Berlin's words—"God Blessed America for me"—but by the time he'd finished the song, he'd turned that line, and the title, into "This Land Was Made for You and Me." The lyrics were now voiced from the perspective of an endless traveler like Guthrie, who "roamed and rambled" from "California to the New York Island," and who saw in his journeys America's faults as well as its virtues.

Guthrie did not perform his new composition at the Forrest Theater that night. But the songs he did sing, those tales of Dust Bowl deprivation that he had been steadily composing these last five years, and the distinctly plain(s) drawl in which he sang them—"laconic, offhand, as though he didn't much care if the audience was listening or not," according to Pete Seeger—made him an immediate hit. Guthrie had about him a natural wit, a way of conversing with the audience that put them at ease. He related his failures with the New York subway as if he were any other first-time visitor—but he ensured not to be taken as a rube. "The capitalist papers are so far ahead of the news that they know tonight what happened tomorrow," he joked of the evening editions of the following morning's newspapers, "but they never do go to the trouble of informing their readers what they really knew yesterday."

Alan Lomax, whose song-collecting travels with his folklorist father, John, had seven years earlier yielded the "discovery" of Leadbelly, languishing in the Angola Penitentiary in Louisiana, stood in the wings, transfixed. He had been waiting—hoping, certainly—these last few years for just such a musician to emerge from the Dust Bowl, someone full of integrity as well as intellect, a folk singer who was truly of the folk. The twenty-five-year-old Lomax, who had a day job at the Library of Congress (Pete Seeger working as his assistant), immediately invited Guthrie to visit him there, in the nation's capital, where the singer discussed his life and recorded his songs for the Archive of American Folk Song. Lomax also hosted Guthrie on his nationally syndicated radio show and introduced him to RCA Victor. The label bosses appeared bemused by the newcomer, whose clothing, cleanliness, demeanor, and intonation were hardly those of the typically prospective popular music star. Looking, as always, for an angle, they agreed to record him on condition he write a song that related specifically—or, perhaps, yet *more* specifically—to *The Grapes of Wrath*.

Guthrie accepted the challenge. And having befriended twenty-year-old Pete Seeger along with everyone else that night at the Forrest, he found himself composing it at the East Fourth Street walk-up where Seeger lived and a typewriter was available, showing up for the task with a half-gallon jug of cheap red wine. Seeger, a songwriting lightweight by comparison and even less of a rival drinker, watched and learned as Guthrie stood up "every few seconds" to test out a verse on his guitar. When Seeger and his roommate finally turned in for the night, Guthrie was still at it—and when they awoke in the morning, the newcomer was fast asleep under the table, the jug of wine all but empty next to the typewriter, from which extended the seventeen verses of "Tom Joad."

Unprecedented in its length, the ballad had been set by Guthrie to the tune of the Carter Family's "John Hardy." (Adding new words to an old tune was a venerable folk tradition, and would prove particularly popular in coming months and years as singers looked for easy ways to make a political point.) RCA Victor took the equally unusual step of separating its seven-minute recording over two 78 rpm sides, as part of what became the singer's *Dust Bowl Ballads*, volumes 1 and 2, released that summer. (Albums of this time typically collected three 78 rpm singles—six sides—together in a folder. The *Dust Bowl Ballads* therefore featured twelve sides in two separately bound sets.) These recordings were just Woody and an acoustic guitar, and the occasional wail of his harmonica, and they were nearly relentless in their subject matter—"The Great Dust Storm," "Dust Bowl Refugee," "Dusty Old Dust," and so on. But every one of these songs was haunted by the ghost of its authenticity, Guthrie tossing off tale after tale of Dust Bowl hardship—farm devastation, bank repossessions, police brutality, migrant abuse, chronic unemployment, union busting, you name it—with the disarming ease of a man who had witnessed every line and somehow lived to sing the tale.

Was it essential to experience adversity to sing about it with feeling? This soon became the central argument of the "folk revival," which would pit the great formal singers of the day—Burl Ives, Richard Dyer-Bennet, and Paul Robeson—against the great instinctive songwriters, among whom Guthrie had no parallel. And while in years to come "folk" would be considered a white man's music, and "blues" a black man's, in 1940 the distinction was not so clear-cut. *Dust Bowl Ballads* included the titles "Dust Bowl Blues," "Dust Pneumonia Blues," and "Talking Dust Bowl Blues," and nobody questioned Guthrie's right to compose or sing such titles any more than Leadbelly and Josh White were criticized for popularizing songs that became indelibly associated with collegiate white folksingers. What all three were doing, in their own way, was bringing their experiences to bear on a New York audience and peer group that had little true understanding of the suffering, or even the upbringing, that infused such songs.

Dust Bowl Ballads did not sell well: reportedly, fewer than a thousand copies. But Guthrie's personality proved an instant hit in Manhattan, and by late 1940 CBS radio hired him for two nationally syndicated radio shows. "They are giving me money so fast I use it to sleep under," he wrote to Alan Lomax of his $350 weekly income, and he wrote, too, to his wife, urging her to bring the family to New York. Guthrie had stopped writing his column for the *People's World* when he took the CBS gigs; it was hard to declare one's Communist sympathies while earning so much money from a national radio network. Then, just as abruptly, he began doubting himself. The show *Back Where I Come From* he could just about defend, though he argued relentlessly with its director, Nicholas Ray, largely over the inclusion of his new friend, Leadbelly. But the other show, *Pipe Smoking Time*, sponsored by Model

Tobacco, complete with a product friendly rewrite of "Dusty Old Dust" as its theme song, was a complete sellout of his principles, and he knew it. When the *New York Sun* came to his newly rented four-room apartment just off Central Park and wrote an almost palpably sarcastic profile under the headline "Wrath's Grapes Turn to Wine?" everyone else came to know it too.

In just ten short months, Guthrie had experienced the archetypal—but always atypical—New York rags-to-riches story. Except that he hadn't come to the city to get rich and famous. Now, recognizing that he had compromised himself, he compensated in the way of so many who find themselves suddenly out of their depth: he quit. Early in January 1941, he loaded up the brand-new Pontiac he'd just bought with his wages, and drove his newly arrived family "home" to Texas. New York City and all the musician friends he'd met there would have to sing their songs of justice without him.

In March 1941, a select group of what John Hammond might have called "left-wing intellectuals" received an invitation to a singing performance at a private house north of Washington Square Park, for the express purpose of financing a recording session. "We want you to come and hear the songs, give your suggestions, and contribute toward underwriting the albums," read the invitation. "Those who join us in pledging money will receive a corresponding number of albums which may be distributed to the cause of peace, and in the cause of a new music which has arisen out of the people."

The event, it tuned out, was organized in large part by Hammond himself, along with the composer Earl Robinson ("The Ballad of Joe Hill") and Eric Bernay, publisher of the *New Masses,* who had underwritten Hammond's Carnegie Hall concerts and now ran the Keynote record label out of his store on 44th Street. As for the performers, they were called the Almanac Singers, and the extent to which they represented "the people" was open to dispute; their concerts so far had done little more than attract publicity in the *Daily Worker.* Nonetheless, the private event in the Village raised $300, and an album called *Songs for John Doe* was duly recorded. Those who appeared on it were Pete Seeger, Lee Hays, and Millard Lampell—and, invited by Seeger at the last moment to add some much needed color to the proceedings, Josh White and his singing companion Sam Gary.

None of the five was named on the sleeve. And though *Songs for John*

Doe was ostensibly issued by Keynote, it bore only the imprint of the pseud-onymous Almanac Records. This was largely in advance recognition of the album's potential for controversy (and backlash), for *Songs for John Doe* did much more than just "Sing Out for Peace," as was proclaimed on its sleeve. It vehemently argued against waging war on Hitler's Germany—at the very moment the American government was gearing up the public to do just that—from the thinly veiled perspective of American Communists, who opposed such intervention exclusively because of the Soviet Union's nonag-gression pact with Nazi Germany.

If such a stance was provocative in itself, the actual lyrics to *Songs for John Doe* were nothing short of incendiary. On "The Ballad of October 16," for example, named for the date on which Congress had passed America's first peacetime draft, the ensemble chorus dared put into President Roosevelt's mouth the refrain "I hate war, and so does Eleanor / But we won't be safe 'till everybody's dead." Josh White, who had just sung at President Roosevelt's recent third inaugural, took the role in "Billy Boy" of an enthusiastic propo-nent of the war and Millard Lampell as a conscientious objector, the latter singing, "You can come around to me when England's a democracy." (There was no mention of the Soviet political system.) "C for Conscription" and "Washington Breakdown" demonstrated their agenda in titles alone, while "Plow Under" took the New Deal policies of the Agricultural Adjustment Association and likened them, with brazen cynicism, to a plan to "plow under every fourth American boy."

Forty years later, such vehemently stated antigovernment themes would form a subgenre of rock music known as "anarcho-punk"; at the time—and especially given the *mood* of the time, what with continental Europe's democ-racies having all fallen to Hitler's empire—there was nothing with which to compare it. As a result, *Songs for John Doe* received press coverage way beyond its likely sales base, the reviews understandably focusing more on the message (and messengers) than the medium. (Indeed, so dominant were the lyrics that it was nearly impossible to critique the music, other than to note that, on "Billy Boy," Josh White at least made polemics sound pretty.) *Time* magazine called the Almanac Singers "a carefully anonymous Manhattan Communist ensemble"; the *New York Times* noted, "If you do not hold with the isolationists, this album will be anathema to you"; and *Atlantic* ran an editorial that said of the songs, "They are strictly subversive and illegal."

And then, on June 22, only a month after the album's release, Germany tore up its nonaggression pact and invaded Russia, leaving the Almanac Singers (and other American Communists) abruptly bereft of their major motive for "peace" and acutely embarrassed in the process. Eric Bernay destroyed remaining copies of *Songs for John Doe* and, under his more familiar Keynote logo, issued a second Almanac Singers album, *Talking Union*. This session featured Guthrie's song "Union Maid," written in Oklahoma while traveling the preceding year with Seeger, and it represented the fruition of that pair's desire, along with Lee Hays, to issue a songbook of union anthems. Subtlety of voice was never these Almanac Singers' strong point—Hays had a booming basso profundo, and Seeger's and Lampell's conversational styles tended toward the overly earnest—and they benefited on "Get Thee behind Me Satan" from the distinct tenor of Pete Hawes. But the sparse musical arrangements this time around indicated a better understanding of the different musical forms that formed America's vast "folk" movement, be it Josh White's delightful blues guitar on "Get Thee behind Me Satan," Hays's gospel vocals on "Union Train," or the chatty style of "Talking Union" itself.

Although he had run away from his success in New York, Guthrie clearly missed his New York friends, and although he had rediscovered his purpose by writing songs for the Bonneville Power Administration in Oregon, he jumped just about the first cattlecar back east when the letter came inviting him to join the Almanac Singers on a summer tour. He seemed almost relieved that the Nazis had invaded Russia; now he could resume his hatred of fascists in general, Hitler in particular, and begin working that virulence into song. Not that he had much chance on the two albums he recorded with the Almanac Singers in one night before they went on tour. *Deep-Sea Chanteys* and *Sod-Buster Ballads* (both produced by Alan Lomax) comprised mostly traditional numbers true to the album titles, best remembered for the first recording of Guthrie's "Hard, Ain't It Hard," and his rendition of a little-known New Orleans ballad, "House of the Rising Sun." Paid $250 for the two sessions, Hays, Seeger, Lampell, and Guthrie spent the money immediately on a gas-guzzling Buick and took it cross-country, singing primarily at union halls, staying mainly with hospitable workers, unaware that the FBI had opened files on them and was monitoring their performances.

The Almanac Singers appeared to hide little. Upon return to New York, they rented a building at 130 West Tenth Street, near Greenwich Avenue, named it Almanac House, and turned it into a commune. "People came and went all the time," wrote Seeger. "The cuisine was erratic but interesting, the furniture and decorations almost non-existent, the sleeping done at odd hours." But, he noted, "the output of songs was phenomenal." So was the turnover of residents and singers, a veritable who's who of the folk revival that included Alan Lomax, his sister Bess, her future husband, Butch Hawes, and Butch's brother Pete; Agnes "Sis" Cunningham and her husband, Gordon Freisen, hardened Communists from Guthrie's home state of Oklahoma; Burl Ives; Nicholas Ray, the radio director, who took residence on the couch while estranged from his wife; the singer Arthur Stern; the actor and ballad singer Cisco Houston; Sam Gary and Josh White; and two new arrivals from the South, Sonny Terry (who had played at "From Spirituals to Swing") and his musical and social companion, Brownie McGhee, a polio-ridden blues singer and guitarist, both of whom lived at Almanac House until they could find permanent accommodation.

This cross section of class, race, gender, and geographic roots personi-fied the Village ethic of inclusion, and the collective quest for equality led the Almanac Singers, whose lineup varied not just from day to day but from day to night, to perform at all manner of benefits and rallies, taverns, and even the occasional theater. Much of the singing was conducted at Almanac House itself, where, McGhee recalled, food consisted almost exclusively of eggs and pumpernickel bread (usually baked by Hays); others noted that resi-dents got by mostly on cigarettes, red wine, and whiskey. All income earned by any resident was meant to be placed in a central kitty, but there was never enough to go around, and so rent parties doubling as song festivals were held in the basement. Guthrie and Seeger took the name for these sing-alongs from a word they'd picked up at a similar event in Seattle at the end of the tour, and the term "hootenanny" entered the Village vernacular.

Given the town house's central location, the hootenannies soon devel-oped an air of celebrity. Earl Robinson and John Hammond brought people from uptown, said Lampell, "and before it was over we were even getting a smattering of Junior League debutantes who thought it was so colorful to go down to Greenwich Village and see these folk singers." The Almanacs became such a cause célèbre that a former lover of Joe Hill donated to them the singer's private papers, as if passing on the martyred singer's torch.

Harmony singing at such continued close quarters inevitably led to discord. Guthrie received all due respect at Almanac House as the pre-eminent songwriter-in-residence, but rarely returned it, refuting Seeger's demands that songwriting credits be shared equally, and constantly needling his singing partners for their comparatively comfortable upbringings. He sub-jected Lampell to relentless abuse, both because he was an easygoing, north-eastern, middle-class liberal (and therefore an easy target) but also because he was a great writer, the only obvious threat to Guthrie's literary dominance. Lampell eventually moved out, the better to maintain his friendships. (He later became a successful playwright, novelist, and screenwriter.) Nor did Guthrie spare Hays, who, for being a preacher's son, was derided as "middle class," even though he hailed from Arkansas and had been politicized by the depression. Hays rarely made things easy on himself: he had quit the sum-mer tour complaining of various illnesses, and he continued to misdirect his priorities, reserving his strength for in-house debates while frequently crying off from outside bookings. He was also a heavy drinker, and though he had better girth for it than Guthrie, who spent much of his spare time at the nearby White Horse Tavern, Hays was belligerent when steamed. He was eventually asked to leave the Almanac Singers, and his place on bass vocals was taken by Arthur Stern, who knew better than to live in the midst of so many competing personalities, and maintained his residence in Queens.

Only Pete Seeger escaped the infighting unscathed—and that was because everyone knew that, without him, the entire enterprise would fall apart. It was Seeger who fulfilled bookings when nobody else seemed capable of the task; Seeger who communicated between and on behalf of the various Almanacs; Seeger who ensured that the bills were paid. Such organizational skills were surely in his blood. His parents, Charles (a profes-sor and pianist) and Constance (a violinist), were classical music aficionados driven from the University of California at Berkeley by Charles's leftist poli-tics. Back on their native East Coast, they'd lingered just long enough for their (third) son, Peter, to be born before they built themselves an automobile trailer, packed up the children, and set off on the road, intending to promote and perform their classical music to rural Americans. Instead, the opposite occurred: Charles was converted by the locals' own folk music, which he then set about collecting and disseminating with a vigor later inherited by his son Pete—but not by his wife, who left the family for pastures new. Back in New York, Pete had taken up the ukulele and, at age sixteen, after attending a square dance festival in Asheville, North Carolina, the five-string banjo, too, at which he came to excel. He then gained entry to Harvard on a journalism scholarship, but left after two years, at least in part because of his politics: "I ended up joining the Young Communist League, I let my marks slip, and lost my scholarship to Harvard," he explained years later.

When the United States finally entered the war in December 1941, it found itself fighting the same enemy as the Soviet Union. To the extent that this put America and Russia on the same side, the relieved Almanac Singers accordingly, gratefully—and, it has to be said, quite earnestly—changed their tune. On the title track of the 1942 album *Dear Mr. President*, Seeger admitted directly to Roosevelt, as if they had a personal relationship, that although they hadn't always agreed in the past, "we got to lick Mr. Hitler and until we do, other things can wait." (Being Pete Seeger, he then listed his grievances anyway.) And if Woody Guthrie's famous slogan "This Machine Kills Fascists," scrawled across his guitar, did not speak for itself, then the title of the songbook *Anti-Fascist Songs of the Almanac Singers* certainly did. Such was the fervor of the Almanac Singers' newly discovered prowar ethic that they were recruited to sing *Dear Mr. President*'s instantly enjoyable banjo-led square dance, "Round and Round Hitler's Grave," on the propaganda radio show *This Is War* in February 1942. Three days later, the *New York World-Telegram* revealed their various Communist affiliations and— communism being now further derided in the States for its two-year tacit defense of fascism—they were dropped as if they had been some highly contagious disease.

Conscription also played its part in their downfall. Seeger, who in early 1941, on the song "Washington Breakdown," had declared, "Franklin D., listen to me, you ain't a-gonna send me 'cross the sea," was drafted into the Army and promptly sent to the Pacific. Guthrie joined the Merchant Marines, repeatedly, to put off a similar fate until he was finally inducted into the Army—on the very day that Germany surrendered. The group at Almanac House had moved in the interim, after falling behind on rent, to a loft at 430 Sixth Avenue, just down Tenth Street, a less glamorous location for the Sunday "hoots." And then some of the other Almanacs migrated to trouble-torn Detroit in an attempt to spread the pro-union message, and the Singers fell apart completely. Their reputation as folk music's first protest group would live on much longer.

•   •   •

And what of Leadbelly and Josh White, the two other key figures from
that night at the Forrest? In 1940, Leadbelly was already fifty-two,
twice Josh White's age, yet their backgrounds contained many shared experiences. Each was born in the South: Huddie Ledbetter in Shreveport,
Louisiana, Joshua White in Greenville, South Carolina. Each claimed to
have worked with the great Blind Lemon Jefferson—Ledbetter as his elder
and apparent equal, performing together through the Texas Panhandle,
White as the blues guitarist's occasional "lead boy." Leadbelly had traveled
the South, playing windjammer accordion and twelve-string guitar, picking
up a treasure trove of songs along the way that he sang with a voice that
matched the volume of a foghorn with the cadence of a great preacher. All
but an indentured child servant to his blind singer employers, White nonetheless developed his own skills on six-string guitar, aided by a voice as soft
as lamb's wool. Leadbelly was a champion cotton picker, a dedicated womanizer, and a brutal fighter; convicted of killing a man back in 1917, he had
nonetheless won release from two jail terms thanks to his musical talents
and his ability to ingratiate himself with authority figures. White had no such
criminal blemishes to his record, but was every bit the womanizer himself,
and had ample experience of the perils of southern living for a black man:
with his employer John Henry Arnold, he had witnessed a double lynching
in Georgia after lying down to sleep in a nearby field.

Moving to New York at different points in the 1930s, White settling in
Harlem, Leadbelly on the Lower East Side, both men had been signed to the
budget ARC label, singing a blues that was fast falling out of favor with a
young black audience that preferred newer trends in jazz and vocal music.
Each fared better performing to an educated, white audience that coveted
the traditional music of the poor, black South—and if there seemed something vaguely distasteful about this, they accepted that it was the means not
only by which they could put food on the table but by which the folk music
of their roots could be preserved.

And so, in 1940, as Guthrie was putting his *Dust Bowl Ballads* on tape
for RCA, each man accepted a major label commission to record an album of
(evidently fashionable) prison songs. Leadbelly had done the crime and
served the time and could sing with greater authenticity, but for *The Mid-*

night Special and Other Southern Prison Songs, he was backed by the Golden Gate Quartet, whose gospel gloss on songs like "Alabama Bound" and "Pick a Bale of Cotton" was just a little too forceful. White's album benefited from the involvement of John Hammond, who shepherded the project through Columbia, and on songs such as "Nine Foot Shovel" and "Trouble" was better served by his own Carolinians, whom he had assembled mainly from the cast of the short-lived Broadway production *John Henry*, in which he had played Blind Lemon Jefferson opposite Paul Robeson's title role. That these prison song albums were intended for white liberal audiences was demonstrated by the sleeve notes for *Chain Gang*, which claimed, without a hint of self-consciousness, that its "seven Negro laments" offered "perhaps the most genuine folk music of our times."

But White then came into his own. His next album, *Southern Exposure: An Album of Jim Crow Blues*, tackled, head-on, American's institutionalized racism in the buildup to the war against fascism. Crucially, the lyrics came not from White (who was always stronger as an interpreter) but from the Harlem Renaissance poet Waring Cuney. The liner notes, similarly, were penned by the prominent black writer (and Communist Party member) Richard Wright. *Southern Exposure* was (no surprise) issued by Keynote, which launched it at a party in Harlem in late 1941 attended by such musical dignitaries as Teddy Wilson, Earl Robinson, Burl Ives, W. C. Handy—and Lee Hays, whose Almanac Singers must have suddenly seemed inconsequential by comparison.

Southern Exposure succeeded where *Songs for John Doe* failed, in part because White had such a gorgeously endearing voice and an equally attractive way with the guitar, but also because it had been carefully crafted, its lyrics the work of a published poet. It was political, certainly—that was the point of it—but the issues had been thought through without quite such a provocative stance as the Almanac Singers had taken. Its most obvious talking point was "Uncle Sam Says," written after White visited his brother in boot camp at Fort Dix, New Jersey, where he was appalled at the third-class accommodation in which the black troops were being housed; Cuney elaborated on White's experience to incorporate the wider issue of segregation throughout the armed services. When Roosevelt heard the song and understood that as president he was the current stand-in for "Uncle Sam," he requested that White come to Washington and perform it in private—an astonishing invitation for a man of White's humble background. The singer subsequently developed a close personal friendship with the first family, one publicly cemented when Eleanor Roosevelt became godmother to his son, Josh White Jr. In 1942, the first lady's fascination with progressive Greenwich Village induced her to take an apartment of her own on Washington Square Park West.

Leadbelly followed up his own prison album by heading in a direction entirely different from White's. In May 1941, he recorded an album for the New Yorker Moe Asch, the son of a famous Yiddish writer who had started an eponymous record label two years earlier, initially to supply minority radio stations with foreign-language folk music. *Play Parties in Song and Dance as Sung by Leadbelly* served as a high-profile introduction for Asch into the world of American folk music: the notion of a convicted murderer engaging an audience of children to "Skip to My Lou" and "Swing Low, Sweet Chariot" proved just as press-worthy as *Songs for John Doe*. (The ruling columnist Walter Winchell had a field day with it.) Asch was unbowed, describing Leadbelly as "the most wonderful gentleman you'd ever want to meet." The album, on which Leadbelly entertained and educated—but never patronized—his young audience, became a steady seller, launching the endlessly lucrative market for children's folk music.

Inevitably, White and Leadbelly were paired onstage together—at Max Gordon's Village Vanguard, at Nicholas Ray's suggestion and direction. Leadbelly had that deeply resonant voice and picked with deceptive casualness at the twelve-string guitar, an instrument of which he was often labeled "the King": "his genius was not so much in the notes he played as in the notes he didn't play," observed Pete Seeger. Josh White sang and played his six-string as if spinning silk with both: "The sound of his guitar stirred me sensually," wrote Eartha Kitt. "His mouth moved as though he was making love to the words he spoke." White played up this sex appeal to its fullest and most provocative extent, performing with the top of his silk shirts teasingly unbuttoned. Leadbelly, on the other hand, though quite the dandy, had proven unable to shake his country mannerisms that, through a combination of deference and eagerness, sometimes appeared to play into racial stereotypes. He even called his greatest fan "Mr. Woody," and Josh White later took him to task for this: "he played up to the Uncle Tom image of the Negro."

On opening night, November 25, 1941, there were no such conflicts on show, and over two hundred people were turned away from the Vanguard. Among those who made it inside was Guthrie, who responded to Gordon's request for comments by composing, from Almanac House, a several-thousand-word critique of remarkable insight. "Josh and Huddie come from my type of people," he noted, a dig perhaps at his housemates on West Tenth Street. Recognizing nightclub assimilation of traditional folk blues when he saw it, he damned Gordon and Ray's presentation of the duo with faint praise: White sang "too mush [*sic*] in the same movement and temp, all too slow beat, and smooth and sweet," while Leadbelly, he said, was afforded a disservice by being placed below White, off the stage. (The Vanguard had only the one microphone and decided that Leadbelly was loud enough to do without it.) He decried the lack of protest music in the set and encouraged the performers to be allowed to go at each other with their guitars; the word around town, he suggested, should be: " 'Let's go down to the Vanguard and watch Leadbelly and Josh carve each other out.' "

The engagement proved an enormous success either way, extended for three months in all, and when it was done, Gordon moved White into his new midtown cabaret, the Blue Angel. Soon after that, White embarked on a lengthy residency at Café Society, which had itself opened a second, "uptown" location—even though the irony of its name was often lost, as was much of White's political material, in the glamour of the new venue and the upscale audience that it attracted.

White's parallel personalities were captured on records he made in 1944 for Moe Asch. The title *Josh White Sings Easy* indicated the singer's desire to promote his mainstream nightclub persona and included a breakthrough hit, "One Meatball." Yet the same album concluded with "The House I Live In," a patriotic anthem with lyrics by Abel Meeropol/Lewis Allan and music by Earl Robinson, about a multiracial America that offered "the right to speak my mind out." (Frank Sinatra would later adopt the song.) White also recorded for Asch an album named for *Strange Fruit*, complete with a blood-strewn sleeve design. Billie Holiday was furious that White covered "her" song—to the point of supposedly holding a knife to his throat backstage one night at Café Society—but as a black man who had actually witnessed a lynching down south, White explained that he had every right to sing it, too, "until we never have to sing it again."

For his own part, Asch insisted that he "was never involved in the political system." Rather, he was more concerned with his role as "docu-menter," to which end he enthusiastically favored quantity over quality. "It's more interesting for me to sell two each of 1,600 records than 3,200 of a single release if I have not got the facilities to press them," he once explained, and over a forty-year period he proved his point. In 1944, Asch was almost obsessively prolific, cutting acetates on glass when he couldn't access shellac. Among the many sessions he cut that year was an all-star lineup, assembled by Alan Lomax around various singers' work and services leave schedules, featuring Bess and Butch Hawes, Burl Ives, Tom Glazer, Pete Seeger, Sonny Terry, Brownie McGhee, and Josh White. They took the nom de plume of the Union Boys, although, other than the AFM, which had just spent two years preventing its members from making records, it's hard to know which "unions" these "boys" claimed to represent; the album's title, *Songs for Victory: Music for Political Action*, was a more honest indication of their intent. The album concluded with "Jim Crow," on which Josh White sang, bluntly, "Why is the Negro still in slavery?"

A month later, Asch brought Woody Guthrie into the studio to record a pair of songs. Energized by the experience, Guthrie returned with Cisco Houston and, on one occasion, Sonny Terry too, to record a phenomenal 123 more songs over three days in April, including what would become forever known as "This Land Is Your Land." "I was my own recording engineer," said Asch. "There was one mike, we set it up and they just sang, one song after another. Every one was perfect. And if there was a mistake, that was all right too."

Indeed. Guthrie sang about social issues with comic ease, as on the war-related ballads "Lindbergh" and "The Biggest Thing Man Had Ever Done." He recorded his own children's number, "Riding in My Car," full of horn and engine noises. And he put to tape a song he'd written back in 1940 that observed how, if Jesus was to preach in New York City, "they would lay Jesus Christ in his grave." Asch, who noted that Guthrie was "anti–New York" and "a very hard man to get along with," released "Jesus Christ" as part of a six-song album at the end of the year; the many other cuts found their way into public hands only in increments over the next fifty years.

The indefatigable Asch even managed to bring Leadbelly and Josh White into the studio to duet on "I've Got a Pretty Flower" and "Don't Lie Buddy," a song they'd performed together at the Vanguard. It's interesting to ponder what might have become, without Asch's enthusiasm, of the folk revival, specifically of the four key figures who first joined together at the Forrest in 1940. What we do know is that, with Seeger and Guthrie at war, and Leadbelly ageing fast, White became the most successful. "By 1944," wrote his biographer Elijah Wald, "Josh rivaled Burl Ives as America's most popular folksinger." Less out of jealousy than a misguided determination to break into the movies, Leadbelly upped and moved to California.

5

MAMBO MADNESS

Machito and Mario Bauzá had a problem. The war was over, and the Afro-Cubans had just started what should have been a rewarding residency at the newly opened Palladium Ballroom, on the northeast corner of 53rd Street and Broadway. But it was not going well. Tommy Morton, the manager of the second-floor venue, insisted Machito play not just the rhumbas and congas, which came instinctively, but fox-trots, tangos, and waltzes too—every possible dance style for every potential customer. Machito's orchestra, currently recording for the tiny Latino label Verne, was happy for the steady work at a time when the big swing orchestras were breaking up on a weekly basis, but the ballroom audiences were heading instead to the Arcadia, on the other side of Broadway, and to the Roseland, around the corner, and that was not so pleasing.

Frustrated, Machito and Mario Bauzá leveled with Morton: the Palladium should put its faith in Afro-Cuban music, not just in the Afro-Cuban Orchestra as all-around entertainers. A compromise was reached: to test the waters, the Palladium would host a bill featuring nothing but Latin music—but on a Sunday afternoon, so as not to interfere with the regular crowd.

Machito recalled what happened next: "I went to 110th and 5th and I brought Federico Pagani to the Palladium. On the train I asked him how much he earned. He said, 'Don't worry about the money, I'll prove to these people I can blow off the roof.' "

Pagani had every reason to be confident. The forty-year-old Puerto

Rican, a resident of Spanish Harlem since 1925, was a prominent example of an eternally optimistic New York subset—the freelance promoter, the man who brings the crowd. Pagani's methods were shameless: he organized zoot suit contests, advertised a "dance of the bald head" night for which male entrants willingly shaved their scalps, and when pitting Cuba's Xavier Cugat against Puerto Rico's Noro Morales for the "King of the Rumba" crown, dressed them up in boxing gloves for the poster. He even once promised a Harlem audience the appearance of Joe Louis—and rather than the world heavyweight champion and minority hero, brought out one José Luis onstage in the middle of the evening. The audience was having so much fun dancing to Machito's orchestra that they took the hoax in the spirit in which it was intended.

But all that was on home turf, in Harlem and also the South Bronx, which in the 1930s had begun absorbing the overflow of the city's black and Latino population. The Palladium was in midtown: the big time. And so Pagani took no chances. He hired five additional bands, including one led by Machito's biggest rival at the time, the outsized Puerto Rican pianist Noro Morales. He named the event the Blen Blen Club after the Chano Pozo composition and had fliers distributed at bus stops and subway stations across Harlem. Come that all-important Sunday, Pagani, Bauzá, and Machito arrived together, nervously, at lunchtime—to find a line snaking around the block.

"All the blacks came from the Barrio," said Pagani. "There were more blacks than white." (Pagani's "blacks" included Latinos.) This posed something of a problem to Morton and his bosses. "The Italian owner was happy but he said there were too many blacks at the dance. He wanted less of them. I bought [band leader] Pupi Campo for my second dance, and even more blacks came. The owner said, 'I appreciate the good job you did, but hold it down a little. There are more blacks than whites.' I said, 'OK, I'll try.' For the third dance, even more blacks came. He said, 'I can't take it. There are too many blacks. You're going to ruin my business.'"

It was time for Pagani to call Morton's bluff. What do you care about more, he demanded to know: the color black or the color green? Morton, preferring a healthy bank balance to any racial exclusion, told Pagani to keep doing what he was doing.

So began one of the great chapters in New York nightclub history. From that day in 1947 until its doors were shuttered in 1966, the Palladium

Ballroom would be known as the home of Latin dance music. And whatever fears Tommy Morton may have harbored about the influx of "blacks" proved completely unfounded, for the Palladium brought creeds and colors together onto its dance floor as had never been witnessed before in midtown.

The Sunday afternoon matinees were such a success that the weekday nights picked up too, ensuring the Machito Orchestra's financial security. Pagani, meanwhile, was instructed to fill the lower matinee slots with "pickup groups." He offered such a position to Tito Puente, the popular and talented *timbalero* for Pupi Campo, and, watching Puente rehearse his group, was instantly impressed by a number they were working up. Asked its title, Puente shrugged it off as a *picadillo*—a mish-mash—and with that, he had his Sunday group's name: the Picadilly Boys. ("Picadillo" became a staple of Puente's live and recorded set.)

Their debut at the Palladium got everyone talking. "Tito was incredibly good," said Pagani. "He had a fresh sound with a jazz influence," one that was otherwise apparent in Latin music only in the Machito Orchestra. The Picadilly Boys received repeat bookings at the Palladium, inspiring Puente to make the most of the moment: he left Pupi Campo, taking many of the musicians with him, placed himself up front on the timbals and vibraphone, hired a singer, and secured his seven-piece Tito Puente Orchestra a booking at El Patio Club on Long Island's Atlantic Beach for the summer of 1949. When Labor Day rolled around and the other groups came back from their own summer bookings—mostly at the Catskills resorts—an expanded Tito Puente Orchestra joined the roster of weeknight Palladium headliners. All of a sudden, Machito and his Afro-Cubans had some real competition.

He was born at least forty years before the term "Nuyorican" came into fashion. Yet if anyone embodied the spirit of that word—as someone who melds his Puerto Rican roots with his New York home into a singular way of life—it was Ernesto "Tito" Puente, the greatest Latin bandleader New York City ever produced.

Puente's parents had arrived in New York in 1921—drawn, like so many other Puerto Ricans, by their new status as U.S. citizens and the accompanying ideal of American prosperity. The reality in Spanish Harlem was quite different, however, and Ernestito, as his mother called him, born in Harlem

Hospital in 1923, bounced around schools as his family searched for affordable rent, their hardships worsened by the death of Tito's younger brother in
a fall from a tenement fire escape.

Yet Tito and his sister, Anna, never suffered for support. Their mother
enrolled them in the Stars of the Future program at La Milagrosa Catholic
Church, on 115th and Lenox, where they learned to dance and sing. When
Tito started picking out on piano, by ear, lines from the Cuban pianist
Anselmo Sacasas's records, she took him to the Manhattan School of Music
on the Upper East Side, paying for the 25-cent lessons by removing a quarter
from her husband's pocket while he was sleeping. And when the family
rented a room to a music teacher who played alto sax, the family bartered
lessons for young Ernestito on that instrument, too.

Like almost any teenager in Harlem, Puente was a fan of the Ink Spots,
singing their songs in the school stairwells with his friends. "I went to black
schools. I never had any conflict with them," he recalled. "We listened to the
great bands of the day on the radio—Goodman, Artie Shaw, Duke Ellington,
and I'd go to theaters like the Paramount and the Strand to see them perform." Like so many jazz fans of the late 1930s, Puente was infatuated with
Gene Krupa's flamboyant drumming on "Sing Sing Sing," and he took trap
drum lessons to imitate the master. According to Puente, he then won a
"Gene Krupa drum contest" at the Paramount judged by Goodman and
Krupa themselves. He did it by playing "Sing Sing Sing" "note for note, just
like the record," he said, adding, "I put a little Latin shit in there, too." If the
teenager Puente had an abundance of talent, he was hardly lacking for confidence, either.

Come 1939, the Puente family was living on East 110th Street, between
Madison and Park Avenues, in the heart of Spanish Harlem. There Tito
made friends with another sixteen-year-old, who had just moved in five doors
down and with whom his path would cross for much of the next thirty years:
Pablo "Tito" Rodriguez, from Puerto Rico. Following the death of his mother
while giving birth to her tenth child, and that of his father soon thereafter,
Pablo had recently been sent to New York, where his older brother Johnny
employed him to sing and play maracas in his own, active orchestra. That
was but a stepping stone for young Pablo, who had the looks of a movie star
and an ego to match; before he turned twenty, he inherited Miguelito Valdés's
singing position in Xavier Cugat's orchestra—and he might have held on to it

had America not entered World War II. Tito Rodriguez, as he became known, was drafted into the Army in the summer of 1942.

Tito Puente's ascent proved no less rapid. Dropping out of school at sixteen to pursue music full-time, he quickly met José Curbelo, a pianist newly arrived from Cuba who hired Tito as a percussionist for a three-month run in Miami. There they roomed together and became close friends—a relationship that would serve Puente well in years to come. Back in New York, Puente found himself following his neighborhood friend Pablo into Johnny Rodriguez's orchestra, before moving on to accompany Anselmo Sacasas—the same pianist whose solos he had once copied by ear—and the giant Noro Morales. But it was when playing briefly with Machito's Afro-Cubans in 1942 that he came into his own: the teenage *timbalero* proved such a sensation that Machito brought Puente up front to perform alongside him. Then, just when it looked as if he was set to become a star, he too was drafted.

Tito Rodriguez spent only a few months in the service. Tito Puente spent three full years at war, much of it on the aircraft carrier USS *Santee*, from which he saw action in nine battles, earning himself a presidential commendation in the process. In between combat, Puente played alto saxophone in the ship's band, from whose (peacetime-era) professional musicians he picked up important lessons in American jazz. Puente sent arrangements and compositions back from the *Santee* to Machito, but though the GI Bill guaranteed returning servicemen their former jobs, Puente learned upon discharge that his replacement in the Afro-Cubans already had five children to support; he used the Bill to finance tuition at Juilliard instead. Adding the vibraphone and marimbas to his long list of instruments, he also studied the Schillinger method, a mathematical system of composition of which Stan Kenton was one of the better-known practitioners.

Puente's studies paid off quickly. José Curbelo hired him in 1946 to provide the arrangements for his RCA sessions, for which Tito Rodriguez was featured singer. The two Titos continued to work with Curbelo until Rodriguez was fired, under a cloud, just a month after he became a father, around the same time that Puente took the job as Pupi Campo's musical director. Rodriguez gradually regained his reputation, making his debut as a bandleader in 1948 for Gabriel Oller's new Spanish Music Center label. By the following summer, ready to try out a new act, he hired his good friend Tito Puente to provide the arrangements. With the certainty of someone who has recognized a new trend and determined to be a part of it, Rodriguez called his new group the Mambo Devils.

"Anarchy in tempo." That was how Arsenio Rodriguez (the blind *tres* player) referred to the mambo, and he was fully qualified to do so, having helped formulate it in Cuba as a particularly fast and furious exchange between the percussion instruments (especially the conga) and the brass (especially the trumpets) during a song's *montuno* (improvisation) section. The Cuban bass player Israel Lopez wrote an instrumental called "Mambo" in 1938, and the word began showing up more frequently in the title of instrumentals, both in Cuba and in New York—until, in 1950, Perez Prado had a major North American hit with "Mambo #5," and suddenly everyone was talking about the new sound. New York's Puerto Ricans and Cubans alike were already well affiliated with the mambo, and remained somewhat cool toward the commercial style of Prado, who was Cuban-born but a Mexican resident. "That music wasn't dance music," said Puente years later, with a rare lack of diplomacy. "That wasn't Rodriguez's sound or Machito's or my sound." He explained, "It was more authentic music we were trying to play, from the Caribbean."

As Puente described it, the mambo differed from its antecedent, the rumba, "in that it concentrates more on the off-beat, the after-beat, like modern jazz—whereas the rumba is mostly on the beat. And the mambo has much more syncopation in its melodic form than the rumba." This helped explained some of its popularity in New York City, the international head-quarters of jazz, but it would be restrictive to define mambo purely in techni-cal terms; like any dance that grows so famous as to become a self-sufficient genre—think disco in the 1970s—mambo was a highly sensual rhythm that liberated its listeners, from both the constraints of their own hardworking lives and those that society tried to impose upon them.

When the mambo first swept New York, Machito's Afro-Cubans were in the midst of their Cubop period: they reached a pinnacle of respectability when Norman Granz invited them to play at Carnegie Hall in February 1949 as part of his Jazz at the Philharmonic series. Arguably the hardest-working band in New York show business, the Afro-Cubans could be found later that same night broadcasting from Bop City, one of three new bebop venues on

Broadway, not far from 52nd Street. Bop City had been opened by some of the people behind the Royal Roost, where Machito's Afro-Cubans also held court in the spring of 1949, engaging in an electrifying series of broadcasts for "Symphony" Sid Torin's radio show on WMCA, with a number of key beboppers in their ranks—and, on at least one occasion, Harry Belafonte on vocals. There was a third bebop venue, the Clique, at 1678 Broadway, almost next door to the Palladium, which in December 1949 changed its name to Birdland. Among the initial headliners was the musician it had seemingly been named for: Charlie Parker.

But Bird had no financial stake in Birdland. The venue was fronted instead by Moishe "Morris" Levy. Born in the Bronx, Levy had been childhood friends with the future Genovese crime family boss Vincent "the Chin" Gigante; he got his start in nightlife at fourteen (after being thrown out of school for assaulting an elderly female teacher) as a hatcheck boy at the Greenwich Village Inn, where he "won the favor" of Thomas Eboli, who later headed the Genovese family himself. Levy claimed to have been a partial owner in the Royal Roost who felt betrayed when its backers opened Bop City without him, and who was then redeemed by the success of Birdland. Given that Levy was just twenty-two years old in 1949, it's unlikely he could have financed the venture himself, and nobody ever suspected him, at that point, of being more than the day-to-day manager. But he was certainly doing a good job of it: at Birdland, the booking policy ran the gamut from blues musicians to vocal groups as well as Latin and jazz orchestras—and it was rarely less than packed.

Within weeks of Birdland's debut, the Palladium closed for renovations, reopening on March 17, 1950, in grand style, with Tito Puente as headliner, and with a new owner, Max Hyman, whose wife belonged to the family of the Otis Elevators fortune; together, the couple had deep enough pockets and sufficient love for Latin music to ensure the Palladium's survival. Indeed, in a city known for short-lived nightclub ventures, both the Palladium and Birdland proved unusually resilient, each of them thriving until well into the sixties.

Their proximity to each other facilitated regular interaction between the musicians. Jazz artists playing Birdland, if they were of Dizzy's or Bird's caliber, would occasionally be invited to sit in and jam at the Palladium; but the Latin orchestras were *hired* to play Birdland. Tito Puente, who led some memorable radio broadcasts from Birdland in 1952, credited this unequal flow of traffic to the fact that "Latin musicians can play better jazz than jazz musicians play in Latin."

The Latin orchestras' popularity was further aided by the demise of bebop, a music you couldn't dance to, and one that fell victim to its own image of carefully studied cool, complete with the birth of the "hipster" who, as Marshall Stearns described him in *The Story of Jazz*, "played no instrument," but "became more knowing than his model," a definition that still held good fifty years later. As Miles Davis literally turned his back on the audience, steering modern jazz ever farther away from the mainstream, bebop's founding father Dizzy Gillespie found himself suddenly rudderless. Within six months of the groundbreaking "Manteca" and "Cubana Be/ Cubana Bop," his orchestra was recording corny big band numbers like "In the Land of Oo-Bla-Dee," complete with Dizzy's wretched vocal deliveries, which sounded more like a vaudeville send-up of bebop than the real thing. A move from Victor to Capitol only accelerated Gillespie's artistic decline. It fell to Dizzy's old friend Charlie Parker to talk some sense into him—in public, via an interview in the jazz bible *Down Beat*. Stung, Gillespie broke up his orchestra a few months later. In June 1950, proving that there were no hard feelings, he joined Parker, Thelonious Monk, Buddy Rich, and Curley Russell for a one-day session, produced by Norman Granz, that yielded half a dozen great new cuts, of which "Bloomdido" and "Mohawk" served to remind long-term listeners what bebop was about.

Granz then brought Parker back together with Machito's Afro-Cubans in December 1950, with Flip Phillips and Buddy Rich among the nineteen-person orchestra. Providing something of a climax to the whole Afro-Cuban/ bebop crossover, they recorded the *Afro-Cuban Jazz Suite* written by Chico O'Farrill—the Irish Cuban who had been so taken aback by Dizzy Gillespie's "Things to Come" a few years earlier. O'Farrill divided the seventeen-minute suite into five parts, the titles of which spoke more crudely to their styles than did the deft performances. Buddy Rich's full trap drum solo on "Jazz" provided a highlight for those desiring a break from the clave rhythms, but it was Parker's sublime alto sax playing on "Mambo" that proved the most enduring contribution—and suitably so, given that genre's impending omnipotence. For the next few years, it would be difficult for the Latin orchestras to think of much else.

· · ·

Marlon Brando put it best: "No one who went to the Palladium could think about anything but dancing. . . . People moved their bodies in incredible ways to the rhythm of the mambo—the most beautiful dance I had ever seen."

Brando, whose passion for the conga drums led him all the way to Cuba to purchase a pair once owned by Chano Pozo, was joined on the Palladium's Wednesday night dance floor—"exhibition night"—by the likes of Kim Novak, Bob Hope, Sammy Davis Jr., even Marlene Dietrich. Wednesdays were a big night with Jewish people, too, who were familiar with the orchestras from their summer vacations at the Catskills hotels, where dancing lessons were part of the daily activities. Indeed, Wednesdays were particularly popular for the floor show by professionals like Augie and Margo Rodriguez, Carmen Cruz and "Cuban" Pete—and especially the free mambo lessons directed by "Killer Joe" Piro, an Italian from East Harlem and former champion Lindy Hop dancer at the Savoy, who became an enduring dance floor legend. (Tito Rodriguez celebrated him on record with one of his finest cuts, "Mambo with Killer Joe.") It was the night that, by many accounts, saw some of the greatest moves ever witnessed on a New York dance floor.

Friday nights brought "more of a Latin crowd," said Eddie Palmieri, whose older brother Charlie was one of the top pianists of the era (playing with Tito Puente before breaking out on his own), and who would later lead his group La Perfecta through lengthy Palladium residencies. "Tough guys with big names that were well protected in the streets. Gamblers. All the sharp dressers, they came in with their ladies to dance." Saturdays were dominated by Puerto Ricans, who by 1952 were arriving in New York at the rate of 1,135 per week, most of them working in factories and other minimum-wage jobs; lesser-known Puerto Rican orchestras featured lower down the bill to cater to them. And on Sundays the audience was primarily a black crowd, from Harlem, Brooklyn, and the Bronx. Though the demographic split across these four nights suggested a kind of voluntary segregation, the truth was that, in the 1950s, mambo became a universal language across the city's racial and ethnic groups, all of whom gathered on the integrated dance floor to practice and perfect their moves. "The only time you actually stood in front of the stage," said Joe Conzo, who worked as Tito

Puente's publicist, confidant, and subsequent archivist, "was when they had a floor show on Wednesday. Other than that, you *had* to dance."

In such an environment, the orchestras had a role much like that of the future club DJ: they were paid to keep the dancers moving by playing the latest fashionable sounds, and working flat out to do so in a manner that would distinguish them from those who came before and after. Throughout the 1950s, the three masters at this game—and in the Palladium's early days, some were lucky enough to see all three on the same bill—were Machito, Tito Puente, and Tito Rodriguez.

Asked one time which orchestra he preferred playing against, Tito Puente or Tito Rodriguez, Machito replied, "The two of them together. Because Tito would beat the heck out of Tito, Tito would beat the heck out of Tito, and by the time they got to me they were exhausted and I could take them easy." This was the perspective of the headliner, who knew he would be closing out the night; it was to the eternal credit of Machito and Mario Bauzá that, fifteen years after their orchestra had first begun wowing audiences at La Conga, and a full decade after they had pioneered Afro-Cuban jazz and Cubop, they were still revered as New York's premier mambo act despite the younger competition.

Down the bill, however, the battle between the two Titos became so intense that the teenage friendship turned into professional competitiveness and then genuine rivalry. Rodriguez was a multi-instrumentalist, a singer, a looker, and an extraordinary dancer, too: surviving film from the era shows him bouncing himself backward off the floor one hand at a time, just like the hip-hop break-dancers of a quarter century later. Tito Puente did not, initially, sing, but he could certainly dance, and his skills on the timbals mesmerized audiences even as he made it look effortless. He was also his orchestra's musical director, beholden to no one but himself, and his arranging skills enabled him to attract some of the era's greatest musicians.

The confrontation between the two Titos appeared to have been instigated by Rodriguez, who, believing he had pushed ahead in album sales, demanded that his name go above Puente's on the Palladium marquee. Puente refused, and the pair broke with protocol by declining to introduce each other as they swapped places on the bandstand. After that night, they rarely appeared on the same bill together.

Top billing at the Palladium was seen as compensation for the low pay, which was actually *below* union scale, on the basis that the acts were receiving bulk bookings. Similarly, the summer residencies at the Jewish resorts in the Catskills were poorly paid, on the assumption that the musicians were enjoying a vacation, too. The orchestras worked relentlessly, performing two, three, even four sets a night (and sometimes during the day), at least six days a week, most weeks of the year, without ever seeming to get rich. Recording sessions in New York studios were hurried affairs unlikely to yield royalties; and such tours as existed were not guaranteed profitability. Only one-off private concerts, for which a leave of absence had to be granted by Max Hyman or whatever other clubs at which they were "resident," ever produced real paydays. This constant financial struggle ensured that Puente, Rodriguez, Machito, Bauzá, and all the other Latin "stars" remained a familiar presence in Harlem and the Bronx. "You would see these musicians," said Joe Conzo. "And not only would they say hello to you, they were family. Tito was a street guy, so was Tito Rodriguez, and Machito the same way." The city eventually recognized as much: years later, the intersection of 111th Street and Third Avenue was named Machito Square, while East 110th Street became Tito Puente Way.

Throughout the early 1950s, the demand for mambo was such that the orchestras created or brought in basic "head" arrangements, as they were called (Puente picked them up by the caseload from Havana), for which they then quickly cast out titles as rapidly as they could think of them: "Mambo La Libertad" (Rodriguez), "El Nuevo Mambo" (Puente), "Mambo Jambo" (Machito). (At one point, as if throwing his hands up in despair, Rodriguez simply recorded a track called "El Mambo.") Around 1954, the *cha-cha-cha* took hold: essentially mambo at half speed, it was ideal for those who could not master the original dance, and marked for many the inevitable watering down of the music just in time for the Palladium to become a tourist destination. Not that this deterred the orchestras: Tito Puente, who developed an uncanny ability to jump on board bandwagons for just the right length of time, made many *cha-cha-cha* albums. In the late 1950s, a craze emerged for the *pachanga* dance, led by a New Yorker of Dominican roots, Johnny Pacheco, and Tito Puente and Tito Rodriguez both made albums with *pachanga* prominent in their titles.

At the end of the 1950s, around the time that the Cuban revolution saw communication with the American mainland dry up overnight, to the detri-

ment of both countries' musical cultures, José Curbelo shut down his orchestra and opened a booking agency instead, signing up almost every Latin
group and orchestra of note. Gradually, contracts with the ballrooms
improved. The rivalry between Puente and Rodriguez did not. Rodriguez had
been temporarily banned from the Palladium after rumor spread of an affair
with Max Hyman's wife; exiled to the Park Plaza in Spanish Harlem, he
eventually smoothed over the scandal, won back his spot at the midtown
ballroom, and then, in 1960, recorded a best-selling album for United Artists,
At the Palladium. Unable to curb his ego, he cited its success in a demand for
top billing over Puente when they appeared together at the Palladium for a
one-off dance in the spring of 1962. Puente refused, and the matter went
before Local 802. The union ordered equal billing; Puente refused that as
well, handing in his resignation to the AFM. Curbelo, agent for both band-
leaders, sided with Puente. Rodriguez, he said, "was jealous . . . and wanted
billing over Puente. I did not agree to that, since Tito Puente is a composer,
a music arranger, and a record producer, and plays several instruments. If you
want to know why Puente got the best gigs or top dollar, just listen to his
recordings." Dropped by Curbelo, Rodriguez found New York bookings
almost impossible to come by. He moved back to his native Puerto Rico,
where he became a television star and performed regularly, as well as throughout South America, until shortly before his death of leukemia, in 1972.

   In truth, the glory days of the Palladium ended before this final showdown. Though the venue had once enjoyed a reputation for harmony on the
dance floor, a police raid on the Palladium in April 1961 netted enough drugs
and weapons to have the venue's liquor license rescinded. The Palladium
soldiered on gamely for another four years, but with dwindling numbers, for
if it was true that audiences had come primarily to dance, they had always
expected to fuel that passion with alcohol. Birdland, after its own impressive
run, closed in 1965, and Max Hyman cut his losses on May 1, 1966; Eddie
Palmieri was part of the final bill.

Tito Puente released over 110 albums during his fifty-year recording
career; Tito Rodriguez managed almost half as many during a much
shorter life span. Other than a one-off in 1950, Puente's first 18 full-length
albums were all for the Tico label; so were the first 6 by Rodriguez. The man

behind Tico was George Goldner; of all the entrepreneurs to grace the New York music scene over the years, he was arguably the most colorful, the most influential—and also the most self-destructive. Through the forties, fifties, and sixties he would launch label after label, from one genre to another, picking, producing, and promoting hit records with the unalloyed dedication of an infatuated teenager. A gifted dancer, a fancy dresser, committed womanizer, and compulsive gambler, Goldner was a singular character in a business and at a time when it was full of them. "When you met George, you never forgot him," said Art "Pancho" Raymond, a radio broadcaster who became Goldner's initial partner in Tico. "And you wanted him as a friend."

Born in New York in 1918, Goldner was the son of a successful real estate developer on Manhattan's East Side, and a mother who doted on him; from them, respectively, he appeared to inherit a sense of entrepreneurship and entitlement. But he was every bit his own man, building a profitable business in the midtown garment industry, which afforded him plenty of time to pursue his real love: going out dancing at night to Latin orchestras. "He was into that music up to his neck," said Raymond. "He ate it, he slept it, he was just crazy about it." (Shortly after they met, Goldner divorced his first wife for a Puerto Rican woman, Mona.) Raymond, who began broadcasting as a twenty-year-old announcer in New Jersey in 1942, became heavily committed to the music himself. By the late 1940s, he had parlayed his enthusiasm into the premier Latin music show on New York radio, *Tico Tico Time*—named for a hit samba, popularized first by the organist Ethel Smith and then by Xavier Cugat—broadcast on WBYN in Brooklyn. Working freelance, finding his own sponsors, and splitting the proceeds with the radio stations that were exploding in number and format as the FCC opened up the airwaves, Raymond emerged as a leading host for the increasingly popular Latin music format, bouncing different shows around various stations. Along the way, he became master of ceremonies at the Palladium. It was there that he first met George Goldner, who, after opening—and, lacking a liquor license, rapidly closing again—a Latin nightclub in Newark, decided that the record industry might be a better way to indulge his love of the music.

With financing from garment business friends—Artie Fineman and Jackie Waxman, with whom he shared an office on 41st Street—Goldner asked Raymond to become a partner. The pair liked each other, and that counted for plenty, but Goldner also knew—as he would prove time and again over the years—that the best way to gain airplay, and therefore the record sales that ought to follow, was to get disc jockeys on his side. To that end, why not name the label for Raymond's radio show?

Tico Records launched in 1948, right around the time of another AFM ban—this one prompted by the popularity of personality-based disc jockeys (like Art "Pancho" Raymond and "Symphony" Sid Torin) who were fast taking over the airwaves from the more sophisticated, scripted announcers who preceded them, relegating (as the AFM's James Petrillo saw it) the records that they played to the status of "canned" music. As compensation, Petrillo wanted the AFM paid every time a record was played on air. But the record companies were better positioned to hold out this time: they stocked up on recording sessions in the weeks leading up to the strike, which started on January 1, 1948, and were equally quick to return to the studios when the ban was rescinded, after concessions from both sides, twelve months later. Just as important, Columbia unveiled its 33 rpm long-playing album (and accompanying record player) during the strike, and RCA Victor responded from the other end of the spectrum with the 45 rpm 7-inch single early in 1949. Thanks in large part to the popularity of these new formats (for which multispeed players soon hit the market), the record industry would grow in profitability every single year until 1979.

Tico, like most independent labels, stuck with the 10-inch 78 rpm disc for the time being. Its first signing of note was Tito Rodriguez, who was lured away from Gabriel Oller's SMC label in 1949. Soon after, Tico began issuing Rodriguez's more up-tempo recordings under the group name Los Lobos del Mambo (the Mambo Wolves), deliberately close to the Mambo Devils name he had used for SMC.

In late 1949, in between these releases, Tico brought Tito Puente and His Orchestra, still a new act, into the studio, primarily to back the singer Johnny Lopez on the bolero "Un Corazon." Puente was also allowed to record a couple of up-tempo cuts of his own; for the second of these, he dismissed his saxophone and trombone players and recorded José Curbelo's "Abaniquito" with just the blaring sound of his four trumpet players (Mario Bauzá among them), bongos (played by Chino Pozo, Chano's cousin), piano (his former teacher Luis Varona), and bass, along with vocals led by Vincentino Valdés, backed by Frankie Colon and Machito's sister Graciella. Though "Abaniquito" was clearly based on Dizzy Gillespie's Afro-Cuban hit "Manteca" (which preceded it by about six months), especially in its ensemble trumpet lie, the performance by Puente's team of Latino greats exuded a syncopated, sensual complexity that even the finest beboppers could not hope to emulate without some Latin blood in them.

Art Raymond played "Abaniquito" on his *Tico Tico Time*, as he did other Tico releases and those of Seeco, SMC, Coda, and Verne. The public, he insisted, in what would become a common disc jockey refrain, was the ultimate arbiter of taste—and in the case of "Abaniquito," the public made it a local hit. Tico was helped, however, by the Puente Orchestra's hit recording of "Ran Kan Kan" for RCA at the same time and, even more, by the fact that RCA did not then attempt to sign Puente under his own name, but allowed the new star to bounce back and forth between the labels for the next year until he settled into a permanent relationship with Tico.

The early days of Tico were typical of the everyday hustle evinced by the pioneering independent labels. Goldner would take his garment industry orders in the morning, put their production and delivery into motion, and then help load up Raymond's car with the Tico releases he stored in his office alongside garment sundries, before the pair headed off on a sales pitch around the specialty record stores. Raymond would drive over to Newark in the afternoon to present his radio shows at WVNJ, while Goldner would work the phone, meet with artists, and conduct recording sessions. After midnight, they'd meet for dinner—either at the popular music hangout Lindy's or at the cafeteria next door to the China Doll, known in the industry as the "Spanish Lindy's"—and then hit the clubs.

Bolstered by the success of "Abaniquito"—"it took off like wild fire," recalled Raymond—Tico Records embarked on a release schedule that would put its peers to shame. During the early 1950s, Tico released close to two hundred 10-inch 78 rpm singles, plus a series of fourteen four-song Mambo *Volumes* that alternated between the two Titos. In 1952 alone, Puente delivered Goldner some thirty-seven sides. No wonder Tico ran the words "El Rey del Mambo" alongside its logo on the record labels.

Indeed, just as the performers at the Palladium served a similar function to the latterday dance club DJ, so these 10-inch 78s can be viewed as archetypal dance music "white labels." Tico's *Volumes* were aimed directly at the Latin music aficionados, those who wanted to throw their own mambo dance parties at home, who craved a souvenir from their nights at the Palladium, or who just got a thrill from hearing the two Titos come alive on record. Rodriguez's mambos were sophisticated and languid, as typified by his "Mambo Gee Gee," named in honor of Goldner's initials as well as, possibly, his growing love of horse racing. Puente's mambos were fast and frenetic, led by the timbals and distinguished by the galloping trumpets (to the exclusion of other brass), as in "The Drinking Mambo." The occasional track would become some sort of hit—Tito Puente's "Vibe Mambo," in 1951, which brought that instrument to the fore in Latin music, was a prime example, or Tito Rodriguez's "La Renta," a subject of common enough complaint among Nuyoricans—but rarely outside the confines of the Latin music audience. Most 78s sold only in the hundreds. Tico simply did not have the wherewithal to compete with the major labels for chart positions.

Eventually, of course, Raymond's boss at WVNJ—a privately owned station—discovered that his Latin music disc jockey was part owner in a Latin label whose records he frequently played, and yanked him off the air. Raymond secured a new job in Philadelphia (one that would lead him into television) and opted to sell out his interest in the label to Goldner, who, he stressed, "never missed a payment." Raymond's place at WVNJ was taken by Bob Harris, who continued to play Tico's releases. So did Dick "Ricardo" Sugar, who became arguably the most influential of all Latin music disc jockeys in the later fifties, at the Jewish station WEVD. Goldner ensured the support of these various hosts—none of whom was actually Hispanic—by sponsoring blocks of their airtime.

In 1954, Tito Rodriguez left Tico for RCA Victor, for which his first LP was, perhaps predictably, entitled *Mambo at the New York Palladium*. Goldner's response was to sign the original Latin heavyweights, Machito and His Orchestra, and move Tico into concert promotion. In the first few months of the year, he promoted a "Mambo/Rhumba Festival" at Carnegie Hall, sent Tito Puente on the road with the pianist Joe Loco, and packed Machito's Afro-Cubans off on tour for three weeks. All this was in preparation for the "Mambo USA" package tour, which set off in late October from a sold-out Carnegie Hall show with Machito's vast orchestra, the Joe Loco Quintet, the Mambo Aces dancers, and assorted other musicians. But in echoes of Dizzy Gillespie's experiences almost a decade earlier, audience attendance was dismal, and the racism that had all but disappeared from

New York City nightlife reared its ugly head on a daily basis. Some shows played to fewer than twenty people, and the tour came home early; yet again, it appeared that the New York music scene operated in a vacuum, at odds with the rest of the country.

Tico made up its losses by entering the long-playing (LP) market with a flourish at the end of 1955, releasing a dozen albums almost all at once. Eight of them carried the word "mambo" in their title, three of them the "cha-cha-cha," and the other one, *Puente in Percussion*, compensated for this blatant repetitiveness by breaking new musical ground—quite literally, with the appearance of a pneumatic drill on the album's cover. Puente's idea to record a Latin album that lacked piano and horns had not initially sat well with Goldner, a voracious Jewish dancer rather than a student of Caribbean culture. Puente had to explain "the significance of the drum in Africa, its use in religious dance rituals and communication and how the tradition was handed down to us in Latin America," before getting the go-ahead to record with his fellow percussionists Willie Bobo, Carlos "Potato" Valdés, and Mongo Santamaria, and the bassist Bobby Rodriguez, "on the condition that we use the studio late at night to keep the cost down."

From this disputed commission, *Puente in Percussion* became something of a musical milestone, a welcome deviation from the commercial norm. The project opened with six minutes of rhythmic minimalism entitled "Tito on Timbales," Rodriguez's near endlessly identical bass line creating a hypnotic template, and the set continued from there in similarly avant-garde style, through self-descriptive titles like "Stick on Bongo" and "Congo Beat" and on to the pure *montuno* of "Swingin' the Mambo." For many, it represented the debut of Tito Puente as an *artiste*, rather than just another bandleader recording the popular dance rhythms of the era.

Yet directly after its release, Puente left Tico for RCA Victor, this time on a long-term contract that would yield results, initially with *Puente Goes Jazz*, which built on the foundations laid by Machito's Afro-Cubans with the beboppers, and later in the fifties with *Top Percussion* (a follow-up to *Puente in Percussion*) and *Dance Mania*, which introduced Puente to a larger and more lucrative audience. (Tito Rodriguez, languishing at RCA in Puente's shadow, promptly returned to Tico.)

Puente may well have left Tico in frustration at Goldner's penny-pinching. It might have been for a shot at better distribution and promotion. Either way, the move was guided by Morris Levy, for whom Puente had regularly performed at Birdland and who had parlayed his success with the club into tour promotions—sending Birdland packages out on the road with greater success than Goldner and packaging a series of Birdland releases to RCA Victor. In addition, Levy had learned the value of publishing. As he liked to tell it, an ASCAP rep paid Birdland a visit to inquire about its (lack of) performance license, and once Levy realized that he was not being shaken down by a rival mob, but that ASCAP (and BMI) did indeed collect for its members every time one of their songs was played in a nightclub, he commissioned George Shearing to write "Lullaby of Birdland," copyrighted it to his brand-new company, Patricia Music (named for his wife), and duly banked a fee any time the track was performed at his club—which, he ensured, became a nightly occurrence.

Morris Levy later claimed that he "never met" George Goldner until the Tico boss, seething at the loss of Tito Puente, came by his office to complain, at which point Levy apologized for any misunderstanding, and Goldner then suggested that Levy could help him on the promotional front. In recounting this story (to Frederic Dannen, for a *Rolling Stone* feature that later formed a chapter of the best-selling book *Hit Men*), Levy may have gotten his facts mixed up, since the label he then discussed the two men setting up together predated Puente's departure to RCA Victor by two years. But although one suspects they should have met each other earlier in the fifties, given their similar interests in the Latin concert business, and allowing that Goldner would have needed enormous *cujones* to storm into Morris Levy's office and complain about *anything*, that's not to suggest that the general gist of the story is incorrect. By 1955, Goldner had bigger things on his plate than just Tico, the Titos, the mambo and the *cha-cha-cha*: he had one of the most important labels in rhythm and blues. And Levy was looking to cut himself a slice.

6

THE TEENAGERS SING
ROCK 'N' ROLL

George Goldner kept his ear to the streets, and while he would never fall out of love with Latin music, he knew that vocal rhythm and blues groups were becoming all the rage. Inspired by the sounds and successes of the Orioles, Clovers, Dominoes, and others, singing groups were forming on street corners from the Bronx and Harlem out to Brooklyn and Queens, and new independent labels established for that very purpose were snapping them up. Bobby Robinson, whose record store on 125th Street placed him in the heart of the action, had set up Red Robin and scored an immediate top ten R&B hit in 1952 with a ballad sung by a group of grammar school boys, the Mello-Moods, out of the Harlem River Houses. (They didn't follow it up, however, because the singers' parents put homework ahead of paid performing work.) And Morris Levy's childhood friends Hymie and Sam Weiss had set up Old Town, operating out of a cloakroom office farther east on 125th Street in the Triboro Theater.

Goldner, like any good music entrepreneur—and more than many entrepreneurs, Goldner loved good music—wanted a piece of this action. And so, rather than confuse his Tico customers, he established a fresh imprint, Rama Records, early in 1953, and set upon the Harlem vocal scene with the same effusiveness that previously enabled him to sign up the Palladium's big names. Within weeks, he had himself one of the most important releases in all of rhythm and blues.

Five teens from around West 142nd Street who came together in 1951, the Crows named themselves in direct homage to the Ravens and the Orioles, and arranged themselves in a similar manner of ballad-style harmony, while taking on board—because who could ignore it?—the more effusive elements of the Dominoes' excursions into ribald rhythm and blues along the way. They were, from lead tenor down to bass, Daniel "Sonny" Norton, Harold Major, Jerry Wittick, Bill Davis, and Gerald Hamilton, and they followed an entirely conventional route to success, starting out on the neighborhood streets, singing the hits of the day, working their way up to school dances and private parties, and, finally, daring to enter Amateur Night at the Apollo. There they won first prize and, precisely according to script, were approached backstage by Cliff Martinez, one of the agent-managers in attendance.

Martinez took the Crows to the Jubilee label, owned by the former band-leader Jerry Blaine since his original partner Herb Abramson left to cofound Atlantic. Blaine had enjoyed enormous success with the Orioles, and his profits were boosted by the fact that he distributed his label through his own Cosnat company—as he did Red Robin, and others. Blaine had the Crows record as backup on a session for a trumpet player and for the singer Viola Watkins. Neither single was a success, and Blaine released them from their contract. Martinez, unperturbed, took both Watkins and the Crows, who by now had lost Wittick from the lineup, to Goldner.

The Crows were initially no more successful when they released a single under their own name in April 1953 on Rama. In June, Goldner released the two remaining songs from that initial session. In the fashion of the times, one was a ballad—the painstakingly earnest "I Love You So"—and the other a "jump" tune, called "Gee." Both were written by the Crows themselves, "Gee" supposedly in just ten minutes.

The recording could hardly have taken much longer. Over a phonetic four-part harmony, the lead tenor, "Sonny" Norton, reiterated the song's title over and over in a frenzied attempt to explain "why I love that girl." Along the way, he attempted the occasional melisma à la the Harlem vocal hero Clyde McPhatter, but his voice was thin and reedy; he could barely hold a tune, let alone stretch a syllable across several notes. His fellow Crows' harmonies came similarly unstuck the longer the song progressed—which was all of two minutes, a significant chunk punctuated by a bluesy guitar solo.

In short, "Gee" was a mess—but it was a gloriously cheerful mess, encas-ing the thrill of juvenile passion in the fervor of rhythm and blues, in a way that had rarely been captured before inside a recording studio. Still, given that ballads were typically the forte of the vocal harmony group, "Gee" was initially put on the B-side. Though its vocal performance was only marginally more professional than that of "Gee," "I Love You So" generated sufficient interest to keep the single on playlists through the fall.

Then something curious happened. One by one, the nation's rhythm and blues radio DJs flipped the single over, embracing "Gee" as something fresh—a musical extrapolation of what would soon be called teenage. Legend has it that Dick "Huggy Boy" Hugg, a young white guy who aired his radio show from a record store window on Central Avenue, Los Angeles's main black thoroughfare, started the trend by repeatedly airing "Gee" to win back his girlfriend. But the fact that "Gee" made the chart in Detroit before it did so in LA suggests that Hugg was not alone. As if by osmosis, radio stations appeared to grasp that this jump tune, amateur though it might be, had more appeal with adolescent listeners than the sentimental ballads that had previously dominated the vocal group genre.

By the start of 1954, "Gee" had sold 100,000 copies, and Goldner, who held the publishing copyright, commissioned Joe Loco to record a mambo version on Tico. Then, in March, "Gee" entered the pop (generally considered the white) chart—*before* it made the (black) R&B chart. This was unprecedented for a black vocal group, and it indicated that white kids were not only listening to rhythm and blues DJs like Huggy Boy across the country but pestering their neighborhood pop record stores to stock the music. It also suggested that the conventional standards by which record companies and radio stations had long judged popular songs—singing in key, proper English lyrics—no longer held firm. As "Gee" rose all the way to number 14 on the pop charts, it became evident that the emerging teenage market would gladly substitute youthful exuberance and monosyllabic choruses for such old-fashioned values.

A similar story surrounded the success of "Sh-Boom" by the Chords. Hailing from the Boston Road–Jennings Street intersection of the South Bronx, which by the early fifties was predominantly black and Latino, the quartet came together, also in 1951, out on the streets, where kids had a habit of greeting each other with the expression "Boom!" "If you were standing on the block for five minutes, you'd hear that slang word fifteen times or more," said the second tenor, Floyd "Buddy" McRae. Growing up with the atomic terror of the Cold War, the Chords adopted this "boom" greeting for a song, but made it sound more like a nuclear explosion: "Sh-boom." Just like "Gee," "Sh-Boom" was at heart a love song. The first verse opened with the singer's assurance that "Life could be a dream" (if only the object of his affections would promise him her love). But for the second verse, the Chords ad-libbed random nonsense rhyming syllables that they had picked up subconsciously from the bebop era, and consciously from hanging out on the streets. Keen to make something of what they thought was a decent song, the Crows took "Sh-Boom" to Bobby Robinson. He deemed it "not commercial enough," and who could blame him: his major R&B hits until now—with the Mello-Moods and then with the Vocaleers, a group from the same 142nd Street area as the Crows—had been ballads, not jump tunes that celebrated street slang.

Atlantic Records wasn't interested in "Sh-Boom" either. When the label agreed to sign the Chords, it was because it was specifically looking for an act to cover Patti Page's "Cross Over the Bridge." The quartet members, already all in their early twenties, weren't about to turn down that opportunity. They were grateful just to be allowed to record "Sh-Boom" and ecstatic when Atlantic included it as the flip side.

Recognizing the new tide in rhythm and blues, Atlantic established a "Swinging New R&B Label," Cat Records, in the spring of 1954, with the Chords' single one of its four debut, simultaneous releases. (One of the other three was by an eighteen-year-old Sylvia Vanderpool, already a veteran of the Savoy label and shortly to hit the charts as half of Mickey and Sylvia.) All the Chords' promotion was focused upon the Patti Page song—until, in an exact replica of the Crows' story, Huggy Bear flipped the single and played the hell out of "Sh-Boom," and his fellow R&B DJs quickly followed suit. "Gee" and "Sh-Boom" were of a pair aesthetically, each of them jump tunes with slang words of the era used to express the singers' infatuation in a way that both compensated for and improved upon the reality that they weren't honed poets. Professionally, however, the singles were leagues apart: while "Gee" revealed George Goldner's lack of studio experience with rhythm and blues, "Sh-Boom" showed Atlantic's total affinity with the genre—a comfortably trotting rhythm track provided the bedrock for Carl Feaster's tightly honed tenor lead, the bass singer William "Ricky" Edwards's bold interjection in the middle eight (reminiscent in its deep tone of the original Ricky, from the Ravens), and a floating sax solo like that which had worked so well for the Drifters.

By June, Atlantic had pulled the original Patti Page A-side, placed another Chords composition from the original session on the B-side (all the better for publishing purposes, as Atlantic, like any independent label, made sure to own the copyrights wherever possible), re-released the single, and toasted its quick thinking as "Sh-Boom" overtook "Gee" in the charts, rising to number two at R&B and number five at pop, the most successful R&B crossover to date.

As was customary for the era, both the Crows' and the Chords' hits were widely covered by white acts, with "Sh-Boom" infamously beaten to the top of the charts by the Canadian group the Crew Cuts' recording on Mercury. (Purists frequently denounced this policy, though clearly it cut both ways: the Chords had only been signed to Atlantic in the first place because the label wanted to record an R&B cover of a successful white pop song. In addition, because Atlantic owned the publishing rights on "Sh-Boom," it profited handsomely from the Crew Cuts' version without having to spend a penny.) The success of "Sh-Boom" inspired further examples of nonsense syllables in song titles ("Oop Shoop," "Shtiggy Boom") and led to public discussion about how this represented some kind of breakdown in juvenile intelligence. Along the way, "Gee" and "Sh-Boom" helped make 1954 the year that vocal rhythm and blues went mainstream. In fact, both "Gee" and "Sh-Boom" earned their role as (two among many) candidates for the title of first ever "rock 'n' roll" singles.

That raises the obvious question: what was rock 'n' roll and how did it differ from rhythm and blues? The answer lies with a DJ who arrived in New York City in September 1954 to launch a nightly rhythm and blues show on a 50,000-watt station best known for broadcasting the Yankees games. His name was Alan Freed, and the airwaves would never be the same again.

American radio in the postwar years was reminiscent of the frontier years in the Wild West. Having weathered the two strikes brought by the AFM—one over the playing of recorded music, the other over the increasing dominance of the disc jockeys themselves—the medium exploded as the FCC opened up the airwaves, leading to a nationwide increase from 930 AM stations in 1945 to 2,350 in 1952. The long-standing NBC and CBS networks, joined in 1943 by ABC, had a share in many "affiliate" stations across the country, but although they were credited with popularizing vocal groups like the Mills Brothers and the Ink Spots, they were not interested in catering to minorities or in fostering the new style of hep "disc jockey." That they left to the thousands of other stations, many of which learned that rhythm and blues appealed to people of all colors—not just in the bigger, more integrated cities like New York but across the entire nation.

This concentrated interest in new black music was due in part to the Korean War, which broke out in 1950, two years after President Harry Truman had (finally) ordered the desegregation of the armed services. In Korea, blacks and whites lived and fought (and died: the United States lost over 36,000 men in the war) alongside one another for the very first time. In doing so, they gained a greater understanding of one another's culture—and, specifically, one another's music. As the soldiers came home from war and shared that music, their younger siblings emerged as a first generation of "teenagers." Created out of America's postwar wealth and prosperity, teenagers no longer followed a path that ran directly from childhood to adulthood; rather, they were afforded the opportunity to pause and enjoy the years in between. And they exhibited their spending power and leisure time with an obsessive enthusiasm for music, especially the newly explosive sounds of rhythm and blues—readily available to them in short bursts, thanks to the development of the 45 rpm 7-inch single, and in all-night sessions via the portable transistor radios that quickly became the rage.

In the meantime, back in the world of broadcasting, the larger sponsors were gravitating to the new medium of television; as a result, note Bill Brewster and Frank Broughton in *Last Night a DJ Saved My Life*, "radio advertising became much more local. There was a need for snappy talkers to sell up the virtues of chewing tobacco and patent chest tonic." Among the "snappy talkers" was Alan Freed, a twenty-nine-year-old classical music DJ on WJW in Cleveland, Ohio, at the point in 1951 that he embarked on a rhythm and blues show for the station at the suggestion of a willing sponsor, a local record store owner who saw the newly integrated R&B market opening up at his very counter. Freed seemed something of an unlikely candidate for the task, knowing little—if anything—about the music in question. But he certainly had the ego and drive for it: during his short time on air, he had managed to solicit a court-upheld one-year ban from broadcasting in the Akron area after quitting a popular station (over his income) to go straight up against his old show with a rival broadcaster. With somewhat admirable obstinacy, he spent the year that he was banned from radio playing the popular records of the day on late night television instead.

As well as exhibiting both greed and determination, Freed was a heavy drinker, whose alcoholism would leave him open to outside manipulation. But he was also a contagious enthusiast, who could easily carry audiences along in his wake—traits he exemplified on his WJW rhythm and blues show, for which he adopted his persona from an avant-garde record he used as his introduction music, the "Moondog Symphony." Unleashed from the constraints of his earlier radio career, Freed as Moondog howled along to the latest R&B hits while banging on a telephone book and a cowbell, delivering rapid-fire endorsements for a local beer company, and swigging from a bottle of liquor he kept by his side. He quickly became one of the new music's loudest on-air proponents and most intriguing broadcasters. Indeed, because of his apparent affinity with the music (if nothing else, he was a quick study) and his outsized on-air personality, his audience came to assume, initially at least, that Freed was young and black, as opposed to being relatively old and white.

In fact, like radio itself, Freed was color-blind. His first profitable forays into concert promotion in Akron and Cleveland were notable in that they attracted an audience of mainly black youth to hear the likes of Fats Domino, Big Joe Turner, and Billy Ward and His Dominoes. But his listenership clearly crossed the color line—so much so that by 1953 WJW claimed it as "the nation's number one rhythm and blues show."

That title, one might have thought, should have gone to a station in New York City, not only a hotbed of rhythm and blues activity but by far the nation's biggest city, in which 10 percent of its nearly eight million people, according to the 1950 Census, were black. And yet, according to a *Variety* report in early 1953, barely a dozen "Negro jocks" were catering to the demand. (And that was considered "one of the largest concentrations in the country.") The majority of those DJs were carving out their audience during odd hours on left-leaning stations, like WEVD, owned by the *Forward*, a Jewish newspaper; WLIB, owned in the late forties by what was then a staunchly liberal *New York Post* and broadcasting in the fifties from the Hotel Theresa, in Harlem; or the privately held WWRL, which broadcast from Woodside, in Queens, in several different languages. Like the Latin music disc jockeys, who appeared on many of the same stations, the rhythm and blues announcers were encouraged to attract their own sponsors and split profits with the stations, and they bounced from one end of the dial to the other according to the various deals they could make. In this environment, much of the AM frequency remained in a state of constant flux, with two dozen new stations setting up shop in the metropolitan area in the postwar years, and others frequently changing hands and formats as their owners tried to figure out a money-winning formula amid all the competition.

One of the few constants in all of this was "Symphony" Sid Torin, the jazz enthusiast who not only backed Machito and Tito Puente on air alongside the beboppers but had championed the Ravens on the station WHOM as early as 1947. His popularity, combined with the respect he commanded from the musicians, led Torin to WMCA in 1948. But in the meantime WHOM expanded its *After-Hours Swing Session Show* to include broadcasts by (black) Willie Bryant and (white) Ray Carroll from the Baby Grand club in Harlem, as part of its own outreach to the growing R&B audience.

Come 1953, Bryant and Carroll's command of that audience was giving way to younger, more overtly outgoing and predominantly black disc jockeys, the most influential of whom was Tommy "Dr. Jive" Smalls, broadcasting late at night on WWRL. A major shift then occurred over the river in Newark, where the 5,000-watt WNJR changed hands in September 1953, and the new owner immediately converted it to "all-Negro programming." Suddenly, WNJR's airwaves were filled, eighteen hours a day, with shows hosted by Hal Jackson, Charlie Green, and Danny "the Cat Man" Stiles, who had a theme song of his own ("Jeep's Blues") that invited his listeners to wail along like so many alley cats. This made WNJR a perfect fit for Alan Freed and his growing army of Moondoggers, and Freed mailed in transcripts of his shows for WNJR to test the metropolitan waters. He was a hit, and if the local audience had any doubt about Freed's ambitions on their market, they were surely put to rest in May 1954, when Freed promoted a dance at the Newark Armory that included the Clovers, Muddy Waters, and New York's own Harptones. Some eleven thousand people attended the two performances; approximately 20 percent of them were white.

At the same time that WNJR changed hands, so did WINS in Manhattan, which with 50,000 watts of power and a perfect placement in the middle of the dial, at 1010 AM, could blow most rivals out of New York Harbor—if only it could find a format with which to entice them to listen. The station's new owner, J. Elroy McCaw, based in Seattle despite his company's title as the Gotham Broadcasting Corporation, began in a confrontational manner, refusing to renew a WINS contract with the AFM that required the station to hire studio musicians. The AFM responded by throwing up a picket line at Yankee Stadium for the 1954 season's opening game in the South Bronx. Mayor Robert Wagner, a Democrat elected to office the preceding November, refused to cross that picket line, which made for considerable news coverage—though it failed to deter McCaw.

While continuing to focus on inexpensive sports and talk, McCaw set about looking for a marquee disc jockey for the increasingly lucrative rhythm and blues audience in the heart of Manhattan. All in all, it was no accident that while the R&B genre had been building in New York primarily through minority disc jockeys on left-leaning stations, it would come to prominence via a white disc jockey on a white-owned, hard-nosed corporate station in the heart of Manhattan managed from three thousand miles away. For on the eve of the Fourth of July holiday, WINS announced that Alan Freed would be moving from Cleveland to New York City to host his "Moondog" show from 11:00 p.m. to 2:00 a.m., six nights a week.

The heavily hyped launch took place on September 7. Among those who stopped by the WINS studio to offer Freed their best wishes was Bobby Robinson, whom Freed invited to hang out for the evening and help man the phones. The first track Freed played on air on WINS, however, was the number one R&B song in the country, "Oh What a Dream," by Ruth Brown on Atlantic. New York's leading independent label cast an impressively long shadow.

Within weeks of his arrival at WINS, Alan Freed was dominating the New York airwaves, commanding a teenage audience that stretched throughout the five boroughs, across all color lines. Thanks to the WINS 50,000-watt transmitter, teenagers who had struggled to tune into "Dr. Jive" on WWRL could hear the "Moondog" with ease. "You didn't have to put your radio on the back of the sofa and tilt it to get reception," recalled Arlene Smith, at the time a twelve-year-old black chorister attending convent school in the Bronx, who would soon find herself swept up into the world of the vocal groups.

"The transistor radio came in in the 1950s," noted Richard Gottehrer, a future songwriter and producer raised in a Jewish Bronx family. "So not only could a kid listen to radio; he could take the music with him." This was useful if your parents weren't keen on disc jockeys' "mixing the races," as Gottehrer put it. "I would listen under the pillow. When you think of the significance of Alan Freed and what it meant to the world of a teenager, what sounds today pretty simplistic was overwhelming. To hear Alan playing a song, banging on a phone book, yelling 'go go go.' . . ." For many teenagers, it was the sound of freedom itself.

The only initial hurdle in Freed's takeover of Manhattan was that of the original Moondog: Louis Hardin, a blind avant-garde musician who, in the 1940s, came to New York, where, "dressed in thong sandals and a blanket," as one newspaper rather disparagingly put it, he befriended the likes of Charlie Parker and Benny Goodman as he played the "oo," "utsu," and "uni," his own instruments, in doorways along 52nd Street. One of those doorways turned out to belong to the Latin label boss Gabriel Oller, who liked what he heard and released "Moondog's Symphony" (and three other records) on his SMC label, around 1950. Though Moondog was a musical and visual novelty (for a while he wore Viking helmets to protest the fashion industry), he was no idiot savant. Nor was he particularly obscure: when Alan Freed came to town, Moondog had just released an album on Columbia's subsidiary Epic. Hardin sued for copyright infringement, and in late November 1954 a judge ordered Freed to refrain from use of the Moondog name; though WINS threatened to appeal, Freed, demonstrating the empathetic aspect of his nature, told them he would sooner come up with a new title for the show and move forward.

It was an easy enough process: Freed had been labeling his broadcasts a "rock and roll party" for years, as the lyrical euphemism for sex showed up in more and more rhythm and blues songs. Now he made it official: as of Thanksgiving 1954, his radio show became *Alan Freed's Rock 'n' roll Party*, and to celebrate the change in name, Freed announced he would host a "Rock 'n' Roll Jubilee Ball" at the St. Nicholas Arena in Harlem over two nights in January 1955. A letter duly sent out to his fan club members mentioned "rock 'n' roll" some ten times, and rhythm and blues not once. Almost overnight, out of legal necessity, Alan Freed introduced and cemented—in New York City—the most important new term in popular music in perhaps fifty years.

Such was Freed's proprietary relationship to the term "rock 'n' roll" that he immediately set about trying to copyright it. His three partners in a new company, Seig Music, that filed the claim were his radio station, WINS; his long-standing Cleveland-based concert promoter Lew Platt; and his new manager and New York concert promoter, Morris Levy.

Quite how Morris Levy got from Birdland's jazz and Latin formats to Alan Freed's rock 'n' roll parties has never been fully explained. It can, however, be surmised. As a nightclub promoter, Levy knew that just as bebop had given way to Latin dance music, so rhythm and blues was becoming the next big thing, and that Freed offered a way to make money from it. Levy was already highly successful in sending Birdland packages on tour, hiring local disc jockeys in each town to emcee the shows. (These tours were typically road-managed by Tommy Vastola, nephew of Dominick Ciaffone, a.k.a. Swats Mulligan, a Genovese family foot soldier whom, according to Fredric Dannen in *Hit Men*, "Morris is thought to have fronted for.") Whether or not he had bought Alan Freed's favor in Cleveland on such a tour, Levy knew the concert business better than most. He was, on the face of it, an ideal partner.

Once in partnership together, Levy and Freed acted quickly. The success of the Rock 'n' Roll Jubilee Ball at the St. Nicholas Arena gave way to a weeklong Rock 'n' Roll Easter Show at the Brooklyn Paramount, on Flatbush Avenue just over the Manhattan Bridge, a revue presented in the Apollo style (several shows a day, complete with movie as inducement to "turn the house") but almost exclusively devoted to the new music. Featured artists included LaVern Baker, the Penguins, the Moonglows, and Mickey "Guitar" Baker, along with the debut of Freed's Rock 'n' Roll Orchestra, composed of former big band swing musicians forced to adapt or die. The format proved an instant winner, selling 97,000 tickets over the course of a week for a record-breaking gross of $107,000. Tommy "Dr. Jive" Smalls, showing no signs of surrendering to Freed's overnight dominance of the New York City market and, pointedly, no intent of adopting the new terminology, immediately set about hosting his own rhythm and blues revues at the Harlem Apollo.

Despite the instant popularity of Freed's Paramount revues, the Apollo remained the cathedral of black music in New York. "Nobody, absolutely nobody, went out and started recording records that was not familiar with the Apollo, that didn't go there on a regular basis," said Gene Tompkins, a future singer (and R&B archivist) from the fertile Morrisania area of the South Bronx, which by 1953 had already produced local stars in the Wrens and the Crickets. "You would go there and the setting was so electric. You're sitting in the audience and you're looking onstage and you see your friends up there performing, and you're seeing the reaction and you're loving what they're doing, and you say, 'Gee, I'd like to be up there too.'"

As groups like the Crows had discovered, there was a dedicated path to follow before getting onto that Apollo stage. The vocal groups sang first in apartment buildings. "No matter what neighborhood, you'd go into one or two hallways on the block and you'd find a group singing," said Tompkins. "We didn't have microphones and, of course, we didn't have any sound system. So when you would sing, you would hear the bass ringing around the sounds of the concrete walls and that brought out the harmony. And you could actually hear the bird sound of the tenor because it was all in the hallway."

"You learned by trial and error," recalled Bobby Jeffers, who attended James Fenimore Cooper Junior High School, on 120th Street and Fifth Avenue in Harlem, as did members of the Jesters, the Schoolboys, and the Desires. Jeffers sang in many semipro local groups and would later become well known as the CBS radio DJ Bobby Jay. "We'd listen to the records. Someone would come in and say, 'I'm the lead,' and someone else would say, 'I'm the second tenor.' You wouldn't argue or fight, because you didn't know any better."

Benjamin Nelson, who as Ben E. King would enjoy a level of success unique among his contemporaries, was one of the thousands who sang with his friends on the sidewalks on a nightly basis. "Our territory was around 119th Street," he recalled. "There were a lot of groups within those blocks, and we used to challenge guys somewhere up on 134th Street and Lenox Avenue. We would get a group up there and challenge them with our sound. It was a friendly rivalry. We didn't have knives or guns or chains in our hands. We just went to challenge groups vocally. We'd go down that area, maybe run into one or two of the guys, and talk to them, let them know who we are and where we're from, and we'd say, 'We hear you're good.' Before you know it, they've all got together and they're harmonizing."

The battles were driven by pride in vocal performance. "You could tell how good your harmony is against someone else," said King. "You could tell how good your lead vocal is against somebody else. You would know. You could tell the way someone had interpreted a song they had heard on the radio, whether it was the Platters or whoever, whether that singer had taken ownership of that song and sung the hell out of it."

The reward, however, was driven by hormones. "When you challenged someone in their territory, you were also trying to get their girls," said King. "And the girls determined the victory."

"It was never about the money," recalled Bobby Jay. "We were enjoying ourselves, and when you looked around, there were girls. That was the motivating factor. It attracted girls like flies to honey."

As "Sh-Boom" soared up the charts, the Chords signed with Atlantic Records' house manager Lou Krefetz, acquired a brand-new DeSoto limousine with the words "Chords/Sh-Boom" painted across its doors, and headed to California, where, in October, they appeared on CBS television's nationally broadcast *Juke Box Jury.* Yet, for all the attention, they could not secure a follow-up hit, a problem accelerated by an enforced name change (another Chords already existed), first to the Chordcats and later, desperately, to the Sh-Booms. Krefetz, the group complained, paid closer attention to his original clients the Clovers; Atlantic Records, perhaps, felt that the group had dangerously high expectations. Either way, by early 1956, the Chords had left label, management, and a number of unreleased recordings behind them and were, effectively, finished.

The Crows had suffered an even quicker demise. In April 1954, just as they were breaking into the charts, Goldner honored them with three simultaneous releases. One was an R&B single on Rama ("Baby" and "Untrue"), intended to follow in the wake of the successful "Gee." Another was the debut single on a brand-new label that he named both for their breakthrough hit and his own initials, Gee, on which the Crows backed a female singer on the pop standard "Perfida." The third was on Tico, "Mambo Shevitz," a send-up of a commercial for Manischewitz wine that was running, perhaps not coincidentally, on Alan Freed's show. None of the singles took off. But the ongoing success of "Gee" enabled the Crows to acquire a brand-new Chrysler, with their name on the side, and parade around Harlem in it before taking off to Las Vegas, way ahead of the market for such a move. Their final single was recorded before Alan Freed even moved to New York City; and in early 1955, when it too failed to take off, the Crows called it a day.

Although their careers were over, the two groups should have been able to anticipate some financial security, not so much from record sales (royalties were notoriously low in the fifties) but from publishing: after all, they themselves had composed each of their lone hits. The writing credits for "Sh-Boom" were indeed evenly distributed among the five members of the Chords, affording them regular annual income over the decades. The Crows, however, were not so fortunate. The sheet music to "Gee" listed the song's three composers as Viola Watkins, Daniel Norton, and William Davis. The Rama single label removed Norton and listed only Watkins and Davis. And when the song was registered with BMI, the only credit that counted for financial remuneration, George Goldner's name replaced that of Watkins.

The Rama boss was hardly the first industry figure to pull such a move. Even a seemingly noble folklorist like John Lomax had not been able to resist taking a 50 percent credit alongside Leadbelly for "Goodnight Irene." (And what a windfall that turned out to be!) And Goldner could perhaps have argued, had it come to it, that his contribution in the studio had proven sufficient to merit his cut (though clearly not to insist upon it on the sheet music). But he never had to make that claim, for in the fly-by-night 1950s world of rhythm and blues, songwriting credits were routinely requested, demanded—or simply taken—from the original artists, while the copyrights themselves were often assigned by the independent labels to publishing companies owned either by DJs or other businessmen on whose largesse they depended.

In New York, such assigning frequently (though not exclusively) involved Alan Freed. Back in Cleveland, Freed managed a vocal group called the Moonglows, without much success; immediately after his move to WINS, however, Chess Records signed them, and Freed was declared a cowriter of their single "Sincerely." The following year, he was assigned a cowriting credit for another release on Chess, "Maybellene," which came as news to its actual composer and recording artist, Chuck Berry, who had never met the disc jockey. Because such songwriting credits had the potential to raise questions, many other songs of the era were simply copyrighted to Freed's publishing company, Jackie Music. (Not only was this less overt; it was more lucrative: the publisher earned a full 50 percent of a song's profits, whereas the remaining 50 percent was divided between the various songwriters.) When Freed starred in the movie *Rock, Rock, Rock* in 1956 (having already appeared in *Rock around the Clock* and *Don't Knock the Rock*), fifteen of the twenty-one songs included just happened to be assigned to a new publishing company, Snapper Music, that he established specifically for the project. (The others were assigned to Morris Levy's publishing partner, Phil Kahl.)

For the New York indie labels attracted by Freed's increasingly alluring aura, such freewheeling distribution of writing and publishing credits was simply the cost of doing business—along with paying DJs in cash for their support. Atlantic Records' Jerry Wexler justified these payments as "what you would call a normal business expense." (Besides, he added, "we paid everybody.") "Sure, it was payola," he elaborated in an interview. "But it's my firm belief that payola never created a hit. What it did was open access to the airwaves. A hit is a hit is a hit. It was like a horse race, what we were paying for was being in the starting gate on an equal basis with the other horses in the race."

Perhaps because it had deep enough pockets to outpayola the rest, Atlantic remained the undisputed leader of the New York indies. Beneath it, literally dozens of independent labels competed with each other, and though to the casual eye they may have seemed interchangeable (acts tended to bounce from one label to another), they were each indelibly associated with the character(s) of their founders: George Goldner with Gee and Rama; Jerry Blaine with Jubilee and Josie (and Cosnat Distribution); Hy and Sam Weiss with Old Town and Paradise; Bobby and Danny Robinson with their catalog of labels Red Robin, Whirlin' Disc, Holiday, Fury, and Everlast; Morty Craft with Melba; Leo Rogers and Marty Bruce with Bruce; and Paul Winley, brother of the Clovers' singer Harold Winley, with a Harlem-based label in his family name.

From the outset, all these labels downplayed any expectations the artists might have about getting paid. And the artists generally went along. Raoul Cita, the highly respected writer, arranger, and Harptones singer, said that he agreed with Bruce Records' argument that recording royalties from the Harptones' debut ballad, "A Sunday Kind of Love," should be plowed back into promotion—and that he saw the results. "Every time you went in the store, there were Harptones posters. And what were you going to get [in royalties]? Two cents a record. Besides, all the money was in personal performances."

From there, it was a short leap of faith to give up songwriting royalties for the same end result. So when Bruce folded and the Harptones went over to Old Town, and Hy Weiss took a songwriting cocredit on "Life Is But a Dream" (another stirring ballad starring Willie Winfield's exemplary tenor), Cita again accepted it as the prevailing practice of the era. "If you're a struggling songwriter and you want someone to record your song, you've got to give them a piece of your song."

When the Harptones bounced from Old Town to Rama, at least the new label boss was up-front about his intentions. "George [Goldner] came up to me and said he wants to make a payoff to these different disc jockeys. So in order as he didn't have the money, he wanted to put his name on these songs."

The Harptones appeared on more of Alan Freed's revues than any other non-national New York act, suggesting that Cita's various compromises paid dividends. But even when they played Alan Freed's Labor Day concert at the Brooklyn Paramount, three or four shows a day and six on Saturdays, for ten days straight, in 1956, at the very peak of the vocal group craze, they received just $1,100 for the entire five-piece group. "And out of that came the booking agent's 10 percent, and the manager's 15 percent," said Cita. So much for all the money being in personal appearances.

No wonder, then, that vocal groups would sometimes put their foot down (so they thought) and demand recompense for their hit records—in response to which the label bosses might provide them with a fancy new car. That was a lot easier and ultimately cheaper than coming up with or accounting for royalties. And the bosses saw nothing wrong with it. "What were these bums off the street?" Hy Weiss complained to Fredric Dannen years later. "You had to have *credit* to buy the Cadillac."

Weiss's Old Town exemplified the conveyor belt, music-as-product approach to the vocal groups, holding midnight auditions at the Triboro Theater. Similarly whereas Atlantic would use top professional studio musicians—Connie Kay, a former regular at Minton's who joined the Modern Jazz Quartet in 1955, played drums on many a recording—and Goldner would work relentlessly on arrangements, Old Town rushed through its recording sessions to get as much material in the can as possible. "A typical

Hy Weiss session," according to Jerry Wexler, would be "after midnight in a shadowy studio, which the engineer had to be bribed to open up. Hy had three or four groups waiting in the wings. In the recording room would be three pieces: a piano player, a drummer, and a saxophone. Hy Weiss would hit the Talk button in the control room and say, 'First group,' and the group would trudge out and the piano player would say 'Where's your music?' 'We don't got no music.' 'What key?' And Hy Weiss would hit the Talkback and say, 'We don't study keys, motherfucker, play the music.'"

Under such competitive, high-pressure circumstances, it was all too easy for the labels to play hardball with the writers. It was not uncommon for groups to be invited into the control room after an exuberant take and be told their song would see release—provided they agreed to the "standard" half share of their songwriting. If they objected, suggesting perhaps that the label had never heard the song before the session, they would be met with a simple ultimatum: do you want the record to come out or not?

"We had a writer called Buddy Walker wrote a great tune for us called 'Talking to Myself,'" said Gene Tompkins of the Limelighters. "And it was taken to Jerry Blaine. He liked it and made Buddy the offer of 50 percent. Buddy said, 'You have to be crazy.' And of course the record never came out."

Not every label acted like this. And not everyone agreed with those who did. "The bastards who put their names on songs which they didn't write and who stole the birthright of songwriters and singers, and put themselves on royalties as members of groups," said Jerry Wexler, were "corrupt, venal, grasping, simian-intelligence lowbrows, and pieces of dirt."

And yet there remained a begrudging respect for the label founders. "Hy Weiss did not play an instrument, but he had an ear," said Bobby Jay. "Goldner had a talent for discovering talent. Paul Winley, up in Harlem, didn't make the best-sounding records, but his records have a charm. Bobby Robinson can't play anything, but still, the music they created. . . ."

Indeed, some of it was sublime. Even though New York vocal music was formulaic—the ballads were almost all in 6/8 time, and the jump tunes were essentially twelve-bar blues with an obligatory sax solo, while the words "I love you so" appeared to be mandatory for inclusion regardless of format— there were many moments of studio magic. In fact, for the generation that grew up with them, the songs captured the essence of the era as much as a faded wedding photograph or a sports souvenir. In 1955, the artists and labels alike responded to Freed's new rock 'n' roll format by getting their up-tempo recordings down to a fine art: "Come Back My Love" by the Wrens, who formed at Morris High in the South Bronx (which they attended alongside a future secretary of state, Colin Powell), was so polished that it could have emerged from the Atlantic label, proving that Goldner had gotten to grips with the genre; Earl Carroll's boastful performance, along with a typographical error in the title, rendered "Speedoo" by Harlem's Cadillacs on Josie one of the more enjoyable and unusual songs of the era; and with its perfectly spread four-part harmonies, the Valentines' "Lily Maybelle" more than compensated for its lack of lyrical depth. (And yes, all three had a honking sax solo.)

Everything came together at the end of that year with Frankie Lymon and the Teenagers. Their backstory was almost painfully familiar. The core group—including two Puerto Ricans, Herman Santiago and Joe Negroni—met at Edward W. Stitt Junior High School, in the Sugar Hill/Washington Heights neighborhood, entered talent contests, rehearsed in the school function room, and sang in the apartment hallways—to the point that one exasperated neighbor gifted them some old love letters in the hope that they might serve as inspiration for lyrics. The Premiers could hardly have expected to qualify as poets: their youngest member, Frankie Lymon, was just twelve years old in 1955. Frankie, who had been invited on board after the others saw him play bongos for a mambo group at their school talent contest, came from solid musical stock—his father sang with the Harlemaires—and not only could he play the drums but he could sing, he could dance, he exuded charisma and confidence, and he was cute as a button to boot.

Though legend has it that the Premiers were discovered singing under a street lamp, the more prosaic truth was that they shared rehearsal space at Stitt with the newly successful Valentines. The driving force behind that group was the Philadelphian Richard Barrett, who had moved to the area after twice winning the Apollo Amateur Night contest without breaking through. Having now secured success with his composition "Lily Maybelle" for the Valentines at Rama, he was keen to move up in the business. Barrett brought the Premiers to Goldner's midtown office, where they auditioned, with Herman Santiago taking lead. Among their material was "Why Do Birds Sing So Gay?" which Santiago had extrapolated out of their neighbor's old love letters.

Goldner liked what he heard—up to a point. After asking to hear

Frankie Lymon sing the same song, he offered the group a deal, on condition that Lymon take lead in the studio. By the time their debut recording session had concluded, the Premiers had also been renamed the Teenagers and their song retitled "Why Do Fools Fall in Love." And when the record hit the streets, it was Goldner's name that shared writing credits alongside Lymon's, not Santiago's. The publishing copyright itself was assigned to Patricia Music, Morris Levy's company.

And that's where the "initial" meeting between Goldner and Levy comes back into play. "Why Do Fools Fall In Love" was recorded right around the time that Tito Puente left Goldner's Tico Records for RCA Victor. In addition, according to Goldner's daughter Linda, who was around her father's business and made a point of learning his life story from him while he was still alive, Freed had recently all but stopped playing Goldner's rhythm and blues records. (It's true that there had been no major hits on Gee or Rama since the Crows' "Gee.") Certain that Levy had a hand in the first of his business problems, if not necessarily the second, Goldner might well have gone to visit the Birdland proprietor with a bee in his bonnet. According to both Levy and Linda Goldner's accounts, when Goldner came by to complain, he found Levy apologetic for any inconvenience and eager to make amends. ("I really didn't do it to hurt the man," Levy told Dannen about bringing Puente to RCA.) So began what appeared to be a friendship between two of the most important figures in the independent music world, and plans may well have been laid that day that resulted in their soon forming another record label that was to draw on Goldner's A&R talents, Levy's publishing and promotional muscle, and Freed's broadcasting might: Roulette Records. In the meantime, whether as an act of friendship or otherwise, Goldner allocated Levy's right-hand man Tommy Vastola a cowriting credit for both the Valentines' "Lily Maybelle" (recorded in August 1955) and the Wrens' "What Makes You Do the Thing That You Do?" (recorded in October 1955), topped off with the assigning to Levy's publishing company of the copyright for the Teenagers' "Why Do Fools Fall in Love."

That last was a gift that could be measured in gold, for "Why Do Fools Fall in Love" proved arguably the greatest single of the whole vocal group era. In just 138 seconds, it offers every essential element of the genre: a classic "doo-wop" bass vocal introduction, a lead voice so resonant that no one could forget it, a lyric of universal appeal, and a suitably contemporary rock 'n' roll backing, with the drums prominent in the mix and Rama's musical arranger Jimmy Wright's usual sax solo raging in the middle. Facilitated by maximum support from Freed, not so coincidentally, it duly exploded on the streets and radio alike, reaching number six on the pop chart and number one on the R&B chart. All around New York (indeed, all over the country), harmony fans could be found talking about the lead vocal, saying they couldn't tell whether it was a boy or a girl. When they discovered that it was the former, they set about imitating his success by the hundreds.

"I would be listening to Alan Freed," said Arlene Smith, who was entertaining the idea of a proper vocal group with fellow choristers from Saint Anthony of Padua in the Bronx, "and the day he said Frankie Lymon was thirteen, that was *it*. From then on, rehearsals, instead of just saying, 'Come on over to my house,' had a different purpose. Every kid wanted to cut a record."

Or, as the future R&B historian Marv Goldberg, then an eleven-year-old schoolboy in the Bronx, described it: "Frankie Lymon unfortunately unleashed upon an unsuspecting world some of the most horrendous kids-sound music ever. Everybody wanted to sound like him—and almost none of them could."

The one who came closest at the time was Frankie's own younger brother, Lewis, who walked into Bobby Robinson's store in June 1956, looking for an audition. Robinson did not need to be asked twice. Yet it was several months before he released Lewis Lymon and the Teenchords' debut single, his own composition "I'm So Happy," complete with near-mandatory "I love her so" lyric and sax solo. The delay was in part to allow the group to learn more songs—and the dance steps to go with them—to take to the promotional live circuit; it was also because he was setting up a new, solely owned label—Fury—on which to release them. (Red Robin was no more, and Whirlin' Disc was a partnership with Jerry Blaine.) "I'm So Happy" was inane in the extreme—its bracketed subtitle "Tra-La-La-La-La-La" pretty much summing it up—and Lewis, twelve years old at the time, lacked his sibling's vocal dexterity. But at least it exuded a lasting juvenile joy, which was more than could be said for many of the other preteen groups that were snapped up by majors and indies alike to cash in on the Lymon sensation.

As their second single, "I Want You to Be My Girl," raced up the charts, the Teenagers became superstars. In 1956, a year they should have spent in school, they appeared in all of Freed's New York rock 'n' roll revues (Goldner's acts the Wrens and the Valentines, those with the Vastola cowrites, also joined the revues), traversed America on three separate tours, and visited the United Kingdom twice. They also performed the star turn in Freed's movie vehicle *Rock, Rock, Rock*, in which their "I'm Not a Juvenile Delinquent" was the nearest that vocal groups came to social consciousness in the 1950s. (A hit in Europe, it did not take off in the States.)

Lymon's unique star power must have appeared a potentially endless gold mine to his handlers. But they proved too greedy, too quickly. Lymon was moved swiftly to the middle of the marketplace: by early 1957, he was already recording pop standards backed by an orchestra. This, of course, negated the need for fellow vocalists, and so—just eighteen months after the release of "Why Do Fools Fall in Love"—Frankie Lymon and the Teenagers went their separate ways. Their final release under that name, "Goody Goody," only their third top 20 hit, was in fact a Frankie solo effort.

The Teenagers continued a while on Goldner's Gee label, while Lymon's solo outings were released through the new label, Roulette. Lymon was introduced as a solo artist on Freed's latest broadcasting bonanza, the ABC television show *Big Beat*, but as the credits rolled and the audience mixed with the performers, the naive teenage star broke protocol and grabbed a white girl to dance with. Amidst uproar from affiliates below the Mason-Dixon line, Freed was told to book only white acts in the future. He refused, and the show was canceled after just four episodes.

Freed had other lucrative avenues to exploit; Lymon did not. Inevitably, Frankie's voice broke, and when it did, his audience (and backers) lost interest. He embarked on a rapid downfall that ended with a heroin overdose at just twenty-five years of age. It was one of the great tragedies of popular music: not just the manner in which he died, but the sense that such a unique talent was so improperly handled. Certainly, Lymon's rapid rise to fame at the age of thirteen, from the Harlem streets to Hollywood in under a year, informed an ego that was difficult to control. (Among his other achievements, Lymon was known for bedding women twice his age.) He hailed from an era and a genre that didn't bank on longevity, that lacked personal management, that chewed up its talent and spat it back out. Lymon's musical impact on a generation was profound. Any moral from his brief life story was less easily learned.

. . .

n the spring of 1957, around the time Lymon went solo, *Billboard* reported that George Goldner had sold his three record labels, Rama, Gee, and Tico, along with his Tico Distributing Company and his publishing interests—plus his share in the new label Roulette—to Morris Levy and his partner Phil Kahl for $250,000. A week earlier, the same industry magazine had reported that Alan Freed, having expected a 50 percent share in Roulette, had fallen out with Levy when he saw the actual contract, and severed all ties. Although the pair supposedly made nice again a couple of months later, by the time the dust had settled, Freed had off-loaded his own publishing companies Jackie and Snapper Music, along with any interest he held in Roulette, to the same Levy/Kahl partnership. Levy now was not only in the promotions business and the nightclub game, and laden with lucrative publishing copyrights, but he had a handsome record catalog, too.

It's impossible to know all the reasons why Freed and Goldner chose to cash in their chips at the same time, especially given that both men were at the very peak of their powers and that neither should have been in need of quick cash. Linda Goldner denied that her father was addicted to gambling, which would later become an acknowledged concern. Rather, she said, "Morris went to a lot of trouble to create an atmosphere to attract George to go into business with him." That business was Roulette, but Goldner had not anticipated being anything but his own boss. "He was very self-assured and never thought he would have a partner disagreeing with him in reference to studio budgets or spending money on the road when he promoted their records. No one was going to dictate an opinion to George, including Morris Levy." Walking away from the relationship rather than putting up with inter-ference meant leaving his other companies behind: the end game, she said, of "a deliberate setup." Levy described it differently: "George got disillusioned and we bought him out."

Regardless of the reasons, George Goldner signed over not just his pub-lishing copyrights but also his own songwriting claims. In an act of audacity rarely rivaled in the history of the music business, Morris Levy promptly replaced Goldner's name on such major hits as "Gee" and "Why Do Fools Fall in Love" with his own. Many of those credits survive to this day.

• • •

George Goldner took several weeks off from the music business to recover, and then he bounced back. He rented an office at 1650 Broadway, set up two labels, End and Gone, and brought Richard Barrett from the Valentines in as a producer and A&R man. Barrett's reputation as "the one that took Frankie Lymon to George Goldner" was enough for Arlene Smith and her friends, who had now organized themselves as the Chantels, to wait for him outside a Valentines show, and sing him a song that they had written, "The Plea"—a cappella, of course.

Until now, teenage girls had rarely sung street harmony, in large part because they were the *objects* of the music. Frankie Lymon, with whom the Chantels were so hopelessly infatuated that they "stalked" his neighborhood in the hope of meeting him, helped change all that, his prepubescent voice bringing the soprano register into popularity. In the summer of 1957, Atlantic Records had a top ten single with a group of girls from Harlem called the Bobettes, so it was no surprise that Barrett not only listened to the Chantels but took Smith's contact information. A couple of nights later, he visited her household in the Bronx to secure her parents' permission to work with her. Consent granted, he arranged for the choristers to audition for Goldner, who signed them immediately.

Like many others, Smith gave up songwriting credits she later believed she should have held on to: both "The Plea" and the A-side of the Chantels' debut single, a minor hit called "He's Gone," ended up as a split credit with Richard Barrett. "They add a sentence to it, and all of a sudden it's their song, or they're half writer," she said. And yet she recalled of Barrett himself, "He had just a fabulous personality. Guys emulated him and girls loved him, and hoped to be in the ray of his attention. There was this side of him that I will always love and appreciate." Such were the inevitable contradictions of such an unruly era.

As for Goldner, Smith described him as "a perfectionist to a fault." This suited her just fine. "He would always ask me, 'Do it again?' And I would say, 'Yes.' I *never* complained about doing it again."

For the second Chantels single, Barrett brought Smith a demo of a 6/8 ballad called "Maybe" and some gospel albums to study: as a convent chorister, Smith had missed out on that integral aspect of the vocal groups' influences. She proved a quick study: on the master recording, her sixteen-year-old voice soared above her fellow singers' (who avoided the usual nonsense syllables and concentrated instead on choral harmony), so high and yet so graceful, engaging in frequent vibratos. The song hit the top 20 of the pop charts in early 1958. The fact that Goldner (who shared the writing credit with Barrett) cut out the middlemen—he was not exactly on speaking terms with Morris Levy—and assigned the song directly to Freed's new publishing company, Figure Music, surely didn't harm its success.

n this world of almost endless one- or two-hit wonders, the only New York group that appeared to have true chart consistency in the 1950s was the Drifters. "Appeared" is the operative word. The original Clyde McPhatter lineup had quickly followed up the 1953 number one R&B hit "Money Honey" with a double pairing, the beautifully sung falsetto of the ballad "Lucille" (recorded at McPhatter's first and otherwise unused Atlantic session) with the more ribald, up-tempo "Such a Night"; the latter was banned from some airwaves for its bold lyrics, though that did not stop Elvis Presley from later covering it (as he did "Money Honey"). Subsequent singles continued to give full vent to McPhatter's gospel-trained range while running the gamut from raunchy rhythm and blues—"Bip Bam" and "Honey Love"—to reverential ballads like "The Bells of Saint Mary's" and a nearly note-for-note copy of the Ravens' own interpretation of "White Christmas."

In May 1954, a year to the day after McPhatter signed with Atlantic, the singer received his draft papers. McPhatter was stationed at Fort Dix, in New Jersey, and this enabled him to record and perform with the Drifters while on leave. Yet by the time he came out of the service, a decision had been made by the Drifters' manager George Treadwell (who had played trumpet in the Monroe's Uptown house band of the 1940s and gone on to marry and manage Sarah Vaughan) to take McPhatter solo. The singer promptly embarked on a phenomenal run of solo hits on Atlantic (including "Treasure of Love" and "A Lover's Question") that, unlike his R&B classics for the Drifters or the Dominoes, crossed over to the higher reaches of the pop charts.

Not surprisingly, the Drifters floundered without their golden lead voice. They were reduced to making an answer single to the Teenagers, "Fools Fall in Love," to maintain relevance; it failed to make the R&B charts. With morale at an all-time low, Treadwell—who with his partner Lou Levish held the trademark on the name, affording complete control over the group's lineup and its finances—was forced to rehire two previous members to round out a surviving trio for a Dr. Jive revue at the Apollo in late spring 1958. Topping the bill was Atlantic's biggest star, Ray Charles, whose game-changing blend of R&B and gospel had actually come *after* the Dominoes and the Drifters had pioneered the formula. Somewhere near the bottom of the bill was a group from 115th Street that had, for all its local respect, struggled to find lasting success of its own: the Crowns. The Drifters did not perform well over the course of the week, which ended with one drunken member cursing out the Apollo manager Frank Schiffman. The Crowns, on the other hand, especially their baritone Benjamin Nelson, the former neighborhood street singer who had only recently joined the group, impressed everyone. In a move comparable to that of Levy replacing Goldner's writing credits with his own name, Treadwell fired the remaining members of the Drifters and replaced them wholesale with the members of the Crowns.

And what of Alan Freed? He came, he saw, he conquered New York, and then he succumbed to one of the most fabled downfalls in musical history. By the spring of 1958, Freed's movies, tours, TV shows, and various side deals had made him a very rich man, but they necessitated his increasing absence from the microphone at WINS headquarters, much to the frustration of his employers, who came to view his growing ego (and widely known alcoholism) as a liability. In addition, having eagerly promoted himself as the public face of rock 'n' roll, a music that was widely regarded as a scourge by those who could not understand it, Freed had set himself up as its obvious whipping boy. So, when his *Big Beat* tour of 1958 (which included the Chantels, Chuck Berry, Jerry Lee Lewis, Buddy Holly, and, despite Freed's earlier denouncement of the genre, the Canadian R&B "cover" act the Diamonds) hit Boston, and street gangs fought it out in the audience, the media jumped on the disturbances as front-page confirmation of their elder readers' worst fears. Freed was subsequently charged by the Boston authorities, with a rare sense of rhythm for the legal process, with "unlawfully, wickedly, and maliciously inciting to riot during a rock and roll show," and WINS took the opportunity to fire him that same day.

The charges were ultimately dropped, and Freed briefly switched over to WABC radio, but it was too late to turn things around. The disc jockey was soon swept up in—and brought down by—a growing payola scandal. A Senate hearing that had started out examining the rigging of television quiz shows widened—at the suggestion of none other than ASCAP, furious at the way BMI artists had come to rule the airwaves—to include the methods by which radio DJs chose to air records, and Freed found himself at the eye of the storm.

"Why me?" he asked directly of the Senate subcommittee at his hearing on April 25, 1960. "Why should I be the scapegoat?" His question was intended to suggest that Dick Clark—the Philadelphia-based DJ and *American Bandstand* host whose popularity and influence now towered over Freed's, and who had only just divested himself of those of his thirty-plus companies that clearly revealed a conflict of interest—had been far more egregious in taking kickbacks. But the answer to Freed's question was evident by the very fact that he asked it.

"He invited it upon himself," said Jerry Wexler. "Dick Clark did the same things that Alan Freed did, but Dick Clark was a presentable Christian. Alan Freed was a nefarious Jew: [it was] very much the congress of the local DA to nail this obvious detestable malefactor."

As the scandal became front-page news, Clark insisted on his innocence to the committee, assuring the senators, in the face of all evidence to the contrary, that his business deals were strictly legal. Freed, by comparison, older and no longer a hipster, was by turns combative, defensive, and overly generous with his information, admitting that he was on the payroll of three distribution companies in which he held no shares or job title (one of which, Superior, was owned by Sam Weiss), and that he had received monthly cash payments from the record companies Atlantic and United Artists and from Blaine's Cosnat Distribution.

The committee members were astonished by his honesty, but Freed had little left to hide. A concurrent New York district attorney investigation into payola had already handed down a charge of commercial bribery, during the process of which Morris Levy had taken the stand and, under protection of immunity, admitted that his Roulette Records held a mortgage on Freed's estate—and that the company had also lent the DJ $10,000 in early 1958, with the "tacit understanding" that Freed need not repay it. (As Freed cast about for cash to pay his ever-mounting legal fees, he sold his share in Figure Music to Levy, and with it control of the Chantels' big hit.)

Freed was not the only DJ brought down by the payola scandal. The New York district attorney also charged Tommy Smalls, Hal Jackson, and Jack Walker with commercial bribery. (This left "Jocko" Henderson, who broadcast in the mornings on WLIB, as perhaps the only one of the city's major R&B jocks to avoid embroilment in the scandal.) Though none served jail time, each was indelibly tainted by the charges, and Freed embarked on a succession of ever more lowly radio gigs, his body succumbing to alcohol poisoning within five years.

Not surprisingly, Goldner also figured prominently in the hearings. In January 1960, the Federal Trade Commission charged him with bribery of disc jockeys. A year later, he found himself as a witness in the prosecution of one of those disc jockeys, Peter Tripp of WMGM, who stood accused of taking $30,000 in payola in one year. Tripp admitted that he had tapped Goldner for $4,000, but held that it was intended purely as a loan: Goldner seemed "nice," said Tripp. Asked to clarify the word *nice*, he said, "In my business, you've got people stabbing you in the back every day of your life. He was polite, cordial and not a back-stabber."

Goldner was by this point quite used to being called for testimony. In April 1960, he had appeared in front of the Senate subcommittee directly before Dick Clark, where he admitted that he had given copyrights to both Clark and Freed in "the hopes of having those songs played on the air." At the end of his testimony, he thanked the senators for what they were "doing for the industry," declaring, "A lot of good will come out of what you are doing." Having given away so much of his profits over the years to the disc jockeys and their managers—indeed, having taken songwriting credits from his artists to do so—it is quite possible that he was being completely serious.

7

FROM BROOKLYN
TO BROADWAY

At the other end of New York City from Harlem and the South Bronx, the 1950s produced, on first inspection, a generation of teenagers very different from those who popularized vocal rhythm and blues. The postwar kids of southern Brooklyn—at least those who went on to quietly revolutionize the music world—were white, Jewish, and raised not on gospel, blues, jazz, Amateur Night at the Apollo, and Tommy "Dr. Jive" Smalls but on Broadway musicals, sentimental singers, pop standards, and Martin Block's *Make Believe Ballroom* on WNEW. Until 1954, theirs was a world of Perry Como, Patti Page, and Frankie Laine, of classical piano lessons, summer vacations in the Catskills, and the knowledge that they were coming of age in the postwar years of peace and prosperity.

"You could keep your door open, drop in at neighbors, there was hardly any crime or robbery," said Neil Sedaka, born in 1939, of his Brighton Beach neighborhood, which adjoined Coney Island and its amusement parks. The streets, he said, were full of "stoop ball, and kick the can, and stickball."

Barry Mann, born that same year, recalled his Gravesend neighborhood similarly: "It was very friendly, you didn't need a parent to walk you to school."

"The fifties were innocent," said Carole King, who was born in 1942 and, like Mann, attended James Madison High School, in the gridded Brooklyn streets where Midwood and Flatbush give way to the more saline-sounding climes of Ocean Parkway, Marine Park, and Sheepshead Bay. "We believed government was as advertised, and we believed anybody could achieve anything, and we should just pursue our dreams."

Those dreams served to bring these three characters together to work at a company in midtown Manhattan, where, along with other Jewish kids mostly of their age and background in similar offices, they rewrote the American songbook. Their success rate was astounding: no fewer than sixteen of America's number one hits—by some fifteen different artists—over a five-year period at the dawn of the 1960s were written, recorded, or produced by graduates of three neighborhood high schools: Abraham Lincoln, James Madison, and Erasmus Hall. We know it as the Brill Building era, but really it's the sound of Jewish Brooklyn as filtered through the prism of rock 'n' roll.

Brooklyn, founded by the Dutch in the seventeenth century as Breuckelen, after a town in the Netherlands, had been its own city until 1898, when it was incorporated into the new Greater New York. By 1930, it had overtaken Manhattan as the most populous of the five boroughs; just a decade later, its population close to peaking at 2.7 million people, it could have counted as the fourth-largest city in America. Moreover, with nearly a million Jews living within its eighty-one square miles, it contained what has been called "the largest Jewish community of any city in the history of the world." Some were new immigrants, fleeing the European attacks on Jews that would culminate in the Holocaust. But the vast majority were the children of earlier immigrants, many having escaped the overcrowding of New York's original Jewish enclave—Manhattan's Lower East Side—following the opening of three East River bridges and the extension of several subway lines through the borough, in the very late nineteenth and early twentieth centuries.

That influx from Manhattan made its way only gradually across Brooklyn, the Borough of Kings: at first to Brownsville and Williamsburg, then to Greenpoint, Borough Park, and Flatbush. Through most of these years of migration and settlement, the coastline on the southern tip of the borough remained distant enough to qualify as a vacation destination. Indeed, Brighton Beach was originally developed, late in the 1870s, by a railroad magnate who envisioned a middle-class alternative to neighboring Coney Island, which even then had earned itself the sobriquet Sodom by the Sea.

Erecting a hotel on Brighton Beach from which he proudly excluded Jews, that same developer then built the Brighton Rapid Transit elevated train line to attract guests from Manhattan, inadvertently enabling city dwellers, Jews among them, to taste the sea air and dip their bodies in the Atlantic Ocean for the price of a five-cent train ride. Inexpensive rental bungalows sprouted around the Brighton Beach Hotel and quickly attracted families for summer vacations. A horse-racing track, a summer theater, and the famous Reisenweber's Hall all helped create an environment that would sound familiar to later denizens of the Brill Building: many a vaudeville performer was known to earn his wages at the theater, blow them at the race track, and have just enough left over to drown his sorrows at Reisenweber's, all in the course of a summer's day.

During the real estate boom of the Roaring Twenties, Brighton Beach was graced by the rise of thirty elevator-furnished six-story apartment buildings, offering "a year-round resort lifestyle." The subsequent depression turned that lifestyle into one of struggle and overcrowding, as families doubled up with each other to make the rent. But the evictions that were commonplace across the rest of America didn't take hold in this corner of Brooklyn, where the women of the Emma Lazarus Council ensured, by any means necessary, that residents remained in their apartments regardless of a landlord's intent.

The area's creed was evident when, in dedicating a new Brighton Beach synagogue in 1937, Dr. Maxwell Ross proclaimed, "Brighton Beach, not Europe or Palestine, is the real promised land for Jews . . . where we may practice the religion of our forefathers without interference from narrow minded bigots or maniacs." But patriotism for the nation that afforded these freedoms ran high: the residents of Brighton Beach fought in considerable numbers during the war, with death rates reaching as high as 50 percent. Factor in the massacre of family members caught in the Holocaust, and it was no surprise that the neighborhood's first postwar generation, too young clearly to understand the horrors of the war itself but imbued with an inherent sense of injustice and fortitude, proved themselves ready to make their mark on the world.

"We were fighters, we were survivors," said Neil Sedaka, who grew up in one of those thirty Brighton Beach apartment buildings. "The Jewish people from New York had chutzpah, we had push, we had drive." He saw those qualities come together in a love of music and the arts. "The Jewish families bought a piano; they wanted their children to grow up with culture."

"It wasn't like our parents said, 'You have to be successful,'" said Barry Mann, "but it was maybe something to do with that immigrant mentality, of striving to do better without being told you had to do better."

Fifteen miles northwest of Brooklyn's beaches, at 1619 Broadway, on the corner of 49th Street in midtown Manhattan, stood the Brill Building. Opened in 1931 and named for the company of tailors who originally occupied its ground floor store, the ten-story structure featured Art Deco touches above its entrance and a long, mirrored hallway to the elevators. These fancy furnishings signified its intended glamour and belied its eventual status as the home of Tin Pan Alley—the name for the Broadway-based music business that, in the mid-twentieth century, followed the theatrical shows up from an area clustered around 28th Street, to their new home just north of Times Square. By the 1950s, in any number of office cubicles furnished with little more than a desk, a phone, and, of necessity, an upright piano, there could be found the song pluggers, publishers, promoters, arrangers, and other impresarios, rogues, and thieves who constituted the independent music business, as it had long been known. The big shots had their offices there, like Hill & Range, major music publishers of the day, and Frank Sinatra, the most popular singer of his era. Alan Freed took an office in the Brill Building as soon as he moved to New York.

And yet, following the explosion first of rhythm and blues and then of rock 'n' roll, the real action moved over to 1650 Broadway—the Music Building—which, although it lacked the Brill's distinct façade and opened ignominiously onto 51st Street, was preferred for its cheaper rent, and its absence of established old-timers and their inevitable disdain for the new rhythms. (You could even break it down by affiliation: the Brill Building was ASCAP, while 1650 was almost exclusively BMI.) Those without sufficient clout or rent money for the Music Building took space even farther up the street at 1697 Broadway, in what later became the Ed Sullivan Theater, and a few more moved into 1674 Broadway. All these buildings hummed continually with the sound of pianos and deals being struck alike, and the availability of so many businesses in so few buildings made for a one-stop shopping experience. Apart from minimizing phone bills and telegram costs, the congruence of the independent music business in such close-quartered buildings made for a hive of constant buzz and activity. Elevator conversations were closely guarded for fear of releasing secrets—yet office doors were routinely left open so as not to miss out on a hit that came in off the streets.

"You could actually walk through the buildings, all of them, and knock on doors," said the Bronx-raised songwriter Richard Gottehrer. "People would see you, they'd listen to you, you'd play piano, and they would either kick you out quick or, in some instances, say, 'I like your song,' and take an option on it, and give you twenty dollars."

For those who didn't have reason to pound the halls, it was as convenient to spend the day on Broadway itself. "You would always see a lot of interesting guys just standing out front to network," said Arlene Smith of the Chantels. "If you knew what you were looking for, you could find it without going into the Brill Building."

Likewise, you could find it over lunch at restaurants like Jack Dempsey's, Lindy's, or the Turf, where the hierarchy of the music business declared itself through its unwritten but keenly noted seating (or counter) arrangements, and where phone booths served as offices for those who couldn't afford rent in one of the main buildings. After work, the current hit makers would celebrate their successes at eateries on Broadway's Restaurant Row (46th Street, west of Seventh Avenue) or at Al & Dick's on 54th Street. The failures would go home and dream of another day and another possible hit—often enough via a subway ride back to Brooklyn.

As far as one can put a date on it, the saga of the young Brooklyn writers began on October 11, 1952, when sixteen-year-old Howard Greenfield knocked on thirteen-year-old Neil Sedaka's door, at the apartment building they shared, 3960 Coney Island Avenue, right by the beach. Greenfield's mother had heard Sedaka playing classical piano that summer at the Kenmore Lake Hotel in the Catskills and wanted the boys to write together in the Jewish tradition. "She said her son was a sixteen-year-old poet," recalled Sedaka, who was not thrilled with the idea. "I didn't like him very much. He was very, *very* obese. Kids could be cruel—they called him Fat Howie."

Sedaka was hardly a matinee idol himself. "I had feminine tendencies, I held my books like a girl," he said, which didn't aid his own popularity at the 2,000-strong Abraham Lincoln, "a pretty tough high school" filled primarily with Jewish and Italian teenagers, just a few blocks away on Ocean Parkway. But he was already known as a musical prodigy, and by the time "Fat Howie" came knocking, Sedaka was spending his Saturday mornings at Juilliard, just west of Harlem. He started writing with Greenfield, and remembered their first composition, "My Life's Devotion," as a "ruptured rhumba—something stuck in my subconscious from a Xavier Cugat movie." Rhythm and blues might as well not have existed in the early 1950s, for all that it influenced Brooklyn teenagers.

And then along came Alan Freed. "I was intrigued," said Sedaka. "Howie was not. I found it very exciting, very spontaneous, very homespun. But most of the singers sang off-key, and that bothered him." The lack of pitch was not lost on other future songwriters from the neighborhood. Barry Mann, whose mother saw to it that classical music formed part of his upbringing, too, was told about Moondog by a friend, and tuned in. "And I remember thinking at first, 'Everything sounds flat.'" As for many others, it was merely a matter of retuning his expectations. "After a couple of weeks, it grew on me."

Mann's future friend Carole King had a more visceral reaction to Freed's show. "Oh God," she recalled thinking when she first heard it. "This has something that we are not familiar with."

That something was blackness—and it was not, one might have thought, an attribute that white, lower-middle-class Jewish kids from the southern Brooklyn beach neighborhoods could acquire overnight. But they could certainly try. The same month Freed came to town, Mortimer Shuman, who had been a year ahead of Sedaka at Abraham Lincoln, entered City College, where, in his own words, he started to "dress black, talk black, walk black, and eat black." The following year, he began dating the cousin of Doc Pomus, a white blues singer ten years his elder who had been crippled by polio as a child in Williamsburg. Supported on crutches, buried at the bottom of the social heap, the resolute Pomus had taken to singing in the most dangerous of low-rent clubs. If Shuman aspired to blackness, Pomus had long been living it. Indeed, he had already seen his compositions recorded by Ray Charles and Big Joe Turner on Atlantic.

Shuman and Pomus bonded over late night sessions around the latter's record collection. "Doc was into urban blues, and I was into 'tenement music,'" said Shuman years later, citing a euphemism for street harmony singing. As they began writing together, they melded their interests into a blueprint for a more populist rhythm and blues. And when Atlantic recorded some of their initial offerings—though none were immediate hits—Neil Sedaka, who had always looked up to Shuman as a genuine hipster, convinced Greenfield they should write a rock 'n' roll number, too. Sedaka sang the result, "Mr. Moon," at a school "Ballyhoo," and it made him "a school celebrity." The self-confessed sissy was suddenly welcomed by what he called the school "toughies," into the back room of the Sweet Shoppe, the local candy store (and hangout, complete with juke box) opposite Abraham Lincoln.

Elsewhere at Lincoln, Hank Medress was so smitten with the new music that he would write down his predictions for the following week's pop charts as the new positions were announced. But, he said, "I wasn't a great singer, I couldn't play an instrument, and I hadn't yet approached writing songs." Sedaka could do all three, which made him "the guy that had all the cards." Medress approached Sedaka about singing together and, along with their classmate Eddie Rabkin and a girl named Cynthia Zolotin, they formed a vocal group, the Linc-Tones, that soon began performing at bar mitzvahs, weddings, and record hops. A Zolotin family contact then got them into the Brill Building, where they met what Medress called "a shady manager" by the almost impossibly colorful name of Happy Goday, who quickly took them to one Morty Craft, busy setting up his own vocal group label, Melba Records. "We went up there, we auditioned, he set up a meeting, we had a record deal. It really was that easy."

It's a comment often repeated by the youth of Brooklyn. For these Jewish kids—and they *were* just kids—the process of breaking into the music business in the late 1950s was amazingly, almost guiltily uncomplicated. They had come to the right place—Tin Pan Alley, built by Jewish songwriters and entrepreneurs—at the right time, just as rock 'n' roll was declaring itself the first mass teenage movement. Almost every Jewish Brooklyn teenager knew someone who had a family member working the Alley, and an audition carried little risk: unlike aspiring singers and writers from the hinterlands, only a subway ride separated their hopes from their homes.

Success itself did not come quite as easily for the Linc-Tones (renamed the Tokens by Craft) as the initial record deal. Their early 1956 debut single,

"While I Dream" / "I Love My Baby"—ballad and jump side both composed by Sedaka-Greenfield—got the group on a local version of *American Bandstand*, and Sedaka played the chimes on the label's big hit of the time, "Church Bells May Ring," by the Harlem group the Willows, but that was it for the Tokens. They broke up once Sedaka and Medress graduated from Lincoln High.

But the vocal group bug had by now taken hold all across the whiter shades of the borough. Bob Feldman and Jerry Goldstein, two of the Lincoln High teens who hung around the Sweet Shoppe, formed a group called the Choir Boys; they would "go to other neighborhoods and challenge other doo-wop groups," recalled Feldman. At Kings Highway on a Friday night, "everyone would try and outdo each other. There were some wonderful groups that came out of Brooklyn."

Feldman was not referring to Brooklyn's Paragons, Continentals, or Shells, black vocal groups that all recorded for the labels on 125th Street. Admitting that he was "into more white doo-wop"—and by use of that term, the point would be understood—he was thinking instead of groups like the Neons from Borough Park, the Passions from Bensonhurst, and the Bay-Bops from Sheepshead Bay. For as the 1950s moved into their closing years, Jewish, Italian, and other white vocal groups became as prevalent in their own neighborhoods as the black vocal groups had been in theirs, until it was merely a matter of time before one of them charged into the charts in pursuit of the Chords, the Teenagers, the Drifters, and all the others.

When it happened, the breakthrough came from the Italian part of Bronx, where the Belmonts had named themselves for the avenue that ran through the heart of their neighborhood. There was a genuine blue-collar street toughness about them—the lead singer Dion DiMucci was a member of the Fordham Baldies gang—but they had a sweetness to their harmonies far beyond the reach of most white vocal groups. Their first hit single, "I Wonder Why"—released on the independent label Laurie in the spring of 1958—was a classic of its kind: an up-tempo number introduced by a cheerfully nonsense baritone that quickly gave way to clear harmonies spread a cappella across the primary chord, with Dion's pining tenor then singing a frenzied query to romance that typified the teenage experience. If not black enough to be rhythm and blues, it could certainly pass for what was by then considered rock 'n' roll.

Meantime, Atlantic Records had been on its own search for what Ahmet Ertegun called "our answer to Elvis Presley—a white artist who could sing in a black mode." The label pinned its hopes on Robert Walden Cassotto, an Italian boy from the Bronx born with such a rheumatic heart that he had not been expected to make it to adulthood—a diagnosis that, when he inadvertently overheard it, inspired in him an almost pathological quest for stardom in whatever time he had left. Cassotto's initial run of recordings under his stage name Bobby Darin—seven consecutive flops across three record companies—would have destroyed most contenders. But with single number eight, "Don't Call My Name," Darin got onto *American Bandstand*, and in the spring of 1958 he struck gold with his own composition "Splish Splash," a corny—though in that sense, perfectly contemporary—rock 'n' roll song that peaked at number three on the pop charts.

Bobby Darin's interaction with any New York scene was fleeting: almost as fast as his rheumatic heart could carry him, he left rock 'n' roll behind, first for pop ("Dream Lover"), then for cabaret ("Mack the Knife" and the Copacabana), and soon for Hollywood. His original partner and promoter, Donny Kirshner, however, would stay put in New York City, at least for the time being, playing a pivotal role in the lives of the Brooklyn songwriters. The son of a Harlem tailor, and the owner of an ego that could swallow up most of his rivals, Kirshner had entertained a fascination for the world of songwriting ever since he saw the Cole Porter biopic *Night and Day*. And when he met Cassotto in a Washington Heights candy store, Kirshner—despite the fact that he could not read or write music, play an instrument, or carry a tune— quickly introduced himself as a potential lyricist. The pair's first published composition was called, appropriately for Kirshner's future, "Bubblegum Pop." They also wrote "Don't Call My Name," Darin's near-hit, and later a flop single for Connie Francis, famous for her appearances on Arthur Godfrey's *Startime*, and Darin's girlfriend at the time. (Darin's conquest of Francis surely helped convince him of his eventual stardom.) When Darin then acquired Francis's manager, it ended his partnership with Kirshner. Their friendship, however, persisted: Kirshner named his son for the singer, who was also the best man at his wedding.

Donny Kirshner was never a great songwriter. But he learned from his experience with Darin (and Francis) that there was money to be made for someone who could connect the new breed of what could now be called "post–rock 'n' roll" singers with a new generation of aspiring songwriters. He found a willing partner in Al Nevins, the forty-something member of an oldtime "schmaltz" group, the Three Suns, whose 1944 hit "Twilight Time" was on its way to number one in the spring of 1958, as reinterpreted by the Platters. As that song's composer, Nevins knew firsthand the financial value of a hit, and he could similarly see for himself how, in the absence of fresh material, the new acts were relying on old songs. And so he bankrolled a new company, named Aldon Music, a blend of his and Kirshner's first names, and set up shop—not in the Brill Building, where all the old-timers were, but on the sixth floor of 1650 Broadway.

Neil Sedaka, now a full-time Juilliard student (taking advantage of the school's location west of Harlem to attend R&B shows at the Apollo and buy records from Bobby's Record Shop), and Howie Greenfield (stuck working as a messenger in midtown) were still busy shopping songs to any company that would listen. A few sales to Atlantic were all B-sides and flops; Sedaka's own attempts at solo success were dismal. On the way out of a par- ticularly fruitless audition with Hill & Range, whose role as Elvis Presley's publishers had rendered them the new industry powerhouse, they bumped into an ascendant Mort Shuman. The fellow Lincoln alumnus suggested they visit Aldon on their way home.

Sedaka and Greenfield had nothing to lose. They made their way to the Music Building's sixth floor and asked the youthful man who let them into the Aldon office whether they could meet with the publisher. The twenty- three-year-old Kirshner replied that they were looking at him. After getting over the shock, Sedaka sat down at the piano—about the only piece of fur- niture in the room—and began singing the same songs that had just been rejected at Hill & Range. Now it was Kirshner's turn for astonishment: "I'm sitting there with my mouth open, almost thinking someone's putting me on," he recalled. Unable to understand "how anyone with any imagination could turn these songs down"—in his recollection, the songs Sedaka played that day included several future hits—he offered the pair a long-term publishing deal on the spot.

Lesser talents might have accepted the offer. But Sedaka and Greenfield were previously published, well educated, and wisely wary of signing their lives away to an unproven start-up. They insisted on a trial period instead—four months to produce a hit—and Kirshner promptly set out to make his first sale. Playing his ace card, he set up an appointment, at her New Jersey home, with Connie Francis, who had finally hit the top five with "Who's Sorry Now?" about as ancient as any pop standard could be.

The audition was truly frightening for Sedaka, who was the same age as the teenage idol but a world removed from her glamour and fame. Playing Francis his "best ballads" on her piano, as per Kirshner's instructions, he could hardly help noticing that "she was bored to tears." As he and Greenfield felt their opportunity slip away, Sedaka decided to use his own ace card: he introduced "Stupid Cupid," a blunt pseudo-rocker promised to another prospective artist. He got through what he recalled as about eight bars when Francis interrupted: "That's my next record." The teenage singer, it turned out, had no desire to be constricted by the standards of pop ballads: she wanted to rock, as Darin had with "Splish Splash."

The subsequent single, on which Sedaka played piano as if a nervous apprentice to Jerry Lee Lewis, was so tame that it barely qualified as rock 'n' roll—even by the increasingly limp standards of the era. But such definitions depended on the audience, and "Stupid Cupid" aimed its arrow straight at the hearts of white teenagers, for whom the lines "I can't do my homework and I can't think straight" resonated with just as much clarity as the generic blues arrangement. Besides, it was *fun*, a totally harmless, totally teenage, sing-along love song. By the end of the summer, Aldon Music had its first top 20 hit, and when Francis followed it with another Sedaka-Greenfield song, "Fallin'," Sedaka quit studying music at Juilliard to earn his living writing it. Soon after that, Greenfield came out of the closet. Among its other virtues (and for all its many vices), the entertainment business did not judge one's sexual preferences—at least not to the extent of the straitlaced culture back in Brighton Beach.

A pivotal—though at the time underreported—turning point in the shift from black vocal groups to white pop singers took place later that summer. It revolved around two distinctly different sets of Brooklyn youth. Jerome "Anthony" Gourdine, an eighteen-year-old from the Fort Greene projects, close to Manhattan, was already a veteran of two groups (the Duponts and the Chesters), four independent labels (Winley, Royal Roost, Roulette, and Apollo), and no hit singles by the time he brought the Chesters to the attention of Richard Barrett—and, by extension, George Goldner, who had set up his new labels' offices at 1650 Broadway. End Records already had success with the Chantels, and Goldner and Barrett now applied their make-over talents to the Chesters, renaming them the Imperials and, in the studio, rejecting both their intended single and its singer at the last moment, putting Gourdine into lead position for the ballad "Tears on My Pillow." If all of this sounded suspiciously similar to the story of Frankie Lymon and the Teenagers, well, that was surely part of Goldner and Barrett's plan: to prove that they could do it again. Thanks to Gourdine's exquisite delivery—and Alan Freed renaming him on the radio as "Little Anthony"—"Tears on My Pillow" went top five in the pop charts, proving, so it seemed, that the black New York vocal group genre was still alive and well.

But "Tears on My Pillow" was not a group composition, as had been common until then with the Harlem and Bronx vocal groups. Rather, as if demonstrating his enthusiasm for his new location and a new way of doing business, Goldner had picked up the song through the interconnected offices of 1650 Broadway. He now commissioned another of his fellow Music Building tenants, Aldon Music, to supply the follow-up, and Kirshner came back with a tailor-made song for the Imperials, "The Diary," written by Sedaka and Greenfield.

Supplying a song on demand for a black vocal group represented a significant step for the Brighton Beach duo, neither of whom had acquired any of Mort Shuman's hipster status. Yet it didn't faze them. "There was a certain similarity between the Jewish culture and the Negro culture, the suffering, the music in minor keys," said Sedaka. "Some of the chords and harmonic rhythms were similar." Besides, Gourdine sang in a quivering high tenor that, if it didn't necessarily pass as female, as Lymon's did, certainly had some of Sedaka's "feminine tendencies." As with "Tears on My Pillow," Gourdine imbued his performance of "The Diary" with clear enunciation modeled on Nat King Cole's voice, engaging in several melismas à la Clyde McPhatter and fading out with a birdsong falsetto. There was no reason it should not have been another hit.

Except that, while Goldner was out of town, Barrett switched out "The Diary" for one of his own compositions. Nevins and Kirshner were infuriated, twice over, for the only thing they hated more than the waste of a good song was someone going back on his word. And so, having become increasingly impressed with Sedaka's musical skills, his voice, and his evident hunger for fame, and determined to prove a point, they sold him to RCA as a solo artist. Sedaka's rendition of "The Diary"—sung with equally overstated pronunciation, vibratos, and complete with key modulation for dramatic effect—became a top 20 hit at the start of 1959. The Imperials' Barrett-composed single having been a flop by comparison, End Records rushed out its own version of "The Diary," but it was too late. No longer could white artists be accused of "covering" and diluting black R&B singles, not if, like Sedaka, they had written them to begin with.

When ASCAP helped instigate the Congressional payola hearings in 1959, it claimed that BMI, in tandem with the disc jockeys and broadcasters, had acted "to suppress genuine talent and to foist mediocre music upon the public." The notion that kids bought "mediocre music" only because it was shoved down their throats became a self-fulfilling prophecy (depending on one's taste) when the scandal took Freed and his peers off the air: the radio stations, cowed into submission, took to playing a bland form of pop music, almost all of it sung by pretty young white boys and girls, and the kids, hearing no alternative, duly lapped it up.

Kirshner and Nevins benefited enormously from this gradual homogenization of the business. Kirshner's tastes were shamelessly conventional: his idea of the perfect song was "Little Darlin'"—not as originally sung by the Gladiolas, black teenagers from Nashville, but as delivered by Canada's white "cover" group the Diamonds. He had no desire to usurp the status quo, musically or lyrically, no wish to be controversial or stoke any fires of discontent. All he wanted was for his writers to keep (re)constructing the perfect love song.

Just as important, he played by the rules. The Aldon writers were never asked to share their credits with DJs, record company bosses, or Mafia-related figures. And none of them were bought off with Cadillacs. Instead, Nevins and Kirshner gave these writers their own cubicles (windowless cubicles, admittedly, but who needed a view when one had a piano on which to gaze?), encouraging them to mix and match their talents to find a winning formula.

And because royalties could take a couple of years to work their way through the system, the company's contracted writers were given weekly salaries as "advances."

For the black groups of Harlem and the Bronx, those who had come knocking at record company doors throughout the 1950s, their songs near enough completely written, who had recorded hits that sometimes sold in the millions, and who had often failed to see even a penny by way of royalties, this sudden legitimization of the business must have seemed so cruel as to appear racist. For here was Aldon playing fair with publishing in a way that Levy, Goldner, Weiss, and their likes had almost never done—and yet Aldon signed almost exclusively white, Jewish writers, whose songs were then recorded almost exclusively by white artists, for sale to the lucrative white teenage market.

It's a difficult complaint to refute. It may provide only scant comfort that the two- to three-year period that followed the payola scandal is considered by many as rock 'n' roll's lost years, the period during which it effectively ceased to exist as a creative form. New Yorkers could take a certain refuge in the fact that the era's most prominent new stars emerged from Dick Clark's Philadelphia, which enjoyed a season in the sun as home of everything good and wholesome (and, years later, repudiated) about American popular music. But that does not explain how so many dubious hits of this era came to be written by Doc Pomus and Mort Shuman, a pair whose integrity had not previously been found lacking. Throughout 1959, the former black music denizens turned out one formulaic song after another for white-bread teen idols like Bobby Rydell, Frankie Avalon, and James Darren, reaching an almost existential peak when they gave the fifteen-year-old manufactured star Fabian his first top 40 hit with a song called, of all things, "I'm a Man."

Along the way, they were also hired to write a song for Laurie Records' Mystics, five Italian teens from Bensonhurst. Perhaps because Shuman recognized them from his Brooklyn streets, he and Pomus pulled out a bona fide classic from their slew of otherwise anodyne hits. Unfortunately for the Mystics, "A Teenager in Love"—a further dissertation on the watershed Lymon hit of two years earlier, but with a distinctly contemporary arrangement and haunting melody—was *so* good that Laurie's boss, Gene Schwartz, gave it to his previously proven hit makers, Dion and the Belmonts, instead.

Dion was fortunate to be alive to sing it. As part of the Big Winter

Dance Party Tour, he originally signed on to the chartered plane that took Buddy Holly, Ritchie Valens, and the Big Bopper to their deaths in an Iowa cornfield—rather than to the next night's concert—on February 3, 1959. "But," he later wrote, "I couldn't bring myself to spend the thirty-six dollars for a short flight . . . . This was my parents' whole month's rent back in the Bronx. I heard them fight over that amount, more often than not, as to where the money was coming from." His frugality saved his life. And when "A Teenager in Love" charted top five in the spring of 1959, Dion became a true star, a proud New York retort to the saccharine Philadelphians. Meanwhile, Shuman and Pomus brought the Mystics a freshly written song, "Hushabye," as compensation. Formulaic to the point of vapidity, it nonetheless charted top 20. Shuman made the hit-writing process look easy.

The second hit, as Laurie Records knew all too well in allocating "A Teenager in Love" to Dion and the Belmonts, was the one that counted; at that point, you could start talking "career." And Neil Sedaka was lacking for one: several follow-ups to "The Diary" had hit a brick wall. Deciding that plagiarism was the most sincere form of inspiration, he set about writing a song utilizing every theme currently filling the charts. One of those was to name a song for its subject: Sedaka chose the foolproof name of "Carol," by which title Chuck Berry had had a hit just a year earlier, and added a grammatically catchy "Oh!" to the front of it. In the studio, Sedaka then laid it on thick, with a falsetto vocal introduction, multiple harmonies, double-tracked vocals, flamenco guitars that sounded like plucked violins, and Greenfield's almost entirely monosyllabic lyrics that concluded, "if you leave me, I will surely die"—the lone verse then repeated as spoken word, for added effect. The end result bore more than a passing resemblance to "Little Darlin'," but the apparent simplicity of it all masked the genius of its mathematical approach and propelled the single into the top ten in late 1959. Sedaka was up and running again—and would never look back.

Barely a couple of miles across Brooklyn from Sedaka's Brighton Beach neighborhood, on East 24th Street in Sheepshead Bay, seventeen-year-old Carol Klein heard "Oh! Carol" and suspected that the title might have been influenced by more than just a Chuck Berry song. Klein, a gifted pianist, singer, and writer herself, had admired Sedaka and the Linc-Tones to the point of forming her own group, the Co-Sines, at James Madison High. She even went out with Sedaka: he claimed it was "for about a year," while she insisted they had just the "one date." This considerable disparity in memory suggested perhaps some wishful thinking on Sedaka's part, but by the time "Oh! Carol" hit the charts, the issue was moot. In August 1959, Klein married her boyfriend—and songwriting partner—Gerry Goffin. She was by then three months pregnant.

The couple had met at Queens College, where Goffin was already a senior, majoring in chemistry, when Klein enrolled as a freshman. Though Goffin could not play an instrument, the Queens native's childhood exposure to *Make Believe Ballroom* and Rodgers and Hammerstein had inspired dreams of becoming a Broadway lyricist. On meeting Klein, whose abilities were so evident that she had been accepted to Music and Art High (though she left after a single semester), Goffin invited her to help write a musical he had in mind. It was indicative of the times they lived in that, within weeks, he was writing lyrics for her rock 'n' roll songs instead.

Klein, as Carole King, was already known as an inexpensive hire for "demo" recordings, in which capacity she frequently worked with another Queens College student, Paul Simon, who had himself briefly tasted teenage chart success with his friend Art Garfunkel under the name Tom & Jerry. Atlantic Records, ever in the vanguard, was quick to take a chance on the new couple's co-written compositions. But the songs weren't hits, and King's solo career on ABC-Paramount—one of the Hollywood record labels that sprang up to cater to the teenage pop market—did not extend beyond two flop singles. Goffin took a job at a local chemical plant to pay the rent on a Sheepshead Bay apartment as the couple prepared, somewhat fearfully, for their baby.

"Oh! Carol" arrived, and none too soon, like a gift from the gods, and the newlyweds wasted no time issuing an answer record, "Oh! Neil." Goffin, known for his brooding personality and uneven temper as well as a wicked sense of humor, teased his wife's former suitor with a deliberately hokey Nashville rearrangement, and the introduction of a "grand pappy" who "don't like your records." The whole thing sounded less like teenagers in love than teenagers poking fun at each other's expense—and that was itself something new in the pop music field.

Given that the melody went unaltered, it needed Aldon's approval as a "rewrite" before it could be commercially released. Kirshner, understandably intrigued, invited Carole and Gerry to the Music Building to submit more songs; they left with the firm offer of a publishing contract and Kirshner's typically effusive—and equally sincere—promises of unfathomable riches. His endorsement proved important in other ways, too, for female writers were rare around the Brill and Music Buildings, romantic couples even more so. As for teenage mothers masquerading as professional women in a man's world—well, let's just say that the seventeen-year-old King was staring up at a glass ceiling.

With his former flame Carole King now part of the Aldon stable, Neil Sedaka helped promote "Oh! Neil," released on Epic, but it was too much of an inside joke to cross over. Sedaka was always better at promoting himself: under his own name as a solo artist, "Oh! Carol" was followed by a rapid run of four massive hits that ended with the criminally catchy "Calendar Girl." Each was recognizable for its almost minimal lyrical simplicity and its upbeat melodies, which were accentuated by Sedaka's now pervasive use of chimes— a sound that, as Ken Emerson wrote, "conjure[s] up images of prancing majorettes."

"People wanted happy songs," said Sedaka in his defense. "People wanted uplifting feeling, and our songs were very happy, they were positive—they were naive, but they were melodic; they had hooks." They were, it's true, emblematic of their time, and through 1960 Sedaka was so busy taking them up the charts himself that Greenfield began writing with another Aldon staffer, the affable Jack Keller. In the spring, this partnership delivered for Connie Francis "Everybody's Somebody's Fool," written in a country style, as was that year's craze, and it became Aldon Music's first number one hit. That summer, their follow-up for Francis, "My Heart Has a Mind of Its Own," which sounded more like a Hank Williams imitation than anything to do with R&B, also went to the top of the charts. The sixth floor of 1650 Broadway suddenly became the "go-to" place for hit songs, and if Sedaka, Greenfield, and Keller were the industry's new wunderkinder, Kirshner was something bigger, a wunderkind executive.

"Donny Kirshner was, sort of without knowing it, a disciple of George Goldner," said Jerry Leiber. "They were the only two guys in the business that really knew early on, like a psychic, what was going to be a hit. They both had the heart and soul of the twelve-year-old girl."

. . .

Of all the working-class Jewish songwriters and producers who took over the hit factories of midtown Manhattan, Jerry Leiber had perhaps the least illustrious introduction to the music world: he had worked for his mother's store, "delivering kerosene and charcoal to black families in the slums of south Baltimore," where electricity was beyond most people's means. "I really became a welcome character in the neighborhood," he said. "I was bringing them essential stuff, and I was well liked and treated very well. I was brought up with black culture from daybreak in the morning to sundown in the evening, and a tremendous amount of the culture was absorbed by me: the language, the rhythm, the feeling, the attitude, down to my cooking." Leiber, whose mischievous glint was highlighted by mismatched eyes—one brown, one blue—left the Baltimore streets behind when his family moved to California in 1945.

There he met his future partner Mike Stoller, the more calm and reserved of the pair, who had enjoyed, by comparison, a quintessentially liberal New York childhood. Raised in Sunnyside, Queens, he was packed off to an interracial summer camp in 1940, where he "fell in love" with the sounds of boogie-woogie piano introduced to him by some of the black teenagers at the camp. Back home, the seven-year-old took up that style of performing instantly, becoming good enough, quickly enough, that a neighborhood friend, who moved in appropriately leftist circles, secured piano lessons for him from James P. Johnson, the great stride pianist. Stoller learned from Johnson "the structure of the blues" and was smitten by it.

Stoller and his best friend, Al Levitt, became voracious devotees of live music, attending the 1947 Carnegie Hall concert that brought Dizzy Gillespie, Charlie Parker, Ella Fitzgerald, and Chano Pozo together; frequenting the bebop clubs of 52nd Street and neighboring Broadway back when nobody "carded" a fourteen-year-old; and spending their Easter 1949 vacation, six nights in a row, at the Clique, watching Machito's Afro-Cubans alternate with George Shearing's quartet, thrilling to what Stoller called a "very beautiful and very exciting" and brand-new "Asia Minor." And then, later in 1949, he too was whisked off to California, the promised land—where, without missing a New York beat, he promptly became the only white member of a Latin dance band.

James P. Johnson, composer of "The Harlem Strut" and master of the stride piano, with the band he led at Harlem's Apollo Theater and Small's Paradise in 1934–35.

Ella Fitzgerald joined the Chick Webb Orchestra in 1935 and assumed its leadership upon the drummer's death in 1939. The pair are seen here at the Paramount Theater in midtown in 1938.

The earliest known photograph of Machito and His Afro-Cubans, taken between 1940 and 1942. Mario Bauzá is second from right, back row. A teenage Tito Puente is in center, at back, on drums.

Charlie Parker and Dizzy Gillespie, the pioneers of bebop, "used to play lines together just like each other," said Miles Davis. John Coltrane is on the right.

Top left: The Ravens were the first major vocal group to emerge from Harlem after World War II. Seen here in 1947, *clockwise from top left*: Jimmy Ricks, Warren Suttles, Leonard Puzey, Maithe Marshall. *Top right*: The Chords put the Bronx vocal scene on the map with "Sh-Boom," a major hit for Atlantic Records that was initially a b-side. *Bottom*: The Harptones, seen here in 1953, appeared on multiple Alan Freed revues. *From left*: Billy Brown, William "Dicey" Galloway, Claudie "Nicky" Clark, William "Dempsey" James, Willie Winfield. Pianist and arranger Raoul Cita is at bottom right.

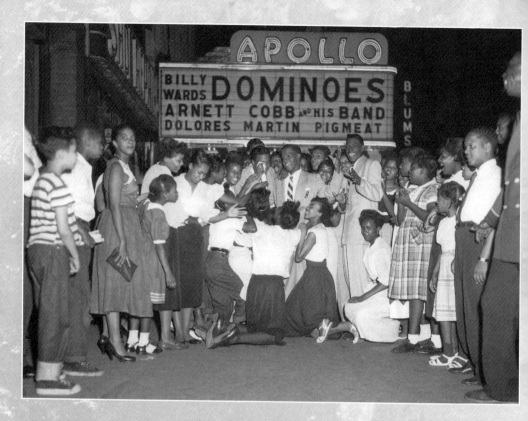

Top: Billy Ward and the Dominoes, shown outside the Apollo Theater on 125th Street on August 19, 1952, hamming up their fans' hysteria for the camera. *Bottom*: Harlem multiracial vocal group Frankie Lymon and the Teenagers became a phenomenon upon the release of "Why Do Fools Fall In Love" in late 1955. Shortly after this show at the Paramount in February 1957, as part of an Alan Freed revue, Lymon went solo.

Left: Founded in 1947, Atlantic Records soon became the biggest and most influential of the New York independent labels. Partners Jerry Wexler, left, and Ahmet Ertegun are shown directing a session for Clyde McPhatter in February 1958.

Bottom: The married songwriting couples, *from left*, Cynthia Weil and Barry Mann, and Gerry Goffin and Carole King (seated at the piano) were best friends—and competitors.

Top left: Josh White, seen playing the Village Vanguard in 1946, was a master of the six-string guitar. *Top right*: Huddie "Leadbelly" Ledbetter was the King of the 12-String. Shortly after he died in 1950, Leadbelly's "Goodnight Irene" became a number one hit for the Weavers, shown below. *Bottom, from left*: Pete Seeger, Lee Hays, Fred Hellerman, Ronnie Gilbert.

The big three mambo orchestras—those of Machito, Tito Puente, and Tito Rodriguez—occasionally shared the stage together at the Palladium, as seen here in the early 1950s. Puente is in the middle of the back row, facing sideways; Machito is leading the session with his back to the camera; Rodriguez is at the microphone alongside Graciella, Machito's sister and vocalist.

Tito Puente, the Mambo King, in full flight on the timbals circa 1954. Trumpeter Jimmy Fresora and *conguero* "Mongo" Santamaría are on the left, vocalist Gilberto Monroig to the right.

Sunday afternoons in Washington Square Park. *Top*: Mike and John Cohen, early 1950s. *Right*: A fourteen-year-old Eric Weissberg, his parents behind him, with Roger Sprung, circa 1954. *Bottom*: The Folksay Trio of Bob Carey, Roger Sprung, and Erik Darling, who first popularized "Tom Dooley," circa 1953.

Leiber and Stoller quickly became two of the only white faces in the clubs and bars of LA's main black thoroughfare, Central Avenue. Their love of rhythm and blues—which in Los Angeles was more "influenced by the southern Delta blues," said Stoller, and therefore dirtier and more guitar-based than the jazz-inflected R&B back east—led them to write songs for Jimmy Witherspoon, Johnny Otis, and, most notably, Big Mama Thornton, for whom they penned and produced a suitably dirty number called "Hound Dog"—before Howie Greenfield ever summed up the courage to knock on Neil Sedaka's door.

Four years later, in the summer of 1956, Elvis Presley took "Hound Dog" to the top of the charts. Leiber and Stoller had no idea it was coming. In fact, Stoller, who was on his honeymoon at the time, a journey rendered extra memorable by the fact that his ship home from Europe, the *Andrea Doria*, sank in fog off New England at the cost of forty-six lives, was so immersed in black music that he had never even heard of Elvis. But the timing was fortunate: the pair had already decided to see out the year in New York, and "Hound Dog" now gave them their pick of professional options. Naturally, Atlantic Records hustled to the front of the line, hiring the pair to write and produce for both the Drifters and the Coasters. Presley's publishers, Hill & Range, invited Leiber and Stoller to write songs for the star's next movie; the following spring, they turned out "Jailhouse Rock," "Treat Me Nice," and two others in one afternoon. RCA offered them a nonexclusive production deal, too. At the end of 1957, the pair of twenty-four-year-olds moved full-time to New York, where Hill & Range supplied them with offices on the ninth floor of the Brill Building, from which they could have looked down on the rest of the music business, if they hadn't been so busy leading it.

By mid-1959, the new, "Crowns" lineup of the Drifters had been touring for several months with unpredictable results. "Promoters would put up the pictures of the original Drifters," said Ben E. King. "Then when the curtain came up here would be these five young guys. We got booed off stage almost everywhere we went!" But the Crowns were serious about adopting their new persona, and King started tinkering with song ideas. He found himself mouthing the words "There Goes My Baby" to another popular tune of the day. When he sang it for Leiber and Stoller, who were just coming to terms with the group's brand-new lineup, they heard something else—a string arrangement that, if not entirely unheard of among vocal groups, was still enough of a rarity to raise eyebrows at Atlantic Records, which had to hire an orchestra *and* a bigger studio to accommodate it.

In addition to the strings, Leiber and Stoller restructured the song with a Brazilian influence, a gentle *baion* rhythm. As for the vocals, twenty-year-old Ben E. King belted the words out with impressive force, though with an equally notable lack of subtlety. The result was an anomaly: the rhythm swung in the summer breeze like an R&B *cha-cha-cha*; the vocals were drenched in enough echo to satisfy a dozen Brooklyn doo-wop groups; the strings swooped and soared as if orchestrating a Broadway weepy; and tympani, used for no other reason than that they had been left behind from a previous session, rumbled hesitantly around the edges. None of these parts seemed to be in tune with any of the others; it was questionable at times whether they were even playing the same song. "But the total effect," Leiber came to realize, after initial doubts, had "something magnetic about it." Indeed, it was one of those songs that come along every few years and rewrite the rules by disregarding them: by introducing the string section and the *baion* tempo, "There Goes My Baby" helped resurrect rhythm and blues, in a new, more sophisticated, Latin-styled fashion. In the summer of 1959, it rose to number two on the pop charts, the first big crossover hit any Drifters lineup had experienced.

In the wake of its success, every Brill and Music Building staffer from Brooklyn to the Bronx angled to compose for the Drifters. The immediate spoils fell to Pomus and Shuman, whose subsequent run of consecutive hits— "Dance with Me," "This Magic Moment," "I Count the Tears" and "Save the Last Dance for Me," all featuring the suddenly mandatory string section— compensated somewhat for their sojourn in the depths of Philadelphia. The last of these songs proved especially majestic: its lyrics, written by Pomus around the time of his wedding two years earlier, represented in part the pain of their author, a man who could not dance unaided. As interpreted by the public, however, they told of a man secure enough in his relationship to allow his woman to dance with others. The two meanings were not mutually exclusive, and the sincerity of the song, along with King's dexterous delivery and Leiber and Stoller's meticulous production, took it to number one in the late summer of 1960. For anyone keeping count on the graduates of Lincoln High, that made three chart toppers in almost as many months.

. . .

King and Goffin aspired to write for the Drifters, too, and they came close when their "Show Me the Way" was assigned as the debut single for Ben E. King, who broke from the group over lack of fair pay. "It was like indentured servitude," said Jerry Leiber of the Drifters' business setup. "They got a weekly salary and they never got, as far as I know, royalties. And every year, they would change personnel. The management was reprehensible." Neither Atlantic Records nor Leiber and Stoller had a say about this management arrangement, and all chose to keep recording the act rather than risk losing it to another label. But the arrangement, a little bit doo-wop, a little bit Broadway, and overly sentimental, was simply too ambitious to connect with the public. Goffin kept his day job at the chemical plant, writing lyrics by night; King tried to write music by day, whenever their infant daughter, Louise, born in the spring of 1960, took long enough naps to allow it.

Then came the evening that Goffin returned from a round of bowling to find his wife out at her local mah-jongg evening: such was the social life for a young married couple in Sheepshead Bay. A note from Carole placed atop the Norelco tape recorder they used for their compositions alerted Gerry that Kirshner needed a song immediately, for which King had already worked out a melody. Goffin might typically have waited until the next day to start on the lyrics. But the assignment was for the Shirelles, and that was too important an opportunity not to seize immediately.

Even before Goffin and King got involved, the story of the Shirelles, the leading girl group of the era, had become one of the great Brill era legends. It dated back to 1957, when one of the girls' fellow students at Passaic High School in New Jersey raved to her mother, Florence Greenberg, about their performance at the school talent show. Greenberg seemed an unlikely fairy godmother: an accountant's housewife, a former Republican campaign worker, she was already well into her forties. But with her children growing up, she had begun to relieve her suburban boredom by hanging out at the Turf restaurant, on 51st and Broadway, hooked by the atmosphere surrounding the Brill Building, seeking a way into the music business. As impressed by the high school singers as her daughter was, Greenberg quickly signed them to her record label, named Tiara in recognition of her fantasies, renamed them the Shirelles (combining lead singer Shirley Owens's name with that of the Chantels), recorded and released Owens's talent show song, "I Met Him on a Sunday," scored some local airplay, licensed it to Decca, watched it become a minor hit . . . and then saw follow-ups flop and the group get dropped.

But Greenberg, who doubled as the Shirelles' manager, wasn't the type to quit. She set up a new label, naming it Scepter with continued mock majesty, and took an office at 1674 Broadway, the least illustrious (and least expensive) of the Tin Pan Alley buildings, determined to do her girls right. Florence Greenberg was, by her own admission, "a white woman who was in a black business," which might explain why the Shirelles' career fully turned around only when she invited Luther Dixon, a former vocal group singer and ongoing hit writer, into the company: his arrangement (and cowrite) of Owens's "Tonight's the Night," complete with string accompaniments à la the Drifters, edged into the top 40 in October 1960. Scepter celebrated its success by moving a block down Broadway into the Music Building. From there it was but a short walk along the hallways to Aldon Music, in search of a surefire follow-up—which was where Goffin and King came in.

Back in Sheepshead Bay, Goffin listened to his wife's piano melodies on tape and knew that she had hit on "something new, something different." As lyricists were wont to do, he took the theme of the act's current hit "Tonight's the Night," in which Owens expressed her fears about (and never quite committed to) putting out for her boyfriend, and brought it over the lines of pre-marriage abstinence. Now he had Owens deciding to give herself "completely" for one night's intimate passion, but returning repeatedly to ask her boy, "Will you still love me tomorrow?" It was later celebrated as being a remarkably mature, groundbreaking lyric, but Goffin didn't have to intellectualize the process: he and Carole were already living its consequences. When his wife came home from her mah-jongg, they stayed up into the early hours completing the song, adding a memorable bridge in the process. The finished composition was everything the pair had overreached for on Ben E. King's solo single—a perfect marriage of traditional pop sentiment and contemporary teenage mores, of schmaltzy Broadway melodies and urgent urban angst.

In the studio, it exceeded even these attributes. Though Owens's initial reaction was, "It's not a Shirelles song," she imbued it with a captivating balance of doubt and devotion. And the production—arrangement credited to Carole King, artful string section "conducted by Luther Dixon"—proved

every inch the match of the Drifters' masters Leiber and Stoller. It was recognized as a first "teenage symphony" by radio stations and record buyers
alike and ,renamed "Will You Love Me Tomorrow," it became the first number one by a black girl group, in late January 1961. In a story that has been
told often but is no less enjoyable for it, Kirshner took Carole King in his
limousine to Goffin's chemical factory and presented the lyricist with a
$10,000 check. And, said Goffin, with truly false modesty, "I've never had to
do an honest day's work since."

Barry Imberman's journey from Brooklyn to Broadway was less poetic
than that of Sedaka, Greenfield, Shuman, Goffin, and King, a fair
reflection of a workmanlike commitment to his craft that would make him
the most successful of them all. Turning from classical to popular music
in childhood and on to rhythm and blues and rock 'n' roll in his teens, he
first figured he had something going for him when he performed his compositions during a working holiday in the Catskills and a publisher promptly
handed him a business card. Less than a year into advanced education at
Pratt Institute for the Arts, in Fort Greene, he took some money he had
saved for tuition, financed his own demo recording, and started knocking on
doors at the Brill and Music Buildings. Imberman was personable and perceptive, good-looking and hardworking, and, by his own admission, driven
to succeed. Soon he was singing other people's songs as the prospective teen
idol Buddy Brooks, writing his own songs for a company called Round Music,
and then recording the standard "All the Things You Are" for Epic—none of
which ventures took off. It was only when he supplied the music to accompany a deliberately dumb lyric for the Diamonds, "She Say (Oom Dooby
Doom)," that he enjoyed his first top 40 hit—in February 1959, the week of
his twentieth birthday. Soon after, he bumped into an acquaintance from the
Catskills, the songwriter Jack Keller, who told him he was pulling $10,000
a year in advances from Aldon Music. Imberman took a walk over to 1650
Broadway, where, as a hit writer for the Diamonds, Kirshner's favorite act, his
audition was a mere formality.

For the next year, as Barry Mann, the talented tunesmith, wrote with
every lyricist in the growing Aldon stable. The anglicization of his name was
no more a big deal for Imberman than it had been for his fellow Jew Carole

Klein to become Carole King, the Italian Robert Cassotto to become Bobby Darin, or Aldon's Greek signing Anthony Cassavitis to become Tony Orlando. Though the homogeneity of the Eisenhower era may have partially inspired these adaptations, it was less about denying one's roots than about looking for a simple, catchy name by which to be remembered in a pop business that did not aspire to great complexity. It was also part of a time-honored musical tradition of reinventing oneself: in his new guise, Barry Mann had carved out a professional career that afforded him almost total independence, while not necessarily jarring with his parents' high expectations. He had every right to feel proud of himself.

In early 1960, Mann scored his first top ten hit with "Footsteps" for Steve Lawrence, another Brooklyn Jew who was already well known from his appearances on *The Steve Allen Show*. As a result of this success, he was commissioned, with Greenfield as his lyricist, to write for Teddy Randazzo, who was still searching for his first hit despite his appearance in *Rock, Rock, Rock* back in 1956. When Mann walked into the manager's office to play the prospective single, he saw, standing behind Randazzo, a "beautiful blonde." He assumed her to be Randazzo's girlfriend.

Cynthia Weil, the blonde in question, whose association with Randazzo extended no further than cowriting the other side of the singer's new single, took one look at Barry Mann and figured: this might be my partner. The product of a wealthy Jewish family, raised on Manhattan's Upper West Side, she had attended the private Walden School and the esteemed women's college Sarah Lawrence. It was not a childhood without problems—her father died when she was seven, and she felt emotionally distanced from her mother. She found refuge in a love of Broadway musicals and was particularly influenced by an aunt, Toni Mendez—a former Rockette who became a successful literary agent and, thought Weil, "understood the creative soul." As a result, she found herself singing in Manhattan nightclubs during college downtime, adding her own lyrics to Cole Porter songs. From there, she got a foot in the door as a lyricist at Hill & Range, where it was a relatively simple step to writing with Teddy Randazzo. It was not the Broadway of her dreams, but it was a start. After all, she was still only nineteen.

In hot pursuit of Mann, Weil made an appointment at Aldon, where Kirshner, impressed by her writing, put her on trial as a lyricist with King. (Goffin and King were still a few months away from writing "Tomorrow.")

The two women worked through their initial discomfort with each other's backgrounds to become close friends, but when Mann and Weil met each other (again) in the Aldon lobby, the inevitable course of events followed.

From the beginning, the Mann-Weil relationship was about more than just romance. "I remember asking to see her lyrics," said Mann, "and when I saw them, I felt they were very interesting because there was a sophistication about them, but at the same time they were soulful. I thought that was very fresh for the music business." Indeed, like her fellow Broadway fan Goffin, Weil would bring a remarkably mature lyrical quality to the midtown songwriting game. In turn, Mann played her the Drifters and the Everly Brothers, and "she picked up the pop genre very quickly." The two started writing together, and soon Mann vacated his family home, on Homecrest Avenue in Brooklyn, for Weil's apartment on 52nd Street. "I was no fool," he recalled.

The couple became Aldon Music's second married songwriting team— few other publishers could boast even one—when they tied the knot on October 29, 1961, amid a phenomenal run of chart action for Mann. In the summer, he had made the top ten under his own (adopted) name, singing a deliciously goofy number he had written with Goffin, "Who Put the Bomp (in the Bomp Bomp Bomp)?," which not only celebrated the preceding several years of nonsense song syllables but served as a farewell to such tactics, too. For Mann (who would never have another solo hit) and Weil embarked on their own songwriting partnership at this time, and it opened up for them a very different musical direction. Their first hit together, "Bless You," as sung by Kirshner's handpicked seventeen-year-old protégé Tony Orlando, evinced an epic structure, including a sense of self-confidence that allowed it to dispense with the first verse and get stuck into its chorus, all within twenty seconds; it went top 20.

But the song that was making the most noise at the time of Mann's nuptials with Weil was his co-write with Aldon's Larry Kolber, "I Love How You Love Me," a deft little monosyllabic ballad that reached the top five as sung by a trio of Californian siblings, the Paris Sisters. The girls themselves, though easy on the eyes, had one foot firmly in the pre–rock 'n' roll era of the Brooklyn writer's *Make Believe Ballroom* upbringing, and they were not set to make great cultural impact. But the song's producer was a different story. His name was Phil Spector.

8
THE BALLAD OF WASHINGTON SQUARE PARK

n the immediate aftermath of World War II, Greenwich Village renewed its reputation as a hotbed of optimistic idealism. "The Village was as close in 1946 as it would ever come to Paris in the twenties," wrote the literary icon Anatole Broyard. "Rents were cheap, restaurants were cheap, and it seemed to me that happiness itself might be cheaply had. The streets and bars were full of writers and painters and the kind of young men and women who liked to be around them."

George Sprung discovered the pleasures of the Village for himself when, as a young man fresh out of the Army, he headed downtown from the Upper West Side one spring Sunday in 1946. Wandering through Washington Square Park, he encountered George Margolin, a printer by trade, leading a small but enthusiastic crowd through chorus renditions of leftist songs like "It Takes a Worried Man" on his guitar. Sprung also met a young banjo player and sandal maker by the name of Allan Block, singing English ballads and other less overtly political folk songs. There was something joyous about the simplicity of it all, and Sprung made a point of returning the next week. He was not a musician, but that didn't seem to matter. He could hold a tune, which was the most important thing, and he had some organizational skills, and that was useful too. He began collecting songbooks; down at the Park on a Sunday afternoon, he'd pass them out to anyone who wanted to sing along. In the process, he got to know the other young musicians; alongside Block, their number included the five-string fretless banjo player Woody Wachtel and the guitarist and banjo player Tom Paley.

Just a few doors down from the park, the prewar generation of folksing-ers began to converge at the basement apartment Pete Seeger shared with his wife, Toshi (whom he had met during Almanac days, attending Margaret Mayo's American Square Troupe, a mainstay of folk activity in Manhattan), on MacDougal Street, by the Provincetown Playhouse. There they strove to regain the momentum they'd enjoyed before the war, while also seeking to maintain friendships made with other musicians in the armed services, now scattered across the country. To this end, in January 1946, they incorporated People's Songs—"to distinguish it from the scholarly folklore societies," according to Seeger, who welcomed Lee Hays back into the fold, alongside a long list of familiar names as sponsors, directors, and/or advisers.

Oscar Brand, a Canadian-born singer, writer, and broadcaster living in the city, began hosting the enduring *Folksong Festival* on WNYC radio around the same time, providing the musicians with a broadcast outlet. "The pervad-ing atmosphere in those early postwar days was a 'progressive' one which resembled the 1932–35 period," he later wrote, in *The Ballad-Mongers*. "The worst was over, the future was filled with infinite possibilities, and the com-mon man was to be once again enthroned. The unions, Communists, Socialists, and progressives began to hire folk singers again for every party, dance, and meeting." After Seeger, Hays, and Guthrie were flown to Pittsburgh to perform for ten thousand striking Westinghouse workers, Seeger began talking of a future in which, just as every church had its choir, every union would have its folksingers, and soon People's Songs begat People's Artists, its own booking agency.

In the meantime, Seeger determined to share the music with a younger generation, too. He frequently took his guitar to the Little Red School House, on Bleecker Street, named for the color of its original building but an apt description of its progressive politics, to lead a classroom sing-along. He held what he called "wing dings"—Saturday morning hootenannies for the under-tens—at his basement apartment on MacDougal Street. Eric Weissberg, an elementary student at Little Red at the time, was among those who attended, at a cost of fifty cents for two hours, as he recalled. His mother would drop him off with his guitar and go shopping on Eighth Street, while he and his friends sang along at the feet of Seeger and his weekly guests: Woody Guthrie, Leadbelly, Cisco Houston, Brownie McGhee, Sonny Terry, and the like, the cream of the New York folk scene. "Think of it, man!" recalled Weissberg years later. "We were listening to these people when we were little kids, barely playing."

In the spring of 1947, George Sprung persuaded his teenage brother to join him in Washington Square Park. Roger Sprung, a pianist, found himself equally inspired by what he encountered there—not just the singing, but the general air of bohemian freedom—and set about learning the guitar and then the banjo, taking lessons, in the spirit of park camaraderie, from Tom Paley. In October of that year, they were joined by a sixteen-year-old, Billy Faier, who had recently relocated to Manhattan from Woodstock with his mother. Faier found himself in the park only because he decided to ride the Fifth Avenue bus, on a Sunday whim, from his home near Harlem to the end of the line, Washington Square. "When I got off, there they were, playing and singing," he recalled.

Faier viewed the elder musician George Margolin as being motivated primarily by communism—"He never sang anything but a left-wing song"—and preferred the company of his fellow teens. "It was a very intensely social event," he said. "I was new to New York at the time, and here I was making friends." Familiar with many of the songs from living in Woodstock, he was inspired to learn the banjo by the example of Block and Wachtel. He was a quick study: Roger Sprung recalled Faier's turning him on to the music of Earl Scruggs, after which Sprung became what he assumed to be the youngest proponent of bluegrass in New York City. Since it was an instrumentation rather than a genre, Sprung found he could play any song in the bluegrass style, including the classical music he'd learned on the piano, and quickly became a focal attraction in Washington Square Park on Sundays. For all these young men, the fact that girls were attracted to the sound of their guitar and banjo playing didn't harm any, either.

Meanwhile, Pete Seeger, one of the best five-string banjo players in the city—though not in the bluegrass picking style—decided to write and film an instruction manual for the instrument. Given that he'd never taught a lesson before, he gathered up some of the children from his wing dings, those who had shown promise on the guitar, and tried out some tactics on them. For eight weeks in a row, ten-year-old Eric Weissberg found himself among the select few taught the five-string banjo from the master. "Pete was a fabulous banjo player," recalled Weissberg. "He played his ass off." Seeger was always sure to return the compliment.

Weissberg was an extreme example of what Pete would often be referred to as "red diaper babies," children of those on the far Left (extending to Communist Party members and their sympathizers) from the 1930s, who enjoyed a liberal and integrated education before the Cold War could shake such accrued values. In New York, these kids attended the likes of Little Red and its affiliated Elisabeth Irwin Middle and High School, and/or the city's elite public high schools, Music and Art in Harlem, Stuyvesant at 15th Street, Bronx Science, and Brooklyn Tech. Typically, these children then spent their summers, first as students and later as counselors, at the progressive summer camps in the Catskills or New Jersey.

Of his own education (Little Red, Elisabeth Irwin, Music and Art, and Camp Woodland, outside Phoenicia, which hosted the Catskills Folk Festival), Weissberg acknowledged, "it was progressive and liberal, it was integrated," but he "never once heard the word 'Communist.' " Rather, he maintained, his teachers—the musicians included—instilled in him the core concept of "brotherhood," a value that came to be closely associated with folk music.

"Folk music was a very integral part of the liberal Left experience," confirmed Mary Travers, born in 1936, who attended the Little Red School House and Elisabeth Irwin High School. "It was writers, sculptors, painters, whatever, listening to Woody Guthrie, Pete Seeger, the Weavers. People sang in Washington Square Park on Sundays, and you really did not have to have a lot of talent to sing folk music. You needed enthusiasm, which is all folk music asks. It asks that you care."

In the late 1940s, folk music was still merely a small part of the park's Sunday scene. There were fire-eaters and violinists; what George Sprung called the "last of the bohemians," a drunken Maxwell Bodenheim, selling his poems by the sheet; and Italian bands performing traditional songs for spare change. The Italian immigrants and their descendants, who considered the Village their own, were not pleased by the singing youth who gathered around the fountain on Sundays, and soon the police put pressure on the musicians to either show up with a permit or not show up at all. George Sprung, with his friends Joe and Jean Silverstein, promptly went up to the Parks Department, filled out the necessary paperwork, acquired a permit, and effectively called the police's bluff. But as crowds increased further, the police began closely enforcing the precise wording of the permit, until it was agreed, after a period of give-and-take, to allow for both singing *and* stringed instruments, limited to four hours on Sunday afternoons, spring through fall, with the permit renewed monthly. (That process would later become annual.) For several years, Sprung, as the most prominent nonmusician among the regulars, was happy to supervise its acquisition.

"It was very egalitarian," said Erik Darling, one of dozens of young singers and guitarists who became a fixture. "If you knew the songs, you were in the center of the crowd. If you didn't have the slightest idea what you were doing, you were on the outside of the crowd. And some people just didn't give a shit, didn't know what they were doing, and sang anyway."

As the musicians broke up into different groups around the fountain, Roger Sprung took lead of the bluegrass contingent, along with the fellow banjo player Willie Dykeman and fiddle player Danny Zemickson, who played his instrument Appalachian style, across the stomach rather than under the neck. Around 1951, eleven-year-old Eric Weissberg came to join them, abandoning Seeger's folk style to learn bluegrass, both from these older youths and from records he picked up at a store on 14th Street. Soon he was good enough to hold a corner of the fountain area down with a fellow banjo player his own precocious age, Marshall Brickman.

A lot happened outside the park during those few short years, notably the deepening of the Cold War and, with it, the ostracism of the American far Left. The American union movement purged itself of known Communists, and the uptown Café Society closed in December 1947, after the proprietor Barney Josephson's brother was accused of acquiring a fake American passport for a senior foreign Communist, the Café was mentioned in various high-profile newspaper stories, and the crowd dropped in half overnight. Josh White, Josephson's main draw, then severed all ties and, choosing to go with the political flow, simultaneously withdrew his name from the People's Songs advisory board. By early 1949, the finances of People's Songs were in disarray, and when a fund-raiser at Town Hall failed to make a dent in the $3,000 debt, the company disbanded.

By that point, Seeger and Hays, close friends despite occasional fallings-out, had already decided to form another group. The initial plan called for a multiracial, coed sextet, but by the time they performed in public, it was with the committed core of three white men and "a brilliant alto," as Seeger described Ronnie Gilbert, who, like the fourth member, Fred Hellerman, was a Brooklyn-born child of eastern European immigrants, and an alumna of People's Songs. "She could hold off the three of us men." Naming themselves the Weavers, the quartet embarked on what remained of the left-wing circuit. "We still had the feeling that if we could sing loud enough and strong enough and hopefully enough it would make a difference," said Gilbert.

It wouldn't—as proven by the ugly scenes at a fund-raising picnic in Peekskill, north of New York City, in the summer of 1949, where Paul Robeson and Pete Seeger were among those attacked by a right-wing mob numbering in the thousands. A People's Songs supporter recorded the chaos that day (sample abuse: "White niggers, get back to Russia!") and helped script a small performance piece, *The Peekskill Story*, which Fred Hellerman narrated and on which the (uncredited) Weavers were heard singing for the first time. Meanwhile, an offshoot of People's Artists, Hootenanny Records, paired a Weavers protest song, "Banks of Marble," with "The Hammer Song," written in solidarity with the Foley Square Twelve, American Communist leaders being tried under the antisedition Smith Act. In a reference to the judge's gavel, the Weavers declared their desire to "hammer out love between my brothers and my sisters, all over this land." "The Hammer Song" was featured, the following spring, on the first front cover of *Sing Out!*, a magazine started by former members of People's Songs, but was otherwise little heard of for several years.

Seeger later dated 1949 as the year he "drifted out of the Communist Party," though he remained a focal part of a struggling Left. Indeed, at the end of that year, he and the Weavers campaigned on behalf of the American Labor Party's 1949 mayoral election campaign, adding to Leadbelly's "New York City" blues a verse about racial discrimination in Stuyvesant Town. In a feat of political sloganeering rarely matched in the history of protest music, they committed to melody the words "On November 8, Vote Row C." The American Labor Party was soundly defeated at the polls.

J ust a year later, the Weavers were the most popular singing group in the nation, performing in suits at, of all unlikely venues, the Waldorf-Astoria, as their songs blasted from pop radio stations coast to coast. Their remarkable transformation in fortune (and values) began shortly after the mayoral election, when Max Gordon approached Seeger, the group's only bankable solo member, about a booking at the Village Vanguard for the holiday season, and was talked into taking on the Weavers instead. (Seeger sold him the group for the same price.) The quartet dressed for the occasion in matching corduroy jackets and, just like the Josh White/Leadbelly double bill at the Vanguard earlier in the decade, dropped the political content to focus on traditional folk numbers like "The Johnson Boys" and "The Fireship," along with Hays's gospel-tinged "Washington Square Blues," which gave full vent to his booming bass. They closed every night with "Goodnight Irene," the waltz that Leadbelly had recorded for John and Alan Lomax in Angola Prison back in 1933. It served as a tribute to a great man who had just passed on; having recently returned to New York after two years in California, Leadbelly died of Lou Gehrig's disease in December 1949.

Absent the polemics, the Weavers displayed an admirable balance of musical skill (Seeger on banjo, Hellerman on guitar), vocal prowess (Gilbert and Hays in particular), and humor (Hays especially, whose dry wit is evident on surviving recordings from radio broadcasts with Oscar Brand). Positive reviews appeared in the nightlife columns, and the initial booking was extended several times over, Max Gordon running ads proclaiming them "the most exciting act I've discovered at the Village Vanguard in 10 years." By the end of an extended six-month residency, the Weavers had signed with Decca Records and taken a dance song from the young Israeli nation, "Tzena, Tzena, Tzena," dressed up like a Hollywood show tune and accompanied by the orchestra of their bandleader/producer, Gordon Jenkins, to almost the very top of the charts. Radio DJs then flipped the single and made the B-side, "Goodnight Irene"—on which mournful violins served to emphasize Hellerman, Gilbert, and Hays's rotation of verses and the ensemble chorus— the very biggest song of the year, touching a nerve with an audience that reached far beyond the folk traditionalists. The Weavers' rendition of the song would never die; the only regret was that Leadbelly had not lived to enjoy it.

As Woody Guthrie had discovered a decade earlier when he took on those CBS radio shows, the Weavers' overnight success placed the act in a quandary, caught between their beliefs and their prospects. As popular music stars, they had an opportunity to promote material written by friends. This they achieved when they recorded "So Long (It's Been Good to Know Yuh)" (the former "Dusty Old Dust") late in 1950, and Guthrie was advanced

$10,000 in publishing royalties. Guthrie had been in a bad way since 1947 when, in a repeat of his sister's childhood death, his four-year-old daughter, Cathy, succumbed to injuries sustained in a fire at his Coney Island apartment on Mermaid Avenue. Wracked with grief, his days of clarity and productivity grew ever more infrequent, and he was even jailed briefly for sending obscene mail to a former female friend. The publishing advance got him out of Mermaid Avenue and into a bigger apartment, but could not inspire a return to his earlier rate of writing.

Nor did the recorded version serve Guthrie's legacy well. Jenkins's orchestra turned it into a sing-along more suited to the decade's omnipresent chorus, Mitch Miller and his "Gang," which might explain why it became a top five hit. (That Guthrie had rewritten the lyrics to remove any references to the original Dust Bowl setting surely didn't harm. This was doubly ironic, since it was the same song he'd rewritten for Model Tobacco ten years earlier.) Subsequent Weavers recordings of "Kisses Sweeter Than Wine" and "When the Saints Go Marching In," made with a different orchestra, tempered the excesses, affording the gifted individual singers room to breathe. But they were the exceptions: the lengthy orchestral buildup for the group's adaptation of a South African song, "Mbube"—which Seeger misheard and thereby renamed as "Wimoweh"—exaggerated its jungle connotations to the point of parody.

Success proved short-lived, anyway. In the summer of 1950, as the Korean War broke out, the anti-Communist *Counterattack* issued "Red Channels," a dossier that named 151 alleged Communists active in show business. Half of those names had connections either to Almanac House or to People's Songs, among them non-Communists like Oscar Brand, Josh White, and Burl Ives, as well as more openly sympathetic characters like Earl Robinson, Judy Holliday, and Millard Lampell—and the Weavers, who were promptly picketed at concerts and TV shows, more gradually boycotted, and eventually blacklisted.

The Weavers did not suffer alone. As the Red scare took its own frightening hold on America, and media executives used "Red Channels" as a guide for whom not to hire for fear of losing sponsors, entertainers were frequently subpoenaed to appear in Washington or at highly publicized subcommittees elsewhere, where they were expected to give names of other "sympathizers." Burl Ives "gave up" his fellow cabaret folk star Richard Dyer-Bennet so as to continue his career in Hollywood, and became persona non grata in Greenwich Village as a result. Josh White went before the House Un-American Activities Committee (HUAC) of his own accord in September 1950 and, while not apologizing for his songs or his stance, lost fans on the left for his actions while failing to appease critics on the right.

Then, in early 1952, a former People's Songs employee, Harvey Matusow, came before the HUAC and offered, as part of well-publicized testimony about communism in the *New York Times* and the Girl Scouts, his apparent knowledge that three of the Weavers remained Communist Party members. Barely eighteen months after "Goodnight Irene" had made them a household name, the Weavers found themselves reduced to singing in a nightclub on the outskirts of Cleveland and, given their own doubts about their elaborate studio productions—and Seeger's particular discomfort with appearing in nightclubs and hotels—decided to retreat. They closed out the year with a hometown show at New York's Town Hall, as was just starting to become a tradition, and took a sabbatical. At the end of 1953, at the height of the Red scare, a defensive Decca Records released the group from its contract—and deleted the Weavers' entire back catalog. "We lost our livelihood, we lost our careers," said Ronnie Gilbert of being blacklisted. "But we lost much more than that: we lost the sense that we were living in a democratic society."

Seeger, who moved his family to a log cabin he hand-built in upstate New York in the early 1950s, was rarely seen in Washington Square Park on Sundays, but Woody Guthrie made the occasional visit. He was photographed there with a protégé of sorts, Jack Elliott, the son of a Brooklyn dentist whose fascination with cowboy life had inspired him to run away and join a rodeo earlier in his teens. When Guthrie suffered a burst appendix in early 1951, Elliott was among those who visited him in the hospital. Guthrie subsequently took Elliott under his wing, bringing him to parties around New York and inviting him on his last two cross-country trips to California. Acquiring the nickname Ramblin' Jack, as much for his lengthy discourses as for any hobo instincts, Elliott learned to mimic his hero's style with almost painful accuracy. He would not be the last.

As the public gathering space for the village on the left of New York, Washington Square Park thrived through the early fifties, a refuge for the red diaper babies coming of age. "There were a lot of different factions," said Happy Traum, who attended Music and Art and, with his brother Artie, became a guitar-playing Sunday regular. "There was a group of people who were really into finger-picking blues guitar. There was the whole group of kids who went to summer camp and sang 'Kumbayaa' till the cows came home, and then there were the people [for whom], if it wasn't pure Appalachian folk music by some obscure ballad singer from the hills somewhere, it wasn't any good."

Such industriousness was not for everyone. Dave Van Ronk, a Brooklyn-born, Queens-raised jazz aficionado with a caustic wit, saw the park gatherings as "essentially summer camp music, songs these kids had learned at progressive camps that I came to think of generically as Camp Gulag on the Hudson. The sight and sound of all those happily howling petit bourgeois Stalinists offended my assiduously nurtured self-image as a hipster." But even he could not stay cynical for long. He soon noticed such people as Tom Paley, Fred Gerlach, and Dick Rosmini "playing music cognate with early jazz, and doing it with a subtlety and directness that blew me away." He started bringing his guitar to the park on Sundays and found himself switching from jazz to folk and stepping up as a leader of sorts. John Hammond—the son of the A&R man/producer, and himself a park regular with his guitar—looked up to Van Ronk in the park as "a *presence* there, a teacher."

Hammond had been raised in the Village and understood that his was not a normal neighborhood. The same applied to John Sebastian, whose liberal family (father a revered harmonica player, mother a radio show scriptwriter) lived on Washington Square itself, and who started frequenting the park from a young age with his harp in pocket. "I certainly had an awareness that where I lived was unique," he said. "I was comfortable having two uncles in one family or maybe [as friends] a couple that didn't racially look like they were a couple in that era. . . . And I did understand that . . . if you were in other places, you might not have that same freedom."

Inevitably, as the summers rolled by, the original generation of park musicians began forming groups. The first of note was the Folksay Trio—Roger Sprung, Erik Darling, and Bob Carey—who released a record on the Stinson label in 1953. Among its four songs was "Tom Dooley," introduced to them by a MacDougal Street resident, singer, and folk collector, Frank Warner, who heard it in North Carolina. Despite Darling's insistence that "the music wasn't that good," the trio's rendition of "Tom Dooley," propelled by Sprung's furious bluegrass banjo playing, demonstrated distinct possibilities for both the song and its format.

More immediately crucial to the scene was the release, on the indefatigable Moe Asch's new Folkways label (his original company Asch and a subsequent label Disc both having gone bankrupt as a result of his enthusiasm), of the six-album *Anthology of American Folk Music*. Assembled by Harry Smith, an iconoclastic Village-based filmmaker and musicologist, the collection was in effect a bootleg compilation of eighty-four recordings that stretched back through every variety of rural blues, country, folk, gospel, and Cajun music. The LP was still a brand-new format in 1952, and Smith made the most of its potential, meticulously sequencing his choices into three double-album packages (*Ballads/Social Music/Songs*), each of which subtly created a lyrical and musical narrative. Nobody had ever contemplated releasing such an all-encompassing collection in one fell swoop, let alone putting them into what seemed such an eccentric order. The *Anthology* was therefore received as something of a revelation in the Village (and in other pockets of urban America), opening listeners up to new (old) styles, new (old) songs, and new (old) performers—some of whom suddenly enjoyed revived careers, once it was discovered that they weren't long dead and buried.

Surprising though it seemed, none of the recordings was more than a quarter of a century old: Harry Smith had purposefully assembled the collection from the period between 1927, "when electronic recording made possible accurate music reproduction," and 1932, "when the Depression halted music folk sales," wrote Greil Marcus. That the *Anthology* was assembled from old vinyl releases, purchased by Smith on his own cross-country travels, and duly covered in crackles and hiss, only increased the sense of physical and chronological distance, whether it was the melding of violins and vocals into the unique square-dance calling of Hoyt Ming & His Pep-Steppers' "Indian War Whoop" or the Reverend F. W. McGee's jubilantly jazzy affirmation of salvation on "Fifty Miles of Elbow Room." The *Anthology* offered a glimpse of a joyfully eccentric and idiosyncratic America that had existed prior to the public conformities of the Eisenhower era—and perhaps was still out there. For the kids of the new Village generation, it was nothing short of a new musical bible, and it was treated with all due reverence. It would be no exaggeration to call it one of the most influential album releases of all time.

Back in business in a big way, Asch now opted to re-release the Almanac Singers' 1941 album *Talking Union*. But since the 33 rpm album had replaced 78 rpm discs in the interim years, he needed more material to fill it out. Seeger assembled an ensemble chorus from Elisabeth Irwin seniors, including Travers, and several of the park regulars, among them Darling, who noted, "A chance to work with Pete was something nobody would have passed up." As Pete Seeger and Chorus, they recorded seven "new" songs (including "We Shall Not Be Moved" and "Casey Jones") for what became *Talking Union and Other Union Songs*, and it proved more influential the second time around, reviving the political discourse within folk music. Its popularity led the recruits to acquire their own name, the Song Swappers, and for Seeger to direct and produce them through three more albums in 1955—two representing music from around the world, the third focusing on the enduring format of children's music: *Camp Songs with 6 to 11 Year Olds*.

Gradually, the political pendulum swung back from the extreme right. Seeger dated the changes to the stalemate conclusion of the Korean War, in 1953: "Ending that war," he said, "made it possible to speak your mind a little more clearer." Senator Joe McCarthy was censured by his own peers in 1954, the same year that *Brown v. Board of Education* opened up America's schools to integration. And so it was that in 1955, when Seeger was finally called before the HUAC, he declined to follow Lee Hays's example in pleading the Fifth Amendment (his right not to incriminate himself), and engaged instead in a fabulously brittle exchange with his interrogators.

The confrontation began as soon as a committee member quoted from the *Daily Worker* of June 1949, dating the first performance of "If I Had a Hammer" to a testimonial dinner for the Foley Square Twelve (eerily ironic, given that the hearings were themselves taking place in New York's Foley Square). Asked repeatedly whether he had performed for Communists, Seeger offered to explain the song, to sing it even—"It is a good song"—but refused to answer the committee's direct question. "I am proud that I never refuse to sing to an audience, no matter what religion or color of their skin, or situation in life," he said. "I have sung in hobo jungles, and I have sung for the Rockefellers."

Asked then to identify the figure, presumably himself, wearing military uniform at a 1952 May Day parade, Seeger threw out a particularly bold retort: "That's a little like Jesus Christ, when he was asked by Pontius Pilate,

'Are you King of the Jews?' . . . Let somebody else identify it." For his refusal
to directly answer the questions, Seeger was charged with contempt of
Congress, and for the next several years remained but a short step ahead of a
jail sentence.

His testimony made front-page news, and between his hometown status
as a hero for standing up to the committee, the success of *Talking Union*, and
the shifting political tide, the Weavers' former adviser Harold Leventhal suggested the group re-form for a Christmas concert. Town Hall was booked
already; Leventhal took a risk on the bigger Carnegie Hall. Come Christmas
Eve, New York's leftist folk lovers lined up around the block by the thousands; the Weavers concert was recorded and released, over a year later, by a
small label on West 14th Street called Vanguard, which soon grew rapidly in
size as it continuously shipped out copies of what it advertised as "the most
successful folk album of all time."

Fortune would not reverse itself for Woody Guthrie. The singer's apparent alcoholic ticks and wayward behavior had been diagnosed, in 1952, as
Huntington's chorea, the same debilitating disease that had destroyed his
mother; he had been hospitalized almost continuously since his last cross-
country trip, with Jack Elliott, in 1954. At a benefit concert at Pythian Hall
in the spring of 1956, Seeger and Hays led an all-star cast through a finale of
"This Land Is Your Land," a frail Guthrie looking on from the balcony. The
Weavers used it to open their next album, guaranteed strong sales following
the success of their Carnegie Hall souvenir, and it spread rapidly across a
new generation of folksingers, from the kids in Washington Square Park to
those who played professionally. The song written on notepaper at a Times
Square hotel was fast on its way to becoming America's alternative national
anthem.

By 1957, what some Villagers sardonically labeled "the folk scare" had
begun in earnest. Moe Asch's Folkways, Maynard Solomon's Vanguard,
Bob Harris's Stinson, and Jac Holzman's new Elektra Records were tripping
over one another to release albums by the "folk blues" icons Sonny Terry and
Brownie McGhee, Big Bill Broonzy and the Reverend Gary Davis; the young
Appalachian traditionalist Jean Richie; local mainstays such as the Weavers,
Pete Seeger, and Oscar Brand; and some of the new Washington Square Park

players like Tom Paley. Leadbelly's "Rock Island Line," as recorded by Lonnie Donegan, went to number one in the United Kingdom as the key song of a "skiffle" movement that stripped rock 'n' roll down to folk basics. (Ramblin' Jack Elliott seized the opportunity to tour Europe with an album called *Woody Guthrie's Blues*.) And Sundays in Washington Square Park continued to attract vast audiences of professionals, amateurs, and tourists alike.

"The whole thing had an aura," said Happy Traum. "You felt like you were in the vanguard of something new. It was a definite feeling that anybody who was interested in folk music in those days was on the forefront of something. And it was a paradox, because all this music was the old traditional stuff."

What the Village needed now was some indoor performance spaces for the winter months, other than the nightclubs with their age restrictions and hefty cover charges. What the Village got first was something more profound. In the spring of 1957, Izzy Young, a former Bronx Science student who, already in his late twenties, had built up a successful mail-order book business, opened the Folklore Center on MacDougal Street between West Third and Bleecker. He did so without any other plan than "to be part of a scene," and because he "was not competing with anybody," he said, "it was an instant success."

Overnight, those with the money had somewhere to buy folk albums, both obscure and commercial, to pick up new editions of *Sing Out!*, and to acquire old songbooks. Those without the cash took to treating the store as job center, mailbox, and social club combined. Young had no problem with this. He would occasionally close the doors to hold hootenannies with the store's assembled musicians; at other times, he would entrust patrons, whether he knew them or not, to look after the Folklore Center while he put on his harness and bells and folk-danced his way down the street.

Prior to the center, the only other public meeting places had been the coffeehouses on MacDougal Street. The most famous was Caffe Reggio, with its vast espresso machine imported from Italy; the most bohemian was Café Figaro, with its French newspapers hanging from wooden racks; and the only one that allowed the musicians even to think about unpacking their guitars, in its tiny back room, was the forward-thinking Caricature. Then, in the summer of 1957, the future folklorist Roger Abrahams's landlord Rick Allmen opened Café Bizarre on West Third Street, the first "coffeehouse" purpose-built for live music. It proved so swiftly successful that it was able to persuade several local musicians to open for national performers for free. Headed by the increasingly ubiquitous Dave Van Ronk, a group of energetic young park regulars, who differentiated between going unpaid in the park and unpaid in a club, formed the Folksingers Guild. "The implication was that we were trying to organize and become a little union for folksingers," said Happy Traum, himself an active member who wrote a term paper about it while attending New York University, which held so much real estate in Greenwich Village that its students viewed Washington Square Park as part of their campus. Yet with only Café Bizarre to protest, "it was more of a social club, and a place to show off your new songs."

But the Folksingers Guild also promoted concerts, primarily at the Sullivan Street Playhouse, and could thus be viewed as a minor People's Artists for the new generation. Likewise, a rival to *Sing Out!* emerged: reflecting the youthful energy of the new crowd, *Caravan* was less earnest than its predecessors, running extensive Village gossip and opinionated essays. Van Ronk and a couple of friends also produced *The Bosses' Songbook*, parodying the earnest lyrics of the previous political generation of singers; in "The Ballad of Pete Seeger," they reminded the Village icon, "This is not '38, it is 1957 / There's a change in that old Party Line."

Seeger knew as much. In the late 1950s, he quit the Weavers, preferring to focus on solo albums and social activism. Erik Darling, while simultaneously leading the Tarriers with Bob Carey and Alan Arkin, took his place. For an independent label, Glory, the Tarriers had recorded a song they had learned in Washington Square Park from another of the regulars, Bob Gibson. It was a West Indian number called "The Banana Boat Song," and when it charted in 1956 (rising to number four, the biggest success for a Village folk group since the Weavers' heyday), RCA quickly had Harry Belafonte record his own version. Belafonte, though widely viewed as a pop musician, carried considerable status in the Village set by dint of his political commitment and frequent performances at the local nightclubs, and his single was also a big hit; a subsequent album of Caribbean songs called *Calypso*, afforded the promotional push that only a major label can offer, became reputedly the first LP ever to sell a million copies.

On their own debut album, released in 1957, the Tarriers included not just "The Banana Boat Song" but "Tom Dooley," familiar to its members Darling and Carey from their earlier recording as the Folksay Trio. Absent the banjo, the recording was much more clearly "folk" than "bluegrass." Yet the album didn't meet expectations. "Our songs and arrangements were quite different from one another, and didn't lend themselves to each other," said Darling. "No two songs were really alike."

Less than a year later, however, three clean-cut college graduates called the Kingston Trio, who had worked the Californian coffeehouses to the point of securing a record deal with Capitol, released a delicate, polished version of "Tom Dooley" not dissimilar to that of the Tarriers. And this time, the song clicked. Just as "Goodnight Irene" had dominated the radio stations at the start of the decade, so "Tom Dooley" seemed omnipresent at the tail end of the fifties, reaching number one late in 1958 on its way to three million single sales.

Harry Belafonte's success with *Calypso* had been applauded in the Village; the Kingston Trio's sudden stardom was not. After all, Greenwich Village artists had introduced "Tom Dooley" on record; they considered the song their own. Worse, the Kingston Trio, as its live set's excursions into Broadway and cabaret revealed, was never accepted as a proper folk group; its members had only ever stuck their heads into the New York scene for a brief spell at the Vanguard. And to add insult to injury, their 1958 best-selling album appeared to have based its cover image on that of the Tarriers from the year before. (This suggested that they had surely heard the Tarriers' version of "Tom Dooley," though it didn't stop their publishers from trying to claim a copyright on it.) The Villagers felt that, having founded the urban folk revival, they had suddenly been robbed of its moment in the spotlight.

The music's newfound popularity countrywide was closely tied to the explosion in college enrollment. Prior to World War II, higher education had been the province of the privileged. But with the passing of the GI Bill for the benefit of returning servicemen, the number of college graduates trebled in just a few years. In 1955, 2.6 million Americans were in college; by the end of the decade, that number had increased by a third again. Many of these campuses mirrored the conformity of the Eisenhower era: Peter Yarrow, by his own admission a red diaper baby who in 1955 graduated from Music and Art to attend Cornell in upstate New York, recalled the shock of entering a "conservative world that was at that point very alien." But increasingly, these same colleges became bastions of liberal thought and support systems for the growing civil rights struggle. Equally, as America's first generation of prosperous teenagers left for universities often thousands of miles away, many brought their instruments and music with them. Yarrow, who stayed on after graduation in 1959 to help teach a Cornell course on folklore and folk music, "saw these young people . . . who were basically very conservative in their backgrounds opening their hearts up and singing with an emotionality and a concern through this vehicle called folk music." He came back to the Village a few months later, vowing to give himself two years as a folksinger before settling down to a career in psychology.

In the wake of the Kingston Trio's success came the predictable explosion in similar-sounding groups, many hailing from the West Coast and landing on major labels. In Greenwich Village, the groups were more eclectic and entwined. For almost two years, Darling did double duty in both the Weavers and the Tarriers, before committing permanently to the former. Eric Weissberg and his friend John Herald returned from a single year at the University of Wisconsin to form, with Bob Yellin, the bluegrass group called the Greenbriar Boys, who performed mostly at the nearby American Youth Hostel on Sunday evenings, after the Washington Square Park gatherings wound down, and to much the same crowd. (The Van Ronk set would head from the park to Roger Abrahams's apartment on Spring Street; the traditionalists ventured down to the Municipal Building, near the Brooklyn Bridge, where Brand's *Folksong Festival* was recorded before a live audience.) The Clancy Brothers arrived from Ireland with the singer Tommy Makem and immediately found a welcome stage in the Village clubs, and a regular table at the White Horse. Roger Sprung formed the Shanty Boys with two other long-term park regulars, Lionel Kilberg and Mike Cohen. And Cohen's brother John, with Pete Seeger's half brother Mike, and Tom Paley, formed the New Lost City Ramblers, who focused on the "Old Timey" music of 1920s and 1930s Appalachia.

All these groups, East Coast traditionalist and West Coast opportunists alike, engaged in rehearsed comic interaction that Weissberg described as "sophisticated corn." The tradition extended back to the Weavers and beyond and would continue with many singer-songwriters of the early 1960s. This humor, archaic and forced though it came to sound, offset the dour sincerity of so many traditional folk songs, some of which could never fully shake their origins as children's lullabies. Besides, in the inclusive atmosphere of Greenwich Village, there was considerable overlap between folksingers, comedians, blues musicians, and cabaret performers—as when Art D'Lugoff opened the Village Gate in 1958 and booked artists of all these stripes, or when Noel Stookey arrived from Philadelphia the following year and found himself, by his own admission, working as "everything from a maitre d' to a standup comic to a traditional folk artist."

To this flourishing Village scene in the late 1950s were added the beatniks, and those who saw themselves as such. Allen Ginsberg, Gregory Corso, and Lawrence Ferlinghetti were all born in or around New York City (Corso on Bleecker Street itself), and Jack Kerouac had briefly attended Columbia University. When they weren't living in San Francisco, or traveling elsewhere, they could often be found at the San Remo Bar on MacDougal and Bleecker; Kerouac recorded a live album of his poetry, with jazz accompaniment, at the Village Vanguard in 1957. Media coverage of the beatniks brought goatees and bongos onto the streets and served, as the folk crowd saw it, to clutter up and even caricature their scene. Yet it was those very newspaper reports on "the poetry and Beatniks in the Village" that moved a teenage Richie Havens to travel in from Brooklyn with his friends. "We thought maybe we could fit in there somewhere," he said, "because we sure didn't fit into Bedford-Stuy writing poetry." Havens and his friends found themselves drawn to the Gaslight Poetry Café, which John Mitchell, the proprietor, carved out of a MacDougal Street tenement basement in 1958. Mitchell, later referred to by the *New York Post* columnist Al Aronowitz as "a master carpenter, a star con man, a resourceful innovator, a proud individualist and a cagey entrepreneur," learned reluctantly that the only way to keep an unlicensed entertainment premise open on a residential street in a heavily trafficked tourist part of town was to pay off the people who had the power to close it. His vocal enmity toward the local enforcement agencies—uniformed and otherwise—became legend, leading to a general feeling on MacDougal Street that he was destined for a premature demise. Yet despite regular raids on the Gaslight, his lack of necessary permits, and his willingness to speak up about police corruption and local protection rackets, Mitchell stayed visible on the scene for many years. In the interim, folklore—an apt term here—has it that noise complaints from the Gaslight's residential neighbors led to one of the great beatnik clichés: the audience applauding a poet by clicking its fingers.

The only pop culture that seemed not to have an impact on the Village scene was rock 'n' roll. A music that had changed the entire national status quo in the mid-1950s, one that was vibrant in Harlem, in midtown, in Brooklyn, and in the Bronx, one that turned so many white New York kids on to black music, seemed somehow to have met a blockade at the metaphorical gates of Greenwich Village. There was certainly a degree of intellectual snobbery behind the folk crowd's notion that rock 'n' roll, even though based on the (rhythm and) blues, was somehow not real music. But, then, by the end of the 1950s rock 'n' roll no longer really existed, and given the see-through vapidity of most of what came to pass for it, as heard through prepackaged Philadelphia teen idols, the young Village intelligentsia had every reason to believe that folk was in fact the true rebel yell.

Notice of the movement's growing depth was served nationally in the summer of 1959, when the Newport Jazz Festival expanded to include a concurrent Folk Festival and when Bob Gibson brought eighteen-year-old Joan Baez onstage. At the time, Baez was essentially unknown outside of Cambridge, Massachusetts (Boston's own Village), but her soprano voice with its trill vibrato and her plaintive beauty instantly made her a marketable female folksinger. Turning down an offer from John Hammond at Columbia Records, Baez recorded her eponymous debut album for Vanguard—which included "House of the Rising Sun" amid its thirteen traditional numbers— in the ballroom of the Manhattan Tower Hotel, with the Weavers' Fred Hellerman playing second guitar. Released in late 1960, it made an immediate impression on the folk movement and also on a national music scene that was not familiar with teenage singers as something other than a malleable marketing tool. Almost immediately, Vanguard's rival Elektra signed Judy Collins, a photogenic ballad singer and guitarist who had come east from Colorado in 1958 and maintained a continued presence in the Village coffeehouses. The success of her album *A Maid of Constant Sorrow,* in 1961, demonstrated that Baez was not merely a female one-off.

With the exception of Hammond at Columbia, the only established record label to show any interest in the burgeoning folk scene was, typically, Atlantic. In 1960, it signed the Tarriers, whose lineup now featured Bob Carey, the stirring gospel voice of Clarence Cooper, and the flamboyant banjo playing of a grown Eric Weissberg. The trio's racial integration intrigued Atlantic, which recorded their album *Tell the World about This* that spring, with the Weavers' Ronnie Gilbert supplying sleeve notes that bemoaned the lack of authenticity in the current folk scene.

In so doing, Gilbert inadvertently helped define a generation gap that was growing between the Weavers and their offspring. "The traditionalists resented people changing things," said Weissberg. "I grew up in the traditional environment listening to Pete and Woody and those guys, but I learned new chords when I was in school. Learned a sixth chord or a ninth chord and thought, 'That sounds nice.' We weren't trying to belittle anything that we were singing." It remained one of the folk scene's inherent contradictions that such an open-minded, inclusive culture could prove narrow-minded and reactionary when it came to the music. For with the exception of Harry Smith's remarkable *Anthology*, the same old songs were constantly regurgitated by the same old (and young) artists on the same old (and new) labels: *Ramblin' Jack Elliott Sings the Songs of Woody Guthrie*; *Dave Van Ronk Sings Ballads, Blues and a Spiritual*; Pete Seeger's *Folk Songs for Young People*. Elektra Records even signed Josh White and issued a fresh album of *Chain Gang Songs*, fifteen years after the original. In such a climate, *Tell the World about This* was arguably ahead of its time, and Atlantic, unable to figure out the market, gave up without releasing a single.

Back in the Village, the new coffeehouse owners, like generations of entrepreneurs before them, found themselves up against the byzantine New York City licensing laws. A cabaret license was generally required for providing live entertainment, but because the coffeehouses didn't serve alcohol, they considered themselves exempt. The police thought otherwise, and raids were commonplace. The venues came upon the simplest of solutions: they neither officially hired nor paid the performers, who, instead, passed a basket around for donations. Although some found it demeaning to ask directly for money, others readily accepted the tax-free income: according to Van Ronk, the better names on the scene could draw $100 or more a week from playing the "basket houses."

With demand still outstripping supply, Izzy Young, already promoting one-off concerts, was dragged to an Italian restaurant called Gerdes, on Mercer and West Fourth, by an advertising executive who saw the potential for a folk club there. The pair launched the Fifth Peg in January 1960, and over the next three months, Young's connections enabled him to book almost every major act on the scene. But Young was neither the world's best businessman nor its most savvy promoter, and the Gerdes owner Mike Porco suggested they take a break; Porco then reopened the venue in June, as

Gerdes Folk City, with Charles Rothschild as promoter, Logan English as MC, and Carolyn Hester—who had first shown up in the Village from Texas back in 1955—as opening performer. Young felt betrayed and took out advertisements stating as much, demanding his patrons take his side. But soon enough the dust settled, and Young went back to promoting his concerts, writing for *Sing Out!*, and hosting a radio show on WBAI. Folk City, meanwhile, became one of the Village's preeminent venues, especially noted for the Monday night hootenannies, when, it often seemed, all performers in town gathered in the basement, guitars and banjos at their side, waiting their turn to head upstairs and play a song or two that just might make their name.

Folk City was quickly joined by a slew of other venues: the Bitter End on Bleecker, Café Wha? on MacDougal, and, across the street from the Gaslight, John Mitchell's latest coffeehouse, the Commons. Mitchell's confrontational attitude was matched on MacDougal only by his neighbor Young, who plastered the Folklore Center's windows with the names of those clubs that weren't paying performers, for which he soon found himself paying for new panes of glass. Eventually, according to a future coffeehouse proprietor called Joe Marra, the city issued a zero-alcohol version of the cabaret license, a coffeehouse license that allowed a strictly limited number of venues—the Bitter End, Café Wha?, Café Bizarre, and Gaslight among them—to provide live entertainment, legally.

Occasional bureaucratic hassles aside, the Village was enjoying a golden age. Tourist buses began rolling through the local streets on weekends (partly in search of beatniks); not far behind them, aspiring musicians disembarked from distant cities, lured if not yet by the hope of fame and fortune, then by the prospect of performing opportunities, good times, and new friendships. When Noel Stookey moved up from Philadelphia in 1959, Mary Travers quickly showed him around town. Occasionally she even joined him onstage. But Travers disdained public attention and never imagined herself as a career singer.

With slightly greater ambition, Tom Paxton graduated from the University of Oklahoma in 1959 and figured on either New York or California to pursue his musical career. "We generally had a rule of thumb," he said, "that folk artists in the East were more concerned with the song and the ones in the West were more concerned with the performance." When drafted by the

Army and sent to New Jersey's Fort Slocum, the decision was made for him: he took a train into the Village on his first weekend and found himself at the Fifth Peg's opening. For Paxton, the Village "was magical." He stood with his face pressed against the window of the Village Gate, watching Pete Seeger perform. He recalled an "amazing bill" at One Sheridan Square: Logan English, the Clancy Brothers and Tommy Makem, and Josh White. "I just absorbed it by osmosis, I just drank it." In September 1960, released from Army duty, he moved full-time to the Village, gradually shedding his military mannerisms—Van Ronk had pegged him as a narc—for those of an easygoing folk musician.

The subsequent winter was famously harsh even by New York standards: snow fell by the foot, temperatures remained below freezing for days on end, and the denizens of the Village scene huddled ever closer around their drinks, smokes, and instruments in the compact bars, basket houses, and clubs. For the teenagers who didn't belong in such places, the arrival of spring—and with it, the return of the Sunday gatherings in Washington Square Park— was more keenly anticipated than ever.

George Sprung, who still religiously attended the park on Sundays with his brother Roger, had long since handed over the task of acquiring the park permit; in 1961, Lionel Kilberg turned it over to Izzy Young. There was a new parks commissioner that year, too, Mayor Wagner having recently replaced Robert Moses—after twenty-seven years in that role among many, *many* others—with Newbold Morris. This hardly set off any alarm bells: Morris had founded the New York City Opera and, before that, as chairman of the Greater New York Committee for Russian Relief, had promoted a Carnegie Hall benefit concert featuring all the usual left-wing suspects. Yet Morris sent down word to deny the park permit. Young suspected that it was because "they really wanted to clear up the Village for real estate," a perennially plausible argument.

Young was probably the very last person Morris should have provoked. On Sunday, April 9, the first official singing day of the spring, several hundred regulars gathered in Washington Square Park. Young led a group of about fifty protesters—"many in beatnik clothes and beards," noted the *New York Times*—from his store to the park, with a cello serving as a mock coffin in the lead. As Young remembered it, the police captain on duty warned him, "You can go into the park, but you can't sing," and allowed the protesters to gather at the fountain. Ever the libertarian, Young promptly handed out song-books to the assembled crowd. The police moved in to close down the sing-ing, several of the youths fought back, and a two-hour scuffle broke out, leading to ten arrests, several injuries, and what the following day's *Times* described in its front-page headline as a "folk singers riot," a phrase that surely, until that moment, had been considered an oxymoron.

For the next few weeks, the battle over Washington Square Park stayed close to those front pages. Morris admitted that he intended to make the park more "attractive," and, between coded comments about how the roving troubadours had attracted elements from "the Bronx and so on," offered the singers use of the East River Park and its amphitheater, demonstrating a remarkable lack of understanding about the culture of Greenwich Village. Mayor Wagner spoke up from his vacation in Florida to support his appoin-tee's "ban" on singing, while Young enlisted the New York Civil Liberties Union, which took the case direct to the state supreme court.

New organizations sprouted up to take sides. Some local residents formed the Committee to Preserve the Dignity and Beauty of Washington Square Park, while the Reverend Howard Moody of Judson Memorial Church, which overlooked Washington Square Park, became chair of the Greenwich Village Right to Sing Committee. Moody, a forty-year-old civil rights crusader from Texas, also took the case of the singers to his pulpit, welcoming five hundred of them the week after the "riot" for a church rally, where he lambasted Morris as a "petty bureaucrat with autocratic tenden-cies," who had set the police against "carefree young people whose only crime is that they want to strum a guitar or sing a tune."

On Sunday, April 23, a crowd of two thousand gathered on Thompson Street, just outside the park, where they sang and played guitars. The police did not attempt to shut them down. The following week, an emboldened crowd of similar size, though mostly of high school age, attempted to storm the park, leading to one arrest. And just a few days later, the state supreme court announced that it would not overrule the parks commissioner, effec-tively upholding the ban. At this point, close investigation of city small print by the singers' advocates revealed that a permit was in fact required only for "minstrelsy," that is, singing with instruments, and the first Sunday in May duly found the Reverend Moody and Izzy Young leading six hundred singers, sans guitars and banjos, into the park, where they broke, almost predictably, into a chorus of "This park is your park, this park is my park."

Common sense ultimately prevailed. Despite the initial show of support, Mayor Wagner overruled Commissioner Morris, and the singers and their instruments returned to the park on May 14 for three hours, under police scrutiny but without disturbance. The Reverend Moody dissolved the Right to Sing Committee, Young vowed to keep the legal battle going "on principle," everyone except the beatnik wannabes agreed to ban the bongos, and the Sunday sing-alongs in Washington Square Park resumed, without need for permits, as the best-attended hootenannies in New York City.

9

LAY DOWN YOUR
WEARY TUNE

The story has been told so many times that it can be boiled down to a couple of simple sentences. In January 1961, the Minnesota college student Robert Zimmerman, nineteen years old, hitchhikes his way to New York City, where he introduces himself to Greenwich Village as Bob Dylan, after Dylan Thomas, the Welsh poet who had drunk himself to death several years earlier at the White Horse, on Hudson Street. The impoverished, waiflike folk musician weaves tales of a hobo lifestyle, maintains a mystery regarding his relatively stable family background, and displays such a fascination with Woody Guthrie in his mannerisms and music alike that, by comparison, Ramblin' Jack Elliott looks positively original.

New York had long been known as a place where young men and women could make a name for themselves, could succeed beyond the imagination of their difficult childhoods: think of Dizzy Gillespie, Tito Rodriguez, or Josh White, career examples of the Great American Dream, proof that fortitude, fortune, talent, and timing can transform status in society. Dylan, however, was arguably the first such prodigious musician successfully to seize upon the Great *New York* Dream, the possibility that one could leave one's past behind and arrive in the city, suitably emboldened by its sheer energy to start a completely clean slate. And this time not as just another hick from the sticks but as a poet, a lover, a fighter, a hobo, any role one wanted to claim for oneself, in the process of which mythmaking one could attain ever greater confidence and admiration until perception became reality, and stardom— on the New York level, at least—was assured.

At the time he released his first album, Dylan's story was full of fanciful lies: he was an orphan, he'd come to New York City on a freight train, and so on. It all made for good press, and Dylan knew as much; he was an early master of the media. Years later, he was able to confess to some sort of truth. Born in Duluth, Minnesota, and raised nearby in what he considered a nondescript mining town, Hibbing, the son of an electrician felled by polio, he listened to Johnny Ray and Hank Williams as a young boy and dreamed of playing guitar for a living. Graduating from high school in 1959, he attended the University of Minnesota at Minneapolis, and immersed himself in its bohemian district, Dinkytown, where he experienced the tail end of the beatnik explosion. Influenced, like countless others, by *On the Road,* he made it out to St. Louis, Kansas City, and Denver, running into the familiar faces of fellow travelers in each town.

Soon enough came the realization that he'd outgrown his midwestern roots: "When I arrived in Minneapolis it had seemed like a big city. When I left it was like some rural outpost that you see once from a passing train." After a seemingly unadventurous stay in Chicago, he hitchhiked with a passing friend to New York, fully aware of its gravitas as "some place which not too many people had ever gone, and anybody who did go never came back." Dropped off on the Manhattan side of the George Washington Bridge, on January 24, 1961, during the harshest winter in years, he took a subway to the Village, walked into Café Wha? carrying the recommended name of its resident musician Freddy Neil (a journeyman guitarist and writer with considerable musical mileage from a childhood spent in both the South and the West), and got a job accompanying Neil on daytime gigs playing to tourists for whom the Wha? represented the height of bohemia.

Dylan quickly discovered that the real action took place elsewhere on MacDougal Street: at the Gaslight, where Dave Van Ronk held down a key Tuesday night residency, and at the Folklore Center, where Izzy Young held court all week long. While Dylan was hanging out at the center one afternoon, Van Ronk—who by virtue of his strong physique, voice, political convictions, and drinking prowess, his steady record releases, stable marriage, and recent *Village Voice* cover story, was fast becoming the mayor of MacDougal Street—stopped by to try out a guitar. Dylan seized the moment and asked how to get a gig at the Gaslight. Though he did not suffer fools gladly, Van Ronk had a generosity of spirit and an instinct for talent that made him a natural mentor to the new arrivals. He invited Dylan to join him onstage at the Gaslight that very same night.

Clearly, Dylan was both ambitious and opportunistic. But Van Ronk, who with his wife, Terri Thal, soon allowed the newcomer to sleep on their sofa, was convinced that Dylan did not land in the Village to jump on any bandwagon. "What he said at the time, and what I believe, is that he came because he had to meet Woody." The great white godfather of the American folk scene, Guthrie had been holed up now for almost seven years in hospitals, Huntington's chorea slowly eating away at his capacities. By the time Dylan hit New York, Guthrie was at Greystone Park Psychiatric Hospital, in New Jersey, and the newcomer took to visiting him there. Dylan also became part of a select group that met at the nearby East Orange apartment of Bob Gleason, a friend who was allowed to take Guthrie out on day release. That Dylan so desperately sought to sit at the ailing singer's feet and play for him his own—that is, Woody Guthrie's own—songs suggests that his admiration bordered on sycophantism, and there were some in Greenwich Village who wondered about his motives. Few could say, however, that he was wrong to make the journey.

Dylan's career got its first major boost when he was booked as the opening act for John Lee Hooker's two-week residency at Gerdes Folk City in April, three months after his arrival in town. Terri Thal had taken up an ad hoc role as his manager, and her endorsement might have been enough for Mike Porco. But the restaurant owner, not otherwise well known for his musical expertise, also had been struck by Dylan's manners (and, literally, his hunger) at the Monday night hoots. It was Porco who took Dylan to the AFM's Local 802 and signed as the twenty-year-old's legal guardian, the singer still trumpeting the myth that his parents were dead. Dylan later described Porco as "the Sicilian father that I never had."

The residency at Folk City (which commenced barely forty-eight hours after the "riot" in Washington Square Park) and gigs at other Village venues those first few months only succeeded in dividing the audience, often—though not always—along generational lines. There were many who heard his rasping voice, his staccato harmonica playing, and what he himself called his "incessantly loud strumming," and assumed, as did Oscar Brand, that Dylan was "a pale version of Woody." Indeed, there were few who would deny that Guthrie was Dylan's primary influence. John Cohen of the New Lost

City Ramblers, himself part of the group that met with Guthrie at Gleason's apartment, noted how Dylan "would suddenly swing and throw his head back, and it was something that I'd never seen—except that I'd seen Woody do that in his convulsions. He was reflecting, internalizing, at least in my mind, all these things from Woody."

Dylan's peers better recognized his distinctive qualities. "There was a buzz about him the minute he came to New York," said Happy Traum. "I just *got* it. After listening to Woody Guthrie and Leadbelly and all these people, you weren't put off by a rough voice. And he had this incredible charisma, and he had the phrasing that would send chills up your spine."

"Dylan was absolutely transporting," said Peter Stampfel, a singer and guitarist in downtown Manhattan who would shortly offer his own take on traditional music. "He was an amazing clown. When he had his little hat on [the Huck Finn cap that served as something of an early trademark], he had all these Chaplinesque moves." Twitching nervously, Dylan would hesitate at the microphone as if he had no idea what he was about to say, then issue a one-liner, strum a chord on the guitar, hum a few notes on the harp, readjust it, hum a few more notes, strum the guitar again, issue another seemingly off-the-cuff quip, twitch nervously a little more, and then break into a riveting delivery of a song that would indicate he had been fully in control of his actions all along.

"I'd either drive people away or they'd come in closer to see what it was all about," wrote Dylan in his memoir, *Chronicles*. "There was no in-between. There were a lot of better singers and better musicians around these places but there wasn't anybody close in nature to what I was doing."

What Dylan was doing, in particular, was daring to write his own songs. Folk music had for so long been defined as an oral tradition that very few people on the scene, not even those with record deals, felt the need to come up with their own material. (Besides, as everyone from Alan Lomax through the Weavers and the Kingston Trio was all too aware, you could earn nearly a writer's royalty by claiming copyright on an arrangement of a "traditional" song.) If a singer had even one composition on his or her own album, it was considered a creative achievement. The new arrivals in town—people like Tom Paxton and Bob Dylan—seemed blissfully ignorant of this status quo and set about writing, if not always original melodies, then at least fresh lyrics to old tunes.

Like almost any songwriter, Dylan's initial compositions paid slavish devotion to their influences: the title "Song to Woody" left little room for imagination, although Dylan had the good grace to name Cisco Houston and Sonny Terry and Leadbelly, too. But he proved a quick learner—and an even faster writer. In June 1961, at the Gaslight, Noel Stookey showed Dylan a newspaper story about a boat, the *Hudson Belle*, that should have taken hundreds of picnickers up the Hudson River to Bear Mountain but had ended, at its New York dock, in a dangerous stampede because of overcrowding. "And he brought a song back the next day," recalled Stookey. "Astounding." More to the point, on "Talkin' Bear Mountain Picnic Disaster Blues," Dylan revealed a wicked humor, sing-speaking his way through an imagined account of the tragedy, concluding that in the future he would just "stay in my kitchen . . . have a picnic in my bathroom." If he was still beholden to Woody, he was at least adopting his icon's greatest assets.

Thal took a demo tape of Dylan's up to Cambridge, hoping to get him gigs there, but was rejected. Izzy Young, impressed by Dylan's lyrics as much as by his music, tried shopping him to the obvious independent folk labels: Folkways, Vanguard, Elektra. He, too, was turned down. (It was the first—and last—time he tried getting someone a record deal.) In the meantime, John Hammond at Columbia, frustrated at his failure to sign Joan Baez, acquired Carolyn Hester, who had recently married a Cornell graduate and aspiring writer, Richard Fariña, and fulfilled many of the same criteria, although she was four years older than Baez. In the close-knit world of the Village set, Dylan became fast friends with the newlyweds and, following a successful trip to Cambridge together, where he got to join them onstage at Club 47, was invited to play on Hester's album.

In September of 1961, Porco gave Dylan a second residency at Folk City, opening this time for the Greenbriar Boys. Enter into the picture Robert Shelton, a *New York Times* music critic who had taken to championing the Village music scene. Shelton knew of Dylan, believed in his potential, and wanted to help him—though few expected his review to be quite so glowing, and some wondered at his motives. "A bright new face in folk music," Shelton gushed. "Only 20 years old . . . one of the most distinctive stylists . . . a cross between a choir boy and a beatnik . . . composes new songs faster than he can remember them . . . bursting at the seams with talent."

By a coincidence so perfect it qualified as serendipity, the same week he was playing Folk City at night, Dylan was recording with Hester by day: his jagged harmonica playing on her album's opening cut, "I'll Fly Away," gave it a distinctly raw edge that proved (too) far ahead of its time. Dylan himself later joked that as he greeted Hammond at the studio, he pressed a copy of the *Times* review into the A&R man's hand. Certainly, an impression was made, for "right there in the studio," recalled Hester of what was meant to be her own recording session, "Hammond starts talking about taking Dylan on his own." To what extent Hammond had seen Dylan perform was never fully clarified, but as a former journalist, he knew full well the power of a positive *Times* review, and he signed the singer to Columbia later in October. Barely eight months after arriving in New York City, Dylan had won himself not only the favor of the Village folk scene and that of an influential *New York Times* music critic but also the rarest of trophies: a major label record deal. Fairy tales could scarcely be better plotted.

As produced by Hammond, Dylan's debut album played it safe. There was barely any accompaniment to his voice apart from his guitar and harmonica playing, and the final sequencing of thirteen songs included eleven nonoriginals. One of those, *another* version of "House of the Risin' Sun," reportedly took its jazzy 6/8 arrangement directly from Dave Van Ronk's repertoire. This "theft" caused a temporary rift in the pair's friendship, only soothed when Van Ronk heard the unrefined recording and concluded that it was so bad that it would surely be ignored. Of Dylan's original compositions, "Song to Woody" was, though endearing, easy fodder for the critics. "Talkin' New York" better revealed his inventiveness, Dylan using his harmonica for comically erratic punctuation as he recounted his arrival in New York that past cold winter, the dollar-a-day gigs at coffeehouses, the club owners who told him he sounded like a hillbilly, on to joining the union and getting robbed "with a fountain pen." (This line was a direct steal from Guthrie's "Pretty Boy Floyd.") "Talkin' New York" was placed confidently up front, as the second song on the eponymous album.

Columbia had high hopes for the album, released in the spring of 1962. Joan Baez's second album for Vanguard had touched a national nerve, rising to the top 20 without benefit of significant airplay or a hit single; there appeared to be a market for fresh young folk musicians. The album was packaged accordingly, with a close-up shot of Bob and his guitar, his expressionless face framed by turned-up coat collar and Huck Finn cap; the ragamuffin vagabond of a year earlier now looked more like a well-fed collegiate cherub. Yet upon its release *Bob Dylan* shifted barely five thousand copies. His rise had been rapid. It seemed for a moment that his fall might prove just as swift. Around the hallways of Columbia, they began referring to Dylan as "Hammond's Folly."

Ever since moving his management business to New York from Chicago, where he had run a successful folk club, the Gate of Horn, the ruthlessly ambitious Albert Grossman (who also cofounded the Newport Folk Festival) had dreamed of managing the perfect folk group. Nothing like the Kingston Trio or any of the imitations that had followed that act's lead, his act would be evenly triangulated: one member firmly rooted in the folk tradition, a photogenic female singer in the center, and a comedic element at the far end. Failing to find such an act in the clubs, Grossman set about creating it. An attempt to align Bob Gibson with Carolyn Hester lacked chemistry; Logan English and Dave Van Ronk were approached, but they declined. So Grossman turned to Peter Yarrow, whom he had acquired as a managerial client in 1960 and who had yet to taste major success; together they sought out the necessary female counterpart.

Yarrow found her on the wall of the Folklore Center, where Izzy Young posted photographs of everyone on the local scene. "I saw a picture of Mary [Travers], and I said, 'Who's that?,' because she was just bursting with energy and very beautiful and all that, and Albert said, 'Oh, she's terrific, if you could get her to work.'" Travers, the former Song Swapper, had remained, by her own admission, "terrified" of performing, but she entertained a visit from Yarrow to her apartment. They immediately hit it off and agreed to work together; when it came to finding the third person, the "funny man," they both thought of the Gaslight regular Noel Stookey.

With Stookey agreeing to a name change for reasons of alliteration, Peter, Paul and Mary introduced themselves to the public at Gerdes Folk City, during Yarrow's booking, in the autumn of 1961. They moved straight on to the Bitter End under their group name, where they quickly proved their mettle, establishing the venue as their home base. There was plenty of skepticism about the trio among their peers—folk was not a musical form that generally supported the cold, calculated creation of an act by a business manager—but equal respect for their credentials. Yarrow and Travers were archetypal red diaper babies and, accordingly, dyed-in-the-wool folk fanatics; Stookey was not only funny but could sing, play guitar, and write songs, too. As for the stage performance, what Travers excused as "nervous energy" Stookey correctly noted came off to audience members as "caged intensity." Early in 1962, Grossman bypassed the New York labels and signed Peter, Paul and Mary to the distinctly unproven and still relatively new Warner Brothers company, on the West Coast.

Like the lineup itself, the sequence of songs on Peter, Paul and Mary's eponymous debut album was calculated to cover all bases. There were a few of the trio's own compositions, a children's song, a number written by Van Ronk, and a handful of traditionals. There were also a couple with Pete Seeger's name on them: "If I Had a Hammer," which had been written for the Foley Square Twelve, and "Where Have All the Flowers Gone?," which Seeger had written over the course of several years, integrating extra verses gathered from the children at Camp Woodland. In the process, it had become a disarmingly powerful antiwar ballad—and a current top 30 hit for the Kingston Trio.

On the surface, Peter, Paul and Mary was all lightness and love: musical director Milt Okun spread the trio's harmonies evenly across the stereo spectrum (relevant only to those who had the new stereo record players, of course), while keeping their playing simple and restrained, unencumbered by orchestras or drums. (In deliberate contrast to this pastoral sound, the cover shot for Peter, Paul and Mary portrayed the trio leaning against a brick wall at the Bitter End.) Radio stations quickly warmed to the act, jumping on its updated version of "The Lemon Tree," giving the trio a top 40 hit and propelling the album onto the charts. Perhaps, in the wake of both the Kingston Trio and Joan Baez, and allowing for Grossman's meticulous management, this was to be expected. What could not have been anticipated was the enthusiasm with which the radio stations then adopted "If I Had a Hammer." The song that the Weavers had never recorded for Decca because of its political content became a top ten hit in the autumn of 1962, and suddenly the whole country was singing about "love between my brothers and my sisters, all over this land."

Along the way, "If I Had a Hammer" became part of the civil rights movement's soundtrack. So, too, did "We Shall Overcome," the popularization of which told a cultural story of its own, as it mutated from a southern gospel number "I Will Overcome," through use on a picket line of South Carolina tobacco farms in the 1940s, to adoption by the Highlander Folk School, where Pete Seeger (a regular visitor ever since his cross-country travels with Woody Guthrie) picked it up, added extra lines, and changed the title word "Will" to the softer vowel "Shall." In the meantime, a fellow folk traveler of Seeger's, the Californian Guy Carawan, became the Highlander's musical director, spreading the revised song by playing it at every civil rights gathering he subsequently attended.

There was no shortage of such events as, from Rosa Parks and the Montgomery bus boycott to the Little Rock Nine, the issue of racial integration came to dominate the news. In 1957, Dr. Martin Luther King Jr. helped found the Southern Christian Leadership Conference (SCLC) in Atlanta; in 1960, the SCLC itself gave birth to a youth group, the Student Nonviolent Coordinating Committee (SNCC). It was at the founding meeting of SNCC, when Guy Carawan played "We Shall Overcome" as always, that the entire body of attendees spontaneously stood up and linked arms—and the civil rights movement found its anthem.

Carawan also proved instrumental in bringing the urban folk singers of the North to visit and sing at the civil rights battlegrounds of the South. Gil Turner and his group the New World Singers, which included the black female vocalist Dolores Dixon, were among the first to travel to Mississippi, forming an alliance with SNCC and its Freedom Singers. The suddenly rejuvenated relevance of the old workers' ballads and campfire songs had a galvanizing impact on Greenwich Village folkies, who were now inspired to write protest numbers anew when they weren't otherwise engaged in all-night drinking and singing sessions.

It was a hedonistic, hectic, halcyon period, civil rights issues notwithstanding. Musicians were flocking to the Village from all over—like the newly married Ian and Sylvia Tyson from Toronto, and Phil Ochs from Ohio. (Both acts would become Grossman clients.) At some point in 1962, Dave Van Ronk noticed that two-thirds of his playing friends were from outside New York— and later concluded that they were hungrier than the homegrown players. The influx of newcomers raised the bar to the extent that the younger John Hammond, the A&R man's son who had taken up playing folk blues, left town in 1961, to get his chops together away from the prying eyes and ears of his peers.

Throughout this period, three Village venues remained preeminent: Folk City, especially for its Monday hoots; the Bitter End, all the more so once Peter, Paul and Mary made it famous; and the Gaslight, the cognoscenti's club. No alcohol was served at this tiny basement venue, with its dangerously low ceiling and double entrance either side of the stoop above it, but patrons often brought their own liquor and, according to Van Ronk, marijuana. After a typically exuberant night of poetry and folk, many of its patrons and most of the performers headed next door to the Kettle of Fish, where hard-drinking musicians from all over the Village gathered for gossip. At closing time, the elite on the scene would retire to Van Ronk and Thal's apartment on Waverly Place for poker and yet more drinking.

In such a charged environment, newcomers like Paxton, Dylan, and Ochs grasped that fortune had put them at the vanguard of a new songwriters' movement, and they were determined not to waste the opportunity. "It was collegial and competitive at the same time," said Paxton. "I don't recall ever hearing anybody do something brilliant and thinking, 'Goddamn it, I hate him.'" Paxton found himself influenced by Van Ronk's and Dylan's both singing the traditional song "He Was a Friend of Mine." "I just thought it was such a beautiful song. And it was only about a month later, in between shows, I wrote 'Rambling Boy,' and that turned out to be my take on it. The lyric was totally unalike, and so was the melody. But it was that feeling. And that type of thing would happen—if you were receptive." "Rambling Boy," a more rounded composition than many of the folk numbers that informed it, helped establish Paxton's reputation as one of the finest new writers on the scene and a true all-rounder: during this same period he also wrote the enduring children's song "Goin' to the Zoo" and simultaneously drew inspiration from his Army days for "The Willing Conscript."

Phil Ochs was never so multidimensional. He had left Ohio State in a fury, one semester short of graduation, when passed over for editorship of the student newspaper because of his strident political views. Arriving in the Village, he fell in with the unreconstructed leftists of the Communist days at *Broadside*, a paper launched early in 1962 by Sis Cunningham and Gordon Freisen, both now in their fifties, as an outlet for the new, politically charged songs. Ochs wrote an editorial for the magazine headed "The Need for Topical Music" and complaining of the hit parade's obsession with romance: "If the powers that be absolutely insist that love should control the market, at least they should be more realistic and give divorce songs an equal chance." Ochs did not write a song about divorcing the (pregnant) girlfriend he had only just married at City Hall, but blunt folk anthems like "The Power and the Glory" and "Where There's a Will, There's a Way" assured attention from among his peers.

On April 16, 1962, just after the release of his debut album, Dylan publicly introduced one of his own new songs, and it would itself prove almost as popular and enduring a civil rights anthem as "We Shall Overcome." He had been working on it for a while: David Cohen, another of the Village insiders (later known as David Blue), recalled spending that afternoon accompanying Dylan on guitar as the writer honed the song lyrics for its debut performance. That evening, in the basement of Gerdes Folk City during the hootenanny interval, Dylan played the completed composition, "Blowin' in the Wind," to Gil Turner, the Monday night host. A crowd circled around the couple, and its conclusion was met by stunned silence. Turner asked if he could play the song in public, then and there. Dylan acquiesced, showed the MC the chords, gave him a copy of the lyrics, and Turner bounded upstairs to launch the second half of the show. "When he was through," recalled Blue, "the entire audience stood on its feet and cheered."

Word spread rapidly through the Village grapevine: Dylan had written a classic. The fact that the melody was taken from a nineteenth-century Negro spiritual, "No More Auction Block" (which Dylan often played at the time, as if inviting comparison), mattered not, for there seemed to be a finite number of tunes and chord changes to accompany a folk stanza. The English language itself was far broader, and "Blowin' in the Wind" drew on symbolism from the ages, raising questions that weaved between mountains and seas to ultimately ask, "How many years can some people exist / Before they're allowed to be free?" In this sense, it was clearly a civil rights song, ripe for the times; and yet Dylan seemed to have already learned that topical songs could enjoy longevity if they maintained mystery. As he wrote in *Chronicles*, "What I did to break away was to take simple folk changes and put new imagery and attitude to them, use catchphrases and metaphor combined with a new set of ordinances that evolved into something different that had not been heard before." "Blowin' in the Wind" did all that and more, even though Dylan would later dismiss it as "one-dimensional."

Gil Turner was doubling as an editor for *Broadside*, where he helped make "Blowin' in the Wind" the cover song for the very next issue, published in late May. Just a few weeks later, Dylan recorded it for his second album, and then . . . silence of sorts. Onlookers could be forgiven for thinking that the young poet's career had been put on hold. As it turned out, events were under way behind the scenes that would guarantee his subsequent success. Most prominent among them was the hiring, in June 1962, of Albert Grossman as manager. Other than trying to wrangle Dylan away from Columbia (the singer had been under twenty-one when he signed to the label, but Hammond was not easily cowed by Grossman and the contract held), the manager's first objective was to establish Dylan the songwriter before moving forward with Dylan the singer. At that point, it was still not accepted that a man of music could be both.

To that end, Grossman gave an acetate of "Blowin' in the Wind," to the musical director Milt Okum, who had the Chad Mitchell Trio include it on an album released in March 1963. (The first to actually record it, apart from Dylan, were Turner's New World Singers, for a *Broadside* compilation that was not released until later in the year.) That album passed by relatively unnoticed—which was good news for Peter, Paul and Mary, still sufficiently connected to the Village grapevine to have caught the buzz on Dylan. "I thought 'Blowin' in the Wind' was just about the best song I could have imagined at the time," said Yarrow years later. Recording it with their typical clarity, ensuring that no word could pass misunderstood, the trio released it as a single in the summer of 1963, ahead of their third album.

Peter, Paul and Mary were, at this point, arguably the most successful recording act in the country: their debut album was still riding high in the charts (where it would reside for three and a half years), their second album, (*Moving*), had gone straight to number two on release in early 1963, with "Puff, the Magic Dragon," Yarrow's allegoric ballad about youth and myth, matching it in the singles charts. "Blowin' in the Wind" now climbed rapidly to the same position, and the name Bob Dylan began being spoken in reverent tones from campus to street to radio station and boardroom.

Indeed, in 1963, folk became the new national music movement, vindicating all those years of Village-centered preservation and protest. Events got off to a celebratory start when Erik Darling's new group, the Rooftop Singers, topped the charts with "Walk Right In" on Vanguard. An old "jug band" number that dated back to the 1920s, the single was notable for its use of twelve-string guitars, which had gone so far out of fashion since Leadbelly's day that Darling and his fellow guitarist Bill Svanoe had to have a pair built on commission by the Gibson company. The song's other standout ingredient was the vocalist Lynne Taylor, an experienced jazz singer, "the difference between Elizabethan ballads and gospel," as Darling put it. "She sang more from the crotch, and the girl folksingers were singing from the very top of their heads. They weren't even down to their nipples."

That spring, ABC launched the TV show *Hootenanny*, milking two dominant youth movements by visiting a different college campus each week to host folk groups in concert. But when the *New York Times* noted Pete Seeger's continued absence from its lineup, suggesting that the old "Red Channels" black list was still in operation, the core members of the Village scene all boycotted *Hootenanny* unless Seeger, who had been signed to Columbia by John Hammond in the interim, was booked. He was not, and the lack of credible artists soon turned *Hootenanny* into a network joke (albeit one with high ratings). Dylan went a step further: in May, as his second album, *The Freewheelin' Bob Dylan*, was finally released, he was booked onto Ed Sullivan's TV show on CBS. At the last minute he was denied permission to sing "Talkin' John Birch Paranoid Blues," his wry poke at the whole "Reds under the beds" witch hunt. Dylan walked out in disgust, and the move did his integrity no harm at all.

The Weavers seized the moment to stage another Carnegie Hall reunion, bringing back not just Seeger but those who had taken his place: Erik Darling, Frank Hamilton, and Bernie Krause. Paxton's "Rambling Boy" was included in the set, and it gained an additional boost when the concert was (inevitably) released by Vanguard as a souvenir album. Seeger recorded a solo show at Carnegie Hall a month later for what would prove his most successful album, *We Shall Overcome*, which helped popularize not just the title track but Paxton's "What Did You Learn in School Today?" and two songs by Bob Dylan. One, "Who Killed Davey Moore?," he had written about the featherweight champion who died following a major boxing bout, introducing it at a Town Hall concert just eighteen days after the fight. It served as excellent evidence of his abilities as a topical songwriter. The other song, the apocalyptic "A Hard Rain's A-Gonna Fall," was assumed by many to be of the same ilk, as a reference to the Cuban missile crisis of late 1962 that brought the world to the brink of nuclear war. It had in fact been doing the rounds of the Village for longer than that already—which revealed the advantage of writing in metaphors. More so than any other number he had yet composed, "A Hard Rain's A-Gonna Fall" became celebrated for its poetic depth, inspiring almost religious reverence for a figure who, at that point, could still be seen propping up the neighborhood bars most nights.

In July of that year, Paxton, Ochs, and Ian and Sylvia were introduced at the Newport Folk Festival, where Dylan closed out the main stage with Joan Baez, Peter, Paul and Mary, and the Freedom Singers, who joined him to sing "Blowin' in the Wind." And then came the movement's crowning moment. On August 28, 1963, a twenty-two-year-old Dylan stood at the Lincoln Memorial in Washington, D.C., alongside Joan Baez, Peter, Paul and Mary, Odetta, Harry Belafonte, Josh White, Sammy Davis Jr.—and Dr. Martin Luther King Jr., who gave his "I Have a Dream" speech in front of a quarter of a million people. The march and its speeches were televised live by CBS, allowing the nation to see and hear not only the speeches of civil rights leaders and activists alike but these songs of the Greenwich Village folk movement: "If I Had a Hammer," "We Shall Overcome," and "Blowin' in the Wind."

Such consistent and credible exposure guaranteed success for *The Freewheelin' Bob Dylan,* the cover of which became an enduring image of Village cool: Dylan and his girlfriend Suze Rotolo, huddled tight, walking arm in arm down a snow-covered Jones Street, a stone's throw from Dylan's apartment at 161 West Fourth Street. The album itself was no less iconic, serving as the declaration of a new folk movement, one in which the singers wrote their own songs. Dylan offered up a dozen of them, of which "Don't Think Twice, It's Alright" and "Blowin' in the Wind" were already perfectly proven as top ten hits for Peter, Paul and Mary, and "Masters of War," "A Hard Rain's A-Gonna Fall," and "Talkin' World War III Blues" suggested themselves as arguably the most overtly socially conscious songs—of any genre—to be released on an album since the days of *Songs for John Doe* and *Southern Exposure.* Dylan would have his share of detractors; but most everyone could agree that he was shifting the musical landscape, proving that one *could* be both a singer and a songwriter—and even something of a spokesman, too. Fully aware of this role, and brimming with confidence, on "Talkin' Bob Dylan Blues" he threw a barb at the midtown hit factories, just two miles uptown from Greenwich Village.

"Unlike most of the songs nowadays that are being written uptown in Tin Pan Alley," he stated, "this is written somewhere down in the United States."

IO

CRYSTALS, ANGELS, AND RAINDROPS

n the spring of 1960, Jerry Leiber, who was about as close as anyone to being King of Tin Pan Alley at the time, had a favor called in by Lester Sill, a Los Angeles power broker who had helped with his and Mike Stoller's early career. "I've got this real crank of a crazy thing here," Sill told him. "He's really very talented, he's dying to come hang out with you and Stoller. . . . Do a man a favor, bring him in and show him how to make records."

The "crazy thing" was Phil Spector, and he knew New York already, having been born and raised in the Bronx. But after his father committed suicide, when Phil was eight, his mother had moved him and his sister out to California, hoping for a fresh start. At Fairfax High—Leiber's old alma mater—the asthmatic, insecure, but keenly intelligent and quick-witted boy found himself at odds with the body-beautiful Californian teenage culture. He took refuge in music, forming, writing songs for, and playing guitar in a trio called the Teddy Bears, and in late 1958, at only the second attempt, they scored a number one single. Set at the 6/8 ballad pace, the sentimental vocals were sung by a neighborhood girl, the title cribbed from the words engraved on his father's tomb stone: "To Know Him Is to Love Him." Spector was seventeen years old at the time.

For various reasons—personality had a lot to do with it—the Teddy Bears were a one-hit wonder, but Spector had no intention of giving up on music as a career. If anything, he wanted to get deeper inside it, work his way into the middle of the business, establish himself as not just another teenage sideman but, as Tom Wolfe would famously put it several years later, as a

Tycoon of Teen instead. And so Spector befriended and then leaned on Lester Sill to find him a new role. Arriving in New York, he took up residence at Leiber and Stoller's office, bringing his considerable guitar skills to their many recording sessions while consistently begging to write with them, which was tantamount to asking a happily married couple if he could sleep with them. Leiber found Spector "not very likable," but "extremely talented," and finally put aside an evening for the three of them to compose. Spector seized the moment: he and Leiber completed "Spanish Harlem" before Stoller could even finish his dinner and join them.

"Spanish Harlem" became a top ten hit for Ben E. King in early 1961, and Spector soon had a number of personal production credits to his résumé, among them a cover of the Lewis Lymon song "I'm So Happy" by the vocal act the Ducanes for yet *another* Goldner label, Goldisc. Yet Spector was never really comfortable working in the male vocal harmony genre, which he may rightly have seen as a sound on the way out. When he produced the Mann-Kolber song "I Love How You Love Me" for the Paris Sisters, however . . . Perhaps it was the softness of the girls' voices that afforded him the artistic license, for he overdubbed strings onto the vocals and instrumental track, a process unheard of at the time, and it helped take the song into the top five. He then parlayed his success with the Paris Sisters into a label deal financed by Sill—Philles, a play on their first names, like Aldon Music—and sought out exclusively female artists. Thanks in large part to his efforts (and those of Berry Gordy in Detroit), "girl groups" would become the dominant sound of the next few years.

The singers themselves grew to hate that term, complaining that the words "girl group" pigeonholed half the human race into one musical genre. Truth is, the "girl group" genre was every bit as rooted in a time (the early sixties) and space (the gap between rock 'n' roll and rock music) as had been the male harmony groups of the later fifties that helped turn rhythm and blues into rock 'n' roll in the first place. And yet, as author Gerri Hirshey noted, "there was nothing homogenized about the lyrics or the looks of these singers. Girl groups sold well because they were the ultimate variety pack, with something for all tastes. And like the best pop music, girl group songs— those $2^1/_2$ minute passion plays—found endless ways to conjugate that troublesome verb *to love*."

Exulting from coast to coast in their vocal and lyrical freedom, the girl groups were a generational phenomenon rather than a regional one. And yet New York turned out more such acts than any other city in the world, Detroit included. This disproportionate claim on the genre had its roots in the city's reputation as the primary source for male vocal groups (which many New York girls then set out to emulate) and in its status at the center of the music industry. For, as had been the case in the fifties, it was cheaper for the industry to hire groups of local high school teens than set off on cross-country scouting trips. To that end, the girls would have no more contractual rights or songwriting credits than the male groups that preceded them, and there would be ample tales of duplicity and poverty to keep the courts busy for decades to come. The difference was that, while the male groups of the fifties had been hired and fired by independent record labels, the girls of the sixties were controlled primarily by independent *producers*—people who took enormous pride in their work, ensuring that the girl group recordings were not just more polished and sophisticated than their male antecedents but frequently served to break new musical ground. That was in large part due to the songs themselves: whereas some R&B labels had made their fortunes on male vocal groups' original tunes quickly bolstered with a cowrite by a label boss (or a "disc jockey"), most producers placed absolute priority on securing the right song to begin with. (Sexism masquerading as tradition surely played a part in the fact that just about none of the singers ever wrote their own songs.) Some of these songs were certainly candy-coated to the point of excess, but as fans of the genre—and they were legion—would readily agree, that didn't stop them from aspiring to art.

By the spring of 1961, the Shirelles were on their third top ten hit in just six months, and the market was clearly ready for more such music. Phil Spector found himself perfectly placed to help provide it. His first act on Philles, the Crystals, came from Brooklyn, where they had been carefully assembled by a former bandleader, Benny Wells (who recruited his niece, Barbara Alston, initially as a background singer), and a local songwriter, Leroy Bates (who added his sister-in-law, Pat Wright, and after whose baby daughter the group was named). By the time Wells and Bates brought the Crystals up to the Brill Building and the attention of the publishers Hill &

Range, it was with a Bates composition, "There's No Other," that Spector, hired to produce it as a demo, instantly heard as a possible hit.

In an early sign of his perfectionist nature, Spector rehearsed the Crystals fastidiously, slowing the song—with Alston, reluctantly, on lead—until it was a 6/8 ballad bordering on a dirge, a throwback in pace to the song that had started it all, the Chantels' "Maybe." But he recorded it in midtown Manhattan in June 1961—three of the girls coming straight from their prom at Commercial High School for Girls in East New York—"There's No Other" looked forward in style: the production included a semisung introduction, and Spector treated both the chorus and the string section with a heavier touch than was typical of the era. Hill & Range were furious when they discovered that Spector had signed the Crystals to his Philles label and promptly fired him as a house producer. With "There's No Other (Like My Baby)" taking both label and act straight into the top 20 early in 1962, Spector, who had secured himself a cowriting credit on both sides of the single, could hardly have cared.

Yet, as with Florence Greenberg and the Shirelles, Spector did not want to rely on the Crystals' original composer, or even his own proven talents, for a follow-up: the stigma of the one-hit wonder was too great to risk upon such hubris. He could hardly raid the closet at Hill & Range, and Leiber and Stoller were none too happy about Philles, either. ("He should have, by right, just in terms of the way we behaved and helped him and started him, invited us in," said Leiber.) And so Spector beat a path to Aldon Music, where he was offered a song called "Uptown," which had an alluring complexity similar to that of "Spanish Harlem," exuding the steaminess of a sweltering summer night on the stoop. Yet the words to "Uptown" were not so simplistic as most of the lyrics on offer. They spoke of a lover who labored all day downtown as a "little man," after which he came home to the singer's uptown tenement—where rents were low and he was "king." They were the work of Cynthia Weil, the music was by her partner, Barry Mann, and between them, the song "broke a barrier," as Mann put it, for being "different than what was being written before."

This was true, to some extent. Yet "Uptown" was not entirely successful as a tale of class and/or race; Weil's upbringing was too evident in the patronizing (and, in the case of New York's Harlem, historically inaccurate) observation that folks uptown "don't have to pay much rent." But the intent was noble, and practice would soon enough make perfect for Mann and Weil. In the meantime, Spector matched its lyrical ambition with a grandiose arrangement that included flamenco guitar, castanets, smoothly cascading strings, a wistful lead delivery by Barbara Alston, and distant but resonant harmonies from the other Crystals. Though it was not a hit on the scale of "Will You Love Me Tomorrow," which it resembled in both words and music, "Uptown" improved on "There's No Other," coming close to the top ten, ensuring that Spector would be recognized as a genuine hit maker. It didn't do Aldon Music any harm, either.

At the point that "Uptown" made the charts in the spring of 1962, the average age of Goffin, King, Mann, and Weil—rapidly defining themselves as the most consistently adventurous and successful songwriters in America—was just twenty-two. Their Aldon boss, Kirshner, was only twenty-six—and yet that small age gap made all the difference. "I was their mentor, father, doctor, friend, psychiatrist," said Kirshner, and the writers were inclined to agree with at least some of this self-serving assessment.

"We wanted to satisfy our father figure, Don Kirshner, even though he was only three or four years older than us," said Mann. "Truthfully it was a very unhealthy atmosphere to grow up in if you wanted to grow up. Because all we cared about was getting the next record, and if we didn't get the next record we were depressed. If Carole and Gerry got the next record instead, we were even *more* depressed. That was our lives."

Kirshner encouraged this competition, relentlessly playing the couples off against each other. Mann and Weil's first hit, "Bless You" for Tony Orlando, had come right on the heels of Goffin and King's own hit for the teenager, and with the Crystals, those roles were now reversed, with a Goffin-King song chosen to follow "Uptown." And not just any Goffin-King song. "He Hit Me (And It Felt Like a Kiss)," as the title made emphatically clear, was a harrowing tale of physical abuse and the girls who put up with it. The Crystals were appalled: Barbara Alston called it "absolutely, positively the one record that none of us liked." Sill was equally horrified. He demanded to know why Spector insisted on releasing it, and recalled being told "that he himself pictured himself doing that shit." The single ran into a wall of not so much controversy as revulsion, especially from radio, and Spector, though seemingly surprised at the reaction, withdrew it rather than risk damaging his reputation. Perhaps he was not invincible, after all.

King and Goffin had overstepped the boundaries of acceptable taste with "He Hit Me," but at least they were writing from experience—that of their babysitter, Eva Boyd, who had shown up at their apartment "all black and blue," as Goffin recalled, but insisted of her physically abusive boyfriend, "He really loves me." Boyd had recently moved to Brooklyn from North Carolina, where she found the babysitter job via her friend Earl-Jean McRae of the Cookies, one of only a few black students to attend Abraham Lincoln High. A group of Coney Island–based studio singers whose history extended back to Ray Charles (he poached their original lead for his Raelettes), the Cookies had released some Sedaka/Greenfield–composed singles on Atlantic, but they hadn't charted, and Aldon Music kept them busy singing lead both on its writers' demos—recordings that could be sent out to prospective hit artists—and on master recordings, backing up the likes of Sedaka, Tony Orlando, and Connie Francis.

Eva Boyd, no mean singer herself, joined the Cookies on many of these sessions, and when Goffin and King—who could do silly songs as easily as lyrics of conscience—wrote "The Loco-Motion" as their take on the current craze for dance anthems, they hired the eighteen-year-old babysitter to sing the lead on the demo, the other Cookies chug-chugging the chorus along behind her. Boyd's sassy delivery so captured the spirit of the song that all involved stopped to wonder whether they hadn't made a definitive recording already. The timing (as well as the musical rhythm) turned out to be perfect, for Kirshner and Nevins had just established their own record label—a not entirely ambitious King as flagship artist—the better to maximize the profits generated by their songwriters. Duly released with a minimum of overdubs, "The Loco-Motion" gave the new Dimension imprint an immediate number one hit. In fact, it dislodged Sedaka's "Breaking Up Is Hard to Do" from the top of the charts in August 1962—affording the Cookies the rare honor of going unaccredited as singers on two successive number one singles, adding to the number of Abraham Lincoln alumni to top the charts, and enabling Aldon Music to reap its sixth number one single in three years.

"The Loco-Motion" 's success aside, Goffin and King continued to write songs of romantic confrontation, as was evident from the songs they now foisted on the Cookies, who were rapidly unleashed as Dimension's own response to the Shirelles and Crystals. First up was "Chains," which viewed love as a tie that binds, and which charted top 20; fast on its heels was the cheerfully confrontational "Don't Say Nothing Bad about My Baby," on which McRea warned her nemesis, "Girl, you better shut your mouth." The girl singers were not only becoming more prominent; they were toughening up. There would soon be an extraordinary irony to "Don't Say Nothing Bad about My Baby." In the fall of 1963, Gerry Goffin went on tour with the Cookies and embarked on an affair with Earl-Jean McRae that resulted in an out-of-wedlock, mixed-race baby. Understandably, the affair was kept quiet, and in public, at least, Carole King stuck by her man.

As a singer, the New Yorker Gene Pitney had worked already with Phil Spector, who produced his minor hit "Every Breath I Take." As a songwriter, he was so riveted by the Crystals' "Uptown" that he sat down to compose what he hoped would be its follow-up, complete with soaring bridge section and appropriate "outsider" lyrics. Spector heard Pitney's song, "He's a Rebel," and agreed. Working at a pace that distinguished him even from his fast-moving competitors (Pitney's publisher sold the song to another record company at the same time), Spector rushed out to California: he had decided to abandon Mira Sound in Manhattan for Gold Star studios in Los Angeles, not only for its unique echo, but to escape the AFM's Local 802 and its enforcement of the rules against overdubbing. (From now on, Spector would bounce back and forth between the two cities, typically picking up songs in New York that he would record in Los Angeles.)

As it turned out, on the session for "He's a Rebel," which marked the true flowering of what would become his "wall of sound," Spector cared less about overdubs than doubling up—demanding, as an unprecedented example, that two bass guitars play in unison. Recorded without the strings that Pitney had initially imagined (as had just about every midtown composer since the Drifters' "There Goes My Baby"), "He's a Rebel" instead relied on a boogie piano and a wild sax break as a throwback to the urgent rhythm and blues sounds of the fifties. And yet just as the sheer weight of the instruments heralded a new sound, so did the full-throttled lead vocal performance and meticulously harmonized backing vocals, which were much more aggressive than anything the girl groups had recorded before, the Crystals among them.

That was partly because the recording didn't feature the Crystals' voices. At Gold Star, Spector used LA's equivalent of the Cookies, the session group the Blossoms, and their lead singer, Darlene Wright, instead. Given that "He's a Rebel" became a number one hit, the wisdom of Spector's decision could not be second-guessed. But for the Crystals, of course, the experience proved painfully embarrassing, all the more so as they knew nothing about it until they heard the song on the radio, while on tour.

The girl group lifestyle was certainly problematic. Not only could producers like Spector take their name in vanity, but women ran the risk of getting pregnant if they lived out enough of the lyrics. And nobody but nobody was going to entertain the sight of a pregnant teenager singing on the package shows of the era. Fortunately for the Crystals, when such an incident befell Myrna Thomas early in their recording career, they were able to quickly replace her with fifteen-year-old Dolores "La La" Brooks, who had been raised singing gospel in the neighborhood. Better yet, said Barbara Alston, Brooks was "what we wanted—a lead singer. I was ecstatic to say the least." Spector was less impressed, said Alston. "He didn't like her voice for some reason and he kept coming back to me."

Brooks confirmed as much. "I didn't excite him at first, because he came from the Teddy Bears," she said. Spector seemed so uncertain how to handle a powerful singer raised on gospel that he initially placed Brooks a few feet behind the others in the studio. Onstage, however, where Spector was nowhere to be seen, and audiences required energy, it was a different story. "If Barbara would come out singing 'There's No Other (Like My Baby)' at the Apollo they would just look at us," said Brooks, who took to the front of stage instead, "with a big voice singing 'Ol' Man River.' " Brooks's voice enabled the Crystals to cover for themselves onstage on "He's a Rebel"—and again, when Spector used Darlene Wright for its follow-up, a Mann-Weil song called "He's Sure the Boy I Love."

Somewhere in the midst of all this, Spector finally came to understand what the girls had been trying to tell him—that La La Brooks was now their lead singer. Upon which, acting with typical haste, he made up for lost time by flying the fifteen-year-old out to Los Angeles, where he had only just recorded Darlene Wright and the Blossoms singing what was to be the next

Crystals single. Brooks now reclaimed the Crystals name for their Brooklyn hometown, replacing that lead vocal on a song called "Da Doo Ron Ron," and with it began a new chapter in the girl group saga.

Thirty miles east of Manhattan, the first generation of children raised in the former potato fields of the original Levittown suburb had been coming of age. And though there were no black kids among them—William Levitt had said he "could not take a chance on admitting Negroes" when he launched the Long Island community out of nothing in 1948—they turned out to be just as infatuated with rock 'n' roll as the kids in the city. Such was the case with Ellie Greenwich, born in Brooklyn in 1940 and moved out to Levittown at age eleven by her Catholic father and Jewish mother, where she grew up on the corner of the idyllically named Starlight and Springtime Lanes. Like her future songwriting peers in southern Brooklyn, her musical tastes were forever changed by WINS's 50,000 watts of power. (Specifically, by the Penguins' "Earth Angel": "I thought I had died and gone to heaven when I heard that.") By her midteens Greenwich had formed her own vocal group, the Jivettes, and chosen to play the accordion, on which she soon began writing songs. Her first effort typified the absolute clarity of purpose that would mark her later, more famous compositions. Written for her high school crush, it was named "The Moment I Saw You."

After the owner of the record store in neighboring Hicksville recommended her to friends at RCA, a seventeen-year-old Greenwich, under the name Ellie Gaye, recorded and released "Cha-Cha-Charming," another sign of the easygoing wordplay for which she would become renowned. It was no more a hit than King's or Mann's first records. Greenwich went to college and embarked on a teaching career, which lasted all of three and a half weeks before she decided, as she put it, "Naah, I gotta try music. I'll always have this to fall back on." A blond bombshell with a vivacious personality to match, she easily secured a few appointments at the Brill Building. Jerry Leiber liked what he heard, partnered her up with the male writer Tony Powers, and offered the pair a "first refusal" contract, meaning that anything he and Mike Stoller decided not to use for their own Trio Music the couple were free to take elsewhere.

So, when Leiber and Stoller rejected "(Today I Met) The Boy I'm Going to Marry," she and Powers, knowing that it was too good to waste, took it to Aaron Schroeder, the publisher who had just supplied Spector with Pitney's "He's a Rebel." Schroeder played it for the producer, who promptly used it as the official coming-out single for Darlene Wright (as Darlene Love). And that was about as far as the Powers-Greenwich writing partnership went. For Greenwich had already met the boy she was going to marry—and write her future songs with, too.

Other than hailing from Brooklyn and being Jewish, Jeff Adelberg had nothing in common with Mann, King, Sedaka, Shuman, and company. His childhood was a tale of crushing hardship, moving out to New Jersey at age seven when his parents divorced, and back to Flatbush four years later—almost exactly the time his future wife, Ellie Greenwich, left the neighborhood—where he lived in a one-room apartment with his mother, his mentally disturbed sister, and his grandfather. There was no room for a piano in that apartment, and no money for it even if there had been. Music came courtesy of a donated turntable—"with a needle that was more like a nail," he recalled—and some big band 78s. His memory of forming a vocal group at Erasmus Hall High, the oldest public school in America, was similarly inscribed with that of his poverty: "Doo-wop is making music if you have nothing to make music with."

Adelberg made it through school and went on to the publicly funded City College to study industrial design. But, convinced that he could sing, he called his one family connection in the music business—and found himself sitting across from the powerful Arnold Shaw at EB Marks Music. Shaw thought Adelberg might be better suited as a writer and partnered him up with Ben Raleigh. From then on, said Adelberg, who changed his pen name to Jeff Barry, "I never had to struggle. Before I knew it, we had a big hit." That hit was 1960's "Tell Laura I Love Her," a wryly written "death" song, as was the craze at the time. (So too was cowboy chic, which Barry, tall and ruggedly handsome, was able to carry off in his dress and demeanor; the original lyric for "Laura" was set in a rodeo.) The song went top ten in America, and number one in the United Kingdom; Shaw rewarded Barry with a $50 increase in salary to $125. "I used to give my mother most of my money, I didn't really need it," recalled the writer. "[That week,] I gave her another fifty dollars. And the look on her face was, did you rob a bank?"

With a hit song behind him, Barry found himself in demand. An offer to manage Bobby Darin's publishing company in Los Angeles proved less alluring than one from Leiber and Stoller to come to the top of the Brill Building and write at Trio Music, all the better as it put him in company with his girlfriend Greenwich, whom he had met at a Thanksgiving dinner hosted by mutual friends. After divorcing his first wife, Jeff married Ellie in late 1962, and the newlyweds started churning out hits at a rate unmatched in New York in the 1960s—even by their married competitors across the road at 1650 Broadway.

For the first year after their marriage, the couple was joined at the hip—in all senses of the word—with Phil Spector, a process that got under way in early 1963 with the Crystals' "Da Doo Ron Ron." It was an archetypal example of their output, for the songs of Jeff Barry and Ellie Greenwich eschewed the (relative) social commentary and Broadway arrangements of those Aldon writers for topics that suited their own newlywed personalities: deliriously dizzy pronouncements of love, loyalty, lust, and—on those rare occasions when their artists, almost entirely female-fronted, needed a change of tack—loss, too. The tunes tended to be similarly upbeat, and none the worse for it. Barry and Greenwich wrote not only some of the most blatantly commercial songs of the sixties but some of the most enduring, too.

For La La Brooks, who recalled that Spector kept her singing through the night in the studio without feeding her, and that he even kept his own mother waiting in the hallway for hours on end when she showed up with sandwiches for him, the experience was less glamorous than it seemed. "Phil didn't care about nobody but Phil," she said. And yet she knew that the performances appeared to justify the means: on both the frenetically simplistic "Da Doo Ron Ron" (a number three hit) and then its epic follow-up "Then He Kissed Me" (number six), Spector wrangled from her an almost frightening combination of fragility and ferocity, while doubling up on studio musicians at an unprecedented rate until the vast conglomeration of instruments (complete with string sections that came on now more like a chorus of electric guitars) could barely be isolated by the listener, but instead had to be digested as a raging, roaring, hormonal whole.

The partnership between Spector, Greenwich, and Barry provided nine consecutive A-sides for the Philles label, the run with which the wall of sound gained its name. Barry never questioned Spector's one-third share of all these hits, most of which were written at Spector's East Side apartment:

"If someone said to me, 'You have to write a hit song this afternoon or you will die, *but* you can call someone to cowrite it,' I would call Phil Spector."

That's what the Ronettes did when they ran out of options: call Phil Spector. That they were just teenagers and had never met him made no difference: though they faced many hurdles on their path to the top, lack of self-confidence was not one of them. Nor did they have to worry about their appeal to the boys, thanks to sisters Veronica and Estelle Bennett's exotic mulatto look, the result of a half-black, half-Cherokee mother and a white father. It was alluring enough that, a few weeks after Lewis Lymon attended Veronica's thirteenth birthday party, his brother Frankie, then at the peak of his popularity and the idol of the local streets, came around to the Bennett home on West 149th Street. Barely fourteen years old himself, Lymon hit on Ronnie—as most people called her once she was in her teens—who recalled that he smelled of drink. She recognized the aroma from her alcoholic father, a jazz drummer who never got over his lack of success and who had recently split from the family, and soon showed Lymon the door.

The disarming experience didn't dampen the Bennett girls' enthusiasm for singing the Teenagers' "Why Do Fools Fall in Love" on Amateur Night at the Apollo. With their younger cousin Nedra Talley rounding out the trio, a supportive Mrs. Bennet afforded them singing lessons in midtown. Hanging around the coffeeshops near the Brill Building, they were talent-spotted (looks-spotted might be more appropriate) by a small-time scout who secured them a successful audition with Col-Pix Records. Named Ronnie and the Relatives, they emerged on record, backed with a steady beat, nearly a symphony orchestra of strings, and the songs "I Want a Boy" and "What's So Sweet about Sweet Sixteen?" Both aspired to the artistry of the Aldon Music teen idol hit makers but missed by a Manhattan mile, the powerhouse delivery of seventeen-year-old Ronnie notwithstanding. Col-Pix then shifted the girls sideways to its rhythm and blues label May, but with no better results. As recording artists, the Ronettes were going nowhere.

Down at the Peppermint Lounge, however, the girls were kicking up quite the storm. A mob-owned joint on 45th Street that had previously been the domain of sailors, the hookers who serviced them, and other lowlife of the Times Square backstreets, the Peppermint had been reborn a-hip by the popularity of its house band Joey Dee and the Starliters. A group of suburban Italian Americans with a deep love of southern black dance music, the Starliters represented a New York rebirth for the culture of rock 'n' roll. Early in 1962, they knocked Chubby Checker's "The Twist" off the number one spot with their own response, "The Peppermint Twist," a simplistic sing-along dance anthem punctuated by a deep saxophone and released on Morris Levy's Roulette label. In the wake of the song's success, the Peppermint Lounge became arguably the hottest nightspot in the nation—the new Palladium, effectively—complete with celebrities like Noël Coward and Greta Garbo, all of whom came to do a dance that had been born in urban black neighborhoods. The popularity of club, dance, and house band alike would play a pivotal role in the New York music scene—not least because the Ronettes, as they took to calling themselves, became the Starliters' dancers, which meant lining the stage and "twisting" their nubile bodies, bras stuffed with Kleenex, for hours on end, stealing the occasional guest vocal in the process. The Starliters even asked them to appear in their movie *Hey, Let's Twist* as the group's girlfriends, but race intervened: the producers figured that the public wouldn't know whether the girls were black or white, and weren't willing to take the chance that they wouldn't care either way.

Murray "the K" Kaufman, the WINS DJ who had succeeded Alan Freed both on air and as New York's leading revue promoter, had no such reservations. After seeing them with the Starliters, he hired the Ronettes on the spot as part of his revue package at the Fox Theater, on Flatbush Avenue in Brooklyn. As unadvertised dancers, and determined to differentiate themselves from the Shirelles, whom they considered "stuck-up," the Ronettes took their ambition into their own hands. Inspired by what Veronica called "the look of the girls we'd see on the streets of Spanish Harlem, the Spanish and half-breed girls who walked around with thick eyeliner and teased hair," the Ronettes squeezed themselves into the tightest skirts they could find, dolled themselves up with excess doses of mascara and eyeliner, and worked their way up Murray the K's bill. It helped that Ronnie had a voice like a foghorn in heat, but she never doubted the importance of image. "The Ronettes were what the girls wanted to be," she wrote, "and what the guys dreamed about."

Whether or not Spector even knew of their existence when they cold-called him, looking to kick-start their recording career, he responded with unusually unguarded enthusiasm. After an audition in which they sang their way through the Frankie Lymon and Little Anthony catalogs, Spector invited himself to dinner at the Bennett household on West 149th Street. There he courted Mrs. Bennett with sufficient conviction that, at his request, she called Col-Pix to inform them that the girls, forlorn at their many small failures, were quitting the business. Once the Ronettes, all still attending George Washington High School at the time, were released from their contract, Spector immediately signed them to Philles—and waited patiently for that perfect song with which to reintroduce the trio, but especially Ronnie, in his image.

When it came along, Spector duly gave it his all. "Be My Baby," another three-way writing split between himself, Barry, and Greenwich, lays permanent claim to being the greatest of Spector's girl group productions—a record that, with its pounding syncopated drum intro, Ronnie's growling kitten vocals, and that great climax of a chorus, was as much rock 'n' roll anthem as pop single. It shot to number two in the charts and established the Ronettes as a distinct, instantly identifiable force within an otherwise often opaque world of interchangeable girl groups and their rotating lineups. It also marked the end of Spector's interest in the Crystals. Though he continued recording them, they were left under no illusions as to who were his favorites, especially once Phil and Ronnie became a couple. The Crystals would ultimately leave Philles with a more impressive chart history than the Ronettes, but after "Be My Baby" they never had another hit record.

As Spector's shuffling of songs and singers demonstrated, the girl group genre was absolutely a producers' market. It was one that served to furnish a fresh career for Hank Medress, who, a couple of years after graduating from Abraham Lincoln in Brooklyn, had reformed the Tokens with another graduate, Jay Siegel, and taken the Weavers' "Wimoweh" to the top of the charts at the end of 1961, rewritten as "The Lion Sleeps Tonight." Moving sideways into an A&R role at Capitol under the production name of Bright Tunes, Medress and Siegel had little success until the day the songwriter and arranger Ronnie Mack walked in their door. Mack had a group of Bronx high school girls, the Chiffons, and a song, "He's So Fine," that Medress and Siegel were instantly convinced would be a hit. Along with their musically proficient band members Phil and Mitch Margo, they rushed to record a demo at the Capitol studios, where the engineer suggested they pull a Phil Spector move and place the backing vocal "doo-lang-doo-lang-doo-lang" hook up front. Yet Capitol rejected it. Medress said that he "ran around all the majors, all the independents," until he ended up at Laurie Records, original home to Dion and the Belmonts. There, he said, "I played the exact record that was sent to Capitol, and they literally locked the door, wouldn't let me out."

Less than two minutes long, "He's So Fine," the playful vocals and shifting rhythm trumping any of the demo recording's aural deficiencies, reconfirmed what listeners knew (and major labels failed to learn) from falling in love with "The Loco-Motion"—that the demo was often the master. It could even be argued that the immediacy of it was part of the reason "He's So Fine" went to number one in the spring of 1963—and why the follow-up, which required more forethought, flopped. Medress and his Tokens then took that familiar walk over to Aldon, where they were asked to consider a Goffin-King demo, "One Fine Day," on which King played piano as Eva Boyd sang lead over the Cookies' archetypal phonetic doo-wop backing. Determined not to second-guess himself again, Medress simply replaced the Cookies' voices with the Chiffons', "in three or four takes," and had another top five hit without need for an expensive recording session. "In those days it was much more organic," Medress noted. "There was a built-in urgency that doesn't exist today. Your instincts ran everything; you didn't have time to intellectualize it into the toilet."

Similar success came with equal ease to his fellow Lincoln High graduates Bob Feldman and Jerry Goldstein, the former Choir Boys. Up and running already as professional songwriters, they hooked up with the Bronx writer Richard Gottehrer when both parties were kept waiting too long for appointments with the same publisher and decided instead to go off and write together. They soon found they had a knack for it, turning out almost a hundred songs in all.

"You'd look for a real-life event that you could draw on," said Gottehrer, of the writing process, "and you would close your eyes and say, 'Can I see this song in the top 10?'" When Feldman told his friends how he'd seen a girl screaming, at his Brighton Beach candy store, "My boyfriend's back and now you're gonna get it!" it got the others thinking, "about somebody saying bad things, mistreating her. And now, wherever that person came back *from* made no difference. The boyfriend's back, you're going to get what's coming to you." Then came the attempt to put that into song. "Instead of saying, 'You'd better run away,' you say, 'If I were you I'd take a permanent vacation . . . ' Something that was never said before."

Feldman, Gottehrer, and Goldstein had become tight with a rather straitlaced white girl trio from New Jersey, called the Angels, who'd recently had a relatively forgettable hit, "Till." Figuring, as Gottehrer put it, "we're so good at making demos, why don't we just do it ourselves, with this girl group that already has a bit of a following?," he and his partners formed FGG Productions. The master recording of "My Boyfriend's Back" might as well have been a demo, propelled as it was by handclaps that barely stayed in tempo with the brisk drums and brass, and topped by the girls' tinny voices, but it had a joyous simplicity that enabled it to be easily replicated on any beach, stoop, or playground. It spent three weeks at number one as the summer anthem of 1963.

The floodgates had opened, and in the rush to fill the public's demand for exuberant female-fronted pop songs, many of the production teams and artists doubled up on themselves. FGG, which always had a mischievous streak, plagiarized "My Boyfriend's Back" several times over, never more blatantly than on "Lookin' for Boys," by the artfully named Brooklyn act the Pin-Ups. Aldon Music kept the Cookies so active in the studio that they had to issue the masters under the pseudonyms the Honeybees and the Cinderellas, with song titles like "Baby Baby (I Still Love You)" now rivaling Greenwich and Barry for promises of eternal love. And when the Tokens recorded several great numbers with the Chiffons' Sylvia Peterson on lead, they released them under the name of the Four Pennies rather than confuse a public that had come to identify with the voice of Judy Craig.

The best of those Four Pennies singles was the debut, "When the Boy's Happy (the Girl's Happy Too)," and it was written by Greenwich and Barry, the hyperactive newlyweds who appeared incapable of doing wrong. In mid-1963, they recorded a demo of their composition "What a Guy," on which Barry played a rapid-fire, almost overpowering snare drum as a base for his comically precise and emphatically basso profundo backing vocals and Greenwich's multitracked vocal harmonies. The result was so odd that Jerry Leiber, no doubt noting the success of similar projects with Aldon and Bright

Tunes, recommended that it serve as a final production. Released on the Jubilee label, under the studio name of the Raindrops, "What a Guy" was not a major hit, but when a similar-sounding follow-up, "The Kind of Boy You Can't Forget," rose into the top 20, the Raindrops became a "real group," consisting of Ellie, her younger sister Laura, and Barry. They hardly lacked for material: to complete a debut album in time for Christmas, they simply covered their own Spector hits "Da Doo Ron Ron" and "Not Too Young to Get Married."

But while Greenwich reveled in her long-overdue moment as a bona fide pop star, Barry discovered he had lost the urge for public gratification and quickly gave up attending lip-synch "live" shows, hiring a stand-in to take his place. Content with writing hits and increasingly enjoying his role as a studio producer, Barry continued to produce singles for the Raindrops through 1964 but otherwise allowed the project to disintegrate. That was a shame: differentiated by the presence of Barry's deep vocals and his nonsense phrasing, cemented by Greenwich's pristine vocals—and aided, of course, by having the entire Greenwich-Barry catalog to draw from—the Raindrops were among the more innovative and entertaining of what could be called the second tier of girl groups.

Meantime, on February 9, 1964, an estimated 70 million Americans tuned in to watch the Beatles perform on *The Ed Sullivan Show* and, so history has it, change pop music forever. But while it was true that America had no male beat groups at the time with which to compare the Beatles (the closest would have been Joey Dee and the Starliters), Britain had no girl groups, no Svengali producers, no songwriting couples like those of the Brill and Music Buildings. So, when the Beatles landed at JFK that February, it was with Spector on board as talisman, and as they tried to settle into the Park Plaza in Manhattan on that historic visit, they were more than happy to entertain the Ronettes, with whom they had just toured in the United Kingdom. They also invited Goffin and King to come visit, having included the young couple's "Chains" on their debut album. (They had followed it on record with "Boys," the B-side to the Shirelles' "Will You Love Me Tomorrow.") While thousands of young girls gathered on the Manhattan streets outside and distended their larynxes into the night air in hormonal worship of British male genes, up in the penthouse it was the New Yorkers who were being treated like royalty.

"I didn't see it as a threat," said Jeff Barry of what came to be called the British invasion. "First time I heard 'I Wanna Hold Your Hand' [the Beatles' first American hit], I thought, 'Okay, I could have written that.' Not that I don't *get* it, but I'm not intimidated."

Nor should he have been. For, amid all their other successes, he and Greenwich had just become part of the most successful new record company in the country.

George Goldner's gambling habits had finally gotten the worst of him. Apparently driven to depression by the ongoing breakup with his second wife, he had managed to take the fortunes he had earned, this second time around (with End, Gone, and Goldisc, and associated publishing and distribution entities), and wind up with racetrack debts that could be surmounted only by offloading those companies to an interested party. That party turned out to be—surprise—Morris Levy, who for the second time in only six years relieved Goldner of his entire catalog to add to Roulette's growing mountain of copyrights. Considering that End's roster included the Chantels, the Imperials, and the Flamingoes ("I Only Have Eyes for You") and early recordings by the Isley Brothers and the Miracles, it was presumably worth some money. But whatever he got from Levy was barely enough to get the bookies off his back, and one night in early 1964, Goldner could be found at Al and Dick's, the music business hangout on West 54th Street, dejectedly entertaining a job offer from another former rival, a gloating Hy Weiss.

Leiber and Stoller were also in a state of transition. They'd fallen out of favor with Atlantic after asking for an audit, and although they had bounced back with hits for two New York vocal acts, Jay and the Americans and the female-fronted Exciters, a pair of new boutique labels, Tiger and Daisy, had charted only once in nearly a dozen releases. When their benefactor at the parent company United Artists fell out with his own bosses, "We were left with a stack of unreleased masters that we had paid for," said Stoller, who, in early 1964, felt compelled to tell Leiber that they were running out of cash so rapidly that he was set to quit the business. Certainly, he was finished with Tiger and Daisy. A depressed Leiber headed over to Al and Dick's for sustenance.

"The place was jumping," Leiber recalled, "and Hymie Weiss stood up at a table and waved at me saying, 'Down here. Let's have a drink.'" Leiber accepted the invitation and found himself face-to-face with Goldner, whom he claimed never to have met before. (Goldner and Leiber worked in different buildings, and although Goldner had often hit up Aldon Music for songs, he appears never to have done so with Trio Music.) "Hymie was blowing cigar smoke into George's face. George was asking Hy to cut it out, and Hy was laughing and really debasing him." When Weiss headed off to the men's room, Goldner explained that Weiss was delighting in offering him an insultingly low salary to come work at Old Town, which was doing very well out of the doo-wop revival of the early sixties. "I can't survive on that," Goldner told Leiber. "But I can't survive without it."

Leiber and Stoller were revered producers and songwriters, and respected businessmen, but as their own label bosses, they were repeated failures. Goldner had some of the best ears in the business; he just couldn't be trusted with money. Together, however, they had the makings of the perfect partnership. When Leiber told Goldner about the unreleased masters, Goldner offered to listen to them immediately, through the night if need be. They left Weiss at Al and Dick's, and Leiber showed him into the office.

"I came back the next morning," said Leiber. "There he sat, every hair in place. His tie up where it belonged, his jacket on, and he's waving this acetate in my face. 'Leiber, on my mother's grave . . .'" The record was "Going to the Chapel," by the Dixie Cups. "I said, 'George, I hate this fucking record.'" Stoller, who joined Leiber for that morning meeting—it was the first time *he* had ever met George Goldner, too—felt otherwise. "I liked it very much," he said.

"Chapel of Love" had been written by Barry and Greenwich together with Phil Spector, who had recorded it with both Darlene Love and the Ronettes, but at the morbid pace that he sometimes adopted, which called into question the apparently joyous intent of the title. Spector shelved both versions. Barry, still convinced it was a hit, produced a new recording by a New Orleans girl group brought into the ailing Tiger and Daisy setup. As sung by the Dixie Cups, "Going to the Chapel" was suddenly sweetness itself, a song of eternal devotion delivered free of cynicism or fear. Now, as the debut release on the brand-new Leiber-Stoller-Goldner label Red Bird, "Going to the Chapel" confirmed both Barry and Goldner's instinct, rising straight to number one, a first for Greenwich and Barry as songwriters—with the additional bonus that it knocked the Beatles off the top of the charts. In fact, British acts riding the Beatles' coattails onto the American charts were frequently doing so via the American song catalog. Herman's Hermits got going with Goffin and King's "I'm into Something Good" (as originally recorded by the Cookies' Earl-Jean); the Moody Blues debuted in the top ten by reviving a Tiger single "Go Now," by Bessie Banks; and Manfred Mann had a number one with a new version of the Exciters' "Do Wah Diddy Diddy," composed by Barry and Greenwich. Why *should* Jeff Barry feel threatened by the British invasion?

Back out on Long Island, in Hicksville, one municipality over from Levittown, George Morton watched Ellie Greenwich's success with admiration only starting to border on envy. Like Greenwich, Morton had been transported by his parents from Brooklyn at a young age to suburbs so new that "the streets had not been paved yet," as he put it. In his case, the relocation came about after he joined a local motorbike gang, but the move backfired on his parents, so to speak, when he discovered the local Hicksville diner scene, full of "motorcycles and hot rods and girls dancing in the lot." It turned out that "there were kids being yanked out of Staten Island, the Bronx, Brooklyn, all being dropped in Hicksville, Long Island." His adolescence ended up being a blast, after all. Morton even formed a singing group with Italian friends who often found themselves on the same local stages as Greenwich's Jivettes.

But there the similarities ended. Now Greenwich was happily married and writing hits for a living in Manhattan. And Morton was not. He decided to go visit. "I didn't want to be in the music business," he said. "My only reason for going to see Ellie at that time, beyond saying hello and congratulations, was to be able to leave there, go back to Hicksville, Long Island, and say, 'Guess who I was just with?,' so that the girls would want to be with me."

Greenwich was happy to bring Morton up to her office, where Barry was also present, typically hard at work, seated at the piano. "It never dawned on me that that's what he was *supposed* to do as a songwriter," said Morton. "It dawned on me that he was ignoring us. I'm Irish, I'm from Brooklyn, and I'm an alcoholic, so I get paranoid!" When Barry finally joined the conversation and asked Morton what he did for a living, the visitor "took that as a put-down" and responded that he was a songwriter. (Morton's vocal groups had recorded the occasional independent single, so he was not quite lying.) When Barry politely asked him what kind of songs, Morton replied, bullishly, "hit songs." Barry, casually, invited Morton to come back with a demo. Morton, insulted, determined to do just that.

He hired a recording studio owned by one of his Italian friends. And he recruited a group of girls from Andrew Jackson High School, in Cambria Heights, at the point where eastern Queens gave way to the Long Island suburbs. The girls had established a name locally and had just started recording demos for a Manhattan company, Kama Sutra. Calling themselves the Shangri-Las, they were visually distinctive, consisting of two pairs of sisters: Mary and Liz Weiss, and the identical twins Margie and Mary-Ann Ganser. They were also white, still a rarity in the girl group genre, unless you counted the aptly named Angels. Moreover, they were good-looking but in a bad-girl kind of way. And they had attitude to back it up. Morton quickly hired them.

The song that he composed for them, "Remember (Walkin' in the Sand)" was, said Morton, a "sad song: girl falls in love, boy has to go away." The way he wrote it, however, was less like a song and more like a play. To this end, Morton elevated Mary Weiss to lead singer, a role typically taken by her older sister, and directed her as if she were an actress. That she rose to the challenge "was a stroke of good fortune," he admitted. "I didn't know that I was making such unusual demands of a fifteen-year-old girl. I thought I should say what I want and I should get it. I didn't know that if it hadn't been Mary Weiss from the Shangri-Las in that room, I would never have gotten the sound I wanted."

With piano contributed by another Hicksville fifteen-year-old, Billy Joel (who had himself been "yanked" out of the Bronx, had recently fallen in love with the Beatles, and was adding to his reputation as a troublemaker and budding pianist with a career as a welterweight boxer), the recording of "Remember" was not lacking for rebellious suburban character. Jeff Barry heard it just once before he took it to Leiber and Stoller, who immediately commissioned a professional recording session—and put Morton on the payroll.

Three weeks later, a re-recorded "Remember," complete now with dramatic sobs and the sound of flocking seagulls, was released on Red Bird. Aided in no small part by the visual appeal of the Shangri-Las, it was an instant top five hit. For the all-important follow-up, Morton raised the stakes.

This time, the girl would fall in love with a moody biker (like himself), her parents would disapprove, and the girl would be forced to break it off, whereupon the biker would ride off into the sunset—and die.

That song, of course, was "Leader of the Pack," which Barry and Greenwich ended up cowriting. Barry's ability to "come up with key lines," as Morton described it, was "incredible"—and no surprise, perhaps, given that he already had "Tell Laura I Love Her" to his credit. Having completed a riveting playlet structured unlike anything going on in the girl group genre, the writers produced it with similar imagination, Barry even running a cable from the studio window down to 47th Street and recording the sound of the engineer's Harley-Davidson. Weiss, as the tragedy-struck lead singer—and the other Shangri-Las, as her neighborhood friends—similarly rose to the occasion, imbuing their vocal performances with such personal intensity that it sounded to all the world as if the narrative were being lived out in real time.

"I had enough pain in me at the time to pull off anything and get into it and sound believable," said Weiss, who had lost her father when she was a young child. "You can hear it on the performances. The recording studio was the place where you could really release what you were feeling, without everyone looking at you." And yet, as Morton pointed out, "Mary had a sincerity and a fragility about her; she wasn't *hard*. She sounded like the young girl next door."

The combination was enough to take "Leader of the Pack" to the top of the charts—and beyond, into a certain category of classics reserved for records that seem never to lose their ability to astonish. Spector had become famous for his teenage symphonies, but "Leader of the Pack" was a teenage psychodrama. (Its authors, specifically Morton and Barry, viewed it as a serious composition, rather than as the novelty listeners often took it for over the years.) It was also the third number one composition for Greenwich and Barry in just five months—none of them were Spector productions. Spector was hurt commercially and offended personally by Greenwich and Barry's defection to Red Bird; he was just as bruised by the arrival on the New York scene of Morton, whom some people were starting to regard as his replacement. Morton was not among them. "I did not think of anybody when I was producing," said Morton. "Never. Ever. Not another group. Nor a production." But, he said, "I do know that throughout history I have got a lot of laughs and a lot of smiles from what Mr. Spector has said about me."

Morton acquired a nickname from Barry, who saw in him a similarity to the pulp radio/print character "The Shadow" 's ability "to cloud men's minds." As Barry described it (and others concurred), "You could be talking to him, and you'd turn around, he's gone. You'd have to watch him all the time. He would disappear for days." Mary Weiss confirmed that while Morton was "one of the most colorful, unique people I've ever met in my life . . . he used to be very difficult to get into a room at a scheduled time."

But when present, he made a critical difference to the proceedings. Footage of "Shadow" Morton in the studio with the Shangri-Las shows an impeccably cool young man in his element, living out his unexpected creative windfall with innate savoir faire. And what a crowded scene of constantly inspired lunacy it must have been at Red Bird in 1964, what with the self-taught alcoholic newcomer Morton, the perpetually inventive and permanently hurried Barry, the go-getting queen bee Greenwich, the original R&B storytelling producers Leiber and Stoller, the "twelve-year-old" fan and addicted gambler Goldner, not to mention additionally renowned characters like the arranger Artie Butler, the Mira Sound engineers Brooks Arthur and Joe Venneri, and the PR man and future industry mogul Seymour Stein, all in the same milieu as the Shangri-Las themselves, who dressed for photo ops and stage shows in their own choice of high boots, hipster sweaters, one-piece black leather leotards, men's waistcoats . . . anything that made them look like the toughest, hippest, sexiest bunch of jailbait the teen market had ever set its eyes on. ("Looking back at the old video clips, doesn't it seem silly when you compare it to today?" asked Mary Weiss. "Maybe that image helped us kids survive in a very difficult adult business.")

The Angels, the Chiffons, the Raindrops, and their ilk epitomized girl groups as a celebration of pop music for its own sake. The Supremes, the Marvelettes, and the Vandellas out of Detroit, along with New Jersey's Shirelles (who stopped having hits in 1963 but continued to make great records for several years thereafter), embodied a new, young black American soul music. But the Shangri-Las and the Ronettes represented something else, the spirit of a new form of rock 'n' roll that was growing all around them. Both acts benefited from the monumentally ambitious dreams of their producers: they befriended and toured with the major rock stars of their day (most notably the Beatles and the Rolling Stones); they became idols and heroines for generations of New York rockers to follow.

And both groups had a relatively short run of permanently memorable hit singles. The Ronettes' top 40 status concluded with an underperforming Mann-Weil classic, "Walkin' in the Rain," at the end of 1964, after which Ronnie Bennett suffered five years of captive misery as the wife of Phil Spector (whose name she would keep), to emerge shaken and not entirely unbloodied on the other side, but with her voice and reputation intact. The Shangri-Las stayed in the charts as the Ronettes dropped off, with "Give Us Your Blessings" and the artfully painful ode to daughter-mother bonds "I Can Never Go Home Anymore," each continuing the "death" theme. But they were careful never to overplay the formula and were equally renowned for the almost conventionally upbeat (and exceptionally well-crafted) "Give Him a Great Big Kiss," with its memorable opening line, "When I'm in love you'd best believe I'm in love, l-u-v." (All involved preferred to forget their commercial swan song, "Long Live Our Love.") They even delivered a piercing cover of the Chantels' "Maybe," the song with which Goldner had launched the whole girl group genre a decade earlier.

"We were crazy about George [Goldner]," said Mary Weiss. "At the end of our first year, we bought George a huge television set. We gave it to him with a big gold plaque on the front as a thank-you present. He was a kid who never grew up." Shadow Morton agreed: "Like a lot of the people in the music business, he was a little boy playing in big man's clothes."

Barry described Goldner as "maybe the most enthusiastic person [he] ever met," given to a familiar routine when brought into the studio to hear the finished mix of yet another hit. "He would be wide-eyed. He would look angry, but it was his emotion. He would say, 'That's a fucking *smash*,' he would pick up the chair he was sitting on . . . and smash it." Barry and company got into the habit of supplying him with a disposable chair at the right moment, and Goldner took it in good humor.

Leiber and Stoller, however, grew tired of him, and quickly. In large part, it was because Goldner's uncanny ability to pick hits in the studio was countered by his persistent habit of backing losers at the track. His gambling, said Leiber, was "a real serious disease," and it had begun attracting the wrong kind of business associates to the Red Bird offices—"the heavies," as Leiber called them.

Stoller had a different, though not unrelated, concern. "He was like an idiot savant when he came to numbers," said Mike Stoller. "If you said, 'We

sold thirty-seven thousand records at nineteen cents with a 6 percent discount,' he could give you the total figure in a second." Yet Goldner was apply-
ing that math off the books, selling records to his shady distributor contacts,
whether to offset his debts or simply because he couldn't help it. (His daughter Linda wondered whether he wasn't bipolar.)

More than anything else, though, Leiber and Stoller felt removed from
the marketplace. "We were babysitting," said Leiber of Red Bird's output, the
endless girl group hits that Jeff and Ellie wrote and produced as effortlessly
as thank-you notes to BMI for the checks that they generated. "We really
couldn't tolerate that stuff any more. I like Muddy Waters, I like Little Walter,
I like Memphis Slim and Lightnin' Hopkins. I don't like that big city trash."
He and Stoller had set up Blue Cat as a side label through which to indulge
their love of R&B, but its one hit, the Ad-Libs' "Boy from New York City," was
so perky it might as well have been issued on Red Bird anyway. Still in their
early thirties, the partners decided to "get away from this baby music" and
pursue grander plans for more adult material. Secured by the "million-dollar
bonds" from their many classic compositions, they opted to quit. They sold
the label to Goldner for a dollar and walked away.

Red Bird lasted a few more months before Goldner's gambling habits
brought him down one final time. "He got caught with some bad people," said
Morton, who described Goldner as "a very generous man," but also noted,
"No true gambler ever wants to win. He has nothing to look forward to.
Nothing to dream about."

The marriage of Jeff Barry and Ellie Greenwich collapsed even before
Red Bird. The demands of the couple's writing partnership, and Barry's
workaholic nature, left no time for romance. An unsuccessful Greenwich
solo single on Red Bird in 1965 entitled "You Don't Know," written by her and
Barry with Morton, seemed in retrospect more like a cry for attention.
Although they held on to their professional relationship for a couple more
lucrative years, during which time they discovered, published, and produced
Neil Diamond, Greenwich never fully got over the demise of a world in which
marriage and music had once been so perfectly entwined. "I had a hard time
for many years trying to adapt because I had only ever known one thing and
it was so wonderful," said the woman who typified the era's youthful energy,
its joie de vivre.

At least she had her songwriting royalties to cushion the fall. For the singers, having neither written their songs nor produced them, there was almost nothing in the way of residual income once the hits stopped coming and the package tours ceased running. Worse yet, many artists lacked control of the most basic aspects of their legacy—as the Shangri-Las discovered when a rogue manager (legally) put a totally unrelated lineup on the road years later.

Some singers set out on the oldies circuit themselves, often reinvesting meager appearance income in lawyers' fees, hoping to gain long-overdue remuneration. Others settled down to motherhood and/or a "proper" career, knowing that nothing could ever replicate the magic of the early to mid-sixties, when hit songs were written, produced, and charted in the space of just weeks, and the artists learned to live in a searing spotlight that, even if it singed them, was still worth the experience.

"I agree that we grew up differently than other people," said Mary Weiss, whose Shangri-Las moved to Mercury Records after Red Bird folded in 1966, but lasted just two singles. "I would not change a minute of it. I missed out on nothing. Other kids were going to proms; I was in London at a press conference. It was just a very different life than most kids live."

And yet attempting to leave it all behind was not always that easy, especially for those who had been icons. "When I could no longer record, I just wanted a regular life like everyone else," said the singer who was barely eighteen years old at the time the Shangri-Las called it a day. But, she added, "it took me twelve years to be able to get lost in the street and have a normal life."

11

PLUG IN, TUNE UP, ROCK OUT

The Beatles' effect on the folk scene proved much more instantaneous and dramatic than their effect on the girl groups, the Brill and the Music Buildings, and it was typified by the experience of Eric Jacobsen. A young banjo player in a bluegrass group called the Knob Lick Upper 10,000, managed by Albert Grossman, Jacobsen called up a Beatles single on a jukebox in early 1964 while on tour in Washington, D.C., eager to know what the fuss was all about. What he heard, particularly in Paul McCartney's melodic and syncopated bass lines, provided nothing less than an epiphany: "I decided, kind of then and there I think, that I was gonna quit the Knob Lick Upper 10,000, and go to New York City, and produce electric folk music." Jacobsen moved into a fifth-floor walk-up on Prince Street, in the Little Italy neighborhood, just south of Greenwich Village. There, by one of those happy coincidences that prove quite common in such a confined and crowded city as New York, his next-door neighbor turned out to be the Village-raised musician John Sebastian.

The twenty-year-old Sebastian had himself just left something called the Even Dozen Jug Band, whose musical smorgasbord of banjos, guitars, fiddles, washboards, and, yes, the actual water jug itself—easy to laugh at, all too hard to play—had briefly been the toast of the Village, recording an album for Elektra consisting of old-fashioned rags and blues. But Sebastian, occasionally employed by Elektra as a session harmonica and guitar player, recognized that the writing was on the wall for all this folk music.

"I'd had this funny double upbringing," he said of the juxtaposition between his Village childhood and his four years at a New Jersey prep school, where he had learned the Chuck Berry and Duane Eddy songbooks. Having also spent time up in Cambridge, "where the snooty folksinger traditionalists were," he had additionally witnessed how "several groups, including Jim Kweskin's Jug Band, suffered tremendously by *not* picking up an electric instrument." By 1964, with the advent of the Beatles, he recognized that "there was a new dawn."

Sebastian and Jacobsen became instant best friends, bonding over each other's record collection, and their affinity for marijuana. Jacobsen desired to pursue electric folk music primarily behind the scenes, to which end he published, managed, and produced demos for Tim Hardin, a Boston singer-songwriter who shocked everyone in the Village by accompanying himself not with the regulation acoustic guitar but with an electric one instead. Along with Fred Neil, who was pushing thirty but whose experience playing electric guitar down south in the fifties provided an important connection to that past, and Peter Childs from the Knob Lick group, Sebastian served as Hardin's backing musicians at the Café Playhouse, on MacDougal Street. There they made the acquaintance of twenty-one-year-old Jim McGuinn, who was employed at Bobby Darin's Brill Building publishing company, churning out copycat rewrites of contemporary hits. And though he preferred hanging out in the Village, McGuinn nonetheless noted that folk "was getting very commercial and cellophane-packaged." This comment was perhaps inspired by his boss, who in late 1963 released an album entitled *Golden Folk Hits*. McGuinn concluded that folk "was a low-quality product, and [he] wanted to get into something else."

His opportunity arrived when he listened to *Meet the Beatles*. Like Jacobsen before him, he was captivated by the group's musical complexity, in this case the "modal harmonies" and what he recognized as folk chord changes applied to a rock-'n'-roll rhythm. Learning the Beatles' songs on an acoustic twelve-string guitar, McGuinn won a residency for his "Beatles impersonations," as they advertised it, at the Café Playhouse, where Peter Tork and Tiny Tim were among the other young musicians who chose to hang out there. All involved could feel that something new was on the rise—and "not just the Beatles," said Sebastian, "but Carnaby Street, the whole London explosion." As the World's Fair opened in Flushing Meadows, in Queens, in the spring of 1964, this loosely arrayed coterie of misfit musicians fantasized about a New York just as happening as London or Liverpool.

Exposure to psychedelic drugs enhanced these ambitions. Whether they were sourced from the peyote plant (mescaline) or dried mushrooms (psilocybin) or synthesized in the laboratory as LSD (acid), the emergence of mind-expanding drugs in the Village, and their instant popularity with a younger generation, had lasting effects on the surrounding music scene. An enthusiastic participant, Sebastian found himself, at some point in 1964, "summoned to drive some dried vegetables" to Washington, D.C., where mutual friends were holding down a residency under the new name of the Mugwumps. Among their members were the singers Dennis Doherty and "Mama" Cass Elliott—and the guitarist Zalman Yanovsky, an exuberant nineteen-year-old native of Toronto, who "amused the hell out of me," said Sebastian. "He inhaled and exhaled people and conversation and jokes and theater. He was this kind of cultural weathervane—and people gathered around him." Staying in town with the Mugwumps, Sebastian found himself taking to their stage with his harmonica, trading licks with Yanovsky rather than sticking to the script. "Yanovsky and I were both aware of the fact that this commercial folk music model was about to change again, that the four-man band that actually played their own instruments and wrote their own songs was the thing."

And so, when the Mugwumps fell apart, Sebastian and Yanovsky returned to the Village, itching to form not so much a rock band in the Beatles' image but an electric jug band. They kicked around with the crowd they'd met at the Playhouse—now including the guitarist Felix Pappalardi—until they recruited a good-looking, hard-playing bassist from Long Island, Steve Boone, and a first drummer. Fritz Richmond of Jim Kweskin's Jug Band suggested they name themselves the Lovin' Spoonful, from a reference to cunnilingus in a Mississippi John Hurt song, and it proved typical of midsixties insider hipness—or rather, outsider squareness—that such a sexually charged moniker became associated instead with the band's genial positivity.

For their debut booking, the Lovin' Spoonful headed over to MacDougal Street's Night Owl, a former after-hours bowling joint under the new ownership of Joe Marra, and otherwise functioning as a coffeehouse and restaurant. Their residency opened in late January 1965—and it closed just two weeks later, on a Sunday night when the total gross fell to just $7.15. "Even their girlfriends weren't there to watch this debacle," recalled Marra of that final night. He resumed booking folk acts.

The Lovin' Spoonful took their unceremonious debut on the chin—except for the drummer, who quit. Replacements were auditioned at the Albert Hotel, a popular musicians' flophouse on Tenth Street, and Joe Butler got the job after breaking his sticks and then playing with his hands until they were bleeding. It was no coincidence that the hard-hitting Butler was a friend of Boone's, from a Long Island cover group—for while the Village folkies were still coming to terms with the very notion of playing electric instruments, the suburbs were already turning out loud "garage bands," inspired mainly by the British invasion, by the dozen.

The Albert became the Spoonful's lair (as it did for many other groups of the sixties). A couple of blocks away, meanwhile, at the Earle Hotel, on Waverly Place, where Bob Dylan had first stayed when he came to New York, the Mugwumps' Dennis Doherty teamed up with John and Michelle Phillips, the former a moderately successful folksinger staring at his thirtieth birthday, the latter his beautiful young Californian bride. Their initial plan was to resurrect John Phillips's group the Journeymen, which their banjo player, Marshall Brickman, had recently quit for a career as a writer, but the folk trio craze was now dead in the water. John truly grasped this only when Doherty, with Cass Elliott in tow, turned the married couple on to LSD, during which trip the married couple opened up to the multifarious beauties of (what John Phillips had perceived as) the Beatles' seemingly simplistic pop songs. By the time they came down from their collective high, Cass and Michelle were best friends, and the New Journeymen had determined to take themselves to St. Thomas in the Virgin Islands, where, joined later by Cass, they were to write some Beatles-style songs of their own and get a short-term club booking. Two years later, that venue's location, Creeque Alley, would spawn the title of a poetic and amusing song about the early days of the folk rock movement, how "Sebastian and Zal formed the Spoonful / Michelle, John and Denny gettin' very tuneful."

For their part, the Spoonful secured a residency just across MacDougal Street from the Night Owl—at the Café Bizarre, the original commercial coffeehouse. Unlike the earnest singer-songwriters elsewhere in the Village, the group thrived on playing to tourists, and worked up their live show by playing several sets a night, six nights a week. The experience was enervating.

"We learned more at that crappy little club than almost any other gig," said Sebastian.

Eric Jacobsen began shopping the Lovin' Spoonful to the record labels. But the only one that would bite was Elektra, and Sebastian turned them down, believing—erroneously, it transpired—that his occasional employers were too ingrained in folk to either understand or market rock music. Still, a compromise was struck: the group recorded four songs that Jac Holzman vowed to hold on to until "you guys are big." Their payment came in the form of a trip to a midtown music store to load up on powerful new amplifiers such as other groups didn't own.

In May, the new and improved Lovin' Spoonful talked themselves back into the Night Owl. Taking no chances after the earlier failure, Joe Marra booked two other groups embracing electric instrumentation, Danny Kalb's Blues Project and, visiting from the West Coast, members of the Modern Folk Quartet, under the pseudonym Fat City Four and featuring a drummer who painted his drumsticks Dayglo, for that moment when the lighting—and yes, at the Night Owl, there was something approaching a light show—was reduced to all-black. The stage having been moved in the interim toward the front window, the energy and excitement of this triple electric bill carried into the street. As it was now early summer, those streets were filled with young people looking to experience the musical changes that seemed to be taking place on a weekly basis in 1965, and the all-electric booking was an immediate hit.

The Lovin' Spoonful took great pride in shaking up the Village folk scene. "We were the first guys to go in with a Super Reverb and a Magna Tone amplifier and be told that we were so loud that it was ridiculous," said Sebastian. The 125-capacity Night Owl was neither designed—nor had a cabaret license—for dancing: church pew benches lined the space from the stage to the back wall, with the exception of a three-foot "aisle" to meet city code. (The front pew soon became known as the "crotch watcher's bench.") Still, recalled Sebastian, "it was not beyond the third or fourth evening that we looked out into the audience, and there's this beautiful sixteen-year-old girl dancing like *we* danced—and not like the last generation danced." Glancing across what there was of the stage, Sebastian saw Yanovsky indicate that he had sensed the same thing: whether they'd stumbled upon the hip new audience or the hip new audience had sought them out, they'd found themselves at a time and place that defined a generational shift. The next day, Sebastian sat down to write a song about how their music had connected with the teenage beauty. "Do you believe in magic," it began, "in a young girl's heart? / How the music can free her, whenever it starts?" (As important as its opening line was the assertion that magic could be found whether "it's jug band music or rhythm and blues.")

Word quickly spread about what was going on at the Night Owl. Phil Spector showed up, professing interest in bringing the Lovin' Spoonful to his Philles label, but though the group adored the Ronettes (Sebastian began every day with a blast of "Be My Baby"), they were determined to use Jacobsen as their producer. They signed instead to the MGM-distributed Kama Sutra Records (the label that had made the first Shangri-Las recordings), which not only had the marketing dollars to compete in the singles market but also was willing to give the group artistic control. Crucially, they were encouraged to record "Do You Believe in Magic" as their debut single.

They did not squander the opportunity. Following the group's desire to use what Sebastian called "familiar instruments to get an unfamiliar sound," Jacobsen aligned the singer's acoustic Gibson (the face of which had been sanded down "so it was really loud") alongside a piano part played by the Modern Folk Quartet's Jerry Yester, in conjunction with an autoharp— affixed with a ukulele pickup. Run through an amplifier, these components were all arrayed sonically so that listeners would hear them as a unique whole. Jacobsen's studio tricks served to elevate "Do You Believe in Magic" above the usual limitations of the pop single. Though barely two minutes in length, it captured the feeling of optimism that was running through the younger Village scene in 1965, and it hit the top ten that fall.

As part of the promotional process, the Lovin' Spoonful were flown out to the West Coast—only to find their former friend from the Village, Jim McGuinn, was being hailed as the Californian leader for this new music they were all calling folk rock. McGuinn's journey had been straightforward enough. Having failed to gain attention as a solo artist in the Village, he had accepted a booking at the Troubadour Club—the Los Angeles equivalent of Folk City, complete with Monday night hootenannies—and never returned. Instead, making a name on Sunset Strip with his one-man Beatles show, he fell in with a Californian crowd of former folk musicians and aspiring rockers who, after a series of false starts, settled on the deliberately Beatles-like name of the Byrds and wrangled a deal with Columbia Records. Their producer then got his hands on an unreleased Dylan song, "Mr. Tambourine Man," and although McGuinn was the only Byrds member considered proficient enough to play an instrument on its recording, his contribution proved epochal. Inspired by George Harrison's use of the newly invented twelve-string Rickenbacker on "A Hard Day's Night," McGuinn had acquired an identical guitar, and on "Mr. Tambourine Man" he married the sonic structure of the Beatles' "jingle jangle" guitar sound to the "jingle jangle" lyrics of the Bob Dylan song; the Byrds number one hit truly embodied the best of both, creating a new sound in the process. A few months later, the Byrds topped the charts again, recording Pete Seeger's adaptation of a biblical verse, "Turn! Turn! Turn! (To Everything There Is a Season)," which McGuinn, as a session musician for Elektra in New York, had arranged and played on Judy Collins's last album. Theft in folk music was always the most sincere form of flattery.

Clearly, folk was going electric with or without Bob Dylan. Already burdened by his reputation as America's foremost protest singer, Dylan determined that it would be with him—especially after the Animals took his arrangement of "The House of the Rising Sun," the one from his debut album that apparently nobody had bought, the song that already had been recorded by almost every folk singer in New York, electrified it, and promptly had a number one single. Dylan hung out with the Beatles when they came to New York in the summer of 1964, turning them on to marijuana (even though he, like most in the New York music scene, had already progressed to acid). And he hung out in the studio with John Hammond, the guitar-playing son of his A&R man.

Hammond had found his niche in the wake of the folk explosion, when a fascination with traditional blues music sprang up, bringing the likes of Mississippi John Hurt, Son House, and the Reverend Gary Davis to join John Lee Hooker, Brownie McGhee, and Sonny Terry in the Village clubs. "The blues has always gotten a bit of a short shrift," said Hammond of the music's acceptance among the folk musicians, for which its birthplace and growth far away from New York City surely played a part. Hammond had hoped to redress that balance on his second Vanguard album, *Big City Blues*, but his skin color worked against him: "If you weren't black, you weren't authentic." Undeterred, for his fourth album, *So Many Roads*, in late 1964, Hammond brought to New York from Toronto the musicians Levon Helm, Robbie Robertson, and Garth Hudson from the Hawks, who were doing what Hammond observed as "phenomenal blues and R&B." Hammond also hired the white blues players Michael Bloomfield and Charlie Musselwhite from Chicago—and invited his "good friend" Bob Dylan to view the proceedings.

When next Dylan entered the studio, in January 1965, it was with his own, electrically amplified musicians (including John Sebastian and Steve Boone). That album, *Bringing It All Back Home*, represented a seismic musical shift: it opened with a purposefully abrasive and gloriously quick-witted electric recording, "Subterranean Homesick Blues," which had about it an additional kind of electricity—a vitriolic anger, a sense of injustice and frustration, laden with dark humor, that could not have been so easily propelled by a simple beat-up acoustic six-string. It became Dylan's first proper solo hit, grazing the top 40. His fame, however, was already out of all proportion to his singles success, and after an exhausting, speed-ridden first tour of Europe that spring, filmed by D. A. Pennebaker for the legendary documentary *Don't Look Back*, an increasingly embittered Dylan retreated to Peter Yarrow's cabin in Woodstock, where he wrote furiously. He imagined that he might even abandon music for prose: "I found myself writing this song, this story, this long piece of vomit, twenty pages long, and out of it I took 'Like a Rolling Stone.' . . . It suddenly came to me that this is what I should do."

"Like a Rolling Stone" would merit endless study over the coming years, but much as the song's put-downs and allegorical rhymes made it a work of great marvel and mystery, it was the performance that rendered it such a seminal midsixties moment. And as so often with Dylan's recordings, there was very little planning behind it. Rather, Dylan, Mike Bloomfield, and a familiar core of session musicians simply entered the studio in June, with Dylan's long-term producer Tom Wilson at the helm, and set about the process. Wilson invited to the session, though only as an observer, another young guitarist, Al Kooper—and he helped make all the difference.

Kooper's résumé was near enough a prodigy's summation of the New York music scene of the last several years. Sang in vocal groups in Queens. Attended Birdland as underage jazz fan. Turned professional at fourteen, joining the hit act the Royal Teens as guitarist. Worked the Music Building, where he teamed up with proven songwriters. Got turned on to Dylan by his fellow Queens native and teenage hit maker turned Brill Building songwriter, Paul Simon. Began playing folk under a pseudonym at a club in Queens. And in the middle of this transition, cowrote "This Diamond Ring," which, as recorded in a Mersey Beat style by the new California group Gary Lewis and the Playboys, became a number one hit in early 1965. By rights, Kooper was on top of the Music Building game. But, at age twenty-one, he intrinsically understood that the days of midtown offices dictating national tastes were on the way out. Dylan going electric, on the other hand . . .

With Mike Bloomfield in the studio, Kooper was hardly going to get a chance to play guitar on "Like a Rolling Stone." But then Wilson excused himself from the control booth, Paul Griffin shifted from the Hammond organ to the piano in an attempt to find the song's groove, and Kooper seized his opportunity. Wilson returned to the booth, saw Kooper sit at the Hammond, and asked, "What are you doing there?" Dylan, with whom Kooper had immediately bonded, told Wilson to just roll the tape. The session musicians in the room kept the six-minute song moving that day (though just barely, for the finished version was the only one out of fifteen takes ever completed), but it was Bloomfield's circular guitar lines and Kooper's organ part that lifted the performance out of conventional studio methodology and into ethereal territory.

"I was trying to play something that would complement what everyone else was playing," said Kooper. "But I had a very very *very* limited palette." Creating for himself a suitably simple melody, he played it slightly behind the rest of the band, in order to be certain of landing on the right chord. As the song progressed, Kooper grew in confidence, hitting the note on time with the rest of the band, until by the third chorus, he was playing a kaleidoscopic part reminiscent of the Animals' Alan Price on "House of the Rising Sun." Throughout this process, Dylan was snarling rather than singing the words, "How does it feel . . . to be on your own?," sounding more like a misogynist Mick Jagger than a protesting Woody Guthrie.

Dylan's former college town friend Paul Nelson, who later became an editor at *Rolling Stone* (named, in part, for the song), and later still an influential A&R man, remarked that the song's "negative statement" ran counter to everything folk music represented. He had a point: the folk movement had always relied on affirmation to get through its struggles (e.g., "We Shall

Overcome"), or at least fell back on spiritual possibilities ("Blowin' in the Wind"). By comparison, "Like a Rolling Stone" was not just negative but nihilistic, even plain nasty; as such, and not just because of its amplified arrangement, it was in no way, shape, or form a folk song.

Posterity, then, appeared to demand some formal farewell to folk music from Dylan, and it came at the end of July when he headlined the Newport Folk Festival, accompanied by a full electric group that included Kooper, Bloomfield, and members of the Paul Butterfield Blues Band. Under-rehearsed and overamplified, performing on a stage not designed for electric acts, the group encountered a smattering of boos amid cautious applause for a nearly indecipherable "Maggie's Farm," and only a marginally more posi-tive response for the brand-new "Like a Rolling Stone," which Columbia had just released, split across two sides of a 7-inch single. When the group left the stage after only one more song, the discontent grew louder—and it hardly subsided when Dylan returned with an acoustic guitar, to play "It's All Over Now, Baby Blue."

"That was an incredible fucking watershed moment," said Kooper, who watched the encore from the wings. "I thought, 'This is unbelievable, he's saying goodbye.' And what better way to say it?"

During that momentous summer of 1965, at the point when Kooper was first feeling his way across a Hammond organ onstage, a group called the Rascals was proving that the tonal capabilities of the double-registered keyboard could dominate an electric group format, to the extent that bass guitarists were unnecessary. For now, they were doing so at an elite nightclub on a barge on the far eastern end of Long Island; within a few months they would be doing so from the top of the charts.

Growing up in the 1950s in the suburb of Pelham, just beyond the Bronx, from where his parents had migrated, Felix Cavaliere had discovered early on how it felt to be an outsider. "We were in a town where there were no other Italians," he said of a community that was dominated by WASPs, who refused Jews, blacks, and Italians alike entry into the local country clubs. That envi-ronment of denial, he said, "spurred me from the get-go to be involved in what I guess you'd call civil rights."

Cavaliere studied classical piano as a child. But in the late 1950s, in neighboring New Rochelle, he saw a black R&B trio called the Mighty Cravers who utilized just organ, drums, and sax, the organist playing bass with the foot pedals, and it resulted, he said, in "a complete metamorphosis." Cavaliere immediately switched from piano to Hammond organ, the choice of churches and R&B musicians alike. In the meantime, he put together an integrated singing group, embarking on the rounds of the Brill and Music Buildings; nothing biting, he enrolled at Syracuse University, in upstate New York, where he found himself leading a cover band, Felix and the Escorts. Through a friend of its lone Jewish member, the group secured a booking for the summer of 1963 at the Raleigh Hotel, known as one of the hipper resorts in the Catskills—a reputation proven by the fact that its main attraction that summer was Joey Dee and the Starliters.

This provided Cavaliere and the guitarist Mike Esposito with further inspiration, for here was a group of fellow suburban Italian Americans—Joey Dee had been born DiNicola and, like his guitarist Dave Brigati, hailed from New Jersey—who had managed to take their own love of black music to the top of the charts. Cavaliere decided to go for it: he quit Syracuse at the end of the summer and hit New York City with members of the Escorts instead.

The city was jumping. "It was very fertile, very active," Cavaliere recalled. "It was really like a melting pot." The action was based largely around the midtown dance clubs, many of which had sprung up in the wake (and in imitation) of the Peppermint Lounge's success, including Joey Dee's own Starliter Lounge. These venues were filled with hardworking dance groups; the ones that Cavaliere was interested in were the black ones, from the South. On the cusp of turning rhythm and blues into something called soul, these acts were inspired by the likes of Ray Charles, whose use of the organ was prominent, or James Brown, who showed how to keep the audience on its feet all night. They would perform the dances that had followed in the footsteps of the twist—the mashed potato, the jerk, the swim, the watusi. (The Starliters' hit that summer of 1963, "Hot Pastrami with Mashed Potatoes," indicates the extremities of the craze.) More than that, they all indulged in "The Show"— that part of the performance where band members engaged in shameless acrobatic stunts, something the local white groups were typically too uptight to imitate. "They did all these tricks—like playing guitar behind their backs," said Cavaliere. "It was so entertaining—and people just ate it up."

It was so entertaining that Felix and the Escorts struggled for bookings, and when Cavaliere received a call from Joey Dee's manager in October, looking for a replacement keyboard player in the middle of a European tour, he took the next available flight. In Germany a few days later, Cavaliere found himself sharing not only the stage with the Starliters but a bill with the Beatles. There were ample similarities between the two groups. Both were white, working-class bands raised on a genuine love of black American rock 'n' roll, and each had hit the top of their home country's pop charts. But there was one significant difference. The Beatles were writing their own songs—and not just dance numbers, but love songs of surprising intricacy. "When they did the American music, I was not very impressed," said Cavaliere of the Beatles' cover versions, "because I came from the R&B school, and they just didn't have the feeling for it that we were used to having. But when they did *their* music, it was like a breath of fresh air. It was, 'Oh my goodness—what is *that*?'"

Reenergized by the European tour (and by the good fortune of being "passed over" for the draft), Cavaliere assembled a new group from the overflow of great musicians on the thriving midtown scene. The guitarist Gene Cornish came through a similar path as his own, via an upstate cover band that broke up when it hit the city, after which, just as all roads once led to Rome, Cornish found himself hired by the Starliters. The second singer Eddie Brigati was brother of the Starliters' permanent guitarist Dave Brigati; he had a searing, soulful voice, could double on percussion, and had the kind of front man moves that had been popularized by the British invasion bands. And Dino Danelli was busy making a name for himself at the Metropole in midtown, with "these spinning and twirling and throwing tricks that he had picked up from the jazz world," as Cavaliere recalled it.

With Cavaliere playing the bass lines as well as the keyboard parts on the Hammond, the new quartet allowed itself to be named the Rascals by the comedian Soupy Sales, with whom they had struck up a friendship. Then they took their extensive list of contacts and, in the early months of 1965, hit a metro area club circuit governed by one simple rule: "If you don't get the people up and dancing, you don't get paid." The Rascals were doing just that out in Garfield, New Jersey, when they were headhunted by representatives of the leading Manhattan discotheque Ondine, who were converting a disused barge in the Hamptons, on the eastern end of Long Island, into a nightclub, and offered the Rascals the summer residency.

The group took one trip out east to look at the place and immediately signed on. "It wasn't a working ship, but it looked like it and felt like it. The decoration was gorgeous; it was that gay influence that was just impeccable. I knew it was going to be great. First of all, we were going to have a lot of fun, and number two, the publicity we were gonna get out there would be amazing."

The Rascals hired Adrian Barber, a British sound engineer Cavaliere had met while on tour with the Beatles, who had recently moved to New York, to maximize the PA system. They also brought with them their image. Dance clubs at the time still insisted that groups play in suits and ties, which for a sweat-inducing band like the Rascals was tantamount to torture. The Rascals attempted to circumnavigate the requirements with some creative touches: big "knickerbocker" pants trousers and short ties with ruffled collars designed by Danelli.

At the Barge, the Rascals in their Little Lord Fauntleroy clothes performed current R&B/soul hits like "Mustang Sally" and "Land of 1,000 Dances." In almost every case, they felt they were bringing something to the original. "The band was really good," said Cavaliere. "It achieved what I wanted. You didn't have to concentrate on one guy. I had no clue from a business point of view; all I knew is that if you play well and people pay attention to you, sooner or later someone's going to discover you."

For the Rascals, that someone turned out to be the textile millionaire Walter Hyman, whose main claim to musical fame was that he had bankrolled the long-standing Latin nightclub promoter/agent Sid Bernstein's ambitious ideas. Considering that one of those ideas had been to book the Beatles into Carnegie Hall months before most Americas had heard of them, that was about as good a connection as there was in the summer of 1965. Hyman invited Bernstein to come see the Rascals for himself.

But Bernstein could not spare the time. Thanks to his foresight with the Beatles, he had become the biggest promoter in New York City. During May and June, he had hosted the Rolling Stones, the Kinks, the Moody Blues, the Dave Clark Five, and Herman's Hermits, all at the New York Academy of Music, on 14th Street. And on August 15 of that year, he would be promoting the Beatles at the Mets' Shea Stadium, in Queens. With all 55,000 seats already sold, it was to be the biggest pop concert in global history. Hyman had to "kidnap" Bernstein and drive him out to Westhampton to see the Rascals, upon which the promoter understood why his friend had gotten so excited. Felix Cavaliere, said Bernstein, "was like Tito Puente. When he sat down at that Hammond organ, it was his guts pouring out. He was singing black."

Blown away by their "ruggedness," Bernstein agreed to comanage the Rascals with Hyman, and declared his intent by flashing the words "The Rascals are coming" at Shea Stadium just before the Beatles took the stage that memorable day in August. The post-Shea buzz was enough to bring Phil Spector to the Barge. The Rascals represented a rock 'n' roll version of the "blue-eyed soul" sound Spector had helped introduce earlier that year, with Mann and Weil's epic composition for the Righteous Brothers, "You've Lost That Lovin' Feelin'." And the Rascals knew that they had blown him away. "Adrian Barber wired the place, and there was no escaping us. When you came into that atmosphere, you were totally enveloped in sound. Phil was literally turning in circles when we saw him in the dressing room, because we got him, we totally reached him." But, just like the Lovin' Spoonful, the Rascals wanted control over their finished sound. They, too, turned him down.

Instead, after Labor Day, the Rascals came back to residencies at short-lived midtown clubs like the Phone Booth. Then they signed to Atlantic, which was desperate to find a viable white rock 'n' roll band—its *first* all-white band—and were that much happier to find one that sounded black. The admiration, certainly, was mutual. The Rascals were assigned a producer, Tom Dowd, a new arranger on the scene by the name of Arif Mardin, an A-side, "I Ain't Gonna Eat Out My Heart Anymore," via a pair of midtown songwriters, and were all set to go—but for the discovery of a Harmonica Rascals band that forced a name change. In their rush to release a record, they agreed to a poorly chosen modifier: the "Young Rascals" in their knickerbockers glory would struggle for the kind of credibility that ensures recognition by posterity.

A sterling example of energetic blue-eyed soul, with Eddie Brigati's voice wailing in the lead, "I Ain't Gonna Eat Out My Heart Anymore" was only a minor hit. But the group's second single more than made up for it. They had been including in their live set a recent minor hit by a veteran R&B vocal group, the Olympics, for which they quickened the song's tempo. The reaction was instantaneous. "The first time we did 'Good Lovin',' people jumped out of their seats and started dancing," said Cavaliere, and that was all the critique he needed. Recorded with contagious effervescence on February 1, 1966, a Hammond solo prominently placed in the middle, and with Cavaliere singing lead this time, the stars aligned. Aided by a couple of television performances that transported the Young Rascals' stage energy into millions of living rooms, "Good Lovin'" soared up the charts. By the end of April, it was number one across America, and the cover bands of the metro New York area had themselves a set of local heroes to emulate.

As all six minutes of "Like a Rolling Stone" blared from radios and record players throughout New York in the summer of 1965 (Columbia had been encouraged to condense the whole song to fit onto one side of a 7-inch after radio stations took to segueing the two sides together), Al Kooper found himself very much the man of the hour, his services on the Hammond in great demand. In September, he was invited by the producer Tom Wilson to participate in a session with Danny Kalb's Blues Project, the act that had opened at the Night Owl with the Lovin' Spoonful six months earlier and been bouncing around the Village coffeehouses ever since. Kalb immediately extended an invitation to permanent membership, and Kooper, not yet fully comfortable on the organ, accepted, figuring that, with the act's regular gigs in the Village, he could "improve [his] skills on a daily basis."

The Blues Project was not, by nature, a blues *band*: Kalb and his fellow guitarist Steve Katz came from a folk background (Katz as a member of the Even Dozen Jug Band), the drummer Roy Blumenfeld from jazz, and the bassist/flautist Andy Kulber from classical music. Along with Kooper and the vocalist Tommy Flanders, the blues served mainly as a mutual musical meeting point from which they could expand in different directions. They were heavily influenced by John Hammond's *Big City Blues* and by the subsequent *So Many Roads* set that had utilized the Hawks and Mike Bloomfield. The Hawks were now playing with Dylan, and Bloomfield had joined the Paul Butterfield Blues Band from Chicago. So when, in November, the Blues Project embarked on a residency at the Café Au Go Go, on Bleecker Street— another long, narrow coffeehouse, with its stage against one wall, forcing the audience to the side and rendering amplified sound especially hard on the ears—they found they had the white New York blues scene to themselves.

Playing six nights a week, two sets a night, they quickly jelled as a band, attracting a younger following keen for a local version of British white blues bands like the Animals and the Yardbirds. And over four memorable nights during Thanksgiving 1965, the Blues Project shared its residency, as part of the "Blues Bag" promotion, with Big Joe Williams, the Seventh Sons, David Blue, John Hammond, Fred Neil, and John Lee Hooker. "We were so loud that nobody could really go on after us," said Kooper. "But we were very embarrassed to have to close the show."

As the new year dawned, the Blues Project was still ensconced at the Au Go Go, playing now to packed houses, and Tom Wilson recorded the group's set there for a debut album on Verve, where he had ended up in a producer/ A&R position after falling out with Columbia. (For reasons that have remained unexplained, Dylan never worked with him again after "Like a Rolling Stone.") Released in early 1966 (by which time Flanders had left the band), *The Blues Project Live at the Café Au Go Go* comprised mostly covers, with one song by the British Dylanite Donovan alongside Eric Andersen's "Violets of Dawn." Lacking the material and studio setting for a hit single, it was not a best seller. But it served to establish the Blues Project as a forebear of an emergent New York City rock "underground," a position cemented later that year when the Blues Project released its only studio album, *Projections*— sleeve notes by its new manager, Sid Bernstein. By then, however, Kooper had determined to take control. "I was writing songs and arranging songs. Nobody else was doing that in the band. I wrote a song for the bass player so he could play flute. I recycled some gospel songs. I couldn't just sit there and watch the chaos that would have ensued had somebody not tried to organize it." With vocals taken mainly by Kooper, and again with a disregard for the singles format, *Projections* hinted at the shape of sixties music yet to come: the lengthy jam "Two Trains Running" clocked in at eleven minutes. Hailed by critics, fans, and, most notably, other musicians on both coasts and many points in between, the Blues Project had begun stretching rock music out onto the distant horizon.

Released in the spring of 1966, the Lovin' Spoonful's debut album, *Do You Believe in Magic*, served as a celebration of the Village streets and the music that permeated them, past and present, from a jug band version of the perennial *Anthology* favorite "Fishin' Blues," through a Fred Neil song ("The Other Side of Life"), a Ronettes number ("You Baby"), Sebastian's witty future number two hit about choosing between two sisters ("Did You Ever Have to Make Up Your Mind?"), and on to an instrumental tribute to the venue that had established them, "Night Owl Blues."

The little venue on Third Street was suddenly the hottest in the Village, as electric bands with names like the Strangers, Fugitives, Myddle Class, Magicians, and Blues Magoos flocked to the Night Owl from all over, hoping to acquire some of the magic that had served the Lovin' Spoonful so well. All heavily influenced by the British invasion groups, some of them by the new black soul music, and only peripherally by the folk that once dominated the Village streets, these groups inadvertently (and with varying degrees of artistic success) conspired to produce a colorful new sound, the early thrashings of psychedelia. A prime example was "An Invitation to Cry," the 1965 debut release by the Magicians, themselves reputedly named after the Spoonful's hit single; formed by a company mischievously called Longhair Productions, and possessors of a record deal with Columbia even before they took up a Night Owl residency, they signified the feverish pace at which the industry was attempting to keep up with new sounds. The Blues Magoos' Mike Esposito—Felix Cavaliere's former college friend and Escorts guitarist—was soon looking back on the Night Owl as "a contract workshop. You'll see a band three or four times and all of a sudden they're gone, with a recording contract in their hands." No longer afforded the time and space to build up their live show away from the spotlight, few of these groups proved capable of going the distance.

If it seemed contrary to the key New York electric groups' original influences, and even their aspirations, that this blossoming new rock scene consisted exclusively of white guys, then around the corner at Café Wha?, beginning June 1, 1966, with the residency of Jimmy James and the Blue Flames, there was some vindication for the black musicians who had made the midtown clubs jump and first scared Felix Cavaliere's Escorts into submission. Hendrix, as James had been born and was set to become better known, was not a native New Yorker, though he put down (short-lived) roots in the city. An experienced backing guitarist for some of the bigger names in R&B, including Little Richard, the Isley Brothers, and Jackie Wilson, Hendrix had hit New York in 1964 and 1965 with the King Curtis band, whose big hit, "Soul Serenade," was tailormade for the midtown dance clubs. Hendrix set himself up at the Theresa Hotel in Harlem, behind the Apollo, and at the end of 1965, almost inevitably for a master exponent of "the show," was brought into the lineup of Joey Dee and the Starliters. Still, when it came to finally launching his own band, Hendrix recognized that the best action was happening not in Harlem or midtown but in the Village.

That said, the Wha? was still vying with the Café Bizarre as the *least* hip of all the Village coffeehouses and was unlikely to provide him with his big break. That came instead when he joined John Hammond onstage at the Café Au Go Go in front of a star-studded audience, including the Rolling Stones' Keith Richards and his girlfriend Linda Keith. When Richards took off on tour, Linda Keith stayed behind, feeding, housing, and constantly talking Hendrix up to everyone she knew in the business. She finally struck gold with Chas Chandler of the Animals, and at the perfect moment—just as he quit that band to move into the business side of the industry. Chandler and the Animals' manager Mike Jeffery quickly signed Hendrix to a management and production deal, upon which, in mid-September 1966, Hendrix moved to London, leaving Café Wha? and the Village rock scene gratified by the experience.

For those already at the top of the game, the mood of the era was one of constant inspiration. "I was involved with people that were changing music," said Al Kooper, "and I started to feel like *I* was involved in changing music. And that every day I could get up and go work to try and change music. And that I could succeed in doing that. And that was a wonderful feeling. It was sort of a renaissance period." The mood of infinite possibilities was reflected at Steve Paul's the Scene, located in a labyrinth of basement space along West 46th Street. A former publicist for the Peppermint Lounge, Paul ran the kind of place where the Blues Project could headline—but only after an opening set by Tiny Tim, the former Café Playhouse regular now becoming famous for his ukulele-accompanied falsetto singing, and then an exhibition of karate chopping. The Scene embraced the kids who clung to the coattails of its hanging-out rock stars, affording them their own room with free sodas—and it was the only venue in New York at which the Blues

Project, Young Rascals, and Lovin' Spoonful all performed live, though the last of these bands remained so rooted in Village culture that it viewed anywhere above 14th Street as "uptown."

Further signs of changing times appeared in early 1967, when the Blues Project participated in Murray the K's "5th Dimension" package in midtown Manhattan, which featured the American debut of both Cream and the Who. It was a last hurrah for the revue formula that had lasted several generations. That summer, when the Who returned to America, it was alongside Jimi Hendrix—a star in the United Kingdom already, and about to become one in America, too—at the Monterey International Pop Festival in California, the first ever "rock" festival, and a harbinger of the forthcoming summer of love.

Monterey featured its share of prominent New York artists (the Blues Project, Simon & Garfunkel, a solo Al Kooper) and emigrants (the Byrds and, as headliners, the Mamas and the Papas), yet conspicuous by their absence were the Lovin' Spoonful, who only the preceding year had taken "Summer in the City," a celebration of gritty urban life cowritten by Sebastian's younger brother, to the top of the charts, the highlight in an impressive run of seven consecutive top ten singles. Yet, if they believed that they warranted an invitation to an event that was about to shift the power base from the East to the West Coast, they blew it in the spring of 1967 when Zal Yanovsky, in the company of Steve Boone, got himself arrested in San Francisco with enough newly purchased pot to face either a jail sentence or deportation back to Canada, either of which would mean his departure from the Lovin' Spoonful. The police gave him only one alternative: make another drug purchase so they could bust the dealer—and, taking bad advice from those around him, he agreed.

The Spoonful's game plan in doing so, said Sebastian, was to get the dealer "the best lawyer that pop music money can buy. But instead, the dealer, counterculture guy that he was, said, 'I don't want your lawyer to represent me, I'm going to have *my* lawyer represent me.' And this particular guy tried to make the case around legalizing pot, in 1967. Which was too out of touch to believe." Or perhaps, given the idealism of the San Francisco scene at the time, it was the Lovin' Spoonful who were out of touch—for the result of turning in the dealer was the band's ostracism. "There were fliers that said, 'Groupies: Don't fuck the Lovin' Spoonful—they're finks,'" recalled

Sebastian. For Yanovsky, it was the end of a dream. "His thoughts about the band, and music and the business, and the generation of love, was shattered," said his founding bandmate. Yanovsky began drinking (more) heavily, to the point that he became a burden onstage. A showdown ensued, with the result that Yanovsky left the band anyway and, with him, the magic that had carried the group so far. A year later, John Sebastian quit the band, too; something still called the Lovin' Spoonful struggled on without him for a few more rather embarrassing months, until it reached the obvious conclusion and called it a day.

Nor was the San Francisco drug scene beneficial to the Blues Project. At some point in 1967, Danny Kalb had what Al Kooper called "an incident with Owsley," the underground chemist and Grateful Dead soundman who manufactured LSD tabs in the thousands. "Owsley dosed him, and that was the end of Danny," said Kooper. "That changed his life radically; he never came back from that acid trip. It was a very bad reaction, and for years he was a changed man. And he couldn't play for a long time." Kooper and Steve Katz had already quit the Blues Project by then; determined to push the group's sound forward into the late sixties—specifically, determined to use a horn section in the manner of the jazz artist Maynard Ferguson—they set up shop at the Café Au Go Go in the summer of 1967 and emerged with the bulk of a new band, Blood Sweat and Tears, which would further push at the rock music envelope as the sixties concluded.

Felix Cavaliere was never tempted by the West Coast. "I had this muse enter my life, this young girl I fell in love with, and I wrote all these songs for and about her," he recalled. "It's amazing how in love I was. I was just ridiculously in love, I was just *gone*." The relationship did not last: in a few months, Cavaliere would write the song "How Can I Be Sure" about the same relationship. But before that could happen, in the spring of 1967, he wrote "Groovin'," the lyrics to which reflected the fact that Sunday afternoons were about the only time he had off from the gigging routine to take full advantage of the romance. "Groovin'" marked a musical detour in the Cavaliere-Brigati writing partnership; a sweetly soft number, with a lazy Latin rhythm and delicate backing harmonies, it found them at the vanguard of a new direction in soul music. To many who heard it for the first time, "Groovin'" sounded as if sung and performed by a black group—and that was about the highest compliment the Young Rascals could ask for. As a crowd of 200,000 headed to Monterey in June 1967, it was the New York act that had the number one single in the country.

A nd there, perhaps, the story of how New York City plugged in, turned on, and rocked out might end. Except that, if one wanted a single—a solo—parable to define the journey the city took in those few short years, one that was not built around the all-male electric bands of the Village and the suburbs, it could be found in the saga of a girl who came from the suburbs and helped realign the Village, bringing together not just the worlds of folk and rock but that of the Brill Building, too.

Raised in New Jersey, a self-confessed red diaper baby, Janis Fink—not the name by which she would become famous—attended summer camps that typically concluded with a group trip to Washington Square Park, where "all the counselors would play guitars and we would all sing." Taking up the guitar at the age of eleven, she "started going down [to the park] and playing songs and singing [her]self." This was 1962. That her family lived in East Orange, and that she traveled to the Village by bus, on her own, seemed of little import. "People forget how much safer it was then. Nobody would bother me." Besides, the Village of the early sixties was still a step short of becoming a tourist attraction. "You knew who your friends were by the way they dressed," and Janis, a child genius who had begun speaking at seven months, had no shortage of them. "There was a time when I knew every store owner in the Village, and every guitar seller and everybody who would regularly hang out." Dave Van Ronk and Odetta took Janis under their wings, and the Reverend Gary Davis gave her guitar lessons.

In 1964, still just thirteen years old, Janis submitted her first songs to *Broadside*, and the magazine responded by publishing "Hair Spun of Gold," a brazenly mature lyric written from the perspective of a grown woman lamenting the giving up of her creativity for married life and motherhood, and promising to protect her baby daughter from making the same mistake. It was one of the first—indeed one of the only—truly feminist songs to emerge from the Village era of "protest music." Fink, adapting her brother's middle name Ian in its place, played that song and others at *Broadside*'s monthly concerts at the Village Gate, where Buffy Saint-Marie, perhaps the only established performer on the scene tackling similar subject matter, became an inspiration.

Janis Ian's immersion in the Village culture at such a young age enabled her to experience what she called the midsixties "blossoming of creativity"— without the jaundiced perspective of the long-standing folk purists. "There was this great transition in the Village. Groups like the Lovin' Spoonful who were coming out of folk but playing electric music. And they were having hits, and they were playing the Village. So you started seeing a lot of cross-fertilization. Pure folkies and pure rock 'n' rollers getting together, and each learning from each other's world."

Yet Ian struggled to fit into this new world. Elektra Records signed her for one of its many compilation albums, this one a singer-songwriter project, but didn't use her recordings. "Jac Holzman told me I would never make it as a singer, but I would make it as a writer. And that same afternoon Harold Levanthal [manager of Pete Seeger, the Weavers, and others] told me I would never make it as a writer, and I should concentrate on being a singer." She disregarded both men. "I knew I wasn't going to make folk records, I was going to make folk-*rock* records. I was listening to the Stones and the Beatles. It was a whole different thing from these people who were ten years older and committed to this very narrow vision of folk music, a very codified music. I never felt that way. I didn't have the peer pressure. I was living out in East Orange, which was all black. Got the early side of Motown there. I was hanging out with my friend who had a blues band."

Fate was waiting to play the right hand. It happened after performing at the Gaslight one night, when Ian was commandeered by a prospective manager who promised her the earth—and met her after school the very next day to bring her to his attorney: Johanan Vigoda, who later managed Stevie Wonder. "Johanan listened to two or three songs," she recalled, "and took me straight up to Shadow Morton's office."

That was an inspired move. Red Bird was falling apart, and Morton had lost interest in trying to follow the same formula with the Shangri-Las at Mercury. There had been some efforts to bring the girl group sound up to date with rock—the Chiffons' 1965 single "Nobody Knows What's Goin' On" was only one step short of psychedelic—but the public was looking for *artistes*. Now here was Janis Ian, fifteen years old—the same age as Mary

Weiss when Morton first recorded her—and not only were her songs built on the lyrical narratives with which Morton had made his name, but she wrote them herself.

Still, Morton, who had told everyone he was quitting the music business, was none too thrilled to have Vigoda walk in on him all but unannounced, "pushing little Janis, saying, 'Here she is—play something for him.'" He took refuge behind that day's *New York Times*, his way of "shutting down."

"He was sitting at his desk, reading the *New York Times* with his cowboy boots propped up on his desk," recalled Ian, "so Johanan told me to pull out my guitar and start singing. I did, and the newspaper stayed up. So I kept singing, and the newspaper stayed up. And I finished the song, and the newspaper stayed up." Ian did what any normal fifteen-year-old would surely have been tempted to do in the face of such rudeness. "I took a cigarette lighter out of my pocket, lit fire to the newspaper, and left."

While she waited for the elevator with Vigoda, Morton rushed out, embarrassed and apologetic, calling himself an "idiot," begging to hear the songs again. A frustrated Ian obliged, and they hit it off. "He literally listened to everything I'd written to that date, picked 'Society's Child,' and said, 'Great, we'll go into the studio next week.' And we did."

Morton initially heard "Society's Child" as similar to his own "Leader of the Pack:" "Girl falls in love, mom and dad don't like it," as he put it. Only in the studio, using much the same team as on the Shangri-Las records, did one of the musicians, the bass player George Duvivier, stop everyone, saying, "I don't think we should record this anymore until we listen to the words." Once they did so, they identified the line that differentiated "Society's Child" from everything else out there in the pop music world. It was a reference to the boyfriend's face, "shining black as night." That brought a totally different meaning to the narrator's mother insisting that, "he's not our kind." "Leader of the Pack" suddenly seemed tame by comparison.

Led by the veteran arranger Artie Kaplan, the subsequent recording owed much to the Red Bird studio style, full of dramatic breaks and tempo changes, but still it held back, paying respect to the song's folk roots. And if Ian's voice lacked the addictive vulnerability of Mary Weiss, it was more classical and certainly belied its tender years. But when it came to the final vocal take, Morton took her outside. He told her, "I cannot guarantee the success of this record as it stands, but I can guarantee that if you change just that one word, I will get you a top ten record. It's your call." Ian "thought about it for all of two seconds," as she recalled, and told him, "It stays."

And it did. As a result, Morton recalled, no label wanted to touch it, including the one that financed the session: interracial teenage romance appeared too hot even for the musically interracial label Atlantic to handle. Eventually, after dozens of rejections, Jerry Schoenbaum at Verve Records (which had recently taken over Folkways) decided to take a chance with his new Verve Forecast imprint. There was, initially, very little radio action other than on the burgeoning New York FM stations, which is not to say that nobody noticed it—for as Robert Shelton wrote on the eventual debut album's sleeve notes, "Censorship was clearly keeping the song from wider air-play, but censorship on this level cannot be proved or determined. You just know it is there."

Support eventually came from Leonard Bernstein, of all people, who in April 1967, several months after the single's initial release, invited Ian to perform it on a Sunday night network television special entitled *Inside Pop: The Rock Revolution*. The next morning, newspapers and magazines picked up on the story of the fifteen-year-old with the lyric that adults didn't want to hear. As embarrassed radio stations decided that the song was playable after all, it became a top twenty hit. Yet the controversy was far from over: Ian was castigated by some of her original supporters in Greenwich Village for appearing to embrace the old enemies of the Brill Building, and hounded by teachers at her new school, Music and Art (her parents had moved to Manhattan in the interim), for managing to "make it" without their help. Of even greater concern, both she and Morton endured hate mail and death threats from racists because of the song's subject matter. When Ian was on tour, strangers would come up to her in the street and spit in her face.

"Society's Child" was, then, a pivotal musical moment—and not just for its content. It also represented a crucial shift in the power base, from producer to musician. At their very first session together, Ian recalled, Morton, who had famously "directed" the Shangri-Las, "just put me in the studio and said, 'Okay, tell the guys what you want them to play.' " She spent a lifetime trying to figure out "whether he was drunk or tired or bored or just trying an experiment . . . because he was part of what was rapidly coming down, and I was the era that was coming up, and he may have thought that this is a way to be a part of that."

"She was on the right path," said Morton. "In this case, from the time that she first played her songs for me, on that huge guitar that nearly covered her body, it seemed obvious to me that this girl knew where she was going, The only thing that could have hurt it then was my ego or someone else's ego getting in the way, trying to prove that they were smarter than her."

Morton was himself smart enough to stay out of the way. As a result, Janis Ian received a co-arranging credit with Artie Kaplan on her eponymous debut album, a precocious masterpiece (and a major hit) on which she wrote all eleven songs, even though she was only sixteen by the time of its release. The material, all of it performed with the studio band, ranged from "Society's Child" through the amusingly juvenile "Younger Generation Blues" and a self-admitted "controversial" song about the cult of the pop star, "New Christ Cardiac Hero." It also included the song that had started it all off for her, "Hair of Spun Gold." Janis Ian, sixties child, was not going to go the way of her narrator.

12

ALL TOMORROW'S PARTIES

By the dawn of the 1960s, the reputation of Greenwich Village had put an end to one of its original attractions: cheap rents. The real estate agents' solution was to recommend that hard-pressed would-be bohemians search the other side of Broadway, beyond the bookstores that dominated Fourth Avenue, and into something they called the Village East. By 1961, they had switched those words around and, as realtors have a habit of doing in New York City, declared a new community: the East Village.

The invention of the East Village came as news to those who had long lived there and known it by a different name: the Lower East Side. Not that anyone needed a degree in city planning to understand the thinking. The East Village, carved out of an area between two major cross-streets, 14th and Houston ("0" Street for those who were counting), had no prior connotations, which offered something of a blank slate. The Lower East Side, on the other hand, generally understood to run as far south from 14th Street as the Brooklyn Bridge and beyond, was associated worldwide with poverty and overcrowding, infamous for having once contained almost a million immigrants within barely two square miles of tenement slum land. That was not necessarily the stuff of realtors' dreams—and yet for the bohemians who already made it their home, the Lower East Side had an equally rich history of creative culture and political activism, and they were none too keen to surrender its name.

What the realtors announced as the new East Village had its roots in the old Bowery Village, where a windmill once stood on the corner of modern Tenth Street and Third Avenue. That land had belonged at the time to the private estate founded by New Amsterdam's final governor, Peter Stuyvesant, who was buried underneath what became St. Mark's-in-the-Bouwerie, New York's second-oldest surviving church (and a mainstay of Lower East Side activism), on the corner of Second Avenue and Stuyvesant Street.

What the realtors were happy to leave aside, for now, as the Lower East Side, also had its roots in private land, that belonging to members of the Rutgers family, who made their fortune primarily in brewing, and the descendants of Lieutenant Governor and Chief Justice James De Lancey. In the late eighteenth and early nineteenth centuries, these landowners built solid masonry row houses for an aspiring middle class on comfortable 25- by 100-foot lots. But after the opening of the Erie Canal in 1825 made New York's docklands the busiest in North America, the initial homeowners swiftly headed north to quieter communities, and absentee landlords stepped in to cater to the new hourly wage earners, subdividing the old row houses for tenancy or else tearing them down and replacing them with cheap wooden structures.

In the subsequent population explosion—between 1830 and 1860, Manhattan's inhabitants quadrupled, from barely 200,000 to over 800,000—it was the lower eastern part of the island, with these new tenement buildings and their easy access to dockland employment, that bore the brunt of the increase. Landlords further divided the row houses into ever smaller rooms, many without light or ventilation, and then built additional tenements in the gardens out back, until a plot of land initially designed for one family might now be occupied by as many as thirty. Around the notorious Five Points intersection of the old Sixth Ward, the Irish huddled twenty-five and more to a room, a solid thousand of them in a single building known as the Old Brewery. The mostly German residents of the Tenth Ward, bordered by Division, Norfolk, and Stanton Streets and the Bowery, were no better off: reformers found babies literally dying from suffocation in the fetid air of the apartments.

Yet still the city kept growing, still the immigrants kept coming. Joining earlier waves of Irish escaping the potato famine, English chartists avoiding persecution, and Germans in the wake of a failed revolution came more, predominantly Jewish Germans, escaping antisocialist legislation, until New

York was the largest German "city" outside of Berlin. Half a million Russian Jews, fleeing pogroms after they were held responsible for the assassination of Czar Alexander in 1881, arrived, in just two decades, settling mainly in the Tenth Ward, pushing the Germans north across Houston Street. Southern Italians, mostly single males escaping poverty after their nation's unification, and Chinese, themselves mainly escaping depression-fueled racism in their original American home state of California, added to the numbers.

What united this polyglot community—which included also the freed black slaves and their descendants who had long made the area their home— was a desire to escape persecution, and it metamorphosed on the Lower East Side of Manhattan into a valiant fight for their rights. The Irish and Germans established unions and co-ops in the 1840s and 1850s and frequently took to the streets to protest for better conditions. Tompkins Square Park—named for the New York governor who had championed the abolition of slavery— saw its first major confrontation in 1857, and its worst in 1874 when, following a serious economic collapse, a crowd of seven thousand gathered to demand that the mayor install a public works program, only to be cleared out of the park by baton-wielding police. Among the twelve hundred members of the German Tenth Ward Workingmen's Association who stood their ground and fought was a young Justus Schwab, brandishing the red flag of the Paris Commune as his weapon.

Inevitably, the immigrant groups carved out their own distinct locales: a Little Italy in the streets south of Washington Square Park; a Chinatown around Canal Street. After Germantown was decimated by the 1905 sinking of the *General Slocum*, at the cost of over a thousand lives (most of them children), it left behind a core Lower East Side that was 95 percent Jewish, albeit of every ethnic variety: Eastern European Jews, Sephardic Jews, Galician Jews, and, especially, Russian Jews. In 1908 Israel Zangwill's play *The Melting Pot* imagined the tribes of different Jewish immigrants "smelted" in America into one, and in the process popularized a term that became ever associated with New York City.

The density of the Tenth Ward was measured at over 450,000 per square mile in the 1900 census, making it the most crowded corner of the world, and a fiercely political one at that. Abraham Cahan founded the Jewish newspaper the *Daily Forward* in 1897 as "the conscience of the ghetto." Emma Goldman took up part-time residence with the other socialists and anarchists at First on First, a bar owned by the riot veteran Justus Schwab, brought her oratory to Union Square, where she extolled anarchy and women's rights, and launched *Mother Earth* magazine in 1906. (She was deported in an anticommunism drive in 1919.) Meyer London arrived from Russia as a twenty-year-old in the 1890s, became a lawyer, fought for workers' rights, and was elected New York's first Socialist congressman in 1914, inspiring all-night revelry in Rutgers Square.

Yet the majority of European and Russian Jews could not wait to escape the great New York ghetto. Some took their families out to Brooklyn, where so many of the Brill area's pop songwriters were later born and raised. Others settled in the Bronx, where by 1930 fully half of the 1,265,000 population was Jewish. The new generation of bohemians who took advantage of the cheap rents left in the wake of their exodus quickly discovered that the Lower East Side's history of activism had instilled in the neighborhood a pervasive laissez-faire attitude. For here, in the heart of the old ghetto, it seemed, one could truly live according to one's own rules—or lack of them. For many, it was an urban nirvana. Left alone by the tourists and folk singers west of Broadway, by the city bureaucrats and mobsters alike, they created for themselves a more singular, idiosyncratic, and risqué version of Greenwich Village.

Allen Ginsberg, for example, the most consistently active and engaged of the original beat writers, lived on East Seventh Street, on the far side of Tompkins Square Park. Fellow poets like Denise Levertov and LeRoi Jones read at the American Theater for Poetry, on East Fourth Street, and Mickey Ruskin's café Les Deux Megots on East Seventh. The Five Spot on the Bowery played host to legendary residencies by Ornette Coleman, Thelonious Monk, and John Coltrane. Stanley Tolkin's Thirteenth Street Bar on Avenue B attracted the hard-drinking painters and writers of the day. And the Dollar Sign on East Ninth maintained a pair of frequently copulating monkeys in the window alongside a prominent sign advertising "Peyote for Sale."

When underground and avant-garde filmmaking boomed in the early sixties, it was briefly centered on the Charles Theater on Avenue B and 12th Street, in large part thanks to Jonas Mekas, a Lithuanian-born concentration camp survivor who formed a New American Cinema Group movement in late 1960s and took over booking at the theater. Significantly, when the celebrated pop art painter Andy Warhol decided to start making such films in 1963 (for, as would become evident, there was no cultural movement in New

York in which he could not prosper), he screened his debut movie, *Sleep*, at a Bowery apartment, with Mekas as the guest of honor; he then shot much of his next film, *Kiss*, at an apartment on Avenue B.

In the meantime, Tenth Street around Third Avenue, where the Bowery Village windmill had once stood, became known for its largely black, co-operative art galleries, with some 250 dues-paying members spread across eight galleries by 1962. In a similar spirit, Elaine Stewart opened the non-profit La MaMa Experimental Theater in a basement on East Fourth Street, inspiring St. Mark's-in-the-Bowery to follow suit with its Theatre Genesis, which attracted new playwrights like Sam Shepard, a former waiter at the Village Gate. The church, lovingly referred to as "St. Marx's" in the 1930s, began hosting poetry readings, too: Allen Ginsberg and Ted Berrigan were regulars.

And then, in 1965, Don and Allan Katzman started a local publication that they filled with provocative political essays, commentary, and cartoons, all laid out as if under the influence of mind-altering substances. They named their paper the *East Village Other*, not so much in (grudging) recognition of the neighborhood's apparently "official" new moniker but as an ironic com-ment on every local bohemian's favorite French poet, Arthur Rimbaud: "Je est un autre."

Peter Stampfel, a Milwaukee boy who dropped out of the University of Wisconsin to pursue the bohemian lifestyle, visited New York City for the first time on his travels in 1959. There he discovered that the Lower East Side "was much more hip than the Village. Everybody said it, everybody knew it." Satisfied that the area's eclectic mix—older Jews and Ukrainians, younger Puerto Ricans, a variety of blacks, and bohemians of both geographi-cal and lifestyle origins—was not as unsafe as strangers would have him believe, the twenty-year-old Stampfel returned later that year for good, find-ing an apartment on Clinton Street. "The whole world knew about Greenwich Village," he said. "But only New Yorkers or bohemian types were aware of the Lower East Side as a bohemian center."

As a fan of the Harry Smith *Anthology of American Folk Music*, Stampfel had come to New York hoping to immerse himself in the folk scene; being "wildly enthusiastic about bluegrass," and knowing Eric Weissberg and John

Herald from the University of Wisconsin, he eagerly visited Washington Square Park, only to find that "all the bluegrass guys sounded very much like the same person." By comparison, the performers on the *Anthology*, he noted, "weren't as fancy, but they sounded like they were on different planets. The variety and the weirdness trumped the technical precision, as far as I was concerned."

Stampfel switched from the banjo to the fiddle to better distinguish himself, and when, in the spring of 1963 his girlfriend invited to their East Houston Street apartment her former boyfriend Steve Weber, a poet and guitarist from Pennsylvania with a wild reputation, the pair hit it off "like long-lost brothers." Propelled by a copious supply of crystal methamphetamine, which, Stampfel said, exploded in popularity on the Lower East Side in 1962, they stayed up playing guitar and fiddle together for three days and nights. Toward the end of the binge, they headed to the Village, and an impromptu set at the Café Raffio, on Bleecker Street, where there was a mirror opposite the stage. Seeing their sleep-deprived, drug-addled reflection, Stampfel decided, "Me and Weber playing together was just weirdness beyond any dreams of weirdness I could ever possibly have dreamed. I thought, 'We have to do this, we must do this, this is just too fucking outlandish for us not to shove in everyone's faces for ever.'"

Convinced that a niche existed for an act that presented the *Anthology* eccentricities with a rock 'n' roll attitude, Stampfel and Weber, as the Holy Modal Rounders, worked up a set of traditional songs. Whenever Stampfel struggled to decipher a lyric from a recording, he simply inserted his own, relevant to the present day. Later he might learn the original words, but "in every case," he said, "I thought my words were better. I wasn't trying to be nutty. I just thought it was an improvement."

The duo's spirited attitude came across in their coffeehouse performances. "Part of it was we were really having a good time," said Stampfel, "and most people who were playing folk music were serious. Or else, if they were having a good time, it was a faux good time. They were *acting* jolly." Stampfel had an infectiously cheerful, comedic charisma; Weber had actual star power: "Guys were interested in his guitar playing, and girls were interested in fucking him." Weber was especially renowned for his constitution. "People would see Weber taking all these drugs and carrying on in this totally crazed Dionysian way, seemingly without effort," said Stampfel. "And people would try and emulate him—and tend to come to very bad ends very rapidly."

With the folk boom in full swing, the Holy Modal Rounders, though atypical, were offered their share of recording contracts. They chose the minor label Prestige. On November 21, 1963—the day before President Kennedy was assassinated—the duo recorded an album that filtered the eccentricities of rural American folk music through the contemporary drug culture of the Lower East Side. Courtesy of Stampfel's lyrical adjustments, there was now a reference to "sniffing glue" on the *Anthology*'s "Blues in the Bottle," the prevalent use of the word "cocaine" on "Hey, Hey Baby," and a rewrite of the old standard "Hesitation Blues," on which Stampfel sang, "I got my psychedelic feet and my psychedelic shoes, / I believe Lord o'mama I got the psychedelic blues."

It was the first known use of the word "psychedelic" in song. "I wanted to do it before anyone else did," said Stampfel. "At the time I really felt that hallucinogens would lead to a major worldwide breakthrough in consciousness." Stampfel was not alone in this belief, though it would be at least two more years before "psychedelic" started to be used as a musical adjective. Upon release in the spring of 1964, the cheerfully ambitious *Holy Modal Rounders* was widely misinterpreted (*Sing Out!* denounced it for being disrespectful to tradition) and widely ignored, though with all its eccentricities it would endure far better than many of its contemporaries. Weber and Stampfel were less innovative on *Holy Modal Rounders II*, but by the time of its release, they cared little, for they had just about abandoned any pretense to folk music and instead joined up with the Lower East Side's first and foremost rock band: the Fugs.

ike Stampfel, Ed Sanders came to the Lower East Side from the Midwest, in his case Kansas City, a central location that exposed him to jazz, classical music, R&B, rock 'n' roll, and country and western. He was blessed, too, with literary parents, and a high school English teacher who encouraged him "to write anything [he] wanted." This upbringing helped instill a lifelong fascination for Greek poetry and history, but Sanders also fell headlong for beat poetry, especially Ginsberg's *Howl*: "It changed my life. I memorized it. I went to New York a few months later and I immediately went to all the poetry readings I could. I loved the Beats."

In New York, Sanders took classes at NYU, drank with the painters, poets, and writers at the Cedar Tavern and Stanley's, joined the civil rights marches down south, and was imprisoned for trying to board a Polaris nuclear submarine during a protest in the summer of 1961. In his cell, he wrote the lengthy "Poem from Jail," smuggled out on toilet paper and cigarette foil, establishing his own career as a celebrated beat poet. Moving to an apartment on 11th Street between Avenues A and B—the eastern bulge of the Lower East Side often referred to as Alphabet City—he launched the inimitable *Fuck You / A Magazine of the Arts*. Here he mixed quasi-pornographic imagery with his idiosyncratic "Egyptian freak-doodles," along with poetry by the likes of Ginsberg, Weber, and Tuli Kupferberg, a "beat hero" known for hawking his own magazine *Yeah* on the Village streets, and for reputedly being the character who, in Ginsberg's *Howl*, "jumped off the Brooklyn Bridge this actually happened and walked away."

Late 1964 found the "free-formist" Kupferberg, forty years old already (he dismissed much of his twenties and thirties as a blur of "mystery and history"), living above a wholesale egg market on East Tenth Street between Avenues B and C, recording his poetry to tape in song form. When Sanders, newly graduated with a degree in classics, rented the store next door to open a vegetarian coffeehouse and bookstore, the pair began collaborating on these poem songs: the Beatles and the Stones had opened up new avenues of creativity for two men who were hardly restrained to begin with. "Ed was a wild, crazy, mid-Western young man," said Kupferberg, "and I was a New York radical Jew. So together we had everything or, as some people would say, nothing."

Soon enough the pair had written over fifty songs. Most were sexual, scatological, topical, or simply surreal. But Kupferberg couldn't play an instrument, and Sanders did not want to be stuck behind the drums and piano that he had learned as a child. They recruited a Texan, Ken Weaver, to play bongos and maracas, after which Weber and Stampfel, smitten by what the latter called the trio's "crazy anarchist ideas," came to the rescue, volunteering their services as guitarists and fiddlers.

In doing so, the pair "gave us the illusion that we were musicians and a band," said Kupferberg. "We didn't give a fuck actually. We weren't out to do high art." Appropriately, Kupferberg came up with the name of the Fugs—a sexual euphemism taken from *The Naked and the Dead*, by Norman Mailer, a native of lower First Avenue in the 1950s—and the five-piece group played its first show at the opening party for Sander's bookstore, Peace Eye, on

February 24, 1965, with an opening set by the Holy Modal Rounders. Among the artistic celebrities in attendance were William Burroughs, George Plimpton, James Michener—and Andy Warhol, who supplied canvas prints of his flower designs as decorations.

The Fugs drew inspiration from what Sanders paraphrased, in part, as a tradition that extended from "the dances of Dionysus in the ancient Greek plays and the 'Theory of the Spectacle' in Aristotle's Poetics . . . to the jazz-poetry of the Beats, to Charlie Parker's seething sax, to the silence of John Cage, to the calm pushiness of the Happening movement, to the songs of the Civil Rights movement, and to our concept that there was oodles of freedom guaranteed by the United States Constitution that was not being used." They brought this mixture onstage to the American Theater for Poetry; the Bridge Theater, on St. Mark's Place for a run of Saturday night concerts; even the opening for Izzy Young's newly located Folklore Center, on Sixth Avenue. The *Anthology* producer Harry Smith, still making movies, still collecting music, still just about scraping by at the very pit of the underground, saw in the Fugs at these shows a genuinely urban jug band—or at least that's what he told his original benefactor, Moe Asch at Folkways, who agreed to put out an album. In April 1965, Smith helped the Fugs record twenty-three songs in one fell swoop, after which he and Sanders narrowed the selection down to ten, discarding (so they thought) several of the most patently outrageous. In the fall of 1965, they released those ten as *The Village Fugs—Ballads and Songs of Contemporary Protest, Points of View and General Dissatisfaction.*

Every bit the oddity of its title, the album was neither beat poetry, jug band, protest folk, folk rock, nor rock 'n' roll, only vaguely the sum of such ingredients, and as inventive and truly magical as it was both hilarious and, at times, plain dumb. The material ranged from Weaver's hard-driving trib-ute to the "Slum Goddess of the Lower East Side" (a perennial neighborhood character promptly taken up by the *East Village Other* as a fashion spread), through two William Blake poems set to music by Sanders, to the puerile humor of Weber's "Boobs a Lot" and Kupferberg's minimalist dirge, "Nothing," the bongo accompaniment of which did not clarify whether it was poking fun at the group's beatnik roots or just playing along.

If there was one issue the Fugs were eminently serious about, it was their pacifism. In late 1965, they packed themselves into a Volkswagen van and embarked on a national tour—no easy feat to pull off at the time—in opposition to a Vietnam War that few young people clearly understood and yet was on all of their minds that summer, given that President Lyndon Johnson had just abruptly doubled the number of draft calls, to 35,000 per month. Comparatively few New York musicians ended up serving—during the first years of the war, they were hardly the kind of fighting men that the forces were looking for, and, besides, they taught each other how to get around their draft interviews by hook or by crook—but opposition to the war became the one issue on which all of them could agree. The Fugs were the first to embrace this opposition, without apology or concern for etiquette. Their position was most clearly stated in a classic line from "Doin' All Right," contributed by their poet friend Ted Berrigan: "I ain't ever gonna go to Vietnam / I prefer to stay here and screw your mom."

"That was enough to get us beaten up if we did it in the right place," said Kupferberg—as was his aptly titled and brilliantly stated "Kill for Peace," as close as the group got to a conventional rock anthem. Over time, it also became the Fugs' most theatrical stage presentation: a typical performance might find Kupferberg dressed as a U.S. general, force-feeding a limbless doll, doing duty as a Vietnamese baby, with chocolate-covered candy, then pouring spaghetti sauce over the doll as a metaphor for American mass murder.

Upon return from their tour, the Fugs set Steve Weber free: his position became untenable the night he lay down to sleep, onstage, in the middle of a Fugs set, using his guitar as a pillow. (Weber, said Sanders, was the only person he ever saw take LSD as a cure for toothache.) Peter Stampfel had already broken from Weber for missing a series of Holy Modal Rounders shows and being overly generous with his drugs in crowded restaurants. That had meant breaking from the Fugs, too—just before they attracted the attention Stampfel craved. "Weber was fine and dandy until the Beatles hit," said Stampfel. "And when that happened, he realized, on an unconscious level, we had the opportunity to have some degree of success, and that's when he started sabotaging things because . . . well, gee, why does a creative person start sabotaging things?"

The mercury hit a balmy 61 degrees Fahrenheit on January 1, 1966—which was just as well, given that the Republican mayor John Lindsay's brand-new administration was welcomed to office by a transit strike, forcing revelers to walk off their hangovers and Lindsay to cancel the inaugural parties he had scheduled in each of the five boroughs. As the strike dragged on through the first twelve days of January, the image of New York City as an almost mystically functioning world capital took a serious hit.

New Year's Day did not bring tidings of joy to Ed Sanders, either. A few hours after the Fugs performed at the Bridge on St. Mark's, his store Peace Eye was raided. Confiscating copies of *Fuck You* and other magazines, the police arrested Sanders and charged him with "possession with intent to sell pornography." The American Civil Liberties Union took up the case, and Sanders was ultimately acquitted, but not until a year and a half later, during which time Sanders's faith in the First Amendment would be frequently tested. In the interim, the Fugs recruited new musicians, turned fully electric, and signed to the avant-garde jazz label ESP, named for its founder Bernard Stollman's fascination with the international Esperanto language. Stollman arranged for hire of the Astor Place Playhouse, one of the historic Colonnade buildings on Lafayette Street, as a home venue for the Fugs' increasingly elaborate performances, and also hooked the group up at a four-track studio, a rarity in 1966. The Fugs embraced both opportunities, and upon release in the spring of that year, *The Fugs*, liner notes written by Allen Ginsberg, astounded onlookers by entering the top 100 albums chart.

Success came not so much despite the presence of "Kill for Peace" and "Doin' All Right" as because of it. Similarly, many record buyers were drawn to, rather than repelled by, songs like "Group Grope" and "Dirty Old Man." The discussion of sexual freedom sometimes bordered on degradation in the newly emboldened "freak" culture, not just in Fugs songs but also in the increasingly lewd cartoons of the *East Village Other* and associated underground comics. And yet the line on "Doin' All Right" that "we get more sex than spades" was so offensive on so many levels that it could be digested only with the intended sense of humor. "The whole sexual thing the Fugs put forth was an idealized exaggeration," observed Stampfel. "On one hand there was certainly a great deal of sexual acceptance, which had been going on in a bohemian sense since there was a bohemia. But it really wasn't actually as rampant as depicted in Sanders's poetry and in the songs of the Fugs." Indeed, lost in the Fugs' giddy celebration of "group gropes" was the fact that Sanders (married with a child) and Kupferberg were involved in steady relationships.

Police raids and obscenity charges, on the other hand, were a very real consequence of Lower East Side activism, and when an American flag was burned onstage during an antiwar play called *LBJ* at the Bridge, the city's License Department immediately tried to revoke the theater's license. The Fugs attempted both to show solidarity with the Bridge and to demonstrate the strength of the First Amendment at their next show by setting fire to a flag emblazoned with words they held more dear than the image of the Stars and Stripes: "Lower East Side."

Two days later, on April 18, Sanders joined Ginsberg and Mekas at the Bridge for a press conference to launch the New York Eternal Committee for Conservation of Freedom in the Arts. It was, the *New York Times* journalist Sidney Zion observed, a "rambling" affair, with Ginsberg accusing "petty officials" in the new Lindsay administration of deliberately harassing the avant-garde movement as part of what Mekas called, somewhat hyperbolically, "a desperate gathering of evil or sick forces to delay the development of man." Zion noted from talking to Sanders that the Fugs "burned an American flag at a performance last Saturday night and that nothing had happened as a result." But the reporter's (inadvertent?) substitution of an "American" flag for that of the "Lower East Side"—the difference between sacrilege and art—immediately resulted in exactly the harassment the new committee was bemoaning. The Fire Department and building inspectors descended on the Astor Place Playhouse, citing code infractions in the Fugs' multimedia performances. After playing nine shows a week for almost four consecutive months, the Astor Place residency was abruptly canceled, and the Fugs, at the peak of their popularity, were suddenly without a home. So much for those oodles of freedom.

f a visitor to New York that same day in April 1966 had been looking for a scenario that truly represented a midsixties collision of past and present, East Village and Greenwich Village, Long Island and Lower East Side, commercial and avant-garde, mainstream and counterculture, film, music, poetry, art, drugs, *and* the cult of personality, he needed only to walk across St. Mark's Place and halfway down the block from the Bridge, venture into the hall known as the Dom, and wait for the 9 p.m. commencement of the Exploding Plastic Inevitable.

There, against a backdrop—and two side walls—on which were projected Andy Warhol's avant-garde films (*Sleep, Kiss, Vinyl, Eat, Couch, Banana*, etc.), themselves overlaid with both slides and film of the night's band, under a mirror ball off which bounced colored pin lights so that the room was swimming in stars, spotlights and strobes picked out the dancers Gerard Malanga, Mary Woronov, Ingrid Superstar, and Ronnie Cutrone as they moved around the stage. Warhol himself watched impassively from the balcony, while the Hungarian/German model/actress/singer Nico, dressed in virginal white, sang in a voice one writer described as "like a 'cello getting up in the morning." Alongside her, in contrasting black clothes, two electric guitarists, an electric viola player, and an androgynous-looking drummer attacking tom-toms with mallets created a feedback-driven drone such as had never been heard on a New York club stage. They were the Velvet Underground, they were in the midst of their first fully fledged residency, and they were embarking on one of the most fabled of New York musical stories, a supposed morality tale of how innovation does not necessarily reap reward—at least not within a group's lifetime.

The key to that story, to the music they made, and the manner in which they played it, lay in the contrasting paths of the group's two main members, both of them twenty-four years old at the time. John Cale, whose sonorous voice revealed his upbringing in the valleys of Wales, had come to New York from his London college via an unsuccessful scholarship in Massachusetts. Sharing an apartment in a thriving artists' building on Ludlow Street, just below Grand Street in the heart of the old Tenth Ward, Cale had thrived on the Lower East Side's avant-garde scene: in September 1963, he had been one of several performers who repeated an Erik Satie piano piece 840 times over, turning an 80-second composition into a 19-hour epic. With his roommate Tony Conrad, the minimalist composer La Monte Young, and Young's partner Marian Zazeela, he was also a member of the Theatre of Eternal Music, in which each musician held an individual note for two hours at a time.

The wiry-haired, tautly built Lou Reed came at his music from a more conventional direction. Born in Brooklyn but then whisked out to suburban Freeport, Long Island, by his upwardly aspiring Jewish parents in the early fifties, Reed found salvation in the rock 'n' roll radio of Alan Freed and Jocko Henderson. Learning to play guitar, he was soon writing songs, playing in bands, and spending his high school lunch hours hanging out at the local radio station. Like many of his sixties contemporaries, he had a precociously early start in the music business, recording a copycat doo-wop song for a Mercury subsidiary when barely sixteen. It wasn't a hit, but Reed's obsession with writing—both words and music—was now thoroughly ingrained.

So too was his combative nature. At home, he played his electric guitar late into the night, smoked pot, was given to serious mood swings, and, though he dated girls, told his parents he was homosexual. Despairing at such behavior, they sent him in 1959 to a psychiatrist, who recommended a cure increasingly in vogue at the time: electroshock treatment. For antisocial behavior that would become commonplace in the sixties, Reed underwent eight weeks of thrice-weekly electroshock treatment at Long Island's Creedmore State Psychiatric Hospital. The long-term result was an instinctive antipathy toward authority, a removal from emotional attachment, a need to manipulate relationships, and a further embrace of the renegade lifestyle.

Reed decamped to Syracuse University, where he fronted a couple of cover bands (crossing paths with Felix Cavaliere and the Escorts), published a literary journal, saw Bob Dylan in concert, and learned to play the harmonica. He jammed with his fellow guitarist and Long Island native Sterling Morrison during down time, broadcast his own eclectic radio show on the college station (so eclectic that it was forced off the air), started selling soft drugs (marijuana) and delving into both hallucinogens (peyote, LSD) and hard drugs (heroin), and experimented sexually. He also befriended Delmore Schwartz, the poet and prose writer who had once been a permanent fixture on the Village literary-social scene, from where, to paraphrase Ginsberg, he had been one of his generation's best literary minds to slip into alcohol abuse and madness. Now teaching creative writing at Syracuse, Schwartz became the younger writer's mentor as they read through Shakespeare, James Joyce, and Dostoyevsky. Schwartz, determined not to let Reed squander his potential, threatened to haunt the younger writer from the grave if, as Reed recalled, he "didn't really try to write well and never sell out."

Yet, back in New York, Reed promptly went to work for Pickwick Records, writing imitations of contemporary hits for cheap supermarket compilations. When he penned a cash-in dance song, "Do the Ostrich," the label released it under the band name the Primitives—and when it looked like it was taking off, sought musicians to fulfill public appearances. Cale and Conrad, approached at a Manhattan party, agreed to join the faux band for the performance art experience of it. At the company's warehouse in Long Island City, Cale and Reed met for the first time and, opposites in attraction, quickly hit it off.

They performed some gigs together as the Primitives, but as the act ran its course ("The Ostrich" was no mashed potato), Reed played Cale his more "serious" songs, and Cale saw, as he put it, that "what Lou was singing about was not what rock 'n' roll was generally about." In particular, Reed was carrying with him from Syracuse two stark songs of honest drug talk. "I'm Waiting for the Man" had Reed's narrator, a lone white boy on 125th Street, fending off street hassle while waiting for his dealer, an account of such precision that it seemed it could only have been written from experience. "Heroin" found Reed not just daring to name a song for the most addictive of narcotics but appearing to extol its apparent virtues in the lyrics.

In much later years, Reed would attempt to distance himself from his strikingly detailed first-person account of self-injected narcotics abuse. Citing the likes of William Burroughs's *Junky*, he insisted that "in novels it would be a big nothing." This was not true: Burroughs, like Ginsberg, was charged with obscenity for his writing. Besides, Reed did not necessarily deny his early drug songs' autobiographical streak: " 'Heroin' is very close to the feeling that you get from smack," he said.

On the group's earliest surviving home recordings, from the summer of 1965, "Heroin" lived up to Reed's claim; even in acoustic form, it served as an oppressive rush to the nervous system and therefore all too easy to (mis)interpret as an endorsement, rather than merely an account, of a fix. The other songs were less potent. "All Tomorrow's Parties" sounded as if it had been written at a Folk City hootenanny—just as a track called "Prominent Men" came across like a Bob Dylan outtake from 1964, complete with harmonica solo. Cale, who hated folk music—"every song's a fucking question," he caustically stated—steadily eradicated Dylan's influence; Reed's harmonica playing was never heard on a Velvet Underground record.

For his own part, Reed, who "didn't know from La Monte Young," and generally set his literary lyrics to conventional chord patterns, found himself instantly attracted to Cale's work with the Theatre of Eternal Music, also known as the Dream Syndicate. "That drone stuff was really fun," he observed. "I got into it because of distortion, getting a feedback tone."

Tony Conrad quickly stepped out of their way, vacating the Ludlow

Street apartment so Reed could move in with Cale: for all his suburban upbringing, Reed proved perfectly suited to the Lower East Side lifestyle. A chance encounter on the D train brought his Long Island/Syracuse connection Sterling Morrison back into Reed's orbit, straight over to Ludlow Street, and right into the burgeoning musical partnership as a second guitarist and the group's rock 'n' roll heart. Angus MacLise, another resident of the same Ludlow Street building and occasional member of the Dream Syndicate—a poet and free spirit who had journeyed as far as Nepal—completed the quartet, playing bongos and tablas. His influence showed when he and Reed wrote a treatise that summer in which they proclaimed, "Our music is the western equivalent to the cosmic dance of Shiva."

MacLise secured the unnamed act its first engagement, in the spring and summer of 1965, at the Cinematheque (in the same building as the Astor Place Playhouse) for the filmmaker Piero Heliczer's project *Launching the Dream Weapon*. A prototype of the Exploding Plastic Inevitable, the group performed from behind a screen onto which several of Heliczer's experimental movies were projected at once, through veils lit by slide projectors, while dancers swirled around them. The relationship continued almost until the end of the year, by which point MacLise was no longer part of the project. When the *Saturday Evening Post* journalist Al Aronowitz, who had brokered the preceding year's meeting between Dylan and the Beatles, invited them to open for his first managerial rock clients, the Myddle Class, at a high school gig in Summit, New Jersey, the drummer was confused by the very concept. "Do you mean we have to show up at a certain time—and start playing—and then end?" he asked. Rather than succumb to convention, MacLise quit.

He did his friends a favor. They were younger and hungrier and truly believed that they had something to offer the rapidly expanding world of rock 'n' roll. They found a drummer through their Long Island/Syracuse connections: nineteen-year-old Maureen Tucker, a short-haired tomboy, whose simplicity and stability proved the perfect foundation for the others' experimental tendencies. As the Velvet Underground—their name taken, in an exercise of serendipity, from a pulp novel found on the Bowery by Tony Conrad—they played their first gig at that New Jersey school, on December 11, 1965, opening with arguably their most contemporary and commercial song, "There She Goes Again," before embarking on the sadomasochistic "Venus in Furs" and then the self-explanatory "Heroin." "Half the people walked out," observed Morrison. A few days later, they began a residency at the Café Bizarre.

Bad idea. Not for the tourists of Greenwich Village the extended freak-out "Black Angel's Death Song." Not for the Lower East Side group several sets a night to a half-empty room, playing endless cover versions and enduring demands from club management to tone down their wilder material. The group was rescued when a filmmaker friend, Barbara Rubin, stopped in with Gerard Malanga, a handsome young poet and part of the crowd that hung around Andy Warhol's Silver Factory studio, on East 47th Street. Malanga loved to dance—with a bullwhip, in a prototype of the Lizard King persona soon perfected by the Doors' Jim Morrison, and his interpretive moves proved particularly suited to "Venus in Furs." Excited, he returned to Café Bizarre a couple of nights later with the key Factory figures in tow: the film director Paul Morrissey, actress Edie Sedgwick, and Andy Warhol himself.

Like everyone else in the arts world in late 1965, Warhol—who had recently announced that he was giving up painting—knew that the real creative action was taking place in rock 'n' roll music, and in the Velvet Underground, he saw an opportunity to get involved. Within days, he and Morrissey offered to "manage" the group. Recognizing that the patronage of New York's most talked-about multimedia artist would surely trump his inexperience in actual management, the Velvet Underground accepted. They quit the Café Bizarre residency before it ran its course and left Al Aronowitz behind in the process.

Reed often claimed that Warhol's fascination with the Velvet Underground could be distilled as follows: "We were doing with music . . . the same thing he was doing with movies and painting: i.e., not kidding around." Certainly, Warhol and Reed were kindred spirits: keen observers of the human psyche, known for emotional detachment and manipulative personalities, they liked art that shocked and were, despite a propensity for the pills of the day and their image as late night carousers, given to relentless hard work. Those shared tendencies might explain why Reed accepted Warhol's managerial caveat: that the Velvet Underground take on board as a second lead singer his other new discovery, Nico. A former model, she'd recently played in Fellini's La Dolce Vita, released a single on the Rolling Stones' label, and came to the Factory with a song given to her by Bob Dylan in Paris that past summer ("I'll Keep It with Mine"), reputedly the result of an affair. Though hardly the most commanding of stage performers—Richard Goldstein of *New York* magazine described her delightfully as "half Goddess, half icicle"—her presence was undeniably hypnotic. The group agreed to set aside some songs for her to sing.

If it seems almost incredible—or at least evidence of the era's fast-moving times—that Warhol was able to unveil the Velvet Underground and Nico in concert just one month after their debut show at a suburban high school, it's worth remembering that the group came to his Factory with almost all the components in place. They were already old hands at performing in front of, behind, or alongside movies. They understood the concept of music as theater, of art as avant-garde. Cale had worked with the major minimalist composers of the day, John Cage and La Monte Young. Warhol, then, served primarily (and effectively) as the catalyst by which the Velvet Underground could attract an audience—or at least public attention, as he proved by having the group perform at a plush midtown hotel in lieu of a speech he had been invited to give the New York Society for Clinical Psychiatry. That event was reviewed in the *New York Times*, mostly in the words of the psychiatrists themselves. Several appeared horrified and insulted, though one described the performance with apparent fondness as "a repetition of the *concrete* quite akin to the L.S.D. experience."

A claim can certainly be made for the Velvet Underground as America's first truly psychedelic rock group. The collision of lights, films, and slides, the combination of drone and repetition, volume and intensity—all were designed to confuse the senses and create what the Byrds' Jim McGuinn called, in his own definition of psychedelic rock, "music that bleeds together." But the Velvet Underground declined to accept that role. "We were never into psychedelics," said Morrison. Uppers and downers were more the drugs of choice. The Factory employee Brigid Polk (real name Berlin, daughter of the Hearst company's chairman), who would remain close to Lou Reed for years, recalled of the early Velvets days, "Everyone was taking speed. Everyone was drinking a lot. Nobody went to sleep at night. We used to stay up for eight or nine days without going to bed."

The residency at the Dom, for which the space was renamed the "Open Stage," began on April 1 as the Erupting Plastic Inevitable, offering, in the words of a half-page ad in the *Village Voice*, "movies, food, dancing, lightworks, ultra sounds and multiple films." The paper returned the favor the following week, printing a picture of the Velvet Underground from opening night on its front cover and running an entire page of photographs inside. There was no description of the music, perhaps because it was so difficult to define. After all, Cale fashioned his electric viola out of two guitar strings on the low end, two mandolin strings up top, and used a double bass bow to achieve a sound he described as "very similar to a B-52." Reed and Morrison down-tuned their guitars by as much as a full note, to allow for additional sustain, meet the pitch of Cale's strings, and match Reed's natural singing tone. Each guitarist used his amplifier as if another instrument, introducing feedback and distortion into the set at a time when such ideas were unheard of in American music. (Crucially, John Cale had gone back to the United Kingdom in 1965, when acts like the Who were just beginning to experiment with this idea.) "We put three chord rock into one chord rock," said Cale. "We just had the drone into everything. We were very insistent on breaking the rules."

Word went around town that the group's performance bordered on violence, as if out to deliberately aggravate. Factor in the black clothing, the sunglasses worn onstage (to shield the group from the epileptic effects of their own light show), and the dark choice of subject matter, and such a conclusion was understandable. But it was misplaced. The Velvet Underground were capable of extreme tenderness, as evidenced by the two songs Lou Reed wrote for Nico in the midst of their brief and turbulent affair at the beginning of 1966: "I'll Be Your Mirror" and "Femme Fatale" were ballads of such simple, astounding beauty that, had Reed never written anything else, they would have secured his songwriting legacy.

Typically, a band of the times sought the sponsorship of a record company before recording an album. But Warhol, who had famously commoditized painting with his silk-screen process, was used to doing things the other way around: creating the art first, mass-producing it later. He and Paul Morrissey now applied this philosophy to the Velvet Underground, taking the profits from the Exploding Plastic Inevitable residency and spending them at the Scepter Records studio in midtown, where, as "produced" by Warhol, the hum of the amplifiers bled across "All Tomorrow's Parties," augmented by Cale's repetitive piano lines and Nico's double-tracked vocals; feedback was used as coloring on the garage rocker "Run Run Run" and "European Son"; and the viola drone rose to an almost caustic squeal on "The Black Angel's

Death Song." Throughout, vocals were frequently submerged by the instrumentation as the faders were pushed deep into distortion territory—even on
a ballad like "Femme Fatale."

Despite later assertions of mass rejection, Tom Wilson at Verve quickly
snapped up the album. He produced one brand-new song: the dreamy ballad "Sunday Morning," sung by Reed, which would be released as a single
later in 1966 and serve as the album's atypical opening track, too. Wilson
also remixed several of the most controversial songs, although none of the
words were altered. Reed again cited Warhol's role: "Andy made a point of
trying to make sure that on our first album the language remained intact.
He didn't want it to be cleaned up and because he was there it wasn't."

The finished album was staggering in its originality and intensity, and
also in the diverse energy of its arrangements. "I'm Waiting for the Man,"
unrecognizable from the acoustic demo of a year earlier, was now a sinister
electric guitar blues strut, joined in its hard-rocking nature by the comparatively palatable and unquestionably jaunty "There She Goes Again" and "Run
Run Run." At the other of the spectrum "The Black Angel's Death Song,"
"Venus in Furs," "Heroin," and "European Son," ranging from three to almost
eight minutes in length, respectively, all incorporated various degrees of
viola, drone, feedback, and distortion to initially harrowing effect. Scattered
throughout were the Nico-fronted ballads, of which "All Tomorrow's Parties"
now sounded so ideally suited to Nico's deep, detached, voice, and seemed so
perfectly to describe the Factory crowd's obsession with the nightlife circuit
that it was easy to forget it had predated even the naming of the Velvet
Underground.

Yet Verve delayed release of the album, hoping that the singles "All
Tomorrow's Parties" and "Sunday Morning" would chart first. They did not,
and in the interim, Verve focused its attention on Frank Zappa's West Coast
group the Mothers of Invention, whose debut set *Freak Out!* (the first ever double album) it released in July. There was no love lost between the two groups,
who had shared a bill at Bill Graham's Fillmore in San Francisco when the
Velvet Underground traveled to the West Coast late in May. Relations hardly
improved when, at the end of 1966, in the glow of the acclaim afforded *Freak
Out!*, the Mothers came into New York, down to St. Mark's Place, and right
into the Dom (now rechristened Balloon Farm), to hold court for a month as
the newly hailed leaders of the rock underground.

The Velvet Underground had reflected a certain zeitgeist through 1966, during which time they toured the Exploding Plastic Inevitable, taking it into ballrooms and art institutions across the country, attracting copious press cuttings as they went. (And who would not have wanted to be in attendance at the Action House on Long Island on December 4, when they performed alongside the Young Rascals, the Ronettes, and the Fugs?) But by the time *The Velvet Underground & Nico* was released in the spring of 1967, eleven months after being recorded, the zeitgeist had moved on. In the interim, the Beatles had unleashed *Revolver*, the Byrds *Fifth Dimension*, and the Beach Boys *Pet Sounds*, each album pushing music forward in leaps and bounds, leading to the new musical definition of "rock" music as a result. *The Velvet Underground & Nico* would never sound dated; but its uncompromising recording techniques were certainly in danger of going unappreciated in all the attention afforded these major artists' gilt-edged productions.

Matters were hardly helped by Verve's painfully embarrassing press ads, which read as if they had been dictated by movie marketing people at the parent company MGM: "What happens when the daddy of Pop Art goes Pop Music? The most underground album of all! . . . Sorry, no home movies. But the album does feature Andy's Velvet Underground (they play funny instruments). Plus his this year's Pop Girl, Nico (she sings, groovy). Plus an actual banana on the front cover (don't smoke it, peel it)." The last was a reference to a prevailing (but unproven) belief that banana skins had hallucinogenic properties when smoked. Warhol considered his banana skin cover a work of art, and his was therefore the only name printed (in large type) on the front cover. To the extent that he had coveted a role in the rock world, he had achieved his goal; perhaps the Verve marketing team could not be blamed for relegating the music to a sideshow after all.

Over the years, *The Velvet Underground & Nico* would serve as one of the most influential albums ever released: though the assertion that every person who bought it formed a band was somewhat apocryphal, its relevance could be measured in any number of ways, including the fact that every song, however initially challenging, was eventually covered by other artists. But any traction it gathered upon release quickly came to a halt when the Factory actor Eric Emerson discovered that his image from the Warhol movie *Chelsea Girls* had been used on the back cover without his permission, and demanded payment. MGM-Verve refused and, instead, recalled the album. While Emerson's image was being airbrushed out of future pressings, *The Velvet Underground & Nico* lost its lowly hold on the charts, never to return.

I n the summer of 1966, Lou Reed came down with hepatitis and was confined to Bellevue Hospital; across the aisle, suffering from the same illness, lay another Brooklyn-born musician (of sorts), Jim McCarthy. A Beatles fanatic, McCarthy had fronted a cover band that regularly played the Dom's basement bar—until the day he and his friend Larry Kressler saw the Fugs at the Astor Place Playhouse. "They changed my life," he said. Watching them, McCarthy realized, "I didn't want to sing other peoples' songs that were important to them, I wanted to sing songs that were important to me, that meant something to *me*. And hopefully that were kind of meaningful, that were not just pop. And the Fugs were the embodiment of that."

But then he caught hepatitis. And shortly after he was released from Bellevue, his girlfriend kicked him out. He moved into Kressler's apartment, farther down Avenue B, where the two of them, with their friend Jay Dillon, spent much of their time sitting around getting stoned. "I was in bad shape," said McCarthy, who one day stood up abruptly in the apartment, grabbed a tambourine and some maracas, and started shrieking, "just letting it all out." Kressler and Dillon joined in on other instruments lying around, and they enjoyed the cathartic experience so much that they decided to make a habit of it.

After Kressler took a job as sales manager at ESP, the label boss Stollman agreed to finance a single by the Godz, as they now called themselves with the addition of a fourth member. They recorded nine "songs" at the session instead, most of it consisting of atonal singing, hesitantly strummed guitars, and polyrhythmic percussion. ESP, which had built its reputation on avant-garde jazz prior to signing the Fugs, promptly released it as a 25-minute album, *Contact High with the Godz*, in late 1966.

Five years later, the rock critic Lester Bangs wrote a retrospective on the Godz in *Creem* magazine and noted that while they might "well be the most inept band" he had ever heard, nonetheless their debut was "a perfect artifact of New York in its period." As usual, he was right. Contemporary reaction split largely along geographical lines. With shows that verged on what

McCarthy called "total anarchy," the Godz were banned from Village venues like the Night Owl, Gaslight, and Café Bizarre. They fared better at the Cinematheque, the Bridge Theater, and the band shell at Tompkins Square Park, where they opened a couple of times for their heroes the Fugs. Along the way, the Godz developed some confidence, in part from McCarthy's experience in cover bands. "Even though it was improvised and chaotic, I would try to direct it with my guitar playing and my vocal. So it took *some* sort of acceptable form within all that chaos. When we got it right, it got you moving."

On 1967's *Godz II*, the quartet dared cover—if that was the right word for it—the Beatles' "You Won't See Me" alongside five-minute violin "solos" and various minimalist near-instrumentals, most of which sounded as if they had been recorded inside a tin can at the bottom of the East River. The Godz were extremely proud of it, considering themselves part of a movement alongside the Fugs and the Holy Modal Rounders, one whose attitude could be summed up in the words "Fuck you, we're going to do it our way," as McCarthy put it. "That was part of the hip scene—breaking the rules."

ESP's own motto, "the artists alone decide what you will hear," appeared tailormade for the Lower East Side musical community. The Fugs, however, had reason to dispute that claim. To their fury, the word "screw" had been faded down on the final mix of "Doin' All Right"; relations became irreparable when Stollman bought up the act's debut album from Folkways for re-release, but also packaged its unreleased cuts as *The Virgin Fugs*. These leftovers included some of the Fugs' funniest *and* most offensive material: Stampfel's "New Amphetamine Shriek" ("If you don't like sleeping and don't want to screw, / Then you should take lots of amphetamine too"), the litany of coarse sexual references that was Kupferberg's "Coca Cola Douche," and the proclamation on "We Are the Fugs" that "we eat pussy, we ain't fussy." *The Virgin Fugs* closed with "I Saw the Best Minds of My Generation Rot," a free-spirited rewrite of Ginsberg's *Howl* that almost prompted the poet to sue ESP for its unauthorized release. His energy was ultimately expended in a more positive manner: having just released a successful album-length reading of his *Kaddish* on Atlantic, he helped persuade Jerry Wexler to sign the Fugs to an album deal.

Those were heady days for a group that had formed with such low expectations (and expertise). After the Playhouse cancellation, the Fugs had moved into the Players Theater in the Village, where they performed twelve times a week for months on end. *Life* magazine put Sanders on its cover in February 1967 as the poster child for "the Other Culture," that is, avant-garde, experimental art. Unable to keep up his commitments to Peace Eye, Sanders passed the bookshop on to a community group led by a local hippie activist, "Groovy," who promptly turned it into a crash pad for the hippie runaways who were flocking to the East Village. A new Fugs lineup (ironically or otherwise, the bassist John Anderson had been drafted) set about making an album for Atlantic, for which Ginsberg and Gregory Corso stopped in to help record a "Hare Krishna" chant. The finished record—*The Fugs Eat It*—was approved by Atlantic executives, as was a cover design. And then Jerry Wexler called Sanders at home and explained, in a "brief, stunning" conversation, that the album would not be released and that the Fugs were free to find another label. No satisfactory explanation was ever offered. Nineteen sixty-seven, of all years, came and went without a new Fugs album.

ippies hit the New York mainstream in a big way that Easter Sunday, March 26, when ten thousand of them gathered in Central Park's Sheep Meadow for a "be-in." The peaceful celebration was organized in part by Paul Williams, editor of the new music magazine *Crawdaddy*, and by Jim Fouratt, a young actor and gay rights campaigner, who described the event as "an affirmation of love and happiness." Unlike its San Francisco forerunner, the Central Park be-in was structured to have *no* structure—no stage, no performers, no leaders, just thousands of people creating their own entertainment, establishing their own good vibe. By those standards, it triumphed, and the scene appeared to flourish. During May and June, an estimated two thousand hippies moved into the tenement buildings surrounding Tompkins Square Park. Local landlords delighted in the sudden popularity afforded the neighborhood, doubling the rents on their dilapidated apartments. Long-term business owners also welcomed the initial influx of suburban white youth, many of whom brought their savings with them for the "summer of love."

The original beats-turned-hippies were more ambivalent; although they welcomed all new constituents to their (counter) culture, they were less enamored with the public drug use that invited police pressure, the "circus" street performances that attracted tourists previously confined to Greenwich Village, and the ever-increasing number of runaways who, as in San Francisco's Haight-Ashbury district, showed up penniless and clueless, expecting the resident hippies to take care of them. The predominantly Puerto Rican population of Avenues C and D, meanwhile, a largely forgotten neighborhood (sometimes called Loisada) blighted by genuine poverty and urban decay, looked with disdain upon the new arrivals in their brightly colored garbs, waxing spiritual niceties while downing large quantities of mind-altering drugs and yet expecting society (mainstream or underground) to catch them when they fell. Racial tensions and petty crime increased in the neighborhood through 1967. Jim McCarthy of the Godz was held up three times on his home block, Seventh Street between Avenues C and D, that year alone.

Matters first came to a head on Memorial Day, when a license was granted for a Tompkins Square Park concert on condition the crowd confine itself to the band shell. When hippies spilled onto a surrounding grassy picnic area, the police moved in to clear them with a display of brute force that harked back to the riot of 1874, guaranteeing a mutual antagonism that would carry over into future generations of East Village others. Though a backtracking parks commissioner immediately yanked the double-entendre sign "Keep Off the Grass" from that corner of the park and replaced it with the comically outdated "Troubadour Area," the incident only served to aggravate the indigenous youth: a concert a few days later was broken up by a Puerto Rican gang.

By the fall, pressure from the police and his landlord had forced Sanders to reclaim the Peace Eye crash pad from Groovy and friends, and return it to bookstore status. On the night of October 8, Groovy was photographed with a young girl in a sleeping bag, on the street outside the local "head" shop Psychedelicatessen on Avenue A and Tenth Street. Hours later, the couple were discovered lying naked on the floor in a boiler-room basement just a block away, on Avenue B, their heads beaten to a pulp with furnace bricks.

The "Groovy murders" dominated the following day's front pages. (Two young drifters were eventually arrested and convicted for the murders, though their motives were left unexplained.) The media already knew the male victim as James Hutchinson, a petty thief and former gang member from Rhode Island who'd gone on to become possibly the most media-savvy street hippie in the East Village. (His only rival was medieval-clad Galahad, with whom he had once hosted a crash pad.) But in his murdered partner, they discovered the *real* stuff of headlines, an instant poster child for what was quickly labeled the "generation gap." Hailing from a wealthy family in Greenwich, Connecticut, eighteen-year-old Linda Fitzpatrick had just finished four years of private prep school; it turned out she had successfully convinced her parents that she was gainfully employed, designing posters in the hippie culture, even as she drifted from the East Village to Haight-Ashbury and back again, gravitating from LSD to speed in the process, sleeping in transient hotels with male hippies, and, finally, taking to begging with the other young homeless on the streets of the East Village to support her drug habit. "I didn't even know there *was* an East Village," her distraught father told a *New York Times* reporter who pieced together her dual existences. "I've heard of the Lower East Side, but the East Village?"

The Velvet Underground, though resident on the Lower East Side, persisted as if the whole hippie era, the Vietnam protests, the be-ins, the rising crime rate and shift in drugs, were taking place somewhere else entirely. They jettisoned Nico, though they supplied music and several songs—including the title track with its many references to various Factory characters—to her debut solo album *Chelsea Girl*. They then set about replacing Warhol and Morrissey as managers, everyone involved realizing that management was actually a full-time job. With Steve Selsnick coming on board in that role, they used the summer of 1967 to record their second album, *White Light/White Heat*, one of the most uncompromising records ever to have stood the test of time.

Tom Wilson produced *White Light/White Heat*, as he did *Chelsea Girl*, and he appeared to thrive in collaborating on a record that, in places, harked back to his own pre-Columbia days working with the free jazz artists Sun Ra and John Coltrane. The album contained only six songs, almost every one of them a challenge of some sort, from the drug references of the title track, through the eight-minute story "The Gift," narrated by John Cale over one relentlessly reworked riff, to the seventeen-minute finale, "Sister Ray." A coming together of the group's myriad influences and the culmination of their artistic impulses, it was emboldened by Reed's account of sailors and transvestites "sucking on my ding dong" while "looking for my mainline"; after several verses it gave way to instrumental combat of such predetermined intensity that the group ran through it the one time only. In the midst of doing so, Cale pulled out all the stops (quite literally) on the organ, drowning the drums in the process; while Morrison switched pickups to try and get back into the race, Tucker, unfazed, held steady behind them all, knowing that her purpose in the group was, as she later described it, to maintain "the same beat we were starting at, and just keep it under there, so that when everyone came back, there was something to come back *to*." The lack of a bass guitar on the track only amplified, if that's the right term, an apparent desire to assault the listener; when compressed with the equally abrasive, though far more conventional, "I Heard Her Call My Name" onto one side of an album, "Sister Ray" became even more of a treble-top feedback squeal.

Again, the album was ahead of—or at least outside of—its time. There was nothing approximating a possible hit single, and the supposedly adventurous DJs of the newly emergent FM radio wouldn't touch "Sister Ray," even though, within a few months, they were all over Iron Butterfly's similarly long "In-a-Gadda-Da-Vida." Released at the top of 1968, *White Light/White Heat* was a commercial disaster. The Velvet Underground continued to tour the nation's burgeoning rock circuit, but after taking the Exploding Plastic Inevitable to Steve Paul's the Scene in May 1967, they would not play New York again for three full years. And when they did, it was in a room above a restaurant.

Max's Kansas City, situated at 213 Park Avenue South, just off the northeast corner of Union Square, opened in December 1965. Like Andy Warhol, who latched onto the Velvet Underground that same month, its proprietor Mickey Ruskin had observed the seismic shifts taking place in popular culture and, following his success with previous gathering places—the Tenth Street Coffeehouse, the Ninth Circle, and Les Deux Megots, sought to gather these freshly cross-pollinating elements of the New York scene into a brand-new venue.

The extent to which Ruskin succeeded spoke in equal parts to his prior reputation, his legendary generosity, and his cultivation of diverse personalities. It spoke, too, to the venue's central location—at the crossroads of East and Greenwich Village, uptown and downtown. And it spoke especially to that which can be neither perfectly planned nor fully explained—the circumstances by which people gravitate to a place (in time) and decide that they like it so much they don't want to go anywhere else.

Initially, Ruskin's customers were the visual artists and their dealers, eager for a new location after the nearby Cedar Tavern had shut down: Willem De Kooning, Leo Castelli, Frosty Myers, and company. Soon, the fashion industry, including its models, gravitated there: the photographer John Ford described Max's as "one of the reasons I didn't like to leave New York." And then, in early 1968, Andy Warhol moved his Factory from midtown to Union Square West, upon which he and his entourage immediately made Max's their after-"work" hangout, and there was no looking back.

Max himself was a fiction, a host name chosen for his universal homeliness. Everyone knew that it was Mickey Ruskin's joint, with the owner's personality stamped all over it. Ruskin hired waitresses who looked good in miniskirts, but ensured that they were equally imbued with charisma. (In 1968–69, their number included Debbie Harry, fresh from an alarmingly brief major label career of a folk rock group, the Wind in the Willows.) He hired as his first bouncer a man who said he'd never been in a fight, working on the theory that "people who like to fight, get into fights" and, therefore, vice versa. For most of the time he ran Max's, Ruskin neither drank nor did drugs, which made him an outsider in his own domain, where copious sexual and drug activity took place not only in the back room and the bathrooms but also in the dining booths, the telephone booths, and even at the bar. Among its many other attributes, Max's was one of the only places in town where openly gay people felt safe in straight company.

Max's was ostensibly a restaurant: "Kansas City" referred to the popular raising ground for steaks in the mid-twentieth century. Its happy-hour buffet was gratefully attended nightly by dozens of otherwise starving artists. Ruskin granted many of these regular patrons a charge card, though few ever got around to settling their tabs. Likewise, he allowed his friends to cash checks at the bar, even as he knew that many would bounce. Though all this appeared like so much business insanity, a growing reputation as the nexus of Manhattan culture soon drew enough free-spending "tourists" (i.e., any-one not a regular) to make up the difference.

On busy nights, when the front room filled rapidly, the tourists were sent upstairs to "Siberia." The cognoscenti, meanwhile, gathered in the back room—a relatively small salon, about 25 feet wide by 30 feet deep, perma-nently bathed in a red glow and thick with smoke, with barely a dozen tables, all occupied by the hallowed elite. (The elite of the elite sat at the large "round table," to the front right of the room as one entered.) Significantly, though Ruskin could frequently be found out front of Max's on weekend nights, limiting entry to those he deemed appropriate, the back room itself was guarded only by what one of its most ardent regulars, Danny Fields, called "a magic invisible force."

Born in Brooklyn, raised in Queens, and educated—short of a degree—at Harvard, Fields had moved to Manhattan in the very early 1960s, just in time to witness the blossoming of the folk scene. In the Village, he learned how to "follow the flow and the film festivals and the bars" until "you become part of a crowd and then you sleep with the right people then you *become* the right people." By the beginning of 1966, Fields was absolutely "the right peo-ple," sharing an apartment with Edie Sedgwick, and socially engaged to the Velvet Underground. He was also, by day, the editor of a music gossip maga-zine called *Datebook*, a role in which he "broke up the Beatles as a perform-ing act" when he reprinted a John Lennon quote (ignored in the United Kingdom, where it was first published) stating, "We're more popular than Jesus now," and America's Christian base harassed the Beatles' subsequent Stateside tour to such a debilitating extent that it became their last. Ruskin cited Fields as one of Max's "key figures," credited for bringing in the "musi-cians and music industry people," and one of a handful whose approval had to be cultivated for acceptance to the back room. Yet Fields's criterion was as simple as it was elusive. "To be in the back room, nothing was required except that you be fabulous. You didn't have to be rich, you didn't have to be beauti-ful, you didn't have to be famous: you had to be fabulous."

By 1968, the year that album sales overtook those of singles, Fields had been hired as the resident "freak" for an Elektra Records that, with the Doors, had become the only New York folk label to successfully cross over to rock. On Sunday, March 31, wandering Washington Square Park, Fields came across a singer, David Peel, performing with a ragtag band of followers labeled for the Lower East Side. Fields found himself drawn to Peel by what he called "this remarkable, thuggoy-accented, brazenly hoarse, and tendentious singer," and also by Peel's energy, which he recalled as "a cartoon of a bouncing ball." Once the Sunday evening curfew kicked in, Fields cornered Peel, took the singer straight to Max's Kansas City, allowed him to order the biggest steak on the menu, and suggested they record an album for Elektra.

The Brooklyn-raised Peel represented a new generation of park singers, far removed from the earnest folkies of the fifties and early sixties. A full-blown hippie who had swapped an entry-level Wall Street job to follow the trail to Haight-Ashbury and back, another New Yorker enlightened by exposure to the Fugs, Peel lived in Alphabet City, where rent was cheap and the area "hadn't been exploited yet," but was drawn to Greenwich Village to play outdoors. "Washington Square Park had a natural amphitheater and its own encirclement, probably one of the best parks in the world for that," he said. By the time Fields saw him, Peel had only just worked his way up through the ranks of the park faithful—from chorus singer to tambourine banger, harmonica player, and now singer and guitarist with his own following. Peel cast himself as a radical compared with the park's old guard: "We're not just going to sing beautiful music; we're going to sing to make things beautiful." But he was not a troublemaker. "Cheap wine was our biggest high," he recalled. That "and smoking bananas."

Peel wrote a song, "Banana Grass" about this trend for banana peels, and when he aired it in Washington Square Park, "it was like Peel mania." He quickly embarked on an entire catalog of similarly contemporary songs. Some were serious: "Mother, Where Is My Father?" was a poetic anti-Vietnam protest that Elektra wisely chose to lead off his debut LP. (Peel had been fortunate enough to perform his military service before the war in Vietnam escalated.) But most were just deliciously silly reportage. "Whatever was happening, I wrote a song about it as a spokesperson, a town crier, rather than what I was experiencing myself." "I'm a Runaway" was self-explanatory to anyone who frequented either Washington or Tompkins Square Park. And "Up Against the Wall, Motherfucker" served to advertise the slogan of the Lower East Side's latest self-appointed rebel group, which was led (to the extent it had a leader) by the painter Ben Morea, one of half a dozen protestors who had broken into (and been beaten back from) the Pentagon during an antiwar protest in October 1967.

The Motherfuckers—as rolled more easily off the tongue—had announced themselves to the media on March 28, 1968, at Grand Central Station, gate-crashing the Yippies' 3,000-strong yip-in. The Yippies (ostensibly the Youth International Party, but more widely viewed as a satirical statement on hippie culture) were themselves just a few weeks old at the time, having come into existence in the new year with the proclaimed intent of hosting a "festival of life" at the Democratic National Convention in Chicago that summer. (This would serve to protest President Johnson's likely renomination as party leader in the midst of the Vietnam War.) Before its cofounder Jerry Rubin started to preach violence, prominent New York musicians like Judy Collins, Dave Van Ronk, and Blood Sweat and Tears all performed at fund-raisers for the Yippies; and Ed Sanders, Allen Ginsberg, and Jim Fouratt became part of the organizational structure, which set up an office on Union Square East the same time as the Factory moved in across the square. Regulars of Max's back room briefly enjoyed the sight of the Yippies' other main founder, Abbie Hoffman, breaking bread with Andy Warhol.

The Grand Central Station yip-in had started out peacefully, but turned sinister shortly after midnight, when a handful of cherry bombs exploded, some revelers climbed on to the concourse clockface, and a banner proclaiming UP AGAINST THE WALL, MOTHERFUCKER was unfurled. As if on cue, the NYPD's Tactical Patrol Force waded into the crowd with billy clubs, searching out Abbie Hoffman, whom they beat to the ground. Fifty-seven people were arrested; over twenty, including Hoffman, were hospitalized.

Time magazine noted that before this, the crowd had been happily snaking through the concourse singing "Have a Marijuana." That was news to David Peel, who had been leading the chorus; the song was actually called "I Like Marijuana." But "Have a Marijuana" had a certain ring to it, and it became the title of David Peel and the Lower East Side's debut album, recorded "Live on the Streets of New York." (This sounded more urbanely glamorous than admitting that it had been taped in good old Washington Square Park.) To Elektra's delight, the album became an immediate underground favorite; something about Peel's simplicity of message, along with the communal feel of the Washington Square Park crowd, appealed, if not exactly to the masses, then certainly to a large number of banana peel smokers.

. . .

The same day that Danny Fields stumbled across David Peel in Washington Square Park, President Johnson announced on television that he would not be seeking reelection after all, thereby derailing the Yippies' raison d'etre; he recognized that the Vietnam War had demonized him among his party's core base. Just a few days later, on April 4, Martin Luther King Jr. was shot dead by James Earl Ray outside his motel room in Memphis. Riots erupted in black neighborhoods across the country, most notably in Washington, D.C., Baltimore, and Chicago, where Mayor Richard Daley gave a hint as to how he would welcome the Yippies that summer by telling his police to "shoot to kill" the arsonists. New York City did not explode on quite the same level, but in Harlem and Brooklyn's Bedford-Stuyvesant the number of arrests, injuries, and buildings set on fire were all comparable to the last time there had been major civil unrest, in 1964. It was just that this time the police held back, under apparent instruction to do so from a mayor who, despite two deaths in the New York violence, flatly refused to classify the disturbances as a "riot."

What, then, to call the unrest at the end of April at Columbia University, in part over its plan to build a private gymnasium on former public ground in Harlem? (For his own part, the Columbia's Students for a Democratic Society leader Mark Rudd defined it as "a stick-up" when he wrote to the president, Grayson Kirk, and warned him, "Up against the wall, motherfucker . . .") Students took over and occupied five buildings on campus for a week, before being evicted by police who used force on a scale forbidden during the Harlem non-"riots" weeks earlier; of 712 people arrested, 148 had head injuries.

And so it went. On June 3, Valerie Solanas, author of a little-known feminist manifesto S.C.U.M. (Society for Cutting Up Men), a woman who had had bit parts in Andy Warhol movies but now held the artist in contempt, marched into the Union Square offices of the Factory and shot Warhol three times. He survived, though barely: pronounced dead on arrival at the Cabrini Medical Center three blocks away, he was only revived after doctors opened up his chest and massaged his heart. The Factory's open-door policy immediately became a thing of the past. And barely twenty-four hours after that, Robert F. Kennedy was assassinated in California, just after winning that state's Democratic primary on what could have been his route to the party's nomination. As with the death of Martin Luther King Jr., and that of John F. Kennedy almost five years earlier, the question of who actually ordered the killing would remain wide open, fueling the quasi-revolutionary movements, from mostly white Yippies to all-black Panthers, that were now in full swing across the country.

Felix Cavaliere and the Rascals were among the millions devastated by King and Kennedy's assassinations. (The group had finally dropped the "Young" in time for its latest big hit, "A Beautiful Morning.") Cavaliere and his fellow songwriter Eddie Brigati directed their pain as best they knew how, recording "People Got to Be Free" in the middle of May. The single opened straight into the chorus of the uplifting anthem, and though the lyrics sounded naive to some, they struck a chord for most. Punctuated by pertinently soulful brass lines (the sax played by Hendrix's former bandleader King Curtis), "People Got to Be Free" spent five weeks at number one in the summer of 1968. "Young" or otherwise, the Rascals were the only American rock group to have three number ones in the latter half of the sixties.

"People Got to Be Free" was the top single in the country in August when the Democratic National Convention opened in Chicago, and Mayor Daley's police greeted the fifteen hundred or so Yippies who attempted to camp out in Grant Park with a brutality previously reserved only for pre–civil rights blacks, on one occasion extending their beating to include dozens of members of the established news media. The rest of the world recoiled in horror at the sight of a country in hate with itself but, in November, American voters elected Richard Nixon as president. The right wing was back in the White House; the war in Vietnam would continue for several more years.

Back in New York, the original Yippies split: Hoffman and Rubin continued the path of most resistance, while the likes of Sanders, Ginsberg, Fouratt, and others chose more peaceful means of opposition. The Motherfuckers filled the void, dumping uncollected Lower East Side trash at Lincoln Center as "an exchange of culture" and demanding of Bill Graham, the West Coast concert entrepreneur who had just spent $125,000 converting an old Jewish theater on Second Avenue into the Fillmore East, that he open its doors for a weekly "community" night. Under considerable duress—he had already tried to buy the *East Village Other*'s support by supplying it with office space above the theater—Graham agreed, and over the course of several weeks in late 1968, such Lower East Side staples as the Fugs, the Group Image, and

David Peel all graced a Fillmore stage otherwise reserved for (and revered by) groups of the caliber of the Who, the Doors, and Jefferson Airplane.

On December 26, Elektra sponsored its own free concert at the Fillmore, headlined by the MC5, whom Fields had just signed along with their Detroit neighbors the Stooges. The intended community celebration turned into a debacle when Fields, who spent more time with the fabulous people in the back room of Max's Kansas City than among the revolutionary hippie freaks of the Lower East Side, made the mistake of sending the group to the venue in a limousine. When the singer Rob Tyner then declared from the stage, "We didn't come to New York for politics, we came to New York for rock 'n' roll," members of the Motherfuckers' retinue invaded the stage, holding the MC5 hostage to explain their lack of revolutionary fervor in a heated "Q&A session." Considering that the MC5 were the only band to play in Chicago at the so-called festival of life (even the Fugs had pulled out), they had every right to consider their treatment unwarranted. They also thought twice about taking limousines to the Lower East Side in the future.

Signed now to Reprise, whose owner, Frank Sinatra, had given his blessing, the Fugs released two albums in 1968 and became an international touring act. But by embarking on suites and masses, even employing Harry Belafonte's backing singers, both *Tenderness Junction* and *It Crawled into My Hand* suffered from overambition—admittedly a common tendency for the era. The group would never again recapture the urgency of "Doin' All Right" and "Kill for Peace." The Holy Modal Rounders' Peter Stampfel and Steven Weber reunited when ESP offered them money to do so; on *Indian War Whoop*, a wonderfully weird album even by the standards of ESP, Sam Shepard joined them on drums. The playwright had given himself a crew cut in protest of "all the bullshit" surrounding the long-haired summer of love— and ESP, figuring that would not sit favorably with the Rounders' hippie audience, left him off the album cover.

The Godz, reduced to a trio, tidied up their sound for their third ESP album, which defeated their very purpose and marked their demise. The esoteric East Village label did far better with Pearls before Swine, the nom de plume of the nineteen-year-old draft resister Tom Rapp, who moved to New York from Florida to record his protest album *One Nation Underground*;

it sold in the six figures and was followed by the more stridently antiwar *Balaklava*, after which, like most acts on ESP, he switched labels. (The acts were all generally frustrated at lack of payment; Stollman claimed that the pressing plant was bootlegging ESP's records, a genuine problem for independent labels dealing with dubious manufacturers.) And David Peel and the Lower East Side moved off the streets and into a recording studio for their second Elektra album: *The American Revolution* opened with the newly empowered rock group's eponymous tribute to their neighborhood, "Lower East Side," complete with reference to "hanging on St. Mark's Place every day and night." Again, it was a success.

As for the Velvet Underground, Lou Reed paid only lip service to the era's madness on the group's third, eponymous album. "There are problems in these times," he sang on "Beginning to See the Light," before adding a jubilant whoop and the emphatic declaration that "none of them are mine." Certainly, he had his own way of handling problems. In September 1968, he met Morrison and Tucker in a Sheridan Square bar, and informed them that he would no longer play in a group with John Cale, who—married now to the cutting-edge New York fashion designer Betsey Johnson and dressing accordingly stylishly—was in danger of becoming the group's focal point. Reed's tactic paid dividends, and Morrison headed off to tell Cale that he was fired. Cale brushed off the dismissal and was soon active both as a producer and a solo artist. His absence was noticed in the lack of musical confrontation on *The Velvet Underground*, self-produced at the end of 1968 and best noted for Reed's ode to the Factory "superstar" Candy Darling ("Candy Says"), the hard-driving "What Goes On," and the ballad "Pale Blue Eyes," which rivaled "Femme Fatale" as his most tender composition.

Like its predecessors, *The Velvet Underground* failed to sell. But the group now had something akin to a catalog, and the "rock press," itself a new phenomenon rising in tandem with FM radio, began to take notice, heaping overdue praise on the band. The act got off Verve and signed to Atlantic, which appointed Adrian Barber, the Rascals' former soundman and recent producer, to oversee production of a new album in the summer of 1970. Proceedings were not smooth. Maureen Tucker, heavily pregnant, went on sabbatical, and was replaced eventually by the seventeen-year-old brother of Cale's own replacement Doug Yule. The recording stretched on for months, the front cover featured the clichéd image of a New York subway station (the designer was European; that was his interpretation of "underground"), and Doug Yule ended up being the only member pictured on the sleeve, yet *Loaded* turned out to be a remarkably cohesive album. It even produced a couple of eventual FM radio hits: "Sweet Jane" and "Rock & Roll," the latter of which was Reed's childhood projected onto a young girl, who "put on a New York station" and had her life "saved by rock 'n' roll."

Yet there had developed a profound disconnect between the Velvet Underground and the New York City streets from which Reed took so much inspiration, as evidenced by their three-year absence from the local live music scene. The announcement of a residency at Max's Kansas City, therefore, to coincide with the recording of *Loaded*, provided an opportunity to regain some local credibility: the Velvet Underground would be the first rock group to play arguably the hippest spot in town. The upstairs dining room was cleared of tables to facilitate audience participation and, thanks in part to the teenage drummer Billy Yule's exuberance (the antithesis to Mo Tucker's steady tom-tom beat) initial reports of the Velvets at Max's cited them as "a genuine rock & roll dance band," the *Village Voice* declaring of their careers that "things are at all-time high." Lou Reed initially seemed content with the proceedings, but then he realized, as the residency dragged on through the summer, that he had allowed himself to be trapped by expectations. Max's was only half a mile from St. Mark's Place, but it was four very long years from the Velvet Underground as part of the Exploding Plastic Inevitable, and those years seemed to be traveling in the wrong direction. "I never thought I would not do what I believed in, and there I was, not doing what I believed in," said Reed. "And it made me sick."

With the ghost of Delmore Schwartz looking down on him, on August 23—a show that Brigid Polk, in the audience that night, recorded for posterity as she did every other aspect of her life—Reed quit the Velvet Underground. In fact, he quit New York entirely, returning to Long Island to live with his parents and taking a day job as a typist at his father's accounting firm.

Tracked down to his father's office by Lester Bangs for *Creem* magazine, Reed denied widespread rumors that he'd had some sort of narcotic freakout. "I'm probably one of the most anti-drug people around," he stated, as if dissociating himself from the Factory-associated night owl of the preceding decade. Then he asked Bangs, conspiracy in his voice, "Don't you think there might be some truth in the idea that marijuana leads to harder drugs?"

13

THE APPLE STRETCHING

omosexuality was not illegal in New York City in the 1960s; it just seemed that way. The New York State Liquor Authority (SLA) had long insisted that merely by serving drinks to homosexuals a bar was maintaining a "disorderly house," which the SLA could (and would) then close; it embarked upon a particularly aggressive series of such license revocations from 1959 through the mid-1960s. Only in 1967, after constant agitation by a handful of openly gay campaigners, were New York bars allowed to knowingly serve homosexuals without prosecution. When, the next year, a state judge decreed that same-sex couples dancing together were not breaking the law, it may have seemed that the tide was finally turning. Yet the New York Police Department continued to enforce an arcane and degrading law that required people to wear at least three items of gender-specific clothing in public. In addition, the police policy of entrapment extended beyond the solicitation of gay prostitutes on the street and frequently involved the arrest of young men on the dance floor.

This discrimination and victimization did not deter gay nightlife. Rather, it sent its potentially lucrative customers into the clutches of the people who knew how best to profit from it: the Mafia. In Greenwich Village, always Manhattan's prime gay neighborhood, the scene's clubs and bars were divided almost equally between the Gambino family (the Washington Square, Purple Onion, and Tony Pastor's) and the Genovese family (the Tenth of Always, the Bon Soir, and the Stonewall Inn). Few of these venues ever had all the correct licenses, but the police were known to turn a blind eye in exchange for

regular payoffs. To keep up appearances, the Sixth Precinct would occasionally launch token raids, typically tipping off the club owners in advance.
After the routine demanding of ID (partly to degrade and arrest patrons who
had dressed as members of the opposite sex), and a bout of homophobic
name-calling, the police would leave, and the bar club would resume its
activities. Neither the police nor the club owners ever expected the patrons
to protest: where else, after all, were "queers," "faggots," or "faeries"—as
they were most commonly referred to in public—permitted to flaunt their
lifestyle?

Of these various Village bars, the Stonewall Inn on Christopher Street,
almost from its opening night in March 1967, proved the most prominent. An
insalubrious double storefront, the Stonewall's windows were painted black
and boarded on the inside, and its decor consisted simply of two connected
rooms, each with a dance floor and a bar, one with the bonus of a few booths.
The Stonewall clientele, according to one of its regular customers, Wayne
Rogers (later to become Jayne County), who had frequented the club since
arriving in the city from Atlanta in 1967, included "drag queens, hippy queens
with long hair down to their shoulders, butch lesbians in men's shirts [and] a
few straight people." Also in the mix were teenagers—blacks, Puerto Ricans,
and whites alike—who fell under the late sixties terminology of "flame
queens," favoring body-hugging male clothing with teased hair and eye
makeup, and who attracted "chicken hawks"—older gays out to seduce them.

Ostensibly a "members-only" club (one of the means by which the mob
could circumvent SLA requirements), the Stonewall's customers would typically sign in under idolized names such as Judy Garland, Diana Ross, and
Joey Dee. Once inside, they were encouraged to head straight to the bar,
where drinks were watered down, and glasses refilled with only a cursory
rinse in a dirty vat, there being no running water behind the bar. Stolen
goods, drugs, and sex were all readily traded under the watchful eye of Ed
"the Skull" Murphy, a career criminal and veteran gay club manager, who
also oversaw activities at the nearby "juice bar," the Tenth of Always, where
the clientele was yet younger. (The drinking age in New York at the time was
eighteen; being alcohol-free, the Tenth of Always could let in those even
younger.) Well known for his own fondness for "chicken," Murphy was
embroiled in various prostitution rings, and alleged to be behind the permanent disappearance of at least one of the young Stonewall regulars.

Despite all this, the Stonewall afforded a certain degree of shelter, espe-cially for the homeless kids who slept in Christopher Square across the street. And many of the young gays admitted that the seediness of the place added to its attraction. But what really distinguished the Stonewall was the free-dom to dance, without harassment, something not found in other gay Village bars. The Stonewall's twin dance floors were fed by a jukebox; in June 1969, when the club was subjected to a police raid that would have major repercus-sions on gay nights and dance music alike, that jukebox was stocked in equal part by Motown ("The Young Folks," by Diana Ross), contemporary hippie hits ("Aquarius / Let The Sun Shine In" from *Hair*), dramatic camp ("In the Ghetto," by Elvis Presley), girl groups ("You Came, You Saw, You Conquered," by the Ronettes), and straight-up dance instrumentals ("Grazing in the Grass," by Friends of Distinction).

There were several reasons why the raid early on Saturday, June 28, proved atypical. For one, it was a ferociously hot midsummer's night on which a full moon rode high in the sky. For another, it was already 1:20 a.m. when the music was halted—peak hour for New York's weekend revelers, when hor-mones are typically raging and grievances well fueled by drink and drugs. In addition, it was the second raid on the club in four nights, the Sixth Precinct having apparently made one of its token incursions earlier in the week. The funeral of the gay icon Judy Garland had taken place in Manhattan ear-lier that day, some 22,000 people filing past her coffin in just twenty-four hours, adding to the foreboding atmosphere. And the raid itself was far from routine, having been launched by detectives of the First Division, a higher authority. "We knew the Sixth Precinct wasn't very effective in keeping these bars properly controlled," the raid's leading detective, Deputy Inspector Seymour Pine, said years later. "We didn't tell them we were going to raid the bar."

Only once inside the club, having halted the music and seized the cash registers, did the officers call the local precinct for backup. The detectives then began inspecting IDs and checking gender. At least three drag queens and one particularly butch lesbian were arrested for cross-dressing; the oth-ers were released slowly, one by one, onto the street outside, where the atmo-sphere turned into something between a carnival and a protest. When the butch lesbian (a "passing woman" by other terminology) was placed inside one of the Sixth Precinct's police cars, she delighted onlookers by proudly exiting from the other door. When bodily handled back into the car, she fought back, physically. "That was the moment," said Jim Fouratt, the Yippie/hippie gay activist who avoided the Stonewall for its chicken hawk reputation but found himself walking down Christopher Street that night on his way home from Max's Kansas City. "That was the flashpoint when people suddenly became conscious that they had power."

First coins, then stones, and finally bottles and garbage began raining down on the police. This came as a surprise: gays were typically seen (by police, Mafia, and media alike) as incapable of defending themselves. But the street kids/flame queens of Christopher Park had long ago learned to fight, quite literally, for survival, and they were the ones leading the attack. While they tried—unsuccessfully—to turn over the police vehicles, Pine's First Division detectives took the unprecedented step of barricading themselves *inside* the Stonewall. Those on the street smelled the cops' fear, and began ripping up loose concrete paving stones as weapons. A parking meter was even freed from the sidewalk and turned into a battering ram on the Stonewall's front door. (The oak door, reinforced with steel for just such an attack by the police, held.) Inside, Deputy Inspector Pine was about to give his officers permission to discharge their weapons when he heard sirens signifying backup.

This was the Tactical Patrol Force, the same police who had cracked so many skulls at Grand Central Station a year earlier, but this time they found themselves on the receiving end of a rearguard challenge by the young Stonewall queens. As the battle became a temporary free-for-all, Pine emerged briefly from the Stonewall to grab the nearest protester, arresting none other than Dave Van Ronk, the distinctly heterosexual folksinger, who had broken from a Friday night of typically drunken revelry at the nearby Lion's Head to see what the fuss was all about.

The streets finally cleared shortly before 4:00 a.m. But the crowds returned to Christopher Street to confront the police the following night, and again the next, by which point a different gay crowd, that which spent summer weekends on Fire Island (where lack of transportation and division of villages had facilitated the first truly gay community on the East Coast), had returned to the city to learn that it had missed out on a historic occasion. Ronnie Di Brienza, a twenty-six-year-old bisexual who had been inside the Stonewall that Friday night, put it best in the following week's *East Village*

Other: "The gay people are the last people anyone ever suspected would violently demonstrate for equal rights. Well, let me tell you baby, you just don't fuck with the gays anymore."

iterally speaking, *discothèque* translates as "record library," which is how the French originally intended it. More flexibly, it came to be understood as a nightspot where people danced, to records played from a turntable rather than a jukebox. Under such definitions, the first New York discotheque would surely have been the stately named Le Club. Opened by the wealthy Parisian scion Olivier Coquelin on Sutton Place on New Year's Eve, 1961, Le Club featured Slim Hyatt "spinning" records to an uptown crowd that paid a hefty annual membership fee for the privilege.

Le Club became an immediate hit with the jet set—the new term for the former café society who, thanks to transatlantic passenger flights, now included aristocratic Europeans as well as wealthy Americans, and who favored French *chansons* and Italian ballads in addition to American rhythm and blues. The jet set could also be found in the early sixties at the Peppermint Lounge, or at Trude Heller's, though at both venues the "spinning" of records still took second place to residencies by the likes of New York's all-girl group Goldie and the Gingerbreads, and the ubiquitous Joey Dee and the Starliters.

Then came Arthur. Founded in 1965 by the Welsh miner's daughter Sybil Burton when her actor husband swapped her for Elizabeth Taylor, funded by a who's who of thousand-dollar investors that included Leonard Bernstein and Julie Andrews, and named for George Harrison's haircut in *A Hard Day's Night*, Arthur, at 54th and Second, rode a perfect cultural wave: part British invasion, part New York melting pot, and equally popular both with aspiring hipsters and with the coveted jet set. Like its contemporaries, Arthur relied heavily on a house band (the Wild Ones), but it also boasted a disc jockey, Terry Noël. A former Peppermint Lounge dancer and consummate record collector, Noël liked to talk of the "feeling the crowd emanates . . . like an unconscious grapevine," and he became arguably the first New York nightclub DJ to serve as something other than a human jukebox.

By the end of 1965, midtown was filled with French-themed discotheques and British invasion nightclubs alike: L'Interdit, Le Directoire, the Phone Booth, and Ondine, the fashionable status of which was amplified by the fact that the Animals' Eric Burdon enjoyed his first acid trip there, courtesy of the Stones' Brian Jones, while under the protective custody of the rising photographer Linda Eastman. In April 1966, Olivier Coquelin and Adlai Stevenson's son Borden opened Cheetah, near the old Palladium at Broadway and 53rd, and the stakes were raised further. Cheetah's opening night included two hundred models sporting both the flowery images of Carnaby Street and the vinyl suits of downtown Manhattan; cylindrical changing rooms hung from the ceiling; a Nathan's vendor cruising the 8,000-foot dance floor; and a series of side rooms offering television broadcasts, avant-garde movies, and even, for those for whom the sensory overload was too much, a library.

A crucial shift back downtown came when the Ondine promoter Bradley Pierce signed on to Salvation, located in the former Café Society space on Sheridan Square. Under Pierce's popular jurisdiction, Salvation became another celebrity haunt, attracting the likes of Liza Minnelli, Mia Farrow, and Faye Dunaway—but unlike the more fashion-conscious midtown clubs with their strict (though rarely admitted) quotas, it welcomed the local gay clientele, too. Also contributing to Salvation's status was Terry Noël's presence as disc jockey—until the night he arrived late for work once too often, to find his place on the turntables taken by a former dancer from Trude Heller's whom he had previously dismissed as a mere "groupie": Francis Grasso.

Grasso, from Brooklyn, and nineteen years old at the time, differed from Noël in two key areas, and they were enough to alter the entire direction of New York nightlife. First was his refusal to see the disc jockey as a support system for the club's liquor sales: where Noël would regularly throw on slow records to encourage visits to the bar, Grasso worked instead to keep the dancers *on* the floor, all the time building momentum, taking listeners on a lengthy, sensual journey toward a memorable musical climax. "Nobody had really just kept the beat going," he said, years later. "They'd get them to dance then change records, you had to catch the beat again. It never flowed."

In addition, Grasso played essentially black music. Where Terry Noël had favored the Mamas and the Papas, the Doors and the Rolling Stones, Grasso took the Stones' and the Doors' heavier cuts as a launching pad into the heavy white groups who aspired to sound black, the psychedelic side of Motown, the emergent anthems of Sly and the Family Stone and the Chambers Brothers, and the ongoing dance sermons of James Brown, the undisputed King of Soul who was held in especially high regard in New York for his seemingly constant appearances at the Harlem Apollo and the live album recorded there. The jet-setters were on the way out, and Grasso helped show them the door. It was not mere coincidence that on June 21, 1969, one week before the Stonewall raid, Arthur closed for good—sold to a consortium led by Bradley Pierce, who announced the intent of turning it into a perfectly ungroovy supper club.

Pierce had vacated Salvation by then—wisely so, for as Salvation became ever more popular with the local gay crowd, it simultaneously became beholden to mobster muscle. Francis Grasso was spinning there the night of June 27/28, when the Stonewall was raided; he recalled that the management locked the doors amid the violence not only to keep the crowd outside from coming in but, especially, to keep the crowd inside from coming out. For as graffiti that showed up within hours on the Stonewall's exterior spelled out—

Gay Prohibition

Corupt$ Cop$

Feed$ Mafia

With the Stonewall temporarily shuttered in the weeks after the raid—the police had, among other things, taken an ax to the bar—the Gambino and Genovese families moved in together on Salvation's putative owner: Bobby Wood, a former used-car dealer from the Bronx, who, lacking other options, decided to keep a detailed record of his payoffs (to police and mob alike) and of on-premises thefts and drug deals. In December 1969, the State Liquor Authority, clearly having its own misgivings about the operation, suspended Salvation's liquor license, but the club merely slipped into "juice bar" mode and kept right on doing business. Then, in February 1970, Wood showed up dead, on a side street in Queens, his body riddled with bullets. Just a few days later, a "letter from the grave" was handed over to senior law officials; in it, Wood named the mob figures who had wrestled control of the club, and two detectives who had shaken him down for $8,000. "Should I meet with a violent death or disappear, certainly one or a combination of these men are responsible," wrote Wood, who also referenced Mafia intimidation of John Addison, operator of the Together discotheque, on 59th Street.

Yet business continued unabated. By the summer, the Stonewall's lease had been transferred to a Gambino representative, Nicholas Di Martino—who had also just reopened Salvation as the Haven, "the ultimate teen club." At the Haven, he brought back Francis Grasso, who was soon joined by twenty-six-year-old Steve D'Acquisto, a long-haired cab driver who stopped in one night on a customer's recommendation and was instantly converted to the music; and then Michael Capello, just sixteen when he first started hanging out at the Haven. The three became best friends.

Part of a cultural continuum that stretched back to the doo-wop era's similar fascination with black music, Grasso and his Italian-American friends were not necessarily "connected." But the experience of shared cultural and neighborhood backgrounds made them an obvious first line of employees on the ever-growing gay club circuit. David DePino, for example, grew up on Mulberry Street, in the heart of Little Italy, where one of his neighbors, "an Italian roughneck" named Nicky Falco, went on to become the front man for Tamburlaine, a dance club inside a Chinese restaurant on a busy stretch of 48th Street. There Falco employed DePino's older sister, who brought David to see the club for himself when he was only sixteen.

DePino recalled of his first night at the club—the entranceway of which featured a bridge over a pond full of goldfish—that he "felt like Alice in Wonderland." Inside, he found "guys humping guys, girls kissing girls, and the music blasting, and lights blinking." Tamburlaine, as DePino discovered, was "*really* gay. It was crazy, it was loud, it was over the top, the drugs were rampant." But there was yet a more crucial distinction. "I always went to little neighborhood places with bands. Music always stopped. Jukeboxes always stopped. But this music was continuous. I remember looking over to my sister's friend and saying, 'This song has been on for an hour. It's the longest song I've ever heard.' She said, 'No, it's a DJ playing music.'" That would have been Steve D'Acquisto, who had secured the residency upon Frankie Grasso's recommendation.

Grasso himself soon progressed to the Sanctuary, on West 43rd Street between Ninth and Tenth Avenues, a former German Baptist church situated, appropriately, given that it had previously displayed a mural of the devil engaged in sexual activity with multiple angels, in the heart of Hell's Kitchen. In a brief late sixties existence, the Church, as it was then known, had a liquor license and enforced a couples-only policy; but as the Sanctuary, fronted by Seymour and Shelley, a pair of flamboyant gay promoters who fronted a number of popular after-hours and/or gay bars from the Village to midtown, it downgraded to juice bar status and shifted sexual allegiance accordingly.

At the Sanctuary, all the ingredients for the new decade's dance clubs came together. "It had a mixer," said Joey Madonia, sixteen years old in 1971, when he was brought to the club by his Brooklyn neighbor Frankie Ramos, the proprietor of the influential Manhattan store Downtown Records. "It had turntables. It had a light show. It had a sound system. It had a DJ booth. The DJ booth was in the center. It was on the altar." For the Catholic-raised David DePino, that was enough to provoke a religious experience on his first visit. He recalled dancing to the music of Grasso when "suddenly the room went pitch-black and everybody screamed, and all the stained-glass windows were lit from the outside. That took you into a whole other world and you realized, I'm really in a church. I was shocked, I was amazed, I felt guilt, I felt every emotion at the same time. I was overwhelmed. And I said, '*I have to be here for the rest of my life.*'" Within weeks, the seventeen-year-old DePino, having figured out he was gay, had secured a job working behind the juice bar on the dance floor, which was surrounded on both sides by church pews that rose up to the stained-glass windows.

Few people ever spoke about the Sanctuary without talking about Francis Grasso; the two became intrinsically connected to each other's legacy. Such was Grasso's unprecedented influence over his audience that Joey Madonia, for one, frequently found himself approaching the altar to find out what was playing. "The Sanctuary was the only club where every record was good," he said. He set about collecting everything Grasso ever played there.

Grasso, a heterosexual in a mostly gay scene, was not, by modern standards, an "underground" disc jockey. His playlist at the Sanctuary was wide and varied, and relatively mainstream. He still played white rock music, from the Doors to the James Gang to T. Rex and Chicago Transit Authority; he bought heavily into cross-cultural experiments like Mitch Ryder's *Detroit-Memphis Experiment*; he played gospel ("Rain," by Dorothy Morrison), soul ("Hot Butter and All," by Lou Courtney), and R&B ("You're the One," by Little Sister, the Family Stone's backup singers). There was James Brown: Grasso named "Hot Pants," released in the summer of 1971 at the peak of Sanctuary's reign, as one of the most popular records he ever spun. Likewise, there was no shortage of the equally prevalent Motown, that label itself reaching with arms outstretched into the musical possibilities of a new decade. And Grasso was an early fan of acts that were, at that time, still filed under R&B: New Jersey's Kool & the Gang and Chicago's Earth Wind & Fire.

But if Grasso became best known for any one style, it was his love of African music. He championed Osibisa, a group of Ghanaians and West Indians living in England, whose eponymous 1971 debut album produced the Sanctuary hit "Music for Gong Gong." And he dug back in time to reintroduce the music of Babatunde Olatunji, an African percussionist living in New York, whose *Drums of Passion*, a major hit upon its 1959 release, included the seminal Sanctuary cut "Jin-go-lo-ba."

To keep the groove going all night long, Grasso taught himself how to "beat mix." Working with singles that featured parts 1 and 2 on separate sides (for years, James Brown didn't release them any other way), he would use the state-of-the-art mixer's new cue systems to splice the beats together from one turntable to the other to create, he hoped, a seamless segue. Soon, he was doing so midsong: Joey Madonia recalled him extending the short drum break in the middle of Steam's 1969 number one single "Na Na Hey Hey Kiss Him Goodbye," switching from one turntable to another and back—a habit that would later take hold in the parks of the Bronx. When it came to records of different tempos, Grasso figured a segue point in his headphones, one record playing in each ear: the Thorens turntables at the Sanctuary did not allow for any kind of speed control.

Given the lack of recorded evidence, we can only guess at the true precision of the mixing. "Steve D'Acquisto and Francis Grasso were the first two people I heard mix music continuously," said David DePino. "Were they in 'beat'? I don't know. All I know is that the music never ended, and back then, that might have been all you had to do." But by playing for several hours at a stretch—the Sanctuary often didn't close until late morning—Grasso learned to teach, read, and react to his audience. "I always played according to what I got from the crowd," he said. "If I saw them maintain the level of intensity, then I'd bring in a quicker record. It always depended on the vibe."

Sanctuary's reputation ensured that it was chosen for the nightclub scene when Hollywood came to New York to make the movie *Klute*, starring Donald Sutherland and Jane Fonda. Grasso recalled the hiring of real hookers and clubgoers as extras, and such flagrant drug use that the police showed up. Indeed, the ecstatic environment that Grasso created nightly often demanded gratification that could not be found on the dance floor, and as sexual acts spread to the street in the early hours of the mornings, the Sanctuary generated unprecedented public attention. By March 1972, the state district attorney was calling for its closure; the end came, predictably, not long afterward.

David Mancuso had no desire to attract the attention Francis Grasso commanded at the Sanctuary—not from the police, not from the city bureaucrats, not from the media, and certainly not from the Mafia. Raised in an orphanage by nuns in upstate New York, Mancuso had arrived in the city in 1962, with an open mind and a limited budget. His subsequent journey through the 1960s involved much temporary employment, considerable immersion in the era's political struggles, major experimentation with psychedelic drugs, and such an intense spiritual quest for self that in 1969 he forswore material possessions, stopped using money, and ended up in Bellevue Hospital, diagnosed as catatonic. But from 1965 onward, there was one constant: his lease on the second of five floors at 647 Broadway, a couple of blocks above Houston Street, in a former manufacturing building in a mostly abandoned part of the city.

"In a lot of these loft spaces, five thousand feet and under," he recalled, "small businesses had started to move out, and the landlords were getting stuck on how to rent the spaces. So they started letting people live in the spaces and looked the other way, even though it was illegal. In my building each floor was a loft. But there were only a few other people along that stretch of Broadway living in lofts. It was extremely rare."

Granted such space and privacy, Mancuso, who had relished the communal environment of his orphanage, began throwing multimedia parties in 1966. "I didn't do it for income, I just did it to have a party." But Mancuso, a great believer in "social advancement" and something of a natural guru figure himself (people would later describe him, with his beard and long hair, as a calmly commanding Jesus-like presence), found that he had a gift as a host. At the start of 1970, following his hospitalization (and after regaining control of the loft space he had briefly lost while swearing off possessions), he recognized that he "had to do something for income" and decided to see if a party could make a small profit. "It was just a way to subsidize the space. And I thought that was legit without getting into a business, without getting into the club scene." Mancuso arranged a Saturday night party around Valentine's, called it "Love Saves the Day," the initials of which carried an invitation to psychedelic participation, sent it to a group of friends, and set about decorating his loft space, preparing food, and fine-tuning his hi-fi equipment. He had no great plan with regard to the music; there appeared to be no need. "It seemed to be that a lot of my friends, we all liked the same records."

That February night, around one hundred people filled his loft to eat, drink, talk, take acid, dance, and otherwise commune through late Sunday morning. It was a roaring success—considered by many as a seminal event in the history of dance music—and Mancuso repeated the process a month later, soon making it a weekly event. This carried it with the risk of visits from both the police and the mob, each with the power to close him down unless suitably remunerated. "I didn't want to make myself a target," said Mancuso, who avoided doing so by keeping the events private. He sent out individual cards marked "Your invitation" to his friends, whose names would be checked off on the night against a master list in the building's vestibule. At the entry to his second-floor loft, his guests would then make a fixed "donation," which guaranteed them virtually everything they needed to enjoy the party—except alcohol, which Mancuso did not serve, partly to avoid legal repercussions and also because he favored (his guests' bringing and sharing) other means of getting high.

Almost every aspect of the party stood in contrast to the nightclub scene. A Christmas tree stayed up all year round, and a yoga shrine filled one wall. The food was healthful and plentiful, not least because some of his friends, actively disenfranchised members of the counterculture, "might not have eaten that day." There would be fruit, cakes, rice, vegetables, and ice cream. Balloons were strewn around to bring the largely tripping collective back to the joys of childhood. "It was all about turning on the senses. If all the senses come together, then maybe you go to another sense up there some place."

Only after eating, socializing, and relaxing would the guests start dancing. Finding himself at the turntables almost by default, as the man who best knew his friends' tastes, Mancuso included in his soundtrack many acts that were ubiquitous at every dance party of the era—Motown and James Brown—and several that were simultaneously finding favor on the Sanctuary dance floor, like Little Sister and Osibisa. But whereas Francis Grasso generally hammered the hard funk for a crowd juiced on uppers and downers, Mancuso extolled the percolating groove for the flowing acid trip. That meant incorporating not only the message music of Edwin Starr and Curtis Mayfield but the blue-eyed soul of Rare Earth and Traffic, while constantly on the lookout for similarly rhythmic acts from across the globe—such as Cymande, a West Indies fusion group whose ode to women's lib, "Bra," mixed funk, soul, African, and Caribbean sounds with infectious ease.

Yet Mancuso refuted the notion of himself as a disc jockey à la Frankie Grasso and others. "I'm a real believer that the music plays *us*," he said. "I really, really see the music as something that is bigger than all of us. When you start thinking you're in control, you miss half of the whole thing. I think that you distance yourself, especially from the healing forces of music and what it's all intended to be." Accordingly, Mancuso mostly allowed records to play in their entirety, without any adjustment of tempo, in honor of the musicians' original creative intent.

Unlike his contemporaries, who lived a primarily urban existence, Mancuso spent half of each week in a cabin in Mount Tremper, in the Catskill Mountains just west of Woodstock. He passed his days there wandering the woods, exploring swimming holes, immersing himself in the crystal-clear sounds of the natural world and how they related to the rhythms of the loft dance music. In 1972, Mancuso asked Alex Rosner, an expert in sound system design who attended the parties, to replace the single hi-frequency tweeters in his speakers with eight apiece, the better to hear the hi-hat cymbals that Mancuso had now identified as the steady pulse of the party music. Rosner, initially skeptical, ultimately hung the tweeters from the ceiling in the middle of the room like chandeliers, facing outward. (The main speakers, with the bass and midrange, faced into the room.) The result was clarity in the top end that had never been heard before on a dance floor.

A similar quest for audio perfection was occurring in the recording studios. The most important release of 1972 for New York dancers was surely that by the former Temptations' singer Eddie Kendricks, whose *People . . . Hold On* album featured the eight-minute "Girl, You Need a Change of Mind." Propelled by a kick drum kept firmly on the midtempo beat, a booming bass line straight out of early seventies blaxploitation anthems ("Shaft," "Superfly," etc.), furnished with tightly punctuated horns and a syncopated piano line that would itself form the template for something known much later as "house music," and rendered ecstatic by Kendricks's effortless falsetto, it seemed to go on forever—and that even before its "breakdown," after which it built back up, instrument by instrument, phrase by phrase . . . only to do the same thing all over again. "Girl, You Need a Change of Mind" was one of those songs dancers could truly lose themselves inside of, but when edited down to a 7-inch single, it lost its emotional depth and failed to catch on at radio. Precisely because it never became a commercial hit, "Girl, You Need a Change of Mind" persisted instead as an "underground" dance anthem, still capable of filling the floor two and three years after its release.

Equally important was the music emanating from Philadelphia, in particular Kenny Gamble and Leon Huff's Philadelphia International Records (PIR) label, which launched itself into the charts in 1972 with the O'Jays' "Backstabbers." Like Tamla-Motown, PIR employed a house band and proven teams of songwriters to fashion a city-associated sound, softer and more seductive than that of Detroit, with greater focus on the strings than the funk, all of which caught on with gay dancers in New York: releases by Harold Melvin and the Blue Notes, the Trammps and People's Choice, all helped focus attention on the City of Brotherly Love as a key supplier to the New York dance floor.

As this evolving new dance music spread across New York, David Mancuso's Loft—lacking any official name, the place became known by its location—emerged as the tastemakers' headquarters. Here, in the early hours of a Sunday, away from the bright lights, ear-splitting sound, and undercurrent of mob violence that was the burden of their paid gigs, the DJs could gather and listen to music that, thanks to Mancuso and Rosner's sound design, was never so loud that they couldn't also talk—especially about records. Steve D'Acquisto shared the debut album by the British progressive rock act Babe Ruth, and Mancuso adopted "The Mexican," its break-friendly reinterpretation of Ennio Morricone's "For a Few Dollars More." Mancuso bought for himself "Soul Makossa," by Manu Dibango, an African record released on a French independent label, with a gently vibrating soul-funk rhythm, tribal vocals, and punchy brass riffs that proved perfect for the all-embracing Loft dance floor. When Frankie Crocker, a radio DJ at WBLS whose rise to airwave prominence tracked that of the club DJs, also picked up on the record, some labels began issuing cover versions to meet the demand—until Atlantic (always Atlantic!) secured the rights from the original French label and took the song into the national top 40 in the summer of 1973.

The experience was almost frightening for the club DJs, who had never considered that they could launch obscurities on a path to hit records. While some relished their newfound influence, Mancuso insisted on seeing the bigger picture. "A record is born when it's born," he said. "A DJ can realistically look at it as being a midwife. But to say that 'This is a Loft record' "—as many have claimed of "Soul Makossa" and others—"is categorizing the music."

Mancuso had other issues to worry about. In 1972, the Loft was raided by a plainclothes cop who, initially turned away for lack of invitation, secured entry by coming in as someone's guest. As his freshly squeezed orange juice was hauled away to the police labs for testing, Mancuso was thankful for his years of alcohol-free caution. Ultimately, the case was thrown out (the policeman lied about how he gained entry), but Mancuso postponed the parties for a month while the case went to court. And then, just a few months later, he caught a couple of young partygoers, Nicky Siano and his part-time girlfriend and full-time collaborator Robin Lord, selling Tuinal. "That was the first and only time at Broadway we had to put someone out," said Mancuso. "He was only sixteen years old, and I understand that, but he didn't understand the spirit of the party. People did *not* like the idea of someone trying to sell drugs."

Aspiring to improve the Loft by putting in a new, more dance-friendly floor, and offered the chance to spend a summer in London, Mancuso gave notice that he would close for three months in the middle of 1973. While in London, he learned from the *International Herald Tribune* that the ancient Broadway Central Hotel, just ten doors north of his loft, had collapsed in the middle of an afternoon rush hour. Several people were presumed dead in the rubble. Fingers were being pointed, given that the building—which had degraded into a welfare hotel over the years—had been cited as "hazardous" in an inspection just months earlier. Within days, Mayor Lindsay was ordering stepped-up inspections on all the city's pre-twentieth-century structures.

Mancuso knew that his own loft would become part of that review—and that he would have a hard time not only explaining why he was living and throwing parties at a space that lacked the zoning for either, but why he had recently taken over an adjoining loft and torn down the dividing wall, doubling his space to over 3,500 square feet. (The fact that his landlord supported all these endeavors would mean nothing to the city's bureaucracy.) That was more than enough to give him pause during his intended holiday. And then, upon his return, there was the small matter of Nicky Siano.

n many ways, Nicky Siano exemplified the new dance generation. Ambitious, talented, flamboyant, handsome, and almost impossibly young to be putting all these attributes to work, the Brooklyn-based teen and the equally extroverted Robin Lord had been first exposed to the New York club scene at Tamburlaine in 1970 and then its successor Tambourine the following year. If the midtown nightclubs offered Siano his first glimpse of disc jockey power, the Loft provided an epiphany of a different kind. "Never, *ever* did [Mancuso] play records," Siano recalled. "He created an *environment* for each record."

Inspired to seek a similar role, Siano landed a job at the cabaret dance club the Round Table, by setting Robin Lord's teenage charms on the club's mob-connected manager. In such sexually permissive times, neither Lord nor Siano considered this to be in conflict with any core values; besides, Siano was in the process of confirming his own homosexuality. The pair's decision to launch their own club was partly the result of being ejected from the Loft for their drug dealing. As Robin Lord put it, "You won't let us in? Fine, we'll open our own club." Siano's older brother, who had the necessary friendships to raise the money and ensure the venture's viability, managed their endeavor.

Situated on 22nd Street between Sixth and Seventh Avenues, the This and That Gallery started as a near–carbon copy of the Loft—the Saturday night party was by invitation only, the sound system was designed by Alex Rosner, balloons supplied part of the decor, and refreshments were provided in return for a fixed "donation"—with the notable difference that it focused on the straight crowd. But after its launch in February 1973, the Sianos quickly learned a lesson of New York nightlife: that while opening night is almost always a guaranteed success (night owls love something new), gaining the crowd's loyalty is another matter entirely (ditto). In addition, Siano and Lord quickly discovered that the straight crowd was nowhere near as much fun as the gay one.

Then Mancuso took off for the summer, allowing Siano's Gallery to refocus itself as a gay alternative. By the time Mancuso returned, the Gallery was easily the hottest "private" dance party in Manhattan. "For a while he had a very cocky attitude that he was going to get the Loft crowd and all that stuff," recalled a bemused Mancuso. "I was thinking, 'What the hell? I'm just having a party . . .'" Yet competition has a way of making nightlife thrive, and as the Loft regulars returned to Broadway in the fall of 1973, the Gallery came to find and define itself. Mancuso was pushing thirty, and his parties reflected his maturity as well as his spirituality. Siano was a vivacious gay teenager of the early seventies, and the Gallery's music mirrored his high energy levels. Siano favored the female vocals of artists like Betty Wright and Brenda Holloway over the international rhythms that permeated the Loft; many credited him with putting the "diva" into disco. "David's room, everyone got down and grinded," said David DePino. "Nicky's room everyone threw their hands up and screamed."

Siano was arguably the first of the disc jockeys to view himself as a musician, playing his records like the strings on a guitar, or the keys on a piano, to create out of them an entirely new performance. He understood that the break in James Brown's "Give It Up" featured the same rhythmic handclaps as the Temptations' "Law of the Land," and he wove them together. He took two copies of Gloria Spencer's "I Got It" and extended the introduction. "Other DJs would play three records to peak a crowd," he told Tim Lawrence. "I'd play ten! I'd play peak records until they were screaming so loud that I couldn't hear the music. I was doing that because if I was on the dance floor that's what I would have wanted."

Siano's mixing abilities were aided by his skilled use of varispeed turntables (still a new phenomenon in the club world, and a controversial one at that); his willingness to isolate the treble, midrange, or bass (plus Alex Rosner's customized sub-bass); and a minimal light system that, like the Sanctuary's and the Loft's, frequently cut to black. The ecstatic atmosphere, further enhanced by the distribution of acid-spiked punch, would inspire Siano to take ever greater mixing risks—and occasional failures, what club land would later term "train wrecks." Though his enthusiasm for drugs and alcohol made him unpredictable, Siano was, in the prime of his youth, readily forgiven his excesses.

Clubs were opening almost every week now, so it seemed, and new resident disc jockeys emerging accordingly. There was Tee Scott at Better

Days, west of Times Square, where some claim that the dance floor "whis-tles" first came into vogue; Richie Kaczor at Hollywood, on the site of the old Peppermint Lounge in midtown; Richie Rivera at the Anvil in the Meatpacking District, a hard-core gay party with an X-rated lower floor. In Brooklyn, Steve D'Acquisto was playing to a hometown crowd at Broadway on Coney Island Avenue, while Paul Casella held court at the Monastery in Queens. The white gay Fire Island crowd began congregating during winter at the Tenth Floor on West 25th Street to hear Ray Yeates. And though Nicky Siano would be most closely associated with his own Gallery, John Addison hired him for weekday nights at Le Jardin, which, upon its open-ing in mid-1973 in the basement of the storied Diplomat Hotel on 43rd Street, became an instant celebrity haunt, the first of the new clubs to aim for the mainstream. For weekends, meanwhile, Addison picked off Bobby Guttadaro—soon known as Bobby DJ, the first to so append his name—from the Continental Baths.

The phenomenon of the gay bathhouse was very much a product of late sixties sexual permissiveness—but, as with the gay nightclub or loft party, that did not necessarily make it legal. Indeed, upon opening his Continental Baths on the Upper West Side in 1968, Steve Ostrow faced the usual rounds of police raids and payoffs. Only after Stonewall and the sub-sequent explosion in gay pride was he was able to conduct business more transparently—and profitably. Unlike most bathhouses, which existed almost exclusively for sexual encounters, the Continental offered rooms for the night, served food and drink, and expanded rapidly to include live enter-tainment around the swimming pool; it remains forever famous as the venue where Bette Midler was first embraced by a gay audience.

By the end of 1972, the Continental Baths had installed a new sound system, and an improved DJ booth around the pool, and had begun attract-ing not only the Fire Island crowd but gay black men, too. Among them were Larry Levan, a former altar boy from Brooklyn, and Frankie Knuckles, from the Bronx; the pair met through the competitive drag ball scene that had long flourished in the Harlem underground, and gravitated to the Loft. Knuckles's recollections of attending Mancuso's parties as a sixteen-year-old were emblematic of a minority that went largely unreported at the time.

"There's always one person that feels like the odd one out, who feels like the black sheep. You feel alone to a certain degree. Well, that's the way I felt until I went to the Loft, and then I realized there were more people in the world just like me. It was the first time I'd actually just let everything go. . . . Just the freedom, it spoke volumes to who and what I was. And that was it: I was hooked."

Levan, nineteen in mid-1973, was first to hang out at the Baths; when Knuckles, then eighteen, joined him, he found it so magical that, he recalled, he and Levan took a room and stayed there for the next two weeks. Over subsequent months, Levan worked his way into Ostrow's favor and secured a resident DJ gig early in the week; when promoted to weekends, he handed his previous slot over to Knuckles. Their approach to DJing reportedly reflected their personalities. "Levan," wrote Henry Kielarowski, another teenager on the gay club scene, "had electric eyes, enormous native intelligence and creativity, and a wild, free, impulsive magnetic personality. Larry lived for the moment. Frankie, on the other hand, was more prudent and future-oriented." Few could have suspected at the time that the pair would go on to become two of the most revered DJs in the entire history of dance music. Most who attended the Baths—which, by 1973, on Saturday nights only, included (clothed) straights—were too overwhelmed by the sexually charged atmosphere. Nona Hendryx, singer with LaBelle, the all-girl vocal act raised on R&B, turned rock, and now embracing the gay crowd, recalled playing there as "an odd, surrealistic experience, performing to guys in towels, and with other activity going on in little cubicles along the way."

The only DJ not evidently enjoying himself during this deliriously hedonistic period was Francis Grasso. After the Sanctuary closed, he found work at a place called the Machine, in the Empire Hotel in midtown, but returned to the Village when Nicholas Di Martino, his former employer at the Haven, offered him partnership in Club Francis, above Café Wha?, the first New York dance club to be named after its disc jockey. According to Grasso's own accounts, his departure sat badly with the Machine's backers, and they took it out on him in a blind alley one night, rearranging his handsome features in a vicious beating. As Grasso sat at home for three months recuperating, unable to attend the new club that bore his name, the initial shock that followed the news of the beat-down settled, among his peers, into a kind of belated acceptance, as if the horrific violence inflicted upon him was perhaps some kind of karmic payback for his previously unimpeded self-confidence, salary, and sexual appetite. Time moved at a furious place in the new dance underground, and it seemed to be passing Grasso by.

n the recreation rooms and "parks" of the housing projects, at one-off parties thrown in colleges and ballrooms all over the city, kids from the street—almost exclusively heterosexual and either black and/or Puerto Rican—were similarly embracing the new multicultural dance music and, especially, the new means by which they could control it. For the most part, these two scenes would follow parallel paths through the 1970s to produce two very different forms of disco, but occasionally someone would jump from one scene to the other to find his calling. Such was the case with Tony Smith, who grew up in the projects that lined the East River from the Brooklyn Bridge on up to 14th Street, learning to play lead guitar, and in 1968, at the age of fourteen, playing in a high school group named, aptly for the era, Soul Sound Explosion. When performing at local churches, recreation centers, or the Henry Street Settlement, in the heart of the Lower East Side, Smith would bring his record player and play music between sets. Then, in the volatile summer of 1968, as city street life took on a new urgency, people began bringing their players outdoors, starting the trend toward "sound systems." Eager to join the party, Tony Smith did likewise. Accessing power was as easy as opening up the base of the street lamps and hot-wiring into the city electricity.

Come the spring of 1969, Smith found that he had competition—and "that's when the battle of the DJs started." There were two ways of winning that battle: create a bigger and louder sound system, or build a bigger and better record collection. Smith chose the latter route—especially once Downstairs Records opened, in the subway station at 33rd and Seventh Avenue in 1970, and he discovered a whole culture of people just like him, each searching out dance tracks that weren't being played on the radio, that were most likely hidden away on albums. Simultaneously, Smith and his friends noted that the parties at schools like Hunter and NYU, thrown mainly for and by black and Puerto Rican youth, were undergoing a significant shift. "What used to happen was the DJ played a record, you danced with the girl, you separated, then the DJ would play another record," recalled Smith. But now that there were two turntables and a mixer available for use, "there's continual music." The result was that, "all of a sudden, no one is playing slow music."

Though he always had white and Asian friends, Smith primarily attended the straight black dance clubs in his part of town: the Dom on St. Mark's, the Third World Gallery, 43 Below. It was only around 1972 that he discovered the West Village gay scene and, with it, a different kind of music. At first, ingrained homophobia had him listening from outside, but when he finally plucked up the courage to enter the Limelight, on Seventh Avenue and Sheridan Square, the eighteen-year-old was overwhelmed by what he saw and heard. "Gays weren't so much about doing the *bugaloo*—it was all about the melody of the song." And then there was the fact that the DJ at the Limelight had a custom-built booth, whereas, "in most black clubs, the DJ had to make his own booth to play music."

The person inside the Limelight's booth was David Rodriguez, a true fan of the underground, of old soul artists like Betty Wright and Brenda Holloway, and someone who loved to tell a story over the course of a night's music. The first Puerto Rican to make a name for himself on the gay club scene, he was also one of the first to promote the idea of the DJ as educator rather than mere entertainer. The discovery of such eloquence sent Smith on a deeper quest, aided, if for different reasons, by the Limelight's doorman—Ed "the Skull" Murphy. "He had a crush on me," said Smith, who resisted Murphy's advances while following him to the various gay clubs he "promoted." That journey took Smith to Hollywood, where Richie Kaczor, even more than Rodriguez, "could play new music that no one ever heard and make you like it," said Smith. "That's when I decided I definitely wanted to be a DJ." By this he meant, a *club* DJ. "One of the things that made me want to leave the street was that the street wasn't progressive enough."

They were, for sure, entirely different scenes. As Joey Madonia had discovered before him with Francis Grasso, the likes of Rodriguez and Kaczor were happy to share details about what they were playing, eager to promote the artists. This was a far cry from outdoors, where Smith had blacked out the label of Billy Sha-ree's "Do It," a two-minute Brooklyn-produced single "that always got the crowd crazy," to prevent other DJs from being able to identify it. The mobile sound system culture that Smith had grown up around now appeared to be controlled by four major names: Cameron Flowers, Maboya, Ron Plummer, and the Smith Brothers (no relation), who had gravitated to places as large as the Audubon Ballroom in Harlem. Smith, who recalled that "the black street DJs were vicious," found he could no longer compete. A friend pointed him to an ad in the *Village Voice* for a new club, Barefoot Boy on 39th Street and Second Avenue, looking for a resident DJ. As a straight black jock auditioning for a white gay club, he figured he wouldn't stand a chance. But five records into his audition, Smith was told he had the job: seven nights a week, from nine until four, at $25 a night.

Smith was in heaven, all the more so when he realized that he had the freedom to create his own style. It meant dropping James Brown from his set and adopting the more relaxed, string-dominated sound of Philadelphia; but having softened up his approach, he found that "you could take way more chances with white gay and black gay than you could straight." He knew he'd made it the night he looked out from the booth to see Richie Kaczor, Nicky Siano, and David Mancuso, together at the bar, nodding their heads to the beat in approval.

Joey Madonia, who later became his deputy at Barefoot Boy, said that Smith was "the only person who could beat mix on Lenco turntables," which could be manipulated only by manually lifting up the lever and setting it in between 33 and 45 rpms. "He managed to do it and do it flawlessly. We were still limited to finding records on our own, and he played a few records that you wouldn't know about unless you'd heard them. And it didn't matter what he picked—his mixing skills were just phenomenal."

Hunting for recordings along Eighth Street one day in 1973, Smith saw a copy of the Philly act Yellow Sunshine's eponymous debut album—good for the opening track only, he knew—but when he reached for it, another teenager, Danny Krivit, grabbed it before him. Krivit had been raised in a nightclub environment, in the heart of the Village, where his parents ran the Ninth Circle with Mickey Ruskin. Sid Bernstein lived upstairs, and Felix Cavaliere would stop in at their apartment after business meetings to play the piano. Around 1969, Ruskin long having moved on to Max's, the Krivits followed local fashion and transformed the Ninth Circle from a straight restaurant into a gay-friendly nightclub, and business flourished. Though slow to invest in turntables, they allowed their underage son to choose the music via tapes. A year later, a music executive neighbor introduced Krivit to James Brown, who gave him a white label of "Get on the Good Foot." With that, Krivit's path in life was determined.

Growing up in the Village in a progressive family, Krivit never harbored prejudices, but he noticed them on the street. Still, from what he dated as the first gay pride march, a year after Stonewall, he saw how "the whole homophobia thing really took a backseat." And as he became swept up in a world of lofts, galleries, and nightclubs, gradually elevating himself to the position of respected DJ, then like Tony Smith, with whom he became best friends after their chance encounter, the teenage Krivit quickly learned the golden rule of the era. "If you had a good club, it was gay." It was that simple. "If someone told you it was a good club and it was straight, you would look at them like, 'Really? How?'"

While in Europe in the summer of 1973, David Mancuso picked up an album, *Wild Safari*, by a Spanish group called Barrabas, and back at his new and improved Loft, the mix of Latin grooves and psychedelic funk on the title track and another called "Woman" became instant Loft anthems. When his patrons clamored for their own copies, Mancuso contacted the Spanish label and imported the first of several boxes, selling the records at cost. He gave a copy to Nicky Siano, and the teenager took it as a peace offering, hammering "Woman" to death. The jungle telegraph between the different club disc jockeys was now moving at such a pace that, with the exception of something as obvious as Barrabas, nobody could be totally sure who was first to play any particular record.

That might explain why several of them claimed such a role with "Love's Theme," a luscious instrumental that opened the initially ignored album by the soul trio Love Unlimited. Written and produced by Barry White, "Love's Theme" further marked the steady marriage of seventies funk and soul into something more orchestral and luscious, heavy on the strings and the hi-hat, but with a deliciously flexing funk guitar pulsating throughout. Endorsed by the New York DJs, "Love's Theme" became a dance floor classic, building up such demand that in late 1973 the record label, 20th Century, released it as a single, credited now to the Love Unlimited Orchestra—upon which it rocketed to the top of the charts. When it came to the industry's back-patting distribution of souvenir gold records, Bobby DJ was among the recipients—the presentation made at Le Jardin by Barry White himself.

This marked only the first occasion that New York club DJs were officially recognized for "breaking" a hit record. The following summer, "Rock the Boat," by Hues Corporation, and "Rock Your Baby," by George McRae, were back-to-back number ones, and each was acknowledged for having been established first on the New York dance floor. That spring, "The Sound of Philadelphia," by MFSB featuring the Three Degrees, on PIR, had also topped the charts. The DJs could not quite take credit for that one, given that it had been commissioned as the theme song for the TV show *Soul Train*, the arrival of which itself confirmed the increasing popularity of the new dance music. But they were so predisposed to MFSB (since they were the house band playing on most of the Gamble and Huff/PIR hits) that they pounced on the accompanying album, *Love Is the Message*, especially its lengthy title track, on which the musicians were afforded freedom to improvise, as if playing modern jazz swing, and on which a second part to the song, a delicate balancing act between sassy saxophones, a mellifluous organ solo, and swooping strings, presented itself almost as a bonus track. Blending melody and groove in symphonic style, "Love Is the Message" became arguably the biggest anthem of the entire musical movement—its endurance aided, surely, by the fact that it was never a radio or chart hit in its own right.

Perhaps it was no surprise that the same summer in which the new "disco" sound topped the charts four times in as many months also saw the closure of both the Loft and the Gallery—at least in their original locations. Mancuso's already precarious status had been further endangered when a few of his loft neighbors, newcomers all, became so rattled by the weekly incursion of what one tenant called "some of the more bizarre segments of our society" that they launched a media campaign against Mancuso. The *New York Times* wrote about the situation in a half-page story in late May 1974, for which Mancuso refused to be interviewed ("I won't play their game," he said at the time, though he later observed of his neighbors, "A couple of them I quite liked"), and it forced the hand of the Buildings Department. On Friday, May 31, citing Mancuso's demolition of the connecting wall between his two rental lofts, it served immediate notice to evict him from the premises because of its "extreme situation." Rather than fight the Building Department over what he considered an errant decision—"I did not want to bring any attention to my landlord about other violations he may have had"— Mancuso folded, proving the effectiveness of his grapevine by canceling the following night's party with just a few phone calls.

And whatever factors had enabled Siano's Gallery to stay in business for well over a year proved insufficient once it, too, was featured prominently in the New York media, in this case a major *New York* magazine story called "The Return of the Disco" in July 1974. The Fire Department hit the Gallery soon afterward and, citing inadequate fire exits, closed it down right there and then.

Siano's Gallery bounced back quickly, reopening on the corner of Mercer and Houston Streets, right at the entrance to the increasingly fashionable SoHo (south of Houston) area, in November 1974. The new location maintained the old ideal of membership cards and invitations, but was, by Siano's own admission, "more like a club," complete with a state-of-the-art lighting system. His big record on opening night was the brand-new "What Can I Do for You?" by LaBelle, perhaps no surprise given that the trio had headlined at the Metropolitan Opera House barely a month earlier, a seminal concert that brought the flamboyant gay disco set right into the heart of New York's cultural establishment. (The audience had been invited to wear silver, and, as LaBelle's Nona Hendryx recalled, "they wore as much as was possible—or as little!")

Just a month later, another discotheque opened down the block, in an upstairs, open-plan loft space on the corner of Broadway and Houston. Whereas the Gallery catered predominantly (but never exclusively) to a gay crowd of color, Flamingo, in the words of its promoter Richard Fesco, attracted the "conceited," "A-List," "very beautiful" white gay people who spent their summers on Fire Island. The different demographics ensured a lack of competition between the two clubs, but the presence of so many young party people—specifically, gay party people—sat uneasily with many SoHo residents, who were busy buying up the largely abandoned area's old industrial spaces and turning them into private lofts. They understood that they were creating a new artists' colony, and that the City Planning Commission had already determined that discotheques would not be a part of it.

So when Mancuso signed a lease for 99 Prince Street, right in the heart of the newly declared locale, he found Michael Goldstein—publisher of a brand-new paper, the *SoHo Weekly News*—waging a high-profile war to keep him out. Goldstein wrote that Mancuso's previous Broadway location was an "after-hours, drug-oriented club," which soon saw picketers on Prince Street demanding "No Juice Joint in SoHo." Mancuso felt that the *Weekly News* was stirring up latent (and outdated) racism and homophobia—"They didn't want my kind of people," he said—and set about a campaign of his own. He published a declaration of intent (sample line: "We did not have a happy childhood, but it has not soured us on life") and secured the support of Vince Aletti, the preeminent journalist of the discotheque scene. In June 1975, Aletti detailed the battle over SoHo in the *Weekly News'* senior rival, the *Village Voice*, revealing that Goldstein had earlier been turned down from renting 99 Prince Street as his magazine's office, suggesting that his motive for attacking Mancuso was personal. The piece served its purpose; Goldstein backed off.

Determined not to be caught in the same legal limbo that troubled his original Loft parties, Mancuso established a limited company and formally requested a cabaret license for his new premises, knowing perfectly well that they were almost impossible to come by. He was thrilled, then, to be denied—on the grounds that the company did not fit the requirements. This confirmed what Mancuso had always claimed: that his parties were private affairs, free of commerce, and therefore outside of bureaucratic jurisdiction. Just six weeks later, in October 1975, he threw his first private, legal, weekly party; though it was a while before they took off (his guests initially missed the magic of the original Loft), they would continue there, growing gradually in size and legendary underground reputation, for many years to come.

Out in the mainstream, driven by media coverage of easy profits, more and more entrepreneurs opened discos; as they did so, ever farther away from Manhattan and its (gay, black, Latino) minorities, they drew their weekend crowds from their local communities, most of which were young, white, and straight. The hits, likewise, were emanating now from the center rather than the fringes of the market: the Bee Gees, former folkies who transitioned into disco that summer with "Jive Talking"; Donna Summer, who emerged from the Munich studio of the producer Giorgio Moroder with the orgasmic (and, in album form, seventeen-minute long) "Love to Love You Baby"; and David Bowie, who switched from glam to soul with his *Young Americans* album. With each of these outside interjections, influential and inspired though some may have been, the sound grew more formulaic and synthetic, farther removed from the orchestral soul of the original discotheque classics.

But that was the inevitable price of popularity, and fighting it was like swimming against a riptide. In 1974, the club programmer (and future *Billboard* columnist) Tom Moulton began "remixing" 7-inch R&B singles into longer, more dance-friendly versions; they were so successful that they enabled less talented DJs to sit back and let the remixes do the work for them. Later that year, Moulton pressed acetates of Al Downing's soaring soul anthem "I'll Keep Holding On" on 12-inch vinyl—the cutting room had run out of 7-inch acetates—and he and his DJ friends quickly discovered how much louder and more clearly the music, especially the bass, came across on the wider groove. Scepter Records—which had maintained its involvement in R&B ever since its early success with the Shirelles, Maxine Brown, and the Isley Brothers, and whose promo chief Mel Cheren had been first to commission Moulton's remixes—promptly began servicing disco DJs with promo-only 12-inch 45s. In the spring of 1976, the new New York dance label Salsoul employed Walter Gibbons, Galaxy 21's resident DJ, to remix "Ten Percent," by Philadelphia's Double Exposure, into a ten-minute dance floor lovefest. It was issued as the first ever 12-inch commercial release, complete with a cut-out in the middle of the sleeve so that the label credits were visible on a record rack. Gibbons's extended mix was soon outselling the 7-inch by ratios of up to ten to one.

By this point, the New York media had thoroughly raked over the disco scene: a major *Village Voice* cover story of July 1975 ("Inside the Disco Boom") was followed almost immediately by similar profiles in the *News*, the *Post*, the *Times*, even the *Wall Street Journal*. So when *New York* magazine commissioned Nik Cohn for yet another story, the gifted British novelist and "new journalist" beat an untrodden path to Bay Ridge, in south Brooklyn, and a disco called 2001 Odyssey. There he honed in on and wrote about eighteen-year-old "Vincent," an apparent Al Pacino look-alike who danced with grace and precision and was the undisputed leader of the local "Faces."

That crowd, as befitted the Bay Ridge/Bensonhurst locale, was almost exclusively Italian working class—the demographic and borough that had produced so many of the founding disco DJs to begin with. But Cohn didn't connect the dots. He never even mentioned the Odyssey DJs. (He talked, disparagingly, instead about a cover band of "blacks from Crown Heights, who played as loudly and as badly as anyone possibly could.") In Cohn's narrative, the Bay Ridge Italian Faces were misogynist ("the female function was simply to be available"), racist ("Latins were greaseballs, Jews were different, and blacks were born to lose"), and, on the dance floor, almost fascist. (Cohn wrote of Vincent leading a retinue of up to fifty people through the ensemble steps of the bus stop dance and its local variation, the odyssey walk, rather than focusing on any displays of individuality.) A scene that had grown out of gay liberation and racial integration, that celebrated originality on the dance floor and the turntables alike, that embraced all music from all cultures, had apparently been reduced to the most reactionary of conservative values—and this barely ten miles from Greenwich Village. It was as if Grasso, Mancuso, D'Acquisto, and Capello had never existed.

As far as Cohn was concerned, they hadn't. Cohn had only just arrived in New York. A highly regarded expert on rock, he didn't know the first thing about the discotheque scene. Though he frequented Odyssey 2001 to construct his story, he based his characters on the west London of his 1960s youth—hence the term "Faces," which was the common parlance for those fashionable "mods" of the sixties who distinguished themselves from the everyday "tickets." There were interesting parallels to be drawn between these two youth cultures, a continent and a decade apart, but Cohn couldn't do so without blowing his cover. "My story was a fraud," he finally admitted in a confessional he wrote for a British newspaper in 1994. Vincent was "completely made-up, a total fabrication."

Fiction it may have been, but Cohn was a compelling writer. Before the ink had even dried on the newsstands, his "Tribal Rites of the New Saturday Night" feature had been optioned for a movie by Robert Stigwood, the Australian-born impresario behind Hollywood's hit interpretations of *Jesus Christ Superstar* and *Tommy*. Stigwood not only offered Cohn, with whom he already had a working relationship, the opportunity to adapt his "fraud" for the screen for a guaranteed $150,000 but also cut him in on a percentage of the movie's profits. As for the soundtrack, Stigwood turned to an act he had discovered back in the sixties, one that still recorded for his record label, RSO. That would be the Bee Gees, whose latest disco single, "You Should Be Dancing," was already on its way to number one that summer of '76, just as Cohn's feature hit the stands. The story of disco was about to be rewritten.

The changing faces of the girl groups. *Top*: The Chantels, Catholic school choristers from the Bronx, whose lead vocalist Arlene Smith, *at top*, cowrote their first 1950s hits. *Bottom left*: The Ronettes from Harlem—sisters Veronica and Estelle Bennett and their cousin Nedra Talley—pictured with producer and Veronica's future husband, Phil Spector. *Bottom right*: The Shangri-Las, comprised of identical twins Margie and Mary-Ann Ganser, and sisters Liz (not shown) and Mary Weiss.

Top: After playing Hammond organ on 1965's "Like A Rolling Stone," Al Kooper, *at left*, became close friends with Bob Dylan. That same year, Kooper joined the Blues Project.

Above: New York's first and foremost folk-rock group, the Lovin' Spoonful, recording their number one hit, "Summer in the City." *From left*: Zal Yanovsky, John Sebastian, Joe Butler.

Left: Janis Ian at 16. Said producer "Shadow" Morton, "From the time that she first played her songs for me, on that huge guitar that nearly covered her body, it seemed obvious to me that this girl knew where she was going."

Rock groups of the Lower East Side. *Top*: The Fugs, whose Ed Sanders (*at front*) owned the Peace Eye bookstore on East Tenth Street and was featured on the cover of *Life* magazine in 1967 as a poster child for the "Other Culture." *Bottom*: The Velvet Underground: Maureen Tucker, Sterling Morrison, Lou Reed, with their patron Andy Warhol at left. (John Cale not shown.)

Hilly Kristal outside CBGBs, his club on the Bowery, in 1977.

Talking Heads as a trio in 1976: David Byrne, Chris Frantz, Tina Weymouth.

The Ramones onstage at CBGBs, 1977. They played the club almost three hundred times in all. *From left*: Johnny, Tommy, Joey, Dee Dee.

Blondie's Chris Stein and Debbie Harry reunited with original bassist, Television's Fred Smith (*far left*), at the *Punk* magazine benefit at CBGBs, May 4, 1977.

Hip-hop pioneers of the South Bronx. *Top*: Afrika Bambaataa, Charlie Chase, and Red Alert on the turntables at the Kips Bay Boys Club in the Bronx, circa 1980. *Above*: DJ Kool Herc (*on right*) with Tony Tone at the T Connection, circa 1978. *Right*: Grandmaster Caz, one of the only DJ-rappers, in 1979.

14
LOOKING FOR A KISS: GLITTER, GLAM, AND NEW YORK DOLLS

As fast as loft parties and discotheques opened up post-Stonewall, rock venues closed down: the Scene in 1969, the Electric Circus in 1970, the Fillmore East in 1971. The Village circuit was reduced to booking inoffensive singer-songwriters, or comfortably mainstream cover bands, its familiar faces of the early sixties scattered far and wide: Bob Dylan, Peter Yarrow, and other former folkies to Woodstock; John Sebastian and Phil Ochs joining the migration to Los Angeles. Al Kooper, kicked out of his own group Blood, Sweat and Tears, left for the United Kingdom, while the Rascals broke in half with pen poised over a lucrative new deal with Columbia and would never have another hit.

Lenny Kaye, a budding rock critic and guitarist who moved over from New Jersey to attend NYU in 1967, recalled of playing for six weeks at the Bitter End in 1969, "You knew you weren't in the center of action. All these clubs were coming to the end of their lifeline." Kaye took a job at Village Oldies on Bleecker Street and in 1970, in the spirit of nostalgia, wrote a story on the a cappella doo-wop groups of South Jersey and Philadelphia for *Jazz and Pop* magazine. Soon after it was published, Kaye, living at the time with Lisa Robinson (another rising music journalist), and her husband, Richard (a record producer), received a phone call from the Robinsons' friend Patti Smith. She had read the piece and, as a product of the Philadelphia–South Jersey region herself, wanted to express her gratitude.

Kaye knew about Smith from Max's, where she stood out as "quite striking, quite ectomorphic, very beautiful and cool," having fashioned her look on Keith Richards—common enough among the boys of the era, unique among the women. Smith usually traveled in the company of the rising gay photographer Robert Mapplethorpe, with whom she had made friends on her arrival in New York in 1967 and taken to living with at the Chelsea Hotel in 1969, where friendships also blossomed with Jim Carroll, a local poet, and a host of others who rendered the Chelsea a constant party. Along the way, Smith cultivated a fixation on two tragic French Symbolist poets—Arthur Rimbaud and Paul Verlaine—and began to write poetry herself.

Smith and Kaye became friends, hanging out after hours at Village Oldies, dancing around the store to vintage 45s. When Smith landed her first major poetry gig, at St. Mark's-in-the-Bowery on February 10, 1971, she asked Kaye to accompany her on guitar. The pair played "Mack the Knife," it being the lyricist Bertolt Brecht's birthday, and a few songs they had put together in a hurry; and Smith read some of her poems, including one called "Oath," with a provocative opening line that Jesus Christ "died for some-body's sins but not mine."

"And that was it," said Kaye. "What we were doing was so unusual that there was no sense of what actually you would do with it or where you could play it." It would be nearly three years before they would take to the stage together again.

Among the many New York scenesters who fled the city at the dawn of the seventies was the actor Eric Emerson, whose photograph on the back of the first Velvet Underground album had led to its initial recall. Warhol had continued making movies after parting company with the Velvets, and Emerson had starred in one of the most successful, *Lonesome Cowboys*. But now Warhol appeared to be tiring of movies, as he did everything eventually, and Emerson wasn't about to sit around becoming another Factory has-been. He accepted an invitation to join the experimental Los Angeles rock group Messiah as its front man.

That he was in the process of becoming a father made little difference. "You don't take a creative person like that and say, 'You have to stay home now,'" said his then pregnant partner, Elda Gentile, who had been gifted a date with him on her eighteenth birthday, in 1968, for which he introduced her to the back room of Max's. Gentile was not alone in her belief that Emerson was "the most beautiful man on the planet," or that he was "really crazy" yet imbued with a certain innocence: his new bandmates in Messiah felt much the same way. "He had charisma, he had the look, he was flamboyant," said Sesu Coleman, the group's drummer. (The group also included a violin player and a guitarist.) "We all loved him right away."

And so, in the spring of '71, after an earthquake in Los Angeles dented their confidence, Messiah accompanied him back to New York. Emerson quickly talked Mickey Ruskin into providing them with a gig at Max's, the first since the Velvet Underground. The Factory crowd all came out (or, at least, upstairs) to see what Emerson had been up to, but although Messiah was visually intriguing, with "feathers in the hair and tin foil on the drum stands, lights in the bass drums, dry ice and candles and skulls," as Coleman described it, no one knew quite what to make of the music. After the show, Paul Morrissey took the band aside and offered an honest assessment. "The Velvets closed rock 'n' roll in this city down," he explained. "There are no clubs to play. New York is cabaret. It's off-Broadway."

He was right. A scene set in motion by the directors/writers/actors John Vacarro, Ron Tavel, and Charles Ludlam in the mid-1960s with their self-descriptive Play-House of the Ridiculous was taking over the downtown scene as the predominant art form. And why not? Rock 'n' roll had grown boring, conceited, and pompous—and the earnest singer-songwriters of the era (Carole King among them, with the multimillion-selling *Tapestry*) were no alternative. The Ridiculous Theater, on the other hand, was colorful, glamorous, flamboyant, and shameless, full of what Lisa Robinson later recalled as "grotesque chalk white masks, kohl-rimmed eyes, sparkly spangly lips and eyelids, amazingly colored wigs of every shape and dimension, shiny g-strings, dildos, extravagant costume jewelry. . . ."

. . . And glitter. Lots of it. The Jackie Curtis play *Heaven Grand in Amber Orbit* opened in 1970 with a group of performers in the lobby singing a song, "Thalidomide Baby," completely covered in the stuff. As was Curtis's wont, lines for the play were primarily taken from old movies: plot was never the most important aspect of the Ridiculous Theater. The Max's crowd loved it, as they did the sequel *Femme Fatale*, for which Curtis hired the director Tony Ingrassia and cast three relative unknowns from among the Max's regulars: Patti Smith, Elda Gentile, and the former Stonewall regular and drag queen Wayne Rogers, newly renamed for the Stooges' home turf in Michigan, Wayne County.

Also cast in *Femme Fatale* were Candy Darling and Holly Woodlawn, who, along with Curtis, formed what Wayne County called the "queen bees" of the Factory-dominated self-anointed superstar drag scene—though it was Curtis, County insisted, who "was the smart one, the most intellectual, the most temperamental," and, crucially, "the first of the glitter queens." County, currently sharing his East 13th Street apartment with Curtis, Darling, and a rising young photographer, Leee Childers, wrote and starred in a play of his own: *World—Birth of a Nation,* directed by Ingrassia, which introduced a former Salvation DJ and self-confessed groupie Cherry Vanilla to the stage. The lines in *World*'s first scene were all titles of Velvet Underground songs. The highlight, if that's what it could be called, was a scene in which John Wayne gave birth to a baby through his anus.

Never one to let a culture develop in New York without his own involvement, Andy Warhol decided, in the words of the theater world, to steal the show. He handed over hours of his tape-recorded conversations with various Factory characters and asked Ingrassia to make a plot out of them. The result, *Pork*, was nonsensical and offensive, proving particularly obsessed with feces. This created great discontent for Brigid Polk (a.k.a. "Pork," the title character), who had been recorded by Warhol describing her wealthy childhood in intimate detail.

Pork opened at La Mama in May 1971, a few weeks before Curtis's latest play, *Vain Victory,* in which Emerson took to the stage as one of the actors and singers, covered in glitter from head to toe; his Messiah bandmates, having taken Morrissey's advice to heart, provided the musical accompaniment. *Vain Victory*, Curtis's first stab at directing, was considered chaotic even by Ridiculous standards; Ingrassia's *Pork*, in large part thanks to Warhol's attachment, was promptly invited to London. In the summer of 1971, the cast and crew members Tony Zanetta, Leee Childers, Wayne County, and Cherry Vanilla were among those flown to London, where their performances at the Round House in Chalk Farm were regularly graced by the presence of one David Bowie.

Cultural interaction between New York and London has always ebbed and flowed according to the trade winds of fashion, and it was now about to enter a particularly turbulent period of cross-pollination. The twenty-four-

year-old Bowie, struggling to escape his one-hit wonder status ("Space
Oddity" had hit the charts back in 1969), was just finishing a new album,
Hunky Dory, that included a tribute trilogy to a New York City he barely
knew from firsthand experience but which he wrote about eloquently. His
"Song to Bob Dylan" served as a plea to the increasingly distant poet to
return to his old self. "Andy Warhol" demonstrated an intrinsic understanding of that artist's thinking, with clever wordplay on Warhol's preferred
method of screen printing. And "Queen Bitch" was clearly an homage to the
Velvet Underground, from Lou Reed–like riff to lyrics about a "Sister Flo."
Befriending *Pork*'s cast and crew brought Bowie a direct link to at least a
couple of his lyrical subjects, and when he flew to New York in September to
sign a new record deal with RCA, Tony Zanetta duly introduced him to
Warhol. Bowie was also fêted with a press dinner in his honor on that visit;
Lou Reed, newly relocated to Manhattan after his Long Island sabbatical,
and Iggy Pop, whose Stooges had just been broken up after two albums on
Elektra, were among the guests.

Inspired by the unrestrained, reinvent-yourself, gay-positive glamour of
New York, and especially by the characters in *Pork*, Bowie now created his
own androgynous persona: Ziggy Stardust. The following January, he told
Melody Maker, Britain's best-selling music paper, "I'm gay, and always have
been," a statement that, though largely a publicity stunt (Bowie was married
and had an infant son), acted as a release valve for an international rock community that had been watching the emerging gay liberation movement with
repressed envy. In June 1972, the album *The Rise and Fall of Ziggy Stardust
and the Spiders from Mars* was released, launching Bowie's alter ego as a cult
of personality. In Britain, they called it "glam rock," a trend that soon reached
down to the preteen set. In America, they called it "glitter rock," and though
Ziggy Stardust had minimal chart impact at the time (the concept was a difficult sales pitch to the vast expanses of middle America), in New York it was
an instant phenomenon.

That same summer, at Bowie's invitation, Lou Reed flew to London to
record his second solo album, *Transformer*. (His first, produced by Richard
Robinson, had been a flop.) Among the songs he brought with him was "Walk
on the Wild Side," for which he spun biographical snippets of the three
"Queen bees"—Holly Woodlawn, Candy Darling, and Jackie Curtis—along
with those of their fellow Factory actors Joe Dallesandro and Joe Campbell,

into a loving tribute to transgressive New York decadence. It was familiar territory for Reed, but "Walk on the Wild Side" was his definitive statement on this culture and its characters, offering meticulous lyrical detail. The "back room" in Candy Darling's verse, for example, was that of Max's Kansas City; the Sugar Plum Fairy's Apollo was the Harlem venue; and Jackie "speeding away" was Jackie Curtis—or, at one point in the sixties, anyone associated with the Factory—on an amphetamine rush to oblivion.

In the studio, Bowie and his guitarist and coproducer Ronson afforded "Walk on the Walk Side" a simple arrangement that enhanced its lyrical intricacy, with both acoustic and electric bass lines, a sax solo straight out of a Harlem street corner at midnight, and a chorus of backing singers imitating the "colored girls" of Reed's lyrics. Upon release in 1973, "Walk on the Wild Side" received unexpected airplay, and, with Reed having adopted the glam look in the interim, slipped into the American singles charts, acquiring classic status not only as a song indelibly associated with the New York streets but as a glitter rock anthem that celebrated some of that movement's founding figures. By the time it charted, however, New York had a new generation of glitter idols.

They were outer-borough misfits for the most part, drawn from the Bronx, Queens, and Staten Island to an Anglophile bar called Nobody's on Bleecker Street, to the Bethesda Fountain in Central Park on Sunday afternoons, to Max's Kansas City on any night they could gain entry. They were not the full-fledged transvestites of "Walk on the Wild Side"—they were all straight boys when it came to it—but they wore the glam and glitter of New York's newly liberated gay culture with as much pride as any queen of the night. They were the New York Dolls and, in their own short-lived manner, they would prove every bit as influential as the Velvet Underground.

Their roots lay in the lifelong friendship between the guitarist Sylvain Sylvain (born Ronald Mizrahi), an Egyptian Jew whose family had been forced into exile after the Suez Canal crisis, and the drummer Billy Murcia, whose family had suffered similar sudden ejection from Bogotá, Colombia, after his father had crossed the wrong business partner. The pair met at Van Wyck Junior High in Queens, and continued together to Quintano's School for Young Professionals, a smaller, more liberal version of Music and Art

High, located behind Carnegie Hall, which thrived from the fifties through the early seventies. There they formed their first band—the Pox, which got as far as a late sixties gig at the Hotel Diplomat—and befriended another Queens native, Johnny Genzale, the future Johnny Thunders, a baseball prodigy whose own debut group, Johnny and the Jaywalkers, had gone nowhere.

All three were obsessed with fashion. Sylvain and Murcia set up their own company, Truth & Soul, making hand-loomed sweaters in a native Colombian style with help from Billy's mother. Betsey Johnson, John Cale's wife, placed orders for her store, and when the pair expanded into psychedelic bikinis, the hipster shop Paraphernalia bought in, too. Soon enough, Sylvain and Murcia sold the company, spending the proceeds on a lengthy trip to Europe, where Sylvain, in particular, indulged his fascination with a London rock scene that seemed far healthier at the time than that of New York.

Johnny Thunders didn't make clothes; he *wore* them. A full-time mannequin identifiable primarily by his Rod Stewart/Ron Wood rooster shag haircut, he was known, in the words of his fellow Queens native Tommy Erdelyi, as "the coolest kid in New York." Jerry Nolan, a future member of the Dolls, recalled how Genzale, while out "profiling" by the Bethesda Fountain, "would have a girl's blouse on, and on top of that a sparkling girl's vest. And then maybe a cowboy scarf. And he wore make-up, which really set him off."

Another future Doll, the bassist Arthur Kane, was given to wearing a tutu, ballet tights, and huge platform shoes, all the more striking given his considerable height and heft. Dropping out of Brooklyn's Pratt Institute for the Arts in 1970, following the death of his mother, Kane and his guitar-playing school friend known as Rick Rivets also headed to Europe, financing their stay in Amsterdam by selling drugs, for which Kane was eventually deported. Back in New York, Kane, Rivets, Murcia, and Thunders (who had taken his own rock 'n' roll reconnaissance trip to England) formed a rock group, Actress—and soon found themselves scouting for a better lead singer than Thunders.

They found him in David Johansen, who had grown up on Staten Island, New York's oft-forgotten borough, with his ear tuned to black soul and his eye keenly focused on the alternative universe that revolved around the Factory. Blessed with charisma and confidence (and looks that resembled

Mick Jagger's, a blessing at a time when the Rolling Stones were considered the keepers of the rock 'n' roll flame), Johansen worked his way into the back room of Max's and, briefly, onto the stage of a Charles Ludlam play. But, as his future partner Cyrinda Foxe, a beautiful blonde who appeared in the American version of *Pork*, acerbically explained, "David was a little more heterosexual than they wanted him to be."

Sylvain returned from Europe to replace Rivets on guitar, by which time the group had renamed itself for an Upper East Side toy repair store, the New York Dolls' Hospital. Rehearsing in the back of a bicycle store, the quintet set about imitating the basic boogie of the Stones and the Stooges, with Sylvain and Thunders swapping simple riffs back and forth. But if the music was straightforward, that was exactly the point. The New York Dolls knew that rock 'n' roll had veered off track—that, in the words of Sylvain, "it had lost its sex appeal." Their plan to set it back on course involved not just an impulsive overdose of glamour but a return to its musical roots. Think of Little Richard during his wildest youth, color him white, transport him to the Lower East Side in the early 1970s, and multiply him by five. That was the New York Dolls.

Thunders, Sylvain, and Murcia, along with Thunders's girlfriend, moved into a decrepit loft on Chrystie Street in the East Village, where their fondness for getting loaded and their disregard for day jobs necessitated a monthly rent party to keep the landlord at bay, which in turn, enabled the Dolls to work out their kinks in front of an avid crowd of friends. By the spring of 1972, the quintet was the kingpin of the local streets. And that seemed like a reasonable accomplishment in itself. "We called ourselves New York Dolls," said Johansen, "but I don't think we ever expected to go anywhere besides New York, per se. We were just the band of the East Village when we started out."

But in the post-hippie comedown of the early seventies, with New York in an apparently endless decline, the East Village was a mess, and there were no clubs to play. The Dolls' first concert took place instead in the Palm Room basement of the Hotel Diplomat on West 43rd Street, at a benefit show attended by Danny Fields, who told Johansen "that he thought the band were great." Warhol himself was peripherally involved in the Dolls' first advertised show, also at the Diplomat, on May 29, entitled "An Invitation beyond the Valley." Jackie Curtis performed in a supporting role, and their friend Jerry

Nolan played drums in the opening band, Shaker. The Dolls also played at a bathhouse in Brooklyn, where Sylvain recalled of the audience members, "They were all looking at Johnny Thunders, and they were all playing underneath their towels. And poor Johnny, he had such homophobia!" The gay scene, for all that the Dolls teased themselves otherwise, was not for them. They needed a venue to call their own.

Sy Kaback, a former racing car driver who made his fortune in air-conditioning, had co-owned the Theater Cabaret, at 240 Mercer Street, since 1966. In early 1971, after one of the project's more successful off-Broadway plays was forced out because of a leaky roof, he took the venue over from his partner, the Village Gate's Art D'Lugoff, and set about expanding the two lower floors, there at the back of the Broadway Central Hotel, into a very downtown version of the Upper West Side's Lincoln Center. The 35,000-square-foot Mercer Arts Center would house, according to its publicity materials, "seven cabaret theaters, rehearsal space, two acting schools, editing rooms, construction space for sets, props and costumes, several small bars, a restaurant, offices, and have access to a 1500 car parking lot." Kaback claimed to be sinking $300,000 of his own money into the project, but not out of altruism. "My motive," he said, "is to make this a financial success."

By the fall of 1971, he had renovated enough space to open up the Kitchen, a room intended for experimental art installations, and booked the pianist Michael Tschudin, who in turn brought by the band Messiah. That group had settled into a Friday night residency of sorts at Max's, primarily as a means by which Ruskin could send exuberant show-offs like Emerson and their penchant for drunken tabletop stripteases and dances (known as "Showtime") upstairs. Gradually, Messiah had come to realize the exclusivity of this environment. "Not everyone was invited into the Warhol scene," said Coleman. "Not everyone made it up to Max's and was let in."

And so they talked themselves into a penurious existence at the Mercer, helping Kaback empty the Broadway Central's ballrooms of various debris and construct stages for the theater spaces by day, in exchange for a practice place by evening—and a performance with Tschudin in the Kitchen at night. By the time the Mercer Arts Center had its official opening party, in November 1971, with a highly rated performance of Ken Kesey's *One Flew over the Cuckoo's Nest* in the main theater (the Hansberry), Messiah had become the Magic Tramps and were performing a nightly cabaret set with Tschudin in the "Blue Room." There Emerson would entertain dinner customers in his leather hot pants, bounding across the stage sprinkling glitter over the audience to the sound of the William Tell Overture. Periodically, Factory stars like Geri Miller, Candy Darling, and Jane Forth would sit in on such songs as "Would You Like to Swing on a Star?" (Emerson embarked on an affair with Forth, with whom he soon had another son.) None of this suggested the Mercer as rock 'n' roll club, but that didn't stop Johansen, who knew Emerson from Max's, from asking for a gig.

Emerson obliged, and the Dolls' first show at the Mercer Arts Center duly took place in June 1972, in the Kitchen, opening (and closing) for the Magic Tramps. Their entourage of dressed-up East Village fans reacted with predictable enthusiasm, and Al Lewis, the Mercer promoter, immediately offered them a Tuesday night residency in the 200-capacity Oscar Wilde Cabaret Room, at the far, Broadway end of the complex. Their first headlining gig was on June 13, 1972—almost the exact day David Bowie's *Ziggy Stardust* album was released.

It would be difficult to exaggerate the impact of the New York Dolls at the Mercer Arts Center. For an entire generation of New York's musical youth, many of whom had attended school in the sixties, when anything and everything seemed possible, and who found themselves now stuck in a city where nothing seemed to be happening, the act was a revelation, the experience almost transformative.

"When I saw the Dolls, I realized you didn't need to be a great musician; it was more interesting if you were cool," said Tommy Erdelyi, who was inspired to form a band called Butch. His best friend from Forest Hills High School in Queens, John Cummings, was similarly impressed by "how great they could be with limited musicianship." Douglas "Dee Dee" Colvin, another Forest Hills alumnus (or, rather, dropout) was equally blown away. "Great songs, great energy, wild stage antics," he recalled. "I couldn't believe what I was seeing; it was the best thing in the world. There was no one could compete with it."

Yet, said Lenny Kaye, who counted himself as a "total fan" and went to see them almost every week, "the Dolls were not these abstract primitivists. David Johansen knew the blues. Johnny Thunders knew how the English stars dressed. They were able to pull all of these aspects of fashion and presentation and energy and amateurism and existentionality in one package."

"They brought hard rock music back in," said Elda Gentile, who, Emerson having flown the nest, soon became partners with Sylvain. "The image in itself, that they wanted to be 'Dolls,' was very attractive to girls. And where the girls go, the boys go."

"The girls liked them more because they had the balls to dress like this," confirmed photographer Bob Gruen. The Dolls "were very macho guys who were wearing what they were wearing to be more beautiful guys. There was nothing gay about them, but they weren't afraid to seem gay, they weren't afraid to seem effeminate, they weren't afraid of anything."

The Dolls' image was not a shock to the group's core audience, those who'd participated in the Ridiculous Theater, gathered around the Bethesda Fountain or hung out at Nobody's, those who read about David Bowie in the American edition of *Melody Maker*, and who saw the Dolls as New York's inevitable (and natural) contribution to a glam/glitter revolution. As Leee Childers aptly described it, "You didn't just go to see the Dolls. You had to be *seen* seeing the Dolls. It was an actual participatory thing. Everybody in the audience was just as outlandish as the Dolls were."

. . . Except, perhaps, for Marty Thau, a thirty-five-year-old music marketing executive who stumbled upon one of the group's earliest shows the very night he quit a job at Paramount Records. As far as he had been concerned, at that point in 1972, "Everybody in America was wearing army coats and earth shoes." Yet "here were these guys decked out in leather and leopard skin with bouffant hairdos, black nail polish, lipstick, six-inch platform boots, chopped jeans, feather boas, armbands and pantyhose."

Peering behind their image, Thau heard "loud and hard ghetto music about girls, sex, drugs, loneliness, heartbreak, and the rites of teenage romance." In particular, in "Looking for a Kiss" and "Personality Crisis," he heard the stuff of hit records, something he knew about from his years at the Buddah label. He invited the group to dinner in the back room of Max's and came away "very impressed with how much they knew about what they wanted to do." He thought, "Maybe I should look into managing these fellows."

Thau called in as his partners a couple of booking agents turned managers, who were already working with Elephants Memory, the holdover hippie-freak band that John Lennon and Yoko Ono had picked as their backing group upon recently relocating to New York City. The fact that the managers had also acquired a group called Aerosmith, whose front man Steven Tyler (another Quintano graduate, by coincidence) shared David Johansen's resemblance to Mick Jagger, seemed no big deal at the time.

With major management, the support of the downtown scene, and effusive, almost weekly coverage in *Melody Maker*, courtesy of Roy Hollingworth, its New York correspondent and American editor, a major record deal might seem to have been in the cards. But "labels were afraid of them," said Thau. "Didn't know what to make of them, immediately perceived them to be gay. They seemed just a little too wild for the record industry to deal with." They were also, at that point, more exciting onstage than on tape: a demo produced by Thau revealed the group's (freely admitted) technical limitations: while Sylvain and Thunders acquitted themselves admirably, it was hard not to hear the Iggy influence in Johansen's voice on the song "Human Being" as pure homage.

So when an offer came to play the United Kingdom, where Detroit's glam rock group Alice Cooper had just reached number one with "School's Out," they jumped at it, heading to Europe in October after seventeen consecutive Tuesdays at the Mercer. The initial highlight of the trip was a prestigious show opening for Rod Stewart and the Faces at Wembley's 8,000-seat Empire Pool. The initial low point was a drive to Liverpool to find that Lou Reed, fresh off his musical face-lift courtesy of Bowie, refused to let them play, for reasons that may or may not have come down to home turf rivalry. In between, the group acquired a cult following among London's groupies, and the management secured several offers of record deals. And then, on November 7, Billy Murcia attended a Chelsea soiree without his bandmates, overindulged in Quaaludes and alcohol, and passed out. The party hosts, rather than call for help, put him in a cold bath and poured hot coffee down his throat. An unconscious Murcia choked to death.

The surviving members, beside themselves with grief, were flown home to New York on the first available flight. Record deals were suddenly moot. There would be brighter days to come, but Murcia's death cast a permanent shadow over the New York Dolls. "We never really got over it," admitted Sylvain, the drummer's closest friend since junior high. His partner at the time saw the collapse for herself. "As much as they tried to keep it together, as much as they tried to protect themselves," said Gentile, "it just drove them into a spiral of destruction."

A self-confessed "outsider," Alan Vega had grown up in Bensonhurst, where as a teenager in the midsixties "you could feel the oppression. . . . Crossing the Manhattan Bridge in those days was like further than traveling the Atlantic. It was more than a distance trip; it was like a time trip. Going to the Village was like being transported three hundred years."

Witnessing Iggy Pop of the Stooges cutting himself onstage at the New York State Pavilion in Flushing Meadows in 1969 convinced Vega he had found a kindred spirit, and helped propel him toward a similar role in life. Simultaneously drawn to creating visual art—"ink drawings, very weird shit, working with plastic and light"—he became a founding member of the Art Workers Coalition, who "wanted to force curators to put in some young artists' work—and get paid for it." In the late sixties, such confrontational activism often got results, and Vega found himself co-running the Project of Living Artists, a downtown loft financed by the New York State Council on the Arts: "About six of us getting a stipend of $100–$200 a month to keep the place open twenty-four hours a day so that any artist could come in any time they wanted." One who did so was "this white guy with an Afro," Martin Rev.

The Bronx-born Rev hailed from "a family of very talented non-professional musicians" who embraced life outside of the mainstream. He learned piano from the bebopper Lennie Tristano, saw Thelonious Monk at the Five Spot on the Bowery, and jammed with the drummer Tony Williams. By the point he met Vega, Rev knew perfectly well how to compose, perform, and record music the conventional way—and that he didn't want to do so. Rev and Vega bonded instead over the Velvet Underground and, especially, Manhattan's pioneering electronic duo Silver Apples—entranced by the hypnotic sound of the "drone," the possibilities for the electric keyboard, and the power of experimental art.

Vega had been taken to Max's Kansas City by a first wife, with whom he lived in the basement of a funeral parlor in Brooklyn's Park Slope. Astutely, he rejected Andy Warhol's offers to visit the Factory. "I had seen a lot of people go into that place as one kind of person and come out a lost soul." Instead, he and Rev set about forming an audiovisual act, taking their name from the comic book character Satan Suicide in *Ghostrider*. Suicide's earliest shows were at the Project of Living Artists, Rev playing drums, Vega alternating between guitar and trumpet. For a year or two, they bounced around any venue that would have them—which were few and far between. Then the Mercer Arts Center opened, and Suicide found their spiritual home.

The week that the New York Dolls left for London, Suicide stepped into the Oscar Wilde Room for a four-Wednesday residency advertised as "a Punk Music Mass." The duo took their terminology from a review of the Stooges in *Creem*, in which Lester Bangs referred to Iggy Pop as a "punk," a euphemism for delinquents dating to *Rebel Without a Cause* and a long way farther back. Suicide's act stood in direct contrast to the celebratory rock 'n' roll of their friends in the New York Dolls. Audiences "were going to come in off the streets, and they were going to get the streets right back in their face," said Vega. While Rev played repetitive, distorted riffs on a pair of keyboards, occasionally hitting out at a snare drum with one hand, Vega half sang poetic prose stories about dangerously lost souls and jumped into the audience à la Iggy—only Vega, dressed as a street gang member in leather jacket emblazoned with the word SUICIDE on its back, wielded heavy chains. "The reputation was that I was a total fucking lunatic, but I was always aware of what I was doing. The only person who would ever get hurt at one of our shows would be me. I knew about the Theater of the Absurd."

The Mercer residency brought Suicide a *Melody Maker* review from Hollingworth ("the starkest trip I have ever seen"), and, before he departed for London that month, moral support from the New York Dolls' manager, Marty Thau, that would much later reap dividends. But what was most important about Suicide's arrival on the stage was that it marked the first known use of the word "punk" as a musical adjective. Little did they know what they had started.

Dismissing them as "a drag act," Chris Stein had initially ignored the fliers for the New York Dolls posted at New York's School of Visual Arts, where he was studying photography. A Brooklyn-raised guitarist whose teenage band the Morticians had opened for the Velvet Underground in 1967, Stein had turned "completely nuts" in 1969, in part as a delayed reaction to the death of his father, but also because of his massive intake of LSD. Yet spending time in Bellevue did not seem particularly unusual. "Flipping out was the norm," he recalled. "Everyone I knew would do their stints in the nut house at some point or another." Living now on First and First, in a welfare-funded apartment as part of his rehabilitation, he went to see the Dolls after a review compared them to the Rolling Stones.

Stein thought that the Dolls "had tremendous charisma and a real star quality about them," but that they "were very much on a pedestal." In short, he found them "unapproachable." He gravitated instead toward the Magic Tramps, particularly Emerson, whom he found "really good-looking, completely crazy, a real vital character in love with life." Stein and Emerson became best friends and then roommates on First Avenue. Still looking for a satisfying musical outlet, Stein attached himself to the Magic Tramps, in a role that fell some-where between roadie, photographer, and occasional guitarist.

Emerson made friends with everyone—even the Hells Angels, who had set up shop in 1969 on East Third Street. Heading home from their head-quarters one afternoon, he and Sesu Coleman stopped in at a favored Angels watering hole, Hilly's on the Bowery. A former manager of the Village Vanguard who owned another bar on West 13th Street, Hilly Kristal appeared to have neither the money nor the inclination to properly furnish or furbish his new space, located in a turn-of-the-century bar underneath the inappropriately named Palace Hotel. (In that stretch of the Bowery, just above and below Houston Street, there were around sixty such single-room occupancy hotels for alcoholics, war veterans, recently released criminals, and others down on their luck.) The place appeared to have been born with the smell of stale beer, dankness, and dog shit with which it would forever be associated.

But Kristal was looking to promote live music, and Emerson and Coleman, also seeking to expand the local scene, offered their services as at the Mercer, this time helping build a stage along the narrow club's side wall. As a result, the Magic Tramps were the first band to climb onto that stage at the "Grand Opening" of Hilly's on the Bowery as a music venue, on October 19, 1972, where they were followed by a trio of solo artists who better fitted the venue's stated menu of "jazz rock blues." The promotion seemed entirely incongruous with the surroundings. "We knew we wanted to get another club opened up, but was this the place?" asked Coleman.

For the time being, the answer was no.

•   •   •

Throwing themselves back into the band as a means of dealing with their grief, the New York Dolls hired Jerry Nolan as a replacement for Billy Murcia. His drumming style was harder and faster, and, feeling suitably reenergized, the Dolls returned to the Mercer Arts Center and its biggest theater, the 450-capacity O'Casey, a week before Christmas 1972. They sold it out.

In the few months that they had been playing the Mercer, the New York Dolls had given birth to an entire glitter musical movement. Some of the performers predated them, others may have come along at the same time, but no one doubted that the former "band of the East Village" was now kingpin of an entire scene. There was Teenage Lust, led by two recent alumni of David Peel's Lower East Side, enjoying a glamorous about-turn of image now that they were backed by four lovely Lustettes; the finely named, if musically derivative, Harlots of 42nd Street; and the former Dolls guitarist Rick Rivets's new band, the Brats. Several Ridiculous veterans similarly jumped on the new trend for musical theater: Wayne County with Queen Elizabeth, featuring songs such as "It Takes a Man Like Me to Find a Woman Like Me," graphically illustrated with a rubber penis; Ruby Reyner (who had starred in *Heaven Grand in Amber Orbit*) with Ruby and the Rednecks, singing the Crystals' "He Hit Me (And It Felt Like a Kiss)," wearing boxing gloves, punching herself out upon its conclusion; and Holly Woodlawn and Elda Gentile with Pure Garbage.

Though there were many musical disparities between the acts, the newly energized downtown scene celebrated its commonality at events like the First International Costume Glitter Ball, held at the Hotel Diplomat on December 30, 1972; the multiband bill headlined by the New York Dolls at the Mercer the following night; or the Valentine's show of February 1973 at which the New York Dolls, Suicide, Queen Elizabeth, and Magic Tramps, offering four of the most magnetic front men New York ever produced, each performed in separate rooms.

But there were also groups that, for various reasons, kept their distance— like the Neon Boys, led by Richard Meyers and Tom Miller, best friends since attending reform school in Delaware. Meyers had come to New York in 1966, at age seventeen, with literary aspirations partially realized by publication of a magazine, *Genius : Grasp*; Miller joined him a few years later to focus on his folksinging. Meyers saw in the Dolls "the first band that valued attitude above anything that was musical." When Miller then showed him how simple it was to play rock 'n' roll bass guitar, the pair recruited Billy Ficca on drums and recorded six songs in the spring of 1973. Despite song titles ("Love Comes in Spurts") and lyrics ("Your boots so pink that I can't think / Your heels so high oh my we'll fly") straight out of the glitter scene, the Neon Boys, for lack of a second guitarist, broke up without a gig; it was not yet their time.

Andy Shernoff, who had attended elementary school with Johnny Thunders, was equally smitten by the Dolls at the Mercer. "They looked great, they were exciting, there were girls there, it seemed like, 'Wow, I can play that.'" Having enrolled in college in New Paltz, ninety minutes north of New York, he brought his city-bred musician friends Scott Kempner and Ross "the Boss" Funicello to a rental house in nearby Kerhonkson, where they practiced hard and partied even harder. Shernoff began writing songs laced with the same madcap humor as infested his "pop culture" fanzine, *Teenage Wasteland Gazette*. "We were big Chuck Berry fans," he said. "And Chuck Berry was about cars and girls and teenage life in general. We took it into the seventies version of that: more TV, a little wrestling, getting drunk." With suitably dumb-but-fun songs like "Weekend" and "Teengenerate," the group named itself the Dictators.

On January 30, 1973, a four-piece group made its debut at an Irish bar turned rock club, the Coventry, in Sunnyside, Queens, the faces of its members coated in lipstick and mascara in apparent homage to the New York Dolls. The few people in attendance could scarcely have known that they were witnessing the birth of one of the biggest rock groups in history. Time, after all, did not appear to be on Kiss's side: the drummer Peter Criss, twenty-eight already, had gigged at the Metropole as far back as 1963. Having gotten married that past summer—his childhood friend Jerry Nolan was best man—Criss had joined the bassist-vocalist Gene Simmons and guitarist-vocalist Paul Stanley in their group Wicked Lester just in time for the band to get dropped by Epic Records.

Yet Kiss represented a new beginning as much as a last-ditch effort. "The premise of the band was that each one was going to be a star," said Israeli-born Gene Simmons, twenty-three years old at the time of their debut. "All of us trim, tall, white, dark haired, no blond guys. It was going to be very, sort of, defined. Every guy had the same-length hair, very much in the mold of the Temptations." But within that uniformity, each member gradually developed his own comic book superhero persona, which in time unraveled as the Demon (Simmons), the Starchild (Stanley), the Catman (Criss), and the Spaceman (the newly acquired twenty-one-year-old Bronx-raised guitarist Ace Frehley). Crucially, every one of them wore that character as a mask. The nature of their overstated image was such, said Paul Stanley, also twenty-one at the time, that "no club would hire us because of how we looked and how loud we played."

Not necessarily so. The New York glitter rock scene initially welcomed Kiss as one of its own, the group joining the Brats and Queen Elizabeth at a couple of Bleecker Street loft parties in the spring of 1973. (Often thought to have hailed from Queens, the Kiss members came from all over New York City and maintained a rehearsal space in Manhattan.) But Kiss soon set their own path; they were perhaps the only New York glitter band of the era *not* to play at the Mercer, or to open for the Dolls, whom Paul Stanley later dismissed as "a great, charismatic-looking band who didn't play very well." Kiss took their musicianship as seriously as their makeup. They constructed ready-made party anthems like "Strutter," "Firehouse," and "Deuce," led by blunt guitar riffs, with Simmons's and Stanley's vocals veering into the high-pitched wail that would become a hard rock trademark. Headlining the Hotel Diplomat in July '73, they secured management, and just a week later, at a club gig on Long Island, were seen by Neil Bogart, who invited them to become the first act on his new label, Casablanca.

Bogart had been Marty Thau's boss at Buddah and, presumably keeping tabs on the glitter scene, would have known all about the New York Dolls and perhaps been seeking his own version. For sheer force of local popularity—boosted, for better or worse, by their notoriety following Murcia's death—had finally brought the Dolls a record deal that spring through Paul Nelson (Dylan's old college friend) at Mercury. Todd Rundgren, a respected young producer for the Band and Badfinger and a recent hit maker in his own right with "I Saw the Light," on being hired to oversee the proceedings, proclaimed, "The only person who can produce a New York record is someone who lives in New York." Reviewing the finished results in *Creem* that fall, Robert

Christgau wrote, "There has never been a band—not even the Velvets—who have conveyed the oppressively close excitement that Manhattan holds for a half-formed human being the way the Dolls do." Rundgren appeared to have achieved his goal.

Certainly, *New York Dolls* was a remarkably confident and accomplished album, the addition of piano and backing vocals helping turn such songs as "Personality Crisis," "Jet Boy," and "Trash" into instant glitter rock anthems. And the group's New York roots were evident throughout: in "Frankenstein" and "Subway Train," each of which referred to New York directly, and in the appropriation of the opening line from the Shangri-Las' "Give Him a Great Big Kiss" for the Dolls' own "Looking for a Kiss." (As if admitting to New York's changes in the few years since the girl group boom, that song then made references to "shooting up" and "looking for a fix.")

Like *The Velvet Underground & Nico*, *New York Dolls* has been hailed over time as one of rock's greatest debut albums, a major influence for future generations of punk, glitter, and pure rock 'n' roll bands. Why, then, was it perceived as a failure at the time? For one thing, expectations ran almost impossibly high: such had been the hype from the Mercer residency that little short of a gold record would have satisfied the cynics. (The album sold over 100,000 copies at the time, but failed to crack the top 100.) The group's hard-partying lifestyle didn't help. It was a problem for Todd Rundgren in the studio, and if that was something that could be kept relatively quiet, it was less easy to hide Arthur Kane's bandaged hand, which prevented him from performing when the group visited Los Angeles in September. (It soon became common knowledge that he had almost lost his thumb in a preflight knife fight with his girlfriend, a street girl known as Connie Gripp.) Nor were the Dolls greatly aided by their choice of album sleeve, on which they splayed themselves across a couch pouting and dressed like full-on drag queens; gay liberation—especially the cross-dressing aspect of it—had not yet pervaded the hinterlands, and record stores and radio stations alike balked at the very sight of them. A tour with Lynyrd Skynyrd hardly changed those perceptions. "When they finally met the youth of the country," Paul Nelson later observed, "that youth seemed more confused than captivated."

Still, most of that was in the future on the evening of August 3, when the New York Dolls opened for the British glam rockers Mott the Hoople at the

Felt Forum Theater, at Madison Square Garden. It must have felt a world away from the Mercer Arts Center just a mile and a half downtown, where the Magic Tramps were rehearsing at five o'clock that same evening when they heard a commotion in the street below. Sesu Coleman went to the window: "there were maybe one to two hundred people shouting, 'The building's falling down, get out!' " On its Broadway side, the eight-story hotel was, indeed, collapsing into the ground.

Four dead welfare residents were eventually pulled from the rubble. Most of the Arts Center rooms, being on the Mercer Street side of the building, survived the collapse, but city bureaucrats, embarrassed by newspaper reports that some 450 maintenance violations had been filed against the hotel in its last thirty months, took no chances, and condemned the entire structure. Just as David Mancuso lost his loft in the wake of the hotel's collapse, Sy Kaback was out the several hundred thousand dollars he had invested in the Mercer Arts Center, and Manhattan was without the most thrilling arts and performance venue it had known that decade.

A talented guitarist who grew up in the Village, hung around Steve Paul's the Scene and was then moved out to New Jersey by concerned parents, Richard Lloyd had, like so many of his generation, lost faith in New York in the early seventies and relocated to Los Angeles. In the spring of 1973, he heard about the New York Dolls and the Mercer and thought, "Maybe something was building and I was now old enough that I could be a part of it." He was in New Orleans, halfway home, the day he heard that the Mercer Arts Center had collapsed. "I thought, 'Now I'm screwed. I'm going to a place where the scene just fell down.'"

Lloyd gravitated instead to Max's, where he was befriended and given refuge by a Factory employee, Terry Ork, who had a huge loft on East Broadway in Chinatown. Ork, said Lloyd, "wanted to have an association of artists the same way that Andy Warhol did with the Velvet Underground," and he heard in Lloyd's guitar playing the possibility of starting down that path. When they went to see the Neon Boys' former guitarist Tom Miller play at the 13th Street cabaret club Reno Sweeney's one night, Lloyd was captivated both by the demeanor of Miller's so-called manager, the former Neon Boys' bassist Richard Meyers, and especially by Miller's song "Venus de

Milo." "Inwardly I recognized: I'm missing something. I'm putting a band together, but I don't have all of it. And he's got 'it,' whatever 'it' is. But *he's* also missing something." Lloyd leaned over to Ork and said, "Put him and me together and then you'll have your band that you're looking for."

That band soon became Television, the name chosen for its social ubiquity, with Ork supplying the seed money for equipment and his loft for rehearsal. Now that Miller finally had a guitar foil, Meyers came back on bass, and Billy Ficca returned on drums. In what Miller called a way of "disassociating yourself from your past," he and Meyers decided on a change of last names. Miller opted for Verlaine, after the French Symbolist poet who, a hundred years earlier, had been Arthur Rimbaud's male lover in Paris and London. Meyers chose the last name Hell.

At the Chinatown loft, Television flourished. It was, said Lloyd, "that feeling as though you've run off and joined the circus. Like the carefree feeling that you have suddenly been released from all fetters: it wasn't about playing rock, or about being in the business, or making great art. It was the sensation you get that gives you chills up and down your spine. It was just this complete abandon."

ike Miller with Meyers, Patti Smith reunited with her former musical partner, Lenny Kaye, in the fall of 1973. The years since the one-off show at the St. Mark's church had been productive, if not necessarily lucrative. She'd collaborated on a play, *Cowboy Mouth*, with Sam Shepard, that reflected the intensity of their brief affair, and appeared also in Tony Ingrassia's *Island*, alongside Cherry Vanilla and Wayne County. She had moved in with Allen Lanier, keyboard player with Long Island's hard rock band Blue Öyster Cult, and supplied a lyric to the group's second album. And she had gained an increasingly strong reputation for her poetry, which was published as an anthology (*Seventh Heaven*), and in *Creem* magazine, and which she performed in regular opening slots at the Mercer's Oscar Wilde Room, relying on her stage presence and rhythmic meter rather on than musical instruments.

"I started getting successful, writing these long, almost rock & roll poems," she later recalled. "And I liked to perform them, but I realized that, though they were great performed, they weren't such hot shit written down." Her friend Jim Carroll concurred: "I always thought that her poems on the page were not as good as her lyrics. I saw right away that she needed a back beat." And so, in the fall of 1973, she reunited with Kaye and they took their "Rock 'n' Rimbaud" double act into Le Jardin, newly opened in the basement of the Hotel Diplomat. Chris Stein, in attendance, recalled it as "very tongue-in-cheek . . . almost a parody of a rock act. I thought it was fantastic, and why doesn't she do it with a band?"

But that didn't happen. "We didn't form anything," said Kaye. "We probably had more in common with the cabaret singers that were going on at Reno Sweeney's than we did with the New York Dolls, even though we all hung out in the same cauldron." It was certainly not your normal rock show. Starting out with understated two- and three-chord riffs to back what Kaye called Smith's "sense of French Symbolist poetry and cinema and appreciation of Bob Dylan's surrealistic wordplay," they frequently segued into the kind of sixties garage rock cover songs ("Hey Joe," "Gloria") that Kaye had recently compiled for an enormously influential Elektra album called *Nuggets*, from which point they would expand into the "open-ended improvisatory field" of the late sixties San Francisco acts. "Once you get 'out there,' you're beyond melody, you're beyond harmony, you're beyond anything but just feeling the pulse of the music and going where it takes you," said Kaye.

The addition of a pianist, Richard "DNV" Sohl, solidified the sound, but audience reaction varied. At the end of 1973, Smith and Kaye secured a slot opening for a downward-spiraling Phil Ochs at Max's Kansas City. "People were digging what we were doing," said Kaye. "We were getting encores, they were understanding it. Then we went up to play a college mixer at Fordham, and they looked at us like we were extraterrestrials—they started booing, and it was like playing into the gale of a wind." Lacking more permanent musical employment, the multifaceted Smith joined Kaye in the world of rock criticism.

With admirable self-mockery, the New York Dolls named their second album *Too Much Too Soon*. Production was initially assigned to Jerry Leiber and Mike Stoller, but at the last moment, the pair backed off, recommending Shadow Morton in their place. That combination could have been a hit: Morton knew New York better than Todd Rundgren, and the Dolls were big fans of the Shangri-Las. But Morton was an alcoholic, a dangerous ingredient to throw into the mix with a group whose "passion for life," as manager Thau politely put it, had turned Thunders and Nolan into heroin addicts and rendered Kane an alcoholic. The team was forced to fall back on covers and early Dolls songs. Just four completely new compositions made it onto the album: "Babylon" and "Who Are the Mystery Girls?" were the best.

As the Dolls partied in the studio, the eponymous debut album by Kiss hit the stores. The quartet had drawn some attention opening for Blue Öyster Cult at the Academy of Music on 14th Street, when Gene Simmons attempted to unveil a fire-breathing stage trick and inadvertently set his hair ablaze. Such theatrics—without the mishaps—would eventually become their career-making calling card, but for now, and even though they toured relentlessly and Casablanca backed them to the hilt, *Kiss* barely dented the top 100. The group would suffer its own bouts of drunkenness, exhaustion, and a sophomore slump before perfecting its glam metal genre and, beginning in 1975 with its third album *Dressed to Kill,* taking it to previously unimaginable heights of fame, fortune, and debauchery.

In the spring of 1974, then, the New York Dolls were still the city's premier band. Their Halloween '73 show in the ballroom of the Waldorf-Astoria, the city's most prestigious hotel, had seen hundreds of ghoulishly dressed glitter kids preening for local television (and hundreds more who couldn't get in causing a near riot). A concert at the Academy of Music for Valentine's Day '74 proved almost as memorable; Bob Gruen filmed the Dolls in gangster cameos as the "Lipstick Killers," driving through Manhattan, enacting their own St. Valentine's Day Massacre on their way to the show. Proven masters of the grand statement, the Dolls now announced *Too Much Too Soon* with a "New York World Tour."

It was nothing so fanciful as it sounded: a couple of dates each at Max's and the Coventry, one on Long Island, one uptown, another at the new showcase venue the Bottom Line Cabaret on West Fourth Street and Mercer— and one a few blocks east, at Club 82, the new home of a slowly waning glitter scene. Situated a few doors down from La Mama Theater, Club 82 had been opened as a lesbian hangout by the Mafia boss Vito Genovese's bisexual wife, Anna, in 1953. By the end of that decade, several locations on that strip of East Fourth Street had been identified as forming a Genovese center for heroin distribution trafficking; yet Club 82 thrived despite these associations, its "femme impersonators" receiving glowing reviews in the nightlife columns for their elaborate productions. (Clearly, there was a distinction between the legality of cross-dressing onstage and off.) Come the mid-seventies, gay liberation had rendered the underground drag club concept outdated, the East Village kids had fallen head over high heels for glamorous androgyny, and so the club's front women—two bull dykes known as Tommy and, appropriately enough, Butch—turned Wednesday nights over to live bands on the glitter scene. Yet Club 82 continued to feature its dominant disco music on the dance floor, meaning that the glitter kids were as likely to hear Hues Corporation as Mott the Hoople. Such a charged melting pot of music and sexual affiliations brought both David Bowie and Lou Reed along for the ride, transvestite dates on their arms.

For the New York Dolls' gig at Club 82, the opening group the Miamis (Queen Elizabeth *sans* Wayne County) performed in three-piece suits, in tribute to Butch and Tommy. Then, in homage to the club's illustrious past, the Dolls played in full drag, Kane in hot pants, Sylvain in a dress and bright leggings, and Johansen stealing the show in a sparkling strapless dress belonging to his girlfriend Cyrinda Foxe. The lone holdout was a bare-chested Johnny Thunders, his homophobia apparently still intact two years since playing the Brooklyn bathhouse. "They still talk about what we did at Club 82," said Sylvain, years later, and it was true that no one who attended that night ever forgot it.

In hindsight, however, the triumphant drag set turned out to be a swan song for the New York Dolls, and also for the glitter scene. Absent national recognition for the Dolls, or record deals for any of the other acts, the glitter scene fell apart, its participants abandoning the makeup and outlandish clothes for more conventional street fashion. You could even, near enough, put a date on the transition: April 14, 1974, Easter Sunday. That was the night the New York Dolls kicked off their New York World Tour on Long Island. That was also the evening that Patti Smith and Lenny Kaye attended a gig on the Bowery, where Television were in the third week of a Sunday night residency at a club that would forever change the face of New York's music scene.

15

THE GLAMOUR OF POVERTY

CBGB and OMFUG, to give Hilly's on the Bowery its full new title, stood for Country Bluegrass and Blues and Other Music for Undernourished Gourmandizers. The second acronym was just Hilly Kristal having a little bit of fun: "I felt CBGBs sounded so pat that I wanted something to go with it that sounded a little uncouth, or crude," said the ex-Marine, in his early forties by this point. It was the first set of initials that begged explanation: what could possibly have encouraged Kristal to believe that his skid row bar, as previously patronized by Hells Angels, Bowery bums, and very few others, would, under a new name, suddenly attract cognoscenti of a traditional American rural music fast falling out of favor in urban New York?

Fortunately, his faith was never put fully to the test, fate intervening almost as soon as he changed the bar's name. In December 1973, Kristal found himself gazing down from "a ladder in front of the club fixing the awning in place . . . to notice three scruffy dudes in torn jeans and T-shirts looking up at him inquisitively." That would have been members of Television who, excited to hear about a venue on the Lower East Side, promptly requested a gig. When Kristal in turned asked what music they played, they responded with the most generic and accurate adjective possible: rock. To which Kristal told them that he had no interest in putting on rock music. Couldn't they see that he had named the place for country bluegrass and blues?

Television had to think on their feet. As Richard Lloyd recalled, "We said, 'Well, really you have no idea, it's completely original, it's not like any rock you're thinking of, it has some country, has some blues, not so much bluegrass but it's really original.' And Hilly said, 'Well, I don't know.'"

I don't know. That uncertainty, hovering halfway between acceptance and refusal, proved to be his greatest virtue. Kristal genuinely *didn't* know— he didn't know from Television, he didn't really know from any of the bands that were about to make CBGBs the most famous little rock club on the planet. What he did know, like any good entrepreneur struggling to make ends meet, was that there are times when you just go with the flow. Though noncommittal at first, he allowed Television's manager Terry Ork to persuade him to let the band play on Sunday nights, when the bar was otherwise closed. Television made their debut—accompanied by a couple of Kristal's preferred "country blues" artists—on March 31, 1974.

The irony of this now legendary piece of hustling was that the roles had somehow gotten reversed. Kristal should have been begging Television—and any other musicians they may have known—to play his club, given that it was effectively bereft of both audience and ambience. But for Television the scenario was perfect. "You're not stepping into anyone else's shoes," explained Lloyd of the band's motivation to play such a dive. (Though with Kristal's dog running rampant around the club, there was always the very real possibility of stepping into shit.) "When you do find your own place it's on your own terms, so you don't have to bring anybody else's baggage." As a band, Television knew that they were different from what else was out there, and that they wanted to be able to cultivate it at their own speed. CBGBs offered that opportunity—especially since, unlike almost every club or bar owner in town, Kristal did not expect them to play covers all night.

Television's opening show was sparsely attended, but the musicians were shameless self-promoters. They designed an advertisement and flier in which a picture of the band looking like refugees from the Beatles' Hamburg era was accompanied by supportive quotes from Danny Fields, now editing *16* magazine; Scott Cohen, editor of Andy Warhol's *Interview*; and Nicholas Ray, the *Rebel without a Cause* director. Such endorsements attracted Josh Feigenbaum from the *SoHo Weekly News,* who wrote a remarkably prescient review of one of their first shows on the Bowery. "The great thing about this band is that they have absolutely no musical or socially redeeming characteristics and they know it," he observed, noting with acerbic accuracy that the very fact that they were "loud, out of tune and pretentious as hell" surely made them "the next big break-through group coming out of New York." Terry Ork immediately used this last phrase for his advertisements; it was soon bettered by one from David Bowie, who witnessed Television at a Club 82 one-off and cited them as "the most original band I've seen in New York."

When Patti Smith and Lenny Kaye attended the third night of Television's Sunday residency, Kaye too, as a journalist of repute, was hit up for an endorsement, and duly obliged. Kaye immediately recognized that "this scene was an 'other' scene, kind of anti-glitter." Smith was struck more viscerally and, though still living with Blue Öyster Cult's Allen Lanier, soon embarked on an affair with Tom Verlaine. Later that spring, in both the *SoHo Weekly News* and Lisa Robinson's magazine *Rock Scene*, Smith would write with unrestrained excitement about Television in general ("sexy sexy as hell") and Verlaine in particular, crediting him with "the most beautiful neck in rock 'n' roll." In the meantime, she invited Verlaine to play lead guitar on her first record, a self-pressed 7-inch single. His contribution was to "Hey Joe," a version of the song Jimi Hendrix had made famous, and which was preceded by "Sixty Days," Smith's poem about Patti Hearst. But it was "Piss Factory," on the flip side, that revealed Smith's true originality as singer, writer, and performer: while Kaye and the pianist Richard Sohl traded riffs with elegant ease, Smith fired off a largely autobiographical tale of her journey from Jersey wage slave, via exposure to the Paragons and the Jesters, to a dream of taking the train to New York City, where "I'm gonna be so big, gonna be a big star, and I'm never going to return," a prodigiously powerful performance that justified her growing reputation.

"It was really an experiment to see what we could do," said Kaye of the unusual decision to release their own single. (The process was bankrolled by Robert Mapplethorpe, now an established photographer.) "It seemed like if you could get it pressed, you could probably find a few places to get it circulated. I was involved in the record geek world. I was a collector. It seemed nice to make an artifact." Visually, the 7-inch single, with its stark black-and-white paper sleeve head shot of Smith and its typed-font lettering, served as a blueprint for a whole generation of do-it-yourself releases. Critically (in all senses of the word), the act had enough friends in the right places to ensure that it would get considerable press coverage. Commercially, who cared? They were pressing only 1,500 copies.

Inevitably, in the summer of 1974, Patti Smith and Television took to the stage together—though not at CBGBs, but for a ten-night residency at Max's Kansas City, a rare exception at a club that typically booked only national acts. This was a tribute to the acclaim Smith, Kaye, and Sohl had wrought from their determination, in Kaye's words, "not to be trapped by definitions." Television, the opening act at Max's, had yet to acquire such displays of confidence; their early performances were noted as much for tuning problems as musical prowess. But the group understood image as keenly as the New York Dolls. It's just that theirs was an anti-image. "The glamour of poverty," was how Lloyd described it. "That look was Richard Hell's baby. Nobody else had it. The spiky hair, the ripped clothes, the glamour of it, the insouciance, it's all Richard, and he deserves to be recognized for that." Lloyd demonstrated Hell's vision by cutting his hair, dying it blond, and wearing a T-shirt hand-painted with the words PLEASE KILL ME.

"We were really unique," confirmed Hell. "There was not another rock 'n' roll band in the world with short hair. There was not another rock 'n' roll band with torn clothes. Everybody was still wearing glitter and women's clothes. We were these notch-thin, homeless hoodlums, playing really powerful, passionate, aggressive music that was also lyrical."

Hell's most notable songwriting contribution would prove to be "The Blank Generation." Though the chord patterns and title stole from the poet Rod McKuen's tongue-in-cheek 1959 single, "I Belong to the Beat Generation," Hell intended to emulate the Who's anthemic statement "My Generation." He would frequently have to stress that it was not the generation that was blank—as in empty—but rather intended as an invitation to a new generation to define itself as it desired. Hell occasionally left the word "blank" unsung to imply as much.

Hell's iconic status was instantly recognized by, among many others, Elda Gentile, who described him as "the first punk, in terms of image and attitude and everything. He was gorgeous, he was raw, and he wasn't anything like what you had ever seen before." In the fall of 1973, Gentile had put together a group with Debbie Harry, the former Wind in the Willows singer and Max's waitress, who had otherwise retreated to her native New Jersey (where she had been raised by adoptive parents), working in a health spa. The two women had bonded over the New York Dolls: "I liked Debbie," said Gentile. "Some of the groupies were backbiting, and pretty vicious, and I didn't like the way they would talk about her—because she *was* prettier than them."

The six-piece Stillettoes—three girl singers and three boy musicians, a cabaret revival of the sixties girl group—had recruited Eric Emerson's friend Chris Stein as guitarist after Gentile invited him to their second show. There he and Harry experienced what the latter called a "psychic connection" and quickly became a couple. At Television's penultimate Sunday night gig, in early May 1974, the Stillettoes (fleshed out by the third singer Amanda Jones, drummer Billy O'Connor, and new bassist Fred Smith) made their CBGBs debut and were immediately taken by the club's homeliness. "It was the kind of place where you felt you could do anything you frickin' wanted, because it was so trashed to begin with," said Gentile. "There was a sense of freedom in that venue. Hilly—who thought he was running a country and western club!—was like a fatherly figure. And he was very nurturing."

Reenergized by the Stillettoes, Harry moved into an apartment on Thompson Street in SoHo, and Chris Stein joined her, subletting his own place on First and First to Tommy Erdelyi. Chris and Debbie formed an unusually tight relationship in a city of constantly revolving musical beds. "He wasn't overly possessive," said Harry. "He didn't have an extreme macho attitude, and we had fun together. We laughed at the same things, yet we had differences of opinion and respect for each other." Inevitably, they started writing songs together, and among those that formed part of the Stillettoes' set in early 1974 was one called "In the Flesh," an obvious throwback to the girl group era set in 6/8 time, and a more upbeat rocker, "Rip Her to Shreds." Gentile had her own material in the set, too, but although she sensed her power base slipping as Stein and Harry became an increasingly committed couple, still she "felt the Stillettoes were really on the edge of being able to push through and have the chance to do something." When they played Club 82 in June, members of the Who were in attendance. So was a representative from Albert Grossman's label Bearsville. After the show, the girls in the group were offered a record deal; the boys were not. Gentile forwarded the offer to Harry, and "the next thing I know," she recalled, "Debbie and Chris are on the fly."

Stein felt justified in splitting. "There was too much catfighting going on. It didn't seem the right kind of thing." He and Harry took the Stillettoes' rhythm section with them, and a couple of months later, with Ivan Kral on second guitar, unveiled themselves at CBGBs, with much the same material but under a new name, Angel and the Snake. They gave the support slot to Tommy Erdelyi's new band: the Ramones.

• • •

Because of their (eventual) revolutionary impact on the international music scene, there's a tendency to wish that the Ramones had arrived overnight, fully formed: Johnny Joey Dee Dee Tommy, "da brudders," white boy, Queens-raised rebels united against the world.

But like the other groups that became synonymous with CBGBs, the Ramones had more than their fair share of history—which in Tommy (Erdelyi) and Johnny (Cumming)'s case extended back to 1966 and their high school band, the Tangerine Puppets. In fact, by the time the Ramones came into being in early 1974, the members had such a catalog of fluctuating friendships that a linear telling of their formation would prove essentially impossible.

The story, certainly, started in Forest Hills, a middle-class Queens neighborhood with tree-lined streets shading detached houses that look as if they belong farther out on Long Island; even the high-rises (in one of which Joey Ramone was raised) appear more comfortably affluent than elsewhere in the city. But in the minds of the future Ramones, each of whom attended Forest Hills High School in the sixties, the neighborhood spawned mediocrity, complacency, and conformity. All but Tommy, whose family had escaped the Soviet invasion of Hungary in 1956, and who had the refugee-immigrant's drive to succeed as a result, served time as social outcasts and teenage delinquents. Or, as Douglas "Dee Dee" Colvin later put it, "People who join a band like the Ramones don't come from stable backgrounds."

Colvin had a particularly miserable childhood: growing up with abusive, alcoholic parents on a variety of Army bases, primarily in Germany (where he was born), he developed low self-esteem that he sought, from too early on, to assuage with drugs. By the time his mother finally divorced and fled to the States (the family lived briefly in Atlanta during Dee Dee's childhood), Colvin was damaged goods. He took to hitchhiking across the country, during which time he was jailed in Indiana for armed robbery, joined a gang of muggers in Culver City, holed up with "a bunch of freaks" in Hollywood, and was jailed again for car theft in Malibu. (All the same, revealing perhaps the core of his naïf personality, Colvin felt he "didn't have much of a criminal mentality.") Finding his way back to New York, he dived into the disco and glitter scene of the early seventies, hanging out at both the Sanctuary and the

Mercer Arts Center, and was seen turning tricks with the male prostitutes on the corner of 53rd Street and Third Avenue. In Queens, he associated with anyone who dug the Stooges and the New York Dolls, a small crowd that included his three future bandmates.

Jeff Hyman also grew up with emotional instability, a result of his ungainly height and ill poise, and his obsessive-compulsive disorder. The only band member actually born in Queens, the only Jewish member, he was a consummate pop music fan, forever in thrall to the Beach Boys, the Beatles, and, especially, Phil Spector's wall of sound. Hyman explored the hippie trail to California, handed out fliers for massage parlors in Greenwich Village, and ultimately combated his insecurities by joining the Queens glitter band Sniper, giving himself the name Starship, and dressing provocatively in, as he once recounted it, "a black satin-like jumpsuit made of stretch material with a bullet chain hanging around the groin . . . pink-lavender boots with six-inch platform heels."

As it did for Colvin, family life proved sufficiently unpleasant for Hyman that he regularly left home, only to occupy his mother's art gallery on Queens Boulevard—where he invited the more genuinely destitute Colvin to join him. Colvin had taken on the persona of Dee Dee Ramone from simple alliteration of his first name combined with Paul McCartney's stage name (Paul Ramon) in the early Beatles; he now suggested Hyman take the moniker Joey, and it proved instantly more appealing to the girls.

As for John Cummings, he was, by his own admission, "bad every minute of the day, from the time I woke up." Even his lifelong friend Tommy Erdelyi said of him that he "could be great fun to be with—or could be mean as a rattlesnake." A baseball fanatic and hard-line conservative, he became so disenchanted with rock 'n' roll in the early seventies that he sold his guitars and his record collection, seemingly content working in construction—until January 1974 when, influenced in part by the New York Dolls, encouraged in particular by Tommy and Dee Dee, he finally walked into Manny's in midtown and spent $50 on a Mosrite guitar. If Mosrite was good enough for the Ventures, it was good enough for him.

It was Dee Dee who brought Joey and Johnny together into a band. Indeed, though he would later come to be seen by most—and idolized by some—as a glorious fuckup, Dee Dee's initial leadership role was such that he fronted the group, too, as singer and bass player, with Joey on drums and

Johnny on guitar. He even contributed the band's name from his own, and the idea of each member "becoming" a Ramone followed—less, perhaps, as a true mark of brotherhood (Johnny and Joey were never best of friends, to say the least) than the marketable perception of such.

The trio had a rehearsal in Queens and there, said Joey Ramone, "we realized that we had something that was exciting, a chemistry." By their own accounts, the trio wrote two songs there and then. One was "I Don't Wanna Walk Around with You," the only other lyric of which was the eventual retort, "So why'd you wanna walk around with me?" The other was "I Don't Wanna Get Involved with You." As Johnny Ramone later told *Rolling Stone,* tautologically perhaps, it was "almost the same song."

Tommy Erdelyi, having broken up his last band, Butch, and now co-running a showcase-rehearsal space called Performance, on East 20th Street in Manhattan, saw himself as his friends' inevitable manager, perhaps even their songwriter. When he offered the trio rehearsal time, they surprised him by showing up with "just absolutely weird songs." Indeed, having hit on their theme, they quickly expanded their repertoire to include "I Don't Wanna Go Down to the Basement," "I Don't Wanna Be Learned, I Don't Wanna Be Tamed," and, in case anyone thought that the list of negatives endorsed a lifestyle of complete nihilism, the perceptibly positive "Now I Wanna Sniff Some Glue." The lyrical approach was either genius, stupidity, or comedy—or, in retrospect, a brazen combination of all three.

Essentially, they were just following standard literary advice: write about what you know. "The songs were about our frustrations and feelings of alienation and isolation," said Joey. (And also their obsessions with B-movies, comic books, and other icons of American trash culture.) That these songs had but few words each was quite deliberate: as far as Dee Dee was concerned, if you couldn't sum it up in the song title, it wasn't worth saying in the first place.

On March 30, 1974, with Erdelyi out of town, the three-piece Ramones invited around thirty friends to come see them at Performance Studios. It was not an auspicious debut, the set collapsing several times into complete chaos. Dee Dee suggested afterward that Joey come up front and sing, and it made all the difference: Hyman had within him one of rock music's most distinctive voices, capable of delivering romantic ballads and crude choruses alike in a genuinely unaffected and yet deeply emotive Queens street tone. And though his gangling posture and wafer-thin face made for an unconventional front man, it ultimately rendered him an icon for thousands of self-confessed outsiders, weirdos, and freaks. Tommy Erdelyi picked up the drumsticks in despair at auditioning would-be rock stars who couldn't seem to keep it simple, and the lineup was complete. "By the second time I tried it, it started to gel the sound of the Ramones," he said. "I guess I instinctively knew what the music needed."

As for image, at least a couple of the Ramones knew of the Dictators playing at the Coventry, sporting a simple uniform of jeans, sneakers, leather jackets, and T-shirts. They were equally aware that this (lack of) image had not kept the Dictators from acquiring a major record deal. All it had taken, in fact, was for Andy Shernoff to hand a demo to Richard Meltzer and Sandy Pearlman, music journalists and creative forces behind Blue Öyster Cult, whom he had befriended through his *Teenage Wasteland Gazette*, after which the group was signed to Epic. The spring of 1974 found the Dictators trying to build a live following at the Coventry, where their roadie, the wrestler "Handsome" Dick Manitoba, would frequently jump onstage, at first for encores of "Wild Thing" and "I Got You Babe," then gradually easing into a role as front man. "We liked it loud, hard, and fast," said Shernoff of their musical direction, which meant they had as much in common with Kiss as with the Ramones. Not that they gave it much more thought. As they settled in to record their debut album that summer of 1974, all they knew was that they were having a blast.

The members of the Ramones were older than the Dictators, and that maturity ended up making all the difference. The Ramones always approached their live shows as a work of art—something that was never questioned by those peers who continued to attend their sporadic "showcases" at Performance Studios.

"When you saw the Ramones for the first time, there was just nothing that could prepare you," said Roberta Bayley, who had arrived in New York just in time for the Dolls' infamous show at Club 82, and was soon running the door at CBGBs. "It was like conceptual art. It wasn't like seeing a band." Elda Gentile thought of them as "the Andy Warhols of rock," because they were minimalists. Richard Lloyd noted of Dee Dee's habit of introducing each song with a shouted "one-two-three-four," that "it was clear by about 'five' that they were onto something."

Yet beauty was clearly in the eye of the beholder. Kristal recalled of their

CBGBs debut, "They were even worse than Television . . . the most unto-gether group I'd ever heard. They kept starting and stopping—equipment breaking down—and yelling at each other. They were a mess." Uncertain that they could ever be quite so bad again, he promptly rebooked them. The Ramones played CBGBs over twenty more times in 1974 alone.

"His reaction was a strange reaction because he didn't know why he was inviting us back," said Tommy Ramone, who tried not to second-guess the process. "We just wanted to play the music that we liked. It wasn't that, 'This is what the world needs,' it was what *we* needed. When we were coming up, we realized that, unless we're kidding ourselves, we're pretty good. Then, by the time we started playing our first gigs at CBGBs, I already knew, or I already felt, that this band was special and that it was great. I figured that if I thought it was good, other people should do, too."

That proved somewhat optimistic. "It's not that there was any interest," stated Joey flatly, years later, of playing to the same handful of people for months on end. And he believed he understood the reasons why. "What we were doing was something totally new and evolutionary and unique. Nobody had done what we had done."

Within the confines of the four-piece rock 'n' roll band, this was, per-haps, true. The singles charts of the era, after all, were becoming increas-ingly dominated by disco, the album charts by concept records often extended over two discs. And though the Ramones were drawing on the familiarity of rock 'n' roll's twin heydays—the late fifties and the midsixties—they were doing so with a thoroughly contemporary and uncompromising attitude, and with lyrics that were so dumbed down that there was therefore nothing with which to compare them.

"It was very confusing to people because they didn't know if we were a put-on, a parody," said Tommy. "If you hear something you've never heard before, the first instinct is to go, 'It's bad' . . . and then you go home and start to think about what you just heard and you say, 'Hang on, that wasn't bad, that was good.' All these things happened when people first saw us. And how short the songs were and the way we dressed. And we did have a sense of humor, so some of the things were tongue-in-cheek. And that was different too. So people would wonder, 'Is the whole thing tongue-in-cheek?' No, it was just a humorous part of it."

The Ramones' songwriting crystallized with "Judy Is a Punk." Joey claimed to have gotten the idea from walking past a Queens apartment house "where all the kids in the neighborhood hung out on the rooftop and drank." It was a work of deceptively complex simplicity, the title itself never quoted in the song. There were a couple of seemingly nonsensical lines about the characters Jackie and Judy going to Berlin to join the Ice Capades, and that was more or less it. Lifting a trick employed by the midsixties British pop stars Herman's Hermits, Joey then chanted, "second verse, same as the first," and repeated the stanza. Tommy Erdelyi—or, now that he was in the band, Tommy Ramone—concluded that they had come up with something "futuristic." To the extent that this was likely the first song ever to include the word "punk" in its title, he was right.

The Ramones were filmed playing "Judy Is a Punk" at CBGBs in September, just a month after their debut gig. Compared with the other songs taped that same night, it was by far the strongest, the group staying hard on the beat, playing with the sense of fury for which they would soon become famous—Dee Dee strumming rather than picking at the bass—and at such a volume that the words proved all but indecipherable. Their image had not fully lost its glitter influence, but the haircuts that would later embody the notion of "da brudders"—bowled at the front, grown out at the back—were all in place. So was the chaos that early gig-goers all recalled: an onstage argument followed the opening song "Now I Wanna Sniff Some Glue" about which number to play next, settled by Johnny shouting, "Hey hey let's go, quick, lively," as they settled on "I Wanna Go Down to the Basement." Whether the quarrel was spontaneous or stage-managed, as a piece of archival footage it was fascinating—and not least because it revealed CBGBs as a surprisingly tame venue, the few audience members seated at tables and chairs in front of the three-tiered stage, emotionally removed from the energy of the show as if, indeed, watching a piece of performance art.

Chris Stein and Debbie Harry had no such predetermined manifesto as the Ramones, no such quest for originality as Television or Patti Smith. They were still very much feeling their way—and were grateful to have a supportive location in CBGBs. Ditching the name Angel and the Snake, they reverted to the style of the Stillettoes, recruiting a couple of additional female singers—each of whom, like Harry, had fair hair—and as Blondie, made their CBGBs debut in January 1975. Playing to this strength, Stein and Harry wrote a song, "Platinum Blonde," about every (bad?) girl's desire to become a Marilyn Monroe, and added to the set both the Shangri-Las' "Out in the Streets" and LaBelle's new single, "Lady Marmalade," on its way to number one in early 1975. The additional members didn't last, however, nor did a partnership with Tish and Snookie, a couple of eminently cool girls on the scene who would later start their own band (the Sic Fucs) and a successful fashion company (Manic Panic). Nor did Ivan Kral, who left to join Patti Smith. Nor, for that matter, did the drummer Billy O'Connor, who, despairing of a stable lineup, decided to pursue a career elsewhere.

Stein and Harry placed an ad in the *Village Voice* for a new drummer—and Clem Burke got the job. A nineteen-year-old glitter kid from Bayonne, New Jersey, who hung out at Club 82, looked up to the New York Dolls as "gods," and had recently moved into a storefront on East Tenth Street with his high school friend Gary Valentine, Burke showed up for the audition wearing red shoes and "a U.S. Navy shirt on like [he]'d seen a picture of Keith Moon wearing." It helped that he could play in the same style as the Who's drummer, and had done so in garage and glam bands for five years already (in venues from Carnegie Hall to Club 82). Having seen the Stillettoes live, he was eager to join Blondie. "We had a common ground, in liking the Velvet Underground, Iggy Pop, the Ronettes, the Shangri-Las. I didn't have to be educated by anyone as to what the aesthetic of this band was going to be. My take was that, being a drummer, I was always looking for my Bowie, my Jagger, and when I saw Debbie, I decided that she was going to be that person for me."

Burke made his debut with Blondie at CBGBs on April 7, a Monday. He felt good about it, too—until, between sets, the bassist Fred Smith told the band he was leaving for Television. Immediately. This not only spelled the demise of Blondie just as they had gotten going again. It also meant that the long-standing downtown rumors were true: Richard Hell and Tom Verlaine had parted company.

Despite beginning 1975 as the band that everyone was talking about at CBGBs (and beyond), the more Television performed, the more evident it became that something had to give. Richard Hell displayed his streetwise convictions in titles like "Fuck Rock & Roll," "Change Your Channels," and the Neon Boys' holdover "Love Comes in Spurts." Verlaine's more conventionally poetic approach was evident in "Enfant Terrible," "Horizontal Ascension," and "Venus de Milo." Similarly, Verlaine was an accomplished guitar player, now thriving off of Richard Lloyd's equally practiced instincts, and this put him increasingly at odds with the untutored bass playing of his childhood friend.

As Roberta Bayley, now Richard Hell's partner, noted, Hell "had his own following, he jumped around onstage, he had his own humor and charisma— and Tom [Verlaine] wanted it to be a serious band. And little by little they kept shaving off [Hell's] songs until all that was left was 'The Blank Generation.' Why be in the band? It wasn't like he was in it for his bass playing anyway."

In early March, Television opened for the New York Dolls at the Little Hippodrome in midtown. The Dolls' star had fallen considerably: *Too Much Too Soon* had sunk like a stone, Mercury had all but dropped the band, Nolan's and Thunders' heroin addiction was out of control, Kane was in rehab, and glitter was on the way out—which is where the British fashion entrepreneur Malcolm McLaren came in. Sylvain had met McLaren at a trade show in 1971 and stayed in contact; McLaren had fallen in love with the Dolls along the way and now decided to manage them. (A bemused Marty Thau received a "Dear John" letter informing him of the decision.) At the Little Hippodrome, McLaren dressed the act in red patent leather, with a communist flag as a backdrop. Three years earlier, when David Johansen had proclaimed himself "trisexual"—as in, "I'll try anything"—Sylvain had warned him never to say anything he couldn't back up. None of the band could back up their use of communist chic, and they knew it. The Hippodrome gigs would be the last shows the original New York Dolls played in New York.

At those same concerts, McLaren saw in Richard Hell's torn shirts and spiky hair a genuine street fashion, and in the song "The Blank Generation" a truly contemporary musical statement. He offered his services to Television. Verlaine vetoed the idea and, when Island Records financed a demo session coproduced by Roxy Music's Brian Eno, insisted that only his own songs be recorded. That proved the last straw, and Richard Hell quit. He and Verlaine had been best friends since running away from boarding school to Alabama together at age sixteen, but no more. "I felt totally betrayed," said Hell.

The split took place in the midst of a six-weekend CBGBs residency Television shared with Patti Smith through March and April of 1975—a pairing that truly put the club on the city's musical map. Smith came to the residency with a record deal under her belt, the first of the post-glitter generation to acquire one, courtesy of Clive Davis at his newly formed Arista label. And with that deal came media acclaim. "Miss Smith has it in her to be as successful an artist as American pop music has produced," gushed the *New York Times* critic John Rockwell, who also noted of her first night (ever) at CBGBs, that Smith chanted "her image-rich visions in a shamanistic rapture."

"Her performances really did give me the chills and raise the hair on the back of my neck," said Chris Frantz, a relative newcomer to New York from Rhode Island. "She was making some kind of quantum leap in the method she was using, the poetry she was performing. I think you could say it was almost like voodoo. It had a romantic side, but it also had a spiritual side. I would say that she was a shaman."

As for Television, when Fred Smith joined halfway through the residency, Verlaine and Ficca's own free jazz tendencies suddenly blossomed, Lloyd's guitar playing flourished, and, almost overnight, songs like "Marquee Moon" and "Little Johnny Jewel" became improvisational masterpieces, edging up toward ten minutes or more in length.

Blondie, bereft of their bassist, were left watching from the sidelines. And when Burke couldn't persuade Stein and Harry that they had a group worth salvaging, he too auditioned for Smith, who was then seeking a drummer to round out the lineup for her debut album. He made the mistake of doing so in Blondie's own midtown rehearsal room, where he was caught red-handed by Harry, who became convinced that Smith saw her band members as ripe for the picking. Burke stayed with Blondie, to everyone's long-term benefit, but animosity continued to simmer between the scene's two lone female leaders.

Lenny Kaye preferred to describe this period as "a big mating dance," and it was difficult, certainly, to keep track of all the partners' steps as they searched for musical monogamy. Richard Hell formed the Heartbreakers with Johnny Thunders and Jerry Nolan, who quit the New York Dolls shortly after the Little Hippodrome shows; as Blondie flailed, Stein tried out, half-heartedly, as their second guitarist. Malcolm McLaren, failing to lure Richard

Hell back to London with him, suggested a musical marriage between Suicide's Martin Rev and Debbie Harry. The couple were firm friends already, but unlikely musical bedfellows. "If you work with a woman," said Rev, "it is natural that you start to soften some of the edges." Undeterred, McLaren returned to his London clothing store Sex, where, later that same year, he projected much of what he had seen and heard in Richard Hell onto a group of teenagers who hung around the store: the Sex Pistols.

The night of May 27, Harry and Stein visited their friend Eric Emerson at the luxury apartment on Greenwich Avenue he shared with his latest partner, Barbara Winter, whose divorce settlement from her musician husband, Edgar, enabled her to play benefactor and, according to Emerson's friends, enabler. That night, "he was shooting massive amounts of dope, sleeping standing up," said Stein, who, like Sesu Coleman and other close friends, lamented how a formerly joyous personality had taken to biting people, pulling their hair, shredding his clothes, apparently mutating from good-natured madness into the real thing. "We left when he was trying to lure us into some sort of orgy with him and Barbara," said Stein. "We went home, and she called the next day to say, 'Eric is dead.'" The newspapers reported that Emerson had been hit by a truck near his apartment, on his way home from a party at the Fashion Institute of Technology in the middle of the afternoon. Emerson had been a major star within the world of Warhol and his films, Max's and the Mercer Arts Center. Those who knew him had always predicted truly global fame. It was not to be. A weekend-long wake drew an A-list crowd of downtown notables and, as Debbie Harry put it, "marked the death of the glitter period."

Spurred back into activity, Harry and Stein auditioned Clem Burke's friend Gary Valentine. He was not a schooled bassist, but he was a poet, a songwriter, and a good looker to boot, and the new, four-piece Blondie returned to CBGBs on July 4, 1975, opening for the Ramones. Debbie Harry had turned thirty just three days earlier.

David Byrne, Chris Frantz, and Martina Weymouth, the future Talking Heads, met in the early 1970s at the Rhode Island School of Design (RISD)—the "Harvard" of art schools—two hundred miles northeast of New York. All three hailed from farther afield: Byrne from Scotland via

Canada and Baltimore; Frantz from Kentucky; Weymouth from California. Byrne claimed a working-class background, while Frantz and Weymouth were both military children—not of Dee Dee Ramone's tortured upbringing, but of an admiral and a general, respectively. Byrne, a guitarist, and Frantz, a drummer, had formed their first band, the Artistics, in 1973: they played mainly cover versions, from Motown to bubblegum, along with a couple of Byrne originals. Simultaneously, Frantz, a big fan of dance music, hosted *Soul Train* parties on Saturday mornings, over which he and Weymouth bonded; they were soon dancing regularly to "Love's Theme" and "Soul Makossa" at a gay discotheque in Providence called, coincidentally or otherwise, the Gallery.

Byrne, dropping out of RISD, was first to make the move to Manhattan, in the spring of 1974, settling into a loft space on Bond Street with another former RISD student. The location put him half a block from CBGBs, and he witnessed the Ramones' debut there that August. Frantz and Weymouth, following in the fall after finishing their degrees, soon found their own space on the ninth floor of 195 Chrystie Street, just south of Houston. They quickly became accustomed to the fact that their building, like many other lofts, was zoned for commercial use, not residential—which meant that during winter, the heat was switched off at 5:00 p.m. Their landlord "knew we were staying overnight but couldn't have cared less," said Frantz.

By early 1975, heat or no heat, Byrne had moved down to Chrystie Street with them, and the trio formed an odd little commuter family, setting off together in the mornings to take the F train from the dirty and often dangerous Second Avenue stop to the comparatively glamorous 57th Street stop in midtown, where Byrne arranged photo stats for an ad agency (giving him the opportunity to print band posters for free), Weymouth sold shoes at the upscale Henri Bendel store, and Frantz worked in the loading department of the equally ritzy European furniture/houseware store Design Research.

This juxtaposition of provincialism and urbanism, downtown and uptown, of freezing lofts at night and pleasant jobs by day, inevitably found its way into Talking Heads' music, helping distinguish them as the first CBGBs paying customers to come back with their own group. "We felt like there was a place for the type of music we wanted to compose and play, and it was a type of thing that wasn't being heard on popular radio," said Frantz. "We were targeting people like ourselves—people who were interested in rock music and loved to go out and dance but didn't really have bands they could get behind."

But first they had to cement a lineup. David Byrne had a contrite wail that, by conventional standards of the day (if not those of other CBGBs singers) was tuneless; he and Frantz even approached Debbie Harry as a possible singer during Blondie's lull. (She politely declined.) Weymouth was not a natural vocalist either, nor could she play an instrument—which didn't stop Frantz from encouraging her to take up bass. Moe Tucker of the Velvet Underground aside, there was no precedent in New York rock for women playing anything as secondary as the bass in an otherwise male group. Weymouth's decision to learn it anyway raised awkward band dynamics: Frantz and Weymouth were now both rhythm section and romantic couple, a majority vote that Byrne soon challenged by seizing the role as lyricist and, absent any other contender, lead singer. Long-term conflicts were subjugated to the collective goal of making "interesting" music together. With no residential neighbors to disturb in the building, then almost every night after work through the first half of 1975, Talking Heads (their name a reference to the pundits on TV) rehearsed at their Chrystie Street loft, working up a set of short, sparse, rhythmic songs. Alongside numbers like "Warning Sign" and "Psycho Killer" (which David Byrne brought to New York fully written), they soon revealed their art school training by placing an arrow in the song title, "Love –> Building on Fire."

In the spring of 1975, Talking Heads finally asked Hilly Kristal for an audition, the success of which was evident by their prominent debut on June 5, opening for the Ramones. If the billing seemed like an odd contradiction between volume and virtue, attitude and art, the two groups nonetheless shared distinct minimalist tendencies: neither desired to outstay its welcome onstage, neither saw purpose in excessive elaboration. As a result, the Ramones fell instantly in love with Talking Heads. So did Kristal and his wife. And so did many in the audience, fascinated by Byrne's frightened vocal yelps and his henlike neck-pecking; by Weymouth's intensely boyish beauty (having just cut her hair, she looked like a sixties mod starlet) and the way she stared from over her giant bass at the back of Byrne's head as if her playing depended on it; by Frantz's funky drumming, personified by his instrumental "Atom à Bomba," influenced by the salsa and merengue he was absorbing on the Lower East Side; and by the curious melodies and the stylist subject matter, titles like "The Girls Want to Be with the Girls" and "I Want to Live." Talking Heads were so instantly popular that they were invited back the following weekend as headliners, and then to play alongside both the Ramones and Blondie on July 16, 1975—the opening night of CBGBs' first Rock Festival.

Prior to the summer of 1975, CBGBs had been something of a secret society. "You could make a list of the first hundred people to perform at CBs," said Clem Burke. "Because the people that performed were also the audience. In the beginning it was this little microcosm of hip culture that was taking place that no one else in the world knew about."

"About 95 percent of the people who came in the beginning were in bands, and they all got in for free," said Roberta Bayley. Even as the scene developed, and she could start charging people admission, almost everyone who came past Bayley at the door had a role of some sort: "band, photographers, band managers, publicists, writers, clothing designers, girlfriends. . . . But within those categories there weren't that many people. You really would see the same people over and over and over again." Many of the participants would liken the tight scene at CBGBs to that of a rock 'n' roll high school, the kind they wish they could have attended in real life.

Inevitably, word of what was happening on the Bowery eventually spread farther afield. Specifically, when Max's Kansas City closed in December 1974, Mickey Ruskin having approved one extensive bar tab too many, its more musical-minded back-room regulars started venturing the mile down the Bowery to CBGBs, where many of the groups had a Max's connection anyway. Key among them was Danny Fields, who enthused about the club in a column he wrote for *SoHo Weekly News*—albeit over a year after the initial reviews for Television and six months after the Ramones had first been written up in the paper. Meantime, John Rockwell continued to champion the scene in the *New York Times*, and Lisa Robinson wrote an influential piece for *Hit Parader* magazine on the new New York bands. No one quite had a term for it yet, in part because the artists were so disparate, but it was evident that some kind of back-to-basics movement was germinating, away from the sort of instant spotlight that had been trained on the New York Dolls.

The effect on the club was notable: what started out as Sunday night experimental bookings had now extended to four-night double bills, two sets a night. (CBGBs didn't turn the house, which allowed people to come and go at different hours, and removed a certain amount of stigma about headliners and opening acts.) The previously shuttered Mondays and Tuesdays were then opened for "new talent," and the poetry nights on Wednesday all but abandoned. The bookshelves at the front of the club still spoke to his beatnik aspirations, but Kristal knew well enough that his club had allowed a brand-new scene to develop, and the summer of 1975 seemed a good time to take it public.

But though it was book-ended by performances from the Ramones, Blondie, Talking Heads, and the Heartbreakers, most of the other "Top 40 New York Unrecorded Rock Acts," as the festival was subtitled, were to remain just that. Who now—or even then—recalls Punch, Dancer, Uncle Sun, or Uneasy Sleeper? What of Day Old Bread or Pretty Poison? By spreading the net so far, Kristal weakened his pool of talent. As CBGBs settled into its role as a venue for predominantly white, male-centric rock groups, Elda Gentile, who continued to bring a form of the Stillettoes into the club, bemoaned what she saw as "the change in values," how "all of a sudden, everyone had to have one boyfriend—and he's a rock star." It could even be argued that CBGBs represented not so much the future of music as its past: the same week that the *SoHo Weekly News* celebrated the launch of the summer 1975 Rock Festival with a center-page photo spread of mostly interchangeable long-haired white rockers playing the perennial guitars and drums, the *Village Voice* published pictures of a multicultural, pansexual scene as part of a cover story that invited readers "Inside the Disco Boom."

Not that there was a complete lack of overlap between these scenes. The CBGBs jukebox featured the Hues Corporation, as well as the Who, Gladys Knight next to David Bowie. Blondie's cover of "Lady Marmalade" and an introduction into their set of something they originally called "The Disco Song"—later to become "Heart of Glass"—spoke to their own enthusiasm for the more dominant genre of the era. As Talking Heads' drummer Frantz recalled, "There was a lot of talk about disco: 'Don't you hate disco?' and 'It's so boring.' But I was able to play beats that were basically beats I heard on disco records, and as long as you had guitar and bass that sounded something like rock, nobody seemed to mind."

Talking Heads found themselves right in the middle of the five leading

"CBGBs bands." They shared artistic tendencies with Television and Patti Smith, but made no claim to those acts' love of poetry or free jazz; they shared a pop sensibility with both Blondie and the Ramones, but were more calculated than the former, more restrained than the latter. Like all the bands, they played cover versions ("I Can't Control Myself," "1-2-3 Red Light," "96 Tears"), and yet Byrne differentiated himself by playing acoustic guitar. They were also shockingly professional, printing up business cards and handing them out with invitations to attend CBGBs as they toured art openings and avant-garde performances. Typically, they would be met with the response: you want us to come to *The Bowery?*

Yet for those in the know, the club's skid row location was always a large part of its attraction. "You could walk over to the Gem Spa," said Gary Valentine of the egg cream palace on Second Avenue. "Or head over to another bar where the drinks were cheaper, or even go to Alphabet City to score some dope, and then come back to catch the headliner." He wasn't being facetious: Dee Dee Ramone even wrote a song about pawning his possessions for some more of those "Chinese Rocks." When Tommy Ramone flatly refused to allow it into the set, Dee Dee took it to the Heartbreakers, whose Richard Hell, himself a user, added a couple of verses (including a reference to Dee Dee) and immediately made it one of the new group's signature songs.

The barely kept secret that heroin could be scored so easily from dilapidated storefronts and apartment buildings on the Lower East Side only further fostered the notion of CBGBs and its surroundings as a no-go zone. In truth, the entire city was in a state of collapse. In less time than it had taken the New York Dolls to crash and burn, Abe Beame had become mayor (in 1974) and ridden New York City to the very brink of bankruptcy. This was hardly all his fault: the warning signs had been there since the sixties, and the national recession in 1973 merely confirmed the inevitable. Put simply, New York was spending much more than it was earning, and banks were no longer willing to lend the difference. But regardless of underlying causes, Beame's leadership skills proved woefully lacking. The embodiment of the earnest, non-charismatic bookkeeping bureaucrat, he seemed hopelessly disconnected when, in the summer of 1975, he enacted "austerity measures" that called for firing 36,000 city workers. The result? Policemen rioted, firemen called in sick, and the Sanitation Department went on strike, leaving 58,000 tons of garbage piled up on the streets. With the city, quite literally, a seething, stinking summertime mess, Beame begged the federal government to bail it out. President Ford refused; Nelson Rockefeller, who had become Ford's vice president after fourteen years as New York's governor, sided with Beame. When Ford still indicated his determination to let market forces have their own way, the *Daily News* on October 30, 1975, came up with one of the most famous tabloid headlines in history: FORD TO CITY: DROP DEAD.

The CBGBs scene barely blinked.

"It made a great playground for us," said Alan Vega, whose Suicide played at CBGBs occasionally, but more often appeared at Max's, which reopened under new ownership in late 1975 and began booking some of the same acts. "We owned the city. We literally felt like we owned that part of New York. You'd see lines of people just walking from the one club to the other. We felt like outlaws, we made the music, we owned the street. There was a sense that we would create something amazing out of this thing, and we did."

Indeed, if it's true that protest music proves most fruitful when it has something to protest against—witness the civil rights era of the early sixties—then it's equally axiomatic that countercultures thrive during times of economic decline. Some would argue that the New York City music world was never more artistically creative than during the economically "bankrupt" period of the middle seventies. Certainly, in tandem with the disco scene, the rock bands benefited enormously from the preponderance of vacant real estate, which translated into cheap lofts that served as both living quarters and rehearsal spaces. Television operated out of Terry Ork's loft in Chinatown. Talking Heads had theirs on Chrystie Street. Blondie secured a loft on the Bowery itself, just below Houston Street right around the corner from CBGBs. (Kristal, who had a moving and storage company on the side, helped them move in.) And the Ramones began doing business out of a loft on East Second Street, right around the corner from CBGBs that belonged to Arturo Vega, a Mexican-born artist who invited Joey Ramone to live there and became the group's artistic director, designing the instantly recognizable presidential eagle logo with the group's first names around its circumference.

Like Talking Heads' place on Chrystie Street, the Blondie loft had no heat at night. It also had an insane "landlord" living upstairs who kept half-full bottles of urine on his floor, and a liquor store out front that sold Nitrane Express and other fortified wines to what Stein called the local "contingent of poor old fuckers," one of whom was found, shoeless, frozen dead on their doorstep on a winter's day. For Blondie, it was nirvana. Stein, Harry, and Valentine all lived there, and with Burke nearby on First Avenue, the group took to regular rehearsing. The effect on their live show proved immediate, although another sabbatical was forced when Burke spent November and December 1975 with his girlfriend in England, where it turned out a similar "back-to-basics" scene was brewing. On his return, Burke's bandmates brought him straight to the Bowery loft for a homecoming party, at which every group member (and groupie), every artist, photographer, journalist, fashion designer, and scenester appeared to be in attendance—the last great party before the record deals kicked in and money took over. Burke had brought home with him the latest album from the English pub rockers Dr. Feelgood, and it barely came off the turntable all night. "If there's one group that could take credit for giving direction to the New York scene, it must be Dr. Feelgood," proclaimed Harry.

That same holiday season brought further proof of the scene's robust health, as Alan Betrock, who had been writing a "Know Your New York Bands" section in the *SoHo Village News,* launched his own magazine, *New York Rocker.* He promptly commissioned Harry to write about the Miamis, the Miamis to write about Blondie, and Richard Hell, under a pseudonym, to extol the virtues of the Heartbreakers, whose dedication to conventional rock 'n' roll values (and its accompanying glorification of excess) challenged the notion that everything taking place on the downtown scene was new and original.

New York Rocker was incestuous, but it was tame compared with *Punk,* a *Mad* magazine for the CBGBs generation, the brainchild of the cartoonist John Holmstrom, and occasional filmmaker "Legs" McNeil. The pair were influenced by *The Dictators Go Girl Crazy,* released that past summer to something less than mass acceptance. In its own way, the debut Dictators album was genius: "(I Live for) Cars and Girls" was a sublime mixture of Chuck Berry and New York Dolls; "Two Tub Man" threw out insults with glee ("Lou Reed is a creep"); and the covers of "I Got You Babe" and "California Sun" must have had some effect, as the Ramones were soon heard playing the latter. It just didn't fit in at the time.

But that only made it more appealing to McNeil. "On the inside sleeve of the record was a picture of the Dictators hanging out in a White Castle hamburger stand and they were dressed in black leather jackets," he wrote in

Please Kill Me, his oral history of punk. "The picture seemed to describe us perfectly—wise guys. So I thought the magazine should be for other fuck-ups like us. Kids who grew up believing only in the Three Stooges. Kids that had parties when their parents were away and destroyed the house. You know, kids that stole cars and had fun.

"So I said, 'Why don't we call it *Punk?*'"

For the debut issue, they interviewed Lou Reed after cornering him in the audience at a CBGBs Ramones gig. Reed acted, even by his own standards, obnoxiously rude—though McNeil was hardly asking him the kind of reverential questions he might have anticipated. Mary Harron, a third member of the start-up team whose own piece on the Ramones filled the center pages, thought the interview a bust. It wasn't until she saw the front cover—a Holmstrom cartoon that captured Reed's vituperative essence—and how the dialogue had been printed verbatim that she realized, "Everything that was humiliating, embarrassing, and stupid had been turned to an advantage. And that's when I knew that *Punk* was going to work."

The second issue of *Punk* featured a photo of Patti Smith on the cover and an interview with New York's leading lady inside, a more conventional approach to music journalism. The third, dated April, had as its cover a Holmstrom cartoon of Joey Ramone sniping round the Bowery streets, an ultimately iconic image. Inside, Holmstrom responded to an accusation that he had named *Punk* after sexually acquiescent prisoners, noting defiantly that the word "punk" had been around since Shakespeare's day. He then defended their previous issue's definition of a punk as a "beginner, an inexperienced hand," and gave a prescient, handwritten appraisal of what it meant musically: "Punk Rock—any kid can pick up a guitar and become a rock 'n' roll star, despite or because of his lack of ability, talent, intelligence, limitations and/or potential, and usually does so out of frustration, hostility, a lot of nerve and a need for ego fulfillment."

That just about summed it up. Punk rock it would be.

The importance of CBGBs and the bands that played there could never be measured in terms of record sales. Whereas previous New York music scenes churned out chart-topping singles with joyous regularity, only one hit pop act emerged from the Bowery club—Blondie, who attained four number ones between 1979 and 1981. Album sales would prove a more assuring barometer of fashion, even though the only act to score a top ten album in their U.S. homeland was, again, Blondie.

Yet the scene's influence proved irrefutable—and not only in hindsight. As the Bowery bands found their way into recording studios in 1975 and 1976, they lit the fuse on an international music scene. Whether referred to as street rock, punk rock, or new wave, the acts of the CBGBs generation fashioned a major turning point in rock 'n' roll, the effects of which continued to be felt ten, fifteen, even twenty years later.

Fittingly, given her long-standing (and revered) status downtown, Patti Smith was first to "graduate." Her debut album, *Horses*, recorded in the summer of 1975 and released that November, was hailed for its ability to balance visionary poetry with lengthy musical improvisation while staying true to rock 'n' roll tradition. Six years after a group of irate New York civil rights activists protested the Miss America contest in New Jersey and launched what was soon short-handed as "Women's Lib," *Horses* also marked the "coming out" of a truly feminine/feminist rock. This was apparent not just in Smith's performance, which defied all male expectations of the female singer, or in the lyrics, which opened with the *Oath* poem's brazen (and, to some, blasphemous) declaration "Jesus died for somebody's sins but not mine." It was especially evident in the Robert Mapplethorpe cover portrait that aped male iconography, showing Smith in white shirt, her jacket strewn casually across her shoulder, her hair ragged, her tie loose, her natural facial hair unneutered. As Vivienne Goldman, a British journalist who later moved to New York, observed, "It was a shock at that time to see a woman be proudly a woman and yet so androgynous, and not caring whether she was gratifying the traditional male expectations of what a woman needs to be to be sexy."

John Cale, among the first of the old guard to attend CBGBs on a regular basis, produced *Horses*, at Electric Lady studios. Lenny Kaye maintained, "By choosing John, what we said was that we wanted to make an artistic record," yet the recording process proved somewhat fraught. The group hoped to create the kind of "moments" in the studio that came about so easily onstage; Cale had to convince them that "recording is also illusion." Despite the arguments, they succeeded in their mutual goals, and nowhere more evidently than on the album's centerpiece, "Land," which expanded from a quietly disturbing poem about a boy called Johnny getting raped against a locker, into a hallucinogenic vision of "horses" that quickly became the Rascals/Wilson Pickett classic "Land of 1,000 Dances" (segue line, "Do you know how to pony?"). It took off from there, Smith's voice overdubbed in and out of itself, the playing members' repetitive three-chord refrain (which echoed Cale's Velvet Underground) encouraged to ebb and flow according to the dynamics of the poem, which concluded with a dream of Smith making out with Rimbaud as the protagonist Johnny met a bloody demise. "Land" brought Patti Smith comparisons to Jim Morrison's musical poems like "The End," but she was already exploring dark corners of musical and lyrical space the Doors never discovered.

Horses was greeted with critical acclaim falling little short of pure rapture. Smith sold out seven shows at the Bottom Line, toured the United Kingdom and other parts of Europe, and was rewarded for three months' solid American touring by seeing *Horses* climb into the *Billboard* top 50, a phenomenal achievement for an uncategorizable record that lacked a hit single. As she returned to the studio to record her second album, *Radio Ethiopia*, the likelihood of Patti Smith's ever gracing the CBGBs stage again seemed slight indeed.

Tommy Erdelyi had produced an album's worth of Ramones demos in late 1974—if one allowed that an album could comprise fourteen songs all under two minutes in length. The recordings were neither as fast nor as ragged as one might have anticipated from viewing the band's often shambolic live shows, but neither were they as charismatic. Major record label executives were not readily predisposed to the CBGBs scene after the expensive failure of the New York Dolls, and the few who deigned to actually listen to the Ramones demo summarily rejected it.

The only A&R person to show any interest was Craig Leon at Sire, the label started by Red Bird's Seymour Stein and FGG Production's songwriter-producer Richard Gottehrer after the decline of the Brill Building era in the late sixties. Leon saw the Ramones at CBGBs and loved that "they were loud and they were uncontrolled," even as he confirmed that "they were more of an art band than a conventional rock 'n' roll band." But Gottehrer and Stein did not express immediate interest in visiting the Bowery to see the group for themselves. At this point, Sire's reputation had been built primarily on progressive rock. Leon found this ironic, as "the Ramones didn't do thirteen songs in twenty minutes. They did one big song. It was actually quite a prog thing."

Marty Thau, meanwhile, having started to check out the CBGBs scene at the urging of his erstwhile clients Jerry Nolan and Johnny Thunders, quickly found himself courted by the Ramones as a prospective manager. That was not a job offer he wanted to entertain—and after the New York Dolls, who could blame him?—but, a talent spotter in truest sense of the term, he offered to produce a single instead, recording the eminently commercial "I Wanna Be Your Boyfriend" and the band favorite "Judy Is a Punk" in the spring of 1975. The single ended up being shelved—mainly because, that April, at Lisa Robinson's enthusiastic urging, Danny Fields finally got to see the Ramones at CBGBs. "We idolized him, because of his close relationship with Iggy, MC5, and the Doors," said Erdelyi, who was feeling overstretched as the band's drummer, spokesman, producer, and manager. For his part, Fields "fell in love" with the Ramones—"I just thought they were doing everything right," he said—and when he volunteered to take the managerial reins, the group readily accepted.

Not that Fields could easily secure them a recording contract, either. The majors didn't want to know, and though Craig Leon kept on at his bosses, it wasn't until Seymour Stein's wife, Linda, went to CBGBs and, like Fields and Robinson before her, fell head over heels for a band that had now honed its act to military precision, that Seymour agreed to attend a showcase at Performance Studios. Seymour's primary mantra in music was as a simple as a Ramones chorus: "The song is everything." He heard the pure pop classicism underneath all the volume, and when Craig Leon promised to produce a Ramones album for "next to nothing," the deal was cemented. Leon took the Ramones into Plaza Sound, the vast studio inside Radio City Music Hall, in February 1976, and emerged less than two weeks later with their eponymous debut album. The session cost $6,000 and change. At a period when rock music was dominated by the extravagance of Fleetwood Mac and the Eagles, this was, truly, next to nothing.

The Ramones wore its economy on its sleeve via a black-and-white shot of the four members standing against a Lower East Side brick wall, courtesy of Roberta Bayley, who had only recently bought a camera. (The shot was initially commissioned for *Punk* magazine.) The three playing members were recorded playing live, with their equipment isolated in different rooms, enabling for stereo separation as on old Beatles records. The drums were sent straight down the middle, in mono, the guitars were panned right, the bass hard left, and Joey's vocals were mostly double-tracked and separated accordingly. In addition, the guitars were overdubbed repeatedly. "I would have Johnny play the same thing six times and take six different EQs and mash them together into one sound," said Leon. Yet ultimately, the album sounded as if it had been recorded in a cardboard box dropped into the ocean, a result of the mastering process: the tapes had to be compressed beyond usual limits because the bass, panned as it was all on the one side, could barely be contained within the vinyl groove.

Its primitivism turned out to be its main asset, and its fourteen songs all became sonic landmarks, the (eventually acclaimed) founding fathers of a new musical movement. Initial pride of place was given to "Blitzkrieg Bop," with a "hey-ho-let's-go" chant lifted directly from the Bay City Rollers' current hit "Saturday Night"; the comically violent "Beat on the Brat" ("with a baseball bat, oh yeah"); and "Judy Is a Punk," complete with old-fashioned handclaps. The finale, "Today Your Love, Tomorrow the World," was a tongue-in-cheek riff on fascism at a time when swastikas had become high fashion. (Dee Dee Ramone, raised in postwar Germany, collected them; Arturo Vega painted them; Wayne County, Johnny Thunders, and Arthur Kane all frequently wore them.) Seymour Stein begged the group to leave it off the album—or at least to remove the "Nazi schatze" reference. When the band refused—Joey and Danny Fields, both Jewish, supported the shock content—the label boss had the good sense not to belabor the issue. It wasn't evident that *The Ramones* would be an instant hit, after all.

And it wasn't. Not in America, where journalists, radio programmers, and concert bookers alike experienced complete culture shock and bemusement—and where an unsatisfying official launch show at the Bottom Line, opening for Dr. Feelgood, revealed the risks inherent in removing the band from its natural habitat. As the Ramones gamely toured the country, they found themselves embarking on an uphill struggle. "They were scared," said Tommy Ramone of the industry at large. "They were savvy enough to realize that what we were doing was revolutionary, and they didn't want revolutionary. They wanted status quo. When revolutions happen people lose jobs."

"People wouldn't let go of their first Black Sabbath album," recalled Joey Ramone. "Or their first Led Zeppelin album. And they wouldn't open up to anything that was different." *The Ramones* stalled just outside the *Billboard* top 100, at exactly the same position, curiously enough (no. 111), as had the heavily hyped debut by the New York Dolls. Given the weight of *The Ramones'* press clippings, however, Sire quickly financed another album. Following their dictum of minimalism—second album, same as the first—the Ramones effectively re-recorded their debut.

On the Fourth of July, 1976, the United States celebrated its two hundredth birthday. Gerald Ford tried to shore up his struggling presidency by hosting Britain's Queen Elizabeth in Washington, D.C., but the public instead cast its collective gaze on New York, where so many millions of their ancestors had arrived as immigrants—suggesting that, financial crisis and crime rate temporarily put aside, it was still the unofficial capital of the country. That morning, a flotilla of tall ships sailed into the city's harbor, watched over by the nation's most popular symbol of independence, the Statue of Liberty; as what seemed like every small vessel from within a hundred miles flocked to join them, a party atmosphere erupted in the city, culminating in the greatest, longest, and most spectacular fireworks display New York had ever seen. Just a week later, the city would be hosting the Democratic National Convention at Madison Square Garden, where Georgia's Governor Jimmy Carter would be nominated as the party's presidential candidate. City workers were on a mission to rid midtown of graffiti and grime, pushers and prostitutes. Taxi drivers were on their best behavior. For that heady couple of weeks, Mayor Beame could forget his troubles and bask in the warm glow of good publicity: New York City, it seemed, just might have returned from the dead.

The Talking Heads members found time to wander down to Battery Park that afternoon and soak up the festive atmosphere—and in the evening they concluded a four-night residency at CBGBs, the prominent booking a mark of their popularity on the scene. The Ramones might have seemed more obvious candidates for the city's celebration of Independence, especially given their presidential seal logo and their lyrical immersion in all-American trash, but the two hundredth anniversary of independence from Britain found them, instead, performing on a British stage for the first time.

The Ramones had been released in the United Kingdom into a desperate political climate that, unlike New York's own fiscal problems, had enveloped working-class teenagers, who accepted songs like "Now I Wanna Sniff Some Glue" on face value, leading to appropriate tabloid hysterics. The audience at their debut show—at the Round House, where *Pork* had played five years earlier—included members of the Sex Pistols, the Clash, and the Damned, pioneers of the contemporaneous British punk rock explosion. The Sex Pistols were already up and running, covering Stooges songs and having taken on board elements of Richard Hell's image. But both the Damned and the Clash quickly seized on the Ramones' voluminous two- and three-chord minimalism as a means by which to convey a message—which, in the economically depressed United Kingdom, was inherently more political. The following spring, the Clash released their debut single "White Riot," and it was impossible not to realize that the Ramones' influence had already jumped the Atlantic.

Blondie's status on the scene seemed to have been a continual case of taking one step back for each one forward. Some critics were convinced that Debbie Harry, who admitted to a certain degree of stage fright, wasn't up to the lead role. "Blondie will never be a star simply because she ain't good enough," lashed Britain's *New Musical Express* in a late 1975 report on the New York scene that lauded their close friends the Ramones; the *Village Voice's* Robert Christgau told Chris Stein personally, "Blondie is a loser's band."

Other journalists came to their support. In the summer of 1975, *New York Rocker's* publisher, Alan Betrock, who later wrote a book on girl groups, produced a five-song demo that included the Shangri-Las' "Out in the Streets," the early version of "Heart of Glass" entitled "Once I Had a Love," and the self-effacing "Platinum Blonde." Though the demos failed to pique label interest, Betrock put Harry on the cover of *New York Rocker's* third issue, under the headline, in deliberately direct contradiction to the band's critics, that she was "the girl most likely to."

By the spring of 1976, the group had added the keyboardist Jimmy

Destri, and the live shows were getting stronger by the night. Richard Gottehrer, having quit Sire, and Marty Thau, with whom he had set up a production company called Instant Records, came knocking—the scene was too big now for all but the laziest of major labels to ignore—and Blondie welcomed their résumés. After all, "Blondie were like a bubblegum band," said Clem Burke, without apology. The addition of Craig Leon as coproducer was the icing on the cake.

"They weren't great players, but they had great enthusiasm," said Leon of Blondie, a widely shared view at the time. "They were an instance where the sum is greater than its individual parts." Leon and Gottehrer set to work on "Sex Offender," a streetwise update on the Shadow Morton/Shangri-Las soap operas, originally written by the bassist Valentine about his statutory rape charge against an under-age girlfriend, now adapted by Harry in the guise of a prostitute entangled with her arresting officer. Recording at Plaza Sound took almost as long as the entire Ramones album. But the result was worth it: big and booming, with tambourines, organ melodies, and Harry's voice as sultry and horny as it ought to be given the lyrical content, "X Offender" (as it was renamed for fear of offending anyone) sounded the perfect alarm. After being sold on to Private Stock, an independent company part-owned by the doo-wop star Frankie Valli (who graced CBGBs with his presence to sign off on his approval), they were commissioned to record an album.

Where *The Ramones* had sounded "lo-fi and arty," as Tommy Ramone described it, the LP *Blondie* came out of the same studio with crystalline clarity. Craig Leon drew on his classical background to bring in "recurring motifs and countermelodies." Richard Gottehrer brought his expertise from producing doo-wop, girl groups, and imitation British invasion bands. On the long-standing set highlight "In the Flesh," he even hired Ellie Greenwich to sing backing vocals. Released just in time for the 1976 holiday season, *Blondie* surprised everyone with its professional polish. Yet Blondie's street roots were still visible: Harry later joked about how all the lyrics featured "someone getting shot, stabbed, degraded, or insulted." The edge was evident from "In the Flesh," which referred to walking on the Lower East Side, and from the reference to a "Miss Groupie supreme" on "Rip Her to Shreds," which Harry delivered in a sassy streetwise tone that made her sound tough as nails. Reviews were almost begrudgingly positive. Now all Blondie needed was radio play.

. . .

As early as the summer of 1975, Television had followed Patti Smith's lead, borrowed her drummer and his tape machine, and recorded a 7-inch single for independent release, manager Ork establishing a label for that very purpose. But Verlaine chose one of the group's oddest and longest songs, "Little Johnny Jewel," which, spread across both sides of the 45, only reinforced the notion of Television as an inherently uncommercial proposition. The group remained unsigned until late 1976, when Elektra Records recognized it had all but slept through the latest downtown scene and snapped up the last of the available leading acts.

Working with Andy Johns, who had engineered almost all the Led Zeppelin and Rolling Stones albums of the 1970s (so much for musical revolution), Television quickly made up for lost time. Richard Lloyd had taken to notating his guitar solos, ensuring that they followed the rhythm of a good story (introduction, elaboration, resolution), and this enabled him to double-track them for unusual sonic effect. Tom Verlaine was given more to free-form extemporizing, and the combination of their guitar styles— often separated to left and right channels—provided *Marquee Moon* with one of its many distinctive calling cards. Another was its deliberate lack of groove; it could hardly have been further removed from the disco era had it been recorded in Arkansas. Rather, the recordings were kept naturally tight (i.e., uncompressed) and without undue effects, providing a blueprint for a form of chromatic, rather than rhythmic, music that would later come to be called angular.

Other than its opening, anthemic songs "See No Evil" and "Venus," *Marquee Moon* revealed a contempt for brevity, and nowhere more so than on the ten-minute title track, which built from the audible hum of the Fender amps into a celestial celebration of the six-string guitar's ethereal possibilities, Verlaine's solo later cited as among rock music's most eloquent. When this unique instrumentation was topped with the author's poetic (though curiously unobtrusive) vocals, delivered in something of a terse, high-pitched wail, *Marquee Moon* proved almost impossible to categorize—and would therefore, on its release early in that cataclysmic year of 1977, be recognized as something entirely original, a new dawn in rock music.

. . .

Seymour Stein never forgot the night he first heard Talking Heads. He was standing outside CBGBs between sets, like just about everyone else: Kristal's club was an exception to the dominant "no reentry" policy. His ear suddenly pricked up to the words "When my love stands next to your love" sung to a divine melody, and he felt himself drawn into the club as if by musical gravity. After the show, he immediately set about promising Talking Heads the earth—or Sire's financially limited but emotionally devoted equivalent. This was November 1975, and it marked, he later said, "the beginning of the longest courtship that I ever had with a band."

While acknowledging Stein's advances, the trio recorded three songs for another ardent fan, Matthew "King" Kaufman of Beserkley Records—home label to Boston's Jonathan Richman and the Modern Lovers, quirky minimalists who had, over the years, played the Mercer, CBGBs, and Max's without ever quite catching on. The session was reported in a major *New York Times* review in March 1976, in which John Rockwell gushed how "the abrupt layerings [of their songs] recall planes of color in minimalist art" and announced that both Columbia and RCA were also interested in the group, sending Stein into paroxysms of panic. The trio did record a demo for CBS: the only track to (later) see the light of day was a suitably sparse (acoustic guitar, bass, drums), yet surprisingly complete, "Sugar on My Tongue." But the CBS bigwigs, like those of the other majors, refused to take the relationship any further.

This was fine by the band, which felt it more important to acquire a fourth member to fill out the sound, and they headhunted the Modern Lovers' keyboard player, Jerry Harrison, shortly after that group broke up. Having just resumed studies at Harvard, Harrison was reluctant to drop them all over again, but decided to do so anyway after visiting the group's Chrystie Street loft in September 1976. Shocked by its decrepit state, the bullet holes in the window, the bathroom down the hall, the genuine danger of the neighborhood streets, and the fact that the group ate only the cheapest of Chinese food now that they had given up their midtown jobs for music, he nonetheless recognized in all this a commitment that couldn't be questioned.

Once Harrison joined, Talking Heads officially put themselves on the market—and soon signed with Sire. In the many months since Seymour

Stein had first pursued the group, he and his wife had come to see them again and again, and he had regaled them—in song, as was his manner—with his own encyclopedic knowledge of music over many an alcohol-soaked dinner. In addition, the Ramones spoke highly of Sire's support. Allowing that Linda Stein was now comanaging that band alongside Danny Fields, that might well have been a given.

Before they signed, Talking Heads asked for one more pause in proceedings. They wanted to release an independent single, as had almost all the other bands on the scene. Stein reminded the group that Sire was, itself, independent and offered to take care of it for them. For their debut single, Talking Heads recorded the same song that had initially drawn Stein through the CBGBs portal, "Love $\rightarrow$ Building on Fire." It was released in the first few weeks of 1977.

16

THE BOOGIE DOWN BRONX

Hip-hop was born in the Bronx. That much has never been in dispute. But of its "four elements," only perhaps the art of b-boying—later reinterpreted as break-dancing—was a pure Bronx phenomenon, and even then its historical connection to jazz and mambo dancing has often been noted. The other three hip-hop elements—graffiti, DJing, and MCing, the last of which would turn out to be the most enduring and profitable once it was renamed "rap"—were all products of several boroughs (or even cities) and took hold only over an extended period of time. What established the Bronx as the home of hip-hop, and rightly allowed it to lay claim to birthing the most important musical movement since rock 'n' roll, was the way in which it took these potentially disparate elements and fused them into a visible, viable, visceral whole.

Isolation had a lot to do with it. For several years in the early 1970s, cultural developments that worked their way up through New York City paused when they hit the Bronx. There they were steadily altered and reshaped, far from the public eye. By the time the rest of the city caught on to what the Bronx youth were doing, their movement was already five years old—and yet, it had still to declare itself on vinyl. Hip-hop, then, was the first American musical movement since the earliest days of New Orleans jazz to define itself outside of the recording studio. To fully understand how this came about, one has to understand how the South Bronx became so isolated in the first place.

. . .

The borough of the Bronx was named—though not until 1898—for the river that wends southward through it, neatly separating the hilly land on the west from the flatter terrain to the east. As part of the town of Westchester, to the north of Manhattan, it first began enticing the city's residential overflow in the mid-1840s. When new railway lines opened up the possibility of a daily commute to and from "downtown," property speculators, seizing on the potential for profit, subdivided the land near these new railway tracks to create instant suburban villages with such enticing names as Woodstock, Forest Grove, and Mount Eden. In turn, as the mainly Irish laborers who built the railways opted to raise families there, the population of southern Westchester exploded, reaching 35,000 by 1870, the vast majority concentrated in communities west of the Bronx River. In 1874, following a referendum in which Westchester voters were promised not just access to the city's water and sanitation but an extension of its elevated transit lines, 12,500 acres of Westchester were annexed by the City of New York.

Residents of the two new wards created by the annexation called themselves "North Siders," indicating the extent to which they viewed themselves part of the city below. Accordingly, despite the wards' ridges and valleys, they adopted Manhattan's grid system, haphazardly continuing dozens of numbered streets over the river from Harlem and Washington Heights. Before they could get carried away doing so, the New York Park Association swiftly set aside permanent green spaces, admirable not only in size (Van Cortland and Pelham Bay Parks were both bigger than Central Park) and scope (Bronx Park became home to both the Bronx Zoo and the New York Botanical Garden) but also for creating a novel network of tree-lined parkways that encouraged intrapark travel. The communities of Mott Haven, Melrose, and Morrisania—the core of the future South Bronx—were not so fortunate; densely populated already, largely with tenement housing catering to the rapid influx of new residents, the Park Association could claim for them only the comparatively minuscule, 25-acre St. Mary's Park.

The new wards doubled in size in 1895 when New York annexed an equal area to the east of the Bronx River, and three years later the Bronx was given its name as one of the five boroughs created by the new Greater City of

New York, the only one connected to the American mainland. Its prospects appeared splendid indeed. In 1905, Borough President Louis F. Haffen proclaimed that the Bronx would become the "most contented and the most progressive borough of the greatest city in the world," and for the next few decades his vision seemed justified: for the Jews who followed the Irish, Italians, and Germans out of the Lower East Side, a Bronx address signaled a realization of the American Dream. The borough's status was boosted in 1923 by the opening of both the New York Yankees Stadium, close to Borough Hall in the lower Bronx, which brought baseball's biggest team over from Manhattan, and the Concourse Plaza Hotel, sitting proudly on a ridge at 161st Street and the Grand Concourse, the latter road modeled on the Champs-Elysées.

By 1940, the borough's population had soared to almost 1.4 million, a third of whom lived in the confined neighborhoods of the South Bronx. Over 90 percent of the residences there were rentals, and as this housing stock began to deteriorate, those who could afford to move out of the South Bronx—Jews and Germans in particular—did just that. In turn, their place in these cheap apartments was taken by the new poor: blacks from the South and the West Indies, Puerto Ricans, and, over time, an additional 170,000 blacks and Latinos who were displaced from Manhattan by that borough's slum clearance. Battle lines were drawn along racial divides, with teenage gangs pitting Irish against Jews, Italians against Puerto Ricans, whites against blacks. By 1945, at least twenty-three gangs had been identified by the 41st Precinct in the neighborhood of Hunts Point–Crotona Park East alone, a sign of things to come.

But nothing divided the borough like Parks Commissioner Robert Moses's Cross-Bronx Expressway, which cut off the South Bronx with razor-like brutality, as it sliced through some 113 streets, seven parkways and expressways, and a total of nine different railway or subway lines during its construction in the late 1940s and early 1950s, forcing the relocation of sixty thousand residents from a dozen established neighborhoods. Unlike the parkways that had used vacant land to connect (and enhance) the borough's green spaces, the Cross-Bronx took the opposite approach, "destroying blocks of apartment buildings at a time when every apartment was needed," as Evelyn Gonzalez noted in her book *The Bronx*, "housing that was newer and better than that in the South Bronx." In its connecting of traffic from New

Jersey (via the George Washington Bridge) to Queens and Long Island (via the Whitestone and later also the Throgs Neck Bridge), "neighborhoods were demolished so travelers could bypass the Bronx completely."

Moses was also at the helm of the city's numerous public housing projects, the "towers in gardens" ideal of the French architect Le Corbusier, which spread like a cancer across many Western cities in the postwar years but proved particularly virulent in New York. In the South Bronx in the 1950s, under the guise of "slum clearance," Moses and the city planners leveled street after street of existing neighborhoods and, in their place, erected soulless tower blocks in concentrated groups, some 12,500 apartments crammed into ninety-six buildings across just five housing projects, every one of them officially designated for low-income families—and none of them with the movie theaters, convenience stores, or lavish gardens Met Life had built for forty thousand middle-class residents in the Parkchester section of the Bronx.

The psychological damage caused to the South Bronx by the new expressways and housing projects proved irreparable. Remaining white families (mainly Italian and Irish) took flight to the edges of the Bronx or the tristate suburbs, facilitated by a 1960 change in law that allowed city employees (including firemen and policemen) to live outside the five boroughs. By the midsixties, the map of the South Bronx had been redrawn to reflect decidedly man-made boundaries: the Cross-Bronx Expressway to the north, the Major Deegan Expressway at the Harlem River, and the elevated Bruckner Expressway (which placed the once thriving Bruckner Boulevard under a literal shadow) at the Bronx River. Socially, culturally, and financially isolated, it was now a poverty-stricken island of mostly run-down tenement buildings, aging row houses, and menacing public projects.

The South Bronx's problems were exacerbated, on almost all fronts, by bureaucratic mistakes, misdeeds, and misplaced faith. While rent control, established during World War II, generally provided an incentive for long-term residents to remain in their neighborhoods, many Bronx landlords found themselves unable to make a profit on their buildings, removing the motivation to maintain them. The buildings became slums, further lowering the quality of the neighborhood, and with no prospect of change in sight, the more unscrupulous landlords took to arson for the insurance money—setting fires in empty apartments, trusting that the Fire Department would arrive in time to save any tenants who hadn't gotten out, but not the building. Seeing the potential for profit, blatantly criminal landlords began buying up depressed buildings at bargain prices, collecting what rent they could, at gunpoint if necessary, neglecting all maintenance and taxes, employing "finishers" to remove and sell whatever fixtures could reap a profit, and then hiring local kids to torch the buildings, pocketing the insurance payments and fleeing for the hills, before the various investigative authorities could catch up to them.

The city directly contributed to the wave of arson when it actively promoted a policy that gave burned-out tenants priority for public housing (*and* replacement money for old furnishings). The new housing projects offered little by way of social interaction, but at least they had hot and cold water, heating in winter, and a roof that did not leak. And so tenants, too, became arsonists. Local ladder companies reported arriving at burning buildings in the middle of the night only to find families fully dressed, suitcases by their side in preparation for relocation; teachers reported students naively announcing "this week is the fire." And yet nobody in power would use the word "arson." The fires burned out of control, their root causes allowed to smolder, ignite, and spread further.

In 1968, as the fires started to spread, a fresh wave of potent heroin hit the streets of the Bronx (as it did those of Harlem, the Lower East Side, Bushwick, and other impoverished areas), creating a generation of junkie criminals desperate to feed their habits. With large elements of the police force involved in the drug trade itself (as was widely known on the streets and finally confirmed by the Knapp Commission in 1972), crime escalated: burglaries in the Bronx rose an astonishing 1,650 percent through the 1960s. Into the security void stepped a new generation of powerful, violent teenage (and even preteen) gangs. Puerto Ricans made up the majority: the Savage Skulls, the Ghetto Brothers, the Roman Kings, the Seven Immortals, the Mongols, and the Dirty Dozens were all active in the southernmost South Bronx. In the major housing projects to the east of the Bronx River, massive numbers of Black Spades ruled the roost. North across Fordham Road, white gangs such as the Arthur Avenue Boys, Golden Guineas, and War Pigs fought to hold what they perceived as their last lines of defense.

The gangs typically modeled their appearances on the Hells Angels, sporting cutoff denim jackets with gang logos—"colors"—on the back. And they demanded of their new members brutal initiation rites, of which the "Apache" lines of bat- and chain-wielding graduates were nothing compared with the Russian roulette forced on thirteen-year-old Michael Corral by the Savage Skulls, who was awarded the street name Lucky Strike for obvious reasons. Those who weren't so fortunate as Corral were left to rot in the abandoned buildings that the gangs claimed as clubhouses: the first division of Savage Skulls brazenly made its clubhouse in an abandoned building just a block from the 41st Police Precinct—or Fort Apache, as it became known.

Though the gangs were glorified by the media for declaring war on local junkies and pushers (often with murderous efficiency), they served primarily to provide members with the camaraderie and security that was lacking at home. This essentially boiled down to the defense of local turf by any and all means possible—and, subsequently, a fear of travel outside one's neighborhood unless in a protective pack. Not only had the South Bronx become an island of its own; its individual neighborhoods were growing increasingly isolated in turn.

Unsurprisingly, the area's remaining jewels rapidly lost their sheen. The Concourse Plaza Hotel, which in 1960 had hosted the presidential candidate John F. Kennedy as he wooed the Bronx Ladies' Club for its endorsement, changed hands repeatedly as it fell on hard times. In 1965, Joseph Caspi, a Bronx native who'd made his money in the garment industry, bought it as both investment and trophy, leaving its day-to-day management and catering to the companies that held leases to do so. That turned out to be a classic case of bad timing, as the new, vast Co-Op City in the far northern reaches of the Bronx was busy drawing thousands of middle-class Jews away from the Grand Concourse, taking their resources with them. That same year, the Plaza's management began accepting families who had been burned out of their apartments in the fires sweeping the eastern South Bronx, once it was discovered it could charge the city more for these temporary residents than its paying guests. Long-standing tenants, visitors, and civic groups, rather than share the hotel with welfare tenants, took their business elsewhere, and the caterers quickly went bankrupt. A desperate Caspi took over the banqueting rooms and allowed local black organizations to rent them for dances, and in December 1971 his son turned the Baroque Room into the Tunnel Plaza discotheque. This, at least, proved a success, and among the disc jockeys who made it so was one who appropriated his name from the movie *Shaft*, and another who went by his own name, John Brown: both hammered, in particular, like almost every discotheque across the city, the good-foot soul of the Harlem Apollo's adopted son James Brown.

Among the regulars on the Tunnel dance floor was a sixteen-year-old Jamaican immigrant, Clive Campbell, known locally as Kool Herc(ules), the title bestowed on him by neighborhood friends for his strong build and prowess in athletics and basketball. Herc had been introduced to the Tunnel Plaza when his family, having emigrated from Jamaica in 1967, was housed at the Concourse Hotel after being burned out of their apartment on East 168th Street, when the youngest of the six children had set the curtains ablaze.

In due course, the Campbells were relocated to one of seven buildings that formed Sedgwick Houses, a project hard underneath the George Washington Bridge. From there, Clive would routinely head back to the Tunnel Plaza. He also attended house parties with his mother, where Motown was the music of choice, and Catholic Church–sponsored "First Friday" youth dances. In Kingston, Jamaica, the Campbells had lived for a while in Trenchtown, the heart of the city's music ghetto, where sound systems reigned. Now, in the Bronx, Clive's father, Keith, bought a PA, complete with large Shure speakers, for a local R&B group. When Clive, who had started taking his records to local house parties, hooked up a speaker wire to a jack, and attached the jack to a preamplifier, he rendered the system so loud that his father forgave him for messing with it in the first place, and Clive Campbell was allowed use of the PA when it wasn't needed for a band gig. "And that's how it started, man!" he said. "That's when Cindy asked me to do a back-to-school party."

Cindy was Clive's younger sister, hoping to raise funds to hit Delancey Street and buy new clothes for the upcoming school year. She threw her "Back to School Jam" on August 11, 1973, in her building's ground-floor recreation room, hand-drawing fliers that advertised 25 cents admission for girls, 50 cents for boys, and party hours running from 9:00 p.m. until 4:00 a.m., the late hours reflecting the midsummer vibe. The night rolled around, a healthy crowd showed up, and once Herc switched from Jamaican music over to the kind of hard soul and funk that had become the music of choice for the city's dancing youth—James Brown, the Isley Brothers, Rare Earth, and others—the party exploded. Sitting back in a chair behind his Garrard turntables, Herc occasionally announced himself, Jamaican MC style, via a microphone plugged into an echo chamber. But the main attraction of the night was the instrumental break sections that the younger teens so clearly favored as a chance to bust their moves—and which Herc quickly chose to focus on. As a result, word spread that DJ Kool Herc had just thrown the party to end them all—or perhaps, to start something new, for the August 11 jam at 1520 Sedgwick is frequently cited as the birth of hip-hop.

There are several reasons why such an apparently innocuous event should have proven so pivotal. First and foremost, Herc brought to the party not just a record player and a couple of home speakers, the sort that powered up most community center jams, but a throbbing *sound system*. As Herc himself said of the newly voluminous Shure columns, "They wasn't something to be looked at, they was something to be *feeling*." Soon enough, the speakers would acquire their own name—the Herculoids—and become almost as famous as their owner.

Second, Herc brought the music. The audience at his parties, which soon became regular events, all said the same thing: Herc played music you didn't hear on the radio. Instead, he hyped tracks that played up the Latin pulse of the South Bronx and Spanish Harlem streets: the Incredible Bongo Band's "Bongo Rock" and "Apache," the Jimmy Castor Bunch's "It's Just Begun"; he pumped black soul like Baby Huey's "Listen to Me" and Booker T. & the M.G.'s "Melting Pot"; he highlighted the international sounds popular on the downtown dance floors, like "Fencewalk," by Brooklyn's Mandrill, and "Bra," by Cymande—plus dozens more that the audience could never recognize and that Herc, who at his father's advice soaked off the labels to preserve their exclusivity, was not about to announce.

And then there was the way he played that music. Whether Herc got it right on the first night or, as is more likely, over the course of the follow-up parties, he quickly saw the popularity of the instrumental sections that enabled the aspiring b-boys—those who would later be called break-dancers—to do battle with each other. Vocals, these kids had discovered, got in the way of their moves; but the rhythm parts, whether at the start of a track, at the end of a chorus, or (best of all) extended as midsong "breaks," set them off. Herc learned to identify the most popular of these, as on tracks like "Scorpio" (by Dennis Coffey and the Detroit Guitar Band), "Apache," and "It's Just Begun," and deliver them one by one as the party peaked. He called it the "Merry-go-Round."

Herc, now eighteen, also brought both respect and security to the party. At six feet six, he was a commanding presence. "They couldn't be looking down at me," he said of the teens that came to his first parties. "They had to look up." Herc was a familiar dancer on the floor of the Tunnel Plaza. He'd run with a graffiti crew called the EX-VANDALS: he'd left the tag CLYDE AS KOOL on many a city wall before realizing that his strength lay in his love of music. In other words, "this was not somebody gonna be stepped on."

But Herc was not a gang member. Never had been, never would be. He lamented their presence, how "the gangs came up and start to terrorize the clubs in the Bronx. Start smack up girls, start feeling them up, disrespecting them, robbing people coats and stuff, [and how] it shut the discos down." So, from his first party onward, he made it clear that he wouldn't brook trouble of any kind. Take it down the block, he'd say not just at the first whiff of aggression but at the first smell of weed or angel dust. His parties were alcohol-, drug-, and weapon-free events, and at 1520 Herc had the muscle (his own and that of his friends) to ensure they stayed that way.

Finally, there was the matter of timing. The year 1973 turned out to be pivotal in the Bronx. In March, the police responded to community pressure and closed down the Tunnel Plaza for operating without a license—all the more reason for Herc to throw his own parties. Meantime, the fires reached new heights that summer: during August, the area around Charlotte Street, just south of Crotona Park, fell victim to fifty-six fires in twenty-two buildings over just two weeks. While some bureaucrats finally broached the term "arson" and questioned how to tackle it, Robert Moses gave up on the South Bronx entirely. He advocated moving its entire half-million population to new housing projects he would build at Ferry Point Park, in the east of the borough. As far as he was concerned, the South Bronx was "beyond rebuilding, tinkering and restoring."

George Steinbrenner, the new owner of the New York Yankees, was similarly dismissive. With Yankee Stadium having fallen into disrepair, Steinbrenner threatened to take the richest team in baseball over the river to New Jersey. Rather than lose the lucrative taxes, New York City, under Mayor

Lindsay, purchased the stadium and set about a two-year refurbishment program, one that it promised, under the auspices of "urban renewal," would also rejuvenate the surrounding South Bronx streets. At the end of September 1973, the Yankees played their last game in the South Bronx for thirty months. From a sociologist's perspective, the South Bronx was about to enter its darkest hour.

Yet for the kids on the streets, a new day was dawning. "The lifespan of youth style in New York City parallels the life-cycle of a neighborhood," Jeff Chang wrote in *Can't Stop Won't Stop: A History of the Hip-Hop Generation*, tracing the evolution of the final Bronx youth gangs to the turbulent year of 1968. "It's about five years, the time it takes for youths to come through their teens, long enough for them to imprint their own codes, styles, and desires on the block." By that reckoning, the gang cycle would have been completing itself in 1973—just as DJ Kool Herc began throwing his parties. A new generation of Bronx youth was primed and ready for a new form of street culture, and Herc, it turned out, was their man.

But Herc was not alone. On the opposite corner of the South Bronx, at the Bronx River Houses, which, like Sedgwick, were (deliberately?) tucked under the expressways—in this case, the Cross-Bronx, the Sheridan, *and* the Bronx River Parkway—the community center had been hosting parties since at least 1970, for residents or their friends exclusively. And from the beginning, a regular presence in their midst had been that of Afrika Bambaataa.

He was born in Manhattan (most likely in April 1957, and possibly as Kahim Aasim: Bambaataa was always reluctant to reveal his true identity) to a family of West Indian descent and radical politics, surrounded by black Muslims and with at least one uncle well known in black nationalist circles. Moving to a ground-floor apartment at Bronx River, he was drawn to the dominant Black Spades gang, where his charisma, strength, and bravery saw him quickly promoted to a leadership position. When he was bused to Stevenson High School in one of the South Bronx's last white vestiges—the far Soundview section—in 1971, he found himself fighting on the front lines of a racial gang war. And when black and Latino gang violence accelerated over the course of that year, culminating in the December murder of a respected leader of the musically minded Latin group the Ghetto Brothers in a Bronx park, the fourteen-year-old Afrika Bambaataa attended the emergency peace summit at the Bronx Boys Club.

Bambaataa never fully renounced his involvement in the Black Spades, nor did he discuss their inner workings; the glorification of the "thug life" would be left to later generations of hip-hoppers. What he did admit to was a desire for conquest rather than vengeance. "I took my things of attacking areas from the history of Napoleon [and] Shaka Zulu," he said. "I used things I was reading in school to attack areas and make them join up with us."

Bambaataa may have learned about Napoleon at school, but his study of Shaka Zulu—the warrior king who, in nineteenth-century South Africa, united numerous subtribes into a formidable black nation—was inspired by extracurricular exposure to the 1960s British movie *Zulu*. That film showed an outnumbered British military outpost as colonial heroes beating back an onslaught of tribal Zulus. (A similar theme would later be explored in *Fort Apache, The Bronx*, about the 41st Police Precinct.) Bambaataa viewed it from the opposite perspective: "to see these black people fighting for what was theirs against the British, that always stuck in my mind."

Inspired, a maturing Bambaataa began to apply his leadership qualities in a peaceful direction, folding first the Black Spades and then other gangs into what eventually became his Zulu Nation. And throughout this period, "Bam always DJ'd," said fellow Black Spade and future Zulu Nation MC Mr. Biggs. "Before and after a rumble, Bam would go in the house and turn on the music full blast, he'd put the speakers in the window and play music all night long."

In due course, as Black Spades disc jockeys like Kool DJ D (from Bronx River) and DJ Mario the Disco King (from the nearby Bronxdale Houses) moved up into the clubs, Bam and his younger friends took over the jams in the Bronx River community center. Their system was primitive: Bam with a record player and speaker on one side of the room, a friend with his own setup on the other. They would use flashlights to signify when their 45s—the popular junior high hits of the day—were coming to an end.

Only a few hundred yards—a no-man's-land of railway tracks, the Sheridan Expressway, and the Bronx River itself—separated the Bronx River Houses from the home turf of the Savage Skulls and the Seven Immortals. By 1973–74, these Latino gangs had become so immersed in internecine warfare that even the most hard-core members were quitting. Lucky Strike of the Savage Skulls dropped his colors after his best friend Blue was found murdered in the clubhouse, making him amenable to the Zulu Nation's peaceful approaches. Soon he was attending meetings at Bronx River Houses. Members of the Zulu Nation began to come through the East Tremont neighborhood handing out fliers for free parties at the Bronx River, promising "Peace Love and Unity" if everyone left their colors at home, and Ray Abrahante, better known by his graffiti name BOM 5, and a youth member of the Savage Skulls, decided to take up the invite. When Abrahante recognized Bambaataa from gang confrontations, the latter extended the hand of friendship, and the former saw it as a seminal moment. "Thank God for Bambaataa realizing that there was too much violence going on."

In 1975, Bambaataa entered a Housing Authority essay contest, and won a trip to West Africa. He talked later of visiting Nigeria, the Ivory Coast, and Guinea-Bissau. But if the African journey helped further his quest to promote black self-determination, an event much closer to home proved equally pivotal. In early 1975, his cousin and best friend Soulski was shot dead by the police on Pelham Parkway, in circumstances Bam felt were unjustified. It could have taken him back down the path of gang warfare, but it had the opposite effect. Turning inward, to his own people, and choosing the path of self-determination rather than confrontation, Afrika Bambaataa—the "Affectionate Chieftain"—threw himself wholeheartedly into his role as leader of the Zulu Nation. Those who attended its parties, which benefited from the turntable set Bambaataa received as a graduation present, and which featured not just the dominant black funk and soul of the midseventies, from James Brown to Parliament/Funkadelic, but white acts like the Rolling Stones, Monkees, and Grand Funk Railroad, were hardly going to argue with the additional title he appointed himself along the way: Master of Records.

I n May 1974, the arrival of spring inspired DJ Kool Herc to take his parties outside to Cedar Park, a playground where Sedgwick and Cedar Avenues intersected, at the foot of Bronx Community College, almost right underneath the Major Deegan. As would a whole generation of future New York DJs, he siphoned electricity off a street lamp.

Among those to attend what would become a series of infamous block parties was Joseph "Flash" Saddler. Born in Barbados on New Year's Day, 1958, raised in the Throgs Neck area of the far eastern Bronx, Saddler became obsessed with the rhythm of dance music at an early age. His father brutally beat him, however, for playing with his extensive record collection; Saddler Senior then abandoned the family, which included four daughters as well as the lone son, and when Joseph's mother went into the hospital suffering from mental illness, he and the two youngest girls were placed in foster homes. After repeatedly running away, they were finally sent upstate, to the Greer School, on Hope Farm near Poughkeepsie—and there, for five years between 1966 and 1971, the prepubescent Joseph thrived, losing much of his city accent, learning to trust authority figures and look beyond the color line, and even getting to play disc jockey at the school dances. But if moving to the country was a culture shock, moving back to the Bronx five years later was an even bigger one, especially as his mother, out of the hospital for the time being, had settled on 163rd Street and Fox, a part of the South Bronx where, a 1969 survey determined, only one in twenty people ever lived long enough to die of natural causes.

Embracing the emerging street culture upon his return, Saddler tried his hand at graffiti: his tag was FLASH, the prefix given him by a friend called Gordon, based on their mutual love of the superhero of that name, Saddler's prowess on the track, and his general hyperactivity. But his heart wasn't in graffiti. Nor could he successfully pull the b-boy moves that would give him credibility on the dance floor. Attending Samuel Gompers Vocational Technical High School even farther in the heart of the South Bronx, he pursued instead his fascination with electronics. From a young age, Saddler had been taking devices apart to see how they worked, wondering how to improve on the design in the process. Now, in tenth grade, he took on an assignment to build a tube amplifier from scratch. Walking home from school through streets reduced by arson and abandonment to piles of rubble, armed with wire cutters and a screwdriver, he'd keep his eyes to the ground, looking for parts not just for the tube amp but also for the rest of a stereo system. The day he saw someone dump what was likely a stolen Thorens turntable that they couldn't pawn, he felt like a prospector striking gold.

Flash generally stayed home in the evenings to work on his electronic projects, but, word having spread through the South Bronx, he was determined to catch Herc's outdoor jam that May. He was still blocks from Cedar when he first heard the familiarly pulsating rhythm of "The Mexican," by Babe Ruth. It was the loudest sound he had heard in his life, so powerful that the streetlights were dimming in time to the bass. For Flash, still trying to build his own amp, let alone his own sound system, that alone was a revelation. But there was also the fact that the crowd was several hundred strong— "folks from four to forty, sweating and bouncing, breakin' and popping."

And that music: Herc was playing Motown and other hits for the old folk and the new sophisticated soul for the adult crowd, but when it came to the music for the teens, he was focusing so closely on the breaks, the parts that sent the kids wild, that few people had a clue what songs he was playing. Other than a few recognizable classics, Flash certainly didn't. All he knew was what everyone else knew, too: that if he wanted to hear them again, he'd have to come to a Herc party to do so.

By the summer, Herc had parlayed his street reputation into a club residency, first at the Twilight Zone on Jerome Avenue in his neighborhood, and then at another nearby spot called the Hevalo. Among those who heard him that summer for the first time was Curtis Brown, the future Grandmaster Caz, who recalled, "No one DJ of that time or before that time inspired as many people to come and do that and get involved in that music as Kool Herc. He's the one that the streets flocked to." After his own exposure to Herc, Brown successfully appealed to his mother to release some money his father had left him, so he could buy a DJ system. It took him two days to figure out how to wire the equipment together. By his own admission, he was just a "toy DJ."

To the extent that Flash did not have a decent setup, and was restricted to playing in basements and the occasional house party in the South Bronx, he was also a toy DJ. But at least he knew how to wire equipment together. And with his scientific mind and his love of beats, it didn't take him long to grasp that Herc, though he had the biggest sound system—and reputation— in the Bronx, hadn't learned how to blend the breaks to their fullest potential. For the few crucial seconds that the records overlapped, the dancers would lose their rhythm. Flash believed that there must be a way not only to identify where the breaks started, but also how to switch between them, to keep the beat flowing, keep the b-boys jumping.

There was: in the bigger clubs, especially downtown, DJs used expensive mixers, like the Clubman, that allowed them to cue up the next record in the headphone without the crowd's hearing it. But the Bronx kids couldn't get into the clubs. And even if they knew about such a device, they couldn't afford one anyway. Flash decided to create his own. He purchased a toggle switch, a couple of little preamps, ran bridges between left and right turntables, soldered all the male and female wires together, and Krazy-Glued the toggle switch to the top of the mixer. And it worked. He then used his knowledge of home electronics to develop a fully functioning cross-fade, one that didn't drop volume as you switched channels. And that worked, too. He was in business.

Herc, Flash knew, ruled the southwest Bronx. Bambaataa owned the southeast. That still left a lot of territory in between. Flash and friends, including his b-boy partner E-Z Mike, decided to stake some of it out for themselves. They took their records and their home-soldered sound system down to the park in the Mott Haven Houses at 142nd and Willis, opposite the even larger Patterson Houses. The Casanovas ruled these projects, ex–Black Spades affiliates nowhere near ready to fold into a peaceful organization like the Zulu Nation. There was every chance that they would chase Flash and his friends off their turf, perhaps even confiscate the equipment in the process. But in part because Flash and his friends had no gang association, and especially because of the music they played and the way they played it, they found themselves adopted by the Casanovas instead. It would prove a difficult affiliation to shed, and there were times when the Casanovas started more trouble than they quashed, but with these local "hard rocks" watching their backs, the budding DJs were soon playing "parks"—to the extent they were anything other than urban playgrounds—all over the South Bronx.

In the process, they gained a following, one that included Nathaniel "Danny" Glover and his younger brother Melvin, who went so far as to wear a T-shirt emblazoned FLASH FAN. Nathaniel recalled seeing Flash on "little makeshift turntables and makeshift cueing that he had built himself," playing records "that we never heard before" and mixing them, too. "Before him . . . nobody really had a technique to bring one record in while the other record was going out, for it to be like a uniform thing. And Flash was doing that back in the early '70s. Extremely revolutionary."

But for Flash, blending wasn't enough. Frustrated at the brevity of the break sections, he determined to, as he put it, "figure out a way to do things to the records that the record just should have had." The way that he had taken apart his sisters' electronics to put them back together, now he took two copies of "A Funky Thide of Sings," by the jazz drummer Billy Cobham (a 1975 release), and deconstructed them, going back and forth over the break, visualizing the individual beats. By holding still the waiting record on the slip mat, while the turntable itself spun underneath, he could cut in from the other fader and, assuming he timed the cut correctly, seamlessly mix from one to the other. To do this back and forth *repeatedly*, however—to extend the shortest of breaks as if on a loop—he needed to know, by sight, where the break actually started. He took to marking out start and end positions on the record label—the "clock theory," he called it—with a grease pencil. All this meant manhandling and dirtying the records themselves, breaking a cardinal sin of DJing, which, until now, considered vinyl sacrosanct. Still, he could now quick-mix the same break beat across two turntables ad infinitum. He could even mix *different* break beats against each other. Flash was ecstatic. As far as he was concerned, he'd just reinvented the wheel.

And yet, the first time he tried out his new quick-mix style and clock theory, in the summer of 1975 at an outdoor park, the response was so muted that "it was like a speaking engagement," as he recalled. "A lot of people ridiculed it. They didn't like the idea of it. I was so excited, but just nobody would get it. I cried for a couple of days." Flash was eighteen years old, in the process of becoming a father for the first time, and his ambitions were moving faster than the scene around him. He was in dire need of a break of his own.

Flash found that break in the person of Pete "DJ" Jones, arguably the biggest name on New York City's black music circuit in the mid-1970s. Jones "epitomized the true meaning of a DJ," said the future star rapper Kurtis Blow, who first heard him at the midtown club McCoys in 1972. "He had the precise timing necessary to enable the partygoer to dance nonstop while keeping the break of a record playing continuously."

Jones, a self-confessed "wallflower" yet an imposing six feet eight inches in height, had discovered early on that he was less conspicuous when he sat behind the decks than when he stood up on the dance floor. Like everyone else, he was a James Brown fan, but as he rose to DJ prominence, he embraced acts that took the big band "funk" of the early seventies and softened it into an improvisational form of early disco. Among them were the New York area's own Crown Heights Affair, Fatback Band, Kool & the Gang, Brass Construction—and B.T. (formerly Brooklyn Trucking) Express, whose "Do It Till You're Satisfied," as remixed and extended by Tom Moulton, rose all the way to number four in the pop charts in late 1974. Jones played "Love Is the Message," by MFSB, the anthem of the gay dance floor, yet he also spun some of the tracks that had been claimed by the b-boys in the Bronx, "Bongo Rock" and "Scorpio" among them. He was perhaps the only DJ in New York who could successfully straddle all styles.

In 1974, Jones was thirty years old, at the top of his game, playing all over New York City at venues where the crowd was typically well dressed, in the highly coveted eighteen- to twenty-two-year-old range. Jones secured their loyalty not only through his seamless mixing style but also by traveling with a veritable harem—among them a glamorous assistant, Miss Becky "DJ" Jones—promoting the notion of the DJ as super stud.

Jones held down a day job as a schoolteacher, and he was known, unlike many of the other mobile DJs, for being warm and gracious, a mentor as much as a master. When he met Flash, in the summer of '75, playing a park in the Bronx (for Jones knew as well as anyone else that your popularity in the clubs depended on your popularity in the streets), he took the ambitious but temporarily stalled teenager under his wing. Jones taught the younger DJ not only how to blend his mixes better, but also how to read and react to a crowd, how to give them what *they* wanted rather than just what *he* wanted. Soon enough, Flash found himself employed as Jones's deputy, playing Nell Gwynn's in midtown, the Stardust Ballroom in the Bronx, even boat rides on the Circle Line. It was a crucial education, for it introduced Flash not only to another audience but to a different style of music and a softer style of DJing. He added Philly soul classics like "Do It Any Way You Wanna," by People's Choice, and "(For the Love) I Gave to You," by the Delfonics, to his set. And soon enough, he'd learned how to balance the expectations of a dance floor (whether in a club or a park) with his increasingly acrobatic skills, which now included the remarkable ability to mix behind his back. "Grandmaster Flowers was the best mixing DJ that I ever saw," said Pete "DJ" Jones, giving credit where it was due, but "Flash was the fastest."

In the way of the vocal groups that preceded them on the same Bronx streets by a quarter century, the new generation of aspiring DJs began forming partnerships with friends and acquaintances—then promptly falling out with each other and forming new ones. A central location for all this activity was the spacious home belonging to "Mean" Gene Livingston's family, on Boston Road and 168th, in the heart of an area known as "the 9" for its 169th Street nexus, where Flash resided for a while, storing his system there while partnering with Gene. A younger Livingston brother, Cordie-O, was DJing his own sound system at the time with a local teen, Arthur Hayward, who'd taken up the name Disco Bee. And an even younger brother, Theodore, thirteen years old in 1975, was watching and learning from his older siblings on his way to becoming the first child prodigy of the new DJ scene.

Theodore would join the others on shopping trips to Downstairs Records in midtown, the same store in the 34th Street subway station where the underground discotheque DJs were picking up their music—which partially explains why so many of the same tracks became popular with both the gay crowd *and* the b-boys. Theodore earned himself free 45s by becoming the "wizard" of the Downstairs pinball machine, and at home he practiced relentlessly on the DJ equipment when his brothers weren't around. Whereas Flash needed to mark out the entry and exit points for a break beat on the record label, Theodore somehow memorized the vinyl, to the point that he could drop the needle on the record in exactly the right place as he cut the crossfades. It was like a magic trick. Soon he was giving lessons to Flash, and the two of them took to playing together at "63 Park," on Boston Road and 168th Street. Envious of the attention afforded his kid brother, "Mean" Gene quit.

Then Theodore went one better. Interrupted in midpractice one day in June 1975 by his mother, he found himself absentmindedly "scratching" the waiting record back and forth—but with the volume in that fader turned up. Only when his mother left the room did it dawn on him that the scratching sounded good. So he kept at it. "What I did was give it a rhythm. I made a tune out of it, rubbing it for three, four minutes." Historically, many of the greatest musical innovations came about by accident. Scratching, like the 12-inch single, turned out to be one of them.

The DJ, clearly, was the pied piper of the new Bronx youth culture. But the audience had also become stars of the show: with the DJs initially focused simply on playing the records, the raucous teenagers turned inward to the dance floor, fully engrossed in each other's style. Nothing said "style" as emphatically as b-boying. And so, much as the kids came out to hear Herc, Bambaataa, and then Flash, they also came out to see the local b-boy legends: Keith and Kevin a.k.a. the Nigger Twins, Tricksy, Bumpy Faced Melvin, Monk, Sinbad, Profile, Sau Sau, Flippin' Mike, and dozens more.

A romantic version of b-boying would compare it to the vocal groups of the fifties, who challenged each other to singing contests on the street corners of Harlem and the Bronx. In reality, the b-boys (the initial "b" has, over the years, been accredited by participants to the Bronx, the beat, the break, and the boogie; the first of these seems most likely) took the element of fierce competitiveness from the waning gangs of their elder siblings, reinterpreting their elaborate, provocative war dances to claim their own street reputations, block (party) by block (party). They engaged in "battles." They "burned" each other. And the losers could sometimes get sore about it. "There was a lot at stake," said Jorge "Fabel" Pabon, who as a Puerto Rican was in the minority of b-boys. "Like your whole neighborhood laughing at you."

At the birth of the block parties, the b-boys primarily engaged in what was called "up-rocking" or "top-rocking." As with the Lindy Hop decades earlier—not that the kids themselves were drawing the connection, their major reference point being James Brown—it was about the pace of one's foot movement. (B-boys even danced on their toes.) Gradually the dancers introduced "freezes"—dramatic pauses in acrobatic positions—that served as victory poses to one's fellow crew, and as provocation to their rivals. And as the freezes got ever closer to the ground—the "chair freeze," the "baby freeze"—eventually the dancers took to spinning on the floor, on their backsides, their heads, whatever worked, laying down cardboard beneath them to prevent cuts and bruises. Back in the midseventies, though, the spinning was still a long way from coming into fashion. You were more likely to see the likes of Flippin' Mike, back-flipping his way off a dance floor like a gymnast.

Almost everyone who came into the early 1970s culture considered himself a b-boy. But only the best could lay claim to actual b-boy*ing*. It was a skill, as DJing had become. As MCing would become. And as graffiti was proving itself to be. Many Bronx b-boys were prominent also in developing graffiti as an art form that soon became ubiquitous across the city. Gathering by day at what they called the Writer's Bench at the 149th Street/Grand Concourse station, breaking into subway yards like "the Ghost Yard" opposite De Witt Clinton High in the North Bronx by night, they saw themselves as civil servants, beautifying a city that had essentially run out of the resources to do so itself. STAY HIGH 149 attached a stick character to his tags as early as '71. SUPER KOOL 223 made a point of hitting every train on the IRT in '72. PHASE 2, who dressed as stylishly as he graff'd, helped develop the bubble letters that became dominant in '73, in part by replacing spray can nozzles with larger ones from oven cleaners and the like, making for fatter lettering and thereby bigger images. PISTOL took credit for the emergence of the 3D look in '74. And so on. Ultimately, as in any art form, greatness was secured not by short-term claims but over the long term, by public recognition and respect.

The above artists all came from the Bronx. But the graffiti movement was not founded in the borough, nor did it achieve its initial prominence in the Bronx any more than it did elsewhere. "It had nothing to do with race or age or size or deformity," said LSD-OM, a white kid who began making his mark in 1969, utilizing city property and city property only. "You wrote, you were a part of the culture, and it was beautiful." PHASE 2, even though he ran with Kool Herc in the EX-VANDALS and later designed fliers for the Bronx parties, acknowledged that "headbanging" music was the writers' sound track of choice in the early seventies: graffiti's close association with hip-hop would come only during the second wave, in the very late seventies and early eighties, once it had been embraced by the downtown art scene.

For those Bronx kids who didn't become artists in their own right, graffiti was merely a rite of passage: Herc (CLYDE AS KOOL), Bam (BAM 117 and BOM 117) and Flash (FLASH 163, for his neighborhood block) all tagged before they became DJs—at which point they immediately dropped the habit. But writing in *New York* magazine in the spring of 1973, Richard Goldstein correctly envisioned the long-term perspective. Calling "the graffiti movement . . . a lot like rock 'n' roll in its pre-enlightenment phase . . . the first genuine teenage street culture since the fifties," he predicted, "If all this begins to seem as compelling to middle-class kids as the J.D. [juvenile delinquent] style did twenty years ago, then we are in for some inventive times."

•   •   •

arlem had fallen on its own troubles through the sixties and early seventies, subject to the same rise in social ills as the Bronx: cheap heroin,
teenage gangs, corrupt cops, anonymous arson, violent crime, welfare depen-
dency, and the like. But, steeped in black history as it was (and the South
Bronx was not), there was always an air of militant defiance and social conti-
nuity to the area—as exemplified, in May 1968, by the coming together of
the Last Poets at a party celebrating the birthday of Malcolm X in Mount
Morris Park. By the time the members of the trio issued their eponymous
debut album in 1970, they had honed their delivery, accompanied only by
bongos and other percussion, into a keenly enunciated style, for which they
would later be hailed as godfathers of rap. Certainly, their language would
become common in hip-hop, if only from the mid-eighties onward. The Last
Poets castigated their own people for a tendency to "party and bullshit" on
the track "When the Revolution Comes"; reclaimed the "n" word on "Wake
Up Niggers" and "Niggers Are Scared of Revolution"; made ample use of the
term "faggots"; and on the track "New York New York" raised the ugly specter
of "tiny fat Jews . . . holding a fiery hoop and watching you burn your ass
jumping through it." Aided by the ferocity of its language, *The Last Poets* hit
the top 30 of the album charts, overshadowing the near-simultaneous release
of *Small Talk on 125th Street and Lenox*, on which the poet, novelist, and
now musician Gil Scott-Heron (who had attended high school in the Bronx),
accompanied also by just a bongo player, tackled similar subject matter,
including "The Subject Was Faggots" and the more enduring "The Revolution
Will Not Be Televised."

This new spoken-word "social consciousness" supplied an important part
of Harlem's rhythm in the early 1970s; but it lost the battle for cultural dominance to the pervasive image popularized by *Shaft* and *Superfly*, that of the
pimp and the hustler making serious paper and bedding beautiful ladies, living large in times of need. This was the milieu into which a teenager called
Hollywood was thrust on his way to becoming a living legend, a self-made
celebrity, and a crucial link in the creation of hip-hop.

Born and raised in central Harlem, learning to sing and dance during
"the talent show era . . . when there were a lot of channels for kids," Hollywood
acquired his stage name for his showbiz personality. (His given last name was

Holloway; his first name fell by the wayside.) At the age of fourteen, at the
dawn of the troubled seventies, he dropped out of school, left home, and took
to the streets. "I slept in basements. I slept on rooftops. I scrounged around
through the streets trying to find a source of getting money." He finally
achieved it by going to work for the hustlers in the after-hours clubs. "That
was the world I wanted to be in. They had the cars and money and jewelry
and all that fly stuff."

Having found his support system, Hollywood quickly progressed from
errand boy to "Dancing Doorman" to fifteen-year-old disc jockey at an after-
hours club, Lovely's, on 148th Street and Seventh Avenue, where he would
play whatever music people wanted to hear from "twelve at night until twelve
in the morning," talking over the segues like a radio jock, earning tips from
men and women alike: "I was getting drugs *and* hugs." But upon visiting the
upscale Charles Gallery, on West 125th Street, he discovered another world:
a DJ whose records were *"flowing."* When granted entry into the smoke-
glassed DJ booth, Hollywood understood why: "This guy has got headphones,
and he's listening to the track before it comes live. I had to *chop* my beats in."
Like the kids on the Bronx streets a year or two later, Hollywood had no idea
the cueing system existed until he saw it in action.

He began playing Sunday nights at the Charles. There, "like a kid in a
candy store," he began "singing my conversations. And it's rhyming, so it's just
like song. There was always a little instrumental before the vocals came in.
And I would time those vocals with my conversation so as soon as I finish
talking, the guy is singing." They were simple enough rhymes—"We gonna
overcome 'cause I'm coming at you"—and they weren't well suited to the
sophisticates of the Charles Gallery. Hollywood took up residency instead at
a new bar, the Bunch of Grapes, on the east side of 125th Street. There he'd
start as early as four o'clock in the afternoon, catering to an after-work crowd.
He'd still be there in the early hours, fueled by his "love of the music—and
cocaine."

In 1975, with disco music on its relentless upswing, the Fatback Band
released "(Are You Ready) Do the Bus Stop," popularizing the line dance of
that name, and Van McCoy (who, signed to Leiber and Stoller's Trio Music,
had written hits for the Shirelles in the sixties) recorded a similar dance tie-
in, "Do the Hustle," which promptly went to number one in the pop charts.
Suddenly, as Hollywood said, *"Everyone* was doing the hustle," and there was

plenty of opportunity for a charismatic DJ like himself to show the people how. When invited to bring his microphone skills to Club 371 in the Bronx, he jumped at it.

Located on 166th Street at Teller and Clay, Club 371 was right in the middle of the territory being carved out by Herc, Bam, and Flash, and yet a world removed from the b-boys. Club 371 had Technics turntables, and a sunken dance floor. "It was an adult venue for real," said Hollywood. "No street gear *whatsoever*. Everyone came in there looking good." And it was there that Hollywood made his name, playing Thursdays through Saturdays and soon earning $400 for doing so.

Hollywood at this point was still very much a disco DJ. But when a Puerto Rican teenager called Junebug stepped up as his assistant, bringing some of the Bronx street vibe both to the choice of music and the way it was played, it freed Hollywood to "get on the microphone, step out the booth and get with the people." The DJ and the MC developed a routine, and Hollywood's warm personality, easy flow, and steady way with party rhymes (many of them delivered to exactly the same break beats and disco classics being played all over New York) made him a superstar among black New Yorkers. Kurtis Blow, who'd travel up from Harlem to hear him, called him "the talk of the town." Flash called him "one of the greatest solo rappers that ever there was." And Disco Bee was among those who dressed up to hear him: "He was sending a happy message, doing what he loved. His stuff just clicked. And made you want to party."

"Nobody else was doing it," said Hollywood. "You had guys who were like announcers, and they were controlling the party so to speak, but they had no polish, they had no flair. I brought this polish to the game, I brought this flair to the game. At six in the morning we doing stuff like 'party time is anytime and anytime is party time . . . shit goddamn get off your ass and dance.' Syncopated to the track. So when I said, 'Throw your hands in the air . . .' I'm the first guy coming with that."

If so, there were others following closely in his wake. From the Douglas Houses in Harlem came both Reggie Wells and Eddie Cheeba, another pair of DJs who rapped to the rhythm on the mike. Theirs was a particularly Harlem style—some people called them "R&B DJs"–but when, at Hollywood's request, they followed him to 371 after the venue added a second room, they too had an influence on the Bronx streets.

"Guys like me and Hollywood, Eddie Cheeba, the stuff that we were doing," Reggie Wells told the hip-hop historian Mark Skillz, "at that time, no one else was doing in any club in New York City. I'd say, to me, rap kind of started there, in that club."

Others might have challenged that last assertion. From the beginning, Kool Herc had surrounded himself with MCs, specifically his close friend Coke La Rock, and a team of support DJs, including Clark Kent and Timmy Tim, who also got on the mic. Yet it was enough for them to offer up the occasional phrase—"and yes y'all, the sound that you hear . . ." or a shout-out "to my mellow" (a friend), drenched in the echo that was a Herc trademark. They weren't thinking of rhyming—of *rappin'*, as the term was used to describe an everyday part of black culture that extended back from Harlem's "R&B DJs" to the radio jocks, through to Harlem's Last Poets and Gil Scott-Heron, the boxing boasts of Muhammad Ali, the bebop culture of Dizzy Gillespie, the scat singers like Cab Calloway, the Apollo comics like Pigmeat Markham, back back back via the "dozens" all the way to the African "griots."

As for Bambaataa, he offered up discussion at the Bronx River Houses as he established the Zulu Nation, and some of the words that came over the mic from fellow Zulus took a cadence that could be likened to the Last Poets, as much as to the ministers from the Nation of Islam. But this was something separate from his DJ sets, which were primarily about the turntables.

And Flash, though he liked to write rhymes, was by his own admission "totally wack on the mic." He'd found his talent, and he wasn't about to lose focus. In fact, late in 1975, he'd been likened to a grand chess master for his turntable skills and acts of pure showmanship, and the prefix stuck. (The craze for kung fu, which manifested itself on the dance floor in some early b-boy battle moves, and in the charts with Carl Douglas's "Kung Fu Fighting," also influenced many adopted names.) In the meantime, Flash let members of his growing fan club get on the mic, talking loud and generally saying nothing, until the day that Keith Wiggins—Keith-Keith, as he would be billed, until he started using the street name Cowboy—stepped up to it at 63 Park and essentially made it his own.

"It seemed like he came out of nowhere," said Melvin Glover, the self-anointed "Flash fan." "Suddenly I heard all this yelling, and Cowboy was on the mic telling people, 'Throw your hands in the air, and wave 'em like you just don't care.'"

"It wasn't the thing, talking on the mic," said Disco Bee, who was equally surprised at the sudden presence of Wiggins in their midst. "He just happened; I guess he'd seen somebody do it." If it was DJ Hollywood at Club 371, then Wiggins, who'd grown up a Black Spade in the Bronx River Houses, never let on. But seeing his popularity, the preteen Melvin Glover and his older brother Nathaniel started writing their own rhymes, working up a routine at home, until Flash allowed them to join Keith-Keith for what now became the Three MCs. Nathaniel eventually adopted the name Kid Creole, and the prodigious young Melvin became Mele Mel, taking the Herculords' stock phrase and elaborating upon it: "A yes yes y'all, to the beat y'all."

The Three MCs brought distinct personalities to Flash, Bee, and Mike, who briefly billed themselves as the Terrible Trio to match. Cowboy was the aggressive type known as a "hype man." Creole was smooth. And Mel managed to be both. When Flash played a record like "Bra," by Cymande, the Glover brothers would go into a back-and-forth. One would stop, the other would come in. That one would stop, the first would come back in. But it was Mel, said Flash, who could "get extremely creative with words," and once his attitude and age—he only turned thirteen in May '75—were factored in, that made him the MC everyone watched out for.

Flash appeared to be on a long run of karmic payback for his troubled childhood, as if others, sensing that he was destined for greatness, wanted to be a part of it. The next in a long line of partners and mentors to come his way was Ray Chandler, a heavyweight from a family that, as Flash said, "*nobody* ever messed with." Chandler saw the excitement surrounding Flash and his crew at 63 Park one day—their home spot, the playground at PS 63 in the heart of "the 9"—and, with the winter of 1975–76 kicking in, decided to become their promoter.

"We were going to stay exactly like everybody else until we got Ray Chandler," said Disco Bee. "When he came along, he was like, 'You boys could be BIG!' We were like, 'Yeh yeh yeah, we already tried.' Turned around and he was throwing a flier in our face. Boom! We're playing at this high school. Boom! We're playing at this place. Boom! We got our own club!"

That club was the Black Door (so called because that was the only way to identify it), at Boston Road and Prospect Avenue, just up the road from PS 63, and it quickly became Flash's and the Three MCs' weekend turf. Club 371 was only ten blocks to the west, but the two clubs were virtual opposites—one upmarket, frequented by well-dressed couples in their twenties; the other, in Flash's own word, a "hellhole" where the local b-boy teens, in regulation sneakers and other street wear, came bounding up the street in large gangs, watched over carefully by Ray Chandler's security detail. At 371, the sophisticated R&B DJs from Harlem held court. At the Black Door, the quick-mixing, hard-rapping MCs and DJs of the Bronx ruled the roost. At both clubs, the party would keep going far beyond official closing hours and into the morning.

In the meantime, Herc had taken his parties off the block and into the Webster Avenue Police Athletic League, up near Fordham Road (the latest unofficial border of an ever-expanding South Bronx), restricting admission to the teenagers who were the main audience of the new culture—and most in need of the diversion from the streets. Bam and his Zulu Nation were starting to hire local schools in the evenings for much the same purpose. As more and more teenagers were exposed to the party scene, they formed "crews," composed now not just of DJs but of MCs, break-dancers, and security. Each would plaster its name across uniform T-shirts or jackets, more for the sake of self-promotion than intimidation; the look was a long way removed from the aggressive denim "colors" sported by the gangs they were now slowly replacing.

In the South Bronx, Mean Gene, Cordie-O, and Theodore Livingston teamed up as the L Brothers, added the MC brothers Kevie Kev and Robbie Rob, plus Busy Bee, and became a prominent name, not far behind Flash in popularity. In the North Bronx, closer to Co-Op City, the DJs Breakout and Baron held court as the Brothers Disco, known for their "garbage can" speakers made out of 55-gallon steel drums, and for adding the first female MC to the scene, Sha-Rock, as part of what became the Funky 4. (Sha-Rock even had her own security, the Sisters Disco.) And the all-around b-boy Curtis Brown awarded himself the name Casanova Fly and formed a DJ partnership with Disco Wiz—Luis Cedeño, a Puerto Rican–Cuban teenager who had broken away from the Savage Skulls to become arguably the first Latino DJ to play the streets. As the names of many DJs and their names indicated, the word "disco" had only positive connotations in the Bronx. Far from rebelling against the dominant dance culture, the b-boys (and girls) were joining in as best they knew how, playing many of the same records as were being hammered by DJ Hollywood, Pete "DJ" Jones, and Bobby "DJ" Guttadaro alike.

Not content with being just a DJ, Casanova took to the mic, too. "Everybody's first introduction to MC/rhyming came from these little phrases that we were saying that were just stretched out. You heard somebody's phrase and you said, 'Well, I'm gonna take that phrase to the next level.'" He took his from the 1973 album *Hustlers Convention*, by Jalal Nurridin of the Last Poets under the name Lightnin' Rod. With Kool and the Gang supplying the music, *Hustlers Convention* was near enough a blaxploitation movie/ Iceberg Slim novel brought to rhyme on vinyl, and it set such a high standard that only a brave or foolish youth would try to match it. Casanova Fly fell into both of those camps. "I always turned the music off and said my best shit a cappella, 'cause I didn't want you distracted."

As they developed their own styles, the crews started taping their live sets (or making pause-button tapes at home) and selling the cassettes on the streets. (Taping someone's set without permission, however, was an invitation to a beat-down.) Livery car services like OJ's served as de facto radio stations and distribution centers, playing and selling the tapes as they drove customers to and from parties and clubs. By this method, reputations traversed territorial lines—and via the city's hyperactive high school kids, and the turfless graffiti scene, the sound traveled even farther, to Harlem and beyond. All of which made the DJs into superstars even though they had yet to appear on radio or record: Bambaataa and Flash both recalled being followed around Downstairs Records in the midseventies by "toy" DJs, hoping to pick up the same "exclusive" records.

And so, barely a year after he'd started promoting them, Ray Chandler booked Grandmaster Flash, Disco Bee, and EZ-Mike, and the Three MCs, with the upcoming Herc fan Kool DJ AJ in support, into the Audubon Ballroom, on Broadway between 165th and 166th Streets, just across the Harlem River from the Bronx. This was the room where Malcolm X had been assassinated, and it could hold three thousand people. The booking was audacious; arrogant, even. Flash and Bee had to borrow giant speakers known as the Refrigerators from a Jamaican sound system to pump up the room. (They'd already commissioned their own enormous amplifier, the Gladiator, from the same crew. It was so heavy it took two people to carry it.) The night started perilously slow, just a few hundred people in the ballroom by midnight, and Flash vacated the building, afraid that he had overplayed himself. When he returned, the Audubon was overflowing, the floor literally heaving up and down. With no radio ads, nothing but fliers and word of mouth, Flash and his crew had drawn almost three thousand people.

That night, as every night, Keith-Keith got on the mike and struck up a rhyme he'd introduced when he first joined Flash, Bee, and Mike. It had originally come into play at block parties on Tinton and 165th, by the Forrest Houses, with Cowboy playing drill sergeant on a friend from the 'hood who was heading into the Army. The friend soon left for the service, but the phrase stuck:

"The hip, hop, the hibby, the hop the hop the hop, hibby dibby hibby dibby dibby dibby, hip hop. . . ."

17
WELL, NEW YORK CITY REALLY HAS IT ALL . . .

New Year 1977 blew in to New York with the city's typical penchant for overstatement, bone-chilling temperatures turning outdoor celebrations into a battle against the elements. At the Bethesda Fountain in Central Park, Debbie Harry dressed in a silver miniskirt over thermal underwear and took to a snowy Parks Department stage alongside the four other members of Blondie. As the clock struck twelve—and with the thermometer reading just fifteen degrees Fahrenheit—four men dressed as eight-foot-tall "Hands of Time" marched down the staircase by the fountain, illuminated by giant klieg lights, and the group launched into Booker T. & the MGs' "Time Is Tight." In front of the stage, a thousand-plus partygoers roared their approval. Via the Joel Siegel show, countless more watched on television. The group was paid $500 for the appearance, far and away the biggest sum it had ever earned. Blondie's prospects were looking up.

Yet as their debut album made its way around America, the group found itself running into the same wall of resistance at radio as had the Ramones. Something about groups from the Lower East Side seemed to strike fear (of change?) into the hearts of the nation's music directors. Elsewhere in the world, however, people heard Blondie for what they were: a back-to-basics rock group in love with pure pop. In Australia, a Bob Gruen–filmed promotional clip for "In the Flesh" (the B-side to "X-Offender") made it onto national television, propelling the single to number two in their national charts. It was on the other side of the earth from the U.S.A., admittedly, but nobody could now claim that the CBGBs bands were noncommercial.

Nor were they trying to be. For the Ramones' second album, Sire Records hired Tony Bongiovi, the producer behind Gloria Gaynor's disco hit "Never Can Say Goodbye." Not surprisingly, *Leave Home* was emphatically more polished than the band's debut—but to Bongiovi's credit, the sheen was not at the expense of velocity. As for the songs, they were of equally high quality; in fact, they were of very similar subject matter and substance (abuse). But to accuse the Ramones merely of repeating themselves would be to miss the point. Who else would have reacted to the storm surrounding "Now I Wanna Sniff Some Glue" by then writing "Carbona Not Glue," in honor of a patented brand of household cleaner? And who could not appreciate the blunt honesty of the album's opening track, a flip-off from Dee Dee to his girlfriend Connie Gripp—the same one who nearly hacked off the thumb of Arthur Kane of the Dolls—called "Glad to See You Go"? Still, lacking the novelty of the debut to justify fresh press attention, *Leave Home* failed to exceed its predecessor's sales.

By comparison, Television (with the album *Marquee Moon*) and Talking Heads (the single "Love -> Building on Fire") were seen as something new, and both were received warmly by the domestic and the international music press alike. In early 1977, John Rockwell noted of the flood of releases from CBGBs groups that, "by any logical criterion, the current New York rock scene is a movement," and no one thought to disagree. That May, Television took Blondie along to the United Kingdom, where, thanks in large part to a ludicrously effusive review in Britain's *New Musical Express*, *Marquee Moon* had broken into the higher reaches of the album charts. And the Ramones returned to Europe for a headlining tour, taking their Sire label mates—and proven friends—Talking Heads along for the ride.

Prior to embarking on that tour, the Ramones recorded a new single: "Sheena Is a Punk Rocker." It was the *third* song—following "Judy Is a Punk" and "Suzy Is a Headbanger"—to explore a seemingly thin theme. But when Joey Ramone played it to Seymour Stein, the Sire boss recognized that it had honed the Ramones' message to the sharpest point yet. Responding with an urgency befitting his Brill Building past, he insisted the group record it immediately. "Sheena" took all the individual components that made the Ramones so exciting—the surf influence, the wall of sound, the handclaps, the vocal harmonies, the sing-along chorus, but also the buzz-saw guitars, the British invasion attitude, the relentless street drive—and wove them into an irrepressible whole. True to the Ramones' style, the initial line adapted a lyric from an earlier song, in this case the debut album's opening anthem, "Blitzkrieg Bop," and then turned it into a memorable adage to the eternal energy of youth culture: "Well, the kids are all hopped up and ready to go." The Ramones were rewarded for their repetitiveness in the United Kingdom—where "punk" was a dirty word to some, but also a confirmed national music trend—with a top 40 single, the first there for any of the new New York acts.

On May 29, as "Sheena" climbed the charts, the Ramones (and Talking Heads) could be found playing at a pub on the outskirts of south London called the Greyhound. Across London, Television and Blondie filled the 3,000-seat Hammersmith Odeon. And back in New York, Patti Smith was embarking on a fresh residency at CBGBs. Her second album, *Radio Ethiopia*, credited to the Patti Smith Group and released late in 1976, had proven less palatable to public and critics alike—not, as in the Ramones' case, because it was too similar to its predecessor but perhaps because it was too different. Loaded with reggae rhythms, an improvised ten-minute title track, and at least one controversial song title, "Pissing in the River," it lacked the imagination that had rendered *Horses* so distinctive.

Then, in January 1977, opening for the mainstream rock artist Bob Seger in a Florida arena, Smith worked herself up into her usual frenzy performing *Radio Ethiopia*'s "Ain't It Strange," and inadvertently tripped over a floor monitor—falling fourteen feet off the front of the stage and breaking two vertebrae in her neck. Smith later attributed her fall to a warning from God—as if, in her shamanistic performances and growing sense of creative self-importance, she had overstepped her earthly boundaries. But if so, she had a funny way of showing it: her return to the stage at CBGBs took place on Easter Sunday, three years after she and Kaye first walked in to the club to see Television. She entitled the performance "La Resurrection."

The South Bronx started the new year of 1977 in a media glare of its own—though not the kind, like that afforded the CBGBs scene, to attract tourists. On January 3, PBS television hosted *The Police Tapes*, a documentary film by Alan and Susan Raymond, the same couple behind the groundbreaking "reality" series *An American Family*. The ninety-minute *Police Tapes* followed officers of the 44th Precinct in the western section of the South Bronx—DJ Kool Herc's territory. "It's like a flowing river and all the garbage is flowing on down through it," said one disheartened cop, in the company of the camera crew, and the events captured on video made for a harrowing viewing experience, for *The Police Tapes* portrayed gang, domestic, and criminal violence in all its ugly and brutal mundaneness; in 1977, sudden death was, statistically, a daily part of the 44th's routine. Two corpses were shown: one, stabbed to death, was surrounded, almost casually, by bystanders when the police showed up. Chief Tony Bouza, the Bronx borough commander, quoted Greek philosophers as he admitted that he was "almost . . . the commander of an army of occupation in the ghetto." And then, noting that there had been no redistribution of wealth in America in thirty years, and embarking on an unusually detailed discourse about the nation's social ills, Bouza wondered aloud whether he might not be better off failing. "That way," he said, "America would be confronting the problem as it had to do during the urban riots of the sixties." He would soon get his wish.

The 44th Precinct's beat—specifically, the Highbridge area—returned to the television screens just a couple of months later in the CBS television special *The Fire Next Door*, which focused on the westward-spreading arson epidemic, finally recognized as such at least a decade after it had begun. The reporter Bill Moyers strove for optimism, especially when he focused on the mainly Puerto Rican homesteaders of the People's Development Corporation, who had taken over an abandoned building on Washington Avenue at 168th Street and, with minimal funding, turned it into a grassroots example of urban renewal. But the general dereliction of the South Bronx—both as a functioning society and a physical neighborhood—was brutally displayed during a street-side interview with Mrs. Sullivan, an Irish woman on Davidson Avenue. Sullivan was moving out after thirty-eight years, the last few spent as the frequent victim of muggings and thefts, a point proven when her tormentors seized the opportunity of her TV interview to burglarize her apartment. After the police arrived and the camera crew followed them upstairs, Mrs. Sullivan started sobbing. So too, no doubt, did many viewers. On March 20, just two days before the CBS special was broadcast, the New York State Assembly had voted overwhelmingly to establish a new crime, "victimizing the elderly." Here, already, was their poster lady.

The young thugs and arsonist landlords were certainly a fixture of the South Bronx. Yet so were the local b-boys and girls, and they went entirely unnoticed by both documentaries, even though the Washington Avenue homestead stood in the midst of, and just a few blocks from, Club 371, the Black Door, "63 Park," the Dixie, and Herc's various residencies on Jerome Avenue. In the middle of horrific inner-city conditions, a new youth culture was trying to turn back the cycle of violence, crime, gangs, and drugs, but the media did not appear to know that it existed. Grandmaster Flash later summed up this contradiction for his generation: "People had their own negative version of what the Bronx was: that was home for me."

The world of disco changed irrevocably on April 26, with the opening of Studio 54. In retrospect, it was inevitable. The disco scene had been receiving simply too much media attention, was making too much money, presented too attractive an investment. Someone was bound to try and launch the discotheque to end them all.

That this "someone" turned out to be the partnership of Steve Rubell and Ian Schrager was also far from surprising, given their backstory. Rubell, slobbish and hyperactive, had set out in 1971 borrowing money from his parents to launch a "Steak Loft" family restaurant on Long Island, wheeling and dealing until he owned half a dozen of them. Schrager, whose father, Louis, a close associate of the mobster Meyer Lansky, had left him a trust fund, opted for a lower profile. The partners were best known for the Enchanted Garden, a discotheque they'd created in a mansion, on a golf course, on the border of Queens and Nassau County. There, working on the dictum that if you spend money, the money will follow, they hired Paul Casella, Queens' most popular DJ via his long stint at the Monastery, Nicky Siano (who laid claim to a brief affair with Rubell), and persuaded the Peruvian-born former Loft baby Carmen D'Alessio to sprinkle some of her promotional magic over Queens. Their investment paid off when *Newsweek* took a break from the presidential election in November 1976 to run a cover story entitled "The Disco Whirl"—and used one of D'Alessio's elaborate weekly theme nights at the Enchanted Garden as its lead.

So when D'Alessio brought Rubell and Schrager to a fifty-year-old opera house and former CBS television studio on West 54th Street, the pair immediately saw the possibilities. Nobody had yet opened a Manhattan discotheque in something so grand as a theater, but the ongoing success of Le

Jardin, Hollywood, and Infinity in midtown only increased the stakes. To help finance the refurbishing, Rubell and Schrager brought in a third partner, the discount liquor retailer Jack Dushey, who invested $333,000 through his construction company. Carmen D'Alessio stayed very much involved as their promoter.

The formula for Studio 54 followed that of the Enchanted Garden, suitably ramped up for Manhattan. D'Alessio was given a blank check to hire the most expensive decorators, florists, and furnishers she could find. Richard Long, who had designed equipment for the Loft among other downtown parties, was hired to install the sound. Richie Kaczor, erstwhile of Hollywood, was brought in as primary DJ, and Siano, still working weekends at his Gallery on Houston Street, as weekday relief.

Thanks in part to D'Alessio's extraordinary access to the A-list and the press that covered them, opening night was a major triumph. The *Daily News* reported that Tennessee Williams, Margaux Hemingway, and Cher were among those seen inside; just as important, it noted that the actors Robert Duvall, Michael Douglas, and Warren Beatty gave up standing in the outdoor drizzle, hoping to be admitted, and went home. The *New York Times* correspondent commented likewise, with words that spoke directly to Steve Rubell's credo: "A surprisingly large number of patrons milling around the entrance chose to wait, apparently on the theory that any place that hard to get into must be worth waiting for."

None of the newspapers mentioned the music. Nor did they do so a week later, when D'Alessio hosted Bianca Jagger's birthday party and staged a Lady Godiva routine, in which a buck-naked beauty entered the club on a white horse—after which Mick Jagger's wife gamely rode around the dance floor a few times for the benefit of the paparazzi. That spectacle made the front page *and* the center pages of the *Daily News*, and with it began the nightly routine of the velvet ropes, Steve Rubell guarding the entrance as if it was his personal fiefdom (which, essentially, it was). With the equally pitiless Marc Benecke serving as full-time guardian of the guest list, Studio 54 invented a new disco pastime. It was called "getting in," and it could easily take up half of one's night out.

To be fair, Studio 54 ensured that, for those who met the criteria, the wait was worthwhile, with an assault on the senses more akin to that of a circus than that of a disco. The man in the moon and his coke spoon; the

outlandishly—and often barely—dressed dancers of both sexes and all per-
suasions in between; the shirtless bartenders; the casual carnal activity on
the balcony; the celebrity shoulder rubbing. Given that New York had yet to
emerge from its fiscal bankruptcy, that crime continued to rise alarmingly,
and that fear ruled the outer borough streets as the "Son of Sam" serial killer
struck with apparent impunity, then Studio 54 represented either the last
days of the Roman Empire or a phoenix rising from the ashes. Or, very possibly, both at once.

Studio 54 was never about the common man: though Rubell talked often
of his door policy as "tossing the salad," he admitted mostly flamboyant and/
or famous individuals (the kind known by a single name: Andy, Truman,
Halston, etc.) peppered by just enough free-spending nobodies and ascend-
ing beauties to spread the false myth of the club as a meritocracy. He also
heralded a new kind of club land proprietor, one who frequently showed up
in the DJ booth to make requests and otherwise dictate the night's musical
direction. Richie Kaczor did his best to break new music, but to the extent
that the crowd came to dance, it was to the disco sounds that they already
knew, and in the summer of 1977 that meant the autoerotic techno blueprint
"I Feel Love" by Donna Summer, the luscious "Native New Yorker" by
Odyssey, the increasingly in-demand Bee Gees.

The formula was a moneymaker. "The profits are astronomical," Russell
told *New York* magazine late in 1977. "Only the Mafia does better." In an
interview of astonishing hubris, he elaborated, "It's a cash business and you
have to worry about the IRS," then added, almost as a taunt, "I don't want
them to know everything." Sure enough, at the end of 1978, a federal raid on
the office yielded several hundred thousand dollars in cash, much of it hidden in the office ceiling, a crime of tax evasion for which both Schrager and
Rubell would ultimately serve jail time. After being taken over by a more
orthodox businessman in 1981, Studio 54 continued to prove profitable for
owner, habitués, and paparazzi alike, basking in its glow as the world's most
famous (if no longer most exclusive) discotheque until it finally shut up shop
in 1986.

The denizens of New York's original disco scene took Studio 54's arrival in
stride. There was quite enough going on below Houston Street to keep

them busy, and much of it revolved around Larry Levan. The former "Loft baby" and Gallery regular had been drawn back downtown from the Continental Baths, first to DJ at the sound designer Richard Long's "SoHo Place" parties on lower Broadway, then to a former dairy factory named for its location on Reade Street, in a thinly populated area south of SoHo (the future Tribeca). Spinning inside Reade Street's giant refrigerator turned dance floor, where the parties were often fueled by a newly discovered empathetic/hallucinogenic drug called MDA, Levan established himself as a musical force to be reckoned with among the black gay set. So when Reade Street was closed as a fire trap (the vast refrigerator's only exit was its entrance), the promoter Michael Brody, himself a former but much older Loft regular, hurried to find another location.

He discovered it in a garage on King Street, just west of SoHo, where another disco had recently failed. Setting up quarters for himself in the building, Brody bought Larry Levan's loyalty to the project by inviting the DJ, now dating David DePino, to live above the (fully functional street-level) garage while they turned it into a vast club. A sarcastic DePino opined how it would one day be "paradise," and the club had its name: Paradise Garage.

The Garage took the membership policy of the decade's earlier parties to an extreme; it subjected applicants to a formal interview, at which heterosexuals stood at distinct disadvantage. ("That I never understood," said David Mancuso, who saw the Garage as his Loft writ large. "What happened to Stonewall? Why does it matter if I'm straight or gay?") The Garage never served alcohol, allowing its parties to start in the wee hours of the morning and end in the early afternoon. And rather than advertising the venue publicly, Brody chose to announce and partly finance Paradise Garage with a series of "Construction Parties," the first of which was held in early 1977. Step by step, the patrons, mostly black and gay, watched the vast garage converted from a dance floor full of sawdust and hay into a sophisticate's dream. (Eventually, a lighted runway ramp would lead up from the garage ground level into a complex complete with movie theater, changing rooms, a kitchen, and a Buddha room.) Involvement in the club's development ensured a relationship that, for its members, went much deeper than paying annual dues.

The music firing up the construction parties at the Garage remained intentionally underground. There was Salsoul's first lady of disco, Loleatta

Holloway, especially Walter Gibbons's remix of her single "Hit and Run"; the French male singer Cerrone's fifteen-minute anthem "Love in C Minor"; the Jamaican-born model Grace Jones's "I Need a Man," as produced by Tom Moulton; and Moulton's epic remix of "Love Is the Message" for a *Philadelphia Classics* album that put the MFSB instrumental right back up there as the most enduring anthem of them all.

Levan became a legend at the Garage not so much for his mixing skills as for the way he used the EQs and other effects on the individual records, and for working the audience with similar command, according to his (volatile) moods. His ability to manipulate physical space, ambient temperature, and audience temperament—those intangibles that so drastically influence a night's popularity—was second to none. So was Levan's capacity to spike the (free) punch with the perfect amount of LSD or MDA, enough to render his followers mildly euphoric, but never overly ecstatic; he would take care of that from the turntables.

In almost every way, Paradise Garage served as the anti–Studio 54. "There were no cameras allowed in the Garage," said David DePino. "No clocks, you never knew the time; there were no mirrors, you could never see yourself. We always felt that if you were dancing intensely to a song and you were sweaty and you were all caught up in it and you looked at yourself in a mirror, you would say, 'Oh my God I look like a nut,' and you would maintain yourself. The floor wasn't air-conditioned, people changed their clothes in the dressing room two or three times a night. Because people really *got down and danced.*" Studio 54 could lay claim to being the most famous club of them all, but Paradise Garage enjoyed a reputation among those who experienced it as the greatest. It would stay open until 1987.

The evening of Wednesday, July 13, 1977, Casanova Fly and Disco Wiz set up their equipment at a park just off the Grand Concourse in the Bronx. It was midweek, so there was little likelihood of a bigger name playing in the 'hood. But school was out, and an oppressive heatwave had just descended on the city, which made for a sizable if possibly volatile audience. The pair hot-wired up to the streetlights as usual and set about rocking the park. Just after 9:30 p.m., while Caz was working the break beat on DC Larue's "Indiscreet" disco 12-inch, the streetlights went out—and as they did so, the turntable ground to a halt. Seconds later, a bodega gate slammed down—loudly—and people started shouting, "Blackout!"

There had been a blackout across the whole of the Northeast back in 1965, but it had taken place in November, when the weather was cold, and at a time of day when many people were still at work. Power was maintained sporadically in different parts of the city, and the blackout lasted only twelve hours. This time was different. It was midsummer. School was out. It was hot as hell. It was already late at night, storeowners had gone home, and many people who didn't have air-conditioning—just about anyone who was poor—were "cooling" themselves on the street. And a lot had happened in New York since 1965: entire neighborhoods had turned into ghettos. People were no longer so peaceful, so patient, so positive—or pleasant.

Out on Valentine Avenue, bottles started to shatter as crowds formed and people ran in all directions. Disco Wiz, the former Savage Skull, drew his .45 to protect the sound system. Run *that* way, he screamed at the crowd, and that's what they did. Within minutes, the six lanes of the Grand Concourse were filled with people looking for action. It was as if someone had released the valve on the pressure cooker of South Bronx living. On Jerome Avenue, just west of Grand Concourse, a crowd smashed the plate-glass windows at the Pontiac dealership, and by 11:00 p.m., less than ninety minutes after the blackout had begun, fifty-five brand-new cars had been driven right off the lot and into the night.

By the time the lights came back on—some twenty-five hours after they went out—looters had inflicted so much devastation on the South Bronx that it was as if they'd been competing with the preceding decade of arson. The Fire Department dealt with 307 fires in the borough during the blackout, 14 of them "all-hands" alarms. Of the 473 Bronx stores looted, one-fifth were set ablaze for good measure. And unlike previous riots in New York, those sparked by racial tensions with the police, black-owned businesses were not spared the wrath of a mob that included housewives, retirees, and children as well as the predictable stickup kids and gangbangers. Everything from diapers to sneakers, televisions to washing machines, had been considered fair game.

Some thirty other poor neighborhoods across New York City reported disturbances during the blackout. Other than the South Bronx, the hardest hit was Bushwick, the heart of black Brooklyn suffering its own wave of arson and degradation. (Harlem also exploded, though the Apollo did not have to worry about protecting itself: the hallowed venue had closed in early 1976, after a shooting death in one of its boxes during a show.) New York City, which seemed to have returned from the brink a year earlier with the bicentennial celebrations and the hosting of the Democratic National Convention, revealed itself that long July night to be just one power outage from the abyss.

Close to a thousand people were arrested in the Bronx. Caz was not among them, even though he admitted to looting. Out with the throng on the Grand Concourse, he saw a crowd descend on a store called the Sound Room, using sheer force of numbers to break the locks on the gates. He joined in, crawled under the gate, and emerged with a Clubman 2, near enough the top mixer of its day. "That was all I really wanted," he justified, thirty years later. "You couldn't just say, 'I want to be a DJ.' You needed equipment."

And Caz was hardly alone. "Before that blackout," said his partner Disco Wiz, "we had literally just four to five legitimate DJ crews. The very next day, there sprung this whole revolution of DJs. That was a huge spark and a huge contribution to the hip-hop culture."

The blackout proved the final undoing of Mayor Beame; the seventy-one-year-old former comptroller was revealed to be lacking the decisive leadership the public desperately needed. Even the arrest of David Berkowitz—the "Son of Sam"—in early August, though it helped put a troubled public's mind at rest, failed to save him. Beame lost out in September's Democratic mayoral primary, along with the Studio 54 "patrons" Bella Abzug and Percy Sutton, to two relative upstarts: Congressman Ed Koch, and New York's secretary of state, Mario Cuomo. The tough-talking Koch, born in the South Bronx back in the twenties, when Morrisania was still heavily Jewish, campaigned on the streets as a pragmatic Democrat eager to reinstall the death penalty in the face of New York's continued crime rise, and it made a difference. By early October, having handily won the runoff against Cuomo, it was all but certain that Koch would become the city's next mayor.

. . .

The fall of 1977 saw a further flood of releases from the CBGBs' set, the final graduation, if you like, of the rock 'n' roll high school's students. Blondie released *Plastic Letters*, produced this time by Richard Gottehrer alone, and embarked on a grueling six-month world tour that took them to Australia and South Asia as well as across America and Europe. A spirited cover of "Denise," a top ten hit for the Queens doo-wop group Randy and the Rainbows back in 1963 (rewritten as the gender-appropriate "Denis"), rose to number two in the United Kingdom pop charts. The album's success elevated Debbie Harry to the status of superstar pinup in many territories, and though there was no suggestion (as yet) of an American hit single, still *Plastic Letters* reached the top 75 of the U.S. album charts.

The Ramones went even better when they released their third album in November. Produced and engineered by the *Leave Home* team of Bongiovi, Erdelyi, and Ed Stasium, and once more sticking with fourteen short songs of familiar lyrical content, *Rocket to Russia* represented the culmination of everything the group had been working toward. Aided by the inclusion of "Sheena Is a Punk Rocker" (re-recorded for the album) and "Swallow My Pride" (another UK hit), it proved something of an American breakthrough, yielding top 100 single success in America for "Sheena," for the tongue-in-cheek tribute to the decaying Queens hangout "Rockaway Beach," and for the cover of Bobby Freeman's rock 'n' roll classic "Do You Wanna Dance?" Backed by heavy touring, *Rocket to Russia* even broke into the top 50 of the American album charts. Almost universally, it would be acclaimed as the pinnacle of an impressively stubborn fourteen-album career.

As crisp and clean as a freshly ironed button-down shirt, 77—as Talking Heads named their debut album, in honor of that momentous year—was everything everybody had hoped for from the group: artful, tuneful, danceable. Intellectual, too, with song titles like "First Week/Last Week . . . Carefree" and "Tentative Decisions," accompanied by a lyric sheet that, compared with that of the Ramones, read like Tolstoy. Still, Talking Heads could be as dry as their Sire label mates: hearing David Byrne sing, "Some civil servants are just like my loved ones / They work so hard, and they try to be strong," on "Don't Worry about the Government," it was hard to be certain of sarcasm. Byrne's detached perspective reached a zenith of icy cool on "Psycho Killer," a song that been written long before "Son of Sam" terrified New Yorkers, though its timing as a summer single—complete with "run run run run run run away . . ." chant—could hardly have proven more apposite.

Byrne's voice, that fragile yelp now quite captivating, and his lyrics, clearly the work of a gifted prose writer, propelled him to the front of the group in the public's eye. And yet nobody could listen closely to 77 without hearing it as a group effort, Tina Weymouth's melodic funk bass lines wedded to Chris Frantz's incisive drums (in more ways than one: the couple got married that summer), with Jerry Harrison's additional guitar work and keyboard parts adding the necessary gloss. 77 had been a difficult album to record: the producer Tony Bongiovi was enjoying a number one single that summer with his disco mix of the *Star Wars* movie theme, and he projected his desire for hits upon a group that, in Frantz's words, "were so far removed from thinking like that." Commercial success would ultimately have to wait, but only a little longer: a cover version of Al Green's "Take Me to the River" became an AM hit the following year.

By comparison, *Blank Generation*, the debut album from Richard Hell & the Voidoids, as he had named his new group after leaving the Heartbreakers in 1976, received a more muted response. (The Heartbreakers had released their own LP, the ragged *L.A.M.F.*, on the British label Track earlier in '77, and broke up soon after.) Richard Gottehrer's production didn't help: his pop instincts, so effective with Blondie, jarred with the Voidoids' artistic impulses, and compared to Byrne's unschooled but endearing voice, Hell's guttural shouts and screams grated more than they soothed. There was also the issue of image. Hell graced the album sleeve in shades and torn shirt, a look he had perfected several years back—but what was once innovative had, thanks in part to the spread of British punk, already become something of a cliché. All this was a shame, given Hell's literary skills and the underlying quality of so many songs—not just the title track, which in more appropriately primitive form had been recorded and released as a single, a year earlier, on Terry Ork's label, but those like "Love Comes in Spurts" and "Down at the Rock 'n' roll Club." After another album with the Voidoids, Hell would quit music and return to writing, reclaiming his reputation as a poet and becoming a novelist, too.

As evidence that New York's various scenes did not exist in isolation from one another, the tireless Marty Thau secured funding for his latest venture, Red Star Records, from Marvin Schlacter, a former Specter and Chess executive who simultaneously launched his own highly influential independent disco label, Prelude. Thau immediately signed Suicide, the act he had first seen at the Mercer Arts Center some five years earlier. This was a brave move: by their front man Alan Vega's admission, Suicide remained "the rotten apple of all the bands in the basket." Nor were they easy to record: Martin Rev's keyboard, drum machine, and effects all ultimately emanated from one amplifier, leaving nothing to mix. To compensate, the producer Craig Leon introduced "dub" techniques he had learned from a recent session in Jamaica with Lee "Scratch" Perry, running effects through the console at the same time as the duo were playing. Schlacter was initially disappointed by the results, citing the importance of the bottom end for the disco market. Thau took the tapes and remixed them as best he could, given the nature of the original recordings; he and Leon eventually split the difference and shared the production credits.

Released in December 1977, *Suicide* was never going to be a hit on the disco floor, but still it set a new standard in electronic music for its incongruous mixture of rhythmic groove and lyrical grime. Nothing like it had ever come out of New York City—the late sixties synthesizer pioneers Silver Apples sounded positively commercial by comparison, the Fugs suitably comedic, and though the Godz certainly rivaled for sheer effrontery, even that act had never abandoned guitars and drums. To do so, especially as part of a celebrated new "rock" scene, was "blasphemy," Vega admitted—and it provoked riots when Suicide opened for the Clash and Elvis Costello in Europe. Songs like "Cheree" and "Girl" were, in fact, perfectly commercial, but nothing, it was true, prepared the listener for "Frankie Teardrop," on which Vega's improvised account of a factory worker who, laid off and evicted, killed his family and then himself, was accompanied by some of the most bloodcurdling screams ever committed to record. Though it struggled for immediate attention given its markedly independent status, *Suicide* would prove just as influential, in its own way, as *Horses*, *The Ramones*, and *Marquee Moon*: it would ultimately be hard to imagine the next decade's electronic pop, industrial, and dance music, especially the proliferation of synth-pop duos, without it.

•   •   •

The world of disco changed irrevocably—for the second time that year—with the launch of *Saturday Night Fever* in December. For this, the movie of his *New York* magazine essay, Nik Cohn's fictitious character Vincent was reimagined as Tony Manero and—of course—given a love interest (a curiously cold and older woman), with whom he set about training to win a dance contest at 2001 Odyssey. (The movie was shot at the original Bay Ridge club, though a lighted dance floor was laid down for additional glitz.) All this provided the necessary cinematic opportunities for John Travolta, as Manero, to hustle, bus stop, and otherwise boogie across the floor in his polyester pants and wide-collar shirts, launching a lucrative business (for others) in disco dancing instruction along the way. Elsewhere on the screen, Cohn's original profile of the Bay Ridge weekend ritual remained largely intact. The Italian "Faces" were just as misogynist and racist on film as in print, helpless to control their working-class destinies and therefore resigned to making the most of them, running in increasingly enclosed circles of wanton hedonism.

By concentrating on these Hollywood clichés of youth culture, *Saturday Night Fever* had more in common with *American Graffiti* and *Rebel without a Cause* than with the Manhattan disco scene—and that, of course, aided its popularity in the American heartland, where most of the *thirty million* double album soundtrack sales were registered on the way to its becoming the biggest-selling album ever, up to that point. (Often decried for its domination by the Bee Gees, *Saturday Night Fever* nonetheless included authentic disco/R&B acts like the Tavares, Kool & the Gang, Yvonne Elliman, the Tramps, K.C. & the Sunshine Band, and even MFSB.) Average American teenagers and twenty-somethings, after all, could not contemplate gaining entry to Studio 54, nor did they care to imagine themselves inside a gay club, but they could easily envision their own 2001 Odyssey—especially as, by late 1977, every hotel operator and bar owner in the country appeared to have converted his quarters into precisely such a space.

The Abbatiellos were among them: an Italian family of shopkeepers and bar and nightclub owners who sat down to watch *Disco Fever*, a television special celebrating the movie's world premiere, and seized on those words as the long-overdue name for a new nightspot they were days away from opening. But there was one major difference between the Abbatiellos' club and all the other Italian-flavored, John Travolta–influenced, Bee Gees–dominated discos that opened around the country in 1977: Disco Fever was located in the South Bronx.

For the Abbatiellos, this was merely business as usual. Al Abbatiello had run a bar on 149th Street and Third Avenue until he was "the only white person in the neighborhood," as his son Sal recalled, at which point he partnered with the black owner of a similarly hard-hit business and, in 1969, opened the aptly named Salt and Pepper Lounge on 168th and Jerome, catering for an older, sophisticated jazz crowd. (He also owned two clubs on Pelham Parkway catering to a white, Italian crowd.) Abbatiello launched Disco Fever, on Jerome at 167th Street, with a Latino DJ playing commercial dance music, hoping to draw the older discotheque dancers. But it was only at the end of each weekend night, when the decks were passed over to a local black kid, George "Sweet Gee" Godfrey, that the crowd got energized, readily following Gee's call to "Wave your hands in the air . . . like you just don't care." Gee struck up a friendship with Abbatiello's twenty-something son, Sal, leading him around the parks and block parties of the South Bronx. Sal went back to his father and told him, "These kids talk over the music, mix the records back and forth, and I've never seen no white kids do anything like this," and said that they should angle Disco Fever accordingly. He was eventually given permission to book such an act—on a Tuesday.

Sal set his mark on the biggest name in the Bronx, Grandmaster Flash, who laughed him off when he heard the fee that Abbatiello had in mind. But then he rethought. Hauling a sound system around the streets to do battle was getting tiresome, his prior residencies at the Black Door and the Dixie had come and gone, and it wasn't as if he had any more lucrative offers for a Tuesday night. He eventually took the booking—and, on the back of a few fliers and word of mouth, six hundred people showed up.

Within weeks, Disco Fever had become the first true b-boy nightclub. "When you stumble onto a movement, if you run with it, something big is going to happen," said Abbatiello, speaking to the same first principle of club management that made Hilly Kristal so successful with CBGBs. Welcoming the teenagers who couldn't get into Club 371 a few blocks away, Abbatiello recognized that they formed part of a new culture. "It had a certain type of dress, a certain type of air about the people, the way they walked, the type of music they were playing. You just saw that it could attract thousands of people."

In time, Disco Fever attracted as resident DJs, on different nights of the week, Love Bug Starski, Reggie Wells, Eddie Cheeba—and JuneBug, breaking from Hollywood to become a DJ in his own right. (Hollywood admitted that hubris prevented him from joining the team, and that the scene passed him by in the process.) Afrika Bambaataa never played, but somewhere around the time that he first hired Grandmaster Flash, who came to "set [his] watch by Tuesday nights," Abbatiello employed Kool DJ Herc. He was disappointed. "Herc was just playing records. Whereas Flash had like five people around him all rapping on the mike. It was a much wilder scene with Flash than with Herc."

Herc was the originator. Without him, there might never have been this thing they were all about to call hip-hop. But he had not kept up with the times. He refused to study the art of beat mixing and blending, even as every kid who'd worshipped at his feet did so. He didn't turn his support team into a proper MC crew, even as those who emulated him did just that. And so, as with Hollywood, events overtook him. Earlier in 1977, at his then resident spot the Executive Playhouse, also on Jerome, he'd agreed to a battle with Pete "DJ" Jones, who brought Flash along as one of his backups—and Flash upstaged him. "He was quick-mixing and spinning around and doing a lot of amazing feats which you ain't never seen no DJ do," said Aaron O'Bryant, a self-confessed "Kool Herc freak" who had taken up the name Kool DJ AJ in homage. "He had skills. He had finesse. He was fast. He amazed Kool Herc's audience. It took maybe two or three weeks, but Flash snatched up all that clientele."

But it was another incident at the same club, now called the Sparkle, later in 1977, that served to truly halt Herc's progress. The DJ saw an altercation developing at the door between his long-standing promotions partner (known as "Mike with the lights") and a trio of aggressive young men he was refusing to let into the club. Herc stepped in as peacemaker, and was stabbed, twice. The wounds were not critical, but still . . . Kool DJ Herc, the man who had done so much to turn kids away from gangs and guns and on to music and dancing, had found that there was no refuge from violence, not even at his front own door. "It made me draw back into a little shell," he said.

The Fever, meantime—regulars dropped the "Disco" after the term fell out of fashion—became the hip-hop equivalent of the Paradise Garage, ground zero for an entire musical movement. Its back room famed as a den of iniquity, its DJ booth as the greatest concentration of talent in the history of hip-hop, its stage equally notorious for showcasing all the upcoming major names in rap, the club remained open until 1986.

December 31, 1977: The annual free concert at Bethesda Fountain has been canceled for lack of funds. Not that Blondie would have taken the booking again. They are on the other side of the world, being paid considerably more than $500 to play "The First Punk Rock Shows in Asia," at the five-star Ambassador Hotel in Bangkok, Thailand. Over in Europe, the Ramones are headlining the Rainbow Theatre in London, their home away from home. It's left to Patti Smith and Richard Hell & the Voidoids to see in the New Year in New York—not on the Bowery, however, but at the brand-new CBGBs Second Avenue Theater. The venue, the former Anderson Theater, holds over fifteen hundred people, roughly four times as many as CBGBs itself, and Kristal, with rumored help from Seymour Stein, has poured over $100,000 into the venture. His reasoning is understandable: the original CBGBs club, he says, has "gotten a little bit hysterical" of late. But what should be a celebration turns into a fiasco, Kristal's beloved laissez-faire attitude letting him down in this more demanding environment. The theater opens on December 27 without functioning heat, sufficient electricity, proper soundproofing, or professional cleaning, and with a flooded bathroom to boot, all of which Talking Heads battle as they try to enjoy the honor of being the venue's first headliners. The following night, Kristal's managerial clients the Dead Boys, whose debut album has just been released on Sire, trash the stage in frustration at the sound, leaving the headliners the Dictators, their second album *Manifest Destiny* also new to the stores, to pick up the pieces.

Patti Smith and Richard Hell then embark on a three-night residency. Bruce Springsteen joins Smith onstage on December 30; the pair sing their coauthored "Because the Night," which will appear on Smith's powerful return to form, *Easter*, and become her first hit single. The night is marred, however, by the all-too-familiar presence of fire marshals, who shut the concert down for unlawful dancing in the aisles. The New Year's Eve performance goes ahead all the same—after which the much vaunted CBGBs Second Avenue Theater is closed, ostensibly to install a new, fully functioning PA. It never reopens.

At Studio 54 in midtown, meanwhile, the New Year is celebrated by a performance from Grace Jones. Though not yet a household name, her stylish debut album *Portfolio*, produced by Tom Moulton, has already made her a "disco-diva," in the words of one *New York Times* reporter. Waiting outside the velvet ropes to see her that December 31 are Bernard Edwards and Nile Rodgers, a pair so entrenched in New York music that their midseventies jazz-fusion outfit was named the Big Apple Band. Now they are leaders of a quintet called Chic, celebrating the success of their debut single "Dance, Dance, Dance (Yowsah Yowsah Yowsah)," a simplistic and sophisticated, funky but fun, contribution to disco overkill. Initially issued on Buddah, it has been bought up and re-released by Atlantic Records, the omnipresent New York label that is snatching up disco records as voraciously as it has every other form of black music over the last thirty years. A top ten hit in Europe already, it's rapidly climbing the American top 40 as the calendar turns over.

But Edwards and Rogers can't get past the velvet ropes. Jones appears to have left their names off the guest list, and though it's a certainty that "Dance, Dance, Dance" is getting hammered on the dance floor, tonight they're just a couple more dressed-up Studio rejects. They head back to Rodgers's midtown apartment, where they exorcise their frustrations with a guitar-and-bass jam session, and as they hone in on the simplest of riffs, they start belittling Studio 54 and its elitist door policy. Rodgers, a veteran of the black activist scene of the sixties, is particularly angry. "Agggghh. . . . Fuck off!" he keeps shouting over the riff, and figures he's on to something, a potential anthem for punk and disco kids, black, white, and all colors in between. Of course, record companies and other business people have something to say about this, and by the time it's recorded, the cry "Fuck off!" has been replaced by that of "Freak Out." But that proves equally universal. Precisely one year later, "Le Freak" will be the number one single in America. In fact, it will be Atlantic Records' biggest-selling single of all time.

The story, of course, does not end there, any more than it started precisely fifty years earlier. The music scene in New York City is one of constant evolution, unwilling to bend to historians and their desires for easy cutoff dates. You can pick a date, choose a place, locate a sound, and call it a movement, but the scene will keep moving regardless, occasionally slipping out of focus and frequently moving off camera, regathering its energies elsewhere. And so, 1977 was the year that disco saturated the mainstream and steadied itself for the inevitable backlash; that punk rock became a media sensation if not yet a commercial proposition; and that hip-hop further got its acts together. But the three dominant New York musical movements of the 1970s had yet to fully connect with each other.

Those pieces of the puzzle came together properly over the following couple of years. In 1978, Blondie recorded "Heart of Glass," the "Disco Song" that had been an occasional part of the live set for three years already; thanks to a meticulous studio sheen and the small matter of good timing, it became a number one hit single around the planet, losing Blondie some of their original "punk" following and gaining them more than enough new fans to compensate. Around the same time, Chris Stein and Debbie Harry met "Fab 5" Freddy Braithwaite, an audaciously overaspiring graffiti artist from Brooklyn who had jumped headfirst into a thriving, downtown Manhattan party scene that mixed punk and disco and art rock and new wave (the more palatable name given to punk by the music industry) at places like the Mudd Club, and on Glenn O'Brien's cable show *TV Party*, which Stein cohosted. Braithwaite brought the now power couple to a hip-hop party at the Webster Avenue Police Athletic League, in the Bronx, where, as they recalled, Grandmaster Flash, the Cold Crush Brothers, and the Funky Four + 1 all performed. Blondie tried to relay some of that night's energy in the song "Rapture," Harry name-checking both Freddy and Flash in what she always insisted was a "homage" to rap rather than an attempt at the real thing. Either way, "Rapture" became a number one single around the world, paving the way for similarly exciting cross-cultural experiments. Chris Frantz and Tina Weymouth, taking a holiday from Talking Heads as Tom Tom Club, embraced hip-hop, funk, reggae, and new wave as they referenced their musical icons on the highly successful "Genius of Love," and then enjoyed a return compliment when Grandmaster Flash sampled the instrumental track for the Furious Five's single "It's Nasty."

Hip-hop had hit vinyl long before then, of course. The credit typically goes to "Rapper's Delight," a multimillion-selling, fifteen-minute travesty of the culture's long-percolating underground roots given the assemblage of its group, the Sugarhill Gang, from whichever interested part-timers the label bosses Sylvia and Joey Robinson could find. (That and the unaccredited use of Casanova Fly's lyrics, just at the point that the MC and DJ had become a respected name in the Bronx.) The former Sylvia Vanderpool, who had hit the charts as half of Mickey and Sylvia in the fifties, and again under her first name in the seventies, was not the only veteran of the original R&B era to hear in hip-hop a comparable form of vocal street music. Paul Winley, who had put out records by the Paragons and the Jesters back in the fifties, and his pioneering neighbor along 125th Street, Bobby Robinson, each recognized the possibilities for themselves.

Winley, who'd already jumped on hip-hop with bootleg break-beat compilations and speeches by Malcolm X, was inspired to make a vocal record by his daughter Tanya, who came home from school with self-composed rhymes in her notebook; he recorded her "Rhymin' and Rappin'" with mom Paulette in 1979, shortly before "Rapper's Delight." The following year he released a 12-inch single by Afrika Bambaataa, doing the "Zulu Throwdown." Bobby Robinson made his own scouting trips to the Bronx clubs, where he picked up several of the leading crews, most notably Grandmaster Flash and the Furious Five, whose "SuperRappin'," also from 1979, was superior in every way to "Rapper's Delight," except that it followed, rather than preceded, it into the record stores. Bambaataa walked after Winley overdubbed musicians onto the records without the DJ's knowledge. Bobby Robinson lost almost all *his* acts to his namesakes at Sugarhill over the Hudson River, who had the promotional muscle—the label was funded by Morris Levy—to take hip-hop into the charts. But just as for any number of Bronx and Harlem acts of the 1950s, getting paid in cash proved that much harder than getting played on the radio.

The New York music scene, then, continued as an unbroken circle of familiar names playing the same old games, with typically new and unpredictable results. Who would have thought back in 1979, when one major label after another dismissed "Rapper's Delight" as novelty, that "rap" would twenty-five years later be the biggest-selling genre in popular music, dominated by artists—many of them, like Jay-Z, DMX, and Biggie Smalls, straight out of the New York housing projects—who could sell four or five million copies of an album in just as many weeks? Who'd have known that punk would become something other than just a byword for sensationalism, and develop into a dominant musical culture of its own, one open to almost as many interpretations as hip-hop? And who'd have banked, back when "disco sucks" badges were doing the rounds in the late seventies, that the music would prove capable not just of going back underground again, at places like the Paradise Garage, but of reemerging in the late eighties, alongside Frankie Knuckle's Chicago-based form of "house," to become a way of life from one corner of the globe to another?

And at the end of 1977, who'd have wagered on New York City's twenty-first-century status as the very model of the thriving big city, a place where tourists could walk safely along 42nd Street at midnight, where Alphabet City would be filled with chic European restaurants, Harlem and Bedford-Stuyvesant would be subject to white gentrification, and the once barren and burned-out streets of the South Bronx would be filled with desirable low-rise housing? Some would argue–vociferously–that this modern New York, for all that it has to offer those who can afford it, lacks the excitement—the highly vaunted edge—of old New York. That aspirants have been priced out. That it's no longer possible to show up with a few dollars in one's pocket, and still expect to have a fair chance of realizing one's dream.

It's a valid argument. But New York City has a fascinating tendency to disprove logic and reason. Somewhere, out of the spotlight, away from the center of media attention, another scene is already developing, just waiting to come into focus.

ACKNOWLEDGMENTS

First and foremost, this book has been informed by the seventeen years I spent living in New York City, and the thousands of people in the school of music and art whom I encountered and shared stories with during those years. Some of the names and faces I recollect vividly; others are a "blur of mystery and history." Thanks to everyone and everything.

Enormous gratitude to Amy Cherry, my editor at W. W. Norton, for buying into the idea in the first place, allowing me to shift my entire period of reference midbook, for gently prodding me to deliver on our many revised schedules without ever rushing me to do so at the expense of quality, and for running a clear pencil mark through some of my "wacky sideroads" while—whilst?—allowing me to justify those tangents I felt were important. Here's to the future. Thanks also to Erica Stern and everyone else at Norton.

Thanks to David Vigliano, Michael Harriott, and Elisa Petrini at Vigliano Associates. To Chris Charlesworth at Omnibus Press in London. Special thanks to Rhonda Markowitz, my research assistant during that phase of the project, for rounding up so many willing interviewees, and for continuing to offer her help throughout the writing process.

With a few exceptions listed below, the hundred or more people whom I formally interviewed for this book have all been either quoted or referenced within the text, and I would like to thank all of them for their time. Extra-special thanks to those interviewees who allowed me to go back to them, time and again, fact-checking well beyond their call of duty. Their enthusiasm and encouragement for the project proved essential, and I look forward to maintaining many of these relationships. In addition, I felt truly humbled by the civility and respect I was afforded by some of the older interviewees, especially those who never made much money from their work, and I hope those qualities show, however subtly, in the writing. I would also like to thank the assistants, publicists, friends, and relatives of my interviewees, some of whom put up with my gently badgering them for months, if not years, on end. In many such cases, my persistence proved fruitful. In some of the cases where it didn't, it was not due to a lack of effort on their part.

I formally interviewed just a handful of people whose names or words have not shown up directly in this book: Eric Anderson, Willie DeVille, Jack Dickerson, Louie "KR.One" Gasparro, Godlis, Michael Holman, Tom Noonan, Steve Paul, Allan Pepper, Randy Poe, Stanley Snadowsky, and Jud Yalkut. They should know that their interviews helped inform the text and that I am grateful for their time.

The following people were particularly helpful in specialized areas: Warren G. Harris for research on theaters; Marvin Goldberg for answering countless queries about the rhythm and blues era; Michelle Zarin for help with Latino acts and contacts; the understandably pseudonymous Bitter Queen for keeping track on the Mafia's involvement in the nightclub industry; Danny Krivit and Tim Lawrence for enormous enthusiasm and contacts on the discotheque scene; Mark Skillz for his help with hip-hop dates and contacts. I came across far too many archival Web sites to mention, but I would be remiss not to make note of the site "It's all the streets you crossed not so long ago," named for a Velvet Underground lyric and which collects "tales of New York City rock & roll landmarks, most of 'em long gone." Additional thanks to all the amenable photographers for enthusiastically sharing such excellent images, and to Holly Cara Price for advice in this area.

In 2005, I followed in the footsteps of many New York City musicians and moved to the beautiful Catskill Mountains. A country call-out to a fellow local biographer, Holly George-Warren, who went through similar deadline hell on her own projects over the same period, for encouraging us to make the move and for additional help with contacts and her music library. Thanks to Ric Dragon, one of our many local jazz men, for reading the first draft of the early chapters and offering such constructive comments. Thanks to David Whitehead for being a good friend, helping locate several contacts, and securing a fair few box sets. Respect due to the Rock Doc crew and our monthly nights gathered around the VCR or DVD player; and to both the Onteora Runners Club and the Zen Mountain Monastery.

I would like to publicize the Mid-Hudson Library System (http://mid hudson.org), which allowed me to easily search, locate, and request books online that were then funneled through to the Phoenicia Library within a day or two, a great marriage of old media and new technology. Extra-special thanks to everyone at the Phoenicia Library itself. I encourage all readers to support and make use of their local libraries—and to support their community schools—lest they be taken away.

I also made plentiful use of the New York Public Library system, especially the research centers: the Humanities and Social Sciences Library on 42nd Street, the New York Public Library for the Performing Arts at Lincoln Center, and the Schomburg Center for Research in Black Culture, in Harlem. The NYPL's Pro Quest system is a thrill, enabling a user to turn selected newspaper stories into e-mailable pdf files—again, a great use of new technology. Thanks to those who put me up (and put up with me) in the city as I embarked on many overnight research journeys after moving upstate, especially my fellow writer Matt McCutcheon.

Thanks to everyone at the www.ijamming.net Pub for the daily communication. I still can't believe we live in a world where a writer can be tucked away in the mountains and yet engage in instant online discussion with old school friends and new acquaintances across several different continents. Thanks to pubber Patrick Carmosino for coming up with the book title. Thanks, too, to the Ramones for writing it (twice, of course).

Finally, love and kisses on the home front to the family for putting up with the writer's whims as always (and the slowdown in income during the final stages of the book): Posie, Campbell, and, especially, our little guy Noel, who went from being a twinkle in his mother's eye to an avid guitarist over the course of this book, playing his first gig (of sorts) before his fourth birthday. This book is for you, Noel. We adore you.

The Rascals, who had number one hits in each of the years 1966, 1967, and 1968, emerged from a New York City club scene where, said organist Felix Cavaliere, "If you don't get the people up and dancing, you don't get paid." *From left*: Eddie Brigati, Cavaliere, Gene Cornish, and Dino Danelli at the Phone Booth in midtown Manhattan, October 14, 1965. The act was known as the Young Rascals through 1966 and 1967.

NOTES

CHAPTER 1: MARIO GETS DIZZY IN NEW YORK

1 **New York City in June 1927:** Bauzá's visit has sometimes been cited as taking place in 1926. The *Encyclopedic Discography of Cuban Music*, vol. 2, *1925–60*, by Cristobal Diaz-Ayala, gives the dates of Antonio María Romeu's recording session in New York as June 7 and 8, 1927 (available in alphabetical pdf files from http://library.fiu.edu/latinpop/discography.html).

1 **an overdue mark of respect:** At the turn of the century, Romeu's introduction of the piano to the *charanga* groups of Havana café society had helped usher in a more populist style of the nation's dominant musical style, the *danzon*.

2 **"We flyin'—just like Lindy did":** Possibly apocryphal, but widely quoted as Lindy lore—e.g., Stephanie Rupp and Kwek Ju-Hon, "Origin of Lindy Moves?" *Blackspeak* 13 (August 2002).

2 **how black people like him can live:** "Negro" was the term commonly used in the 1920s and for many years thereafter. Rather than interjecting the changing terms over different decades ("Negro," "colored," "African American"), I have opted to use the term "black" throughout this book for consistency.

3 **subsequently repressed its dark-skinned majority:** The Independent Party of Color, the Western Hemisphere's first black political party, was brutally extinguished around the time of Bauzá's birth.

3 **"Some Harlemites thought the millennium had come":** Langston Hughes, *The Big Sea*, p. 178.

4 **Langston Hughes's point:** According to Gillian Rodger's biography of Bentley, "one of her songs combined 'Sweet Georgia Brown' and 'Alice Blue Gown' into a bawdy ode to anal intercourse": http://www.glbtq.com/arts/bentley_g .html. Fictionalized in novels by Carl Van Vechten, Clement Woods, and Blair

Niles, Bentley began a recording career in 1928 and later "married" a white woman.

4 **"was where a lot of downtown politicians":** Count Basie and Albert Murray, *Good Morning Blues,* pp. 67–68.

5 **"Slummers; Sports; 'coke' addicts":** Quoted at http://www.nfo.net/usa/harlem.html.

7 **"This . . . is what life had in store for me":** All Bauzá quotes from "how black people" to "had in store for me" are taken from Bobby Sanabria, *The Legacy of Mario Bauzá,* published at http://www.descarga.com/cgi-bin/db/archives/Profile8.

8 **when Louis Armstrong covered it:** Armstrong's version eschewed the claves/maracas/congas combination for less fussy castanets, and swapped the piano for guitar, the better to allow his trumpet to dominate.

10 **"Every time I seen it":** Jairo Moreno, "Bauzá-Gillespie-Latin/Jazz," p. 87.

10 **especially that of Cugat and his orchestra:** Cugat had been born in Spain and, though classically trained in Havana, had left Cuba with his family as a teenager in 1915. In the States he worked first as a cartoonist and then in tango bands, where he perfected his commercial approach to Latin music. He never really had an authentic grasp of contemporary Cuban music—though his well-heeled audience believed otherwise.

10 **"I'm going to teach you":** Sublette, *Cuba and Its Music,* p. 461.

10 **"an incredible teacher and drummer":** Sanabria, *The Legacy of Mario Bauzá.*

11 **"The only time we were bothered":** Stearns, *The Story of Jazz,* p. 204.

12 **"If you were looking at him" and "I'm going up":** From oral history with Louie Bellson, transcribed at the Archives Center, National Museum of American History, available at www.smithsonianjazz.org/oral_histories/pdf/joh_LouieBellson.pdf, pp. 18 and 19.

12 **"Krupa goes to Chick"** Sanabria, *The Legacy of Mario Bauzá.*

12 **"I was never cut":** Bruce H. Klauber, *World of Gene Krupa: That Legendary Drummin' Man* (Ventura, CA: Pathfinder, 1990), p. 24.

13 **playing maracas for El Sexteto Naçional:** A *Sexteto* featured guitar, *tres* (a smaller guitar with three pairs of widely separated strings), bongos, a bass instrument, and two vocalists: a tenor playing clave sticks and, Machito's role, a baritone playing maracas.

13 **"the black man is left alone':** From *Machito: A Latin Jazz Legacy* '87, dir./prod. by Carlos Ortiz.

13 **"American blacks who were living in Harlem":** Ibid.

14 **"Trying to survive in New York'":** Dizzy Gillespie, *To Be or Not to Bop,* p. 60.

14 **Statistics suggested otherwise:** Statistics on Harlem drawn from Roi Ottley,

New World A-Comin'; George J. Lankevich, *American Metropolis; Rhapsodies in Black*, sleeve notes; and Dominic J. Capeci, Jr., *The Harlem Riot of 1943*.

15 **"with some little chick with him"**: Gillespie, *To Be or Not to Bop*, pp. 62–63.

15 **"He must have really liked"**: Ibid., p. 64.

16 **"I thought he was the greatest thing"**: Ibid., p. 64.

16 **"Mario was like my father"**: Ibid., p. 115.

16 **it's hard to imagine Gillespie's career:** Bauzá introduced Gillespie to Alberto Socarras, his own mentor, who employed Gillespie for his New York engagements—and taught him the rudiments of Cuban clave rhythm on the maracas.

16 **when he was just thirty-four:** Webb's birthdate has been an ongoing source of controversy, given variously as February 1902, 1907, and 1909. Eric B. Borgman studied census records of Webb's Baltimore hometown to conclude that the date was, instead, February 1905. http://www.geocities.com/ebbpeg/Webb .html.

16 **referred to Bauzá as an "Indian":** Moreno, "Bauzá -Gillespie-Latin/Jazz," p. 85. Calloway did not even mention Bauzá in his autobiography.

16 **"horse music":** Sublette, *Cuba and Its Music*, p. 463.

16 **his influence on Calloway's music:** Calloway, in both cases, added the Cuban percussion instruments maracas and claves to the sit-down acoustic trap drums that were alien to Latin music. Drummer Chick Webb did not do so when he recorded "Harlem Congo," with Bauzá on trumpet, in 1937.

17 **Gillespie, too, made his mark with Calloway:** As he joined Calloway's group, in September 1939, Gillespie participated in an all-star session led by Lionel Hampton. On "Hot Mallets," he took the first solo, giving way to Benny Carter and Hampton himself on a recording that also featured Coleman Hawkins, Chu Berry, and Charlie Christian. No wonder Gillespie, only twenty years old at the time, later described himself as "nervous as a sheep shitting shingles."

17 **"how to feel some of the simpler":** Ed Morales, *The Latin Beat*, p. 41.

17 **"the importance of Afro-Cuban music"** and **"In those days":** Gillespie, *To Be or Not to Bop*, pp. 115–17.

17 **The orchestra was unveiled as:** It has often been reported that the group's official unveiling took place at the Park Plaza Ballroom in Spanish Harlem on December 3, 1940. A group billed as Machito's Orchestra was advertised as playing the Club Cuba on East 54th Street in October of that year.

17 **"Afro-Cubans":** Though he claimed that it preceded him, the Cuban anthropologist Fernando Ortiz, who traced over one hundred different African ethnicities in Cuba, popularized the term "Afro-Cuban" by including it in a published study in 1906, at http://digilib.nypl.org/dynaweb/ortiz/ortizfin, p. 21.

18 **"one of the bravest acts"**: published at http://www.descarge.com/cgi-bin/db/ archives/Profile8. Sanabria, from *The Legacy of Mario Bauzá*.

18 **"lived by their folkways"**: Salazar, *Mambo Kingdom*, pp. 19–25.

19 **"Our idea was to bring"**: Joop Visser, *Ritmo Caliente*. p. 14.

19 **"From Count Basie and Chick Webb:"** Ibid., p. 14.

20 **"As a kid in Spanish Harlem"**: Steven Loza, *Tito Puente and the Making of Latin Musica*. p. 54.

CHAPTER 2: CUBOP CITY AND ALL THAT JAZZ

22 **"could play anything"**: Ira Gitler, *Swing to Bop*, p. 63.

23 **"playing everything . . . a trumpet man"**: Ibid., p. 75.

23 **taking up semipermanent residence:** A recording exists of Parker playing "Cherokee" at Monroe's somewhere between January and March 1942, accompanied by Al Tinney on piano, Paul Eberneezer on bass, an unknown drummer, and Clark Monroe himself on vocals.

23 **"they would say"**: Parker and Tinney quoted in Gitler, *Swing to Bop*, p. 75.

23 **saxophonist Henry Minton's club:** Henry Minton was celebrated as the first black member of the American Federation of Musicians' (New York chapter) Local 802.

24 **"Cab [Calloway] frowned on"**: Scott DeVeaux, *The Birth of Bebop*, p. 185.

24 **"Dizzy was a devil"**: Dizzy Gillespie, *To Be or Not to Bop*, p. 132.

24 **"There's a big question"**: Gillespie interview with Les Tomkins, archived at http://www.jazzprofessional.com/interviews/Dizzy%20Gillespie.htm.

25 **Dizzy Gillespie and Charlie Parker had met:** Given that he was also touring with Calloway at the time, Mario Bauzá should have been part of this initial encounter, but he appears not to have been invited to the hotel room where it took place.

25 **"was similar to a laser"**: From the documentary *Celebrating Bird: The Triumph of Charlie Parker*, dir. Gary Giddins, 1987.

25 **"It was getting away"**: Gillespie, *To Be or Not to Bop*, pp. 177–78.

26 **"probably the best band leader"**: From *Celebrating Bird*.

27 **"They didn't stop to realize"**: Gitler, *Swing to Bop*, p. 125.

27 **"where all these bad musicians were"**: From *Celebrating Bird*.

28 **"Of all the people"**: Alyn Shipton, *Groovin' High*, p. 121.

28 **"Dizzy had to hum everything"**: Gitler, *Swing to Bop*, p. 119.

28 **"We never labeled the music"**: Gillespie, *To Be or Not to Bop,* p. 142.

28 **"As we walked in"**: Marshall Stearns, *The Story of Jazz*, pp. 224–25.

29 **a citywide cabaret law:** For many years, any employee of a New York venue that sold liquor, from musician to coat check girl, needed an identity or "cabaret"

card, which was supplied by the local police department. Theoretically, the intent was to prevent known criminals from being employed in the nightclub industry, though many saw a racial prejudice to the requirement, given that midtown nightclubs and cafés were increasingly employing black musicians. The strictness of the identity card policy was first revealed when both Charlie Parker and Billie Holiday had their cards rescinded—and therefore their right to work in New York City denied—for drug busts.

32 **"the height of the perfection"**: Gillespie, *To Be or Not to Bop*, p. 231.

32 **"Every time they got on the stand"**: Gitler, *Swing to Bop*, p. 148.

32 **"The Hep-sations of 1945"**: Shipton, *Groovin' High*, p. 147.

33 **"It was very new music"**: From *Celebrating Bird*.

34 **leading black dancer and choreographer:** See "Notes on Shangó" from the Katherine Dunham Collection at the Library of Congress: http://lcweb2.loc .gov/diglib/ihas/html/dunham/dunham-notes-shango.html. Dunham quote from September 2002 video interview in the same archive.

34 **Valdés left for fame and fortune:** Valdés had left Cuba in part because he was unable to employ Arsenio Rodriguez, Chano Pozo, and others onstage, due to their skin color, even though they were renowned composers and had contributed to the success of his recording sessions. See Max Salazar, *Mambo Kingdom*, p. 41.

35 **"If this is the shape of things to come"**: Gitler, *Swing to Bop*, p. 153.

36 **"didn't sit real good":** Brown and McKibbon quotes in Gillespie, *To Be or Not to Bop*, p. 320.

36 **"We'd sing and play"**: Ibid., p. 319.

36 **"the greatest percussionist I ever heard"**: Ibid., p. 319.

36 **was "dynamite" and "probably the largest"**: Ibid., p. 321.

38 **shot him dead:** Muñoz was later sentenced to five years in jail, the lenient punishment a reflection on his war record.

38 **"roughneck" to the core:** Gillespie, *To Be or Not to Bop*, p. 325.

38 **the day before Pozo's funeral:** Chano Pozo biographical details are drawn in part from *The Legacy of Chano Pozo*, a documentary produced by Malanga Films. Also Salazar, *Mambo Kingdom*, pp. 45–47; Scott Yanow, *Afro-Cuban Jazz*, pp. 87–88; and Joop Visser, *Ritmo Caliente*.

CHAPTER 3: THE HARLEM HIT PARADE

40 **admitting black customers:** Several theaters nonetheless maintained a policy of segregation, like the Alhambra, where blacks had to use an alley entrance for admittance to the balcony only.

40 **Outraged clergy and other guardians of morality:** Once he took office,

La Guardia responded to the coalition of interfaith protests, represented by the Catholic archbishop of New York and senior rabbis alike, and set about ridding the city of what he called "incorporated filth." The city's fourteen burlesque theaters had their licenses revoked in 1937

41 **Lafayette had steeped Schiffman:** If it was hard to tell whether the promotion of the Scottsboro Boys, who as teenagers spent years on death row in Alabama for a gang rape that almost certainly never took place, was a statement of solidarity or an act of exploitation, the employment of Charlie Barnet—arguably the first white jazz bandleader to routinely hire black musicians, and ostracized from many white venues as a result—revealed Schiffman and Brecher's integrationist instincts.

41 **"Anti-Jewish sentiment among Negroes":** Roi Ottley, *New World A-Coming,* pp. 122–23.

43 **"The colored people are not whole-heartedly":** Ibid., p. 314.

44 **issued an executive order banning discrimination:** Executive Order 8802 guaranteed "full participation in the national defense program by all citizens of the United States, regardless of race, creed, color, or national origin," and because it had such a tangible impact, the threatened march on Washington is often considered the first act of the civil rights movement.

44 **"the yellow-skinned Jap":** Ottley, *New World A-Coming,* pp. 326–43.

45 **"Hitler has scored":** *People's Voice,* May 8, 1943. Later that year, Powell became the first black New Yorker elected to Congress; a Communist Party member, Benjamin Davis, took his place as councilman.

45 **"to induce insurance companies":** Moses, in a letter to the *New York Times,* June 3, 1943.

45 **"a drop in values":** Nat Brandt, *Harlem at War,* p. 177.

46 **"The riot of 1943":** Jack Schiffman, *Harlem Heyday,* p. 66.

46 **fell by the wayside:** According to Ted Fox in *Uptown,* eight swing bands broke up in December 1946 alone, including those of Tommy Dorsey, Benny Goodman, Woody Herman, and Harry James.

49 **detour from the tried-and-true:** The Ravens didn't see it as anything special at the time, but as Gribin and Schiff later wrote in *The Complete Book of Doo Wop,* " 'Lullaby' gave us, if only for part of one song, the insistent rhythm of the doo-wop genre, nonsense syllables by background harmonizers and a distinct punctuating bass."

50 **"a wonderful designation":** Jerry Wexler and David Ritz, *Rhythm and the Blues,* p. 62.

51 **Jimmy Ricks's star power:** In 1950, Ricks recorded with the Benny Goodman Sextet.

51 **"came up with a handle":** *Soul Man.*

52 **"In 1949, when *Billboard*"**: Nelson George, *The Death of Rhythm & Blues*, p. 26.

52 **"The start of rhythm and blues"**: Additional background on the Ravens is from a Marv Goldberg profile, originally published in *Discoveries*, 93, (Feb. 1996), archived at http://home.att.net/~marvy42/Ravens/ravens01.html.

52 **"It was never explained to me"**: http://www.angelfire.com/biz6/motown Nsou14Ever/ClydeMcPhatter.

53 **the Ques became the Dominoes:** The name of the Dominoes hailed from Ward and Marks's first attempt at a group, predating the Ques, and so named for its multiracial makeup. The idea appears to have been a little ahead of its time.

54 **"slow-witted, sexually obsessed black man"**: John A. Jackson, *Big Beat Heat*, pp. 6–7.

55 **"half the time"**: Philip Groia, *They All Sang on the Corner*, p. 30.

55 **"among the most cultivated cognoscenti"**: Wexler quoted in *Rhythm and the Blues*, p. 69.

56 **"the most soulful singer"**: A. L. Bardach, "Interrogating Ahmet Ertegun," *Slate* magazine, Feb. 25, 2005, http://www.slate.com/id/2114074.

56 **Ertegun tracked McPhatter down:** Various accounts have Ertegun hot-tailing it in a taxi to Harlem, where he found McPhatter in a rooming house; calling the Reverend McPhatter, Clyde's father, from the phone book at Birdland; and sending his employee Lou Krefetz to find McPhatter. The only certainty is that Ertegun acted in haste, knowing that such a great singer would not remain a free agent for long.

CHAPTER 4: THE VILLAGE TO THE LEFT OF NEW YORK

58 **"the American Ward"**: Minday Cantor. "Washington Arch and the Changing Neighborhood," in Rick Beard and Leslie Cohen Berlowitz, eds., *Greenwich Village*, p. 86.

59 **"being independent and being oneself"**: John Wilcock, *The Village Square*, p. 13.

60 **"the first inter-racial nightclub"**: From the documentary *John Hammond: From Bessie Smith to Bruce Springsteen.*

60 **Abel Meeropol:** Meeropol and his wife ended up adopting the children of Julius and Ethel Rosenberg, who had been convicted of espionage for supplying atomic secrets to the Russians and were executed in 1953.

61 **concerts at Carnegie Hall:** The concerts were underwritten by Eric Bernay, treasurer of the *New Masses* magazine.

61 **"from a plantation in Arkansas"**: *John Hammond: From Bessie Smith to Bruce Springsteen.*

61 **"the beginning of the end for Billie"**: Hammond quoted in David Margolick, *Strange Fruit*, p. 78.

62 **"Aw, John's square"**: Ibid., p. 79.

62 **"the beginning of the American folk"**: Elijah Wald, *Josh White*, p. 57.

63 **"laconic, offhand"**: Pete Seeger, *The Incompleat Folksinger*, pp. 42–43.

63 **"The capitalist papers"**: Joe Klein, *Woody Guthrie*, p. 150.

64 **recorded his songs for the Archive:** The recordings were not issued until 1964, at the very height of the folk boom, at which point they were released by Elektra Records.

64 **stood up "every few seconds"**: Seeger, *The Incompleat Folksinger*, pp. 44–45.

65 **"They are giving me money so fast"**: Klein, *Woody Guthrie*, p. 164.

66 **"We want you to come"**: Ronald D. Cohen and Dave Samuelson, liner notes for *Songs for Political Action*, Bear Family Records BCD 15720 JL (1996), pp. 77–78.

66 **the Keynote record label:** Keynote was named for the *New Masses'* own performing revue, the Keynote Theatre.

66 **None of the five was named:** In the *Daily Worker*, Seeger had identified himself as Pete Bowers, to avoid embarrassing his father, who had been forced to resign from the University of California at Berkeley in 1918 for opposing American participation in the Great War.

67 **"a carefully anonymous"**: *Time* review quoted in Klein, *Woody Guthrie*, p. 191.

67 **"If you do not hold with the isolationists"**: Reviews gathered at http://www.woodyguthrie.de/doe.html.

69 **"they are strictly subversive"**: *Atlantic* quoted in David Dunaway, *How Can I Keep from Singing*, p. 84.

69 **"People came and went"**: Seeger, *The Incompleat Folksinger*, p. 17.

69 **"and before it was over"**: Wald, *Josh White*, p. 76.

71 **Joe Hill:** An organizer for the Industrial Workers of the World (the "Wobblies"), Joe Hill had used his guitar and voice to rally union members earlier in the century, with antiscabbing songs like "Casey Jones." He was silenced only when executed by a Utah firing squad in 1915, for a murder few believe he committed. In 1936, the New York–based classically trained composer Earl Robinson, a frequent visitor to Almanac House, put Alfred Hayes's poem "The Ballad of Joe Hill" to music, ensuring that Hill's work lived on in the folk tradition.

71 **"I ended up joining"**: During the same interview, conducted in his eighties for his authorized film biography, *The Power of Song*, Seeger then continued, "A

couple of years later, just before World War II, I think I actually joined, became a card-carrying member."

71 **fervor of the Almanac Singers':** "OWI Plows Under the Almanac Singers," *New York Times*, Jan. 5, 1943, p. 21.

72 **he had witnessed a double lynching:** Or so White claimed; he was his only witness. (His subsequent recording of "Strange Fruit" certainly benefited from the anecdote.) In his biography of White, Elijah Wald disputes several of White's biographical details, but he leaves this one unchallenged.

73 **was better served by his own Carolinians:** The Carolinians included Bayard Rustin, a pacifist and openly gay Communist who would shortly join A. Philip Randolph at the Brotherhood of Sleeping Car Porters and help organize his proposed march on Washington.

73 **that its "seven Negro laments":** Liner notes archived at http://www.wirz.de/music/whitefrm.htm.

74 **"the most wonderful gentleman":** Jim Capaldi, "Conversation with Mr. Folkways: Moe Asch," *Folk Scene* (May–June 1978), archived at http://www.peteseeger.net/fsmoasch.htm.

74 **"his genius was not so much":** Seeger, *The Incompleat Folksinger,* p. 34.

74 **"The sound of his guitar":** Wald, *Josh White,* p. 112.

74 **"he played up to the Uncle Tom image":** Ibid., p. 93.

75 **"Josh and Huddie come from":** Guthrie's letter was published in full by Max Gordon in his memoir *Live at the Village Vanguard,* pp. 45–53. Gordon's heart appeared to be in the right place, but at the start of this chapter (p. 41) he quoted Nicolas Ray as saying that Leadbelly "had just arrived in New York" and that Josh White was "looking for a job." Both men had released major and independent albums that year that had accrued considerable press cuttings and landed them prominent national radio appearances. Unless Gordon was trying to take credit for their "discovery," his recollections perhaps reveal the cultural chasm between the folk circuit and the nightclub world.

75 **"until we never have to sing it":** Margolick, *Strange Fruit,* p. 48.

76 **nom de plume of the Union Boys:** Only six songs out of the sixteen recorded by the Union Boys were released at the time. The most memorably upbeat of them, "Move into Germany," dominated by White, McGhee, and Terry, was not made widely available until the 1980s.

76 **record a phenomenal 123 further songs:** Even the indefatigable Asch was unable to release all this material at the time, and the anthem "This Land Is Your Land" was not made public until 1951. More of it was later collected on *This Land Is Your Land: The Asch Recordings,* vol. 1.

76 **"anti–New York":** All Asch quotes from Capaldi, *Folk Scene.*

77 **"By 1944 . . . Josh rivaled":** Wald, *Josh White,* p. 116.

CHAPTER 5: MAMBO MADNESS

78 **the newly opened Palladium Ballroom:** The Palladium previously served as the Alma Dance Studios, one of several "taxi dance" halls in New York where, in the early 1940s, single gentlemen could buy a dance from a hostess.

78 **"I went to 110th and Fifth":** The Machito and Pagani quotes in this section are taken from the *Machito: A Latin Jazz Legacy* documentary.

81 **Tito and his sister:** Anna Puente died of meningitis while Tito was serving in the Navy. He became his parents' only surviving child.

81 **"I went to black schools":** Steven Loza, *Tito Puente and the Making of Latin American Music*, p. 28.

81 **"note for note":** Tito Puente with Jim Payne, *Tito Puente's Drumming with the Mambo King* (n.p.: Hal Leonard Corp., 2001), p. 13.

83 **"That music wasn't dance music":** Loza, *Tito Puente and the Making of Latin Music*, pp. 37–38.

83 **"in that it concentrates'":** Ibid., p. 134.

84 **"won the favor":** Fredric Dannen, *Hit Men*, pp. 34–40.

85 **"played no instrument":** Marshall Stearns, *The Story of Jazz*, p. 223.

85 **interview in the jazz bible *Down Beat*:** Interview with John S, Wilson, *Down Beat*, Sept. 9, 1949, quoted in Alyn Shipton, *Groovin' High*, p. 209.

86 **"No one who went":** Ernesto Marquez, "Marlon Brando: The Conga Man," *La Jornada*, July 7, 2004, at http://www.blythe-systems.com/pipermail/nytr/Week-of-Mon-20040712/003562.html.

87 **"The two of them together":** Quoted by Joe Conzo in author interview.

87 **compensation for the low pay:** The bandleader's pay was double that of his musicians; for Eddie Palmieri in the 1960s, this meant all of $36 a night, leaving orchestra members with lower pay than that of members of a leading jazz band of the 1930s. In addition, the musicians still had to acquire and carry their police-approved identity cards. In November 1960, the police conducted "inspections" of some 2,400 nightclubs, dance halls, and cafés and suspended the permits of twenty-seven of them, primarily for identity card issues. Among those temporarily closed were the Palladium and the Copacabana in midtown, and the Baby Grand in Harlem. The clubs took their case to the state supreme court, which stayed their suspension; eventually the identity card requirement was abolished.

88 **In the late 1950s:** Puente's "Oye Cómo Va," later covered to great success by Carlos Santana, came from this period.

89 **"was jealous . . . and wanted billing":** Max Salazar, *Mambo Kingdom*, p. 98.

89 **a police raid on the Palladium:** "13 Arrested Here in Ballroom Raid," *New York Times*, April 9, 1961, p. 51.

89 **The Palladium soldiered on:** Additional information on Palladium from Salazar, *Mambo Kingdom*, pp. 87–93.

93 **Most 78s sold only in the hundreds:** Many of these 78s were considered to have been lost to the winds of time. Fortunately, Joe Conzo kept a complete set of Tito Puente's Tico releases; these were issued by Fania, in chronological order, over a series of four double CDs, as this book went to press. Conzo was then set to produce a similar set of Rodriguez's complete recordings, most of which had been completely unavailable on other than on a bootleg called *Mambo Gee Gee.*

93 **Raymond secured a new job:** Art Raymond would eventually come back to New York and WEVD, where he hosted a Jewish community show, *Raisins and Almonds*, for thirty-five years.

94 **releasing a dozen albums:** One of these initial LP releases was Tito Rodriguez's *Mambo Madness*, which included one of the singer's early forays into the English language, "Chiqui-Bop." Interestingly, Machito's orchestra was not billed as the Afro-Cubans on Tico, though it had been on Clef/Mercury.

94 **"the significance of the drum":** Loza, *Tito Puente and the Making of Latin Music*, p. 12.

94 **the debut of Tito Puente as an *artiste*:** It's often said that *Puente in Percussion* was Puente's first LP, but it was preceded in the Tico catalog by four other mambo and *cha-cha-cha* albums, credited solely to Tito Puente and Orchestra.

94 **Tito Rodriguez, languishing:** Tito Puente historically complained about RCA's lack of promotion, and at the dawn of the sixties he returned to a Tico that was then under different ownership. Yet it's hard to deny the success of *Dance Mania* in particular, or to imagine that it could have sold so well on Tico.

95 **that he "never met":** Dannen, *Hit Men*, pp. 40–41.

CHAPTER 6: THE TEENAGERS SING ROCK 'N' ROLL

101 **"radio advertising became much more local":** Bill Brewster and Frank Broughton, *Last Night a DJ Saved My Life*, p. 28.

102 **"the nation's number one":** John A. Jackson, *Big Beat Heat*, p. 48.

102 **"one of the largest concentrations":** Ibid., p. 68.

102 **"all-Negro programming":** Henry T. Sampson, *Swingin' on the Ether Waves*, pp. 1064 and 1128; Jackson, *Big Beat Heat*, p. 59.

104 **Mayor Robert Wagner:** The 1953 election was significant in that Wagner was replaced as Manhattan borough president by Hulan Jack, the first black man to hold such a title in any of the five boroughs.

104 **WINS announced that Alan Freed:** The alanfreed.com Web site has a phenomenal amount of resource information, including contracts, press cuttings, personal and business letters, receipts, invoices, and subpoenas. It was an invaluable aid for this chapter.

105 **the original Moondog: Louis Hardin:** http://www.geocities.com/moondog madness/discography.html and http://www.geocities.com/moondogmadness/biography.html.

105 **"dressed in thong sandals":** Josephine Jablons, "Moondog, Blues, Jazz Disc Ace, Gets NY Show," *New York Herald Tribune*.

105 **mentioned "rock 'n' roll":** Jackson, *Big Beat Heat*, p. 86.

106 **"Morris is thought to have fronted for":** Fredric Dannen, *Hit Men,* p. 37.

110 **"When Freed starred in the movie":** Jackson, *Big Beat Heat*, p. 152.

111 **"If you're a struggling songwriter":** In 1990, Cita enjoyed a payday when "Life Is But a Dream," still cocredited to Hy Weiss, was prominently featured in the movie and soundtrack for *Goodfellas*. "But the Harptones never got paid for the performance itself," he said of recording royalties that, like many from the early days of rhythm and blues, rarely trickled down through the various reselling and licensing of master tapes to the actual recording artists.

111 **"What were these bums":** Dannen, *Hit Men*, p. 49.

114 **"I really didn't do it":** Ibid., p. 40.

114 **a co-writing credit:** Song credits via BMI registrations.

115 **Bobby Robinson's store:** Robinson later changed the name of his store to Bobby's Happy House, in homage to his regional hit with Lewis Lymon.

117 **In the spring of 1957:** *Billboard*, March 30 and April 6, 1957.

118 **set up two labels:** Goldner's original Tico investor, Jack Wiseman, became vice president of Gone.

120 **"unlawfully, wickedly, and maliciously":** Jackson, *Big Beat Heat*, p. 207.

121 **with the "tacit understanding":** Ibid., p. 285.

122 **"nice" . . . "In my business":** "Testimony Ended in Disk Jockey Suit," *New York Times*, May 3, 1961, p. 75.

122 **"the hopes of having those songs":** Jackson, *Big Beat Heat*, p. 287.

CHAPTER 7: FROM BROOKLYN TO BROADWAY

123 **"The fifties were innocent":** *The Songmakers Collection*, produced by Peter Jones Productions for A&E, 2001.

124 **"the largest Jewish community":** David Kaufman, *Shul with a Pool,* p. 248.

125 **"Brighton Beach, not Europe"**: Ilana Abramovitch and Seán Galvin, eds., *Jews of Brooklyn*, pp. 91–92.

128 **"Oh God"**: *The Songmakers.*

128 **"dress black, talk black"**: Ken Emerson, *Always Magic in the Air*, p. 41.

128 **"Doc was into urban blues"**: Mort Shuman interviewed by Stu Colman of Radio London, quoted on *The Drifters: All Time Greatest Hits and More, 1959–1965*, liner notes by Colin Escott.

131 **"our answer to Elvis Presley"**: *The Songmakers.*

135 **"to suppress genuine talent"**: John A. Jackson, *Big Beat Heat*, p. 244.

135 **scandal took Freed and his peers**: When Freed announced his departure from broadcasting during his WABC TV show *Big Beat*, on Nov. 29, 1959, it was to the song "Shimmy-Shimmy-Koko-Bop," by Little Anthony and the Imperials. His last words: "I know a lot of ASCAP publishers who will be glad I'm off the air."

137 **"But . . . I couldn't bring myself"**: Dion, quoted in *King of the New York Streets* (USA: The Right Stuff, 2000).

139 **"conjure[s] up in ages"**: Ken Emerson, *Always Magic in the Air*, p. 105.

142 **"But the total effect"**: Ed Ward et al., *Rock of Ages,* p. 201.

144 **"a white woman who was"**: Robert McG. Thomas Jr., "Florence Greenberg, 82, Pop-Record Producer," *New York Times*, Nov. 4, 1995, p. 54.

145 **"I've never had to do"**: David Kamp, "The Hit Factory," *Vanity Fair*, Nov. 2001, p. 258.

CHAPTER 8: THE BALLAD OF WASHINGTON SQUARE PARK

148 **"The Village was as close in 1946"**: Anatole Broyard, *Kafka Was the Rage*, p. 8.

149 **"to distinguish it from"**: Pete Seeger, *The Incompleat Folksinger*, p. 20.

149 **"The pervading atmosphere"**: Oscar Brand, *The Ballad Mongers*, p. 85.

151 **In New York, these kids attended**: Interaction between the folk community and these schools was an ongoing process. In 1942, a benefit for the Little Red School House was held at Town Hall, featuring Paul Draper and the Almanac Singers. In 1946, Elisabeth Irwin High School hosted a conference entitled "Folklore in the Metropolis," held under the auspices of Camp Woodland, which had founded the annual Folk Festival of the Catskills. Alan Lomax hosted that event, with Seeger, Guthrie, and Margot Mayo among those either speaking or performing.

151 **"Folk music was a very integral part"**: William Ruhlmann, "Peter, Paul and Mary: A Song to Sing All over This Land," *Goldmine*, April 12, 1996, archived at http://www.peterpaulandmary.com/history/f-ruhlmann1.htm.

152 **eleven-year-old Eric Weissberg:** In 1972, alongside Steve Mandel, Weissberg would record "Dueling Banjos" for the movie *Deliverance*; it became a number two pop hit the following year.

152 **"a brilliant alto":** *The Power of Song.*

153 **Naming themselves the Weavers:** Supposedly after a play by Gerhart Hauptmann, though "The Weaver's Song" had been part of the Almanac Singers' repertoire.

153 **"We still had the feeling":** *Wasn't That a Time*, documentary, dir. Jim Brown, 1982.

153 *The Peekskill Story:* Designed as a radio piece, *The Peekskill Story* was released by a tiny New York label, Chart Records.

153 **"drifted out of the Communist Party":** *Wasn't That a Time* documentary.

154 **It served as a tribute to a great man:** Though he recorded for Capitol in LA and engaged in a fascinating series of Manhattan drawing-room recordings in late 1948—making the most of the new long-play magnetic tape while he was still able to walk and sing—Leadbelly was sadly never a major star during his lifetime.

154 **"the most exciting act I've discovered":** Advertisement with these words shown in *The Power of Song.*

154 **"Goodnight Irene":** This was the number that Clyde McPhatter's future Dominoes chose to sing when entering and winning the *Arthur Godfrey's Talent Scouts* on CBS TV that October.

156 **Harvey Matusow, came before the HUAC:** "Agent Calls Singers Reds," *New York Times*, Feb. 26, 1952, p. 14.

156 **"We lost our livelihood":** *The Power of Song.*

157 **"essentially summer camp music":** Dave Van Ronk, *The Mayor of MacDougal Street*, p. 22.

157 **"playing music cognate with early jazz":** Ibid., p. 23.

158 **"when electronic recording made possible":** Greil Marcus, *Anthology of American Folk Music.*

159 **"Ending that war":** Alan Chartock interview with Pete Seeger Collection, Archive of Folk Culture at Library of Congress, 2003/014, for WAMC radio (2003).

163 a **"conservative world that was":** William Ruhlmann, *Peter, Paul and Mary* (1996), http://www.peterpaulandmary.com/history/f-ruhlmann2.htm.

165 **"everything from a maitre d' ":** Ibid.

165 **"the poetry and Beatniks in the Village":** Havens quoted in Robbie Woliver, *Hoot!*, p. 9. The inclusionary attitude that attracted Havens and his black Brooklyn friends to the Village coffeehouses did not extent across the entire neighborhood. In the spring of 1958, the *New York Times* reported on "Johnny

Romero's on Minetta Lane . . . a busy tavern that catered extensively to well-to-do Negroes who often escorted white women." In March, it noted, "toughs entered the tavern and told its owner, John Romero, that he had ten days to wind up his business affairs. Mr. Romero closed his tavern at once and left the country." Reporting on similar harassment of a coffeehouse called the College of Complexes, the *Times* noted, "It appears that the shakedown efforts have been confined to places catering to crowds that are mixed racially."

165 **"a master carpenter, a star con man":** Aronowitz on Mitchell from *The Blacklisted Journalist*, col. Six, Feb. 1, 1996 (link from http://www.blacklisted journalist.com, archived also at http://www.bobdylanroots.com/a11.html).

CHAPTER 9: LAY DOWN YOUR WEARY TUNE

173 **"When I arrived in Minneapolis":** To Cameron Crowe, *Biograph*, pp. 5–6.

173 **"some place which not too many":** Ibid., p. 7.

174 **"What he said at the time":** Dave Van Ronk, *The Mayor of MacDougal Street*, p. 159.

174 **"the Sicilian father I never had":** Bob Dylan, *Chronicles*, p. 64.

175 **"would suddenly swing and throw his head back":** The Cohen quote from a symposium as part of "Bob Dylan's American Journey, 1956–1966," archived at http://www.empsfm.org/exhibitions/index.asp?articleID=33#listen.

175 **"I'd either drive people away":** Dylan, *Chronicles*, p. 18.

176 **"A bright new face":** Robert Shelton, "Bob Dylan: A Distinctive Folk-Song Stylist," *New York Times*, Sept. 29, 1961, p. 31.

177 **"right there in the studio":** Robbie Woliver, *Hoot!*, pp. 76–77.

177 **To what extent Hammond had seen Dylan:** William Ruhlmann, *Peter, Paul and Mary* (1996), http://www.peterpaulandmary.com/history/f-ruhlmann2.htm.

178 **"I saw a picture of Mary":** Ibid.

178 **"nervous energy":** Ruhlmann, *Peter, Paul and Mary*.

178 **Peter, Paul and Mary's:** The name in fact came from Mary Travers's midfifties association with Pete Seeger, a Song Swappers children's number called "I Was Born 10,000 Years Ago," about Peter, Paul, and Moses.

178 **"We Shall Overcome":** *The People's Songs Bulletin* published it in 1947 as "We Will Overcome."

181 **"The Need for Topical Music":** See Marc Eliot, *Phil Ochs*, p. 51.

182 **"When he was through":** Woliver, *Hoot!*, p. 83.

182 **"What I did to break away":** Dylan, *Chronicles*, p. 67.

182 **"one-dimensional":** David Hajdu, *Positively 4th Street*, p. 117.

183 **"I thought 'Blowin' in the Wind' ":** Ruhlmann, *Peter, Paul and Mary*.

184 **as a reference to the Cuban missile crisis:** On the liner notes to *The Free-wheelin' Bob Dylan*, Nat Hentoff quoted Dylan as saying that "A Hard Rain's a-Gonna Fall" was indeed about the Cuban missile crisis. Fact was, he'd introduced it on stage a month ahead of the incident.

CHAPTER 10: CRYSTALS,
ANGELS, AND RAINDROPS

187 **"there was nothing homogenized":** Gerri Hirshey, *One Kiss Leads to Another: Girl Groups Sounds Lost and Found*, liner notes, p. 19, Rhino (2005).

190 **"absolutely, positively the one record":** http://spectropop.com/hspeccrys .html.

190 **"that he himself pictured himself":** Mark Ribowski, *He's a Rebel*, p. 114.

191 **"all black and blue":** Ibid.

193 **"what we wanted—a lead singer":** http://spectropop.com/hspeccrys.html.

194 **"could not take a chance":** Thomas J. Sugrue, *Sweet Land of Liberty* (New York: Random House, 2008), quoted in *New York Times Book Review*, Nov. 9, 2008.

194 **"I thought I had died":** Gee Ellie Gee, interview with Ellie Greenwich by Sheila Burgel, published at http://www.chachacharming.com/article.php?id= 26&pg=2.

194 **"Naah, I gotta try music":** To Charlotte Greig, published at http://spectropop .com/EllieGreenwich2/index.htm.

198 **considered "stuck-up":** Ronnie Spector, with Vince Waldron, *Be My Baby*, p. 37.

198 **"the look of the girls":** Ibid., p. 34.

198 **"The Ronettes were what the girls":** Ibid.

203 **"The place was jumping":** Jerry Leiber's capacity for storytelling is second only, at least in the world of contemporary Brill Building legends, to that of George Morton. But if Leiber's tales ever seem somewhat apocryphal, or perhaps exaggerated, he has managed to convince Stoller of the details along the way. Separate interviews with Leiber and Stoller revealed identical accounts of almost every single incident, transaction, and anecdote.

207 **"I had enough pain in me":** *The Songmakers* documentary.

210 **"Nothing to dream about":** Yet after Red Bird disappeared to his debtors, Goldner dared dream all over again. He set up Cotique Records and returned to the Latin music that was his first love, signing the streetwise and often politicized bugaloo groups of Spanish Harlem, the Lower East Side, and other inner-city areas that no other label would touch: Johnny Colon, New Swing Sextet, Lebron Brothers, and others. His last great act before he was felled

by a massive heart attack in April 1970, at fifty-two years old, was to produce Eddie Palmieri's protest album *Justicia*—for Morris Levy. Nothing much had changed. "Morris Levy had no heat," recalled Palmieri. "It was winter and you either recorded—take it or leave it. I had to record with gloves on." See Louis Laffitte, *Latin Beat* magazine (June–July 2002), at http://findarticles.com/p/articles/mi_m0FXV/is_5_12/ai_87777042/pg_9.

210 **"I had a hard time for many years"**: *The Songmakers* documentary.

CHAPTER 11: PLUG IN, TUNE UP, ROCK OUT

212 **"I decided, kind of then"**: Richie Unterberger, *Turn! Turn! Turn!,* chap. 2, archived at http://www.richieunterberger.com/lovin.html.

212 **the Even Dozen Jug Band:** The band also included Maria D'Amato, who joined Jim Kweskin's Jug Band, wed its guitarist Geoff Muldaur, and later had solo success under her married name; Stefan Grossman and David Grisman, who became well known in their own fields of folk and bluegrass; Joshua Rifkin and Pete Siegel, who went to work as producers; and Steve Katz, who went on to the Blues Project.

213 **"was getting very commercial"**: Robert Shelton, *No Direction Home*, p. 308. Darin also brought McGuinn out to Las Vegas to participate in a folk segment of his show.

213 **his "Beatles impersonations"**: http://rogermcguinn.blogspot.com/2007/04/roadie-report-25-bobby-darin-greenwich.html.

215 **Marshall Brickman, had recently quit:** He would later hook up with the Village comedian and jazz musician Woody Allen, to work on *Annie Hall* and other film scripts.

216 **"you guys are big"**: Holzman was true to his word, ultimately releasing the songs as part of a compilation, *What's Shakin'*, in 1966, that included tracks by Eric Clapton, Al Kooper, Tom Rush, and the Paul Butterfield Blues Band.

216 **the "crotch watcher's bench"**: http://www.petersando.com/mem14.html.

219 **"I found myself writing this song"**: Greil Marcus, *Like a Rolling Stone*, p. 70.

220 **"What are you doing there?"**: Ibid., p. 213.

224 **"It wasn't a working ship"**: Cavaliere probably would not have used the word "gay" back in 1965. But what he called "the gay influence" was indeed being felt within the New York culture at this time—and the Hamptons were already a holiday ground for the Manhattan cultural elite.

225 **They, too, turned him down:** Spector, desperate to find an electric group, ended up working with the Modern Folk Quartet instead, but the cuts were never released at the time.

228 **"a contract workshop":** Interview with Greg Shaw for *Mojo Navigator*, 1 (1967), archived at http://www.lysergia.com/LamaWorkshop/BluesMagoos/lamaBluesMagoos.htm.

234 **"I cannot guarantee the success":** Shadow Morton is one of the music business's great raconteurs, and one of the results of his storytelling—and the rarity with which he gives interviews—is that observers tend to suspect he is being fanciful with the truth. It was a joy to conduct entirely separate interviews with Morton and Ian and have them deliver identical versions of their initial relationship. In particular, Janis Ian's questions about Morton letting her "have her way" in the studio and Morton's explanations for doing so were each entirely unprompted.

235 **"Censorship was clearly keeping":** Bob Shelton, *Janis Ian*, Verve Forecast liner notes.

CHAPTER 12: ALL TOMORROW'S PARTIES

237 **the East Village:** Terry Miller. *Greenwich Village and How It Got That Way*, p. 258.

238 **the old Bowery Village:** *Bouwerie* was the Dutch word for farmland, ironic considering that New York's Bowery subsequently became a byword for an urban skid row. In fact, as the lower part of the Bowery fell into such disrepute that it came to be known as "thieves highway," the wealthier residents above Sixth Street successfully lobbied to have its name changed to Fourth Avenue.

239 **The density of the Tenth Ward:** See http://www.tenement.org/Encyclopedia/lower_landscape.htm. In researching this period, I was unable to find a reliable census study showing a more densely populated area anywhere in the world at any time.

239 **"the conscience of the ghetto":** In 1896, the journalist Cahan had seized on the teeming potential amid the "huddled masses" for his groundbreaking novel *Yekl: The American Ghetto*. The word "ghetto," little known to American gentiles, had originated in Venice, coming to define that part of a European city occupied by Jews. And it was as "the Ghetto" that this part of Manhattan remained known until, by a steady process of repetition, the "Lower East Side" came into regular usage in the twentieth century.

243 **"I wanted to do it before":** Stampfel's accounts can make the Holy Modal Rounders into a comedy act. Wit undoubtedly played a part. But they could be professional even as they were being funny. A live bootleg from 1965, recorded in Detroit, finds the duo consistently in tune, in time, and in tandem, not just with each other but also with their audience.

243 **"to write anything [he] wanted"**: http://www.litkicks.com/Topics/EdSand ersInterview.html.

243 **"It changed my life"**: Like many who came to live in the midst of beatnik culture, Sanders came to disown the term: "Most of my generation laughed when they were called Beats," he wrote in an introduction to *Tales of Beatnik Glory,* a sarcastically titled book of short stories about that period on the Lower East Side; "Beatnik and Beat were two of the great pejoratives of the era." "Nobody called themselves beatniks," said Peter Stampfel. "It was a derisive term."

244 **"Egyptian freak-doodles"**: John Wilcock, "Who the Fugs Think They Are," in Paul Krassner, ed., *The Best of the Realist,* p. 179.

244 **"Ed was a wild, crazy"**: All Tuli repeats this quote from http://www.furious .com/Perfect/tuli.html.

244 **"'gave us the illusion"**: Ibid.

245 **"the dances of Dionysus"**: http://www.thefugs.com/history2.html.

246 **"That was enough to get us beaten"**: http://www.furious.com/Perfect/tuli .html.

246 **Weber, said Sanders:** *The Holy Modal Rounders: Bound to Lose,* documentary, dir. by Sam Wainwright Douglas and Paul Lovelace (2006).

247 **"possession with intent to sell"**: Barry Miles, *Hippie.*

248 **a "rambling" affair:** Sidney E. Zion, "Avant Garde Group Charges Harassment by City," http://www.nytimes.com/books/01/04/08/specials/ginsberg-city .html.

249 **"like a 'cello' getting up"**: Richard Goldstein, *Goldstein's Greatest Hits,* p. 18.

250 **"didn't really try"**: David Fricke, *Peel Slowly and See,* liner notes, Polydor, (1995), p. 9. Schwartz's body gave out on him in 1966; a track on the first Velvet Underground album was dedicated to his memory.

251 **"what Lou was singing about"**: Ibid., p. 21.

251 **"in novels it would"**: *Seven Ages of Rock,* BBC television documentary, pt. 2, *Art Rock* (2007).

251 **" 'Heroin' is very close"**: Dave Thompson, *Beyond the Velvet Underground,* p. 33.

251 **"every song's a"**: Legs McNeil and Gillian McCain, *Please Kill Me,* p. 4.

251 **"didn't know from"**: Rob Bowman, *Between Thought and Expression: The Lou Reed Anthology.* RCA (1992), p. 6.

252 **"Our music is the"**: Clinton Heylin, *From the Velvets to the Voidoids,* p. 11.

252 **in the spring and summer of 1965:** At the end of the year, Cale, Morrison, and Reed, with Heliczer on sax, were shown playing "Heroin" on CBS TV, as Walter Cronkite narrated to middle America this thing called "underground film." Footage appears not to have survived.

252 **"Do you mean we have to show up"**: Victor Bockris, *Up-Tight*, p. 22.

253 **"Half the people walked out"**: Morrison quote from 1990, archived at http:// olivier.landemaine.free.fr/vu/live/1965-66/perf6566.html.

253 **"We were doing with music"**: Victor Bockris, *Transformer*, p. 111.

254 **as "half Goddess"**: Goldstein, *Goldstein's Greatest Hits*, p. 18.

254 **"a repetition of the *concrete*"**: Grace Gluek, "Syndromes Pop at Delmonico's" *New York Times*, Jan. 14, 1966, p. 36.

254 **"music that bleeds together"**: *Rock & Roll*, BBC/WGBH documentary.

254 **"Everyone was taking speed"**: *The South Bank Show: Velvet Underground*, UK television documentary (1986).

254 **"movies, food, dancing"**: The Dom, from Polski Dom Narodowy (Polish National Home), at 21 and 23 St. Mark's Place, had already been a German music hall, a community center known as Arlington Hall, and the scene of an infamous botched Jewish gangland shoot-out. Later, in 1966, it became Balloon Farm and then, the following year, the Electric Circus, the psychedelic discotheque that first served to make St. Mark's Place a tourist trap.

255 **"very similar to a B-52"**: *The South Bank Show*.

255 **"We put three chord rock"**: Cale, *Seven Ages of Rock*.

256 **Verve quickly snapped up the album:** Recording of *The Velvet Underground & Nico* began in May; Verve released "All Tomorrow's Parties" as a single in the summer.

256 **"Andy made a point of trying"**: Rob Bowman, *The Lou Reed Anthology*, pp. 6–7.

256 **the newly hailed leaders:** The prevailing kings of the New York underground, the Fugs, welcomed all comers. A friendship with the Mothers that had formed out west on their 1965 tour grew closer when the groups shared nearby residencies in Greenwich Village in 1967. The Fugs also embraced the Velvet Underground. "There was plenty room in the whole world for both," said Sanders. "I didn't feel competitive about anybody." Quoted in Bockris, *Up-Tight*, p. 33.

257 **"What happens when the daddy"**: Clinton Heylin, *All Yesterdays' Parties*, p. 42.

258 **might "well be the most inept band"**: Lester Bangs, *Psychotic Reactions and Carburetor Dung*, pp. 82–92

260 **in a "brief, stunning"**: Sanders quoted at http://www.thefugs.com/history3 .html.

260 **"an affirmation of love and happiness"**: "10,000 Chant Love," *New York Times*, March 27, 1967, p. 1.

262 **"I didn't even know"**: http://www.nytimes.com/books/97/10/26/home/luckas -fitzpatrick.html.

263 **"the same beat we were starting at"**: *The South Bank Show*.

264 **"one of the reasons I didn't like":** Yvonne Sewall-Ruskin, *High on Rebellion*, p. 14.

264 **"people who like to fight":** Bob Russell quoted ibid., p. 34.

264 **Max's was ostensibly a restaurant:** Ibid., pp. 20–21.

266 **"and smoking bananas":** From Country Joe and the Fish (responsible for announcing it) to Donovan (who sang about it) and to the Velvet Underground (and their debut album cover), the smoking bananas craze was one of the more amusing diversions to the summer of love. When the *East Village Other* surveyed its readers in 1967, some 19 percent revealed that they had smoked bananas; at the Central Park be-in that Easter, one twenty-eight-year-old told a *New York Times* reporter, "It's not as good as a pot high, but what the hell, the cops can't arrest you."

267 **an antiwar protest in October 1967:** This was the same demonstration at which the Fugs brought a flatbed truck to lead a much publicized exorcism of the Pentagon, and then placed daisy stems in the barrels of the guarding soldiers' rifles.

268 **President Johnson announced on television:** From here on, there was constant infighting among Yippies about the point of going to Chicago.

268 **"a stick-up":** http://www.wikicu.com/1968_protests.

268 **Students took over and occupied:** Ed Sanders, *1968: A History in Verse*, p. 106.

270 **The intended community celebration turned:** This incident is recounted with great hilarity, and perhaps embellishment, in Legs McNeil's and Gillian McCain's *Please Kill Me*, pp. 59–62. One strange offshoot of the confrontation was that when the MC5 became infamous for their cry "Kick out the jams, motherfucker," many listeners assumed they were somehow referring fondly to the Lower East Side activists.

270 **ESP . . . left him off the album cover:** The Rounders had the last laugh. Elektra signed them (despite everything), and the act recorded in Los Angeles, where Sam Shepard was writing the script for *Zabriskie Point*. Weber behaved, *The Moray Eels Eat the Holy Modal Rounders* was well received, and "The Bird Song" from the album was picked up by Dennis Hopper for the *Easy Rider* soundtrack.

272 **"I never thought I would not do":** Bockris, *Up-Tight*, p. 118.

272 **Reed quit the Velvet Underground:** Polk's mono recording of the Aug. 23 gig, reputedly Reed's last, was later sold to Atlantic Records and released, in 1972, as *Live at Max's Kansas City*. Despite her drinking partner's persistent requests that someone fetch him a Pernod, and his discussion of a new movie bleeding into the professional-quality microphone, the bootleg recording proved to be of admirable quality.

272 **"I'm probably one of the most":** *Creem*, May 1971, as quoted in Heylin, *All Yesterdays' Parties*, p. 235..

CHAPTER 13: THE APPLE STRETCHING

274 **"drag queens, hippy queens with long hair":** Jayne County, with Rupert Smith, *Man Enough to Be a Woman*, pp. 40–41.

274 **and alleged to be behind the permanent disappearance:** The authors Carter and Duberman both quote Tommy Lanigan-Schmidt as witnessing the street-side kidnapping by Murphy of his friend Tano, who was never seen again. Murphy was said to have kept out of jail in later life thanks to his knowledge, and photographic evidence, of FBI Director J. Edgar Hoover's own homosexual activities.

275 **The Stonewall's twin dance floors:** The full jukebox list is archived at http://www.stonewallvets.org/songsofStonewall-1.htm.

275 **"We knew the Sixth Precinct":** *Villager*, June 16–22, 2004. Speaking to the New-York Historical Society in June 2004, Pine claimed that the raid was conducted in part over an investigation into stolen European bonds. As reported in the *Blade*, June 4, 2004, p. 13, two uniformed Sixth Precinct cops—Frank Toscano and Tommy Noble—have always insisted they were already inside the club, responding to what turned out to be a false call about a stabbing. They accused the First Division detectives of orchestrating the false alarm calls to ensure that some uniformed backup was on hand.

276 **arresting none other than Dave Van Ronk:** According to the *Village Voice*'s Howard Smith, who was barricaded inside the Stonewall with the detectives, Van Ronk admitted to throwing "a few coins," and was beaten to the point of nearly passing out. Van Ronk's arrest was reported in the newspapers but went unmentioned in his autobiography.

277 **"The gay people are the last people":** *East Village Other*, July 9, p. 2.

277 **At the Peppermint Lounge:** The Peppermint Lounge was closed by the State Liquor Authority in December 1965 as part of a crackdown on clubs and bars that failed to disclose their "true"—i.e., mob-affiliated—ownership. The Peppermint Lounge was revealed to be a front for the Genovese capo Matty "the Horse" Ianniello—*New York Times*, Dec. 28, 1965.

277 **the "feeling the crowd emanates":** Albert Goldman, *Disco*, p. 50.

277 **midtown was filled with French-themed:** Eric Burdon and Jeff Marshall Craig, *Don't Let Me Be Misunderstood* (New York: Nation Books, 2002), p. 286.

278 **"Nobody had really just kept":** http://www.djhistory.com/interviews/francis-grasso.

279 **"Gay Prohibition / Corupt\$ Cop\$":** Graffiti on cover of the *Village Voice*, July 3, 1969.

279 **"Should I meet with a violent death"**: *New York Times*, March 18 and March 23, 1970, as archived at http://bitterqueen.typepad.com/history_of_gay_bars_in_ne/gambino_crime_family/index.html. It was probably just coincidence, but that same month, Deputy Inspector Seymour Pine led a raid on the West Tenth Street gay bar the Snake Pit—this time with sufficient backup—resulting in 167 arrests and another outcry from gay activists who believed they were still being victimized by police even as they deplored being under control of the mob.

280 **progressed to the Sanctuary**: The relative short life of the church in its uncensored capacity might explain the lack of photographic evidence of its precise decor.

282 **"Steve D'Acquisto and Francis Grasso"**: Tim Lawrence, *Love Saves the Day*, p. 37.

282 **Sanctuary's reputation ensured**: *Klute*'s Sanctuary scenes show the club much as described in this chapter, though the dance floor is additionally surrounded by some circular tables and the crowd seems predominantly heterosexual. The *Klute* VD comes accompanied by the movie's promotional mini-film of the era, in which Donald Sutherland speaks of New York City as if it were a Third World country: "I think anyone who comes here for the first time is initially appalled. The . . . air is impossible to breathe. There's too many people and it's compressed too tightly. And I was awestruck by the areas of degradation and alienation and squalor."

288 **"Never, *ever* did"**: Lawrence, *Love Saves the Day*, p. 100.

288 **"You won't let us in?"**: Ibid.

289 **"Other DJs would play three records"**: Ibid., p. 107.

291 **"There's always one person"**: Quoted in *The Coolest Year in Hell*, Firehouse Films, New York (2007).

291 **"Levan . . . had electric eyes"**: http://www.djsportal.com/en/articles/index.php?id=disco_history.

291 **and they took it out on him**: Grasso, who died in 2003, consistently told of his beating as summarized here—insisting that the foot soldier who administered it exceeded his orders, which had been primarily to scare the DJ. Such stories from the underworld are inevitably cloudy and open to interpretation. The Machine did not last long enough to leave a traceable history. And whether or not the foot soldier overstepped his bounds, one wonders at the Machine owners' audacity to begin with, given Nicholas Di Martino's powerful reputation. Still, that's the way Grasso told it—and it's always possible that reparations and/or revenge were enacted with considerably less publicity.

293 **the Dom on St. Mark's**: The crowd at the Dom, Stanley Tolkin's bar on St. Mark's Place, above which now stood the Electric Circus, appears to have shifted since the midsixties. "The Electric Circus was the white club, and the Dom was

the black club," said Smith. "That couldn't happen in Brooklyn or Bronx, to have a white club on top and a black club underneath and nobody fighting."

295 **marriage of seventies funk and soul:** Barry White quickly threw together an album, *Rhapsody in White*, of similar instrumentals credited to the Love Unlimited Orchestra; like the re-released *Under the Influence of . . .* , it opened with "Love's Theme." Both albums went top ten.

296 **MFSB featuring the Three Degrees:** The Three Degrees had been discovered and molded, back in his and their native Philadelphia, by Richard Barrett, who had performed a similar role over fifteen years earlier with the Chantels.

297 **"more like a club":** Lawrence, *Love Saves the Day*, p. 134.

297 **"conceited," "A-List," "very beautiful":** Ibid., p. 139.

298 **Aletti detailed the battle over SoHo:** Vince Aletti, "SoHo vs. Disco," *Village Voice*, June 16, 1975.

299 **when *New York* magazine commissioned Nik Cohn:** Nik Cohn, "Tribal Rites of the New Saturday Night," *New York*, June 2, 1976.

300 **"My story was a fraud":** Charlie LeDuff, "Saturday Night Fever: The Life," *New York Times*, June 9, 1996, sec. 13, pp. 1, 14–15.

CHAPTER 14: LOOKING FOR A KISS: GLITTER, GLAM, AND NEW YORK DOLLS

303 **"'The Velvets closed rock 'n' roll":** Quoted by Coleman, in an author interview.

303 **"grotesque chalk white masks":** "Alice Cooper Did Not Invent Glitter," *Creem*, Nov. 1973, p. 50. From the fifties through the seventies, in various countries around the world, the Thalidomide drug caused deformities in the babies of many mothers who were prescribed it during pregnancy.

303 **The Jackie Curtis play:** Jayne County, with Rupert Smith, *Man Enough to Be a Woman*, p. 50.

303 **Ridiculous Theater:** When Charles Ludlam broke from the Playhouse of the Ridiculous in 1967, he started the Ridiculous Theatrical Company. Some people just called the whole scene Ridiculous Theater.

304 **"'was the smart one":** County, with Smith, *Man Enough to Be a Woman*, p. 61.

307 **"would have a girl's blouse on":** Jerry Nolan, "My Life As a Doll," *Village Voice Rock & Roll Quarterly*, July 1991, p. 5.

308 **"David was a little more heterosexual":** Legs McNeil and Gillian McCain, *Please Kill Me*, p. 116.

308 **"it had lost its sex appeal'":** Ben Whalley (director), *Once Upon a Time in New York: The Birth of Hip Hop, Disco and Punk* (2007).

308 **"We called ourselves"**: Ibid.

308 **"that he thought the band"**: Kris Needs and Dick Porter, *Trash*, pp. 44–45.

309 **"They were all looking"**: *Creem*, Oct. 2005, archived at http://www.creem magazine.com/_site/BeatGoesOn/NewYorkDolls/ConfessionsOfADo110510. html.

309 **"seven cabaret theaters"**: Promotional brochure for Mercer Arts Center (1971).

309 **"My motive . . . is to make this"**: "Mercer Stages Are a Supermarket," *New York Times*, Nov. 2, 1971, p. 44.

311 **"You didn't just go to see"**: McNeil and McCain, *Please Kill Me*, p. 118.

311 **"Everybody in America was wearing"**: http://tres_producers.blogspot.com/ 2002_02_10_tres_producers_archive.html#9773615.

312 **"a group called Aerosmith**: Aerosmith eventually enjoyed the success that evaded the New York Dolls. As if shared schooling, looks, and management were not enough coincidence, Steven Tyler ultimately ended up with Johansen's girlfriend, Cyrinda Foxe.

312 **"We never really got over it"**: Sylvain, sleeve notes to *New York Dolls, Live in NYC* (1975).

313 **"a family of very talented"**: David Nobakht, *Suicide*, p. 12.

313 **"I had seen a lot"**: Ibid., p. 18.

317 **"the first band that valued'"**: Whalley, *Once upon a Time in New York*.

318 **"The premise of the band"**: http://www.superseventies.com/sssimmonsstan ley.html.

318 **"no club would hire us"**: http://www.superseventies.com/sssimmonsstanley .html.

318 **"a great, charismatic-looking band"**: http://www.pioneerlocal.com/arling tonheights/entertainment/1103546,db-stanley-081408-s2.article.

318 **"The only person who can produce"**: To Ben Edmonds, *Creem*, Oct. 1973.

319 **"There has never been"**: Christgau ibid.

319 **"When they finally met"**: Nina Antonia, *The New York Dolls*, p. 85.

320 **the eight-story hotel**: Eventually the collapse was blamed on damage caused to a supporting wall during installation of unapproved drainage pipes in the 1940s.

321 **"disassociating yourself from your past"**: Clinton Heylin, *From the Velvets to the Voidoids*, p. 117.

321 **"I started getting successful"**: McNeil and McCain, *Please Kill Me*, p. 161.

323 **bisexual wife, Anna, in 1953**: That same year, Anna Genovese sued for divorce, offering the court detailed testimony about her husband's criminal activities and wife-beating tendencies. Breaking La Cosa Nostra's code of silence was tantamount to a death sentence, but given that Vito was already believed to have arranged the murder of Anna's first husband twelve days before

their own wedding, in the 1930s, and allowing for his central role in New York's bloody gang wars since his return from years of hiding in Italy, he couldn't be so crude as to take revenge on his own wife. He allegedly took it out instead on Club 82's manager, Stephen Franse, who had served as Anna's bodyguard while Vito Genovese had been in exile. Franse was last seen alive at 4:30 a.m. on the morning of June 19, 1953, when he left the club; a few hours later, he was found beaten to death in the backseat of his car. His death was reported at the time, with the sort of media connivance often applied to mob murders, as a "brutal mugging." Anna Genovese's name disappeared from the record soon thereafter, suggesting a change of identity under government protection.

324 **"They still talk about"**: Needs and Porter, *Trash*, pp. 118–19.

CHAPTER 15: THE GLAMOUR OF POVERTY

325 **"I felt CBGBs sounded so pat"**: Grammatically, the club should, by rights, be known just as CBGB, but as Kristal's own account indicates, everyone referred to it in the plural.

326 **"The great thing about this band"**: *SoHo Weekly News*, April 23, 1974.

327 **"sexy sexy as hell"**: Quoted in Clinton Heylin, *From the Velvets to the Voidoids*, pp. 126–27.

328 **"We were really unique"**: Legs McNeil and Gillian McCain, *Please Kill Me*, p. 172.

329 **"He wasn't overly possessive"**: Debbie Harry, *Making Tracks*, p. 14.

330 **"People who join a band"**: Everett True, *Hey Ho Let's Go*, p. 15.

330 **Colvin had a particularly miserable**: Dee Dee quotes and bio from Dee Dee Ramone, with Veronica Kofman, *Lobotomy*, pp. 38–41.

331 **"a black satin-like jumpsuit"**: Jim Bessman, *The Ramones: An American Band* (New York: St. Martin's Press, 1993).

331 **"bad every minute of the day"**: Jim Fields (director), *End of the Century* (2003).

332 **"almost the same song"**: True, *Hey Ho Let's Go*, p. 23.

333 **"When you saw the Ramones"**: http://www.cbgb.com/history/history3.htm.

335 **"where all the kids in the neighborhood"**: McNeil and McCain, *Please Kill Me*, p. 183.

335 **The Ramones were filmed**: Available on *It's Alive*, 1974–96, Rhino DVD.

337 **"I felt totally betrayed"**: Heylin, *From the Velvets*, p. 135.

338 **"Miss Smith has it in her"**: *New York Times*, March 25, 1975, p. 10.

339 **"If you work with a woman"**: David Nobakht, *Suicide*, p. 79.

339 **"marked the death of the glitter period"**: Harry. *Making Tracks*, p. 31.

343 **Who now—or even then—recalls**: Certainly, there were other contenders on

the scene at the time. The Miamis, former playing members of Wayne County's Queen Elizabeth, were considered by many to have the best credentials and best songs. The Mumps were led by Lance Loud, gay icon from the PBS documentary *American Family*, who had moved to New York in part because of the Factory and the Velvet Underground; they offered a highly beloved kitsch view of contemporary culture. The youthful Marbles had emerged from Columbia University with identical "pudding bowl" haircuts and a penchant for classic pop harmonies. Milk 'n' Cookies seemed so impressive at the time that when Alan Betrock launched a "Know Your New York Bands" section in the *SoHo Weekly News*, he made them the focus of his second installment, sandwiched between Television and the Ramones. Such was the initial promise of double drums prog-pop group the Shirts, fronted by Annie Golden, that Hilly Kristal became their manager. There was also Tough (soon to be Tuff) Darts, led by the rockabilly fanatic Robert Gordon. And Willie "Mink" DeVille, who after reading about the Ramones moved from San Francisco to New York, where his streetwise singer-songwriter shtick served him much better.

344 **they played cover versions:** Accepted CBGBs history says that Hilly Kristal demanded of the bands he booked only that they play "original music." Yet most of them also played covers—as, indeed, would any country, bluegrass, or blues group he might have booked under his original vision. It has been suggested that the demand for "original" music may have been a way to get around the license fees to ASCAP and BMI.

344 **"You could walk over":** Gary Valentine, *New York Rocker,* p. 83.

346 **"On the inside sleeve":** McNeil and McCain, *Please Kill Me*, p. 204.

347 **"Everything that was humiliating":** Ibid., p. 207.

347 **"Punk Rock—any kid can pick up":** *Punk* magazine, no. 3, p. 3, at http://www.punkmagazine.com/vault/back_issues/03/letters_a.html.

348 **a top ten album in their U.S. homeland:** Internationally, where markets were more compressed or/and resistance at radio was less, there was much greater success for the leading "CBGBs" acts in the upper echelons of the charts.

348 **"It was a shock at that time":** *Seven Ages of Rock*, BBC television documentary (2007).

350 **Fields "fell in love":** McNeil and McCain, *Please Kill Me*, p. 202.

CHAPTER 16: THE BOOGIE-DOWN BRONX

359 **"North Siders":** Evelyn Diaz Gonzalez. *The Bronx*, p. 17.

360 **the "most contented":** Haffen quoted ibid., p. 5.

360 **"destroying blocks of apartments":** Ibid., p. 116. Though deplored and

decried by residents, especially those whose communities were destroyed in its wake, the Cross-Bronx had the support of Borough President James P. Lyon, and the Bronx Board of Trade, who labored under the misapprehension that it would bring business to the borough. Its very name should have indicated otherwise: expressways were not designed for loitering.

362 **"this week is the fire"**: Jill Jonnes, *We're Still Here*, p. 233.

364 **"And that's how it started"**: Jeff Chang, *Can't Stop, Won't Stop*, pp. 69–70.

365 **"They wasn't something"**: Herc interview archived by the Experience Music Project, at http://www.emplive.org/print.asp?parentCategoryID=2&renderVers=2&articleID=597.

365 **the Incredible Bongo Band's:** Michael Viner, an MGM executive and musician, assembled the Incredible Bongo Band in 1972, originally to provide two songs for a B-movie. When one of them, the highly rhythmic twelve-bar blues "Bongo Rock," became popular with R&B DJs, the team recorded an album of the same name, relying mostly on proven instrumentals that overplayed their claim to percussive magnificence. However, alongside the novelty of "Dueling Bongos" and "In-a-Gadda-Da-Vida," they reworked the 1961 twang guitar classic "Apache" and hit the musical jackpot. From its opening break—a reverb-ridden sound clash between trap drums and bongo—on to its instantly recognizable guitar melody, its Stax-like battle between brass and organ, and then a midway, minute-long repetition of that opening percussive break, during which the bongos were set loose, "Apache" was an instant b-boy anthem. And because it was an instrumental that never let up, unlike so much else that hit Herc's decks, it could be played in its entirety. The *Bongo Rock* album was released by MGM in the summer of 1973. Herc credited a DJ partner, Timmy Tim, with pointing it his way. Whether or not they got hold of "Apache" in time for the first party at Sedgwick is uncertain, but Herc is credited with being the first DJ to expose it to the Bronx b-boys. Over thirty years later, "Apache" was still being relentlessly sampled and remixed, proving far and away the most popular, prominent, and enduring hip-hop break beat of them all.

366 **"They couldn't be looking down"**: http://www.emplive.org/print.asp?parentCategoryID=2&renderVers=2&articleID=597.

366 **"the gangs came up and start"**: Charlie Ahearn, *Yes Yes Y'All*, p. 25.

366 **"beyond rebuilding, tinkering"**: Jonnes, *We're Still Here*, p. 299.

367 **At the end of September 1973, the Yankees:** By the time it reopened, in April 1976, the city had spent some $100 million refurbishing Yankee Stadium. Embarrassed by this overrun, it cut the $2 million that had been earmarked for improving the actual neighborhood. In the meantime, during baseball's absence, a dozen businesses around the stadium that depended on the fans for their traffic closed down.

367 **"The lifespan of youth style"**: Chang, *Can't Stop, Won't Stop,* p. 45.

368 **"I took my things of attacking"**: Ibid., pp. 95–96.

368 **"to see these black people fighting"**: Ahearn, *Yes Yes Y'All,* p. 44.

368 **"Bam always DJ'd"**: Interview with Mark Skillz, archived at http://hiphop101a .blogspot.com/2007/05/you-cant-stop-us-now-birth-of-planet.html.

369 **"Thank God for Bambaataa"**: Ahearn, *Yes Yes Y'All,* pp. 51–52.

369 **a series of infamous block parties:** Though the first parties took place inside the Sedgwick Houses, the outdoor jams at Sedgwick and Cedar became such a part of the hip-hop legend that a group of founding DJs and MCs later started a clothing company named for that intersection.

371 **"folks from four to forty"**: Grandmaster Flash, *The Adventures of Grandmaster Flash,* pp. 46–47.

371 **his street reputation into a club residency:** Chang, *Can't Stop, Won't Stop,* p. 83.

372 **"little makeshift turntables"**: Ahearn, *Yes Yes Y'All,* p. 72.

372 **"figure out a way"**: Whalley, *Once Upon a Time in New York,* BBC 4 (2007).

373 **"it was like a speaking engagement"**: Bill Brewster and Frank Broughton, *Last Night a DJ Saved My Life,* p. 217.

373 **"epitomized the true meaning"**: Kurtis Blow, *The History of Rap,* vol. 1, liner notes.

374 **"Grandmaster Flowers was the best"**: http://www.jayquan.com/pete.htm. Cameron Flowers died in 1992, reputedly as a heroin addict last seen panhandling in Times Square. Whether he beat Flash to the Grandmaster prefix is undetermined, just as his place in DJ history has gone largely uncelebrated.

375 **"What I did was give it a rhythm"**: Ahearn, *Yes Yes Y'All,* p. 63.

376 **"There was a lot at stake"**: Ibid., p. 12.

377 **"It had nothing to do with race"**: Joe Austin, *Taking the Train,* p. 52.

378 **"The graffiti movement"**: Goldstein, "This Thing Has Gotten Completely out of Hand," *New York,* March 26, 1973, pp. 36, 39.

378 **"the talent show era"** . . . **"That was the world"**: Interview with Mark Skillz, archived at http://hiphop101a.blogspot.com/2007/05/straight-no-chaser -dj-hollywood.html (other Hollywood quotes from author interview).

381 **"Guys like me and Hollywood"**: Interview with Mark Skillz, archived at http://hiphop101a.blogspot.com/2007/06/master-mix-those-number-one-tunes.html.

381 **"totally wack on the mic"**: Ben Whalley (director), *Once Upon a Time in New York* (2007).

381 **"It seemed like he came"**: Interview with Mark Skillz, archived at http://hiphop101a.blogspot.com/2008/06/once-upon-time-in-bronx-rise-of.html.

382 **"Suddenly I heard all this yelling"**: Ahearn, *Yes Yes Y'All.* p. 71.

382 **"get extremely creative with words":** Flash, *The Adventures of Grandmaster Flash*, p. 108.

382 **"*nobody* ever messed with":** Ibid., p. 95.

382 **"We were going to stay exactly":** Bee's choice of expression—"Boom!"—harks back to the 1950s, when the Chords wrote the song "Sh-Boom," because "if you were standing on the block for five minutes, you'd hear that slang word fifteen times or more" (see chap. 6). The Chords hailed from the Boston Road–Jennings Street intersection of the South Bronx, in the heart of "the 9." The expression appears to have survived the generations.

383 **first Latino DJ to play the streets:** Honorable mention should go here to Junebug, a Puerto Rican who found himself in the heart of the club scene, as Hollywood's DJ. He was later shot dead over drugs. Mention should also be made of John "Jellybean" Benitez, of Puerto Rican heritage, who grew up on Davidson Avenue in the South Bronx, surrounded by the gang violence of the early seventies, witnessed Bambaataa and others in their element, and decided to become a DJ himself. But once he heard Walter Gibbons at Galaxy 21 in Manhattan, he committed himself to the disco scene downtown rather than the b-boy music of the Bronx. He went on to produce Madonna's first records for Sire.

384 **Grandmaster Flash, Disco Bee, and EZ-Mike:** Tracking the exact chronological progression of midseventies hip-hop culture is exhausting. The movement was seen by its key participants not as a linear development but rather as a constantly circulating series of interlocking developments, the waxing and waning of youth gangs, b-boying, and graffiti all as important to the participants' memory process as specific dates of specific events. Parties were promoted by hand-drawn flyers, if at all, and most of those that predate 1978 no longer exist. The kids didn't carry cameras with them; a photographic legacy to the period 1973–76 appears not to exist. And for several years, DJs and MCs regularly rotated partnerships until they settled into place in a particular crew.

Nobody can expect any memory of this period to be perfect. Flash himself has consistently cited the date of his breakout show at the Audubon Ballroom as September 2, 1976. Yet he has also insisted, including in his own memoir, that "the Furious Five" (as his Three MCs ultimately became known) were with him that night, when it is well known that the lineup was not completed until 1979. Hip-hop historians agree that Flash was capable of filling the vast room before the Furious Five took shape, and so the 1976 date is entirely possible. But it's worth noting that in 1976 September 2 fell on a Thursday, whereas in the following year it fell on the Friday of Labor Day weekend, the more likely occasion for an all-night party. I've gone with 1976 because of Flash's relentless insistence on it.

CHAPTER 17: WELL, NEW YORK REALLY
HAS IT ALL . . .

387 **"Carbona Not Glue":** Predictably, Carbona sued soon after the album's release, and the track was replaced on further pressings.

387 **girlfriend Connie Gripp:** Gripp returned to working the streets and eventually died of an overdose. She was buried in a potter's field.

387 **the flood of releases:** Both clubs had released compilation albums the preceding summer.

387 **"by any logical criterion":** Rockwell, "Report from New York's Rock 'Underground,'" *New York Times*, Feb. 20, 1977, p. 77.

387 *Marquee Moon* **had broken into:** Television's heyday would prove remarkably short-lived. A second album, *Adventure*, recorded in late 1977 but released the following year, was received poorly, and the group broke up after disappointing tours.

390 **"People had their own negative":** Henry Corra (director), *NY77: The Coolest Year in Hell*, documentary (2007).

390 **The partners were best known:** Less frequently mentioned was their ownership of a gay bar in Boston, which they sold in 1975 to a New York discotheque owner.

391 **Siano, still working weekends:** Siano did not last long at Studio 54. Developing a heroin addiction on top of his other pharmaceutical tendencies, he continued to fall from grace when his elder brother Joe, still the guiding business force behind the Gallery, carried out his threat to close the club unless Nicky sobered up. The Gallery shut its doors later in 1977. Nicky Siano was only twenty-one years old. He eventually overcame his addiction and resumed DJing.

392 **the celebrity shoulder rubbing:** Randy Jones, of the camp disco act the Village People, recalled passing a joint along only to find Jimmy Carter's mother, Lillian, sitting next to him. The president's mother herself remarked of her visit, "I don't know whether I was in heaven or hell, but it was wonderful."

392 **to make requests and otherwise dictate:** Tony Smith, who the following year became resident at Xenon, a midtown Studio 54 imitation, noted of this development, "In a mob club they never bothered the DJ. They hired you, you're supposed to know what you're doing. By the time Xenon came out, the owners are in the DJ booth." Smith was ultimately fired "for refusing to play 'Happy Birthday' for Bianca Jagger" at the Xenon owner's request.

392 **"The profits are astronomical":** "The Eccentric Whiz behind Studio 54," *New York*, Nov. 7, 1977, p. 14.

392 **a federal raid on the office:** In a dual bust by the IRS and the Organized

Crime Task Force, Schrager was charged also with intent to distribute cocaine, and the Feds pushed hard for the pair to confirm their ties to a midtown loan shark, Sam Jacobson, for whom payments ranging from $2,500 to $25,000 a week were uncovered in the company's accounts. Rubell and Schrager refused to plea-bargain, and the additional charges did not stick. By the time Rubell died, in 1989, of complications from AIDS, at age forty-five, he and Schrager had opened their first Manhattan boutique hotels, Morgan's and the Royalton. Schrager would go on to become one of the preeminent hoteliers in America.

393 **Levan established himself:** After the Continental Baths closed down in 1976, Levan's former partner Frankie Knuckles moved to Chicago, where he became resident and stakeholder in a club called the Warehouse. There he, too, came into his own, developing an eventually globe-conquering style of dance music eventually known for its founding venue: "house."

393 **The Garage took the membership policy:** There was a temporary hitch in its goodwill when Paradise Garage "officially" opened in early 1978 while the brand-new PA was still being set up, forcing the crowd to wait for hours in the freezing winter cold. Yet that incident had the inadvertent but potentially beneficial effect of alienating the white Fire Island gay crowd that Michael Brody had invited to this opening, ensuring that the core crowd (largely black and gay, and almost exclusively "underground") was able to continue to claim the club as its own.

396 **the hallowed venue had closed in early 1976:** The Apollo eventually reopened in 1985.

396 **"That was all I really wanted":** The Caz and Wiz quotes referring to the Black Out in this section are from *NY77: The Coolest Year in Hell*. Other Caz quotes from author interview.

397 **fourteen-album career:** On their fifth studio album, 1980's *End of the Century*, Phil Spector finally achieved his ambition to produce a New York rock group, with mixed results.

400 **racist on film as in print:** Manero's near-climactic decision to hand the first-place dance prize over to a Latin couple seemed like a belated apology from the filmmakers.

401 **Hauling a sound system:** "I used to do two or three gigs a night," said Hollywood, who once made $900 for half an hour at the armory in Queens, in 1976. "I would do an hour or so, collect my money, and I was gone. Other DJs from that era were working the rest of the night."

402 **to "set [his] watch by Tuesday nights":** Flash, *The Adventures of Grandmaster Flash*, p. 131.

402 **"He was quick-mixing":** Jeff Chang, *Can't Stop, Won't Stop*, p. 80.

402 **"He had skills'":** Charlie Ahearn, *Yes Yes Y'All*, p. 88; http://www.people.com/people/archive/article/0,,20113895,00.html.

402 **The Fever, meantime:** Disco Fever was heavily featured in 1985's seminal hip-hop movie *Krush Groove*, during the process of which it was discovered that the club had been operating all along without a cabaret license. Sal Abbatiello, who saw himself as a community leader as much as a club owner, was furious about what happened. "They used a technicality to close me up after I renovated the park, after I did the United Negro College Fund, I started a youth association, I started a skating rink so all the kids had somewhere to go skate and do their homework. . . . All the Community Board had to say was, 'Yes, he can get the cabaret license.' And they said no. And I just closed up and walked away."

403 **headlining the Rainbow Theatre:** The Rainbow concert was released as the *It's Alive* album in 1979, and the film of the same concert much later showed up on a DVD of the same name. It's generally considered to have captured the group at a creative and artistic peak. Three months after that concert, driven sick by infighting, and never having intended to become a full-time member in the first place, Tommy Erdelyi quit the band to focus on production. His place was taken by the highly capable Marc Bell, who had previously played with both Queen Elizabeth and the Voidoids. By 2004, all three founding Ramones members—Johnny, Joey, and Dee Dee—had died, of cancer, leukemia, and a heroin overdose, respectively.

403 **It never reopens:** Kristal's attention reverted to the club that started it all. CBGBs went on to become a global institution, not only as the birthplace of punk but as a mainstay for a series of subsequent related movements, and as a beloved showcase venue that maintained its reputation for great sound and a homely atmosphere, even though (perhaps because) it never got around to cleaning up the toilets. CBGBs closed in 2006, after a final showdown with the landlord over broken promises and unpaid rent. Patti Smith played the last ever show; Hilly Kristal died of cancer a year later.

404 **a "disco-diva":** *New York Times*, Dec. 30, 1977, p. C1.

407 **"subject to white gentrification":** In 2008, ninety-one-year-old Bobby Robinson's record store was forced to vacate by new real estate interests after sixty-two years in business.

BIBLIOGRAPHY

BOOKS

Abramovitch, Ilana, and Seán Galvin, eds. *Jews of Brooklyn*. Hanover, NH: University Press of New England, 2001.

Abu-Lughod, Janet I.. *From Urban Village to East Village: The Battle for New York's Lower East Side*. Cambridge, MA: Blackwell, 1994.

Ahearn, Charlie, with Jim Fricke. *Yes Yes Y'All: The Experience Music Project Oral History of Hip-Hop's First Decade*. New York: Da Capo Press, 2002.

Antonia, Nina. *The New York Dolls: Too Much Too Soon*. London: Omnibus Press, 1998.

Austin, Joe. *Taking the Train: How Graffiti Art Became an Urban Crisis in New York City*. New York: Columbia University Press, 2002.

Bangs, Lester. *Psychotic Reactions and Carburetor Dung*. Edited by Greil Marcus. New York: Alfred A. Knopf, 1988.

Barfe, Louis. *Where Have All the Good Times Gone?: The Rise and Fall of the Record Industry*. London: Atlantic, 2004.

Basie, Count, and Albert Murray. *Good Morning Blues: The Autobiography of Count Basie*. New York: Da Capo Press, 2002.

Beard, Rick, and Leslie Cohen Berlowitz. *Greenwich Village: Culture and Counterculture*. New Brunswick, NJ: Rutgers University Press, 1993.

Bernstein, Sid, with Arthur Aaron. *It's Sid Bernstein Calling*. Middle Village, NY: Jonathan David, 2002.

Bockris, Victor. *Transformer: The Lou Reed Story*. New York: Simon & Schuster, 1994.

———. *Up-Tight: The Velvet Underground Story*. London: Omnibus Press, 1993.

———. *The Life and Death of Andy Warhol*. New York: Bantam Books, 1989.

Bowman, David. *This Must Be the Place: The Adventures of Talking Heads in the 20th Century*. New York: Harper Entertainment, 2001.

Burrows, Edwin G., and Mike Wallace. *Gotham: A History of New York City to 1898*. New York: Oxford University Press, 1999.

Bradbury, David. *Duke Ellington*. London: Haus Publishers, 2005.

Brand, Oscar. *The Ballad Mongers: Rise of the Modern Folk Song*. New York: Funk & Wagnalls, 1962.

Brandt, Nat. *Harlem at War: The Black Experience in World War II*. Syracuse, NY: Syracuse University Press, 1996.

Brewster, Bill, and Frank Broughton. *Last Night a DJ Saved My Life: The History of the Disc Jockey*. New York: Grove Press, 1999.

Broyard, Anatole. *Kafka Was the Rage: A Greenwich Village Memoir*. New York: C. Southern Books, 1993.

Caldwell, Mark. *New York Night: The Mystique and Its History*. New York: Scribner, 2005.

Cannato, Vincent J. *The Ungovernable City : John Lindsay and His Struggle to Save New York*. New York: Basic Books, 2001.

Capeci, Dominic J., Jr. *The Harlem Riot of 1943*. Philadelphia: Temple University Press, 1977.

Carter, David. *Stonewall: The Riots That Sparked the Gay Revolution*. New York: St. Martin's Press, 2004.

Chang, Jeff. *Can't Stop, Won't Stop: A History of the Hip-Hop Generation*. New York: Picador, 2005.

Cooper, Ralph, and Steve Dougherty. *Amateur Night at the Apollo: Ralph Cooper Presents Five Decades of Great Entertainment*. New York: HarperCollins, 1990.

County, Jayne, with Rupert Smith. *Man Enough to Be a Woman*. London: Serpent's Tail, 1995.

Cray, Ed. *Ramblin' Man: The Life and Times of Woody Guthrie*. New York: W. W. Norton, 2004.

Dannen, Fredric. *Hit Men: Power Brokers and Fast Money inside the Music Business*. New York: Vintage Books, 1991.

DeCurtis, Anthony, and James Henke, with Holly George-Warren. *The Rolling Stone Illustrated History of Rock & Roll*. New York: Random House, 1978.

DeVeaux, Scott. *The Birth of Bebop: A Social and Musical History*. Berkeley: University of California Press, 1997.

Duberman, Martin B. *Stonewall*. New York: E. P. Dutton, 1993.

Dunaway, David. *How Can I Keep from Singing: Pete Seeger*. New York: Da Capo Press, 1990.

Dylan, Bob. *Chronicles, Volume One*. New York: Simon & Shuster, 2004

Eliot, Marc. *Phil Ochs: Death of a Rebel*. London: Omnibus Press, 1990.

Emerson, Ken. *Always Magic in the Air: The Bomp and Brilliance of the Brill Building Era*. New York: Viking, 2005.

Flash, Grandmaster. *The Adventures of Grandmaster Flash: My Life, My Beats.* New York: Harlem Moon, 2008.

Fox, Ted. *Showtime at the Apollo.* New York: Holt, Rinehart, and Winston, 1983.

Frame, Pete. *The Complete Rock Family Trees.* London: Omnibus Press, 1980

George, Nelson. *The Death of Rhythm & Blues.* New York: Pantheon, 1988

Gillespie, Dizzy, with Al Fraser. *To Be or Not to Bop.* Garden City, NY: Doubleday, 1979.

Gillman, Peter, and Leni Gillman. *Alias David Bowie.* London: Hodder & Stoughton, 1986.

Gitler, Ira. *Swing to Bop.* New York: Oxford University Press, 1985.

Goldman, Albert. *Disco.* New York: Hawthorn Books, 1978.

Goldstein, Richard. *Goldstein's Greatest Hits: A Book Mostly About Rock 'n' Roll.* Englewood Cliffs, NJ: Prentice-Hall, 1970.

Gonzalez, Evelyn Diaz. *The Bronx.* New York: Columbia University Press, 2004.

Gordon, Max. *Live at the Village Vanguard.* New York: St. Martin's Press, 1980.

Gribin, Anthony J., and Matthew M. Schiff. *The Complete Book of Doo-Wop.* Iola, WI: Krause, 2000.

Groia, Philip. *They All Sang on the Corner.* New York: Philip Dee, 1983.

Gruen, John. *The New Bohemia.* Pennington, NJ : A Cappella Books, 1990.

Hajdu, David. *Positively 4th Street: The Lives and Times of Joan Baez, Bob Dylan, Mimi Baez Fariña, and Richard Fariña.* New York: Farrar, Straus and Giroux, 2001.

Harry, Debbie, with Chris Stein and Victor Bockris. *Making Tracks: The Rise of Blondie.* New York: Da Capo Press, 1998.

Henderson, David. *'Scuse Me While I Kiss the Sky: The Life of Jimi Hendrix.* London: Omnibus Press, 1990.

Heylin, Clinton. *All Yesterdays' Parties: The Velvet Underground In Print, 1966–1971.* Cambridge, MA: Da Capo Press, 2005.

———. *From the Velvets to the Voidoids: The Birth of American Punk Rock.* 2nd ed. Chicago: A Cappella Books, 2005.

Hoskyns, Barney. *Waiting for the Sun: The Story of the Los Angeles Music Scene.* London: Viking, 1996.

Hughes, Langston. *The Big Sea: An Autobiography.* New York: Hill & Wang, 1963.

Ian, Janis. *Society's Child: My Autobiography.* New York: Penguin, 2008.

Jackson, John A. *Big Beat Heat: Alan Freed and the Early Years of Rock & Roll.* New York: Schirmer Books, 1991.

Jaker, Bill, with Frank Sulek and Peter Kanze. *The Airwaves of New York: Illustrated Histories of 156 AM Stations in the Metropolitan Area, 1921–1996.* New York: McFarland, 1998.

Johnstone, Nick. *Patti Smith: A Biography.* London: Omnibus Press, 1997.

Jonnes, Jill. *We're Still Here: The Rise, Fall, and Resurrection of the South Bronx.* Boston: Atlantic Monthly Press, 1986.

Kapralov, Yuri. *Once There Was a Village.* New York: St. Martin's Press, 1974.

Kaufman, David. *Shul with a Pool: The Synagogue-Center in American Jewish History.* Hanover, NH: University Press of New England, 1999.

Klein, Joe. *Woody Guthrie: A Life.* New York: Alfred A. Knopf, 1980.

Krassner, Paul, ed. *Best of the Realist.* Philadelphia: Running Press, 1984.

Kugelberg, Johan, and Joe Conzo. *Born in the Bronx: A Visual Record of the Early Days of Hip Hop.* New York: Rizzolo, 2007.

Lankevich, George J. *American Metropolis: A History of New York City.* New York: New York University Press, 1998.

Lawrence, Tim. *Love Saves the Day: A History of American Dance Music Culture, 1970–1979.* Durham, NC: Duke University Press, 2003.

Lerner, Michael A. *Dry Manhattan: Prohibition in New York City.* Cambridge, MA: Harvard University Press, 2007.

Loza, Steven. *Tito Puente and the Making of Latin Music.* Urbana: University of Illinois Press, 1999.

Malone, Jacqui. *Steppin' on the Blues: The Visible Rhythms of African American Dance.* Urbana: University of Illinois Press, 1996.

Marcus, Greil. *Like a Rolling Stone: Bob Dylan at the Crossroads.* New York: PublicAffairs, 2005.

Margolick, David. *Strange Fruit: Billie Holiday, Café Society, and an Early Cry for Civil Rights.* Philadelphia: Running Press, 2000.

McNeil, Legs, and Gillian McCain. *Please Kill Me: The Uncensored Oral History of Punk.* New York: Penguin, 1997.

Miles, Barry. *Hippie.* New York: Sterling, 2004.

Miller, Nathan Brad. "Mario Bauzá: Swing Era Novelty and Afro-Cuban Authenticity." M.A. thesis, University of Missouri–Columbia, 2007.

Miller, Terry. *Greenwich Village and How It Got That Way.* New York: Crown, 1990.

Morales, Ed. *The Latin Beat: The Rhythms and Roots of Latin Music from Bossa Nova to Salsa and Beyond.* New York: Da Capo Press, 2003.

Moreno, Jairo. "Bauzá-Gillespie-Latin/Jazz: Difference, Modernity, and the Black Caribbean." *South Atlantic Quarterly* 103 (Winter 2004): 81–99.

Needs, Kris, and Dick Porter. *Trash: The Complete New York Dolls.* London: Plexus, 2005.

Nobakht, David. *Suicide: No Compromise.* London: SAF, 2005.

Ottley, Roi. *New World A-Coming: Inside Black America.* Boston: Houghton Mifflin, 1943.

Partridge, Elizabeth. *This Land Was Made for You and Me: The Life and Songs of Woody Guthrie.* New York: Viking, 2001.

Powell, Josephine. *Tito Puente: When the Drums Are Dreaming.* Bloomington, IN: AuthorHouse, 2007.

Priestley, Brian. *Chasin' the Bird: The Life and Legacy of Charlie Parker.* New York: Oxford University Press, 2005.

Ramone, Dee Dee, with Veronica Kofman. *Lobotomy: Surviving the Ramones.* New York: Thunder's Mouth Press, 2000.

Ravan, Genya. *Lollipop Lounge: Memoirs of a Rock and Roll Refugee.* New York: Watson-Guptil, 2004.

Ribowski, Mark. *He's a Rebel: The Truth about Phil Spector—Rock and Roll's Legendary Madman.* New York: E. P. Dutton, 1989.

Riis, Jacob A. *How the Other Half Lives: Studies Among the Tenements of New York.* New York: Charles Scribner's Sons, 1890.

Salazar, Max. *Mambo Kingdom: Latin Music in New York.* New York: Schirmer Books, 2002.

Sanders, Ed. *1968: A History in Verse.* Santa Rosa, CA: Black Sparrow Press, 1997.

———. *Tales of Beatnik Glory: Volumes I and II.* New York: Citadel Underground, 1990.

Schiffman, Jack. *Harlem Heyday: A Pictorial History of Modern Black Show Business and the Apollo Theatre.* Buffalo, NY: Prometheus Books, 1984.

———. *Uptown: The Story of Harlem's Apollo Theatre.* New York: Cowles Book Co., 1971.

Seeger, Pete. *The Incompleat Folksinger.* New York: Fireside, 1972.

Sewall-Ruskin, Yvonne. *High on Rebellion: Inside the Underground at Max's Kansas City.* New York: Thunder's Mouth Press, 1998.

Shapiro, Peter. *Turn the Beat Around: The Secret History of Disco.* New York: Faber & Faber, 2005.

Shelton, Robert. *No Direction Home: The Life and Music of Bob Dylan.* New York: Da Capo Press, 2003.

Shipton, Alyn. *Groovin' High—The Life of Dizzy Gillespie.* New York: Oxford University Press, 1999.

Spector, Ronnie, with Vince Waldron. *Be My Baby: How I Survived Mascara, Miniskirts and Madness.* New York: HarperPerennial, 1990.

Stearns, Marshall. *The Story of Jazz.* New York: Oxford University Press, 1956.

Sublette, Ned. *Cuba and Its Music: From the First Drums to the Mambo.* Chicago: A Cappella Books, 2004.

Thompson, Dave. *Beyond the Velvet Underground.* London: Omnibus Press, 1989.

Toop, David. *The Rap Attack: African Jive to New York Hip Hop.* Boston: South End Press, 1984.

True, Everett. *Hey Ho Let's Go: The Story of the Ramones.* London: Omnibus Press, 2002.

Unterberger, Richie. *Turn! Turn! Turn!: The '60s Folk-Rock Revolution.* San Francisco: Backbeat Books, 2002.

Valentine, Gary. *New York Rocker: My Life in the Blank Generation.* New York: Sidgwick & Jackson, 2002.

Van Ronk, Dave, with Elijah Wald. *The Mayor of MacDougal Street: A Memoir.* Cambridge, MA: Da Capo Press, 2005.

Wald, Elijah. *Josh White: Society Blues.* Amherst: University of Massachusetts Press, 2000.

Ward, Ed, Geoffrey Stokes, and Ken Tucker. *Rock of Ages: The Rolling Stone History of Rock & Roll.* New York: Summit Books, 1986.

Watson, Steven. *The Harlem Renaissance: Hub of African-American Culture, 1920–1930.* New York: Pantheon, 1996.

Weissman, Dick. *Which Side Are You On?: An Inside History of the Folk Music Revival in America.* New York: Continuum, 2005.

Weller, Sheila. *Girls like Us: Carole King, Joni Mitchell, and Carly Simon—and the Journey of a Generation.* New York: Atria Books, 2008.

Wetzsteon, Ross. *Republic of Dreams: Greenwich Village, the American Bohemia, 1910–1960.* New York: Simon & Schuster, 2002.

Wexler, Jerry, and David Ritz. *Rhythm and the Blues: A Life in American Music.* New York: Alfred A. Knopf, 1993.

Wilcock, John. *The Village Square.* New York: L. Stuart, 1961.

Wilson, Sondra K. *Meet Me at the Theresa: The Story of Harlem's Most Famous Hotel.* New York: Simon & Schuster, 2004.

Woliver, Robbie. *Hoot! A 24-Year History of the Greenwich Village Music Scene.* New York: St. Martin's Press, 1986.

Yanow, Scott. *Afro-Cuban Jazz.* San Francisco: Miller Freeman, 2000.

LINER NOTES

Bauldie, John. *Bob Dylan: The Bootleg Series 1–3.* USA: Sony Music, 1991.

Blow, Kurtis. *The History of Rap.* Vol. 1. USA: Rhino Records, 1997.

Bowman, Rob. *Between Thought and Expression: The Lou Reed Anthology.* USA: RCA, 1992.

Cohen, Ronald D., and Dave Samuelson. *Songs for Political Action* (various artists). Germany: Bear Family Records, 1996.

Crowe, Cameron. *Bob Dylan: Biograph.* USA: CBS Inc., 1985.

Fricke, David. *The Velvet Underground: Peel Slowly and See.* USA: Polydor, 1995.

Gretlund, Glenn N. *The Almanac Singers: Songs of Protest.* UK: Prism, 2001.

Hirshey, Gerri. *One Kiss Leads to Another: Girl Groups Sounds Lost and Found.* USA: Rhino Records, 2005.

Hyde, Bob. *101 Vocal Group Gems from the Golden Age of Rock 'n' Roll.* USA: Rhino Records, 1993.

Komorowski, Adam. *The Ravens: Birds of a Feather.* UK: Proper Records, 2002.

Laredo, Joseph F. *The Weavers: The Best of the Decca Years.* USA: Decca/MCA, 1996.

Marcus, Greil. *Anthology of American Folk Music,* ed. Harry Smith. USA: Smithsonian Folkways/Sony Music Special Products, 1997.

Samuelson, Dave. *The Weavers, 1949–1953.* Germany: Bear Family Records, 2000.

Seeger, Pete. *Pete Seeger's Greatest Hits.* USA: Sony, 2002.

Visser, Joop. *Chick Webb and His Orchestra: Stomping at the Savoy.* UK: Proper Records, 2006.

———. *The Dizzy Gillespie Story.* UK: Proper Records, 2006.

———. *Ritmo Caliente: Machito and His Afro-Cubans.* UK: Proper Records, 2005.

Various. *Rhapsodies in Black: Music and Words from the Harlem Renaissance.* USA: Rhino Records, 2000.

———. *RCA-Victor Jazz: The First Half Century.* Liner notes by Orrin Keepnews, Dan Morgenstern, Steven Lasker. USA: RCA, 1992.

———. *Say It Loud! A Celebration of Black Music in America.* USA: Rhino Records, 1992.

A summer Sunday folk music sing-along in Washington Square Park, 1950. "It was very egalitarian," said Erik Darling. "If you knew the songs you were in the center of the crowd. If you didn't have the slightest idea what you were doing, you were on the outside of the crowd. And some people just didn't give a shit, didn't know what they were doing, and sang anyway."

CREDITS

INDEX